DÖNITZ

The Last Führer

DÖNITZ
THE LAST FÜHRER

Portrait of a Nazi War Leader

BY

PETER PADFIELD

LONDON
VICTOR GOLLANCZ LTD
1984

For Fiona

British Library Cataloguing in Publication Data
Padfield, Peter
  Dönitz.
  1. Dönitz, Karl
  2. Germany. *Kriegsmarine*—Biography
  I. Title
  359.3′32′0924   DD247.D/

  ISBN 0-575-03186-7

Photoset in Great Britain by
Rowland Phototypesetting Ltd, Bury St Edmunds, Suffolk
and printed by St Edmundsbury Press
Bury St Edmunds, Suffolk

'A senior officer who sees his responsibilities and duties in times such as these only within the limited terms of his military duties, without being aware of his grave responsibility towards the whole nation, lacks greatness and a proper understanding of his duty.'

General Ludwig Beck, 1938

'Each soldier has to fulfil the tasks of his position regardless. So our calling and our fate is to fight fanatically, and bound up with it is the task for each of us to stand fanatically behind the National-Socialist State.'

Grand Admiral Karl Dönitz, 1944

Contents

Illustrations

The bomb-proof U-boat bunkers built at all Biscay bases *(Imperial War Museum)*

U-boats berthed at Lorient *(Imperial War Museum)*

HMS *Starling* carrying out a depth-charge attack *(Imperial War Museum)*

U 175 meets her end *(Public Record Office)*

Hitler, Göring and Dönitz *(BBC Hulton)*

Dönitz in Rome, March 1943 *(Professor F. Ruge)*

Following page 450

Dönitz is informed that his government is dissolved *(Süddeutscher Verlag)*

Under arrest—outside the police station in Flensburg-Mürwik *(Ullstein)*

Speer, Dönitz and Jodl *(Imperial War Museum)*

In the dock at Nuremberg *(Süddeutscher Verlag)*

'Number Two' serving his time in Spandau jail *(BBC Hulton)*

Dönitz with his surviving family after his release from Spandau in 1956 *(Ullstein)*

Dönitz in 1972 *(Keystone)*

'Old Comrades' at Dönitz's funeral in Aumühle, January 1981 *(Keystone)*

MAPS

Dönitz's early 1939 war game against British Atlantic supply lines *page 172*

Disposition of U-boats in the Atlantic at the start of the Second World War *page 192*

Acknowledgements

First, I should like to thank David Burnett of Gollancz for encouragement and enthusiasm, so greatly needed over a long haul such as this has been, and Anne Harrel, whose original idea this biography was. I should also like to thank the Manager of my branch of the National Westminster Bank—who kept his nerve.

My great thanks are due to Karl Dönitz's daughter, Frau Ursula Hessler, for her hospitality and ready answers, and to his niece, Frau Brigitte Fidelak, for her very many letters in answer to my queries, and help with pictures. I know both will be hurt by this book, and I am sorry.

From Dönitz's former staff officers, I should like to thank particularly *Kapitän zur See ad* Hans Meckel, *Korv. Kapitän ad* Jan Hansen-Nootbar, and *Kapitän zur See ad* V. Oehrn. I also corresponded with Dr H. J. von Knebel Doeberitz, *Kapitän zur See ad* W. Lüdde-Neurath and from outside the former staff *Flotillenadmiral ad* Otto Kretschmer and *Rechtsanhalt* Otto Kranzbühler. Karl Dönitz's chief of operations, U-boat Command, throughout the war, and former Adjutant, *Admiral ad* E. Godt told me at the beginning he could not assist.

I should like to record my thanks to the late *Konteradmiral* Edward Wegener for much background help and instructive conversation, to Herr Klaus Querling for his tact and initiative in interviewing, to the Daegel family for hospitality, particularly Christian Daegel for his continuing help in finding books and articles; also to Frau Margarete von Lamezan for searching her memory, Professor D. Helmut Gollwitzer, Pastor of Dahlem, and Frau Röhricht, and to Heinrich Jaenecke, who searched his memory and allowed me to quote from his *Stern* article, also to *Admiral ad* Friedrich Ruge, and the late Albert Speer.

While still in Germany I should like to record my great debt to Frank Lynder for his specialist insights into aspects of the Third Reich and the U-boat war and his generosity in making them so readily available, also for his hospitality. From France I should like to thank Maître Denis Jacques for his interesting tour of the château and bunker at Kerneval.

In this country I should like to thank Professor Paul Kennedy of the University of East Anglia and Douglas Botting, both of whom pointed me in the right direction when I started what seemed a daunting task. I owe a great debt of gratitude to Robert M. Coppock of the Ministry of Defence for enormous, creative help with the German naval archive, help with German naval terminology, reading illegible German script and much information besides from his vast knowledge of U-boat affairs, also to Alan Francis of the Naval Library, and Philip Reed of the Imperial War Museum for his creative help. And I am grateful to Patrick Beesley, author of, among other excellent books, *Very Special Intelligence*, Tony Broughton, producer of *The U-boat War* for the BBC, Ludovic Kennedy, who presented it and described his interviews with Dönitz in *The Spectator*, and Jonathan Steinberg, all of whom assisted with recollections. I should like too, to thank Professor Volker Berghahn of the University of Warwick, both for background help from his own works and finding unobtainable books from the National Archives, Washington, and Edwin R. Coffee for detailed examination of the records, and advice.

Mary Paine was most enthusiastic and successful at finding illustrations, and Hugh Young, Helga Cook and Guy Padfield helped ease the burden of translation, for which I am grateful.

I thank the following authors and publishers for permission to quote passages: Paul Kennedy: 'Weltpolitik' in J. G. Rohl & N. Sombart, *Kaiser Wilhelm II: New Interpretations*, Cambridge University Press; A. Dorpalen, *Heinrich von Treitschke*, Yale University Press; M. G. Steinert, *Capitulation 1945*, and K. Neureuther & C. Bergen, *U-boat Stories*, both Constable & Co.; H. Trevor-Roper (Ed.) *The Goebbels Diaries*, Secker & Warburg and Putnams; H. Trevor-Roper (Ed.), *Hitler's Table Talk* and W. Warlimont, *Inside Hitler's Headquarters*, both Weidenfeld & Nicolson; H. Schaeffer, *U-Boat 977*, Wm. Kimber & Co.; G. M. Gilbert, *Nuremberg Diary*, Methuen for Eyre & Spottiswoode; F. Gilbert, *Hitler Directs his War*, Oxford University Press; A. Speer, *Spandau, the Secret Diaries*, Collins; Jack Fishman, *The Seven Men of Spandau*, W. H. Allen Ltd; and for Karl Dönitz's own writings: Musterschmidt for *Mein wechselvolles Leben*; Athenäum for *10 Jahre und 20 Tage*; Bernard & Graef for *40 Fragen an Karl Dönitz*; E. S. Mittler for *Die U-bootswaffe*; Ullstein for *Die Fahrten der Breslau im Schwarzen Meer*.

Finally I should like to acknowledge my great debt to two German historians who charted the ground over which this biography moves, and published so many hitherto unknown documents: Dr Jost Dülffer for *Weimar, Hitler und die Marine*, and Professor Michael Salewski for *Die Seekriegsleitung, 1939–1945*.

If there is anyone I have omitted by oversight, I apologize.

Introduction

Truth is elusive enough at the best of times. To hunt it across a cultural divide such as that between Great Britain and Germany in the first half of the twentieth century presents problems. Race is not one of them: racial characteristics, such as they are—and goodness knows there has been enough seafaring and migration, expulsion and conquest to have mixed up the genes somewhat—are, on the surface, entertaining, even important, in the sense that style and manners are important, but otherwise about as relevant to a man's thoughts and acts as the colour of his eyes. Perceptions of racial differences are another matter; such perceptions played a large part in the later stages of the British Empire, an even larger part in the Third Reich—it was all in the mind.

The real differences between peoples, surely, are caused by the systems under which they live and the habits of mind engendered by the systems—give or take handfuls of dissidents. In that sense there is a chasm fixed by history, geography and beliefs between those brought up in the liberal tradition of the free west, and those from State-centred systems such as Germany's at the time of this story. The western system, arising from the needs of merchants—Bonaparte was right in a more profound sense than probably he realized when he called the British a nation of shopkeepers—sets high values on freedom, without which merchants cannot function properly, contract, which is the essence of trade, and the separation or balancing of power—for once power is concentrated freedom is lost. The Prusso-German system, on the other hand, arose from the needs of soldiers—since Prussia was a continental state without natural frontiers and surrounded by enemies—and placed high values on force and the threat of force, guile and deception, and the concentration of State power to maximize force for internal as well as external purposes. These opposing compulsions pervaded all areas of thought within the two systems, from philosophy and the writing and teaching of history to the popular press and even the pulpit, moulding minds in fundamentally different ways and making it hard for those from either system really to understand their fellows from the other. Tudor and Stuart Englishmen would have understood the group around the Kaiser without much trouble; Asquith's Liberals found it difficult—some never did make the necessary leap—while most Americans were far enough away from the troubled continent—or thought they were—not to have to try too hard. Much the same happened in the 1930s.

The problem of understanding remains; it will always remain so long as there are traders on the one hand and soldiers on the other—and philosophers and historians and politicians who have not grasped the difference. Marxist-Leninists now, Pan-Germans and National-Socialists (Nazis) then, Bonapartists before that . . . the different labels disguise the same product with the same compulsions—just as our labels cunningly conceal ours. We, the west, are the heirs to trade; our freedoms stem from the freedom to trade as their repressions stem from the need to coerce. Merchant power is as corrupt as martial power, but at least we know it and safeguards are enshrined in our constitutions; 'their' constitutions enshrine power, hence corruption—and in the end defeat and destruction.

This is a story of corruption, the corruption of a great nation and its savage destruction. It is at the same time the tragedy of a man with certain qualities born into that great nation and that system of power at one of its climactic periods. That he was a German and I an English-man is beside the point; that I was born into the traders' system, he into the State-centred power system—surely that is the point! There, but for the grace of God . . .

DÖNITZ
The Last Führer

CHAPTER ONE

Ich hatt' einen Kameraden . . .

THE JANUARY MORNING is clear and crisp; sunlight glitters on a snow-laden tracery of branches and the bushes and trimmed hedges of Aumühle, outside Hamburg on the edge of the Saxon forest. Large houses built in the earlier years of the century with ornamented façades and balconies, each commanding its own enclosure of groomed lawn and shrubbery, look out on slow lines of cars and coaches; their drivers, searching for space to park, threaten to jam all traffic in this normally quiet little town. Those who have left their vehicles make their way beyond the houses towards a throng which winds off the road, inching, step by packed step, through a winter fairyland of white-mantled pines and frosted evergreens along the *Kirchenweg*.

The way opens eventually into a clearing before a round chapel built of red and purpling brick in the style of the 1930s; a conical roof showing green copper in places beneath the snow is surmounted by a short tower holding aloft a plain cross. It is the Bismarck Memorial Chapel; we are, in more senses than one perhaps, in Bismarck country. Inside, the last of only six Grand Admirals of the German Navy lies in a coffin draped with the black-red-gold flag of the *Bundesrepublik*; on the flag his service dagger; around the coffin an honour guard of elderly men stand with proud bearing and stern expression, the black-white-red ribbon and the glint of the Knight's Cross over the knots of their black ties between the lapels of civilian overcoats. All are former naval officers. One stands in front holding a black cushion on which the Grand Admiral's decorations are pinned, the Knight's Cross, other Iron Crosses from the Kaiser's time, the Imperial Medal, the U-boat medal prominent among them.

People from the head of the slow and ever-lengthening queue up the *Kirchenweg* are filing past to pay their last respects. Most are of the same generation as the honour guard; neither civilian clothes nor age conceal their bearing. Ribbons and Iron Crosses and here and there the oak leaves of supreme distinction flash at their throats. Some carry naval pattern officers' caps with the badge of the *U-bootfahrer-verband* or one of the Naval Associations; perhaps half of this gathering are old Navy men, but all other arms of the Third Reich are represented—there are former Panzer Commanders, Luftwaffe pilots, silver-haired Standarten-führers and Sturmbannführers of the *Waffen-SS* . . .

'*War das nicht Mohnke?*'

Outside the crowd is still growing.

'*Der Mohnke!*' someone repeats. Wilhelm Mohnke, last SS-Brigade-führer at the Führerbunker in Berlin.

There are queues to sign the books of condolence opened out on tables beneath a long canopy rigged beside the chapel. Old comrades recognize one another; groups have formed; breath rises visibly in the frosty air; voices deplore the government's refusal to grant a State Funeral or military honours to a holder of the Knight's Cross, or to permit official or service representatives to attend, or even to allow the wearing of uniform, others marvel at the multitude who have nevertheless turned out on this freezing morning . . .

'*Mensch, der Rudel! Hast du den Rudel gesehen?*'

Colonel Hans-Ulrich Rudel, the fighter ace with the highest German war decorations, strong sunburned face crowned with thinning white hair, leans on two crutches as he signs autographs for men as old as he who press around.

Those few from younger generations know instinctively they do not belong here; nothing need be said; it is in the bearing, the manner, the voices from another time, used to obey and to command, the vivid, shared experience of young manhood when for a short span they were the masters of Europe—and of the *Niedergang*, the terrible retribution. These are survivors of the German holocaust here to honour their last leader, long since claimed or disclaimed by history, and to reassure themselves of their own honour amid events from which the rest of the world and the government of their new *Bundesrepublik* has recoiled. The few short-haired leather-jacketed youths from *Gau-Hansa* and other neo-Nazi movements who have joined them are probably as alien to them as the curious and sceptical young Press representatives, rather surprised by this great gathering, who seek its meaning.

Perhaps the legends on the wreaths provide a clue: '*Unserem Reichs-präsidenten zum Gedenken*' from an Association of those from German eastern lands; '*Geschichte wertet, Menschen irren*'—history appraises, men err—from a member of the *Bundestag*; a simple wreath from

4

'*Wolf-Rüdiger, Ilse und Rudolf Hess*', another from the U-boat Association Walter Forstmann—the name of a First World War U-boat ace, who was in fact Dönitz's first submarine commander—one from the survivors of U 309, one from 'Crew 36'; '*In treuem Gedenken*' from *Oberleutnant zur See* Kummetz, former Commander U 235; '*Unserem Vorbild an Tapferkeit, Treue und Ritterlichkeit*' our model of courage, loyalty and chivalry from German Youth-leader on a bow of red-white-red, the colours of the former Hitler Youth; '*Er hielt unserem Vaterland die Treue*'—he kept faith with our Fatherland—from the soldiers of the former *Waffen-SS* on a bow of silver and black; '*Treue um Treue*' from *3 Panzerkorps*; '*Deutschland wird leben*'—Germany will live—'*Sein Ruhm überdauert die Zeit*'—his renown outlasts the age—'*Dem Retter von Millionen ostdeutscher Flüchtlinge, dem Grossadmiral, dem letzten Staatspräsidenten in Dankbarkeit und Treue*'—to the saviour of millions of East German refugees, to the Grand Admiral, to the last State President in gratitude and loyalty . . . the messages are legion.

The service has started. It is well over two hours since the doors of the chapel were opened, and the last of those wishing to file through have had to be almost forcibly restrained. Now a loudspeaker relays the words of Rear Admiral Edward Wegener to the crowds outside; he speaks of the Grand Admiral's life, 'grounded on the virtues—now so unjustly reviled—of the Imperial Naval Officer Corps—honour—selfless devotion to duty—patriotism—unswerving loyalty to the government . . .'[1]

Heinrich Jaenecke, one of those listening in the snow, vividly recalling the terror of the last days of the Third Reich when, little more than a schoolboy, he had been quartered in barracks not an hour's drive from Aumühle, has an unequivocal inward response:

'There it is, the word that excuses all. The loudspeaker trumpets it over the wide cemetery: loyalty—the great German lie, the general pardon for all blindness, cowardice, irresponsibility . . .'[2]

'. . . Grand Admiral Dönitz,' from the loudspeaker, 'was a great military leader. His leadership came of tenacity of aim and clarity. He won the hearts of his men through an inimitable charisma . . .

'He had the gift of recognizing the kernel of every problem and of representing its essentials simply to everyone. He had ability in decision and energy to translate into action that which he found right. He was the man of the young generation, innovative and rich in ideas. He was of their spirit. He inspired the young officer corps of the U-boat arm as well as the petty officers and men to fulfil their duty. Even in the hardest phases of the war with huge losses the U-boat arm never wanted volunteers.

'This leadership based on soldierly virtues made the U-boat men of the Second World War a united band which, proud in success, finally made a sacrifice recalling examples from the ancient world.'

When appointed C-in-C of the Navy, Wegener continues, Dönitz had stepped outside purely military affairs and had been drawn into politics. Needing Hitler's confidence to carry out his tasks for the Navy, he had gained it, and it was because of this and his unswerving loyalty to the end that Hitler had appointed him as his successor.

'Today, free from the prejudices of the time, one has to pose the question, whether obedience alone can do justice to the ethical principles of German soldiership . . .'

Towards the end of his oration Wegener comes to the fact that the Federal Ministry of Defence is not represented at the funeral, an implied rebuke vigorously supported by the congregation with whistles of shame.

'The Grand Admiral is even denied the honours due a holder of the Knight's Cross . . .'

More whistles.

'The life of a great soldier is ended. His name is now part of history. We men of the old Navy thank him for his example as leader. We thank him for leading us immaculately in war. We thank him for the firmness with which he brought the war to an end. Beyond the grave he has our affection and our grateful veneration.

'The men of the old Navy are proud that he was one of us.'

Several others add their tributes; finally the parish priest, Pastor Hans-Jochen Arp, speaks of the man who lived his last years amongst them here as 'a quiet citizen' associating with all 'without any sign of rank or dignity'.[3] He had been a Christian, a regular attender at this Church, where he sat in the second row in the middle, covered in a woollen rug. After the death of his wife he had asked the Pastor if he might embellish the family grave with a large carved wooden crucifix.

'I said to him, "That is really not usual here. Why do you want it?" His answer was, "Because He is the only one to whom finally I can adhere."'

Later, discussing his own funeral service Dönitz had told him that he wished to be buried under the colours of the *Bundesrepublik*—'The Imperial flag is out of the question. On my coffin it has to be the black-red-gold flag.'

'That is a "Yes" to loyalty to our State,' the Pastor continues. 'We can only follow him—I believe—if we ourselves therefore say "Yes" and hold to this loyalty. Our activity today is therefore no festival of rebellion, hate or resignation. Be done with madness! Heal what is to be healed! Save men! That was his attitude, which also binds us . . .

'He was, for me, one of the most devout Christians I have met.'

After the orations a hymn; the naval band assembles on the path leading into the cemetery, all members wearing civilian clothes with naval pattern officers' caps. Standard-bearers, holding aloft Naval Association and old Imperial war flags, precede the red-black-gold bedecked coffin carried by former U-boat officers, each a Knight of the Iron Cross. Retired Korvettenkapitän Adalbert Schnee leads with the medal cushion; he was a notable U-boat Commander and member of the late Grand Admiral's staff who, in the last days of the war when everything was collapsing and the allies had complete command of sea and air, took out the first of a new type of U-boat, prepared at well past the eleventh hour to re-open the offensive against shipping.

Through the crowds packed along either side of the path and hiding the well-tended plots beneath the winter mantle of this beautiful woodland cemetery, the Grand Admiral is borne to the drum beat of the funeral march. The path winds among bushes—then suddenly there it is, the great carved crucifix, high above the gathered people, Christ with a crown of snow, sorrowful head bent, arms wide-stretched as if to receive His servant.

Below, a great irregular block of granite like some rune is carved with the single word DÖNITZ; to one side at its base is a memorial tablet:

Ingeborg Dönitz
Geborene Weber
10.12.1893 + 2.5.1962

There is another, larger memorial stone bearing two names:

Klaus Dönitz	Peter Dönitz
Oberleutnant zur See	Leutnant zur See
14 Mai 1920	20 März 1922
14 Mai 1944	19 Mai 1943 Im
Im Engl. kanal	Nordatlantik

The U-boat men turn slowly either side of the fresh earth heaped by the grave and move the coffin from their shoulders. The band is silent as the coffin is lowered in. The Pastor recites the final moving words of the burial service—and then—spontaneously it seems—from a thousand throats the old German song, the forbidden first verse of the *Deutschlandlied* rises from every side.

> '*Deutschland—Deutschland über alles,*
> *Über alles in der Welt . . .*'

The Pastor's lips are closed.

> '*Wenn es stets zum Schutz und Trutze*
> *Brüderlich zusammenhält.*
> *Von der Maas bis an die Memel,*
> *Von der Etsch bis an den Belt—*
> *Deutschland—Deutschland . . .*'

For Heinrich Jaenecke, the song sounds like a blasphemy over the graves. He is transported back to May 1st 1945, when he heard on the radio the metallic voice of the Grand Admiral, 'The Führer has fallen—one of the greatest heroes of German history—but the fight must go on . . .' He and others sprang from the window of the barracks and ran away across the fields.

> We wanted to let the Grand Admiral conduct his war to the end alone. We came through villages in which deserters hung from trees. The farmers warned us against the naval *Jagdkommandos*: 'They are worse than the SS, they do you in without asking questions . . .'[4]

Jaenecke and his companions managed to survive without capture and two or three days later were lying out in a meadow under the spring sunshine when they heard the sound of a motor. It was a jeep with four Englishmen in it, singing.

> We feasted our eyes on the khaki uniforms. A small detail amazed me; there soldiers had no leather belts, only webbing. I thought: the webbing belt has conquered the leather belt. A deep feeling of liberation, of freedom arose. In a second everything, the whole dreadful edifice of fear and destruction in which we had lived, collapsed. It was over. We lay on this meadow in Holstein and looked at

one another. The tears ran down our cheeks, then we laughed until we were hoarse. It was the happiest moment of my youth.

That is what I thought as, 36 years later, the *Deutschlandlied* sounded over the open grave of Karl Dönitz. No, *meine Herren*, nothing is forgotten, nothing is healed over. There is an invisible barrier in Germany over which there is no bridge, and on both sides ever more people are growing up. Karl Dönitz stands on the other side.

Adalbert Schnee wrote an article about the funeral for the U-boat Association. He referred to this moment as 'the moving leave-taking' from the Grand Admiral:

> . . . as spontaneously from the multitude the *Deutschlandlied* struck up. That was the most wonderful parting gift for the deceased. It fulfilled the words, which the three Naval Associations had published in their funeral notices:
> By his soldiers revered, by the enemy respected, in his own land almost forgotten.[5]

Schnee went on to deny the charges frequently levelled against Dönitz, in particular that he had been little more than Hitler's vassal; he knew of no case in the conduct of the war at sea in which his will had not prevailed with Hitler. Finally, he came to 'the last and heaviest reproach':

> Dönitz to the bitter end fulfilled his duty as a soldier and was not the man who could be untrue to his principles. To him refusal of orders would be equivalent to mutiny . . .

Schnee concluded his article:

> Who will not forget the Grand Admiral and be sure that one day under a courageous government he receives an honourable place in German history.

These two views represent opposite poles of opinion; both command wide support in the camps into which Germany remains divided.

CHAPTER TWO

The Imperial Naval Officer

KARL DÖNITZ WAS born in Grünau-bei-Berlin on September 16th 1891, the second son of Herr Emil Dönitz, who came from the small provincial town of Zerbst in the Duchy of Anhalt some 80 miles south-west of Berlin. He was an engineer, specializing in optics who worked for the firm of Karl Zeiss of Jena, a world leader in the field; he was married to Anna, formerly Beyer, from the small town of Crossen on the upper Oder. Anna died on March 6th 1895, when Karl Dönitz was three and a half, his brother, Friedrich, five. Emil Dönitz did not remarry.

This much is certain from the record.[1]

From it one can make assumptions about the influences on Dönitz as a child—his father, his father's station, the spirit of the age and of the city in whose suburbs they lived—Berlin, the imperial capital, where to a greater extent than elsewhere in Germany the strong sap of the new industrial-material age rose in the tough and ancient trunk of Prussian tradition. It was a powerful fusion. The industrial juices forced growth; the spread and shape and purpose was Prussian. Heroic race memories were inscribed in every convolution of the gnarled old bark, and Germans looked up at the magnificent structure and were inclined to dream and tell stories, imagining it would grow and grow for ever. Dönitz's father was one of these, and he raised his two boys—in Karl Dönitz's words—as 'rather one-sided Prussian children'.[2]

His was not an aristocratic or military family—thus not from the strata which set the tone in the *Reich*—nor was there a background of merchant wealth. His forebears, originally small farmers from the upper Saale region, included—according to his own account—pastors, officers, scholars. It can be said that he was of the aspiring middle class; this is probably a useful definition since in those days of earnest German aspiration the middle class, particularly, aspired—to be worthy of the ideals, to imitate the bearing and the outlook and the manners of the Prussian nobility of the sword who stood behind the Kaiser at the head of the empire. They differed from the nobles, however, in their belief in education. And without family wealth Dönitz's father would have aspired to the best education he could afford for his two boys.

As for the younger of these, Karl, it is evident that the absence of a mother from the age of only three and a half must have had a decided effect on his development. What this effect was or whether any woman such as a housekeeper had any counteracting influence as a surrogate loving mother is not clear. Karl Dönitz evidently thought not, for he wrote in his memoirs that his father attempted to take the place of the mother—whom he himself could not remember: 'He is the man whom I have to thank most.'[3]

This picture receives confirmation from the recollections of Dönitz's youngest niece who was close to him in the last years of his life and had been very close to her father, his brother, Friedrich: 'Neither from my father nor from my Uncle Karl did I hear of a woman who took their mother's place. My father stressed to us that his father *never* married again. With much love he had refused to replace the mother.'[4]

In the summer following his mother's death, Karl Dönitz's father took the two boys for the holidays to the small Ostfriesian island of Baltrum; years later he explained to them that he had chosen this lonely place because he had hoped its peace and sublimity would help him to recover from his grief and restore his balance.

There is no doubt that Karl revered his father. 'There is nothing that sticks in a child's memory,' he wrote later in life, 'more than walking with its father and asking him so many questions that he wonders what is coming next.'[5] He kept a drawing of his father on his desk throughout his life—one that he had probably made himself—and when this disappeared in the looting and destruction accompanying the collapse of the Third *Reich* he replaced it with a little photograph. His niece remembered: 'In the last years [of his life] Uncle Karl still spoke to me of his father. Also I recall very well that my father spoke a lot about his father.'[6]

An account of Emil Dönitz, probably based on an interview with Karl Dönitz in later life, states that he had an excellent all-round education including Greek and Latin—which would have been required at the *Gymnasium* he attended in Zerbst—that he was very well-read, possessed a voluminous library, and that his outlook on life was stamped in the Prussian mould; he brought up his boys with a strong sense of their obligations to the State: 'The Monarchy and the German *Reich*, of which

11

Prussia was the core, was affirmed. Young Karl Dönitz grew up in the conviction, as he expressed it, that each citizen had the duty to serve this state.'[7]

Some of the young boy's first vivid memories were of Prussian soldiers. He was five years old, living then in Halensee in what is now a built-up part of West Berlin, but was then separated by sandy fields and pine trees, through which the Kurfürstendamm ran towards the Zoo and the city beyond. The Berlin infantry regiments used this secluded area for training and field exercises, and he often watched them forming line, firing, advancing, storming. One quiet Sunday afternoon here he saw a fairy-tale state coach with retainers in silver livery, and some distance from it the Kaiser and Kaiserin strolling by themselves. 'The Kaiserin had on a lilac dress which I found surprisingly and wonderfully lovely.'[8]

Is this line from his memoirs somehow revealing? Or perhaps he was also captivated, without mentioning it, by the Kaiser's splendid uniform—for it can be assumed confidently that the Kaiser was in uniform. The irreverent said he slept in uniform.

This was about 1897—the precise time that the German monarch was setting the course that shaped twentieth-century Europe and the world. The twentieth century would have taken some frightful turn, there can be little doubt, whatever the Kaiser had done or not done then, for powerful forces were already in motion. They had been set off on the one hand by Bismarck's unification of diverse German-speaking kingdoms and duchies and electorates under the Hohenzollern crown of Branden-burg-Prussia—'those terrible but splendid years'[9]—on the other hand by the 'take-off' of German industry, aided by huge war reparations demanded from France after the last of the Iron Chancellor's three Machiavellian, brilliantly localized wars of unification. On the one hand the Prussian army and Court triumphant, on the other hand German traders and industrialists expansive.

As at all such points of high potential throughout history there was a philosophy at hand—in this case forged from the heroic ethic of the Prussian warrior caste—and sufficient intellectuals and popularizers who would bend to the new wind and create a national will mirroring the attitudes and necessities of the ruling élite. In the case of the German empire created by Bismarck, this national consensus took some time to develop fully for the simple, landlocked view of the Prussians had to be broadened to accommodate the world-wide trading outlook of the new merchant industrialists. At least the attempt had to be made, although it is evident from twentieth-century German history that the soldiers never began to understand the consequences of their changed position. In any case this new Germany of 70 million people was a world power in competition with other world powers and her statesmen were forced to widen their horizons. The first looming object in view was Great Britain, not only the leading trading and colonial nation with a mighty Navy on the 'two power' standard and a world-encircling chain of naval bases, but actually positioned like a giant breakwater across all Germany's routes to the overseas world.

Up until that time Britain had provided German scholars, statesmen and the growing middle classes with a model of individual freedom and constitutional and religious virtue; in the view of the great German historian, Ranke, England had been for centuries the champion of the Protestant-Germanic world, and it was generally agreed, from a study of the languages, that both peoples stemmed from a common 'Aryan' root in India; it was suggested that both had developed their admirable qualities of self-reliance and independence during their migrations.

One practising member of this Germanic cousinly school—in his early days—was the historian Heinrich von Treitschke. 'Admiration is the first feeling which the study of English history calls forth in everyone,'[10] he wrote in the 1850s. In 1874 he succeeded Ranke to the chair of history at the University of Berlin. By that time his views had undergone a radical change exactly paralleling the changed position of Imperial Germany; now he saw that all the time England had been using the Germans shamelessly as continental foils for her own greedy ends and passing off this 'sly and violent policy of commercial self-interest' as a 'heroic fight for the ultimate good of humanity'.[11] The term 'Germanic' had disappeared from his vocabulary, replaced by rival 'Anglo-Saxon' and 'Teutonic' cultures. With the years he grew more extreme, adding anti-semitism to his anti-British stance, roaring out his message to packed audiences composed of military and naval men and civil servants as well as students at the University.

Treitschke was the shock trooper of what came to be dubbed 'the Kaiser's intellectual regiment of Guards'; he was the first to turn so thoroughly against England, the most violently emotional and, from his prestigious position in the Imperial capital, the most influential; above all he told the Prussian ruling caste what it wished to hear, translating their stern creed into historical and fashionable evolutionary terms, and raising their recent conquests and the compulsions that stemmed from these successes into a mystical life-force.

> Unceasingly history builds and destroys; it never tires of salvaging the divine goods of mankind from the ruins of old worlds into a new one. Who believes in this infinite growth, in the eternal youth of our race, must acknowledge the unalterable necessity of war . . .[12]

And echoing the inevitable trend of philosophic thought in a nation such as Prussia, without natural barriers and surrounded by enemies, with only its own discipline and cohesion on which to rely:

> Among the thousands who march into battle and humbly obey the will of the whole, each one knows how beggarly little his life counts beside the glory of the State, he feels himself surrounded by the workings of inscrutable powers . . . Men kill each other who have great respect for each other as chivalrous foes. They sacrifice to duty not only their life, they sacrifice what matters more, their natural feelings, their instinctive love of mankind, their horror of blood. Their little ego with all its noble and evil impulses must disappear in the will of the whole . . .[13]

Treitschke died in 1896. By that time the new consensus had formed. It was popularly described as '*Weltpolitik*' or world policy, and while it could mean many different things to different enthusiasts, the idea in essentials was to build a great fleet to give Germany power in the larger world—in other words to rival the British fleet—so that she could win colonies, spread German *Kultur* and support her traders and manufacturers against the jealousy and active ill-will of Great Britain. While naturally appealing to the commercial community, this policy of overseas aggrandizement was also designed—perhaps primarily designed—to draw the people's attention away from internal strains and by overseas success to create a national pride and spirit which would overcome the particularist tendencies in the various kingdoms and duchies so recently incorporated into the *Reich*, unite the middle classes, who were traditionally liberal and independent, under the Prussian-Hohenzollern yoke, and by increasing prosperity entice the growing urban proletariat from the 'ensnarements' of Marxism as represented by the rapidly growing Social Democratic Party.

In 1897 this new course was set. The two key figures appointed by the

14

Kaiser that year were both disciples of Treitschke; they were Bernhard von Bülow to be the new Foreign Minister, and Rear Admiral Alfred Tirpitz to be State Secretary of the Naval Office, responsible for naval building and manoeuvring the necessary budget through the *Reichstag*. He was to build the fleet, Bülow was to nurse Germany through the 'danger zone' that must ensue once the British divined his intention and before the fleet was strong enough to resist a pre-emptive strike. As Bülow put it, 'in view of our naval inferiority, we must operate so carefully, like the caterpillar before it has grown into the butterfly'.[14]

The policy had too many internal and external contradictions to succeed; the one which had the most immediate impact on the young Karl Dönitz was the need for a tremendous publicity campaign to explain to the German people, land-bound as most of them were, just why they needed a great Navy and colonies and all the apparatus of *Weltpolitik*. In a way this was the greatest contradiction of all, for it alerted the potential enemies inside and outside the country, and for the Treitschkian protagonists made the 'danger zone' frighteningly immediate. Nevertheless, the German people had to be aroused to their world destiny, and Bülow and Tirpitz set about the task with such skill and energy and achieved such success that it was not long before they were trying to restrain the effusions of Pan-Germans, Colonialists and others who had run too far ahead of them.

A modern scholar, Paul Kennedy, has examined this ideological nexus of *Weltpolitik*; he concludes that it bound virtually all who had an influence on German thought, economists, hyper-patriotic Pan-German professors 'who foretold the coming mastery of the German race in the world', colonial enthusiasts, promulgators of the racial theories of Houston Stewart Chamberlain and Legarde, 'who "scientifically" demonstrated the superiority of the Germanic spirit', and was broadcast by all the institutions of the State:

. . . the schools which ceaselessly proclaimed—on the orders of the Prussian Ministry for Education and Religious Affairs—the blessings which all Germans derived from the Hohenzollern monarchy and the need for obedience and patriotism; the universities, whose leading professors, far from being 'above politics', actively commented upon the economic, social and political trends of the day; the Churches—and in particular the Lutheran Church—which preached respect for State authority, distrust of Socialism and an acceptance of one's place

15

in the social order; the patriotic pressure groups like the Navy League, Defence League, Colonial Society and Pan-German League, which together with organizations such as the veterans' associations, also preached the twin messages of domestic unity and external glory; and finally the Press, the greater part of which . . . offered a daily reiteration of the same message.[15]

Such was the atmosphere in which young Karl Dönitz grew; it was as natural to him and he absorbed it as naturally as the oxygen from the air he breathed. It formed a part of the matrix of his brain as fundamental in sparking the paths of his conscious thought as language itself, at the same time providing a focus for his emotional needs, which were great.

In April at the age of six and a half, he went to a preparatory school outside Halensee in a highly fashionable suburb on the edge of the forest known as 'Kolonie Grunewald'. It was known as the millionaires' suburb. Its ostentation belied an official ethic of Spartan selflessness and duty to the State; it was representative of the other half of the German drive—thoroughly despised by the true Prussian officer—which had already turned the formerly austere capital of the Hohenzollerns into 'the most American of European cities'. The dichotomy would not have been apparent to the young Karl Dönitz.

He was only at the school for six months, after which his father was posted to the headquarters of his firm at Jena on the upper reaches of the Saale in the Duchy of Saxony-Weimar. Here was a different Germany, moving at a more leisurely pace. No motors or electric tramcars in the winding streets within the medieval walls of the town nor even gaslight or electricity. Students from the university sauntered from picturesque, timbered houses bedecked with the banners of the different collegiate societies. And outside the gates was a beautiful prospect of wooded hills crowned with towers, testimony to the comparatively recent border warfare between Germans and Slavs. The Dönitzs' house looked out on this splendid view from halfway up a hill aptly named Sonnenberg. 'From morning to evening the south-facing rooms of our house had sun. The view stretched over Jena up the Saale valley to distant Leuchtenburg. Never again in my life was I to live with such a beautiful prospect.'[16]

He and his brother attended the *Realschule*, known as the Stoy'scher after its formidable director, Professor Stoy, who ruled both the public

16

Realschule and an attached boarding department as an absolute monarch. On their first day the Director himself conducted the two boys round, showing them sketches of the old town which adorned the walls and, when they came to engravings of the famous Battle of Jena in 1806 and incidents from the subsequent war of liberation, explaining the scenes to the boys. Karl was thinking what a very genial director he was when they arrived at a cast relief of Bismarck. Immediately the Professor asked his brother who that was. Friedrich had heard a great deal from their father about the great man but failed to recognize the features in the bronze relief. Suddenly angry, Professor Stoy shouted, '*What!* You do not know the greatest German!' and dismissed them coolly.

It is an instructive vignette.

Despite this unscholarly worship of a man whose only morality was power and, like the majority in his influential station, pressing his contributions towards the corruption of Germany, and tragedy in the twentieth century, Professor Stoy ran a splendid school, as it appears from the recollections of Karl Dönitz, one of those who suffered and had to learn a very elementary lesson about the corrupting effects of power very late in life amongst blood, bereavement and ruin.

The school rooms were lofty and bright with many pictures on the walls; each class of the younger pupils had a garden and each boy his own flower bed to dig and sow and delight in the miracle of spring and beauty. Twice a week they had singing instruction, learning children's and folk songs which Karl Dönitz enjoyed enormously; if in later life he heard one of these songs it brought back his childhood pleasure. They learnt about Jena and its history in a practical way, measuring old walls or foundations and working their results up into plans; every year on the anniversary of the Battle of Jena they made a visit to the battlefield after being taken enthusiastically through every tactical detail on maps in the classroom during the previous week. Twice a year they made trips to places of interest, the younger boys spending eight days in the Thuringian hills, visiting Roman ruins and other sites of cultural and scenic value.

All in all the Stoy'scher school sounds a model institution, broadening its pupils' minds by engaging their interest and enthusiasm. Certainly in the school and outside in the small community of Jena which revolved around the university and the firm for which his father worked, Dönitz enjoyed a variety of activities: he played the flute in a youthful orchestra—his brother the violin—attended an art class each Wednesday afternoon in an artist's studio, visited art exhibitions and lectures with

17

lantern slides—several on African, Asian and Polar travel and exploration, no doubt funded by one or other of the societies promoting Germany's place in the wider world—and took part in the fairs and other traditional functions of Jena society.

For their summer holidays every year Emil Dönitz took the two boys to the lonely North Sea island of Baltrum, which they had first visited after the death of their mother. The only inhabitants were a few families of fishermen and sailors who lived in cottages with hayloft and sheep pens under the same roof. They were simple holidays spent strolling in the dunes, investigating wrack washed up on the shore, swimming, boating, lying listening to the rustle of the wind in the spiky grass and the murmur of the sands under the tow of the ever-present sea—or, when the weather changed, thrilling to the roar of the breakers and the spray flying under lowering clouds. On Sundays they attended the small, unadorned, whitewashed chapel with the local men in their best suits and their wives in Friesian costume. The services always ended with a traditional 'God bless our shore!'

At the western end of the island was a small cemetery planted with simple wooden crosses; Dönitz recorded in his memoirs how he loved to lie 'in the peace and sublimity of this place with the bell of the heavens over the flat land' and the view to the dunes and the 'majestic plane of the sea stretching to the distant horizon'.[17]

In September 1908 the Dönitzes moved to the city of Weimar some 20 miles from Jena. Karl Dönitz provides no reason for the move, but since there was a railway connecting the two places, since his father had by now risen in the Zeiss firm to 'scientific colleague', and his elder brother had left school to join the merchant marine,[18] since the twenty-mile displacement from a town in which they were well known and had lived for ten years meant a change of school for Karl at the age of seventeen, it seems reasonable to conclude that the move was *in order* to change his school; it may be that his father or the masters at the Stoy'scher academy considered his intelligence such that he would benefit from the greater scope of the *Gymnasium* at Weimar. That is speculation. The facts as related by Dönitz in his memoirs are that the Stoy'scher taught neither Latin nor Greek but the *Realgymnasium* at Weimar demanded classics and his father informed him that he would have to learn sufficient Latin in private study after school to satisfy the requirements. 'I was literally speechless at first when I received this paternal instruction, seeing a

18

mountain of work before me which seemed to me to be impossible to surmount.'[19]

However, he performed so well in the entrance exam without Latin that the *Gymnasium* admitted him on the condition that he took the Latin paper in six months' time. Practically every day throughout that first autumn and winter in Weimar he crammed the subject in the private rooms of one or another of the *Gymnasium* teachers after school while keeping up with his normal homework in the evenings. He took the paper at Easter 1909 and passed, but recorded in his memoirs that any mention of Latin in later life brought back 'the pressure of those six months of forced learning'.[20]

Weimar had been the home and workplace of Goethe and Schiller, and naturally the *Gymnasium* placed special emphasis on these giants of German literature. The adolescent Dönitz responded with ardour, founding a literary society among half a dozen classmates in his new form. Meanwhile his interest in art, aroused at Jena, was fed by an optional class which he took in the history of art, and he also continued an interest in the fashionable subjects of geology and palaeontology, making excursions to collect rock samples and fossils. One has the impression of a reserved, even withdrawn, youth responding earnestly to the influence of his elders, father, teachers, artists, and committing himself wholly to each enthusiasm. Perhaps this is a back-projection from what is known of his adult life—but perhaps it is not too wide of the mark.

Two things can be said with fair certainty: he was intelligent—not in the highest class of creative intelligence, but with an agile, retentive mind and first-rate ability in expression; and he worked unsparingly at his studies. When it came to taking his *Abitur*, which might loosely be compared to English 'A' level exams, he submitted the best composition on a section of Goethe's verse in the whole school; a harbinger of his later terse reports and memoranda, it was—so he claims, having been told by the Director—'certainly the shortest but also the best, that is to say the clearest and most logical'.[21]

So at eighteen and a half, he came to the end of his schooldays. Half a century later he looked back nostalgically to the 'abundance of experience and stimulation' he had enjoyed in this 'lovely heartland of Germany with its beauty, history and high cultural tradition'.[22]

When he decided he would like to join the Navy is not clear; his stated reasons included a longing to emulate the feats of explorers like Nansen, von Wissmann and Sven Hedin—whose books he read 'with glowing spirits'—and pride in the Bismarckian *Kaiserreich* and a veneration for soldiership 'that lay apparently in my blood';[23] the Navy seemed to offer an ideal combination of travel and the military life. These 'reasons', however, are no more than a reflection of the spirit of Imperial Germany at that date and of Tirpitz's naval propaganda.

The Army was the senior service—until Tirpitz's appointment virtually the only service in Germany. It was the natural destination for sons of the nobility and the higher civil service grades, and consequently the Navy, expanding at a great pace, had to mount extraordinary campaigns to attract suitable officer candidates and had to seek them amongst the middle classes, the new rich merchants and industrialists, and the academics especially. These, for their part, eagerly grasped at the opportunity to wear the Emperor's uniform and cultivate the attitudes and distinguishing signs of the nobility of the sword, for these, not wealth, were the marks of social class and masculinity. Thus were the *nouveaux* and the upper-middle classes, formerly liberal in outlook and looking to England for their attitudes, feudalized and Prussianized—a most satisfactory outcome for the Kaiser whose loyal knights they became, for the Navy which achieved a homogeneous officer corps, and for the new officers and their families anxious for their sons to climb the caste ladder.

This is particularly relevant in Dönitz's case, for in social terms he probably only just made the grade. It is significant that his elder brother had joined the merchant marine which entirely lacked the *cachet* of the arms-bearing services, very significant that he nowhere mentions this fact, even when discussing his own reasons for joining the Navy.

His education qualified him for entry; the decision to admit him or not rested with the Sea Cadet Entrance Commission, which deliberated in private without minutes or necessity to reveal its reasons, basing its judgements on social and financial grounds from information provided by local magistrates, police agencies, district military Commanders and the schools themselves.[24] *Kleine Leute*—the lower-middle and artisan classes—were rejected in nearly all cases, although a few were allowed through the net as a deliberate policy to answer criticism in the *Reichstag*. Any hint of socialist contacts or leanings in the family background, however, operated an automatic bar. Jews were also barred although one or two were taken provided they were both baptized and wealthy—usually members of the so-called 'millionaires' club'. Income was an important factor for everyone; when Karl Dönitz was a candidate in 1910 the parental contribution was calculated at 1,505 Marks in the first year—some 200 Marks above the average industrial wage—and rather over 1,000 Marks for each of the succeeding three years of training, followed by 600 Marks' annual allowance for the next four years as a junior lieutenant in order to keep up the style of an officer—altogether over 7,000 Marks.[25]

Dönitz's father evidently passed the social and financial examination, and on April 1st 1910 Karl reported to Kiel to enter the *Kaiserliche Marine* as a Sea Cadet. There were 206 other lads in this intake or 'crew'; almost half were sons of senior academics—an astonishing proportion and an illustration of how the professorial class had swung their weight behind *Weltpolitik*. A further 26 of the lads were from noble families, nearly all from the lower, usually impoverished and sometimes questionable nobility; a few were the sons of non-noble officers and landowners; 37 had a merchant or industrial background; and 32 came, like Dönitz himself, from other middle-class backgrounds.[26] There was one baptized Jew in this crew and no doubt one or two statutory *Kleine Leute*.

Karl Dönitz entered into his new environment with enthusiasm, so it appears from his Memoirs, from the very beginning: 'How interesting, almost enrapturing was Kiel harbour, where at weekends warships, battleships and cruisers lay at the buoys. How interesting the long mole at Kiel-Wik where on working days torpedo boats lay alongside and cast off . . .'[27] He wrote these recollections late in life, lonely after a series of personal tragedies, and dwelling, according to one discerning visitor, 'increasingly in his wonderful past'.[28] But what sailor in old age does not look back to the innocent days of youth when shared expectation of adventure and new lands and the first indescribable smells of ships and salt-water return sharp-edged and glowing again in the imagination? Certainly for Dönitz the impact of his service initiation by a Spartan regime of infantry drill and hardening physical training in Kiel shone 'in altogether beautiful memory'.[29]

After six weeks acquiring a soldier-like bearing the cadets were sent to schoolships: Dönitz and 54 others went to the training cruiser *Hertha*. Here, during a cruise to the Mediterranean, they learnt the basic sailors' skills practically about the ship and in the boats, also acquiring a grounding in navigation, gunnery and engineroom practice—and spending three debilitating weeks stoking the boilers. It was a strenuous regime deliberately made in the nature of an ordeal. They had to learn in just over ten months what officers in the Royal Navy, who entered at thirteen, picked up over five years. At times they were worked close to the limits of their strength. 'Thus we had opportunity to test and prove ourselves and so gain a better knowledge of ourselves. God be thanked that it was so.'[30]

In such a forcing school comradeship is strong. Dönitz had already struck up a friendship with a cadet who stood next to him in the ranks when they fell in for the initial infantry training. Now they were in the same division and they became inseparable, according to Dönitz, sharing identical attitudes to their new life and their fellow cadets, working together, going ashore together. The youth was Hugo, Freiherr von Lamezan from a Bavarian family descended at some distance from the French nobility.

The two could scarcely have been more dissimilar: Dönitz reserved, deeply earnest, tight-lipped, the younger son of an aspiring father who had brought him up to the stern necessity for hard work and stamped him with the particularist arrogance—to use Karl Dönitz's own phrase—of the North German, in fact Prussian, habit of mind, and von Lamezan, the aristocrat from the more easy-going south, whose darker complexion and features indicated the Latin blood that had mixed with the German in his forebears. Many deep friendships are cemented in just such contrasts. So it was with Dönitz and von Lamezan.

The officers placed in charge of the cadets had a great influence in this strenuously formative introduction to the service. The *Hertha* cadets were fortunate, according to Dönitz, in having first-rate officers, the senior of whom he described as 'a model of quiet, superior, cultured behaviour'.[31] These not only supervised the training but sought to inculcate the ethos and standards of the service. Personal decency, appearance and bearing, Dönitz wrote, were accorded the highest priority, and it is true this was perhaps the most important part of the cadet officers' task, for it has to be stressed the Imperial Navy was very much the junior service, a *parvenu*, and exhibited all the characteristics of the *parvenu*. The compulsions of its officers were to be in attitude and conduct more noble than the nobility of the sword, in professional matters more professional than the officers of the Royal Navy, originally its professional model. Therefore each batch of chiefly middle-class, chiefly North German, but otherwise rather heterogeneous cadets from all regions of the empire had to be pressed into a common mould.

Asked in later life what was the fundamental principle of his training as a sea officer, Dönitz replied that it had been 'the Kantian principle of the Categorical Imperative . . . duty fulfilment was the highest moral value'.[32] No doubt this answer, written after the Nuremberg war crimes trials, was consciously or unconsciously as concerned with his defence—'duty'—as with his training as a cadet. The same can be inferred from his concern to record the decency and fairness with which the naval cadets were brought up. 'Next to the principle of duty fulfilment and bound up with it was the demand for decency, thus to do nothing that offended against the *moral* basis of good behaviour.' And he wrote that he could think back with gratitude to the training and example given by his two sea cadet officers and 'still today with a quiet, sure satisfaction have the feeling: it was all good, as it was managed and as it turned out'.[33]

It turned out a disaster from almost every point of view except perhaps narrow and specialized efficiency. More valuable for any study of German naval training of the period, and more interesting so far as his own character-formation is concerned, is what he failed to reveal in his memoirs: he stressed the extraordinary physical demands made on the cadets but not the brutal punishments still in vogue and practised particularly on the cabin boys, the nucleus of the future petty officer corps, who were also trained in these schoolships. Flogging was still common, and for minor breaches of the regulations cabin boys were still tied to the mast.[34]

Nor, of course, did he describe the conscious drive to foster social exclusiveness in the naval officer corps by stamping the cadets with the style of the Prussian Army officer; this meant adopting a harsh, high, rather nasal barking, a deliberately crude, often ungrammatical mode of speech, a prickly concern for personal and caste honour—the duel, the Kaiser's consent to marry, the Court of Honour to try breaches of the code of chivalry—particularly with regard to the duel and relationships with unsuitable women!—and on board ship insistence on exaggerated marks of deference from specialist officers, petty officers and ratings to the person of the élite executive officer. Perhaps he did not mention these marks of overweening exclusiveness because they were the very things that later blew up in the Imperial naval officers' faces.

Another significant omission was his failure to mention the tense and extraordinary relationship of the Imperial Navy towards Great Britain.

On the one hand the officers of the Royal Navy were respected as blood brothers; as Grand Admiral Prince Henry of Prussia remarked to the British naval attaché, 'other large European nations are not "white men"'—a sentiment with which the attaché entirely concurred: 'His Royal Highness voiced in a peculiarly British way a view that is very prevalent in our own service.'[35] On the other hand, the Imperial Navy was being consciously and very strenuously prepared for *der Tag*, the day of reckoning when the younger, more virile, harder-working, more efficient German Navy, riding the tide of history—as defined by Treitschke—would wrest the trident from the ageing mistress of the seas in a great battle in the North Sea.

None of the cadets could have been unaware of this relationship. The battleship-building competition which Tirpitz had set in motion in 1897 had become the central issue in the external and internal affairs of the *Reich*—quite apart from its dramatic impact on naval affairs. It had forced England to react, first by securing an alliance with Japan and an *Entente* with her traditional rival France, enabling her to bring her battlefleets home from the Far East and the Mediterranean to face the growing German fleet in the North Sea, second by building superior battleships known after the name of the first as 'Dreadnoughts' and forcing Tirpitz into a qualitative as well as a numerical race. This had increased the financial stakes hugely, indeed exponentially, for the Royal Navy stepped up the size with each new class laid down and Tirpitz had to respond or drop out of the competition.

He had no intention of dropping out, and the Kaiser, his master, had no intention of allowing the British to dictate to him what size his Navy should be; consequently the fleet was increasingly built on borrowed money and the national debt and the taxes required to service the debt rose alarmingly. This had the opposite effect on the workers to that originally intended; it also re-opened the natural rift between the traditional land-owning Junkers and the new merchant-industrial class. In short, it had become thoroughly counter-productive, decreasing Germany's freedom of movement in international affairs, drawing Great Britain into the alliance, 'encircling' and seeking to control her growing might, and seriously deepening the tensions within the *Reich*. So much was this the case that in Dönitz's cadet year, 1910, the leader of the Social Democrats, August Bebel, took the extraordinary step of opening a clandestine correspondence with the British Foreign Office to alert them to the dangers.

Though a Prussian myself by birth, I consider Prussia a dreadful state from which nothing but dreadful things may be expected; this England is sure to experience sooner than most people think. To reform Prussia is impossible, it will remain the *Junkerstaat* it is at present or go to pieces altogether . . . I cannot understand what the British governments and people are about in letting Germany creeping [sic] up to them so closely in naval armaments . . .

I am convinced we are on the eve of the most dreadful war Europe has ever seen. Things cannot go on as at present, the burden of the military charges are crushing people and the Kaiser and the government are fully alive to the fact. Everything works for a great crisis in Germany . . .[36]

The failure of the naval policy was plain by now to many in government circles, including von Bülow. But the Kaiser could not be deterred from building his magnificent fleet while Tirpitz—now ennobled—had his gaze fixed on a distant goal which even August Bebel had not fully discerned, and which was so fantastic as to cast serious doubt on his sanity. It was nothing less than a giant battlefleet of 60 ships, each with a lifespan of 20 years *fixed by law*, thus an unalterable building 'tempo' of three great ships a year, which the *Reichstag* would not be able to interfere with! His external goal was to neutralize the Royal Navy, his internal goal to emasculate the *Reichstag*![37]

So the great naval race was destined to continue, the taxes to rise, the Socialists and the Junkers to become more entrenched in their opposition, until the crisis in the *Reich* became unmanageable by peaceful means—while on the other side of the North Sea the British became ever more certain that the great fleet could only be for use against the Royal Navy.

This was the background to Dönitz's training years, the looming struggle with the Royal Navy and the deepening crisis and polarization inside the Bismarckian *Kaiserreich*, to which he was bound both by the moral imperative and by sentiment. As the British naval attaché reported in the same year, 1910, 'The whole Navy without exception are absolutely devoted to HM [the Kaiser], not only as their Emperor but also particularly in a personal sense.'[38]

Two years earlier another British naval attaché had reported on the anti-English feeling that it had been necessary to create in Germany in order to obtain funds for the fleet; this feeling had now grown so out of hand that he doubted whether the Kaiser 'much as he might desire it, could restrain his own people from attempting to wrest the command of the sea from Britain if they saw a fairly good chance of doing so'. He concluded his report:

I believe that at the bottom of every German's heart today is rising a faint and wildly exhilarating hope that a glorious day is approaching when by a brave breaking through of the lines which he feels are encircling him, he might even wrest command of the seas from England and thus become a member of the greatest power by land and sea the world has ever seen.[39]

This was the vision that animated the Imperial Navy; it would be surprising indeed if the young Karl Dönitz remained unaffected by the approach to 'der Tag'!

Of the influences about which he did write, probably the most important was the navigating officer of the Hertha, von Loewenfeld; he was a strong, highly individual character with a wide range of interests who was not afraid of unorthodox methods if the circumstances seemed to him to demand them. Later, in the chaos to which Germany was reduced after the First World War, Loewenfeld was one of those who formed a Freikorps of loyalist officers and men to fight against the anarchic Communist bands, which he put down with complete ruthlessness. There is no doubt that Dönitz hero-worshipped him, while he thought highly of the eager and capable cadet; indeed it is probable Dönitz was his favourite.

Halfway through this first year, while the cruiser lay off the turreted walls of Tangier, the cadets were examined in the professional knowledge they had gained. Dönitz came equal second.[40] He recorded in his memoirs that first place went to Helmut Patzig, but did not mention that Patzig later distinguished himself as a U-boat Commander in the war by gunning down surviving doctors and nurses from a hospital ship he had torpedoed. The three top cadets were included in an invitation to the officers from the German Embassy where they were provided with horses and taken on 'an unforgettably beautiful' ride along the coast to Cape Spartel.

Three other shore excursions from the Hertha remained sharp and delightful in his memory when he came to write his memoirs. For the most part, though, it was unrelenting work, and they returned home

26

after the ten-month voyage with hands made callous from much boat-pulling and physical work and the good feeling that they had passed through a stern apprenticeship and become sailors. They had also had many corners knocked off; in Dönitz's words, 'the egocentricity [*Ichsucht*] of each, the human tendency to regard oneself as the most important, was dampened through the necessity in a community to show consideration for others'.[41] This is an interesting observation from Dönitz, since his later career showed that if the flames of his ego really had been dampened, they were by no means extinguished.

Leave and promotion to *Fähnrich zur See* (midshipman) followed the completion of the training ship voyage. Dönitz went to stay with Hugo von Lamezan in Munich and when they returned after their leave they shared the same four-berth room in the Navy School at Flensburg-Mürwik on the coast of Schleswig-Holstein which was to be their home for the next year. Here the training was almost entirely theoretical, the main subjects navigation and seamanship, which included naval regulations; they also learned engineering, gunnery, mining, hydraulics, mathematics, shipbuilding, ship recognition and had an hour a week of English and French. Dönitz and von Lamezan sat next to each other in all the classes.

It was once again a strict regime, drinking, smoking and making music banned inside the grounds, and outside drinking only permitted at inns used by the officer corps. The same went for the choice of seats at theatres and concerts. They had acquired their sea legs and their introduction to the officer class; now they were at their finishing school. In order to ensure they lacked none of the requisite accomplishments, they were given instruction in fencing, horse-riding and dancing. Dönitz did not mention any of these activities, nor duelling, which was officially approved despite many questions in the *Reichstag*, but records that he and von Lamezan bought a 'National Jolly' dinghy between them and sailed it at weekends.

He did not enjoy the Navy School as much as the *Hertha* since, he wrote, the instruction was so theoretical, and in the final exams at the end of the year came 39th, a disappointing position which he put down to his insufficient knowledge of the service rules and regulations; they were in the service handbooks and he had thought it unnecessary to learn them.

From the school in the early summer of 1912 the midshipmen passed on to specialized courses in gunnery, torpedo work and infantry exer-

27

cises, in which he did rather better. It was during this period on June 23rd 1912, that his father died, apparently in Jena. Dönitz's elder brother was training for the naval reserve at this time and the two young men arranged for their father's funeral on the island of Baltrum which he had loved. Whether this was his wish or a touching act of sentiment by the brothers is not clear. They followed the coffin borne by fishermen through the lonely cemetery past the plain wooden crosses marked with the names of the island families. 'Today,' he wrote late in life, 'my father's grave and my most wonderful youthful memories are joined.'[42]

For the final year of their training the midshipmen served aboard sea-going ships of the fleet. Dönitz was appointed to the modern light cruiser, *Breslau*—a disappointment since his appetite for travel had been whetted and she belonged to the Home Fleet. Waiting on the pier at Kiel to join her, and no doubt gazing out across the harbour to the low, four-funnelled silhouette, he found von Loewenfeld beside him, and learned that he was the cruiser's First Officer.

'Are you glad,' the great man asked, using the familiar and for a midshipman most flattering '*du*', 'to have been posted to me in the *Breslau*? I applied for you.'

'No, *Herr Kapitänleutnant*,' Dönitz replied. 'I wanted to go to the Far East in the cruiser squadron.'

'Ungrateful toad!'[43]

So began a posting which was of great importance for Dönitz in a number of ways. For it turned out the cruiser was despatched to the Mediterranean and he was able to enjoy a culturally and socially broadening life very different from that he would have experienced in the Home Fleet, whose officers lived at the few northern bases in closed societies no different from those of garrison regiments in provincial towns, where monotony manifested itself in excessive drinking, indebtedness and petty disputation over rank and status.

Similarly in professional matters, he obtained a far wider experience and many more opportunities to exercise initiative and judgement than would have come his way in the fleet. Also as a protégé of his idol, von Loewenfeld, his natural ability was fostered in a demanding, often unconventional but rewarding atmosphere. The first officer's confidence in him was revealed immediately he reported to the Captain, von Klitzing, for he was given the important and for an inexperienced *Fähnrich* unusual post of signals officer. This was a particularly significant assignment in a scouting cruiser in those days of the infancy of wireless telegraphy, and says more for the opinion von Loewenfeld had formed of him than a written report. Late in life he could still recall his horror when he was told of his assignment, especially when he learned he had just five weeks to prepare himself for large-scale fleet exercises. He was spared this test at the last moment; war broke out in the Balkans and the *Breslau* was despatched to the Mediterranean to uphold Germany's interests in company with the new battlecruiser, *Goeben*.

This was splendid news for the crew, and Dönitz when he heard the announcement so far forgot his reserve as to launch himself jubilantly at von Loewenfeld's side; the first officer, as pleased as he, overlooked the indiscipline. They embarked stores, coal and ammunition hurriedly overnight and sailed early the next morning.

A few days and they were in milder southern weather, passing Gibraltar, the British lion couchant guarding the entrance to the middle sea; soon afterwards they were steaming through the narrows of Valletta harbour, Malta, to replenish bunkers at this British fortress commanding the centre of the strategic board. What, one wonders, were Dönitz's thoughts as from his mooring station aft he gazed up at the formidable stone walls and battlements sparkling in the clear air and saw inside the basin the White Ensigns blowing from the jacks of the lines of warships of the British Mediterranean Fleet? He would have had more than a passing acquaintance with British naval history; it was studied with some fascination in the German service; Tirpitz and von Bülow had spent a great deal of the first decade of the century mesmerized by the 1807 Battle of Copenhagen when the British fleet had wiped out the Danish Navy in a pre-emptive strike without declaring war—and which the British First Sea Lord, Fisher, had been prepared to repeat, so it was believed, on the German Navy before it grew too large. 'Lord Fisher of Copenhagen' was the name he enjoyed in Berlin and Kiel.

Now a more serious danger threatened. It had been clarified by the very events in the Balkans which had brought the *Goeben* and *Breslau* racing out to the Mediterranean. For the fighting threatened to draw in Austria-Hungary against Serbia; Serbia was supported by Russia; Russia was in alliance with France, and as Germany was bound to support her ally, Austria, the great European war was only one rash step away. While the *Breslau*, after filling her bunkers in Grand Harbour, was on her way to the trouble spot, the German Ambassador in London was informed that in the event of the Balkans war spreading to the great powers, Britain would find it impossible to remain neutral; she had formed links with France and Russia and she would come in on their side. The Ambassador sent a report of the interview to Berlin. The Kaiser erupted, scribbling impetuously in the margin, 'The final struggle between the Slavs and Teutons will see the Anglo-Saxons on the side of the Slavs and Gauls!'[44] And he summoned his naval and military chiefs to a meeting at the Palace. This was not the goal he had sought when the new course had been set in 1897, but it was an inevitable way-station which should have been foreseen: Great Britain was bound by her vital interest to intervene if it seemed the balance of Europe would be altered; now the direct threat posed by Tirpitz's fleet made it certain she *would* intervene. Yet the fleet was not remotely strong enough to influence the course of events—nor could it ever be without bankrupting the nation.

This was recognized by the Army, jealous and annoyed at the vast sums that had already been lavished on Tirpitz. In the fateful meeting that took place in the Palace at Potsdam that December 12th 1912, General von Moltke, Chief of the Great General Staff, called for war: war was unavoidable in the long run, therefore now was the time to strike before France or Russia could complete their preparations. Tirpitz objected that the Navy was not ready; he would prefer a postponement for eighteen months when the widening of the Kaiser Wilhelm Canal for dreadnoughts and the U-boat base in Heligoland would both be complete. 'The Navy will not be ready even then!' Moltke retorted contemptuously. 'War! The sooner the better!'[45]

The Kaiser was no Bismarck; besides, the fleet was a factor that Bismarck had never had to reckon with. He was, however, an absolute monarch in all but name. The constitution he had inherited had been devised by Bismarck to fragment power and concentrate it all in his person, while giving the appearance of a democratic apparatus of lower and upper houses of parliament. In practice the elected lower house, the *Reichstag*, had only limited blocking functions—although too much for Tirpitz's peace of mind—and could initiate nothing, and the upper house, the *Bundestag*, was controlled by Prussia. The Kaiser was King of Prussia and made the key appointments in his kingdom as, under his imperial crown, he made the key appointments in the government of the *Reich*; moreover, as Commander in Chief of the armed forces he made the key appointments in the Army and Navy, both of which were answerable to him alone, not to the civil government, nor to a defence committee of any kind. Tirpitz was one such appointment and it was entirely due to the Kaiser's support that he had been able to distort the finances and the internal and external relationships of the *Reich* to such an alarming extent against the opposition of the Army and—since it had been realized what his policy was leading to—against successive governments. Now the Kaiser was faced with the consequences.

He was incapable of dealing with them. Whether anyone could have controlled the Bismarckian *Kaiserreich* at this potent stage in its development may be doubted; one thing is certain: Kaiser Wilhelm II was not the man.

During his childhood he had been alternately spoilt by his mother, Queen Victoria's daughter, 'Vicky', and tortured by doctors trying to compensate for a tilt to his neck, lack of balance and a deformed arm, while his education had been entrusted to a humourless tutor who had sought to instil with a pitiless regime of work just those 'Prussian' virtues in which Dönitz had been grounded, hard work, self-denial, duty. Earnestly as the tutor had worked, he found the boy unable to concentrate on any subject; he had a lively intelligence and a good memory but his mind flitted. He also showed alarming inclinations to selfishness, vanity, autocracy, traits which his mother had also sadly noted, so it was decided to send him to school to mix with other boys. Far from having the ego knocked out of him, the young Prince had found that he could use his position and a natural aptitude for telling amusing stories to enhance his self-esteem. Meanwhile Bismarck was also shamelessly playing up to his vanity in an attempt to sever him from the dangerously liberal influences of his mother, 'the English Princess'.

From school he travelled the Hohenzollern monarch's inevitable path to the First Regiment of Guards at Potsdam, the vaunting stronghold of all that was most swaggeringly masculine and Prussian, thus most autocratic and most alien to all the ideals his over-zealous mother had tried to instil in him. It is scarcely surprising that he emerged, to all appearances a monster of grotesque vainglory; in fact he lived much of his time in an interior world of Teutonic myth and suffered complete nervous prostration when real events forced themselves in upon him.

The outside world saw only a wilful braggart at the head of what had become the mightiest nation in Europe, one which, in his own inimitable idiom, sought its 'rightful place in the sun' and was prepared to use its 'mailed fist' to get there.

The reality was even more dangerous. Wilhelm was still incapable of concentration, his mind still flitted as it had as a boy; he could memorize details of things that interested him, particularly specifications of all the world's warships culled from *Jane's Fighting Ships*, with a virtuosity that amazed all, and he could tell amusing Irish stories very well all night. But he was incapable of making any synthesis of his store of largely useless information or the signals entering his command post from the different interest groups within the *Reich*. Consequently he was incapable of making coherent policy decisions and sticking to them; he was constantly swayed by whim, vanity and the latest flatterer who caught his ear. The result was that what appeared from the outside to be the most dynamic and highly organized industrial nation in Europe was actually under no supreme command.[46]

This was epitomized in the result of the meeting of December 12th 1912. The civil government was not represented, the Army wanted an immediate Bismarckian war, the Navy was rightly alarmed at such a prospect, and Wilhelm, his vanity outraged by Great Britain once again setting him limits, and in any case compelled to play the compensatory role of 'All-highest' war lord, ordered not war—for that would have been real—but every preparation for war in the near future. Bills were to be prepared for increases in the Army and Navy, plans to be laid by both services for the invasion of England; the Foreign Ministry was to seek alliances wherever it could, the Press to prepare the people, warning them of the imminence of a Slavic invasion so that when it came to the day, they would know what they were fighting for.

Whether, as could be argued, this was a decision for war in eighteen months' time—summer 1914—when dreadnought battleships would be able to traverse the Kiel Canal, or whether it was just another act in Wilhelm's private theatre, is not important; the consequences were beyond measure. It not only violently increased the speed at which the *Reich* was moving towards collision with the rival powers, it convinced the Army which wanted to be convinced that war had indeed been decided on. The Army demanded and succeeded in obtaining the largest peacetime increase in its history, and—as contemptuous of the new enemy, Great Britain, as of the Navy which had brought Great Britain into the ring—finalized its plans for the continental war on two fronts.

In the meantime the Foreign Ministry joined in the great-power diplomacy to contain the immediate Balkan crisis. Such was the position as the *Breslau* joined an international naval squadron giving effect to diplomacy by blockading the coastline of Montenegro. Because of the delicacy of the situation there was no shore leave and it became interminably monotonous and uncomfortable, the ships lying rolling to the steep seas of the Adriatic.

One Sunday when the weather moderated somewhat Dönitz decided to relieve the tedium by taking the ship's dinghy for a pull towards the land, without however setting foot on it. Nearing the shore, he was surprised to see what must have appeared a vision, a woman in a grey-green nurse's uniform perched on a rock in the water, watching him—and smiling. Soon the dinghy was hard by the rock, one moment lifted by the swell to within touching distance, the next deep below her, while he tried to find a few words which she might understand. He offered her some chocolate 'which she immediately popped into her charming little mouth with visible enjoyment',[47] and after some while they managed to agree a tryst at the same time and place on the following Sunday.

He was evidently much smitten, but on his way back to the ship, according to his memoirs, the thought struck him, here they were blockading the Montenegrins, and here he was giving one of them his chocolate! He confessed his error when he reported back to von Loewenfeld, but the first officer only laughed at his 'blockade running'. Taken at face value it is an interesting vignette revealing almost obsessive duty-consciousness. Perhaps it was just bravado to spice up the story for his idol, von Loewenfeld.

The following Sunday he was back in the dinghy paying court, perhaps giving her more chocolate. He was sad when he had to leave and was thinking of her in the loneliness of his watch that night when an Austrian torpedo boat approached at speed and heaved a despatch pouch on to the quarterdeck. It contained an order for the *Breslau* to form a landing party as part of an international naval brigade to occupy the Albanian port of Scutari and free it from Montenegrin occupying forces. At once they roused von Loewenfeld, and the rest of the night was spent in preparations, Dönitz agonizing over whether he would be included in the party as he took down orders dictated by the first officer. He was overjoyed when he heard his name as one of the section leaders.

They weighed with the morning and the party landed the same day at Scutari to occupy the section of town allotted to them by the overall Commander, the British Vice Admiral, Sir Cecil Burney. All the officers were given mounts. That evening as Dönitz was riding between the posts for which he was responsible, trying to discern landmarks in the gathering gloom, his horse shied suddenly at a pack of dogs running at them, snarling; then it bolted, carrying him helplessly through the streets.

Naturally he felt somewhat ashamed of this first patrol, but the following morning it turned out that several officers had had similar experiences. The town was plagued by these more or less wild packs of dogs, each jealously guarding its own territory. Loewenfeld was not the man to permit such a state of affairs in his sector and, as Dönitz put it, he 'arranged for the dogs to vanish',[48] The implication of the sentence following is that they were rounded up and shipped to an uninhabited island. Whatever their fate, it can be assumed that Dönitz was witness to a campaign of the sort of ruthless efficiency that marked von Loewenfeld's actions against Communists in Germany after the war.

As the Montenegrins bowed to the pressure of the powers and marched out proudly by night, the next few months were chiefly spent in infantry exercises distinguished, at least on the *Breslau*, by a strongly competitive spirit towards the other national contingents, British, French, Austrian and Italian. The Germans also had plenty of time to observe the other naval officers as all used the Hôtel de l'Europe as a general off-duty meeting place; Dönitz formed the impression that the German officers could stand comparison with any others—so at any rate he claimed. There is little doubt though that the Germans considered themselves very much better than the 'Latin' French and Italians and the heterogeneous Austrian officers, and in general admired only the British. Certainly a story making this point emanated from the *Breslau* in this year 1913 off Albania and spread throughout the German Navy. It concerned a dinner aboard the German cruiser to which the officers of the other navies had been invited. A British Admiral sat next to the German Captain and at one point raised his glass and gazing directly into the blue eyes of the German, as the glasses clicked, whispered a private toast, 'The two white nations!'

This story so impressed one German officer, von Hase, that when he came to write a book after the war, he called it *The Two White Nations*. To leave no doubt about the moral, he described the French, Italians and Slavs as 'intellectually, physically and morally inferior'; the British and German officers, however, gazing at each other 'with flashing eyes', recognized themselves as 'representatives of the two greatest seafaring Germanic peoples. They felt they were of the same stock, originally members of one and the same noble family'.[49]

Racial ideas, whether calmly assumed by Anglo-Saxons who had half

1 Karl Dönitz as a youth

2a *(above)* Kaiser Wilhelm II inspects the cadets aboard the *Hertha*

2b *(below)* The training ship *Hertha*

2c *(inset)* Karl Dönitz as a *Hertha* cadet with two Albanian children

3a *(above)* The cruiser *Breslau* after commissioning as *Midilli* in the Turkish Navy

3b *(below)* The German officers of the *Midilli*—Dönitz seated front row *(left)* with iron cross

4a Karl Dönitz as watch officer of the 'ace' Walter Forstmann's U 35 in 1917

4b *(inset)* UB 64, a boat of the same class as UB 68 which Dönitz commanded in 1918

the world to prove it, or worked at earnestly by Teutons who wanted—as much in psychological as material terms—what the Anglo-Saxons had, were a part of the contemporary mind. Everything known about Dönitz suggests he would have shared them to the full. But when he came to write his memoirs one war and a holocaust after von Hase, they had, of course, become unfashionable, and he wrote in a very different vein. He did not mention the private toast aboard his cruiser, and adopted the viewpoint that every nationality has its particular strengths and weaknesses; he contrasted, for instance, the 'somewhat indolent' character of the Austrians to 'the duty-obsessed, correct, but stiffer and perhaps also narrower Prussian nature'.[50]

In the autumn of 1913 the *Breslau* was relieved by one of the regular battalions of naval infantry from home and the cruiser left the international force. By this time Dönitz had completed the prescribed three and a half years since entering as a Cadet, and he was formally elected an officer by the officers of the cruiser. This was another custom adopted almost unchanged from the Prussian Army; it was designed as the final bar to any dilution of the social and spiritual homogeneity of the officer corps; one objection was sufficient to prevent anyone being elected and there was no appeal.

Having passed this court, Dönitz swore an oath on the Imperial flag—or perhaps an officer's drawn sword:

'I, Karl Dönitz, swear a personal oath to God the Almighty and All-knowing that I will loyally and honourably serve His Majesty the German Kaiser, Wilhelm II, my supreme war lord, in all and any circumstances on land and at sea, in peace and in war . . . and will act in a correct and suitable manner for a righteous, brave, honourable and duty-loving soldier.'

He was gazetted *Leutnant zur See* (Ensign USN or sub-lieutenant RN) from September 27th and placed 20th in the rank-order for his year. This meant that he had acquired sufficient points in the practical courses in the summer of 1912 before his posting to the *Breslau* to move him up nineteen places from the 39th position he had obtained in the final exams at the Navy School—an obvious indication of practical talent, which was confirmed by the glowing report of the Captain of the *Breslau*.[51]

*   *   *

The *Goeben* and *Breslau* continued to spend most of their time in the eastern Mediterranean, for the Balkans remained an area of dangerous friction and were, besides, the axis of a German diplomatic and commercial drive towards Turkey and the Middle East; the warships were symbols of German power. For the 22-year-old *Leutnant* Dönitz it was a delightful period, rich in a variety of exotic experiences. From Port Said, where the cruiser coaled, he made journeys to Cairo to visit the Egyptian museum, the mosques, the pyramids and the other monuments to that timeless civilization; in the Syrian and Turkish harbours where they showed the flag he acquired a taste for Oriental carpets, and under von Loewenfeld's critical eye developed skill in assessing these exquisite works of art. 'I possessed, for instance, an old "Ghiordes" of such beauty of colour in gold and blue, thus saffron and indigo, that often I could not satiate myself with these colours.'[52]

The officers enjoyed strenuous social activity as the representatives of the German empire in the Middle East, particularly in Constantinople, where Embassy officials dubbed the ship the *Ball-Kahn* (Ball-boat). This did not prevent very thorough training in all warlike exercises; indeed as later events were to prove, both German warships were worked up to hairlines of efficiency.

The *Breslau* spent the first three months of 1914 refitting in Trieste, emerging to escort the Kaiser's yacht, *Hohenzollern*, to Corfu, where Wilhelm spent his annual holiday. For the officers who took part in numerous more or less informal social events graced by a variety of Royals, these were the last days of peace, although none could have foreseen it, the last high days of a social order about to vanish for ever. For after escorting the *Hohenzollern* back to Trieste, the *Breslau* was ordered to join another international squadron off the Balkans, and she was there, lying off Durazzo next to the British heavy cruiser, *Defence*, when news came of the murder of the heir to the throne of Austria-Hungary at Sarajevo just 200 miles to the north.

It is important to clarify the events following the murder at Sarajevo. They were deliberately muddied by official Germany at the time and after the war was lost. The truth is that the murder was seen in Berlin as the opportunity that was sought to unleash a sharp, controlled—Bismarckian—war.

There were many reasons why the German leaders needed war. Internally they were threatened by the steady advance of the Socialists, the largest party in the *Reichstag*, now attacking the three-tier voting system by which the land-owning Junker class retained power in Prussia, thus in the *Reich*. These believed they were in a pre-revolutionary situation but, as August Bebel put it, were not prepared to reform their *Junkerstaat*—on the contrary they were determined to hold on to what a modern German scholar, Volker Berghahn, has called their 'untenable position in a rapidly changing industrial society'.[53] Moreover, they were not prepared to make any more financial sacrifices to meet the huge burden of interest Tirpitz's fleet-building had laid on the exchequer.

The financial-industrial interest which had set the pace for the new course of 1897 had also become disenchanted. Far from fulfilling its internal goal of binding the divisions within the *Reich*, *Weltpolitik* had seriously deepened them and with the withdrawal of the Junkers split even the 'patriotic' consensus; in external affairs *Weltpolitik* had forced Great Britain to join the opposing continental alliance, 'encircling' them and blocking all movement. The Foreign Ministry felt this particularly. In 1911, and again in the 1912 Balkan crisis, Great Britain had given Germany deliberate warnings which had shocked and angered them. They laid the British antagonism at Tirpitz's door. Even Wilhelm II could on occasions be forced into the realization that the fleet policy had miscarried.

By the end of 1912, therefore, when the fateful meeting took place at Wilhelm's palace, Tirpitz and the Navy were very much on their own. The Army, the Chancellor, the Foreign Ministry, the Junkers, the bankers, the shipowners and industrialists—and sometimes the Kaiser— the entire Prussian power nexus was against further naval expansion. *Weltpolitik* was not abandoned altogether, simply discarded as an immediate goal. Thinking had reverted naturally to the traditional Prussian cast of continental *Politik*. In fact it was more than that because the new Germany was more than a *Junkerstaat*; it was a world industrial power, and the new policy envisaged a two-stage attack on the world, first continental hegemony, then world power. This was, of course, the policy later pursued by Hitler; like everything else in that second-hand cerebrum it was taken straight from the Kaiser's *Reich*.

The new policy, discernible at least from 1912 and certainly from the Palace meeting of December 1912, was first to smash France and so reduce her that she could never again either threaten Germany's western borders or finance Germany's eastern neighbours, then form a giant German *Mitteleuropa* including Holland and Belgium, the coastline of

37

northern France, the states of Eastern Europe—thrusting Russia back—
and the Balkan countries down to the Mediterranean. This was the first
stage—in fact a United States of Europe under Prussian leadership. The
second stage was to tack a colonial empire on to this huge power base.[54]

Following the December 1912 meeting, therefore, the Army discarded its alternative plan for a strike east and worked solely on train
timetables and supply programmes for a strike west into France through
Belgium; the government and the Army between them blocked Tirpitz's
further naval expansion plans, and the Foreign Ministry set about using
the threat of further naval expansion as a bargaining counter with Great
Britain to force her to grant Germany a free hand in Europe in return for
allowing Britain a free hand on the oceans; meanwhile they sought allies
in Eastern Europe, the Balkans, Turkey and Italy. Propaganda was
shifted away from depicting John Bull as the jealous arch-rival who had
organized the 'encirclement' of Germany, instead concentrating on the
danger in the east—for Russia was bound to come in when France was
attacked.

It was fairly clear what was going on and both France and Russia
hugely stepped up their military programmes in response. This alarmed
the Army; by the end of May 1914 von Moltke had become very anxious
indeed—so he told the Foreign Minister. In two or three years' time the
military superiority of their enemies would be so great that he did not
know how he could cope with them. In his opinion there was no
alternative to launching a preventive war while there was still a chance of
victory. He asked the Minister 'to gear policy to an early unleashing of a
war'.[55]

Relations with England had improved meanwhile, since the focus had
shifted from the dreadnought building competition, and when news of
the murder at Sarajevo came on June 28th it was possible to hope that
here was the pretext needed for a continental war which England, with
her Liberal, humanitarian government containing several proclaimed
pacifists, would not enter. It was not, however, a moment for reason; war
had become a psychological necessity and it was a time for that touch of
madness—that steeling oneself for the leap into the unknown, necessary
at times in human affairs. To the ministers, 'haunted by the nightmare of
internal chaos and external defeat, war seemed the only way out of the
deadlock'.[56]

For Wilhelm himself, shocked by the murder and in a high state of
emotion, the existence of the Austrian Empire was at stake; it was time

for the Serbs to be 'straightened out' once and for all.[57] When his ministers urged the Austrians to do this and the Austrian Emperor sought clarification, Wilhelm assured him of unconditional German support. He was playing up to the war-lord image expected; he also wanted to believe the war could be localized. Tirpitz, on holiday, received a letter from his 'ears' in Berlin saying that HM did not think it very likely that Russia would help Serbia because the Tsar would not wish to support regicides and Russia was not yet ready militarily or financially; the same was true of France. 'HM did not speak of England.'[58] Whatever plane the Kaiser was inhabiting, on any rational consideration it was evident that Russia could not afford to allow her client Serbia to be overrun by Austria without losing her whole position in the Balkans. She had made this very clear after the previous crisis: she would consider an attack on Serbia as a *casus belli*—'*une question de vie et de mort*'.[59]

So in alternating realism and wishful thinking, optimism and doubt and increasing high nervous tension, as in any great conspiracy, the secret preparations went ahead in Berlin and Vienna behind a façade of normality and calm deliberately created to prevent alerting the other powers prematurely. Meanwhile the fleet was put on a war footing. Of the Mediterranean ships, the *Goeben*, which had not been in dock for two years and whose speed was seriously affected by boiler trouble, had been ordered to Pola in the Adriatic and workmen and materials were sent overland from Germany for the necessary repairs. Cruisers on foreign stations were alerted to the state of tension.[60]

Dönitz, as signals officer of the *Breslau*, must have been aware of the alert. In common with all other German naval officers who wrote of this period, he made no mention of it in his memoirs. To outward appearances there was no change in the international squadron lying off Durazzo; occasionally the *Breslau*'s landing parties went ashore to repel insurgents, from time to time in off-duty hours a *Breslau* team played *Wasserball* against a team from HMS *Defence*, yet 'the continually increasing tension lay like a shadow overall'.[61] This is a revealing sentence if it refers to July as a whole for in accordance with the German policy of complete normality until the very moment to strike, the only 'constantly increasing tension' was in Berlin and Vienna and aboard the *Hohenzollern* and the ships of the High Seas Fleet on exercises in the North Sea and in Tirpitz's hideaway in the Black Forest—and aboard the *Breslau*, now the only Imperial warship in operational condition in the Mediterranean, and anchored close by a British heavy cruiser!

The British position was an enigma. In Berlin the Foreign Ministry pondered the question with the chief of the Admiralty staff: 'How would it be if we threatened England that if she declared against us we would occupy Holland? How would the Admiralty staff evaluate that?'[62]

Tirpitz received a report of this conversation, which could not have reassured him about the competence of the diplomats in charge of the game, and in the same post a letter informing him that Austria would deliver a note to Serbia on July 23rd: 'Private information over its tone differs. Zimmermann thinks Serbia cannot swallow it.'[63] Tirpitz underlined the final words. The letter went on to say that the German Ambassadors in St Petersburg, London and Paris would go into action on the same day to call for localization of the conflict; evidently it was believed Serbia would not swallow it.

The Austrian note was delivered as planned while the French President and Premier were at sea on their way home from a visit to Russia and just a few hours out of Kronstadt. As the deliberately humiliating terms and extraordinarily short time for reply became known in the European capitals and the German Ambassadors went into their prepared professions of surprise and complete ignorance of the ultimatum, and sought to advise their host governments of the 'inestimable consequences' which might arise as a result of the alliance system if they were to become involved, it was clear that Bebel's forecast was about to be fulfilled and they were 'on the eve of the most dreadful war Europe has ever seen'.

The British Foreign Secretary tried desperately to pull the powers back from the edge and into another international conference, but the timetable of the central powers admitted no delay. On July 28th Austria declared war on Serbia, then one after another—although not without prodding from Berlin—the links of the alliance machinery began to clank together. Finally by July 29th only a few large questions remained: would Italy join the central powers, which way would Turkey jump, and above all would England come in?

On the same day the British Admiralty sent out the 'Warning Telegram' to all ships. Aboard the *Breslau* before Durazzo they saw their British neighbour weigh and take up another position far to seawards out of torpedo range. That night she disappeared. She made no signal, 'let alone a personal leave-taking as she broke the long lying-time together. With that the change of our relationship to England became obvious'.[64]

In Pola, meanwhile, the crew of the *Goeben* had been assisting the dockyard men sent out from Germany and, working around the clock in the fierce heat below decks, had replaced 4,000 defective tubes in the battlecruiser's boilers in eighteen days. She sailed down the Adriatic on the 30th, and late on the 31st Admiral Souchon ordered the *Breslau* by wireless to Messina in Sicily, calling on the way at Brindisi to organize colliers for a rendezvous at sea. The cruiser sailed secretly that night, arriving at Brindisi in the early hours of August 1st. Dönitz had been chosen to make the coaling arrangements with the German consul and, after he had been put ashore, the cruiser continued on her way; he was to be picked up later by the *Goeben*.

It was a close, heavy summer's night as he walked through the silent streets looking for the Consul's residence. Finding it eventually, he made his way in to an inner courtyard—it was an old palace—but found he had to shout to rouse the household. At length a man appeared on one of the balconies demanding angrily who it was; when he saw the naval uniform his manner changed. 'His first question, which he put to me without knowing what I wanted of him at such an early morning hour, was: would England take part in the coming war or not?'[65]

After a morning spent in arrangements for the colliers, Dönitz had lunch with the Consul and his family, then went down to the harbour and sat alone on the outer mole gazing out to sea, gnawed by fears that the *Goeben* might be diverted and might not be able to pick him up; he would have to spend the war in Italy instead of in the fighting with his 'beloved *Breslau*'. Late in the afternoon she appeared, 'God be thanked . . .' and he went aboard and reported the success of his mission to Souchon.[66]

She sailed that night, steering south-west for the toe of Italy. The following morning, August 2nd, was fine and hot; the sea flashed and glittered under a blue sky cut grandly to starboard by the heights of Calabria. Rounding Cape Spartivento with Mount Etna ahead shimmering in a heat haze, she steered up for Messina; soon the masts and funnels of the *Breslau* could be made out amongst the assembled shipping; Dönitz transferred to her as soon as they were moored.

By now it had become clear that Italy was not going to come in on the German side; it was also clear that the German squadron was not going to have the support of the Austrian fleet on which Souchon had counted. He had come to Messina to carry out an agreed plan for a joint strike against transports which would carry army units from North Africa back to mainland France, but now he was alone. No doubt it was because of the question mark over England's intentions, but it left his two ships dangerously exposed to the British Mediterranean squadron headed by three battlecruisers, now concentrated at Malta, barely 150 miles to the south.

In Berlin, meanwhile, Wilhelm had collapsed. Monstrous reality had forced itself in, distorted as it was in his egocentric view: 'as a reward for keeping our pledges we get set upon and *beaten* by the Triple Entente as a body so that their longing to ruin us completely can be finally satisfied'.[67] Up to this point France had done her utmost to give no provocation, but von Moltke's heavy artillery and troop trains were precisely timetabled; the Chancellor had been forced to dash off a note to Paris to legalize the declaration of war necessary on the next day.

Souchon, informed of the situation by cable, made the extraordinarily bold decision to strike against the French transports with his squadron alone. The ships were cleared for action, boats, wooden furniture and other inflammables offloaded into a German passenger liner which had been diverted to the harbour because of the threatening situation, while reluctant Italians were prodded by the German Embassy into providing coal. At last at dusk the lighters arrived and coaling began in an atmosphere of feverish excitement.

So I experienced the last day of peace before the First World War. As before the beginning of the Second World War, the hours immediately between peace and war were unforgettable . . . in such fateful periods men's consciousness and subconsciousness are particularly receptive.[68]

Coaling was completed at midnight. An hour later, after washing down, the two ships weighed and left, steering with screened lights first north, then westerly for a position between Sardinia and the French North African coast. After sunrise any smoke seen on the horizon caused them to make large alterations away.

In London that day the government was at last able to unite on the decision that honour—because of its obligations to France—and self-interest both dictated; for the King of Belgium had appealed for help against German violation of his country's neutrality. The Foreign Secretary told a packed House of Commons that he did not believe that if

Great Britain stood aside she would at the end of the war be in a position to undo what had happened, 'to prevent the whole of the west of Europe opposite to us—if that had been the result of the war—falling under the domination of a single power, and I am quite sure that our moral position would be such as to have lost us all respect'.[69] He carried the House, and afterwards composed a simple ultimatum to the German government timed to expire at midnight (Berlin time) on the next day, August 4th: unless the invasion were halted Britain would be at war with Germany.

The invasion could not be halted. The railways and strategically located sidings could not be moved, the plan was inflexible. France had to be crushed inside six weeks so that the effort could be shifted east against Russia before that ponderous colossus should overwhelm Austria and the few German divisions holding the East Prussian borders.

Nevertheless the ultimatum came as a profound shock. Until then all had gone well; the new-found unity of the nation was a particular success. Socialist leaders who had been denouncing the 'patriotic' parties and war only a week before had been wooed by ministers and had submitted without a struggle, suddenly discovering that they were, before everything, Germans. They had swung round almost *en bloc*, declaring in the *Reichstag* that the war was a 'just cause' and plighting their union with the government. As if this was the moment for which they had been waiting, the people followed; everywhere was a fervent, fierce nationalism; for the time for reason was past. 'Brilliant mood,' the chief of Wilhelm's naval cabinet had noted in his diary after the Russian declaration, 'the government has succeeded very well in making us appear the attacked.'[70]

Wilhelm had roused himself temporarily to play up to the mood, but his private world dream had become a nightmare. Those who saw him after the British ultimatum were shocked at his appearance.

In the early hours of August 4th the *Goeben* and *Breslau* neared the Algerian coast, the battlecruiser steering for Philippville, the light cruiser for Bone.

> The picture is clear in my memory as in the grey morning light the hills, houses, light towers, moles and harbour works with ships of Bone came in sight. Obviously as a young soldier I was impressed with this first war action.[71]

43

The enemy were caught off guard as the *Breslau* closed and opened fire, and some 40 miles to the west the *Goeben*'s far heavier broadside came as an equal surprise. It was a token bombardment, though, lasting scarcely ten minutes and doing little if any damage to the troops or transports, igniting one magazine with a fortunate shell; then both ships turned and headed out in a westerly direction as if making for the Straits and the open Atlantic. Out of sight of the land they turned east again for an agreed rendezvous, but scarcely had they joined at ten o'clock than smoke was sighted ahead and shortly over the horizon the tripod masts of two warships. It was a heart-stopping moment; they could only be British battlecruisers. The alarm sounded, 'Clear ship for action!' Souchon altered to port, the British to starboard in response. Souchon, whose last news was that the British would probably be an enemy and he was to be prepared for hostile action, decided to brave it out and came back to his original course.

In tense silence they watched the dark grey shapes lengthening; the twelve-inch gun turrets were lined fore and aft and so far stationary; the White Ensigns, symbols of victory at sea for centuries before the German service was born, fluttered in the black smoke overcast pouring out astern. They passed without exchanging salutes at four miles, and immediately turned and followed, one on each quarter of the *Goeben*. Nerves aboard the German ships would have been even tighter had they known that the British Commander in Chief, aware of their bombardment, had sent a message to London requesting permission to open fire.

The *Breslau*, which could scarcely contribute in action, was ordered to separate and go ahead to Messina to make arrangements for coaling. As she drew away northwards, the entire ship's company of the *Goeben* apart from those on the bridge or in the turrets was sent down to help the stokers in the furnace heat below. To the British it appeared that the battlecruiser made at least a knot over her designed 27 knots, and as they themselves had not had the benefit of a recent docking, they dropped gradually further and further astern through the afternoon. By the time the British ultimatum expired that night both German ships were on their own. They entered Messina unobserved.

Once again the Italian authorities seemed reluctant to provide coal and Souchon ordered the German merchantmen in harbour alongside the two warships to plunder their stock. Through that afternoon as the sun beat down on the metal decks turning the close compartments below into ovens the crews worked to transfer coal from bunkers that had never been designed for the purpose; openings were hacked through bulk-heads and decks, rails torn away, while the *Goeben*'s band played marches to keep up the spirits of the exhausted men. Above in the wireless rooms increasing signals traffic indicated the enemy—as the British now were—concentrating across their exit routes just outside Italian territorial waters.

At noon the following day, August 6th, coaling was discontinued. It was essential the crews should have some rest before the breakout which had to be attempted as the 24 hours allowed Souchon by the Italian authorities ran out. All the men were given postcards to write a few words home. It is said that all the officers made their wills.

Souchon meanwhile confronted another awesome decision: the pre-vious day he had been informed from Berlin that an alliance had been concluded with Turkey, and he was to proceed to Constantinople to join his squadron to the Turkish fleet. He had asked for help from the Austrian fleet, but again he had been refused, this time because the British declaration of war had been against Germany alone and they wanted nothing to disturb this situation. Meanwhile complications arose in Turkey—in fact the Turkish government had never been united on a German alliance—and shortly before noon that morning, August 6th, another message from Berlin stated that entry into Constantinople was not yet possible on political grounds. Dönitz, who had been sent aboard the flagship to clarify some question, saw Souchon after the receipt of this message as he was discussing it with his chief of staff. 'The silent, calm, serious manner of both men' impressed itself indelibly on his memory.[72] The decision had just been taken, despite everything, to run for Constantinople; it was another incredibly bold venture, particularly as Souchon was convinced the British heavy units would be disposed to the eastward to block his way to the Austrian ports in the Adriatic.

As they prepared to sail in the late afternoon every man aboard realized it would be a bolt for life or death; once again they screwed their nerves to the sticking point; the officers, who knew the impossible odds, were possessed of a fatalistic determination to make a gallant fight and die for the honour of the flag.

They went to action stations as they left harbour, the *Goeben* ahead, the little *Breslau* following, and steered south, hugging the Italian coast, lit in the slanting rays of the sun. Soon smoke was seen on the starboard bow and presently the expected shape of a British cruiser beneath. Souchon led around the Cape and steered northwesterly as if making up the Adriatic. The cruiser, the *Gloucester*, followed, nine miles off; in the wireless room they heard her signalling their course and position to the rest of the British fleet.

The evening gave way to velvet night with a low moon hanging over the hills to port; in these conditions the German squadron found it impossible to shake off their shadow, and at 11 pm Souchon turned east. However, the British heavy units had been stationed to the west of the Straits expecting a second attempt to harass the French troop transports, and there was only a cruiser squadron between Souchon and his goal. This failed to find the *Goeben* that night—although passing within a mile of the *Breslau*—and when dawn broke on the 7th only the *Gloucester* was still in touch.

During the morning the *Breslau* deliberately started falling astern of the *Goeben* to draw off the British cruiser or catch her between two fires, and at one o'clock the *Gloucester*'s captain, judging she was endangering his pursuit of the main target, opened fire and increased to full speed to close. The *Breslau* replied immediately with two ranging shots, then went into salvo firing, at which the *Gloucester* altered away, 'as it was found the shooting of the *Breslau* was excellent and a whole salvo of hers dropped along the line on the off-side of the *Gloucester*, not one of them being more than 30 yards over'.[73] She was the first British ship to discover the remarkably accurate gunnery of the Imperial Navy—in this case controlled by Kapitänleutnant Carls, gunnery officer of the *Breslau*. The *Gloucester* kept firing as she altered away, and scored one hit on the waterline armour of the German cruiser. Meanwhile the *Goeben* altered 180° to protect her consort and also opened fire, so while the *Gloucester* drew away the two German ships closed each other, and when Souchon turned back to his easterly course, the British cruiser followed. Such was Dönitz's baptism of fire.

The *Gloucester* finally gave up the pursuit at five o'clock that evening, abeam of Cape Matapan, which she had orders not to pass. In the German squadron it was difficult to believe their good fortune. However, they were by no means out of danger: after coaling from a collier ordered to meet them in the Greek islands, they had to test the attitude of Turkey, which was obliged by international law to deny them entrance to the Dardanelles. If this happened it was difficult to imagine a second escape from the British fleet—indeed strengthening wireless traffic on the morning of the 10th caused Souchon to break off coaling and race for the Straits. If refused permission to enter, he intended fighting his way in, so his officers believed, and as the two ships arrived off the entrance and lay stopped, flying 'G'—'I require a pilot'—in range of the forts clearly visible against the dry, brown hills, the ships' companies went to action stations. Presently two Turkish torpedo boats were seen coming out. Tension mounted. Then the leading boat hoisted the signal, 'Follow me!' and turned to lead them in.

The vineyards and villages they knew so well from peacetime cruises slipped past to starboard bathed in a roseate glow; to port the heights of Gallipoli stood in shadow.

The Turkish government was still divided. A war party led by the most radical of the 'Young Turks', Enver Pasha, a former military attaché in Berlin, now a forceful advocate of alliance with Germany in order to conduct an aggressive policy in the Middle East to retake Egypt and the Suez Canal—which naturally fitted in well with German plans—was strongly opposed by a neutralist party intent on keeping out of the European struggle altogether. The embassies of all the powers in Constantinople were natural centres of influence and intrigue. However, the cause of the Triple Entente had received a serious setback on the outbreak of war when the British government had requisitioned for its own use a huge super-dreadnought battleship which the Turks had purchased earlier that year while it was building at Newcastle on Tyne. This high-handed act was felt keenly at Constantinople and played into Enver Pasha's hands; Souchon's arrival with the *Goeben* provided him with the trump card he needed.

Already, as War Minister, he had taken the powers of Commander in Chief of all Turkish forces on land or sea. The naval forces were actually trained and run by British officers under Admiral Limpus Pasha, a capable and conscientious but at that time worn-down Englishman, badly needing a rest away from the enervating climate and strain. Enver had naturally kept him in the dark about his plans for the *Goeben* and *Breslau*. Then early in the morning of August 10th, hearing that Souchon's arrival was imminent, he had replaced the British Commander of the flotilla forces with his own man; hence the torpedo boats which guided the German ships in. Limpus and his officers in Constantinople remained unaware.

The next day Limpus learned the astounding news from the papers and calling for an interview with the Minister of Marine was told that both German warships were being bought by the Turkish government. This was a device to legalize the Turkish position in admitting them. It was also on Enver's part an attempt to force the government into war by embroiling them with the Entente powers. For the British fleet had at last arrived off the Dardanelles and was being refused entrance while at the other end of the Straits the Russians would naturally be alarmed at the upset to the balance of naval power in the Black Sea which must result from Turkey acquiring the powerful German dreadnought battlecruiser; as Limpus noted in his diary, 'if Russia *wants* an opportunity [to strike] Turkey has now given it to her!'[74] The last thing the Entente powers wanted was to push Turkey into the German camp; instead there was a heightening of diplomatic activity to forestall Enver and the German Army contingent under General Liman von Sanders.

Aboard the *Breslau*, meanwhile, the feeling of release from the extraordinary tensions of the past two weeks had given way naturally to depression and irritability. German warships were uncomfortable steel boxes at the best of times, wasting minimum space and weight on creature comforts, and now, at the height of the Turkish summer with the few pieces of furniture floating somewhere off Messina, the cruiser was scarcely bearable. Added to this was the uncertainty about their position; while their comrades were taking part in the struggle for greater Germany they might be interned here for the duration of what was expected to be a very short war. On top of this feeling of impotence was an unexpressed sense of humiliation. They had been fortunate to escape unscathed, but there was no question they had fled the Mediterranean as fast as they could; it was not what their training had prepared them for. Moreover, the British and French Press, almost the only newspapers they could obtain, raised a howl of derision at the ignominious flight and the failure even to get to grips with the single British light cruiser which had followed them.

Within a few days matters began to improve for it became evident that the two ships were in the front line of the scheme to bring Turkey into the war. The first indication was on August 15th when Limpus and all the British officers were superseded without warning by Turkish officers; the following day both German ships' companies were mustered and the Imperial ensigns were lowered to the strains of the national anthem; afterwards the red Ottoman crescent flag was hoisted. The *Goeben* was now *Sultan Jawus Selim*, the *Breslau* was *Midilli*; officers and crews replaced their uniform caps with the fez. Souchon was appointed Commander in Chief of the Turkish fleet and the two ships, still manned chiefly by their German crews, joined other Turkish units for exercises in the Sea of Marmora. Dönitz's special task in this period of changeover from the British to the German way of doing things was to work with the Flag Lieutenant of the *Goeben*—for the Germans still referred to the ships by their former names amongst themselves—to edit a new international signal book and compile a signal code for joint operations.

Whether Dönitz met his future wife at this time is not clear. Her father, General Weber, came aboard the *Breslau* soon after their arrival; he had come to Turkey with Liman von Sanders' mission and was in command of the fortresses guarding the Straits. It seems he knew as little of the Navy as most German generals: arriving aboard the *Breslau* and looking around, allowing a monocle to drop from his eye, he said, 'So this is the *Goeben!*'—that is how Dönitz heard the story in the mess. Whether General Weber's family was with him at this stage is uncertain; if so, it is probable that Dönitz met his daughter, Ingeborg, at one of the social functions to which the officers were invited. Dönitz himself made no mention of how they first met and it may be that she only came out later in order to nurse at the German Embassy hospital in Constantinople; that, at any rate, was her occupation after Turkey entered the war.

The struggle within the Turkish government grew more critical as Enver and the German mission forced the pace with preparatory troop movements for a descent on Egypt and intrigue within that country. The British government considered the possibility of counteracting the German influence by a show of force with the fleet now off the Dardanelles to fight its way in and appear off Constantinople. However, the Germans had increased both the minefields and the efficiency of the forts and the British military attaché advised against it.

In these circumstances Enver decided to force the issue with his fleet—or perhaps Souchon or the German generals suggested it. According to the German official history he waited for a promised German loan of two million Turkish Pounds before putting the plan into operation;[75] directly the money had been transferred on October 23rd, he gave Souchon his orders; these were dated the previous day and directed the German *Flottenchef* to sail into the Black Sea with all battleworthy units of the fleet, seek out the Russian ships and attack wherever they were found without declaring war. He was to justify his action as retaliation— at least this is what Souchon did, so it may be inferred it was included in his orders.[76]

The fleet assembled at the entrance to the Bosphorus to sail, so it was believed, for a wireless and reconnaissance exercise in the Black Sea; this was for the benefit of the Russian Embassy and other foreign observers in Constantinople. In the early hours of October 27th, as the needle-like shapes of the minarets and the domes of mosques and palaces emerged in the first grey light, the ships awoke to life. Here is Dönitz's description in his first book, *The Voyages of the Breslau in the Black Sea*, published in Berlin in 1917:

Punctually at 4.30 the watchkeeping petty officer calls the officer of the watch. 'Time to wake!' Then the pipe sounds, the watch on deck fall in, and the two musicians drum and pipe their *'Freut euch des Lebens!'* ['Rise and shine!'] in such ungentle tones that the greatest marmot (a hibernating rodent) has to take note . . .

On deck the watch are placing buckets with fresh water. 4.40 is 'Wash yourselves!' Hey, how refreshing that is in the cool of the morning! Snorting and blowing, naked to the waist, the fellows hurry to wash under the foc's'le. Damnation, how cold it is!

At 5.15 is *'Backen und Banken!'* ['Cooks to the galley!'] The tables are released [from the deckhead], the cooks bring coffee, bread and butter—and 'Heinrich and Karl', forgetting their early rising, have powerful appetites.

Their carefree enjoyment is disturbed by the pipe of the Boatswain's mate . . .

The first officer is on the foc's'le, calmly considering the men as they appear from below in a leisurely way. Directly they see the 'First', however, life enters their limbs, and they rush for their anchor stations.

The watchkeeping officer inspects the stations for leaving, confirms the ship is clear for sea. The engineroom reports, 'Engines clear!' The Captain comes on the bridge. Punctually at 5.30 he orders, 'Weigh anchor!'

Over there in the *Goeben* and the other old ships of the line and in [the cruisers] *Hamidieh* and *Berk* it has become equally lively. *Breslau*'s anchor is up, the engines turn . . . [77]

And so they started into the Bosphorus, as Dönitz wrote, 'perhaps the loveliest Straits in the world, whose sloping banks adorned with gardens, parks, country houses and villas begin to light in the reddish glow of early dawn'. After a while the banks began to separate and fall away, the

50

vineyards and summerhouses and old ruined castles replaced by forts and lighthouses, and the Black Sea stretched before them and on either hand, sunlit to the horizon.

The morning was spent in exercises. In the afternoon a signal from the flagship ordered all captains aboard. 'I will never forget,' Dönitz wrote in his memoirs, 'the Captain returning with shining eyes.'[78] Almost at the same moment a flag signal was hoisted in the *Goeben*, 'Do your uttermost. It is for the future of Turkey!' Once again war fever gripped officers and men, this time scarcely even tinged with apprehension; the *Goeben* was the most powerful ship in the Black Sea, and both she and the *Breslau* had the speed to escape from any force that might overmatch them in numbers.

Soon the fleet was steering northeastwards at high speed in divisions gradually separating as they headed for different objectives: the *Goeben* with destroyers and a minelayer to lay minefields across the entrance to Sebastopol, where the Russian fleet was lying, and bombard the ships inside, another division to bombard the port of Odessa, and the *Breslau* and *Hamidieh*, towards the Straits of Kertch leading to the Sea of Azov. Reaching their destination in the early hours of the following morning, the cruiser laid mines, then steamed east to the oil port of Novorossisk, presented a formal demand to surrender and, when it was refused, bombarded for two hours. All the ships there were sunk, the harbour installations destroyed and the petrol storage tanks ignited, the flames sweeping along whole streets of houses. When they left, a huge pall of black smoke hung over the blazing town and the glow could still be seen over the distant horizon that evening as they made their way back to the Bosphorus.

Souchon failed to accomplish anything to compare with this as he was driven off by gunfire and then chased by destroyers! However, he sent the required signal to Constantinople: he had been treacherously attacked by the Russian fleet and in retaliation had bombarded their base and coastal towns. It was such an extraordinary story that he later changed it—he had discovered a Russian minelayer about to lay mines in Turkish waters off the entrance to the Bosphorus, had sunk her, then proceeded to the Russian coast to bombard. This was an equally preposterous tale and although the returning ships were fêted as victors by the local populace, the ministers did not take long to find out the truth; after a violent meeting it was resolved to continue the policy of neutrality. At this point, however, Enver and his German co-

51

conspirators were rescued by the Russian government, which rushed into a declaration of war against Turkey. So the scheme succeeded, with the fateful consequences so well known, the entry of Bulgaria with Turkey, thus securing the southern flank of the central powers, the dissipation of Russian effort, the Middle Eastern campaigns—Gallipoli. As the official British naval historian put it, 'when we recall the world-wide results that ensued it is not too much to say that few naval decisions more bold and well-judged were ever taken' than Souchon's run for the Dardanelles.[79]

The officers of the *Breslau* now received a training in cruiser warfare in the best school of all, continuous active operations. While most of their comrades in the High Seas Fleet, locked up in the Heligoland Bight by the overwhelming superiority of the British Grand Fleet, fretted at inactivity, the *Goeben* and *Breslau* contested command of the Black Sea with the numerically far stronger Russian fleet. The chief task was escorting troop and supply transports across to the Caucasus where the land war with Russia was concentrated. As this involved crossing practically the whole width of the sea from west to east, and as the Russians, operating from their central base, Sebastopol, were ideally placed to cut them off on either leg of the voyage it called for extreme care, particularly in reconnaissance.

It was on one such reconnaissance sortie that the *Breslau* had its first serious brush with the enemy. It was an impenetrable winter's night—Christmas Eve—when suddenly the cruiser found herself in company with several ships. A signal lamp flashed; the *Breslau* trained her searchlights on the vessel in response and found the Russian battleship, *Rostislaw*, horrifyingly close. Immediately the gunnery officer, Carls, opened fire. The 10.5-cm shells could not have penetrated the armoured vitals of the enemy but the Russians were surprised by the rapid and no doubt accurate night fighting technique and the cruiser was able to escape.

The same day the *Goeben* struck two mines which had been laid in deep water across the entry to the Bosphorus. She limped home but was out of action for many months. The *Breslau* was now the principal warship in the Turkish fleet as the old pre-dreadnought battleships were too slow to be risked; she cruised continuously, frequently acting as troop transport herself, at night fighting off Russian destroyer attacks. Here is Dönitz's description in his 1917 book:

52

The water columns stand up like bright fountains suddenly planted outside the searchlight beams.

Now there are flashes from the Russians.

There . . . now our salvo lands and the foremost destroyer sustains three hits!

There, now another five! Suddenly there is only his bridge and foc's'le to be seen. He has had enough!

'Change target right!' orders the gunnery officer, and the second destroyer is engaged.

But a high cone of fire is also rising in our ship from the starboard middle deck . . . Damnation, we have received a hit there—and there another!

It is certainly very different when shells explode in one's own ship . . . the funnels, suddenly lit in the glare, rise from the darkness and under them on deck smoke rolls darkly . . .[80]

On this occasion the badly damaged Russian destroyer sank and the other suffered heavy casualties. The *Breslau*'s own loss was seven dead and fifteen wounded from three hits.

Naturally there was shore leave between the sorties. Here is Dönitz describing a foray into the city in the summer of 1915.

We have ourselves ferried across to Stamboul. Today there is to be a great carpet raid!

First we go to Kaffaroff. He has a pair of sumptuous 'Herats' and a 'poem' of a 'Dschaudjegan'. We decline a 'Buchura' which he repeatedly points out. We do not like a hard pattern; a carpet should be a flower bed. And it does not help to 'push' the wares, even if the praised piece is as finely-woven 'as a handkerchief'.

Finally we agree on our choice of the 'Dschaudjegan'.

Now the bargaining begins to settle the final price. This is to carpet-buying what love is to life.

There is a warm battle, and finally no agreement. We go, we will come back later.

Over in the bazaar Spickbok assails us with a monstrous torrent of words praising the beauty and splendour of colour of his carpets to the heavens.

But the beggar has almost only modern, harsh-coloured wares! He jumps around on his darlings in his small carpet-cave, speaking like a waterfall, assuring us on his word of honour that a brand new carpet from the factory in Smyrna is a hundred-year-old piece, an 'occasion', thus proving he has no idea of his carpets.

He is a true Levantine and the greatest rogue.[81]

Leaving, they wandered through the old quarter to the town walls and the ancient Jedi-Kule, the castle of seven towers, where they were shown around by a Turkish invalid. When told they were from the *Midilli*, he looked pleased, and placing both index fingers together, said '*Alleman Turk biraarder*' (German and Turk brothers). 'We nod,' Dönitz wrote, 'and reach a hand to him with a generous "baksheesh" in confirmation of friendship.'

Towards sunset they visited the great mosque of Santa Sophia, its mighty cupola already filling with the shades of night. 'Innumerable oil lamps in chandeliers hanging beneath the cupola are alight, and shining like stars in the gloom of the cupola heaven.' Impressed by the sight and by the Turks at prayer, they returned aboard.

It seems like a dream to us that in the past weeks we were rolling in the Black Sea having a rough and tumble with the Russians.

Fortunate is the *Midilli*! In peaceful harbour days drawing new strength for new voyages. Should the war last months, the crew will be continually invigorated in the fairy-tale town of Stamboul, and go out into the Black Sea as fresh as on the first day of war.[82]

There is a lightness and sensitivity and a quiet irony in the writing. Not bad, one feels, for a young officer at the height of a war when so many were busy turning out turgid heroics—not that his descriptions of battles at sea are free from heroics. Nevertheless one has the impression of being in the company of a civilized man.

By this time he must have met Sister Ingeborg Weber, his future wife. She was a slim, lively 21-year-old, a fully-trained nurse with a mind of her own; a distinctly 'modern' young woman. One can imagine that the snatched times they found together between demanding duties, and the heightened sense of life and the value of the present moment that goes with wartime gave their courtship something of the fairy-tale, poignant quality of old Stamboul itself. Certainly Karl Dönitz would have contributed temperament.

Here is another vignette from his pen of that summer of 1915. Perhaps

Sister Inge was one of the guests on the 'yacht' the *Breslau* officers had acquired for pleasure cruising:

Before Dolma-Bagtsche the yacht's anchor is let go. For how could the *Breslau* officer enjoy the cool Bosphorus wind alone? He finds his fellow men much too agreeable. In his love for his fellows he has therefore invited the ladies and gentlemen of the German colony. They are already standing waiting before the white Sultan's palace of Dolma-Bagtsche and blinking against the sun towards the *Midilli* yacht with the red half-moon above.

The Breslaus have pity on them and fetch them on board in the dinghy. Then up anchor and we cruise out against the wind and current of the Bosphorus.

Hardly anything is gained. The yacht often drives further downstream than it makes to windward. Finally a man from the Consulate, thinking we are incapable, cannot hide his displeasure.

Quickly we put him to the tiller—but he soon asks penitently for relief. He has brought us further downstream.

In the evening it becomes calm; we have to anchor before Arnautkoij.

Our guests have found it wonderful and set out satisfied for the journey home on the electric railway. The oldest of us delays somewhat at first, then bites the sour apple and telephones the First Officer to ask for the steam pinnace . . .[83]

In July 1915 the *Breslau* ran into a deep-sea mine the Russians had laid off the entrance to the Bosphorus; now both German ships were out of action. While the cruiser was being repaired a naval brigade was formed to assist the Turks in the vital struggle against allied landings at Gallipoli. Dönitz himself either volunteered or was sent to the infant Air Service where he received some training as a pilot and served as observer-gunner in reconnaissance flights over the enemy positions.

He was in high spirits at this period; he had just become engaged to Sister Inge. As he tells the story in his memoirs, the flooded *Breslau* had scarcely made fast inside the Bosphorus after running into the mine, than a Turkish destroyer came alongside to take the cruiser's landing party to the Dardanelles. He had no time to wash or shave before jumping aboard her, whereupon she steamed off for the Sea of Marmora, making a brief call at Stamboul to fill the water tanks.

55

What luck, I thought! I leaped from the deck, ran down a short street to the German Embassy hospital, asked there for Sister Inge, became engaged to her within three to four minutes in my unwashed state and in a temperature of 30 degrees and came running again punctually back to the destroyer in order to travel to the Dardanelles for my war mission as a flyer.[84]

This would have been in character; as his friend, von Lamezan's, wife described him, all his life he was a 'pusher'!

Nevertheless, the early proposal—in terms of his age and rank—raises questions. Was it a need for the feminine element in his life missing since the age of three and a half, a desire to regain something of the permanence lost when his father died, a temperamental need for very close companionship such as had distinguished his cadet time with von Lamezan, even an inner sensitivity that he masked in the masculine ethos of the mess? Such speculations come to mind, particularly as young officers were not encouraged to marry—partly on financial grounds, mainly perhaps because dependants at home might take the edge off their risk-taking aggressiveness in battle. So far as money went, Dönitz was the most junior kind of lieutenant, not yet two years out of his time as a *Fähnrich*, and needing for the next two years, by official estimate, some 600 Marks annually over and above his salary just to keep up the style of a single officer. Then again, it was wartime and he was about to embark on an even more hazardous service than he had been engaged on up to that time. And yet it may be that he was simply very much smitten, a natural 'pusher' and young enough not to count the cost.

Of one thing there can be no doubt: he was regarded by his superiors as a model officer. A personal report on him at this time (dated August 1915) by his Captain, von Klitzing, is the first of a series of brilliant commendations preserved in his personal file in the German naval archives:

I can only confirm the previous favourable judgement. Dönitz is a charming, dashing and plucky officer with first-rate character qualities and above-average gifts. At present he is using the dockyard lying time of the ship in order to train as a flyer in San Stefano and has already as observation officer brought repeated valuable intelligence of the enemy.[85]

That autumn the *Breslau* got a new Captain, von Knorr. Dönitz came to respect him enormously for his first-rate intellect, professional skill and energy. The regard was fully reciprocated, and when the cruiser came out of dock in February 1916 and started working up again to battle readiness, von Knorr chose Dönitz as his Adjutant—after which, he recorded, he had no free time: in harbour, if von Knorr was aboard, Dönitz had to be in attendance, and at sea he never moved from his side. 'If by night we were not in touch with the enemy we sat together above the bridge on the compass platform on two empty soap boxes and kept a look-out. I am very grateful to Captain von Knorr for my tactical education.'[86]

On March 22, Dönitz received his step up to *Oberleutnant zur See*, equivalent to a junior lieutenant in the British or American services. Evidently he thought this gave him sufficient financial base to marry; the Kaiser's personal office which dealt with officers' marriages must have agreed for he received the Royal consent. Perhaps his father had left some investments; certainly Ingeborg brought a marriage dowry with her.

The wedding was arranged for late May. A few weeks before, Dönitz was awarded the Iron Cross first class for his part in an encounter with a Russian dreadnought battleship. She was a new ship, the *Imperatriza Maria*, commissioned during the cruiser's time in the dockyard. She had upset the balance in the Black Sea for she was practically as fast as the *Breslau* and had enormously more powerful guns.

Dönitz described the action in his 1917 book in imaginative style with dramatic pauses marked by lines of dots:

Something unpeaceful, indefinite expectancy hangs in the air . . . All nerves and fibres are tense . . . and as if our ship has a special organ to sense this, the aerials above begin to sing and crackle; it strengthens, rattling gently in the wires.

Wireless traffic!

The voices of the night become gradually livelier; the Russian warships must be in the neighbourhood.

The *Breslau* proceeds cautiously, watchfully as if scenting game . . .

There, four points on the port bow two dark shadows emerge from the westerly night sky—Russian warships. They are only some 60 hectometres [three miles] distant and steering an opposite course.

Rapidly we close . . .[87]

Soon they made them out as the new dreadnought and a cruiser, but the *Breslau* merged into the dark background of the Caucasus coastline and the Russians did not spot her. Dönitz's story spins out the agony as the ships passed each other; in his memoirs a more accurate account describes how von Knorr called down to the engineroom for no sparks from the funnels, and manoeuvred the cruiser so as to open the way clear to the west. Shortly afterwards a light flashed from the Russian battleship. Dönitz answered the signals by repeating the same letters back, and von Knorr called down to the engineroom for the utmost power on both engines. To return to the more dramatic, earlier account:

An ever-increasing rushing movement goes through the whole ship. A monstrously powerful straining seems to develop. The ship's body trembles, the screws hum, buzz, churn, the ventilators howl and roar, and the four bellowing funnels shoot sparkling rain.

A foaming stream of water shoots forth from under the stern, the *Breslau* starts up with its 36,000 horsepower and in short time is raging away at highest speed.[88]

The Russian dreadnought, meanwhile, continued to call up with her searchlight and Dönitz continued to repeat the signal letters back to her; long after the war he learned that the battleship's gunnery officer wanted to open fire, but the Admiral would not allow it in case the unknown cruiser turned out to be one of their own they were expecting to meet that morning. So it went until they appeared to be at extreme gun range when the Russians tired of the game. The dreadnought altered to bring her broadside to bear and they saw the flash of the great guns and counted the seconds—ten, twenty, thirty, forty . . . *'Achtung! Aufschlag!'*

There they are, not 1000 metres short, monstrous water pillars, fantastic giant fountains thrown up from an evil, moss-green ground, out of a poisonous gas cloud surrounding them like a ring, its dirty-coloured smoke hanging over the point of impact for a long time.[89]

Von Knorr used helm to throw the Russian shooting out, but the third salvo fired from an enormous range fell just ahead; the cruiser listed heavily to port, her bows plunged as if she had fallen into a trough in the sea, then torrents of water cascaded over the foc's'le and down on her deck amidships so that those standing to the guns were 'literally up to

58

their waists in water'. Miraculously she came out of it unscathed, and the wild chase continued, the Russian gradually losing ground as she kept on turning to bring her whole broadside to bear instead of firing with her forward guns only. Some time late in the morning she gave up the chase. 'This day will remain unforgettable to us.'[90]

Towards the end of May Dönitz travelled up to Berlin for his wedding—why Berlin is not clear. Perhaps Ingeborg had given up her post at the hospital in Constantinople, perhaps she gave it up in order to return to the fatherland to marry and set up a home. Nor is it clear what brother officers were present to support the slim, tanned lieutenant with the very erect military bearing which appeared to add some inches to his stature, and the Iron Cross, first class, glinting at his chest; his friend von Lamezan had been in a British prisoner of war camp since his ship had been sunk at the battle of the Falkland Islands the previous year; his brother Friedrich had transferred to the Navy and was commanding a U-boat.

The marriage was on May 27th; where the two went on honeymoon and for how long is as unclear as the other details.

Dönitz was soon back aboard the *Breslau* though with his demanding Captain and it was not long before they had an even sterner brush with the *Imperatriza Maria*. She came up while they were laying mines off the Caucasus coast, and as they turned and ran for home she chased, gaining rapidly. The *Breslau* had been provided with smoke chests by this time and as the *Imperatriza* reached long gun-range von Knorr ordered smoke and altered course under its cover. When they emerged they were horrified to see the dreadnought even closer and turning to bring her broadside to bear. Another chest was lit and von Knorr altered again. So it continued down the afternoon, the great ship closing inexorably and opening fire each time they emerged from smoke; one salvo straddled, splinters from a shell only ten metres short severely wounding the watch-officer, signalmate and two others on the bridge,[91] and as another smoke chest was lit von Knorr turned to Dönitz and said he was considering running the ship on the rocks so as to save the crew, at least. Dönitz found himself replying, 'I don't know that we should. Perhaps we'll escape again.'[92] Knorr held on and later in the afternoon they saw, to their inexpressible relief, the dreadnought had sagged astern.

It was plain after this that the cruiser's speed would have to be increased by adapting her boilers for oil-firing. Before that Dönitz was ordered home to train for the submarine, or U-boat, arm, on which the naval High Command now pinned all hopes.

The Battle of Jutland on May 31st, trumpeted as a victory, had in truth finally demonstrated the futility of trying to wrest surface control of the North Sea from Jellicoe's incomparably more powerful force; by contrast, U-boats were not only evading the British blockade but setting up a hugely destructive blockade of their own against allied merchant shipping. Naturally the focus of naval effort had been transferred to them; the chief of the Admiralty staff argued that with sufficient boats and an 'unrestricted campaign'—sinking on sight without warning and stopping and searching—British supply lines could be so reduced as to force her to bow the knee. The U-boat building programme had been stepped up and suitable young officers sought; many were volunteers dissatisfied with the inactivity of battlefleet life. It is doubtful if Dönitz was a volunteer since he never made this claim and was not one to hide anything creditable to himself behind undue modesty. However, as a strong-minded, ambitious officer he would have welcomed the chance for early command and distinction that U-boats offered—and with his new responsibilities as a married man the extra allowances in the branch would have been attractive.

In the middle of September he baled up his precious carpets and took leave of his messmates with very mixed feelings; the cruiser had been home and mistress for four impressionable years packed with every variety of experience; on the other hand he was returning to the Fatherland for a spell of leave with his wife.

Von Knorr gave him another first-rate report as an officer of 'above-average talent, especially good professional ability, great professional interest and a strength of judgement exceeding that to be expected from his age and experience'.[93]

In 1938 Carls, then an Admiral and fleet-chief, apparently said to him, 'Dönitzken, the basis of my tactical knowledge stems from the *Breslau*. I do not believe another cruiser in the last war found itself in such incessant sorties and many-sided tactical situations—always playing cat-and-mouse in that dice-beaker of the Black Sea.'[94]

Dönitz reported to the U-School in Flensburg-Mürwik on October 1st and the following day went aboard the Torpedo schoolship *Württemberg* to begin the course, plunging into the work with his invariable keenness and application. From there on December 2nd he went to the *Vulkan* for the U-boat watch officer's course, passing out on January 3rd 1917 with another exemplary report:

He took part in instruction always with very great interest and showed very good success. In practical duties he was very ardent, he possesses very good practical abilities, in depth steering he was very good. Among his comrades he is very well liked [*beliebt*].[95]

By this time he had set up home in a moderately large house near the harbour at Kiel, Feldstrasse 57; it had a master bedroom, two children's and a maid's rooms, a dining room and a drawing room, which contained his wife's grand piano, his Turkish carpets and probably, to judge by his taste later, a number of engravings on the walls of scenes from Prussian history. Ingeborg's marriage settlement must have helped; probably it formed a substantial part of their joint capital whose interest allowed them to live in a style befitting a general's daughter.

She was expecting a baby in three months' time, and no doubt it was again with mixed feelings that he received his first posting as a U-boat officer to a boat based on the Adriatic port of Pola, U 39. The Mediterranean promised pleasant weather and excellent hunting—indeed the Commander of U 39, *Kapitänleutnant* Walter Forstmann, was an established 'ace'—yet it must curtail the time he could see Inge between cruises.

Dönitz said remarkably little about Walter Forstmann in his memoirs; 'outstanding', and in another place 'one of the best Commanders of World War 1' are the only comments he permitted himself, while the ten months of eventful, at times highly exciting, always brilliantly successful cruising in U 39 he dismissed in one sentence. This is so different from his eulogies to, for instance, von Loewenfeld and von Knorr, so different from the detailed descriptions of excitements and even quite ordinary events during his cadetship, in the *Breslau* and later in the U-boats he commanded himself as to demand explanation. Explanations are hard to find. Judged by Forstmann's favourable report on Dönitz at the end of their time together and friendly correspondence later it seems unlikely to have been caused by a quarrel.

Fortunately, both an account by Forstmann himself and the surviving war diary of U 39 allows a reconstruction of this significant period in Dönitz's career. Before that, though, a brief review of the position reached in the U-boat campaign at this time, January 1917—for just as the Second World War was a continuation of the first, so Dönitz's own U-boat campaign beginning in 1939 was a continuation of this earlier struggle.

Ever since the sinking without warning of the Cunard passenger liner, *Lusitania*, by U 20 in May 1915, and the subsequent sinking without warning of the White Star passenger liner, *Arabic*, en route Liverpool–New York by U 24 in August that year, the sharp American reaction had governed U-boat strategy. The Navy had been forced by the civilian government in Berlin to abandon 'unrestricted' warfare, forced to give instructions that passenger ships were never to be attacked, finally forced to shift the centre of gravity of the campaign from the Atlantic to the Mediterranean where there was less likelihood of inflaming US opinion. This had seriously affected the chances of success, for the approach to the British Isles was the prime area in which to blockade Britain, and the requirement to surface and warn victims before attacking deprived U-boats of their prime advantages of invisibility and surprise as well as exposing them to unnecessary danger from their victims' guns—particularly since harmless-seeming merchantmen might turn out to be disguised submarine hunters, or 'Q' ships with concealed guns or torpedoes and naval crews.

The Navy therefore fought hard against the restrictions. By early 1916 they had found an unexpected ally. The Chief of the Great General Staff, von Falkenhayn, recognized that the Army's plan had failed; the whole strategy of concentrating hammer blows on one opponent at a time to crush each in turn swiftly had collapsed, and trench warfare had led to stalemate in which the central powers were on the defensive. Moreover the allies' total command of the surface of the sea—outside the Baltic—was depriving them of essential food and raw materials. In these conditions von Falkenhayn had come round to the naval view that Great Britain was the main enemy, the support of the weaker members of the alliance, and the power that had to be crushed before anything could be achieved on the continent; as the Navy considered itself too weak to support an invasion across the Channel, the sole remaining possibility was the unrestricted U-boat campaign that the naval staff was pressing for.

So the blinkers had been partly lifted from the eyes of the Great General Staff; somewhat late they had come to realize why Tirpitz and Wilhelm and the civilian government had been so alarmed at Great Britain's entry into the war. However, the larger aspects of naval command and industrial power seem still to have escaped them—or perhaps they had more faith in the professional judgement of the sailors than suited professional soldiers whose own plans had miscarried—for

62

unrestricted U-boat warfare was bound to bring the United States and other important neutrals into the ring against them. On this count the civilian government managed to block the proposals, but the Chancellor was forced to agree to a resumption of operations in the Atlantic so long as the prize rules of stop and search and allowing the crew into the boats were adhered to, and so long as no passenger ships were attacked. Both services continued to press for the 'ruthless' campaign they held essential to defeat Great Britain, and in March 1916 the government gave way another step, allowing attack without warning on all *British* ships within a declared blockade area around the British Isles—though still no passenger ships were to be attacked.

Almost immediately U 29 torpedoed the cross-Channel steamer *Sussex* crowded with passengers. Probably this was a case of mistaken identity rather than the 'Hunnish brutality' portrayed in the allied papers; for instance the British submarine Commander, Nasmith, operating in the Sea of Marmora in E 11 the previous year had attacked a vessel which he took to be a troop transport, only to find she was crowded with women and children refugees; miraculously the torpedo had failed to explode and no harm had been done. In any case, amongst the *Sussex* passengers were US citizens; there were also neutral Spanish citizens, two of whom were killed. As a result of the ensuing international furore the Navy was forced to cut back U-boat operations in the Atlantic and concentrate on the less sensitive Mediterranean area.

That summer Germany's position had grown worse with the entry of Rumania into the war against her and a sharpening of the food and materials shortage caused by the allied naval blockade; as a consequence the delicate balance of power at the top shifted: increasingly a new Chief of the Great General Staff, Field Marshal von Hindenburg, and his Quartermaster General, Ludendorff, became identified in the public mind as the strong leaders needed to rally the nation; the civilian government became more a rubber stamp than before, and since Wilhelm had been cast aside long since, the two Army leaders, repositories of the Prussian tradition, became the real rulers of the *Reich*.

With the Army in power it was only a matter of time before the U-boats were 'unleashed'—the Prussian use of language was always instructive—to conduct a 'ruthless' campaign to knock Great Britain out of the war—for the only alternatives were to submit to slow strangulation and eventual defeat—preceded by internal revolution—or accede to American peace mediation, which would scarcely result in the great

Prussian-dominated *Mitteleuropa* for which so much blood had been spent already. The moment came on February 1st 1917—in fact just as Karl Dönitz was preparing to join U 39. The risk was acknowledged; in the German Foreign Minister's view it was that 'Germany will be treated like a mad dog against which everybody combines'.[95] In the Chancellor's view it would be regarded by the neutrals as an act of desperation, without even any proof that it would succeed.

Nevertheless, to the Admiralty staff, the prospects looked good. Their case was based on the average tonnage sunk daily by U-boats in early 1915 before the *Lusitania* incident and the subsequent 'restrictions'. On this experience it was expected that around the British Isles each U-boat on station would sink at least 4,000 tons per day; assuming four stations continuously occupied, this would give a result of 480,000 tons a month. A further 125,000 tons a month was expected from the Mediterranean— for this had been the average sinking rate after the transfer of the centre of gravity of the U-boat war in the second half of 1915. Thus total monthly sinkings were expected to amount to 605,000 tons—an interesting figure as it is almost exactly what Dönitz set himself to achieve in the Second World War; it is interesting too to see the genesis of what his staff referred to then as the U-boat 'potential', that is, the average tonnage sunk per U-boat per operational day.

The 1916 staff calculation assumed that Great Britain was being supplied by 10¾ million tons of shipping. Therefore:

> . . . basing our calculations on . . . 600,000 tons of shipping sunk by unrestricted U-boat warfare and the expectation that at least two fifths of neutral traffic will at once be terrorized into ceasing their voyages to England, we may reckon that in five months shipping to and from England will be reduced by 39 per cent. England would not be able to stand that . . .[96]

To reinforce this hypothesis, the staff could argue that U-boat production was running well ahead of losses and the enemy had developed no effective counter-measures; in the past six months a mere fifteen boats had been lost, many by accident. Thus the Chief of the Admiralty Staff, von Holtzendorff, convinced himself that the campaign would be decisive, and so short that the entry of the United States would make no difference; it would be all over before she could bring her strength to bear. 'I do not hesitate to assert that . . . we can force England to make peace in five months by an unrestricted U-boat campaign.'[97] His conclusion was unequivocal: 'In spite of the danger of a break with America, an unrestricted U-boat campaign, begun soon, is the right means to bring the war to a victorious end. Indeed it is the only means to that end.'[98]

Having convinced himself, Holtzendorff had little difficulty convincing Hindenburg, particularly as the country was facing the worst food crisis of the war that winter. On January 31st 1917, suddenly in the Prussian style, the unrestricted campaign was announced, to start the following morning. There were something over 120 operational or *Frontboote* with which to launch it, about a third of them on patrol at any one time; 24 were working in the Mediterranean from Pola and Cattaro. One was U 39.

Kapitänleutnant Walter Forstmann had been in the U-boat arm since the beginning of the war. He was a legendary name, holder of the *Pour le Mérite*, the highest award for gallantry, and with 300,000 tons of shipping to his credit. He had a squarish face with dark hair brushed straight across the forehead, vigilant dark eyes, dark straight brows, and a determined mouth. His brain was cool and quick and he enjoyed danger; 'it braces the nerves and strengthens the self-confidence'. He believed the recipe for success as a sub-mariner was 'cool courage mingled with a certain amount of indifference',[99] but knew the thin line between courage and foolhardiness.

He had all the contemporary racial prejudices: Italians were excitable and none to clean 'Macaronis', Portuguese were 'not black nor white men, but half and half'.[100] For the English, to judge by his account of the cruises of U 39, he had the usual German mixture of respect and deep antagonism. The sight of the discipline aboard a British ship he had torpedoed moved him to compare Britons favourably with southern Europeans; the sight of the Rock of Gibraltar aroused his 'anger to see here again how England has established herself at the most advantageous maritime points in every part of the world'.[101]

As for the unrestricted U-boat campaign, he rejoiced in it; the declaration, he believed, had the 'approval and confidence of the whole country, yes, the German people has long demanded that U-boat warfare against England should be utilized to its utmost extent. We are going to meet our enemies with the same harshness and lack of consideration as they have shown us in economic matters and our U-boats will no longer submit themselves to the danger of stopping ships. And within a reasonable time the hour will strike for England to recognize by the disappearance of her tonnage the hopelessness of her struggle.'[102] It is certain that Dönitz, fresh from rationing and shortages in the fatherland, had exactly the same view of the British starvation blockade. It was shared by all hands; here, for instance, is Roman Bader, a U-boat chief petty officer from Bavaria:

> When I travelled about on leave and so often saw children whose angel souls shone through their pale, starved bodies, or soldiers themselves but skin and bone, carrying their last loaf home to their wives whose hour had nearly come, I was seized with fury against this inhuman enemy who had cut off Germany's food imports. And what I felt, all my comrades on the sea felt too.[103]

U 39, flying the black-crossed white flag with the Prussian eagle in the centre and the black-white-red Imperial colours in the upper corner, cast off from her moorings at 3 o'clock in the afternoon of February 12 1917, and steered for the open Adriatic. She was a boat of some 685 tons, 200 feet long overall. An 8·8-cm gun stood on her narrow foredeck, abaft it the conning tower rose, light grey-painted with rails around the top and periscope housings rising from the forward end; abaft them in the minute deck on which the officers and lookouts stood their watches, a heavy circular hatch gave access to a vertical steel ladder leading down to the tower and the control room below it.

The body of the U-boat was a cylindrical pressure chamber divided into watertight sections by bulkheads pierced by narrow thick steel doors. Right forward were the torpedoes, hammocks and kit bags stowed amongst them; in the next compartment aft, above a steel deck over the batteries supplying power for the motors which drove the boat when submerged, crew bunks rose in tiers to the arching deckhead. Forstmann's cabin was a curtained-off cubicle by the watertight door leading into the control room; the officers' accommodation was hard by, soft black leather settees which did duty for bunks at night with other bunks above them, the tiny spaces closed off by green curtains. Next was the control room, a warren of pipes, wires, valves, wheels, levers gauges, with separate warrens for the auxiliary machinery and wireless equipment. Through the watertight door at the after end were the diesel engines, the pistons thudding with a beat so loud that conversation was impossible. Aft of them was the turbine compartment, then the hull tapered to the stern torpedo room.

As this brief description implies, there was little privacy and little comfort in a U-boat. There was no bath and only one lavatory for the use of all 50-odd officers and men aboard. Few shaved, no one changed their clothes from the beginning to the end of a voyage. The officers used eau de cologne to mask body odour and the indescribable damp, oil-laden, stale smells of the sweating interior of the boat. But because of this closeness and the shared hardship and danger, and because there was no room for men who could not be relied on, a U-boat's complement was a uniquely tight brotherhood. ' "One for all and all for one," as it was expressed, we were like a great family isolated on the wastes of the oceans . . . I cannot conceive of a finer or more loyal community of life and labour than that of a U-boat.'[104] Thus one typical description.

Dönitz found it so; in the shared purposefulness, the need for constant alertness and self-discipline, the close camaraderie his reserved nature and ardent spirit found fulfilment.

The day following her departure, February 13th, U 39 reached the Straits of Otranto after dark. This was the narrow bottleneck which the British Naval Commander in the Adriatic, Rear Admiral Mark Kerr, had sought to cordon off with a net and mine barrage protected by drifters, but without sufficient of either and without enough destroyers or aircraft or control over the other anti-U-boat forces in the area. The Italians had by this time entered the war on the allied side, but their naval and air forces for this work were under divided control and did not come under Mark Kerr. He constantly pressed the home authorities for more and better-armed craft. 'All the submarines come in and out of Cattaro,' he wrote. 'We hear them every day by the Telefunken stations here. An Austrian plane flies over the drifters and reports where they are, and as the water is deep and the gaps large, they dive and dodge us with impunity.'[105]

Cruising on the surface under a dark, starry sky with a phosphorescent wash at the bows and eddying up the curving sides of the hull, Forstmann made out a line of eight guardships shortly after eight o'clock, and dived, continuing his course submerged. He came up at 11.15; there was nothing in sight and he continued on the surface. Half an hour later another line of guardships, sixteen this time, reared from the dark; he dived again and motored with the electric engines until 2.25 in the morning. Surfacing, he found all clear. The barrage was behind him.

67

Shortly after sunrise a steamer was reported ahead steering easterly; as it was too far off to get into position for a submerged torpedo attack, he decided on a gun action; probably Dönitz was in charge of the party which hastened up to the foredeck; however, they had no sooner opened fire than the steamer replied from two medium-calibre guns and, running up the French flag, altered course directly towards them. Forstmann dived hastily. When they surfaced again 45 minutes later the ship was nowhere to be seen, but the wireless operator could hear her reporting their position through the 'Allo Funkspruch', as Forstmann called it. She was evidently a French auxiliary cruiser. They proceeded southerly making for a position 36° north 19° east on the steamship route around Greece to Malta.

At a quarter past twelve a smoke cloud was spotted over the horizon in the east; Forstmann ordered full speed and altered southwesterly to get in position for a torpedo attack. At one-thirty he dived ahead of the approaching vessel and 40 minutes later fired from one of the bow tubes. A hit! He watched through the periscope as the crew abandoned her.

Afterwards he surfaced and; steering towards the boats, found that his victim was an Italian steamer. Dönitz on the foredeck called out for her Captain, '*Il capitano venga subito a bordo!*' To his astonishment a woman rose from one of the boats and replied in perfect German that the Captain was in her boat but wounded. Forstmann steered alongside, finding a gentleman in a smoking jacket in charge, the Captain with a broken arm and bandaged head lying across a thwart, and amongst the crew nine women 'regarding us in a by no means hostile manner'. The former spokeswoman explained that they were members of the German *Reich* living in Egypt who had been forced to leave and were on their way home via Italy. Forstmann transferred the sailors into one of the other boats, leaving only three with the wounded Captain and the German women, allowed in a Swiss couple with a pretty daughter 'who had already attracted the attention of my men', and took the boat under tow towards the Malta steamship route he was making for. That evening he cast them off with hearty farewells all round, since, he wrote, it was his practice to spend the hours of darkness submerged.

The next morning U 39 was lying in wait in what Forstmann liked to call his 'lair', 36° north, in the Ionian Sea where on the previous voyage he had sunk a troop transport. As dawn broke, two steamers came in sight; he set course for a position ahead of the easternmost and at 7.15

dived and steered in to attack at periscope depth, but after 25 minutes he realized she was going to pass too far ahead and abandoned the attack. An hour later he surfaced and again lay drifting in wait. It was not long before a steamer came up over the edge of the horizon, steering directly for them, to all appearances a freighter bound for Salonika. He decided on a torpedo attack and at 11.50 dived to ten metres, setting a submerged approach course.

> Bow to bow we approach. We proceed as deeply submerged as possible so that the long periscope when driven by motor power through the cover of the conning tower may only just break the surface sufficiently to permit a survey. Beneath me in the control room the hydroplane crew gaze uninterruptedly upon the water level and pressure gauge, carefully guiding the helm and giving themselves the utmost trouble to 'steer straight', as it is called, in the registering apparatus which shows the depth curve as a straight line when the steering is good . . . Near me in the narrow conning tower the navigating officer is busy with compass and set-square and bending over his small chart works out the course while the Torpedo officer [Dönitz] gives orders through the speaking trumpet to clear torpedoes for action. The second officer of the watch is in charge of the hydroplanes, the engineer superintends the engines, flooding and venting arrangements. Anxious thought, serious reflection at all command stations! And therein the whole management of the ship is carried on quietly and securely, almost noiselessly beneath me, for each individual knows his responsible duty and foresees all possible contingencies.[106]

It was Forstmann's custom to involve his crew in attacks by giving commentaries from time to time of what he could see through the periscope. On this occasion as the steamer was still a long way off, he called men individually to the command position to look through the glass themselves. Meanwhile, up in the bows the torpedo hands flooded the tubes and wished their charges luck.

It was a bright day; a north wind tossed up small white-capped waves, good weather for an attack since it would make the periscope more difficult to spot. As they drew closer Forstmann ran it out more infrequently and only for short periods to check the relative positions. Tension in the boat mounted; they closed within 400 metres, then

Forstmann pressed the black button at his side; immediately the engineer and hydroplane operators went into their routine to regain trim as the bows rose with the release of the torpedo's weight. The officers started counting the seconds. Forstmann himself was confident all the factors were right for a hit.

> With metallic sharpness it strikes the ship's side, crack goes the steamer in every joint. A hit!
> Run out the periscope!
> Every hit causes me pleasure. Motionless, struck to death in the engineroom lies the black-painted steamer, her two masts and a short funnel over the slim hull preen themselves close to us. A feeling of exultation fills our breasts. But what is the matter with the steamer? Good God! A dismal spectacle! Hundreds of men are running about like so many caged deer, crowding together or throwing themselves into the relentless sea in mad terror . . . matchless confusion![107]

They wore grey uniforms and caps; Forstmann realized that what he had taken for an ordinary freighter was yet another troop transport packed with soldiers. He watched in disgust as the few lifeboats were lowered in panic, so overcrowded they capsized immediately they hit the water. After half an hour the ship was still afloat, her wireless aerials undamaged, and he decided to give her the *coup de grâce*; he recorded the reason in his war diary: '. . . there is a possibility she is requesting help by wireless, stern shot fired, hit aft. Steamer sank at once after violent detonation in after part.'[108]

He had never seen such spectacular results from a single shot, and when he surfaced a quarter of an hour later the water was bobbing with wreckage, corpses and struggling survivors. He steered towards the dreadful scene to ascertain details, Dönitz again taking station up in the bows.

'Two men are drifting over there, sir!' he called up.

Forstmann steered towards them; a lifeline was thrown and presently two shivering, half-naked and very frightened soldiers were hauled aboard by the forward hydroplanes. Dönitz shouted up, 'Italians!'

> Of course—organ-grinders. Who else should it be!
> They were brought on to the conning tower . . . the younger looks comparatively hearty in spite of the fact that his lower jaw trembles

70

and his teeth are audibly rattling. With bright dark eyes he takes stock of his strange surroundings . . . and after several *avantis* and *prestos* we get the most important facts out of him. '*A bord de* Minas *un général, beaucoup d'officiers, mille soldats et trois millions en or,*' he jerks out in the excitable manner peculiar to the Macaronis. Great joy on our side, why he speaks French like a book . . .[109]

Forstmann set course westerly with the intention of lying in wait off Malta the following morning, meanwhile taking the two 'sea-faring organ-grinders' down for a more detailed interrogation in his cabin, reporting the satisfactory results in his war diary:

It is the Italian troop transport *Minas*, 2,884 tons, on passage from Naples to Salonika. On board were one general, three colonels, and including a 40-man (motor transport artillery) train, 1,000 battle-ready armed Italians from Infantry regiments Nos 31, 39 and 63. The steamer was freighted with munitions and three millions in gold. She was escorted by a destroyer from noon 14.2 until 6.0 am 15.2. In consequence of the great panic on board and the rough seas all the ship's boats capsized, there was no escort nearby and no wireless signal could be made, we may reckon on the loss of all the troops . . .[110]

In his more popular account, no doubt intended at least in part for propaganda effect at home, Forstmann wrote, 'Help shall come too late! Every soft-hearted act of mercy to the enemy would be foul treason to our own striving people . . .'[111] Apropos the sinking of the troop transport on the previous voyage, he had written:

And yet to be honest I am not quite satisfied! Again and again the thought goes through my head that when the steamer sank only 150 soldiers were lost out of 900, a comparatively small loss to the enemy in comparison to the total strength on board. However hard it may seem to sentimental minds in time of war, one must energetically put aside all sympathy, all pity and every other feeling of the kind, for there is no doubt that their influence tends to weakness. The object of war is to annihilate the armed forces of the enemy whether it be on the battlefield or in a fight at sea . . . No Frenchman ought to have escaped with his life to be taken aboard another transport to Macedonia to be used against and cause loss among our field-grey comrades fighting

71

there. I firmly believe it would have been my duty to them and to the Fatherland to prevent this. I am glad now that I came to these conclusions as I was soon able to put them to practical use when sinking an Italian troop transport.[112]

The similarity with some of Treitschke's maxims is apparent, but the logic is irrefutable; thus had this new submarine weapon changed the nature of war at sea. In previous wars and in surface actions in the present war the victors invariably rescued as many of their enemies as they could from the water. But submarines could not accommodate prisoners. The logic of this simple fact, if pressed to its ultimate conclusion in a life-or-death struggle, gives rise to murderous ideas—as will appear during Dönitz's conduct of just such a campaign in the Second World War.

Most of the remainder of the cruise was spent on the North African coast, where Forstmann sank another four merchantmen with torpedoes and two by gunfire. On one occasion he had to dive for a destroyer which dropped a depth charge—one only. On March 7th he brought the boat back to the depot ship at Cattaro.

'Bravo U 39!' Loud cheers greet the fortunate and victorious returned warriors . . . groups forming on deck are pumped with questions, 'How are you?' 'What is it like?' etc. . . . then we receive on board the most welcome greeting of all, the monthly post. Boatswain's mate Herdecker takes the letters out of the heavy mail bag, made of sail cloth, and distributes them . . .
. . . And there in quiet corners the men sit, dreaming of home, of love, of many faraway things.[113]

Probably Dönitz managed to get home, for U 39 spent some months refitting at Pola and did not sail again until the end of May; it is quite likely, therefore, that he was at home when his first child was born on April 3rd; it was a girl; she was christened Ursula.

April was a month of euphoria for the U-boat service and the Admiralty staff. Despite America's entry into the war on the 6th, the figures of enemy tonnage destroyed had exceeded von Holtzendorff's estimates handsomely from the beginning of the unrestricted campaign—so, at least, it was believed. Now for the month of April they passed the million mark. In fact they had not, but the actual figures were sufficiently great to have caused profound alarm in London; they were (German estimates in brackets):[114]

	allied shipping sunk by U-boats		allied shipping sunk by all means
February	464,599 tons	(781,500)	532,856 tons
March	507,001 tons	(885,000)	599,854 tons
April	834,549 tons	(1,091,000)	869,103 tons

The German figures, although inaccurate, were probably the better indication of the way the campaign was going, for in addition to the ships actually sunk some 300,000 tons had been temporarily removed by damage, hundreds of neutrals had, as von Holtzendorff expressed it, been 'terrorized away', and delays and re-routings accounted for many more thousand tons unused. It is not the place to analyse why the Royal Navy had discarded the lessons of its own and others' past wars and failed to institute a system of convoys which had always proved an effective protection for merchant shipping; it is interesting to note, though, that von Holtzendorff and the German Admiralty staff made a graver mistake by failing to allow for the fact that their campaign might *force* the adoption of convoy—or indeed that it might force any reaction which could have any effect on their precisely extrapolated figures; this egocentricity was a feature of all German naval planning; it had been in Tirpitz's time—indeed *Weltpolitik* itself had been undertaken with almost frivolous disregard for the reaction of the intended victims—it was to be so again in Dönitz's time—a fatal belief in simple, preferably 'ruthless' plans on which the enemy would allow himself to be impaled. It was a facet of the Prussian mind which the Imperial Navy had absorbed unconsciously, unaware that it did not suit naval conditions and that great maritime empires had always acted more pragmatically—indeed one of the chief causes of the Royal Navy's failure to bring in convoy was such excessive pragmatism as to lack any proper planning staff!

Nevertheless, when forced by immediate impending disaster to consider and adapt, the Royal Navy was able to do so; a number of officers, mostly in comparatively junior positions, had been pressing for convoy for some time and trial convoys had been organized; finally the staggering April losses convinced both Admiralty and government that unless something were done unconditional surrender stared them in the face; on April 26th the decision was taken to 'introduce a comprehensive

73

scheme of convoy'.[115] Coming in from June onwards, this radically altered the premises of von Holtzendorff's calculations; strategically and tactically the system was offensive; it forced the U-boats to attack in the presence of escorts instead of diving under patrols or guardships and attacking lone merchantmen; with warships in close contact the U-boats were forced to submerge and in doing so they lost their manoeuvrability—for they could not make more than about seven knots at best on their battery driven electric motors—consequently it was difficult for them to get into position ahead for a second attack. But the most surprising result of convoy was to make the waters suddenly very empty. Instead of a stream of ships at more or less regular intervals there were days when U-boat lookouts saw nothing at all.

Convoy gave the neutrals heart, and by making more effective use of shipping space and buying new ships from abroad the allies gradually overcame the tonnage crisis. Von Holtzendorff could not, of course, overcome the deepening crisis in Germany caused by the American entry he had precipitated.

Clear as it is in retrospect that April 1917 marked the turning point, it was far from clear at the time or for several months afterwards to either side, and when Dönitz rejoined U 39 it seemed that Germany was on course for a sensational turning of the tables and no less a triumph than the awaited breakthrough to world power over the carcase of the British empire. After U 39's next cruise few of Forstmann's crew could have doubted it.

He had decided to strike at the very focus of allied and imperial lines of communication off Gibraltar, and after leaving the Adriatic steered directly for the Straits, steering through on the surface after dark on June 7th. The first target presented herself early the following morning; as she was some distance away Forstmann approached on the surface and engaged with the gun, Dönitz directing the firing. The steamer immediately turned away and replied with a 7·6-cm piece on her poop, but after a brief action Dönitz's men scored a hit amidships which stopped her, and she was abandoned. Before sinking her with explosive charges Forstmann found that she was a 3,800-ton Britisher bound for Italy with munitions. In his popular account he recorded a lively scene in the U-boat's foc's'le after the success: 'the gun's crew and ammunition carriers naturally feel themselves the heroes of the hour'.[116]

That evening he sank two ships by torpedo, the second an 8,000-ton British steamer which brought his total for the first day outside the Straits to 16,597 tons! He admired the 'faultless trim and discipline' of the survivors when he approached the group of lifeboats.

> The man in charge clambers over to us. 'Evening, sir!' he says. An Englishman! With a pleasant smile on his face he comes towards me, 'Oh, you bad man! Oh, you bad man!' he repeats again and again . . . His bearing does not convey the impression that he is depressed by the torpedoing, but rather that he is pleased at the sportsmanlike manner of my night attack . . . This ship's officer is, however, an exception, for being torpedoed usually upsets the strongest nerves. In general those in the boats of a torpedoed steamer are in a very depressed state of mind. I believe the chief factor to be the deep injury to the pride of the English, who up to now have held the undisputed mastery of the seas . . .[117]

Remaining in the area outside the Straits for the next fortnight Forstmann sank a further nine vessels before starting his return passage; he arrived back on July 1st with a bag of fourteen vessels totalling 33,000 tons—as the Naval Staff noted, 'an outstanding performance. With his success in the trade war *Kapitänleutnant* Forstmann stands as ever at the head of all U-boat Commanders'.[118] What appears remarkable today is Forstmann's success rate with torpedoes. Practically every shot was a hit, and it was all done by eye and mental calculation; there were no machine calculators as in the Second World War. Perhaps one of his secrets was the close range at which he fired.

This was very nearly his undoing on the next cruise, and came close to ending Dönitz's story. They sailed on July 19th, passed Otranto without trouble and headed for the Straits, steering through after dark during the night of July 27th–28th; again targets started to appear immediately and by August 3rd he had destroyed six steamers totalling almost 19,000 tons. August 4th was uneventful, then on the morning of the 5th a convoy was sighted in the north-east. The day was fine; no wind disturbed the oily calm of the surface, not ideal conditions for an attack since the periscope and its tell-tale wash would be easily visible to sharp lookouts. Nevertheless, he dived and steered north to intercept, soon discovering twelve merchantmen in three columns of four ships each, a destroyer escort on the bow of the leading ship of the starboard column and an auxiliary cruiser on the quarter of the last ship in the port column. Seventy-five minutes later, soon after eleven, by which time he had made out the leading ship in the column as an empty tanker, he set an attack course for a laden ship next astern of her. Because of the sea conditions he used his periscope sparingly; when he ran it out two minutes later to check his position it appeared that his new target ship had altered course somewhat towards him; he ran the periscope in. Two minutes later he had another look. This time there was no doubt; the ship was bearing down straight for him. 'Because of the flatness of the sea he must have seen the periscope.'[119] He ordered 20° starboard rudder, intending to sheer off and get in a stern shot on the third ship in the column. Moments afterwards at 11.10 there was a fearful concussion from starboard forward and the boat was rolled over and pushed deeper; they heard the steamer's bottom plates grating over them.

. . . The steamer passed over the boat at an acute angle, knocked the gun over, and grazed the port side of the conning tower, breaking the three periscopes and the compass. The boat took a list of 20 degrees. Six rivets holding the gun mounting leaked.[120]

Surfacing 90 minutes later and surveying the damage, he decided to return to base. His difficulties were not over though. Four days later off southern Italy while the crew were lying on deck sleeping or reading in the hot afternoon sun, the engineer, pacing the afterdeck, turned suddenly and ran towards the tower, calling out, 'Two flying machines astern!'

Good Lord! There they are . . . barely 2,000 metres astern.
'Aircraft alarm!' One sees that they are rapidly growing larger. I already hear their angry hum. Damnation! This means that the after lookout has not being paying attention.[121]

The sailors jumped down the forward hatch as the alarm sounded; from the bridge the lookouts and watch officer tumbled down the ladder almost on top of each other, Forstmann following, closing the hatch over his head and locking it. Immediately the tanks were flooded and the hydroplanes set for a crash dive. As the sea washed over the foredeck and up the tower Forstmann heard a desperate banging on the hatch-cover above his head. He shouted down to the control room to blow the forward tanks, and reached up to unfasten the cover. Directly he pushed it up a badly-scared stoker named Hausolte came falling in with a rush of sea water. Pulling him down, Forstmann caught a glimpse of the two flying machines only 50 metres away; he shouted for a crash dive as he closed and locked the hatch again. They had reached eight metres when the first bomb landed some distance away, and fifteen metres when they heard a second, also wide.

... I suspect that the flyers took the 45-degree angled periscope as an anti-balloon gun and thought the man on the turret was serving it, which checked their resolve.[122]

It turned out the man had been fast asleep and had not heard the alarm. He had been woken by the engines of the flying machines and, seeing the sea coming up over the foredeck and no one about, realized they were diving, rushed up to the bridge and banged on the conning-tower hatch with his boot: 'The water rose up to my waist, sir. I just clutched hold of the periscope and thought my last hour had come.'

Forstmann did not record his feelings, nor did Dönitz in any published account, but a manuscript he wrote in 1935, almost certainly intended for publication, does contain a tribute to Forstmann's presence of mind on this occasion—without, however, mentioning him by name!

... my Commander of U 39 had sunk 400,000 tons, was one of the first to be awarded the *Pour le Mérite* and above all had a warm heart for his men. Leave one of us in trouble—no, that would not do—not even in this dangerous situation for the whole boat! That was our Commander's lightning-quick decision: 'Compressed air in all tanks! Surface! . . . Hatch open!'—and with a broad jet of green sea-water in fell a poor, self-conscious stoker and called out in most beautiful Saxon, '*Runter! Runter! Fliecher! Fliecher!*' [Down! Down! Flier! Flier!].[123]

It seems from the account that Dönitz thoroughly approved of this split-second decision to rescue Hausolte at the risk of the boat and the rest of the crew. In the Second World War he would not have done, but by then the flying machine had become the U-boat's most feared enemy.

Three days later U 39 was safely in the Bay of Cattaro; from there she sailed for Pola for repairs, during which time it seems probable that Dönitz went home for a spell of leave and Forstmann wrote up his account for popular consumption; it is notable that although he told the

77

story of Stoker Hausolte and the flying machines he made no mention whatever of being rammed and damaged, or even of attacking a convoy.

The next cruise of U 39 was from September 18th to October 14th, during which Forstmann sank six steamers of around 24,000 tons. The Flag Officer U-boats noted it as a 'model undertaking' which had brought Forstmann's personal total up to 411,000 tons of shipping destroyed. 'He has handed over his command as at present the most successful U-boat Commander.'[124]

Forstmann reported well on Dönitz. Under 'Appearance and figure', he wrote 'very good military appearance, socially very deft'. Under 'General Remarks':

Sailed and navigated the boat calmly and confidently, is reliable as watchkeeping officer and understands the management of his subordinates . . . Lively, energetic officer, who enters into each duty with diligence and enthusiasm. Very good writing-officer.

Popular comrade, tactful messmate.[125]

Years later Dönitz replied to a letter from Forstmann: 'U 39 was a *prima* school and time! Ever your grateful Dönitz.'[126]

Ordered to a month's gunnery training course for U-boat Commanders in Kiel in December, Dönitz also left U 39 at this time. And after the course, at which he was described as confident and determined, he was given a command of his own, UC 25, a combined minelayer and torpedo attack boat of some 417 tons.

'I felt as mighty as a king.'[127]

By now the springtime of confidence in U-boats had faded. It was not admitted that the unrestricted campaign had failed; indeed the officially released figures for sinkings were more wildly optimistic than before and tended to disguise it. But nothing could disguise the fact that Great Britain had not been forced to her knees, and as von Holtzendorff had made a public boast that five months would suffice to bring her to that position public confidence was shaken and morale in the U-boat service had deteriorated—although not to the same extent as in the surface fleet.

In retrospect it is clear that the campaign had been defeated. It was not yet entirely clear to the British Admiralty: sinkings were still high, new construction had not caught up yet, and the destruction of U-boats was

78

depressingly low and only just beginning to catch up with German construction. The losses in the last three months of 1917 (German estimates in brackets) were:[128]

	allied shipping sunk by U-boats	*allied shipping sunk by all means*
October	429,147 tons (674,000)	458,496 tons
November	259,521 tons (607,000)	292,682 tons
December	353,083 tons (702,000)	394,115 tons

These still high figures concealed the fact that the U-boats had been forced to shift their operations away from the ocean routes where convoy had been adopted and into coastal waters where the traffic was still largely independent; a further significant proportion of losses had come from the Mediterranean where the convoy system had not really come in until November—as Forstmann's cruises indicate. The actual loss rate of ships in convoy was only 1·2 per cent or one twentieth of the rate in the worst April days at the beginning of the campaign, and it was this fact, not improved measures to sink U-boats or improved results in that direction—still only 5·7 per cent of operational boats sunk against 4 per cent at the beginning of the war[129]—that indicated the defeat of the unrestricted campaign.

Dönitz, determined nonetheless to pour his all into his new command and win reputation, sailed from Pola on his first cruise at the end of February; his instructions were to lay mines before Palermo and conduct trade war in the adjacent waters, but as intelligence came in that the British repair ship, *Cyclops*, was in Port Augusta on the east coast of Sicily, he was directed to attack her with torpedoes or lay mines to bar her passage out. In his account of the cruise in his memoirs he made much of the risks of passing the Straits of Otranto. It is true that a conference on February 8–9th had decided on a tremendous increase in the numbers and extent of guardship lines, nets, mines and aircraft in the straits at the expense of convoy—since the new British Commander Adriatic did not believe in convoy!—but these extra measures could not be brought in immediately and even after completion the barrage proved no more effective than before. U-boats could always dive under the nets and avoid the surface patrols, which they did with impunity. Only one boat was caught in the nets and two at the most destroyed by surface craft. Nevertheless the possibility of mines and depth charges was ever present while negotiating this bottleneck, and steady nerves were required.

Dönitz was forced under and bombed by an aircraft before he reached the straits, which he had hoped to negotiate on the surface after dark, and he was forced under again by another aircraft before he was out of the danger zone—as he remarked, an extraordinarily heavy air patrol for the time. Once through he made straight for Port Augusta, arriving on the morning of March 17th and lying submerged some way off surveying the harbour through his periscope. Inside was a large ship with seven double masts; he assumed with excitement that this must be his target, *Cyclops*. Waiting until late in the afternoon, he steered towards the entrance intending to find a way in by twilight, but he saw ten buoys running in a line from the fairway mark; these obviously held anti-U-boat nets and, unable to see any gaps, he steered out to sea again, intending to make another inspection in full daylight.

This he did early the following morning, the 18th; the first thing he saw was two tugs, each with two lighters in tow, steering out of the harbour between the buoys and a light-tower standing on a rock to the north of the entrance. The chart showed this passage as being a mere seven metres deep. An hour later he saw another tug with a single lighter steering out hard by the fairway buoy, between it and the first of the net buoys; here the depth was shown on his chart as twelve metres. Since the only sizeable ship in the port was the one he took to be the *Cyclops* and the traffic appeared to be solely in barges and small craft, he decided that the small gap of about fifteen metres through which the last tug had steered was the only way he could get in.[130] This is not how he described it in his memoirs; he made no mention of the lighter traffic he observed, stating simply that near the light-tower to the north of the entrance the greatest depth of water was twelve metres; thinking that so mean a depth would be regarded as impassable by U-boats, and that in consequence no nets would be laid there, he decided to go in by this passage. Many years had passed by then, he was an old man and he made other slips of memory in his description of the voyage; yet his war diary entries had been published in the official account of the U-boat war two years before.

Having chosen his entry point by the fairway mark, he ordered the crew to don lifejackets, had the secret papers placed in a sack with an explosive charge, other charges positioned to destroy the boat itself should they be forced to the surface inside, and steered for the gap at periscope depth at three knots—all his small boat could make under water. There was a stiff northerly breeze pushing up whitecaps on the surface and he passed the line of buoys unobserved shortly before 10 o'clock. He continued westerly, using the periscope as little and as briefly as possible to check his position and quickly scan all round to see if he had been observed, but there was nothing in sight save small sailing craft and he remained undetected. Turning to a northerly course for the inner harbour where the large ship was lying, he reached a suitable firing position at 10.49; 'First tube away!' He fired both bow tubes and saw explosions against the forward third of the ship throwing up high pillars of water; immediately he ordered the rudder hard over for a stern shot. Two minutes later the boat had come round and he fired the stern tube. A hit on the quarter! He steered out the way he had come in.

The steamer began to settle at once. Raising his periscope briefly at 11.00 he saw that she had taken a heavy list and her foc's'le was under water. By 11.15 she had turned over on her side, and a minute later there was nothing of her to be seen. By this time a flying machine had appeared overhead. Three minutes later he turned east for the fairway mark and saw that the flying machine was cruising over the line of buoys and a sea-going tug had placed herself directly across the gap through which he had come in. He had no alternative but to down periscope and steer under her; this he did a quarter of an hour later, touching the bottom at eleven and a half metres, then bumping and sliding over it for some three minutes until at a depth of fifteen metres the boat came free. By 11.35 he was well outside and steering for the open sea. There had been no bombs dropped and no warships had come in sight; even the tug had been where she was by chance, he realized.

> The men removed their lifejackets. The explosive charges . . . were stowed away. My watch officer, *Leutnant z. See* Wempe, placed the secret books from the sack back in the drawer. We all beamed at one another. Everyone received a cognac.[131]

He made for Palermo and laid his mines outside the harbour on the 21st; there was little traffic though and he found no targets for his remaining two torpedoes—the boat only carried five—until he looked into the narrows of Messina. Here he found a two-funnelled steamer escorted by two destroyers. He lay in wait submerged, and fired both torpedoes at her, diving deep immediately because of the escort and, not hearing any detonation, assumed he had missed. As the position of his boat had been given away by the turbulence caused by the discharge of the torpedoes, he was soon under depth-charge attack. It is not clear how long this lasted—such attacks were not often effective at this time because of the want of any efficient apparatus to detect a submerged U-boat's position. Some time after it had finished he made his way up again very cautiously and ran out the periscope; there was nothing in sight.

The failure affected him deeply, as all setbacks did, and he was probably an uncomfortable man to be with on the return voyage. Then, steering in close among the Dalmatian Islands by night to avoid the minefields of the Otranto barrage, the boat ran aground, ramming her open mine hatch on the rocks so hard that no engine movements or alterations of trim could free her. He was forced to call up for assistance, which appeared the following day in the shape of an Austrian destroyer. She towed him off and he resumed course for Pola, as he lightly put it in his memoirs, with very mixed feelings, wondering 'how amiably the Flag Officer U-boats and the flotilla chief would receive me'. Almost certainly he was sunk in deep gloom. However, he found on arrival that his exploit at Port Augusta far outweighed any errors; the Flag Officer U-boats (FdU) noted on his report: The Commander conducted the attack leading to the destruction of the valuable 9,000-ton ship with magnificent dash and great circumspection. The achievement deserves special recognition.[132]

The official announcement of the feat was brought to the Kaiser's attention; he noted in the margin, '*Dekoration!*' and on June 10th Dönitz was awarded the coveted Knight's Cross of the order of the house of Hohenzollern. As it turned out the ship he had sunk was not the *Cyclops*, but a 5,000-ton Italian coaling hulk—not that this detracted from the boldness and cool precision of the exploit.

After UC 25 had been repaired Dönitz took her out for another cruise in July, laying mines before Corfu, then making torpedo attacks on four ships, one of which was beached on Malta and the other three presumed destroyed. This was a good result since two of the ships were under strong escort. His flotilla chief noted on his report:

The undertaking was discharged with much deliberation, competence and energy. The thorough observation of the traffic before the mine-laying before Corfu and the occupation of the waiting position before

Thrace deserve special recognition. The strong escort was out-manoeuvred with skill.[133]

UC 25 was paid off after this cruise and Dönitz was appointed to a larger, faster command, UB 68, then undergoing a refit in Pola after having made three Mediterranean cruises since her arrival from the North Sea in January. In his memoirs Dönitz wrote that the longitudinal stability of these UB boats was delicate; when diving at more than four to six degrees inclination the deck area tended to act as a sheer plane forcing the boats to a deeper angle and unless vigorous action was taken they eventually stood on their heads. He suggested that the tendency was perhaps exaggerated in UB 68 during her refit when her original 8·8-cm gun was replaced by a 10·5-cm piece and to compensate a lead weight was attached to her keel, and additional buoyancy tanks were soldered to her upper deck. How important these factors were in subsequent events is impossible to say.

Probably far more important, although not mentioned at all by Dönitz, was the inexperience of her crew. Due to the steady if unspec-tacular loss of U-boats during the course of the war and the desperate efforts the naval command was now making to overcome the convoy system by throwing as many boats into the fray as they could possibly fit out, crews were diluted with increasing numbers of raw entrants who had received a shorter training than hitherto. The crew of UB 68 was an extreme example of this, as the British interrogation report on her survivors makes clear:

> The crew were almost entirely new to the boat and the majority were also experiencing their first cruise on a submarine. Several of them had suffered sea sickness during the voyage. Some of them had only been in Pola a very short time before the cruise began.[134]

UB 68 sailed on her one and only voyage under Dönitz's command on September 25th, practising diving every day on the way down the Adriatic without accidents or alarms. The Otranto barrage, which had by now been increased to the theoretically formidable combination of nets, minefields and patrol lines in depth involving over 200 vessels equipped with hydrophones, kite balloons and depth charges, and 72 aircraft, was passed without difficulty on the surface at night. As another U-boat Commander expressed it when interrogated, this way of getting through the barrage was 'only an ordinary war risk; I could always sight patrol craft long before they saw me'.[135]

Once through the Straits, Dönitz steered for a position 50 miles south-east of Cape Passero—the southern corner of Sicily—about equidistant from Grand Harbour, Malta, on the latitude of the convoy route. In Pola he had arranged to meet another U-boat Commander here on the evening of October 3rd for joint night attacks on convoys during the new moon period. What he did not mention in his memoirs was that such a strategy of joint attack had been adopted by the FdU, Mediterranean, in response to the increasing number of flying machines appearing over the focal points of trade and making it unsafe for U-boats to operate in these areas, which had been their chief hunting grounds. 'Under these circumstances,' Dönitz's Flotilla chief, *Fregattenkapitän* Otto Schultze, wrote in 1927, 'it was necessary to adapt the tactics of the torpedo U-boats to the common employment of several U-boats in the same sea area. Attempts in this direction were started by the FdU in the second half of 1918.'[136]

Nor did Dönitz mention that his partner on this occasion, *Kapitänleutnant* Steinbauer of U 48, an experienced Commander and Knight of the *Pour le Mérite*, had already carried out two operations in concert with other boats, the first as early as January, 1918, with the 'ace', von Mellenthin, who on the basis of his own experiences had already made a proposal for 'group tactics' by U-boats against merchantmen.[137] Dönitz did not mention these things since it would have prejudiced his own claims as originator of group tactics.

On this occasion his partner, Steinbauer, was not at the rendezvous; he had been held up for repairs. Dönitz remained on the surface that night, steering easterly to judge by his subsequent position. At about one o'clock in the morning (October 4th) some 150 miles east of Malta, the navigating warrant officer who had the middle watch sighted the shapes of a convoy heading towards them on a northwesterly course; he called Dönitz who steered for an attack position. According to Dönitz's memoirs, things now happened very quickly; thrusting through the outer destroyer screen, still on the surface, he found the steamers turning towards him on one leg of a zig zag so that he was now inside the columns. He loosed a torpedo at the nearest ship and saw 'a gigantic bright water-column', which was followed by a detonation; just avoiding the stern of the second ship in the column he saw a destroyer coming at him 'at high speed with a white bow wave'.[138] He dived and made away under

84

water. Surfacing again after a quarter of an hour, he made out the shapes of the ships in the west and chased after them at full speed, only gradually overhauling since wind and sea were against him, and by the time he was in position ahead for another attack it had begun to grow light; he had to submerge for a torpedo attack.

The story as told to the interrogating officers by UB 68's navigating warrant officer is less dramatic; it does not mention penetrating the escort screen, nor the zig zag, nor getting in amongst the columns, nor nearly bumping the second ship; he merely said:

One of the bow tubes was fired and a steamer was hit aft, but not observed to sink. To protect the U-boat from attack by the destroyers seen escorting the convoy, orders were given to dive and to keep periscope patrol. After proceeding submerged for about half an hour UB 68 came to the surface again, and steering a course parallel to the convoy on the starboard hand of the latter overhauled the steamer furthest astern and fired a bow tube at a range of about 500 yards. The torpedo was seen to pass across the steamer's bows, the miss being attributed to an overestimation of the speed of the target (estimated at nine knots, actual speed eight knots). Remaining on the surface the U-boat thereupon took up a position on the port side of the convoy, maintaining an approximately parallel course at a distance of 600 yards. In this position she proceeded till daylight, which appeared to come up with surprising suddenness. As it had previously been decided to proceed submerged during daylight and to follow the movements of the convoy until a favourable opportunity for attack should present itself, orders were given to dive.[139]

Dönitz's official report supports this version as it mentions two unsuccessful torpedo attacks made on the surface between 2.30 and 3.30 after the first attack—which had resulted in the sinking of the 3,883-ton British steamer *Oopack*. This report was in print in the official account of the U-boat war two years before Dönitz wrote the second volume of his memoirs—both volumes contained slightly differing accounts of the attack—and it must be assumed that, like the account of his proceedings before Port Augusta, the inaccuracies were intended to enhance the impression of danger and his own prowess, and in this case hide the fact that he fired either one or two torpedoes which missed—an unnecessary conceit, one would have thought, in the light of his proven daring in

85

entering Port Augusta, and his subsequent record and rise to the rare height of Grand Admiral; for that reason the embroidery is particularly revealing.

At all events, came the dawn light on October 4th he dived in order to reach a position for a submerged torpedo attack. Immediately something went wrong. Here again there are three different versions, Dönitz's in his memoirs, a slightly different one in his report, and a very different one pieced together from various survivors by British specialist submarine interrogating officers. There are several possible explanations for the discrepancies; he might have felt the disaster was his fault or he may have felt it was his responsibility to have trained his crew more rigorously before attempting operations in the face of the enemy, or he may have known it was the fault of the engineer, but decided to protect him; on the other hand, he may simply have shut his mind to the fearful details of the experience. First, here is his own version.

After ordering the dive he noticed suddenly that his engineer in the control room below was having difficulty with the depth steering, therefore he ordered more speed to give the hydroplane greater effect; it was already too late; the boat had lost longitudinal stability and was plunging with steadily increasing inclination until practically standing on its head.

I can still see today the pointer on the depth manometer in the conning tower falling. I ordered compressed air in all tanks and both engines full astern and the rudder hard aport to restrain it. Then, apparently because of the very strong forward inclination causing the batteries to overflow, the lights went out. My watch officer, *Oberleutnant z. See* Müssen, who stood next to me in the tower, lit the depth manometer with a torch. We certainly wanted to know whether we could save the boat before it collapsed under pressure of the depth. At about 80 metres—the allowed diving depth of the boat was about 70 metres— there was a crack from the deck (as we saw later the newly-fitted buoyancy tanks had been pressed in by the water pressure). The pointer of the manometer moved further down. Müssen's torch went out. I shrieked, 'Light, Müssen!' It was light again. (Müssen explained to me later that he could not look at the rapidly falling pointer and thought all was lost.) Then the pointer stood at 92 metres, trembled there a second and then took off rapidly in the direction of less water depth. A shaking went through the boat, it shot apparently from the surface. (The English Commander told me later that a third of the boat's length had risen into the air as the boat shot up.) The compressed air had worked . . .[140]

Opening the hatch, he found himself in the middle of the convoy, destroyers racing towards him, firing. He closed the hatch rapidly and ordered another dive. The engineer called up that there was no compressed air left. He couldn't grasp it at first, then realized that the amount of air required to blow the tanks from 90 metres must have exhausted the cylinders. He opened the hatch again. The situation was as before except the destroyers were nearer; shots were hitting the boat; he had no option but to give the order to abandon ship and to open the sea cocks and scuttle her.

His official report on the loss described the cause of the dive as an unexplained jamming of the depth steering, whereupon the boat sank to 80 metres stern-first, then changing to a forward inclination of 50 degrees went down to 102 metres where water came in through the stuffing of the stern tube before the compressed air took effect and she shot to the surface in the middle of the convoy.

The true story was more complicated. The tanks were flooded in the usual way after Dönitz's order to dive, and she was being trimmed for periscope depth when she suddenly plunged to fifteen metres; to remedy this the hydroplanes were set to rise, but she came up so sharply that the conning tower broke surface. One explanation suggested that the ratings on the hydroplane controls gave them too much elevation; the ratings themselves blamed either excessive ballasting of the compensating tanks or too high a speed of the boat. To prevent the boat breaking surface completely the engineer flooded the tanks and sent all available hands to the forward compartments to weight the nose down; as a result she took an alarming forward inclination and dived at speed. At 60 metres the engineer attempted to check her by blowing No. VI tank and pumping out the regulator tanks, but either the pumps broke down or could not cope with the quantity of water at this depth. Reaching 80 metres all tanks were blown and the boat started rising rapidly with her stern pointing down at a considerable angle. As it seemed she must break the surface again, at 30 metres the tanks were flooded once more and again she started down, but even faster this time and with a forward inclination of 45 degrees. Something in the stern compartment gave way under pressure, water started coming in, and one of the tanks on deck cracked as she plunged to 102 metres. For the second time all tanks were blown and she shot up, still at the forward inclination of 45 degrees, and rose from the sea stern first with her screws racing before she settled back in the water.

The navigating warrant officer claimed that he had then opened the conning-tower hatch and found they were in the midst of the convoy. He jumped in again, slammed the hatch shut and called down to the control room to dive, but the supply of compressed air had been exhausted by then and also the boat had taken a considerable list to port. The escorts meanwhile had opened fire and there were two hits, one on the conning tower, one on deck forward. Dönitz, seeing the impossibility of escape, ordered the crew to abandon ship and sent the engineer below to open the vents. All hands went on deck except for the engineer, and most jumped into the sea, leaving the dinghy which was lashed on deck for the non-swimmers. There was no time to lose as the boat sank within seconds of the cocks being opened. Dönitz himself took a header from the bridge. The engineer, however, was not seen again; it was suggested by one of the engineer petty officers that he stayed below on purpose. 'In the latter case,' the interrogating officers concluded, 'it is hard to avoid the belief that rightly or wrongly he felt himself responsible for the loss of the boat.'[141]

The survivors were rescued by the boats of one of the escorts, HMS *Snapdragon*—all but three who must have drowned, and the engineer. Dönitz, who had divested himself of his heavy leather gear and boots in the water, was picked up wearing a shirt, underclothes and one sock. The Commander of the *Snapdragon* thrust out his hand to him when he came aboard. 'Now, Captain, we are quits. Tonight you have sunk one of my steamers, now I have sunk you!' He sent a sailor to fetch a bathrobe from his cabin and placed it around Dönitz's shoulders.

Naturally Dönitz was deeply depressed; he recorded in his memoirs how he kept on turning the accident over in his mind, wondering how it had occurred and whether his engineer, Jeschen, had escaped from the boat or had been trapped below while scuttling her; she had taken only eight seconds to go down, according to the interrogated survivors.

He and the rest of the crew were put ashore at Malta and marched to the old Verdalla fortress which was being used to hold prisoners of war. His mood at this time is described by the British officer who tried vainly to question him.

At first he refused to answer any questions whatever, and even had to be persuaded to write his name. He was very moody and almost violent at times and it was very hard to make him talk at all. This frame of mind, it appears, has been partly caused by the incidents connected with the loss of his boat, and it seems he was not very cordial even with his fellow countrymen as he had previously said he was done with the sea and ships. It seems probable that the loss of UB 68 was due to a direct fault of the Commander.[142]

This initial deduction was probably not shared by the later specialist interrogators, and while they came to no definite conclusions, it is probable they held it more likely to have been the engineer or the hydroplane ratings who started the chain of disaster. As for Dönitz's extreme moodiness, this was not by any means a normal reaction for U-boat Commanders before British interrogators.

The days in the fortress passed dully, Dönitz still obsessed by the loss of his boat and the death of Jeschen, and no doubt by the fact that he could take no more part in the war which had been his life for the past four years. His despair was deepened by the news the prisoners were permitted to glean from allied papers; the outlook had been gloomy before he had left Pola with Turkey, Bulgaria and Austria-Hungary visibly crumbling before the allied armies; now one after another they agreed armistice terms, while in the north the German armies reeled back from Flanders; there were rumours of open disaffection among the starving German population and, worse, mutiny in some of the ships of the High Seas Fleet, while the humiliating terms the allies were seeking to impose were deeply wounding, particularly President Wilson's 'fourteen-point' proposal with its call for the abolition of the Hohenzollern monarchy and the military and the imposition of a democratic system in Germany. Dönitz found Wilson's attitude quite unintelligible.

On November 4th he was taken down to the harbour and went aboard a British cruiser for transport to England, finding his first lieutenant, Müssen, also on board. On the 7th they dropped anchor off Gibraltar; for the next few days he and Müssen watched the activity in the roads from the cruiser's quarterdeck, seeing:

. . . the abundance of flotillas of destroyers, U-boats, 'Foxgloves' [a U-boat hunter] and sloops of all nations England directed for the

89

Gibraltar patrols. It was clear to me what a monstrous superiority of material and force had been used to defeat us.[143]

The cruiser was still at anchor there on the 9th, when one of their comrades from Pola, Heinrich Kukat, struck the last dramatic blow for the U-boat arm, sinking the old pre-Dreadnought battleship, *Britannia*, while she was under escort by two destroyers within three miles of the concourse of nets and U-boat hunters across the Straits of Gibraltar. Seeing the allied ensigns at half-mast and the destroyers steaming in with survivors, Dönitz gloried in this perfect expression of his own mood of bitter defiance:

Heinrich Kukat, you best among the U-boat Commanders of our year! . . . You bravest of the brave . . . You were a fighter, modest, with slumbering strength, which only danger could awaken. And in that you were a capital fellow![144]

Two days later the scene in the roads was very different. As news came through of the flight of the Kaiser and the German government's acceptance of the humiliating terms of the armistice, fog horns, sirens, steam whistles split the air in a deafening cacophony from the armada in the bay, cheers and calls rolled across the water, hats were tossed high, flags run up, and on a nearby ship a captured German war ensign was hoisted upside down with the white ensign above it. He and Müssen stood together on the quarterdeck, 'a small, defiant band with infinitely bitter hearts'.

The Captain came on the quarterdeck with a group of the cruiser's officers with whom he had been celebrating the victory in champagne, and stepped across to Dönitz; looking at the up-ended German ensign and the yelling sailors on the neighbouring vessel, he said, 'I don't like it.'

Dönitz waved his arm in a gesture to encompass all the ships in the roads, British, American, French, Japanese, and asked if he could take any joy from a victory which could only be attained with the whole world for allies.

'Yes,' the Captain replied after a pause, 'it's very curious.'

Dönitz thought, 'An honourable "front man".' In his memoirs he wrote, 'I will hold the memory of this fair and noble English sea officer in high regard all my life.'[145]

So ended Germany's first bid for world power, and Karl Dönitz's career as an Imperial naval officer. But for both the attitudes were too ingrained to be altered even by the bitter shock of defeat.

CHAPTER THREE

Towards the Second World War

AFTER THE ARMISTICE the cruiser continued its voyage to Southampton, where Dönitz and Müssen experienced the curiosity and horror with which ordinary Britons regarded U-boat men. Thence they were sent to a prisoner of war camp for officers at Redmires, near Sheffield. Again almost the only sources of news were British papers, whose columnists had no doubts about the war guilt of the Kaiser, the German military and the U-boat Commanders, and called for their trial and execution. Dönitz regarded this as enemy propaganda, but it made an impression on several of the younger men in the camp who began to deny the Kaiser; they had, they said, always been Republicans at heart. Dönitz, disgusted, founded a loyal barrack which he called 'Hohenzollern'. He was joined by several U-boat colleagues and many other 'genuine warriors almost all repeatedly wounded' to form a congenial community of unrepentant monarchists.[1]

Weeks in captivity drew into months as the allies thrashed out peace terms to be dictated to the defeated enemy. In Germany a Republic headed by Socialists had been born in revolutionary violence. Dönitz fretted, wondering if he would ever see his homeland again, and if so what kind of a Germany it would be, then in an effort to get himself repatriated, he feigned madness.

Contemporary medical reports are missing, but one version of his assumed 'madness' came from Wolfgang Frank after the Second World War, during which Frank served as a Propaganda Officer concerned particularly with U-boat affairs. According to this Dönitz played childish games with biscuit tins and little china dogs that could be bought in the canteen 'until even his first lieutenant thought he was crazy'.[2] It is scarcely necessary to trust the story of a man schooled by Dr Goebbels; nevertheless the Second World War British Intelligence file on Dönitz states that he was sent to Manchester Lunatic Asylum! This suggests that he either feigned madness rather convincingly or *was* a shade unbalanced. In view of the depth of his feelings, particularly about the loss of UB 68 and his engineer, Jeschen—as will appear—it could have been a combination of both. He himself made no mention of it in any of his books although he did tell a US psychiatrist at the Nuremberg war crimes trials a fantastic story—swallowed whole—about pretending to be a U-boat![3] In his memoirs he wrote simply that he deliberately exploited his poor health in order to get home.

Whatever the truth, he was repatriated with some of the earliest batches of prisoners in July 1919.

Kiel was scarcely recognizable as a naval port when he returned. The great harbour was empty of warships; the only sounds of work came from the destruction under the eyes of a temporary allied control commission of those U-boats which had not been handed over to the allies. The naval station itself presented a dismal spectacle, the sentries offhand if not actively insolent, careless in dress and manner, smoking on duty, allowing their rifles to rust. These were some of the visible effects of mutiny and defeat; the inner scars left on the officers were probably not so apparent, but certainly more permanent.

Mutiny had been brewing in the High Seas Fleet since at least 1917; this was the natural result of inaction and the incarceration of the large crews in uncomfortable steel boxes repeating drills that had come to seem increasingly purposeless; it had been heightened by the loss of many of the best officers to the U-boat arm and by existing tensions between the exclusive executive officer corps and the engineer and deck officers below them, by the impersonal, iron discipline with which the big ships especially were run, above all by new tensions arising from the good food and wine and high life enjoyed by the executive officers while the men's rations were cut and the civilian population reduced by the allied blockade to near starvation, in some cases to scavenging scraps from the fleet's garbage. In November 1918 a new naval High Command under Admiral Scheer, disregarding the warning signs pointed out by more intelligent officers, lit the spark that worked along these powder trains to blow the fleet apart; it was nothing less than a suicide run against the British Grand Fleet; the purpose was rationalized in various ways but undoubtedly the real concern was the honour of the Navy, above all the honour of the officer corps.

To the men of the German battlecruiser squadron which had already experienced a suicide run to extricate Scheer's battleships at Jutland, the idea of sacrificing themselves for their officers' code of honour did not appeal. They refused to turn to; others refused even to return to their ships from shore leave, instead running riot in Wilhelmshaven demonstrating for peace and cheering the name of the United States President, Woodrow Wilson. The mutiny spread to the battle fleet and to the cruisers until only the torpedo boats and U-boats remained loyal.

In an effort to split the mutineers individual battle-squadrons were ordered to separate ports; far from allowing the officers to control the divisions, this merely spread the contagion along the coast. In Kiel the Commander of the Naval Station, Admiral Souchon, was caught unprepared by the arrival of the 3rd Battle Squadron flying the red flag and surrendered his command with scarcely a struggle to a 'Sailors' Council'. The next day Lübeck and Travemünde had fallen to other Sailors' Councils and, the day after that, Hamburg, Bremen, Cuxhaven, Wilhelmshaven; from these bases groups of sailors travelled to other industrial cities and garrison towns throughout Germany, raising the red banner of revolution among workers long prepared by Bolshevik propaganda and inadequate rations. Aboard the ships, meanwhile, deck officers and petty officers combined to control the violence of the men's sudden release from constraint,[4] and it was largely due to their efforts that the fleet was not crippled and was able to sail out on its last voyage on November 21st, under the terms of the Armistice to internment in Scapa Flow, the Grand Fleet's base in the islands north of Scotland. Five battlecruisers leading the way, nine dreadnought battleships, guns trained fore and aft, seven cruisers, 50 torpedo boats, 'the endless funeral procession' as one officer wrote, filed out across the grey North Sea to surrender. It was an unprecedented moment in naval history, and a potent symbol not only of the humiliation of the naval officer corps, but of Germany itself. The former fleet Commander, von Hipper, watched with breaking heart; the sailors themselves wondered what would become now of the Fatherland.[5]

Revolution and hunger stalked the streets together. So far as the Navy was concerned, a sailors' 'Council of 53' had taken over the High Command in Berlin and was not only directing the Sailors' Councils running the naval bases and interfering in the negotiations with the allies, but was planning in concert with Soldiers' Councils thoroughly socialist armed forces in which there would be no insignia of rank and officers would be elected to their positions by the men. In December delegates from Soldiers', Sailors' and Workers' Councils throughout the *Reich* had assembled in Berlin for the first Soviet Congress, and on the 23rd, the

'People's Marine Division', incited by Communist groups, forced its way into the *Reich* Chancellery itself. In these circumstances the Socialist Chancellor called in the military to restore order. So the provisional government of the new Republic with its democratic, socialist aims and the old officer corps with its monarchist authoritarian convictions—which the Soviet Congress and the Councils intended to eradicate entirely from the life of the nation—became partners against anarchy and Bolshevism.

The instruments of internal order were not regular service units, but brigades of loyalist volunteers known as *Freikorps*. Dönitz's former mentor, von Loewenfeld, raised one such at Kiel, and in July as Dönitz came home this brigade was winning itself an awesome reputation for swift and ruthless action against Communists, strikers, looters and rioters. Other officers, shocked by events and the collapse of all discipline in the regular service, resigned their commissions; many more debated whether they could serve a Socialist Republic. But at the highest levels the decision had already been taken that the officer corps was to remain at its post, serving the new State, biding its time. Tirpitz, for instance, gave the new regime about one or two years before a strong reaction set in.[6] Others expected to guide this reaction, topple the government and reinstate the monarchy.

This corps exercise in self-preservation was rationalized as a sacred duty to the German people, who after they had recovered from their present temporary setback would need a powerful Navy to realize their world mission. Nothing had changed. The new head of the Navy, Admiral von Trotha, an ardent disciple of Tirpitz had been one of the leading spirits behind the plan to send the fleet on its death ride for honour, and on June 21st 1919, the day the peace terms were supposed to be signed at Versailles, he had the ships scuttled where they rode at anchor in Scapa Flow to salve that honour. Now he intended nurturing the seeds of a new fleet 'so that when the time comes a useful tree will grow from it'.[7] The material allowed him by the peace terms was minimal—six old battleships, six cruisers, twelve destroyers and twelve torpedo boats, with an absolute ban on U-boats and naval aircraft; consequently his immediate aim was in the personnel field; discipline and pride had to be restored, a nucleus of dedicated officers formed who would be able to guide the later expansion. Under the peace terms he was allowed only 1,500 officers; only the best and most loyal need be selected.

Such was the position when Dönitz reported back to the Navy Station at Kiel in July. He was greeted by the Adjutant, *Korvettenkapitän* Otto Schultze, his former U-boat flotilla chief in the Mediterranean.

'Are you going to stay with us, Dönitz?' Schultze asked.

'Do you think we shall have U-boats again?'

'Certainly I think so. The [Versailles] ban will not remain for ever. In about two years it is to be hoped we will have U-boats again.'[8]

This reply, according to Dönitz's memoirs, finally answered the question he had been debating with himself, his fellow officers and his family since returning home—whether or not he should re-enlist in the new Republican *Reichsmarine*. He decided to do so because, he wrote in his memoirs, he had become 'an enthusiastic U-boat man' and was 'under the spell of this unique U-boat camaraderie'.[9]

Nevertheless, the conversation with Schultze seems extraordinary only a month after the signing of the treaty denying Germany U-boats, at a time when the fleet had virtually ceased to exist. One wonders whether, if Schultze did use the words Dönitz recalled 40 years later, it was off his own bat to entice a fanatically loyal and able young officer back to the colours, or if he was simply repeating official policy at a higher level.

All that can be said is that clandestine preparations for rebuilding a U-boat arm were indeed under way within two years, and that the Naval officer corps was imbued from top to bottom with a thoroughly vengeful spirit against the allies, against the Versailles treaty, particularly perhaps against Great Britain, whose 'poisonous hatred . . . inconsiderate inhumanity, incitement (to revolution) and hunger (blockade)'[10] von Trotha saw as chiefly responsible for their present humiliations, but also against the Republican politicians who, by signing the armistice, had robbed the armed forces of victory—this was the legend which the High Command of both Army and Navy were preparing to preserve the honour and ensure the future of the officer corps.

So Dönitz was carried along in the elemental life-stream of the Bismarckian-Prussian system. His father-in-law, whom he had consulted earnestly about his future, had intimate connections at the very top of the system and had already thrown in his lot with the new *Reichswehr*; he counselled Dönitz in strong terms to do the same: 'You are not permitted to abandon the State.'[11]

No doubt Schultze reinforced the message; at all events he took Dönitz on as his assistant to help him with the task of picking the select band who were to be the nucleus of von Trotha's future Navy; he started on August 14th.

Through the autumn of 1919 internal unrest grew, not so much from the Communist groups, which were routed by the government-backed *Freikorps* whenever they showed their heads, but from the monarchists. In November, during a Public Inquiry designed to prove that the government could deal with the military and there was therefore no necessity for the allies to press the peace treaty requirement for war crimes trials of Germany's former leaders, the generals and Conservative politicians turned the tables, putting the revolutionaries and the government in the dock as the authors of Germany's humiliation. On November 18th Hindenburg in his evidence made the historic pronouncement that the immaculate Army had been given a dagger thrust in the back by the revolutionaries. Talk of an imminent military coup to restore the monarchy became widespread.

In February the allies heightened the tension by publishing a list of nearly 900 'War Criminals' and demanding their surrender to stand trial; the names ranged from the Kaiser and his entourage, Hindenburg, Ludendorff, Falkenhayn, successive Chancellors, and among naval officers, Tirpitz, Scheer, von Trotha down to individual U-boat Commanders. Anger erupted, and not only amongst the monarchists; this ultimate humiliation united the greater part of the nation in defiance. The government, knowing it could not survive if it agreed to the demand, sought to gain time; nationalist hotheads, led by a Prussian official named Wolfgang Kapp and supported by a naval *Freikorps*, felt the time ripe to act. An hour before midnight on March 12th, with the tacit approval of the naval High Command they marched on Berlin. The Army High Command refused to support the Republic and the government fled.

In his memoirs Dönitz described how news of the Kapp *Putsch* broke 'to our complete amazement'; certainly there was confusion at Wilhelmshaven naval station, and officers were arrested by patrols of petty officers and men as they had been in the 1918 mutinies, but at Kiel the Station Commander, Admiral von Levetzow, acted promptly and decisively to maintain order. At first he was successful. He was unable, however, to prevent the workers in Kiel from obeying a general strike call from the government which had re-established itself in Stuttgart; the harbour and works in the town were shut down and all transport came to a standstill. Meanwhile among the naval units deck officers hostile to the executive officer corps and radical Republicans deeply suspicious of the officers held themselves apart from loyalist elements, the most convinced of whom were gathered in von Loewenfeld's brigade, now returned to its birthplace. Between the two extremes many basically loyal men were torn between their service duty and sympathy with family and friends supporting the strike. With such deep divisions in his own forces the situation slipped gradually from von Levetzow's control. Dönitz recalls noon, March 10th, as the decisive moment, when from the tower of the naval signal station a white flag was hoisted, signifying the men were holding themselves neutral between the strikers and the officers.

Of all the naval crews, those in the torpedo boats were considered the most reliable; on the following day these boats were sent in to the inner harbour to watch over the other vessels gathered there, and somehow or other Dönitz was in command of one of them with the half flotilla chief embarked aboard. He made no mention of when or why he was appointed to this boat; according to his personal file his appointment as assistant to Schultze ended on March 13th, the day Kapp entered Berlin, but his official appointment to torpedo boats was dated June.[12]

The same day, March 17th, Kapp, who had no plans or means for dealing with the general strike which paralysed the nation, resigned, leaving the lawful government in control again. In Kiel, however, communist groups stormed the naval arsenal, killing the commanding officer; others occupied parts of the harbour, and fighting broke out between them and the torpedo boats. Dönitz made no mention of this. The next day von Loewenfeld's brigade went into action against the workers' bands, and in the harbour the deck officers and radical sailors and stokers mutinied, ordered the white flag hoisted on all vessels and all officers arrested. The torpedo boats remained loyal, however, and to prevent them from being contaminated or trapped inside, the flotilla chiefs decided to sail out for the Baltic port of Saasnitz. On the way the mutineers' flagship, *Strasbourg*, signalled 'Raise the white flag. Arrest officers'.[13] This was not obeyed and the mutineers did not fire.

Dönitz had already experienced discipline difficulties because of the divided loyalties of his crew, and that evening his leading engineer reported that salt water had entered the fresh-water boiler feed; he could not keep the engines going for long. Dönitz had no option but to leave the flotilla and turn for the nearest port, Warnemünde. He had scarcely entered and made fast in the dead of night when machine-gun fire was directed at the boat. Seizing his megaphone he pointed it at some dark figures he made out on the quay, shouting that he had come in from necessity to change his fresh water and he would leave again the next day. This seemed to satisfy the gunners who had assumed his boat was part of a detachment intended to 'capture' Warnemünde for Kapp!

He never did join the rest of the flotilla at Saasnitz, but returned to Kiel; his explanation in his memoirs was that the cause of the boiler trouble could not be ascertained, but it seems evident that the engines were either damaged deliberately by a disaffected member of the crew or he was forced by the crew to return to base. There he was relieved of his command by the mutineers under their elected Station Commander, formerly a petty officer, and probably arrested, although he says simply, 'the officer corps of the Navy did no more duty'.[14]

For the second time in two years the deck officers, petty officers and men had shown their dislike of the executive; several officers were beaten and otherwise mistreated under arrest; meanwhile new officers were elected, chiefly from non-commissioned and petty officers, by the crews of the various vessels—whereupon those executives still nominally serving the *Reichsmarine* refused duty until their position was restored. It seemed to many that this must be the end of the Navy: the 1918 mutinies were widely held responsible for the outbreak of revolution at the end of the war, now the service was deeply compromised by its support for the Kapp *Putsch*, and the men had once again shown themselves, in Tirpitz's words, 'rotten from the base up!'[15] Dönitz, with his passionate loyalty and personal ego to satisfy, must have felt this deeply and bitterly. No doubt the silence of his memoirs on this period is a measure of the depth of his disgust and despondency.

During this anxious time, on May 14th, Ingeborg had her second child, a boy; he was christened Klaus.

At the end of the month there was a resolution of the crisis for the officer corps. A special committee of the *Reichstag* had been set up to investigage the Navy's complicity in the Kapp *Putsch* and some 172 officers, including von Trotha, either retired or were discharged during the course of the proceedings,[16] but on May 31st, anniversary of the battle of Skaggerak (Jutland), those officers deemed to have taken no part in the affair were formally reinstated—at the expense of the deck officers who were struck from the Navy list as a class. This was a significant moment for the Navy and the nation; the government had graphic warning of where the true loyalty of the officers lay, and it was not with the Republic, yet they reinstated the corps almost *en bloc*. No doubt a part of the reason was, as before, that the Communists, still resisting in the industrial cities of the Ruhr and being suppressed without quarter by *Freikorps* units, were regarded as the greater immediate danger. Another part of the reason was that the Republicans had been unable or unwilling to weed out the old monarchist elements from official posts and big business. Everywhere, despite the democratic Republican form of government, the old guard still held positions of power and influence.

So far as the Army and Navy were concerned, the abject failure of the *Putsch* had demonstrated the impossibility of a purely military take-over without broad backing from the people; it was a lesson the officers took to heart, and from now both services held themselves independent or above politics—at least above party politics as played in the *Reichstag*. In a more fundamental sense they were deeply political, the self-appointed guardians of the Fatherland and of the ancient virtues they had been brought up to venerate. Since these were anti-democratic, anti-liberal, bellicose and now vengeful as well, they formed a cancer in the body of the Republic or, as a Socialist deputy put it some years later, 'a state within a state'.

Dönitz, from May 31st again a serving officer, was appointed to command torpedo boat T 157 of the first half flotilla at Swinemünde on the coast of Pomerania. The first real task of the flotilla was to re-establish discipline and rapport with the men. This was easier in Swinemünde than in Kiel where the old resentments smouldered on, much easier in small craft than in the more formal atmosphere of a cruiser or battleship; to judge by his report at the end of the year, Dönitz succeeded very well.

This was not always apparent to him; he was self-critical, ever straining for better results, pushing himself and his men to the limits. By the autumn his exertions, together no doubt with the strain of the early summer in Kiel on top of his continuous war service, had affected his health and with it his state of mind. Again he contemplated leaving the service. Whether this was entirely due to his health and self-critical feelings, as he seems to imply in his memoirs, or whether it had something to do with the continuing attrition between workers and Navy in Kiel, or a schism that had appeared between the fanatically loyal ex-*Freikorps* officers and men, now back in naval service, and those who

100

had not fought ashore—or whether it was also concerned with the difficulty of supporting a family on his poor service pay, is not clear.

In October, T 157 had four weeks in dock at Stettin, where his father-in-law was Commander in Chief of the northern area Army Command. He brought Ingeborg and the two children, Ursula, now three and a half, and the five-months-old Klaus to stay with his parents-in-law and again sought the General's advice on whether he should remain in the service or seek a civilian job, as he put it 'solely to earn money'. Once again General Weber told him where his duty lay and again he accepted the advice, which no doubt reinforced his real inclinations.

So the critical year of 1920 passed. In January 1921 he was stepped up in rank from *Oberleutnant* to *Kapitänleutnant*—lieutenant commander. He took a house in Swinemünde, again a substantial villa with two children's bedrooms and a maid's room.

As the ice broke in the spring of 1921, the torpedo boat flotilla began tactical exercises off Rügen Island. Undoubtedly this was an important period in the development of his own tactical appreciation, and as it was to turn out in the development of U-boat tactics; there is even a possibility that some of the exercises were actually designed to study the problem of U-boat surface attack. No direct evidence to support this has appeared, but several of the torpedo boat Commanders had been U-boat captains and the Navy had already begun clandestine preparations to rebuild the U-boat arm; there was a U-department concealed in the Torpedo and Mines Inspectorate at Kiel; German U-boat plans were on their way to Japan to assist that former enemy power to build a cruiser U-boat fleet and they were followed by German engineers and constructors who were thus enabled to keep abreast of the technology. Other U-boat experts either travelled or took up positions abroad as advisers to governments which it was hoped might buy German-designed boats.

Then in the winter of that year three of the theoretical studies by German naval officers, known as *Winterarbeiten*, dealt with U-boat topics; one of these by the wartime U-boat commander, Marschall, dealt with U-boat surface attack. After pointing out that the introduction of convoys had forced U-boats to adopt different tactics, Marschall listed the many advantages of night surface attack. 'The coming war', he wrote (!) may or may not involve war against merchant shipping', nevertheless U-boat officers must be trained to attack convoys since a warship squadron was itself a convoy.

101

More interesting than the study itself are the remarks appended to it by the Baltic fleet chief—thus overall Commander of Dönitz's flotilla—Admiral von Rosenberg: '. . . especially noteworthy are the arguments about night surface attack. They are valuable and of interest not only for the U-boat officer, but also for the torpedo boat officer.'[17]

The year this was penned, 1922, three German shipbuilders formed a Dutch company, *Ingenieurskantoor voor Scheepsbouw*—known as IvS—to continue U-boat design work by German experts outside Germany.

The drive to circumvent the Versailles ban was on, and the need for U-boats was evident in the task guiding the Navy's planning. This was to counter a Polish attack on East Prussia—which had been isolated from Germany by a 'Polish corridor' up to the port of Danzig—and prevent Poland's ally, France, from intervening. U-boats were ideal to stop French battle-squadrons getting through the Danish Belts into the Baltic, and to combat a blockade of the German North Sea ports.

But whether any of the torpedo boat exercises were designed to investigate submarine surface attack or not, a surfaced submarine *is* a torpedo boat and since both surface night attack and combined operation between two or more U-boats were ideas with which all U-boat Commanders were familiar, the operation of a flotilla of torpedo boats against a battle-squadron could hardly fail to spark off analogies in the minds of the former U-boat Commanders—especially as all the emphasis in training was on night attack because this was the only possible form of action for the German service, reduced by the peace treaty to virtual impotence in capital ships.

The boats were trained to surprise the enemy under cover of darkness, fire their torpedoes and escape rapidly; for this they had to find the enemy by day, hang on to him at the borders of visibility without themselves being seen, and approach gradually as visibility drew in with twilight. This tactic of finding and holding touch with the enemy until the attack could be launched at night was the principal feature of the U-boat 'pack' tactics with which Dönitz's name is associated. It seems therefore that it was born in these years immediately after the First World War—and not in Dönitz's head alone.

Kapitänleutnant Wassner, for instance, of the *Wehrabteilung*, naval High Command in Berlin, wrote a paper in July 1922, suggesting that in his war experience U-boat surface attacks had been the most successful and that since lone U-boat operations were uneconomic against convoys 'in future it will be essential for convoys to be hunted by sizeable numbers of U-boats acting together'.[18]

At all events, during his time in torpedo boats Dönitz impressed his flotilla chief, *Kapitänleutnant* Densch with both his seamanship and his officer-like qualities. Densch's first report on him in August 1921 described his 'exemplary service outlook and fullest devotion to duty'. He handled his subordinates 'very sharply and militarily; despite this he is respected and popular with them'. And despite a serious outlook on life, he was a good comrade 'full of hearty merriment at appropriate times'.[19]

This confirmed an excellent report on him by Schultze, who had also remarked on his deftness in handling subordinates.

Dönitz stayed in the torpedo boat flotilla altogether for nearly three years. During this time, on March 20th 1922, Ingeborg bore a third child, a boy who was christened Peter.

A year later the family moved back to Kiel as he was appointed *Referent*—literally, expert or adviser—to the Torpedo, Mine and Intelligence Inspectorate there. He was assigned to the U-boat department, his area of work primarily submarine hunting methods and the development of a new depth charge and its ejection device.

Although he recorded in his memoirs that he was not very happy about this posting, since he was occupied mostly with technical matters, his ability and dedication made the usual very favourable impression on his superiors. The Station chief of staff reported on him as 'lively and energetic, an excellent soldier, decided in action, clear and confident in word and writing'. He went on: 'To me he was and is a willing subordinate, an adviser of indefatigable working energy, who performed his written work with a clear head and deftness of expression.'[20]

He recommended him, because of his rounded service as Commander of both U- and torpedo-boats, and the great interest he had shown as *U-Referent*, for further employment in the torpedo arm; he also suggested that his 'exemplary service outlook and superior qualities of character' fitted him for posts where he might influence young officers and officer recruits. He concluded: 'To serious consciousness of his duty he joins in a fortunate way a cheerful joy of life which makes him a very popular comrade. As father of three children he had a considerable economic struggle against the exigencies of the time.'

This referred to the period of hyper-inflation during the Ruhr crisis—

the political arm of the movement to circumvent Versailles. At the beginning of 1923 French and Belgian troops had marched into the Ruhr to enforce payment of arrears of war-reparations, as a result of which the German government had called a strike throughout the area. To finance this passive resistance they printed money and there resulted the notorious period when the value of the Mark fell by the day and hour until trunkfuls of paper were needed for the smallest purchases. It was a disastrous ploy, sweeping away the savings of the middle classes, bankrupting thousands, reintroducing hunger to the streets of the cities, further loosening the ties of society and unleashing a bitterness and restlessness that were harnessed by revolutionaries and nationalists for their own ends.

The Dönitzes were one of the families whose capital was destroyed, and as he was paid by the month he could not even protect current spending; even when the currency was stabilized in the autumn Dönitz's monthly salary bought so little it lasted barely two weeks—so he recounts in his memoirs—after which Ingeborg had to shop on credit. His brother who had no family helped with occasional loans. He had returned to the merchant marine after the war, then set up on his own account in Riga probably with a shipping or export-import agency, but the day came when his business went bankrupt; to repay the loans, Karl Dönitz had to sell his priceless Turkish carpets.

His friend, von Lamezan, also suffered. Returning from four years as a prisoner in England he had not re-entered the Navy—perhaps he had been unable to since he had had no opportunity for distinguished service—but took a training in agriculture, hoping to buy a manor farm by the sea. The inflation eroded his capital and he was only able to buy a small-holding on sandy soil in Holstein.

While the middle classes were ruined and workers thrown on the streets, there were elements who emerged stronger than ever from the inflation; the Army High Command received one hundred million in gold at the height of the crisis for the purpose of rearmament outside Versailles limits; a portion of this was passed on to the Navy and incorporated in two secret rearmament funds, one under *Kapitän zur See* Lohmann of the Naval Transport department, the other under *Kapitan zur See* Hansen of the Weapons department of naval High Command. Dönitz mentions in his memoirs that his department at Kiel worked closely with Hansen. Meanwhile big industrialists who had geared their operations to inflation, which had been a feature of German currency throughout the post-war period, expanded their real assets by discounting huge bills of exchange at the *Reichsbank*, paying them back in increasingly devalued *Reichsmarks* and using the profits to buy up medium and small concerns.

Naturally in the chaos the other elements to profit were the revolutionaries. It is possible now to select one as particularly important, Adolf Hitler, and it is interesting to find that he shared significant peculiarities with the exiled Kaiser. He was not so obviously deformed, but he was a poor specimen with hollow chest, wide hips, spindly legs and appalling posture. However, the most striking similarities with Wilhelm II were in early upbringing and mental characteristics: both were almost certainly over-indulged by doting mothers, in Hitler's case probably because all the earlier children in the family had died in infancy; both were judged by tutors or teachers to have talent but to lack self-discipline or powers of concentration, both later proved to have prodigious memories for facts combined with complete inability in analysis; both therefore accepted the world as it was presented to them, exaggerated the picture in their own uncurbed, ego-centred minds, and when they attained power twisted the real world to their own fantasies.

Of course they came from entirely different backgrounds. Hitler was the son of a minor Austrian official and, after failing to obtain any qualifications at school because of laziness and wayward obstinacy against learning anything that did not interest him, he spent his young manhood drifting around cheap lodgings in Vienna painting copies of picture postcards and absorbing the pseudo-intellectual political ideas of the time from pamphlets, and reading in libraries. He accepted uncritically the two great themes of the age and his milieu—social Darwinism as put forward by Treitschke and his followers—struggle as the essence of life, victory to the strongest—and the racialism of Houston Stewart Chamberlain, Richard Wagner and their followers—the importance of racial purity, the mission of the Teutonic peoples, above all the poison in society represented by Jews. The rider to this was that Jews were at the centre of a subversive Socialist-Marxist world conspiracy.

The World War ended his drift and gave focus and imposed discipline on his life for the first time. He enthusiastically supported Germany's world mission and volunteered for a German—not Austrian—regiment, serving as a despatch runner in the Bavarian 6th Division and winning the Iron Cross, second- then first-class; he did not rise above corporal though, which in view of his loyalty, evident bravery and long service, suggests that he was not judged to command the confidence of his fellows.

He was shocked by the revolutions of November 1918 and the armistice, and the official line that the Army had been treacherously deserted by politicians at home fitted his crude ideas of a Jewish-Socialist-Communist world conspiracy. His loyalty came to the attention of the Bavarian Army Command press officer, who employed him to attend local political meetings and report on their tone and ideology; it was during this work that he found his vocation: he made the discovery that he could sway audiences.

In September 1919 he joined a small nationalist group in Munich called the German Workers' Party, and by virtue of the fervour with which he pressed his few received ideas soon came to dominate the group. His success rested not on power in argument, but on dredging the deepest emotions of his colleagues and audiences. He gave them focus for their personal frustrations and bitterness by making 'Reds' and 'November Criminals'—the government—scapegoats for Germany's humiliation; he touched deep tribal chords by telling them they were members of the chosen race. His message was Messianic. He appealed to blood not reason, and although it is easy to criticize the narrowness and vulgarity of his vision, in such frenzied times and with such audiences who had experienced the terror of a civil war and a Communist regime in Bavaria it is understandable that many responded.

Over the next few years the Party grew and formed branches in other towns, largely as a result of Hitler's impassioned oratory; he also won converts through street fighting against the 'Reds' who had hitherto been the masters of intimidatory public brawling; the spearhead of this movement was the SA, or *Sturm-Abteilung*, formed originally to protect meetings and demonstrations from the assaults of their opponents. The name of the Party was expanded to the National-Socialist German Workers' Party—*Nazi* for short.

By the time of the Ruhr crisis in 1923 the SA had become an armed unit organized on military lines with brown shirts, leather belts, swastika armbands and standards, one of the many unofficial *Freikorps* which supported the nationalist cause; its new leader was Hermann Göring, a World War fighter-pilot ace and considerable prize for Hitler, most of whose associates were from the same restricted background as himself. Hitler also had the support of two formidable leaders of the old guard in retirement in Bavaria, Hindenburg and Ludendorff; they were not members of the Party and regarded the fanatical and socially gauche 'corporal' with proper condescension; they recognized his immaculate political viewpoint, though, and admired the military order prevailing at his rallies—in sharp contrast to the anarchy and chaos spreading throughout Germany in the wake of inflation. It was in these circumstances that Hitler forced on a startled Ludendorff the famous *Putsch* which began on November 8th during a nationalist mass meeting in the *Bürgerbraukeller* in the outskirts of Munich. It was to have resulted in a march on Berlin by the combined *Freikorps* to arrest the 'November Criminals', overturn the Republic and set up a nationalist dictatorship on the lines of Mussolini's fascist regime in Italy, which Hitler admired greatly. But the military had learned their lesson during the Kapp *Putsch* and were besides more monarchical than fascist; thanks to elementary errors on Hitler's part the local *Reichswehr* command and Bavarian police were able to disperse the marchers with comparatively little bloodshed and arrest the leaders.

Their trial began in Munich in February 1924, and for the first time Hitler's name became known outside Bavaria. The most significant aspect of the trial, however, is the light it throws on the failure of the Republic. The government had brought the Ruhr crisis on itself for the sake of protesting against the Versailles treaty and was thus largely responsible for the hysterical nationalism and chaos that ensued. To restore order it was then forced to call on its implacable enemy, the Army, whose handling of the situation showed clear sympathy for the nationalists and against the 'Red' revolutionaries. The results of the trial in Munich demonstrated that the judiciary was equally partial; Ludendorff was acquitted, Hitler sentenced for high treason in attempting to overthrow the government to the absurd term of five years with a recommendation for remission. He served only two of them in very agreeable conditions, enjoying pleasant rooms and better and more regular meals than he had probably ever experienced, and he used the leisure to expose his cosmic fantasies in a manuscript, the first part of which was published in 1925 as *Mein Kampf*.

The trial of Hitler and his colleagues was not exceptional. Three years previously there had been a series of trials at the German Supreme Court in Leipzig which showed similar, even more flagrant violations of justice. These were the proceedings taken against a few of those designated as 'war criminals' by the allies. Only twelve actually came to trial, but one particularly nauseous case must be touched on since it is relevant to

Dönitz's later career. It concerned the hospital ship, *Llandovery Castle*, which was torpedoed and sunk by U 86, commanded by *Oberleutnant z. See* Helmut Patzig—who had beaten Dönitz to first place in the exams aboard the *Hertha*. Patzig himself did not stand trial since he had gone to ground—he emerged later in the Counter Intelligence Organization, the *Abwehr*. In his stead his two watch officers were brought before the Court.

From the evidence of these two it appeared that Patzig torpedoed the hospital ship because he was convinced she was carrying ammunition and combatants, in particular US airmen; why he thought so was not discovered. At least five lifeboats got away from the ship before she went down and Patzig, surfacing, interrogated the survivors of several, apparently intent on proving his assumptions about munitions and US airmen. When he found he was wrong he apparently decided to remove all the enemy witnesses to his mistake—since sinking hospital ships was contrary to the Geneva Convention—and after making two vain passes to ram one of the boats ordered fire to be opened with the after gun, then cruised about on the surface firing at the other boats until he judged that all had been destroyed.

After the incident the crew of the U-boat, who had been kept below during the shooting, were naturally depressed. Patzig swore his officers to secrecy and the log was faked to show a track a long way from the sinking, which was not entered. From all this the Court could hardly avoid the conclusion that there had been a deliberate slaughter of defenceless survivors or, as it was put in the Judgement: 'The universally known efficiency of our U-boat crews renders it very improbable that the firing on the boats, which by their very proximity would form an excellent target, was without effect.'[21]

The Court managed to find that Patzig had been in a state of excitement when he gave his order to fire: 'he had to act quickly: under this pressure of circumstances he proceeded in a manner which the naval expert rightly described as imprudent'![22] This naval expert was to become an Admiral responsible for naval education in the 1930s. 'In view of this state of excitement,' the Judgement continued, 'the execution of the deed cannot be called deliberate.'

However, the passage which was to be significant for the future concerned the responsibility of the two officers brought before the Court; they had been on the bridge with Patzig and had assisted in the massacre, although it had not been proved that either had actually fired the gun. The question was whether they could plead their Commander's orders as a defence:

> Patzig's order does not free the accused from guilt . . . the subordinate obeying an order is liable to punishment if it was known to him that the order of the superior involved the infringement of civil or military law. This applies in the case of the accused . . . it was perfectly clear to the accused that killing defenceless people in the lifeboats could be nothing else but a breach of the law.[23]

In view of this and the 'dark shadow' the action threw 'on the German fleet and especially on the U-boat arm which did so much in the fight for the Fatherland' both accused officers were sentenced for having 'knowingly assisted Patzig' in 'homicide' to four years' imprisonment. The feeling against even this mild punishment was fierce and general, and neither man served the full term: one was allowed to 'escape' after serving four months, the other after six months. There could not have been a better example of the mood in leading circles, nor of how the ground was already prepared for Hitler: patriotism, expressed as defiance of the former enemy powers, was a higher value than justice; mass murderers of medical staff including nurses served terms which would have been lenient for petty larceny, while the officer who gave them their orders went free.

All that was needed in Germany was a leader and a Party to focus the hate and enshrine these values in the constitution.

By this time Dönitz, who no doubt knew and cared little about Hitler—although he undoubtedly knew about the *Llandovery Castle* trial and despised the Court and hated the guilty verdicts as much as every other nationalist member of the armed forces—had been posted to the *Marineleitung* or naval High Command in Berlin. Before taking up his appointment in the autumn of 1924 he attended a short staff-training course run by Rear Admiral Raeder, formerly one of Tirpitz's staff officers who had been close to von Trotha and had been shunted to a backroom for cosmetic purposes after the Kapp affair. He was an able, very correct officer devoted to the service in the manner of Tirpitz, and with the same wide-ranging conception of its future and the future of the German people on the oceans. His comments on Dönitz at the end of the course are interesting:

109

Clever, industrious, ambitious officer. Of excellent general professional knowledge and clear judgement in questions of naval war leadership. Good military as well as technical gifts. I recommend he be employed not in one-sided technical positions but given opportunity for general military-seamanlike further training.[24]

He too recommended him as 'very suitable for the upbringing of officer recruits', from which it can be inferred that Dönitz shared Raeder's views about the future of the Navy, hence of Germany in the greater world, and the naval officers' part in 'the future liberation struggle of the German nation', as it was expressed in a naval memorandum of the time.[25]

Dönitz's appointment in the *Marineleitung* in Berlin was as section head for organizational, internal-political and various general military affairs in the *Wehrabteilung*. In his memoirs he leaves the impression that he was concerned chiefly with service regulations and a new military penal code which had to be thrashed out in *Reichstag* committees, co-ordinated with the Army staff and adjusted to suit actual conditions at the naval stations. This was a particularly sensitive task for the service was still in the throes of the internal rift between the ex-*Freikorps* men and those who had not taken an active part against the internal enemies, was threatened by determined Communist infiltration and subversion in the naval ports, and under constant attack from the Left in the *Reichstag*. None of this is mentioned in any of his published writings.

However, the task of combating Communist propaganda and subversion formed a major part of the work of the *Wehrabteilung*, and there can be no doubt, both from his own later attitudes and copious evidence of the state of mind of his seniors in the *Marineleitung* that this time in Berlin reinforced a hatred of Communism that had resulted quite naturally from the various indignities he and his fellows had been put to in recent years. One of the propaganda exercises his department had to deal with in 1926, for instance, was a crass piece of 'proletarian theatre' staged by the *Rote Marine* (Red Navy) commemorating the naval mutinies and depicting the alleged cruelty of the naval officers and finally the execution of the sailors' leaders.[26] Meanwhile his close involvement with the *Reichstag* reinforced his prejudice against party politics—also quite natural, given his upbringing and indoctrination in the officer corps.

Although his liaison duties within the service and with the Army and his representation of the Navy's case in *Reichstag* committees called for very different qualities to those he had needed hitherto, his department chief, *Kapitän zur See* Werth, reported that as a result of his 'ability', quick perception of essentials and excellent service outlook' he adapted surprisingly quickly. Werth went on: 'In dealings with other ministries and authorities he is deft and, thanks to his objective and sympathetic manner of negotiating, achieves the best possible for his department.'[27]

His character and disposition, Werth continued, made him 'a specially valuable naval officer', and off duty he was 'a popular and respected comrade who, despite economic necessities, never loses gaiety and humour'.

The *Marineleitung* at this time was a powerhouse of clandestine rearmament; the leading characters in the U-boat field were gathered here, Arno Spindler, Wilhelm Canaris, the redoubtable von Loewen-feld, all of whom worked closely with Werth and came under the same chief, Rear Admiral Adolph Pfeiffer. Canaris, later head of the intelligence and counter espionage organization, the *Abwehr*, was the liaison between the *Marineleitung* and Spain, whose co-operation was anticipated, especially in U-boat building; he called for a U-boat department in the High Command, as a result of which U-boat affairs were moved from the Torpedo- and Mines-Inspectorate in Kiel up to Berlin—under cover of U-boat counter-measures—and placed under Arno Spindler.

Spindler's first task was to select which types of boat should be designed for the mobilization plan for Case A—war with France and Poland. He set about it by studying the performances of the various world war types as recorded in the war diaries, and questioning U-boat Commanders; Karl Dönitz's name appears among the list of those he intended questioning; whether he did see Dönitz is not clear but as he was so immediately accessible it would be surprising if he was not among the first consulted; this was in January 1926. Prodded by Canaris, impatient to have firm type specifications for his dealings in Spain, Spindler recommended a small 270-ton type for the Baltic and two 500-ton types, one for minelaying, one for torpedo attack, in the North Sea. It is interesting that although war against commerce was in the ascendant so far as long-term naval expansion was concerned, Spindler based his recommendations for U-boats entirely on operations against enemy warships. The 500-ton boats were to act against ships maintaining a distant blockade of the exits to the North Sea, against French squadrons attempting to enter the Baltic, and against French squadrons and troopships in the Mediterranean.

111

The design teams at IvS in Rotterdam were set to work to produce up-dated plans for the three chosen types. Shortly afterwards, in July 1926, three naval missions were sent to Russia, the first under Spindler, the second under Loewenfeld, to seek U-boat contracts under the mantle of the trade treaties which were already allowing clandestine development and production of tanks, ammunition and aircraft for Germany. This surge of confidence and activity was partly in response to a buoyant economy: the Ruhr crisis had led to an international commission recommending a credit of 800 million gold Marks to support the *Reichsbank*. The greater part of this foreign loan went directly to Krupp, Thyssen, Siemens and other key industrialists for weapons, who had already been drawn into the web of rearmament preparations, and since the government at the same time increased the Army and Navy budgets dramatically, the effect was to boost the secret rearmament.

In public meanwhile the foreign minister, Stresemann, was pursuing a policy of 'fulfilment' of the reparations and other clauses of the Versailles treaty; he was rewarded in January 1927 by the withdrawal of the Allied Control Commission, which had been attempting to monitor the arms limitation clauses; the Commission's final report stated that Germany had never disarmed, never had any intention of doing so and had done everything in her power to deceive and circumvent their efforts.[28] This was common knowledge, but despite detailed exposés by Socialist deputies in the *Reichstag* the key government ministers continued to promote rearmament behind their public protestations of abiding by the treaty.

The Navy, meanwhile, carried on without interruption. Eight of ten *Winterarbeiten* in the winter of 1926–7 were set on U-boat topics. In February Spindler started working with Dönitz's immediate superior, Werth, to have a U-boat course for midshipmen incorporated in the torpedo course, and in April, as the first of the German-designed submarines for Turkey was completed at the Krupp-controlled yard in Rotterdam, a former U-boat Commander, Werner Fürbringer, and a former U-boat chief engineer took it out on trials, reporting every detail to the U-department at the *Marineleitung* via a front company formed by Lohmann with his secret fund.[29]

The main drive of the *Marineleitung* in all this was of course to break the 'shackles' of Versailles, restore autonomy in weapons to the service and to the Fatherland, and regain self-respect. Beyond this was a general disdain for parliamentary government and longing for a return to the old

112

certainties; this had been mitigated to an extent by the election of the old Field Marshal von Hindenburg as President of the Republic after the death of the first President in 1925. He was a man to whom they could give their wholehearted allegiance; nevertheless the manoeuvring and compromising of the party political game in the *Reichstag* and the extent of socialist, pacifist and generally anti-military sentiment that found expression there was deeply distasteful, while the strengths and ideals of democracy itself were outside the view of most naval officers—especially so for this small nucleus, hand-picked after the war for their 'sound service-outlook' and professional competence. They had passed their formative years in the headiest age of the Bismarckian *Kaiserreich*; they remained at heart Imperial officers, believing profoundly in Germany's mission in the wider world, their national and racial consciousness and contempt for parliamentarianism sharpened by the humiliations which they and the nation had suffered since 1918. As a body they were in a dangerous, prickly state of mind.

One of those wielding great influence was von Loewenfeld; his view of the world as expressed at a meeting in 1926 was probably typical. In Europe he saw Russian Bolshevism in alliance with the 'Slavic wave' as the greatest threat to Germany and western culture, although Poland and France were the more immediate threats. On the other hand was Italy under Mussolini, France's rival in the Mediterranean, therefore a potential ally—while Mussolini himself, 'Dictator and outspoken destroyer of Italian social democracy and the Jewish freemasonry'[30] was an enemy of German democracy. As for England; he advised a systematic and tactful attempt to form ties with her since she was 'for the moment' the leader of western culture. The historian, Jost Dülffer, sees implicit in this phrase 'for the moment' the expectation that Germany would recapture this position at some time in the future.

The similarity of von Loewenfeld's and Hitler's world views, as expounded at this time in *Mein Kampf*, is striking. Soon the Navy and the Nazis were to form unofficial ties through the former Kiel station admiral at the time of the Kapp *Putsch*, since retired, von Levetzow, who became Hitler's mentor in matters naval.

Dönitz, according to the widow of his friend, von Lamezan, was apolitical—in contrast to her husband who liked to theorize and argue about world affairs. Dönitz had no time or taste for such speculation; his work was his life, and von Lamezan envied him his good fortune in having a task to which he could dedicate himself so wholeheartedly.

113

However, Dönitz's 'apolitical' attitude contained acceptance of everything the naval officer corps stood for. This is implicit in all the reports on him by his superiors, in his later known attitudes, in his fierce ambition and in his life-long regard for Loewenfeld, the quintessential hardline, anti-Communist, anti-Social Democrat, anti-Jewish, nationalist rearmer.

As to Dönitz's part in the clandestine development of the U-boat arm, he was not a key figure; his name does not appear among the members of the committees which took decisions, but as leader of an essentially co-ordinating section in the *Wehrabteilung*, no doubt he played some part. In 1927, the year that practical U-boat training began with Werner Fürbringer's trials crew in Holland, and his own chief, Werth, became directly involved with Spindler in theoretical U-boat courses, there appeared for the first time among the personal and service details which prefaced the annual report on him:

> Employment in service branch as U-boat's watch officer from 1.iii.1917 to 1.xii.1917 U-boat Commander from 11.i.1918 to 25.ix.1918[31]

Werth endorsed his former excellent report and added, 'His confident, deft and sympathetic manner shows at every opportunity . . .'

He entered his physical appearance as 'tall, slim figure. Very good military and social manner.' In fact Dönitz was not much above average height; his extraordinary leanness and very upright bearing gave the impression he was taller than he was.

Werth's chief, Pfeiffer, noted on this report: 'an especially competent officer who deserves observation.'

Although signs of Germany's increasing prosperity were evident in Berlin, Dönitz was still financially constrained. With three children to support and educate and provide with little extras like tennis and dancing for Ursula, his style to maintain in the usual large-roomed apartment with maid at 4 Bergmannstrasse, he could not afford theatres or concerts, nor any of the 'decadent' night life of the capital. Nor would he have wished for the latter; as his reports indicate, he had a serious outlook on life. If there was any spare money he seems to have been inclined to buy antiques, which both he and Ingeborg liked, or copper engravings of Frederick the Great's generals and battles.

When they went on holiday as a family, usually to one of the North Sea islands, Borkum or Nordeney—never Baltrum where his father was buried—they travelled fourth class on the railway; this meant wooden seats with a wide space between for baggage on which the children stretched out and slept. At weekends his daughter, Ursula, then aged ten—her brother Klaus was seven and Peter five—remembers visits to museums and in the summer sailing on Lake Wannsee or going for family walks. A particularly sharp memory she retains is of her father reading to them in bed the traditional ballads he had learned as a boy, *Königskinder*, *Graf Douglas*, *Redboat* and others. He enjoyed declaiming them with feeling and pathos.

The children were brought up in the Protestant (*evangelisch*) religion and said their prayers at bed-time; probably this was the influence of their mother. Dönitz recalls in his memoirs how the youngest, Peter, looked up thoughtfully at his mother from his cot one evening and said, '*Mutti*, does God also have a telephone?' However, as far as Dönitz and Ingeborg were concerned, the Christian stories and prayers were simply the traditional way to bring up children; neither were churchgoers except on special occasions; Ingeborg was described as a modern woman, and it is extremely doubtful if either was a believing Christian at this stage of their lives.

From time to time they spent days or short holidays on the small Lamezan holding in Holstein—although this occurred less frequently while they were living in Berlin because of the distance. Frau Lamezan is certain that Ursula was Karl Dönitz's favourite child. Ursula herself remembers that on occasions when her father returned home in a bad mood her mother would push her out first to calm him. His first greeting, however, was always for their dog, a little Spitze whose name was Purzel. As a self-critical perfectionist and one who lived for his work and pushed himself to the limit and beyond, Dönitz was naturally subject to moods. Ingeborg was of an easy-going disposition, jolly and outward-going, and Ursula felt that she let Karl Dönitz dominate her; this finds support in Frau Lamezan's recollections; she describes him as a 'duty-man [*Pflichtmensch*] who lived for his work without, unfortunately, caring for others'.[32] However, she described Ingeborg as a strong personality. Of the marriage she believes that the two were considerate towards one another [*herzlich miteinander*], although at times he could not give her sufficient attention because of 'his task'.

The impression is that the usual difficulties of a service marriage with

115

its separations and little money in the lower ranks were exacerbated in Dönitz's case by his extreme duty-consciousness and temperamental nature, but that the family was in every other respect normal and very close. Ingeborg was a lively mother who enjoyed horse-play with her children; he was a fond father on holidays or when his duties allowed at the weekends. Ursula remembers, on one of their holidays at Nordeney, a sandcastle competition in which she took part with her father, he constructing a huge sphinx some six feet long, she making its tail. However, she made it so long—with a bow at the end—that he became exasperated and had her shorten it before the judge came round. They decorated the beast with shells and sprayed it with water to prevent it collapsing. It is a nice vignette, suggesting some imagination, some feeling for that ancient culture, or perhaps just for his own pleasant memories of the Mediterranean.

It is perhaps significant that he never, so far as Ursula remembers, spoke of his own childhood to his children; this may suggest it was not so happy as he implies in his memoirs. Asked about this, Ursula agreed that she found it strange he had never said anything to them about his early years; she thought he had described them as he remembered them in his memoirs, but had perhaps suppressed certain feelings.[33]

He was in general a silent man. In company he could exert himself to charm as most of the reports of his senior officers imply; on duty he spoke clearly and to the point, off duty he was a congenial messmate, but he was not noted as a raconteur, nor as a witty or amusing talker. Both Frau Lamezan and his daughter remember him as a reserved man whose strong inner discipline precluded rash, unconsidered remarks. Perhaps childhood reminiscences came into that category. Nevertheless, the suspicion remains that the masculine home in which he grew up and the pressures from his father and his own inner drive did perhaps shadow his youth and cause him to shut many memories up.

His relationship with his brother appears to have been good. Friedrich's loans to help him support his family during the inflation have been mentioned. Although living abroad, he was a visitor from time to time, particularly at Christmas; Ursula remembers him with great affection as a large, jolly man, temperamentally very different to her father. But Friedrich's own youngest daughter, Brigitte, remembers extraordinary similarities of manner and expression in the two men.

When Friedrich married, Ursula was one of the bridesmaids, but at some time afterwards the brothers quarrelled and became estranged;

116

why and when this happened seems unclear; the survivors of the two families were all children at the time and Karl Dönitz did not mention it in his memoirs—indeed he scarcely mentions his brother. It may have been on account of the loans and repayments, it may, as Ursula believes, have been over money left by an uncle. Whatever the cause, it struck deep for the families ceased to see or correspond with one another and Dönitz probably never saw his brother again.

In early August 1927 the Navy's secret rearmament was exposed in what became known as the 'Lohmann scandal'. It had been known for a long time that rearmament outside the treaty was in progress, but when the financial editor of the *Berliner Tageblatt*, investigating the affairs of the propaganda film company, Phoebus, stumbled on and published details of an extraordinary clandestine network of companies funded through Lohmann's *Seetransport* office at the Navy High Command, it rekindled all the anti-militarist ardour of the Communists and the pacifist wing of the Social Democrats, and once again the Navy became the target for bitter sustained attack. Dönitz was involved in preparing the Navy's case for the *Reichstag*. By this time he was working in collaboration with a department of the Army which had been set up in the image of his own department after it had become evident that the Navy was far more professional in political matters. Its chief was Lieutenant-Colonel Kurt von Schleicher, an officer in the Prussian mould who detested the Republic for its materialism and corruption and longed for a return to the austere ethic and authoritarian certainties of former days. Dönitz made no mention of the Lohmann affair or rearmament in any of his published writings, merely stating that Schleicher was the department chief with whom he worked at this period. However, there can be no doubt that he joined wholeheartedly in the military defence against the attack from the Left, no doubt that his attitude towards Communists and Democrats of any colour gained further reinforcement.

The government tried to suppress the facts of its own involvement in Lohmann's dealing. Meanwhile Lohmann himself was sacrificed, together with the Defence Minister and several senior naval officers implicated in the affair who were discharged, moved to less sensitive posts or retired before time; among these were Pfeiffer, Werth, von Loewenfeld and the naval chief, Zenker, who was succeeded in 1928 by the survivor of a former scandal, Admiral Erich Raeder. Canaris received a sea-going appointment, as did Dönitz, although whether this

117

was as a result of his involvement is not clear. What is clear is that these were cosmetic changes and both the Navy and the government continued their efforts to circumvent the Versailles treaty without a pause. Thus at the height of the uproar in August Pfeiffer held a conference attended by Canaris, Spindler, representatives from the naval construction department and Lohmann's go-between firm, on the funding necessary for Canaris' Spanish U-boat project, then nearing fruition, and in November when the contract was at last signed, Zenker approved the allocation of four million Reichsmarks from the Navy's own construction budget.[34] The following spring Fürbringer and his men, having carried out trials on a second German-designed submarine built for Turkey by Krupp's Rotterdam yard, delivered the boats to Constantinople, and both Fürbringer and his chief engineer stayed on to guide the Turkish U-school.

Dönitz, meanwhile, was serving as navigator of the cruiser, *Nymphe*, flagship of the Commander in Chief, Baltic—none other than Rear Admiral von Loewenfeld! Probably this appointment was far more to his taste than the desk job in Berlin; certainly he records in his memoirs that the crew of the cruiser were 'united in a joyous spirit' forming a community in which 'a young sailor was as happy as the Commander at the success of his ship in an exercise'.[35]

One of the reasons for this happier state of affairs was a rigorous selection policy for the Navy, screening out all applicants whose family had any connection with Republican or socialist politics, and which was especially vigilant against deliberate Communist infiltration and cell-building.[36] The naval ports were still hotbeds of Communism and naval ratings a prime target for subversion, but constant vigilance by the officers and major propaganda drives to make the men aware and motivate them to combat the dangers themselves had had effect. The small size of the service helped. For as Dönitz wrote, the candidates could be selected for high quality.[37] The quality most sought, as Dönitz knew well from his three years' involvement in disciplinary and political matters in Berlin, was patriotism.

The time in the *Nymphe* flew by in individual working-up drills, exercises in company—reconnaissance by day, attack by night—a foreign voyage, and finally the autumn naval manoeuvres. Once again he received an exemplary report from his commanding officer, the cruiser's Captain, Conrad, himself an outstanding navigator;[38] in his memoirs Dönitz gives generous tribute to the lessons he learnt from him.

The report was agreed and countersigned by von Loewenfeld, his last official service for the exceptionally promising junior he had picked out eighteen years earlier as a cadet in the *Hertha*.

Dönitz was now 37 years old. On November 1st he obtained his step-up to *Korvettenkapitän* (Lieutenant Commander); this coincided with his first independent command of a force, news of which had been conveyed to him in July personally by a beaming von Loewenfeld: he was to be chief of the 4th torpedo boat half flotilla—as he wrote in his memoirs, 'a magnificent command . . . I was independent. Some 20 officers and 600 men were under me, a large number for a young officer such as I was.'[39]

Immediately he plunged into preparations for the task, utilizing every free hour permitted by his duties in the flagship to work out a systematic training programme; dividing the first year into sections he assigned a goal to each, working up from individual weapon training to sea training by single boats, two boats in company, finally all four boats and exercises with the fleet. When the date came for him to take over the half flotilla he knew exactly what he had to do, and lost no time in imposing his ideas and indefatigable habits of work on his Commanders, nor in showing them who was chief.

It is evident from Dönitz's memoirs that the basic tactics of forming reconnaissance lines to seek the enemy by day and keeping touch at the limits of visibility until the attack by night were unchanged from his former torpedo boat time. And he mentions that in the autumn manoeuvres of 1929 the object was an enemy convoy which his half flotilla had the good fortune to find and 'destroy' that night. Whether any of the exercises were consciously devised to probe U-boat surface attack is not apparent although it is interesting that the report on him for the year 1930 was countersigned by Rear Admiral Walter Gladisch, one of the leading lights in the clandestine U-boat preparations, who signed himself BdU or Commander of U-boats, a title that was naturally not in any official naval list. It is interesting, too, that the same year, 1930, marked the first practical U-boat training of active service as distinct from retired officers like Fürbringer. This was carried out on a 500-ton Finnish submarine designed by IvS and built in Finland with the help of German technicians. The German officers were disguised as civilian tourists, and carried out trials with the boat from July to September.

Answering questions about his career in 1969, Dönitz said that he 'could have had no better military command for later leadership posts than this task as chief of the 4th torpedo boat half flotilla'.[40] Probably he meant this in general terms; however, a biographical sketch of him in the Navy *Taschenbuch* for 1944 states that in the autumn of 1929 his new position with the torpedo boats 'for the first time gave him the opportunity to put down his experiences and suggestions [for the reconstruction of the German U-boat fleet] in the form of memoranda written for his superiors and other influential personalities'.[41] This may be a propaganda fabrication; none of these memoranda appear in Walter Gladisch's papers and have not so far come to light anywhere else. Yet the citing of a specific date, autumn 1929, rather than a generalized statement about his involvement in U-boat preparations is suggestive, and it is interesting that in 1932 detailed consideration of U-boat types led to a decision to reduce conning-tower sizes to give a smaller silhouette. As a highly ambitious, thrusting officer who undoubtedly knew all about the secret U-boat work, it would have been entirely in character for him to have made suggestions and written memoranda on the subject; considering the close involvement of Loewenfeld and Gladisch in U-boat affairs it is even possible that he was being groomed deliberately for the anticipated U-boat arm.

Whether or not this was so, the reports on him by the flotilla chief, *Korvettenkapitän* Schniewind, could not have been more apt:

Excellently gifted for his post, above average, tough and brisk officer. With his ability and indefatigable, conscientious efforts, brought his half flotilla to a notably high standard of training. Possessed much verve and understood how to get along with officers and men. Extremely duty-conscious and energetic, he placed high demands on himself and his subordinates. Possessed a clear, confident judgement in all professional questions . . . Quick in thought and action, prompt in resolution, absolutely reliable.

Very active and interested in the training of his officers, he brings an especially warm heart to the needs and cares of officers and men.

Cordial, candid and pithy character, always ready to help. Highminded and thoroughly educated. In social intercourse cheerful and open, always in good spirits.

All in all—a splendid officer of worthy personality, equally esteemed as officer and man, an always tactful subordinate and excellent comrade.[42]

120

One of the springs of Dönitz's success was his absolutely whole-hearted commitment to his task and his love of his profession; concluding an account of a day with the flotilla at Lisbon at the end of May 1930—written in 1933—he described how in the evening he and his Commanders sat in a square under palms drinking red wine until the dawn light, 'pleased with our life and our fine profession, the finest there is!'[43]

During the time he was bringing his boats up to a high level of efficiency the country entered another period of crisis. The causes were both economic and political. On the one hand the beginning of a general world trade recession exposed the artificial prosperity Germany had been enjoying from foreign loans, and once again inflation, bankruptcies and unemployment rose; on the other hand a swing to the Left in elections in 1928 had alarmed Conservatives and industrialists and induced in them much the same 'backs to the wall' mood as in the years before 1914 and immediately after the lost war. In their desperation they turned to Adolf Hitler.

Hitler had been using the years since his release from prison to rebuild his Party and secure his own position at its head. His tactics had been simple but brilliantly effective: the *Führer* or 'leader' principle, a pyramid of command modelled on the Army in which each man owed unquestioning obedience both to his own immediate superior and to the supreme leader, had made the Party an extension of his own ego, institutionalizing his own need to dominate and his incapacity to listen to or understand any view but his own. The intolerable annoyances of rational argument or rival leadership were cut off by Führer decree. In the short term this served the practical end of preventing factions splitting the party or diluting its message, thus giving it the tactical flexibility, speed of reaction and concentrated focus of a single will. In the long term, of course, it held the greatest dangers since the Führer must become corrupted by his power; the danger was evident in Hitler's case since he was already accustomed to dominating his close colleagues, men from the same restricted background as himself who were held spellbound by the breathtaking flow of his ideas, silenced by his fits of passion when crossed, stirred in their shallow depths by his dark hatreds while they munched cream cakes in the simpler Munich cafés. Conviction and anger and vengeance are powerful weapons; Hitler used them consciously and unconsciously for the satisfaction of his own naked will.

121

To emotional verbal power he joined an animal-like nose for the secret feelings and failings of others and a peasant guile in his dealings with those socially, financially, intellectually above his own level; for their part these despised or humoured him. It was difficult for anyone with critical faculties to take him seriously. A trench coat thrown over his awkward figure, dandruff from his hair spotting the collar, his face redeemed only by blue eyes with a direct and fervent (short-sighted) gaze, he looked what he was, a street agitator. His unimpressive appearance and haphazard manner, described as typical Austrian *Schlamperei*, a Bohemian casualness at odds with his platform image of concentrated force, together with a genuine gaucheness when mixing in higher social circles, were some of his greatest assets. For he was dismissed by political rivals and powerful potential allies as a small-time demagogue who could be used, manipulated and dropped when necessary.

So probably he would have remained had trade recession and unemployment not hit Germany, increasing the numbers whose resentments and idle time could be harnessed to his will. At this he was supreme. As a propagandist and conduit for directing the frustrations and insecurities of the young and the dispossessed and merging them into the national humiliation of the lost war and the national preoccupation with power and the military spirit, he showed genius. The stage management and special effects of the party rallies at Nuremberg, the standards and banners, marching and counter-marching and shouting, music and mass emotion, the street battles against the internal Bolshevist enemy, the repetition in Nazi newspapers and speeches of the articles of hatred—against the treaty of Versailles, against the November criminals in the government who had signed it, against Bolshevism and the Jewish world conspiracy which had spawned it—never descending from generalities to particulars or remedies, never entering into discussion or argument, simply hammering the message home as he was wont to in his own close circle of the half-educated, shrilly and crudely, with these methods the party grew as one of the more noxious effects of the economic crisis. And it was at this point that an infusion of youth with its aggression and idealism transformed it into a potent movement.

So it was that the leader of the conservative, industrial and Pan-German forces, Alfred Hugenberg, threatened by the simultaneous advance of the Left, turned to the Nazis! Hitler had what he lacked, mass support; he had what Hitler lacked, the financial resources and political patronage of industry and the landed classes. Like so many others before

122

him, he underestimated the extent of the Bohemian corporal's driving need to dominate or the elemental amorality of his nature. In religious terms it was a pact with the devil; the consequences should have been clear; fear of international Marxism, bitterness at the national humiliation represented by the hated terms of Versailles blinded him and the magnates he represented—that at least is the kindest interpretation. With free use of Hugenberg's nationwide propaganda machine Hitler became a household name throughout Germany; in elections in September 1930, preceded by brutal street violence between Nazis and Reds and Republicans Hitler's party increased its representation in the *Reichstag* from twelve to 107 deputies, becoming in one leap the second largest party in the House.

Hitler enjoyed great support in the armed forces, particularly amongst younger officers and men, particularly in the Navy. Senior Army officers viewed the Nazis with as much apprehension as they viewed the Communists, rightly seeing little to choose between them: both were revolutionary forces dedicated to the destruction of existing institutions and social structures, both implied dictatorship by the party. But many senior naval officers were sympathetic, for the Navy was still the *parvenu* and after the stigma of the 1918 and 1923 mutinies and the performance of the battlefleet in the First World War needed more than ever to prove that it was not an expensive, potentially disastrous luxury; and since naval officers had a far harder task than the Army to explain the benefits of a fleet to a still generally land-minded nation they naturally inclined to a party such as Hitler's which promised to break the shackles of Versailles and rebuild German armed strength.

Above all perhaps, the nucleus of the officer corps that had been chosen to carry the seeds of the fleet for the future had been selected for their sound outlook and were particularly likely to respond to Hitler's message; the generalities that he was purveying about the German mission in the world and the racial basis of that mission were the very beliefs in which they had been indoctrinated as Imperial officers. And when Hitler talked of restoring German honour, breaking the shackles of Versailles and regaining autonomy in defence they could identify almost personally with the lost honour of the fleet that had not sortied, and the shameful revolutions. It is significant that support for Hitler seems to have been particularly strong among the ex-*Freikorps* men who had fought the Communists.[44] And as unemployment in the naval ports grew and with it the strength of the local Nazi Party branches, and the

123

message spread to the men of the fleet, officers felt that here was a popular 'loyalist' movement whose aims were their own and whose adoption on the lower deck fitted new ideas of 'man-management' through comradeship and shared purpose, which they had been consciously developing since the various mutinies had exposed the dangers of their old style.

Dönitz himself could not have been unaware of Hitler's message; by 1929, his first full year as chief of the half flotilla, both Kiel and Wilhelmshaven naval stations had been successfully infiltrated by the Nazis, and by the spring of 1932 Hitler's propagandist, Goebbels, reported after a visit to one of these stations that 'everyone, officers and crews are entirely for us'.[45] It can scarcely be doubted that Dönitz welcomed the Party message for the same reasons as other patriotic and ambitious young officers; torpedo boats were for young men, and it is perhaps significant that the Commander of Dönitz's leader boat, *Albatros*, von Puttkamer, became Hitler's naval Adjutant after the Nazi seizure of power.

Another reason to believe that Dönitz supported the Nazi message was his close involvement with the concerns of his men. This was confirmed again in his final report from the flotilla chief, Otto Schniewind. After writing that everything in his first very favourable report remained valid, Schniewind went on:

> He developed his half flotilla, in which he enjoyed great respect and strong popularity, excellently. He knew no difficulties, possessed verve and the gift of getting along with his men, is tough in striving for goals and very thorough. Clear in verbal and written expression . . . genuine, solid character, warm-hearted loyal comrade. Also the welfare of his men claims his very energetic attention.
>
> *Korvettenkapitän* Dönitz is an officer with strong personality who deserves especial observation and promotion.[46]

This was the report countersigned by Rear Admiral Gladisch as BdU— Commander of U-boats.

Of Dönitz's next posting, lasting from October 1930 to the summer of 1934, his memoirs are almost completely silent. It was the critical period for the nation when the Weimar Republic fell to Hitler's assault; virtually his only mention of his activities comes in two brief references contained in answers to questions about his career published in 1969. The first is a statement.

In autumn 1930 I was for four years first Admiralty staff officer and leader of the Admiralty staff office of the High Command of the North Sea station in Wilhelmshaven. That says all there is to say about my activities . . . These four years in Wilhelmshaven with a staff of some 40 officers and men was truly a time filled with work.[47]

It is evident from his first year's personal report by the Chief of Staff that some of this work—whatever it was—was of his own making.

Thanks to his quick comprehension and his untiring industry he very rapidly familiarized himself with the position of first Admiralty staff officer and performed well. A very competent staff officer with thorough knowledge of all spheres. Goal-conscious and systematic.

He worked quickly and reliably. Very deft in oral and written expression. Very intellectually animated and interested in all professional questions.

Very ambitious and consequently asserts himself to obtain prestige, finding it difficult to subordinate himself and confine himself to his own work-sphere. He must allow the officers of the Admiralty Staff more essential independence than hitherto.

His strong temperament and inner verve frequently affected him with restlessness and, for his age, imbalance. Must therefore be brought to take things more calmly and not to set exaggerated demands, above all on himself.

His frequent apparent restlessness is probably in part due to his changing state of health (stomach complaints). Latterly an improvement has taken place.

Despite these limitations I consider him an excellent officer whose character is not yet fully formed and who is in need of strong and benevolent leadership.[48]

This is the most interesting of all the reports on Dönitz, not least because its author was Wilhelm Canaris—a most unusual officer, perhaps the most unusual in the German service. More travelled and worldly wise than the run of career officers who had been sheltered from large areas of thought and experience in the service cocoon, he also possessed a Latin subtlety that was contrary to the brutal directness of the Prussian tradition in which the corps had been moulded. This fitted him for the clandestine rearmament work on which he had been engaged almost continuously since the war, but not for the more straightforward duties of an executive officer—at least this was the feeling; his nickname 'the Levantine' reflected this. At Nuremberg Dönitz described him as 'an officer in whom not much confidence was shown. He was a man quite different from us. We used to say he had seven souls in his breast.'[49]

That is rather a good description; Canaris was an enigma and will no doubt remain one, and Dönitz probably found him as curious a specimen as Canaris obviously found this fanatically diligent young staff officer. His remarks about Dönitz's restlessness and imbalance and his uncertain health may, therefore, be a comment on the visible effects of this incompatibility. Whether or not this is so, they are extraordinarily interesting because, for the first time since the British interrogating officer's report on the loss of Dönitz's U-boat in 1918, with its similar suggestion of temperamental imbalance, we are receiving an impression as it were from outside the charmed circle of like-minded and dedicated career officers. To them Dönitz's fervour was both natural and commendable; to Canaris it was exaggerated, and Dönitz, who had just passed his 39th birthday, had the outlook and emotional instability of a much younger man. This judgement appears to be borne out fully in his later career and was echoed afterwards by another close colleague, Albert Speer.

It is interesting that at Nuremberg an affidavit by the United States Consul General in Berlin for this period, 1930–34, was produced which made the same point: 'Karl Dönitz was always not well mentally balanced.'[50] Dönitz disputed the possibility of the American having known him at that time as he was only a junior officer and working at Wilhelmshaven, and the Consul was unable to reply with chapter and verse of the meetings since he had not kept a diary. Nevertheless the description from a man who could not have read Canaris' confidential report must be considered an astonishing coincidence if it was not founded on observation. It therefore lends some credence to the rest of his comments, which were: 'He became one of the earliest high officers of Army or Navy to completely identify himself with Nazi ideology and aims.'[51] This sentence is suspect since, of course, Dönitz was far from a high officer at the time in question, but there is no doubt it describes his later attitude. Does it also describe his attitude in this period immediately preceding and after Hitler's seizure of power? Certainly in his post as staff officer at Wilhelmshaven, he was intimately concerned with the political situation. He makes this clear himself in his second and only other allusion to this period of his career: 'My tasks included measures of protection against inner [service] unrest. Often these questions were discussed in the Defence Ministry in Berlin with the competent representatives of all service commands.'[52]

This implies that he was not confined to Wilhelmshaven—as he stated at Nuremberg—but joined discussions in Berlin and could therefore have come to the attention of the United States Consul General; he was a thruster.

This is speculation. But in view of his undoubted ambition, fervent patriotism, temperament, personal experience of the dangers of Communism which the Nazis were dedicated to eradicating and his later documented hatred of Communists it would be surprising if he had not attached himself for emotional and practical career reasons to Hitler's rising star.

In his own account of his attitude towards Nazism in replies to questions put to him in 1969 he gives the familiar picture of the Republic threatened from both Left and Right extremes; the middle classes had moved to the support of the extreme Right, Hitler, and the centre was therefore weak. In these circumstances it was clear to the representatives of the armed forces that they could not defend the State against both extremes simultaneously; 'that would mean we would have had to fight against the great majority of the German people'.[53] The armed services, he continued, were inclined towards the Nazis because of their commitment to free the nation from the shackles of Versailles and their attitude towards other questions such as reparations, and therefore welcomed Hindenburg's appointment of Hitler as Chancellor. 'We soldiers also hoped that through this change in the leadership the Communist danger would be removed.'

This explanation is true so far as it goes, but extraordinarily bland; as with all areas of controversy in his recollections, Dönitz skates around the real difficulties. The Army High Command recognized the Nazi Party as a revolutionary organization and Hitler's brown-shirted street army, the SA, and the more recently created élite black-shirted squads of SS as quite as dangerous to the state as the Communists. By Dönitz's own account his position involved him in guarding against these internal dangers and in discussions on these questions between representatives of

127

the services at the Ministry of Defence in Berlin; yet he chose to reveal nothing of the complex process or of the doubts and intrigue by which the armed services and the revolutionary army came together.

Another serious omission in his account is race ideology. This was central to Hitler's view of the world; it was never disguised, it was the Führer's *leitmotif*, infecting both internal and external relationships.

No people have more right to the idea of world mastery than the German people, [he proclaimed in 1933]. No other nation has had such a right to claim world mastery on grounds of ability and numbers. We have come in short to this first world partition and stand at the beginning of a new world revolution . . .[54]

This was a theme close to the Imperial officer's heart. The Navy supported Hitler, not simply to break the shackles of Versailles or annihilate Communists, but to fulfil the world mission that was Germany's by right of racial superiority, and could only be accomplished with the aid of a powerful Navy.

In Hitler's vision this was a two-stage process: first continental hegemony through the colonization of Eastern Europe by the *Herrenvolk*—for which he needed the friendship of Great Britain to secure his western flank—second the struggle with Great Britain and America for world domination.[55] This had been the strategy of the Imperial government in the final years before the First War; it had failed because the threat posed by Tirpitz's fleet had prevented England standing aside during the vital first stage. Hitler did not intend to repeat the Kaiser's mistake; he wanted an alliance with Great Britain, or at least a firm understanding on the lines that Wilhelm's Chancellor, Bethmann-Hollweg, had been striving for from 1912 to 1914—a free hand in Europe in return for allowing Britain a free hand in the wider world. This was also the Navy's view. They too had learnt from the failure of the Tirpitz strategy; in any case they could not compete with the Royal Navy with the minute fleet allowed them by the Versailles treaty; their strategy had to be to build a base for the oceanic future and in the short term to give no possible offence to Great Briatain.

Hitler was a political animal with a nose for the compulsions of those with whom he sought to do business and, despite occasional indiscretions such as publicly criticizing Tirpitz's battle fleet and big ships in general, he used the similarities between his own viewpoint and the Navy's to woo Raeder, who, like the pro-Nazi General Blomberg, whose wife and family Dönitz's daughter, Ursula, remembers meeting year after year on holiday on Borkum, like Hjalmar Schacht, the economist, and Thyssen and Krupp and the other industrial magnates, thought he was winning Hitler over. So National Socialism and naval policy were co-ordinated before Hitler came to power and the Nazis gained the support of another interest group.

Dönitz dropped no hint of these deep currents when he framed his careful replies in 1969; indeed he sought to obscure them by starting: 'It is difficult today to write about the past because we today know things which men then did not know.'[56] If they did not know it was because they did not wish to. The character of the Führer and his party was hideously evident in deed and word. Helmuth James von Moltke of the famous Field Marshal's family was by no means the only member of the landed and military classes who saw before the Nazis came to power that 'whoever votes for Hitler votes for war'.[57]

Dönitz's explanation went on to excuse the armed forces from involvement in Hitler's rise to power on the grounds of their political neutrality; this obliged them 'as soldiers to serve the whole German people and the State, whose form had been given by our fellow countrymen'.[58] This is plainly false. Naval officers' hostility to, indeed incomprehension of, parliamentary democracy is copiously documented. Dönitz had served in the departments in Berlin which had dealt with the *Reichstag* and was therefore intimately involved in the deliberate circumvention of parliamentary democracy by the Navy. Moreover, the myth of political neutrality hides the hard fact that Hitler's racial and world views were nothing more than the propaganda of Imperial Germany rendered more brutally simple in his crude mind, and therefore keyed in with the naval officers' basic prejudices. This is indisputable; apart from the enthusiasm for the Nazi Party, especially noticeable amongst the younger serving officers and in the retired officers' Associations ashore, most naval officers who met Hitler personally were impressed. He had the Kaiser's extraordinary memory for technical detail and interest in ship design and weaponry; he appeared to have the future of the Navy at heart; above all he spoke of the future of Germany in terms they approved. In May 1933, three months after Hindenburg was forced reluctantly to invite Hitler to be Chancellor, the leader of Raeder's staff officer training scheme—a key post so far as the Navy's attitude was concerned—spoke before a gathering of SS, SA, *Stahlhelm* and Nazi Party leaders in terms that might have been used by Tirpitz:

> Now the forces which in the last fourteen years were splintered through struggles in Parliament, are free to overcome . . . all the infamous sabotage attempts of Social Democrats, doctrinaires and pacifists . . . Now we *must* again awake and strengthen the *understanding*, the love of the sea and the *will* of the nation and never again allow the life veins to be cut, which for a *free*, *great* people lie on the *free oceans*.[59]

There was a deeper understanding between the frustrated officers of the *Reichsmarine* and the Nazis than hatred of Communism and the Versailles treaty; it was nothing less than a revival of the national goals of 1914. By seeking to obscure this and over-simplify the service machinations and the intrigues of his one-time chief in the combined services department in the Defence Ministry, von Schleicher, Dönitz completely undermines confidence in his account and leaves a large question mark over his own attitude during this critical period.

During his second year on the staff at Wilhelmshaven, Dönitz apparently calmed down; Canaris gave him a far better report:

> Ambition and the endeavour to distinguish himself remain outstanding characteristics. Nevertheless they have no more exceeded the permissible measure.
>
> In his whole manner he has become essentially calmer and balanced. This is due in great part to an improvement in his health.
>
> A strong personality of great knowledge and ability, who will always give outstanding performances. This depends upon advancing this valuable officer as much as possible, although an eye must be kept on him to ensure he takes things calmly and does not place too high demands on himself and others.[60]

The report was countersigned by the Vice Admiral commanding the naval station, 'An officer of much promise well worth noting'.

There is no doubt that by this time he was recognized as a brilliant officer throughout the service, and the fact received official confirmation in the shape of a Hindenburg travel grant for the following year, 1933. These grants were made annually to one outstanding officer from either the Army or the Navy to allow him to travel abroad and increase his knowledge of the outside world. Dönitz chose to visit the British and Dutch colonies in the east, or perhaps this was suggested to him as a useful idea; in either case it was a natural objective for an officer from a Navy which saw its long-term future as the bearer of German culture outside Europe.

He sailed in February 1933 within days of Hitler's appointment as Chancellor, and was away until the summer, thus missing the first onslaught of terror which swept Germany in the 'March days' as the Nazis settled scores with their enemies and with parliamentary democracy itself—as they had promised.

Dönitz's account of his travels on the Hindenburg grant, apparently intended for publication, but never published and omitted entirely from his memoirs, is the most revealing of all his surviving writings, opening startling glimpses beneath the severely controlled façade he presented to the world. Sections of it have been cut, probably by himself after his release from Spandau prison; one can only speculate about the reason, but it may be significant that of the six obvious cuts—there may be others for the copy is incomplete and the pagination curious—three come directly after mention of things British—a British submarine which his own U-boat missed torpedoing during the war, the inscription over the British governor's palace in Malta, a British cruiser which rescued survivors from a wreck on Cape Guardafui; the other cuts occur on passage down the English Channel, the Red Sea and homeward bound through the Mediterranean. Perhaps the censorship was to hide anti-English feelings—yet these come through between the lines of surviving portions of the script.

The other possible reason for the cuts is that the deleted passages were pro-Nazi; judging by the context an anti-British bias seems the more likely explanation. There may be another.

More striking is the script's revelation of the 42-year-old Dönitz as a fantasist. The first example of this can perhaps be written off as a yarn told to enliven the evening dinner table on board the steamer bearing him to the east. According to his account he was telling an innocuous tale about an experience in U-boats when one of the ladies listening told him not to have so much regard for their susceptibilities; they wished to hear about the *real* U-boat war. On this he launched into what seems to be a complete fabrication of a gun encounter with a 'Q-ship' while watch

131

officer of U 39; chasing a small merchantman through a smoke screen they came upon her suddenly, lying stopped; flaps dropped from her sides and four guns opened on them.

God be thanked, we had dashed out of the fog so close that the shells growled above us. Alarm and crash dive—crashing of shells, whistling of air from the tanks, a stupefying noise on deck—[61]

This exciting encounter is not mentioned by Forstmann, nor in the official German history!

A second description of an encounter, the memory of which was brought on by the sight of Cape Bon as they steamed through the Mediterranean, is equally difficult to believe. It was his own boat this time; he had attempted a submerged attack on an escorted convoy by moonlight, but had not got to shooting range. Seized by 'the Teutonic rage', he had thereupon ordered the boat to the surface and made an approach run.

Cursed [moon]light—the destroyers must be asleep, if . . . still we run nearer, still they do not see us—yet, *ach* man, over there already, flashes and 'Tsing—Tsing' shells fly overhead. 'Hard aport! Alarm! Crash dive!—*Donner!* Will the boat not go under? . . . God be thanked, now she drops, but it seems like an eternity. Already the propeller noise comes, then a stupefying roar, the light goes out. Then we had the salute, depth charges in close proximity! That comes of attempting, like a blind madman, to cruise into a convoy by moonlight.[62]

An interesting observation in view of the tactics of U-boats under his orders in the Second World War. It is more interesting that there is not a word of this alleged encounter in the memoirs he wrote after the war; by that time the official history of the U-boat war had been published and the activities of UC 25 described from his log.

The most revealing of all his embroidered tales, however, concerns his imprisonment in 1918. The memory of this was revived when his steamer called at Malta and he went ashore and revisited the 'old, cold, damp fort with dark casemates' in which he had been incarcerated. He remembered how, dressed in only a shirt, pants and one sock, he had been escorted by 'Tommies' with naked bayonets to stand before an English Admiral.

> . . . however I did not feel small and odious.
> The Englishman: 'What number is your boat?'
> A shrug of the shoulders.
> The Englishman, indignantly: 'Who told me you were the Captain? I will stick you in the men's camp and make you work!'
> Really he was not so unfair as, God knows, I did not look like a captain—I: 'I can't help it!' [in English]
> Then the English staff officer wrote on a sheet of paper the number of my previous boat, UC 25, and the name of the fat English steamer, *Cyclops*, that I had turned over in the Sicilian naval harbour of Port Augusta, and shoved the paper to the Admiral.
> I was amazed how well these people were in the picture. They knew exactly who I was.[63]

This is an obvious fabrication. Apart from the British interrogation report on Dönitz, which makes no mention of UC 25, the *Cyclops* or Port Augusta, there is the fact that the ship he sank there was not the *Cyclops*, but a coaling hulk. Therefore the British staff officer could hardly have pushed a paper with the words UC 25 and *Cyclops* in front of the Admiral.

It is remarkable in view of his actual achievements as Commander of UC 25 that it was necessary for him to boost himself with these fantasy exploits. The final phrases of the accounts are surely significant: '. . . attempting like a blind madman to cruise into a convoy by moonlight', and, pure Walter Mitty, '. . . They knew exactly who I was.' These two lines show that beneath the outwardly diamond tough, gifted, indeed brilliant, dedicated career officer, Dönitz was fundamentally unsure of himself; the revelation supports to the hilt Canaris' suggestion that he was immature and temperamentally unbalanced.

In view of these examples of the fantasy world he indulged in, it is probable that another rather similar tale in his account—again against the English—is somewhat exaggerated. This concerned the immigration authorities in southern India. He had crossed by ferry from Ceylon overnight, getting scarcely a wink of sleep because of cockroaches and other bugs, and in the morning, in a bad mood, found the Customs and Medical officers seated at a long table on deck with the first- and

133

second-class passengers queueing to be examined. He sat himself in a deck chair and watched. Finally, when all had been dealt with, a native official was sent across to summon him to the table. He told the man that if his master wanted something he should come himself. The immigration officer duly came over. '"Passport please!"—then the entry formalities, customs and medical inspection, were wound up comfortably from my deck chair . . . I can recommend this process, only four-square behaviour impresses these people.'[64]

So much for his basic insecurity. Of a general anti-English outlook there are suggestions; British officials in Ceylon whom he referred to as Secret Police: 'apparently still live in a war psychosis—in the matter of decreasing war-incitement the colonies limp far behind the British motherland and believe they are able to treat the Germans still with something of the victor's style.

'But wait, my boy!'[65]

What seems plain is that he admired the Dutch colonies he visited rather more than the English. In old Batavia in the Dutch East Indies he was impressed by the feeling that this was not a distant and alien possession exploited for what it could produce, so much as a community closely bound to the motherland by blood, a model of what a colony should be. It is apparent too that he enjoyed the life he found there as a guest in the high, airy bungalows, waited on by Javanese boys in sarongs and white jackets. And he was captivated by the grace of the native women, 'pole-slender and sinfully lovely',[66] thinking it no wonder if planters on their lonely estates and young administrators settled down with a brown wife and forgot Europe in the magic of this voluptuous land.

From Batavia he went to Bandung, then on a long rail journey to Soerabaya, marvelling at the beauty and abundance of the country and the happiness of the people. After the unemployment, bitterness, violence and greyness he had left in Europe it must have seemed Utopia.

Village follows village. You can't walk 50 metres without meeting a man on the way from one of them. And all have work and their bread, and are quiet and apparently contented. On the whole long stretch this unbroken chain of contented people, who had all they wanted to live, made perhaps the strongest impression on this journey. There is no greater proof that Holland is fulfilling its colonial task: no exploitation, no depressing the conditions of the islanders only to exploit them, no,

134

their conditions of life have been bettered and raised through order, organization, care and hygiene.[67]

His observations on the people are perceptive and sympathetic. After describing how a small white baby in his carriage was looked after by its native 'nanny' who never took her eyes off the infant and attended to its every wish like an 'animal mother', he went on: 'I have also never seen the brown women scold their own children and certainly not hit them—that would be to them, with their strong, animal, natural child-love, quite inconceivable.'[68]

From Java he sailed to Bali.

Dear European, if you yearn for a wonderfully beautiful land, and beautiful, graceful, calm, peaceful men with much inner culture, but untouched by European civilization, who live in union with nature—then pack your bags and go to Bali . . . The longer you are there, the stronger will be the charm which these natural, ideally lovely, quiet people will exert on you . . .[69]

He advised visiting the island alone or in the company of a fully sympathetic person who would not disturb 'the harmony of this fairy-tale land'. And he advised against 'doing the sights'; it was much more important 'that in peace and with an open heart you allow the land and people to work on you. Therefore go to southern Bali where no tourist steamers can approach the coast . . .' He described his own excursions, putting up for the night in village temples, gazing up from his mat at the starry sky as he was lulled to sleep by the music of the cicadas and the village gongs warding off evil spirits. 'I am not certain whether the Balinese have not just as much inner decency and natural culture as Europeans.'[70]

From Bali he went by cargo steamer to Singapore, finding among the few passengers an 'animal-catcher' for the Berlin Zoo, a 'gentleman of education and breeding whose peaceful soul showed in his eyes'. He had his captures with him, and his love and infinite care for them impressed Dönitz greatly. At Singapore he boarded a passenger liner for passage to Ceylon and he found it an unpleasant contrast—'long menus, music, cinema, dressing up, surface table talk, cliques, flirts and antipathies . . . a community of snobbery'.[71]

Judging by his descriptions, the things that impressed him most in

135

Ceylon were the jungle-grown ruins of the ancient capitals of the Sinhalese kings at Anuradhapura and Polonnarua, indeed he describes his days in the jungle there as amongst the best of his journey. He was not so happy when he returned to civilization in Colombo. Nevertheless it was a sad morning when he boarded a steamer for Europe, and had to take his leave of the 'wonderland of India—from all the colourful, picturesque, luxuriant strangeness that weaves such a spell on the European'.[72]

The account of his travels from which these extracts have been taken was probably written in diary form as he went, and worked up into a typescript afterwards; it provides extraordinarily illuminating glimpses of a sensitive and perceptive human being beneath the tight-lipped exterior shortly to be set in stone by the events of the Second World War. Here, before he had to guard every word set down, we can read of his evident delight in children and animals: on the return voyage 'to my joy there is a crowd of children on board. It is charming to listen to how they understand one another and to observe how the little mixture of nationalities play with one another.'[73]

Many of his descriptions reveal a contemplative and even poetic turn of mind; he can gaze up into the black void of the night sky between the Milky Way and Southern Cross and feel his gaze plunging into the infinite breadth of the universe. And he can both admire the precision of a flotilla of dolphins sporting by the bows, and put himself in their place, looking up at the ship:

. . . the comical, immobile passengers. What have we there then? Yes, a passenger is springing into a water pool on deck—and splashing around! So—the poor idiot! He calls that swimming, in such a bowl! Does the fellow know at all what sea space, what boundless distance is? . . .[74]

And we discover with some surprise that this indefatigably conscientious officer can enjoy just sitting in a deck chair in the sun!

How well one can endure doing nothing. I believe that man is lazy by nature—only the cursed striving and ambition stings men to action. O world, how lovely you must have been when only small bands of people threaded through the land, and people were not yet crowded together and life made grey. Sunbathing—thoughts![75]

Perhaps the strongest impression left by the account, however, is of how deeply he had been affected by the loss of UB 68 and the death of his engineer, Jeschen. When the steamer passed the spot in the Mediterranean where the boat had gone down he stood alone at the stern rail while the flag was dipped—an arrangement he had made with the German captain—saluting the dead in silence.

> We survivors of UB 68 greet you, who on the 4th October 1918 gave your lives—you above all, brave Jeschen—without you, we the saved would not be in the sunlight now. How did you die, how often have I put this question to myself in the nights since 4th October . . .
>
> In my dreams I saw your small band, you, Jeschen, first, climbing the steep way to heaven's gate. A damp trail of sea-water was your trace—the salt flood dropped from your hair and leathers . . . your pale, tense faces were raised expectantly towards the longed-for goal. There in the distance in beaming rosy morning light you saw the high, mighty fortress of heaven with turrets and pinnacles thrusting in the clouds. Yes, heaven's portals were opened wide to you because you could not give more to your *Volk* than you have given![76]

One is bound to ask after reading this and the heroic fantasies he indulged and his tender observations on children and animals and simple peoples, whether the key to the extremes in his character, the driving duty-consciousness, the ice-hard ruthlessness that was to be demonstrated in the Second World War, was suppression of his natural sensitivity under the weight of the Prussian ethic that ruled Germany—in his father's home, at the Stoy'scher Academy, in the Imperial officer corps under the tutelage of such a natural epitome of the warrior code as von Loewenfeld.

Dönitz returned to his post in Wilhelmshaven in June. He must have found his internal security duties very much easier since active Communists had been rounded up and thrown into concentration camps. In the nation as a whole there was a new atmosphere of hope; the 'National revival' was under way—this at least was the message broadcast by press and radio, now controlled by Goebbels' propaganda department. On the surface it appeared true: massive deficit financing to cure unemployment by stimulating particularly the armaments industries was beginning to bear fruit and there was a genuine sense of hope and new purpose and liberation after the last confused years of the Republic.

This was especially so for the Navy. Hitler had ratified a five-year plan for rebuilding the fleet which had been sanctioned by his predecessor, von Papen, and had confirmed to the chiefs of the armed services that he would ensure the undisturbed development of their forces. Moreover, the spirit of unity through common goals he promised the nation was a theme corresponding exactly with the naval officers' revised conception of leadership through shared aims. Ambitious, middle-rank officers like Dönitz could look to the future with a new confidence.

In October that year he received his step up to *Fregattenkapitän* (Commander), and in November a new Chief of Staff, who had just replaced Canaris, reported on him with unequivocal enthusiasm—'an officer with magnificent intellectual and character gifts . . . healthy ambition and outstanding leadership qualities . . .'[77] The testimonial, which almost looks as if it might have been designed to dispel any doubts raised by 'the Levantine's' reports, ended: 'Truly military and soldierly in thought, warm-hearted as a man and comrade. A superior sea officer of whom the Navy can expect much.'

In June 1934 Dönitz received orders to take command of the light cruiser, *Emden*, in the autumn. He could have asked for nothing better after his three and a half years as a staff officer—independent command and foreign travel combined.

After handing over to his successor, he went to England for four weeks to brush up his English, staying with 'a Lady of the English gentry in Kensington'. Her name was Handfield-Jones and she lived at 24, Bedford Gardens. Her husband was dead and she had lost her only son in Flanders during the war, but bore no bitterness; in his memoirs Dönitz paid generous tribute to her outlook on life.

Every Friday she would give him her suggestions for the weekend written on blue notepaper; these seem to have consisted chiefly of visits to her many 'county' relatives. One of the first was to her 80-year-old mother, who astonished him by gulping back neat whisky as an aperitif before lunch. When he expressed his 'amazement at her vitality' she replied that it was entirely natural since she had spent half her life in the saddle. Her husband was master of the hunt.

The following weekend his hostess drove him to Portsmouth to visit Nelson's *Victory*. The car was stopped at the gates of the Navy Yard and she was asked some questions by the guard before being allowed to proceed. Inside, as the panorama of British warships of every description opened before his eyes, he asked her what the guard had asked.

'They wanted to know whether we were both British subjects,' she told him. 'Naturally I said we were.'

Alarmed that his appearance and halting English might give him away as a foreigner—'and if into the bargain it came out I was a German naval officer'[78]—he told her he would make one very brief tour of the *Victory*, then leave this dangerous spot! He was unable to enjoy the famous ship fully because of his state of apprehension and breathed a sigh of relief when they left the dockyard.

All in all it was probably a pleasant interlude in England; Mrs Handfield-Jones was solicitous for his welfare, he exerted his quiet charm and evidently made an impression since his daughter, Ursula, remembers a correspondence continuing afterwards. Perhaps it exorcized some of the ghosts of his previous period in England; but perhaps they had become a part of him.

In Germany, meanwhile, Hitler had consolidated his power. Earlier in the year he had made a pact with Blomberg, whereby he agreed to liquidate the SA and its leader Roehm, now threatening to carry the national revolution into the ancient stronghold of the officer corps itself; in return the Army would support Hitler as successor to the ailing President, Hindenburg. The liquidations were carried out on June 30th by Hitler and the SS under Himmler—with additional victims, including von Schleicher—and the massacre explained as a purge of traitors plotting a coup against the State. Two months later Hindenburg died and Blomberg fulfilled his part of the bargain; the office of President was merged with Hitler's post of Chancellor, and on the following day, August 2nd, the leaders of the Army and Navy reaffirmed their loyal oath as 'unconditional obedience to Adolf Hitler, Führer of the *Reich* and of the German people, Supreme Commander of the armed forces . . .' The same oath was repeated at ceremonies throughout the *Reich* by every officer and man of the services.

This series of events had significant psychological consequences: the Army had been drawn further into the blood-stained illegality of the regime, above all the armed forces were bound by oath to the person of the Führer; the party insignia had already been incorporated into their uniforms.

Foreign policy had changed, meanwhile, in line with Hitler's anti-

Bolshevik crusade. Since Soviet Russia was the enemy a non-aggression pact had been signed with the former eastern enemy, Poland. The western 'enemy', France, had re-aligned in consequence and the German armed forces were now being prepared to meet a Franco-Russian coalition. For Hitler the fundamental principle for this new system was the benevolent neutrality of Great Britain. He had spelled it out to Raeder after he came to power: the way to keep Great Britain out of the game was to restrict German fleet building to a level that could not possibly alarm her, and he intended, directly the opportunity seemed ripe, to formalize German naval inferiority in a bilateral treaty with her; this would serve the additional purpose of splitting her from France and the other formerly allied signatories to the treaty of Versailles and the subsequent Washington naval agreements which had laid down ratios of naval strength for each of the powers.

As a result of his determination to come to an agreement with Great Britain, increases in the naval rearmament programme worked out that year by Raeder's staff brought planned German tonnage up to one third of Britain's tonnage in the three larger classes of warship—battleships, carriers and cruisers—as it was believed that Great Britain would feel comfortable with such a ratio. In torpedo craft and U-boats the ratio worked out at almost 100 per cent, but since these were for the most part short-range vessels it was perhaps thought they would not be taken as a threat. In any case 50 per cent, 35 per cent and 33⅓ per cent ratios for U-boats were calculated at the same time.[79] This was a considerable increase on the five-year rearmament programme, 1933–38, that Hitler had inherited and which had been more or less in line with Versailles stipulations.

The fleet was intended in the first line for the same purposes of commanding the Baltic and North Sea approaches and striking at the French lines of communication as the earlier mobilization plans, but the terminal date was 1949, fifteen years hence, and there is every reason to believe that what Raeder was actually preparing and what Hitler agreed that year was the thin end of the wedge of the second stage of the over-all plan for world mastery—the struggle with Great Britain. This is suggested by the size and characteristics of the capital ships, by the strategy of oceanic warfare into which they fitted, and by the consideration that the powerful, vastly expensive units planned were appropriate for use against Great Britain but hardly against France or Russia, where the land battle would be decisive.

Confirmation that the final struggle with Great Britain was at the back of Raeder's mind at least comes in his notes of a talk with Hitler on June 27th that year. It is interesting that Hitler's policy of dividing his opponents and potential rivals from one another by the Führer principle extended to the chiefs of the armed services; they reported to him, not to co-ordinating committees which might gang up on him, and this reinforced the mutual antagonisms and jealousies between branches of the armed forces. Already Raeder was seeking Hitler's ear when Blomberg was not present. On this occasion he seized the opportunity when presenting to the Führer the Commander of a cruiser returned from abroad.

He started by discussing the displacement of two projected battle-cruisers—which became the *Scharnhorst* and *Gneisenau*. Hitler told him they must be described as improved 10,000-tonners, not as the 25,000-tonners they actually were, and the speed of 30 knots should not be given as over 26 knots! For the next part of the discussion Raeder's own cryptic notes read:

Development Fl[eet] later poss[ibly] against E[ngland] . . . Preserve tradition. Myself: from 1936 on gr[eat] ships with 35-cm [guns]. If money yes. Alliance 1899. Situation 1914?[80]

Plainly this is an analogy between the situation before the First World War and the contemporary position: an alliance with Great Britain in 1899, he appears to have asked rhetorically, and what would the situation have been in 1914? In the light of *Realpolitik*, precisely the same: England must have sided with the alliance against Germany to preserve the continental balance and do down her chief trade rival. He therefore asked Hitler whether capital ships from 1936 onwards might be armed with 35-cm guns to match the latest British class; Hitler seems to have said, yes, if the money was available. The battleships of the 1936 and 1937 programmes, *Bismarck* and *Tirpitz*, were so armed.

An official note of the same meeting preserved in the German archives is explicit:

Commander in Chief of the Navy stated his opinion that the fleet would have to be developed later against England, that therefore from 1936 on the great ships would have to be armed with 35-cm guns (as *King George* class).[81]

141

The next topic broached was U-boats. Materials, parts and yard space for the first fifteen, mainly of the smaller type, had been ordered, the first batch of executive officers, engineers and some 70 ratings had passed through a newly-established U-school long course which started in October 1933, and Raeder was only awaiting the Führer's orders to start construction of the boats. Hitler told him he did not wish to upset things before a forthcoming plebiscite during which the inhabitants of the Saar region were to be asked whether they wished to belong to the *Reich*, and instructed him in the meantime to preserve full secrecy over the whole U-boat project.

Such was the position as Dönitz returned from his language leave in England; the nation and the Navy was poised to follow the Führer into unknown and dangerous waters.

Meanwhile the *Emden* had emerged from a major refit; he took her over at the end of September with an all-new complement including 160 officer cadets for training, and spent October working her up with his accustomed rigour. On November 2nd, on the eve of departure, he was introduced to Hitler by Raeder as was usual for a foreign-going Commander; what the navy chief said to him we do not know, but once again Raeder left a note of what he discussed with Hitler. He started by pointing out that the funds available to the armed forces for the following year, 1935, were a fraction of those demanded by the new plans and that the Navy's schedule must therefore be set back. Hitler replied that he did not believe the funds would be greatly reduced and he went on to stress the need to rebuild the Navy quickly:

In case of necessity he would cause Dr Ley to place 120–150 millions from the *Arbeitsfront* at the disposal of the Navy . . . later on in a discussion with Minister Göring and me, he developed this, holding that the rebuilding of the fleet in the planned manner was a vital necessity, since war in general could not be waged if the Navy could not secure the ore transport from Scandinavia.

As I drew his attention to the desirability of having *six U-boats* already assembled for the critical political position in the first quarter of 1935, he said he would keep the point in mind and told me to begin construction when the position demanded it. (Marginal note: If the order was not given first boats were to be launched according to plan in June '35.)[82]

This is interesting for the light it throws on the Führer's belligerent mood at this time and the remarkably matter-of-fact way in which it seems that he, Raeder and Göring viewed the consequences of the forthcoming public repudiation of 'the fetters of Versailles'—'the critical political position in the first quarter of 1935'—and indeed the chances of a continental war in three to four years' time! And not a short war either if iron ore shipments from Scandinavia were a 'vital necessity'. It is also an indication of the strength of the rearmament preparations Hitler had inherited from his Republican predecessors; he had not been two years in office yet here he was planning to unwrap a U-boat arm and a Luftwaffe and considering the chances of war against powerful rivals which had never disarmed.

The German naval historian Jost Dülffer believes that this meeting may have been the occasion on which Hitler told Raeder that the time was ripe for entering negotiations with Great Britain for the naval treaty they needed. If this was so, it is interesting to speculate whether Dönitz took any part in the conversation. He had recently returned from England; he was an ambitious officer, ever ready to push himself forward. Hitler was not stiff or formal and sought opinions keenly, especially from those who had experience of foreign lands, especially England, which he always regretted not having visited. On this occasion Dönitz recorded him saying, 'I have always longed to spend a greater time in more distant foreign countries. Unfortunately it will not be permitted me.'[83] This sounds like a reference to Dönitz's forthcoming cruise, or possibly his Hindenburg journey; even so, both embraced parts of the British Empire and it is unlikely that the ever-fascinating subject of the English was not touched upon.

Dönitz may then have told him of the feeling in English conservative circles that Communism was a greater danger than Fascism, that many indeed looked for a strong Germany as a barrier against the spread of Communism. He may have told him that the notorious English 'fair play' was now operating in Germany's favour; it was thought she had been humiliated enough for a war which after all, 'old boy', had been the fault of others as well! It was time to bring her back into the family of nations. Judging from his description of the circles in which his English hostess moved, this might well have been the impression he gained.

Once again it has to be speculation; Dönitz wrote scarcely a word about this, his first meeting with the Führer. There can be little doubt, however, that he was impressed. The erstwhile agitator with hollow chest and bad teeth had been transformed by success and the trappings of martial power into the semblance of a statesman. His 'hypnotic' blue gaze, as ever, drew attention from the less pleasing aspects of his face, now, in the words of one close observer, beginning to be 'caricatured by furrows along his nose and cheeks and by the start of pouches underneath his eyes and chin'.[84] Beneath the patch moustache, the hard downward thrust of his lips hinting at the petulance of ego he had never outgrown would have been set to suggest iron will. And as always he knew exactly how to suit his manner and conversation to whoever he addressed.

There can be little doubt that Dönitz, like so many others, received an impression of assurance, purpose, volcanic sincerity and quick perceptions. Like them he would not have guessed that the stage front concealed only the street agitator of old with the same cosmic hatreds and naïve solutions, the same Austrian *Schlamperei*, the same incapacity to understand complexity or indeed anything that did not interest him, the same distrust of rational argument and inability to synthesize outside the framework of the survival of the fittest; that in consequence the organs of government were sliding into an even looser, more anarchic state than they had been under the Kaiser. Once again the mighty potential power of Germany was not under control, its people bathed in an even more systematic, hate-filled and destructive propaganda under a leader living in the same kind of Wagnerian fantasy as the Kaiser, but whose will and lust to dominate had been nourished by stronger feelings of inferiority and rejection and hardened in a crueller school; not the First Regiment of Guards at Potsdam, but the poor streets of Vienna and Munich set the new course for Germany.

Whether Dönitz ever realized much of this may be doubtful; it is scarcely conceivable that he glimpsed it in this first interview with the man who was to have such a baleful influence on his life. Long after the war he told the Cambridge historian, Jonathan Steinberg, of his impression of Hitler at this first meeting: *'brav und würdig'*—which might be translated as 'honest and worthy'.[85]

Undoubtedly Raeder apprised him of the delicate situation anticipated the following spring, for the *Emden* would be on her own thousands of miles from the Fatherland. Dönitz must have wondered if he might be faced with a repeat of the situation of the *Breslau* in 1914.[86]

Before sailing Dönitz had the ship's company mustered and gave them a talk on the cruiser's mission as representative of Germany: 'From the appearance of the ship, the bearing and behaviour of the Commander and officers as well as the whole crew, foreigners would immediately draw their conclusions about the German *Reich* itself.'[87] He instructed them on their behaviour and how to answer questions about Germany put to them by foreigners, and he warned them that anyone misbehaving ashore—'i.e. drunk'—would be sent home. It can be assumed that the talk was pithy and terse, couched in language every man could understand and probably containing easily remembered short slogans epitomizing essential points. Afterwards he had the instructions and probable questions they would be asked about Germany, together with the correct answers, printed and distributed to all hands. At musters throughout the voyage he would shoot questions at anyone, sailor or fireman or cadet, to see if he understood, as a result of which, he wrote, most studied the paper 'in order not to be made to look ridiculous in front of their friends'.[88]

This attempt at regimenting minds and behaviour was as much a reflection of the sensitivity of German naval officers as a group as of Dönitz's personal methods. After the humiliations of the war and the mutinies, they were attempting to gain fresh bearings in the new revolution which would restore honour and dignity to Germany; naturally they set store by rules of behaviour. Raeder himself was a most earnest exponent of correct conduct. He had produced one handbook on the subject and another was to come out under his guidance, *The Naval Officer as Leader and Teacher*, which explained, amongst many other topics, the role of chivalry and religion, the officer's task in the struggle against materialism, the necessity for optimism, the use of humour. It is reminiscent of English Victorian homilies on etiquette or self-help, designed for those rising or hoping to rise in the social scale; the reason of course was a similar feeling of insecurity induced by society in flux.

It would be interesting to know how Dönitz dealt with instructions on the burning topic of the time, the Jews. He would have had little difficulty with the other questions, since Nazi social doctrine, crude as it was, incorporated many splendid ideals from the treasure house of the youth and back-to-nature movements that had existed side by side with the yearning for power in the Bismarckian *Kaiserreich*.

The first port of call was Santa Cruz in the Canary Islands, from where they sailed to Luanda in Portuguese West Africa. By the time they reached this torrid port at the end of November it can be assumed the

145

crew had attained a high standard in all warlike drills under his untiring regime. The chief difficulty was that the other two functions of the vessel as training ship and 'lightning clean and cared-for' showcase for Nazi Germany interfered. Undoubtedly this simply meant harder work all round.

From Luanda they steamed for the Cape, on the way performing what must have been one of the first oiling at sea exercises in the German service. Dönitz himself had been involved in the preparatory work during his time as a staff officer at Wilhelmshaven—another indication of the ambitious oceanic war on communications that was at the heart of the Navy's long-term strategy even as Hitler came to power.

From Cape Town, where the crew had a splendid time, voting it the best of their ports of call, they steamed up the East African coast, calling at Lourenço Marques where Dönitz visited German farmers in the interior with his Adjutant, *Kapitänleutnant* Eberhardt Godt, and became infected with malaria which hit him at the end of the cruiser's stay in their next port, Mombasa.

Far worse than the malaria was a snub he received here from the British Governor of Kenya: Dönitz had been given the assignment of visiting German farmers in the former German East African colony, now British Tanganyika, by the Foreign Ministry in Berlin; permission for the visit had been sought before his arrival in Mombasa. Now, however, when he visited the Governor in Nairobi to clear the proposed trip he was told that the British Foreign Office had only agreed to his journey on conditions: he was not to wear uniform nor make speeches! This so incensed him that he decided not to go at all; he remembers his behaviour at breakfast in the Governor's residence that day as cool 'to the borders of courtesy'. Little reliance can be placed on his accounts of such incidents, yet this would have been in keeping with his strong sense of duty, temperamental reaction to setbacks and prickliness as a German; it might also have had something to do with the malaria which struck him just before they left the port and reduced his already slim figure to little more than skin and bone before he recovered as the ship neared the Seychelles.

Here he spent most evenings, according to his memoirs, playing bridge with the Governor, 'a typical English gentleman of unsurpassed correctness', and his ladies who were 'always in great toilette in the best social form'.[89] Meanwhile the entire complement of the *Emden* was sent off in batches of 100 or so to spend four days each camping on one of the idyllic

146

islands fringed with blazing white sand beaches and coral lagoons—an imaginative gesture that acted like a tonic.

From this paradise they sailed to another, Trincomalee in Ceylon. This was the British naval base for the East Indies, and again his official duties and social life brought him into continuous contact with the British; he seems to have had a cordial relationship with the Commander in Chief, Vice Admiral Rose, and his officers with their British counterparts who he records, fully understood the German aspirations to break the fetters of Versailles.

It can be seen that the four weeks he had spent in England had been in preparation for this tour of the empire, for the next port of call was Cochin on the Malabar coast of India, after which he headed west on the return voyage, passing Aden, and through the Red Sea and the Suez Canal to Alexandria, another British base. By this time Hitler had produced two 'Saturday surprises'—on March 9th the announcement by Göring that the German Air Force was in existence and, on Saturday the 16th, his own announcement that conscription was to be introduced and the *Wehrmacht* was to have a peacetime strength of twelve army corps and 36 divisions.

The fact of Germany's secret rearmament had been known for a long time of course, but these contemptuous repudiations of Versailles had sent a shock wave through the European capitals, and in the resulting tension Dönitz was ordered not to complete the remainder of his scheduled calls in the Mediterranean, but to make for the Straits and the open Atlantic. This he did, then, apparently filling in the time before he was due home, visited the Canaries again, the Azores, Lisbon and finally Vigo. Here he received a letter from Raeder's chief of staff to the effect that his next cruise with the *Emden* would be to Borneo, Japan, China and Australia—an alluring prospect, he thought.

In fact it had already been decided to place him in charge of the new U-boat arm. Hitler had ordered the construction of the first boats on February 1st; secrecy was to be preserved by assembling them inside huge, specially constructed sheds.

The following month an important conference was held at Naval High Command, Berlin, attended by nine departmental chiefs, including the U-department, at which organizational details of the now imminent U-boat 1st Flotilla were thrashed out; at this stage no flotilla chief was designated, but it was agreed that whoever he was he should be directly under the fleet chief at Kiel, Admiral Foerster.[90] The arrangements were

147

accordingly sent to Foerster for his approval. On April 8th, Foerster notified the High Command that he was in full agreement and suggested that a *Führer der U-boote* (FdU) be appointed at the beginning of 1936. Foerster had been station chief at Wilhelmshaven in 1933 and had countersigned his chief of staff's rhapsodic report on the 1st staff officer, Dönitz, with the words, 'A particularly competent and sympathetic officer'. His successor as station chief in 1934, Dönitz's last year there, was Vice Admiral Otto Schultze—the officer who had accepted Dönitz back into the service in 1919. He was one of the leading members of what might be termed the U-boat group in the Navy and would have been eminently qualified for the post of FdU on account of his war experience had he not been too senior. His comment on Dönitz in 1934 had been: 'A staff officer with high leadership qualities who deserves special observation and advancement.'[91]

While there is nothing in the records to indicate that either of these men now put Dönitz's name forward, both might easily have done so verbally to Raeder. Of course it may be—as suggested earlier—that Dönitz had staked his own claim while chief of the torpedo boat half flotilla. Whenever and however he was chosen, his name appeared as chief of the first U-flotilla in the list of autumn appointments issued on June 6th. It would be surprising if the list did not reach him at Vigo in June or by radio on his way home.[92]

Meanwhile the British government had swallowed Hitler's poisoned bait, entering into bilateral talks with astounding disregard for friends or principles of collective security, and agreeing everything proposed by a German delegation headed by Ribbentrop. To understand this it is necessary to appreciate the state of mind of the British Foreign Secretary, Sir John Simon, and the members of the Board of Admiralty in London. Simon was resigned to German rearmament, believed nothing could stop it, and thought 'the practical choice is between a Germany which continues to rearm without any regulation or agreement, and a Germany which, through getting recognition of its rights, . . . enters into the comity of nations'.[93] The Admiralty was concerned about the possibility of a German-Italian-Japanese coalition against the British Empire, and the imminence of a new naval arms race—triggered by Japanese ambitions in the Pacific—such as had preceded the first war. They leaped at Hitler's offer to limit the German Navy to 35 per cent of the British as a means of containing the European end of the race.

These attitudes indicated an amazing misconception of German aims and methods; their naïvety and wishful thinking is brought out in the British naval staff memoranda on the talks:

We have also received the impression that the German government genuinely consider that they have made a generous and self-sacrificing decision, and that if the opportunity to close with the offer is lost, it is improbable that they will stop short at the 35 per cent level in building up their fleet . . .[94]

This also reveals the aggressiveness of the German tactics. On the specific question of submarines, for which the German delegation claimed a 45 per cent ratio with the option of building up to 100 per cent, the British Admiralty memorandum stated:

In this case [100 per cent] Germany would have some 50 to 60 submarines, a situation which must give rise to some misgivings, but it is quite apparent from the attitude of the German representatives that it is a question of 'Gleichberechtigung' [equal rights] which is really exercising their minds and not the desire to acquire a large submarine fleet. In the present mood of Germany it seems probable that the surest way to persuade them to be moderate in their actual performance is to grant them every consideration in theory. In fact they are more likely to build up to submarine parity if we object to their theoretical right to do so, than if we agree that they have a moral justification.[95]

A better description of the policy of appeasement could hardly have been penned—nor a crasser misjudgement of the Führer and the German Navy. With staggering lack of imagination, historical perception or up-to-date intelligence, the British naval staff applied its own standards—of the assured possessor of half the world, for whom peace and stability were essential—to the humiliated, vengeful inheritors of *Realpolitik*, whose leader claimed the right to world mastery.

Hitler was overjoyed at his masterstroke and told Raeder after the signing that it was the happiest day of his life. He too was living in a fool's paradise, for as a later British Foreign Office memorandum put it, 'this country is bound to react not only against danger from any purely naval

149

rival, but also against the dominance of Europe by any aggressive military power, particularly if in a postition to threaten the Low Countries and the Channel ports'.[96]

Both sides to the agreement showed an amateurish gullibility about the real interests of the other; of the two the greater mistake was made by the Germans; they conducted the conversations with false information and fundamental deceit.[97] In the event they deceived themselves more dangerously than the enemy—a perception that began to surface within two years.

In Vigo, meanwhile, the *Emden* was joined by the cruiser *Karlsruhe* under *Kapitän zur See* Lütjens, and the two ships made their way home in company, arriving in the Jade off Wilhelmshaven in July. Here, according to Dönitz's memoirs, Raeder came aboard and gave him the surprising news that he was to give up his command in order to take over the new submarine flotilla. It is difficult to believe this story. But in any case he recorded his initial reaction as unenthusiastic: he had been looking forward to the cruise to the Far East and U-boats were relatively unimportant in the new fleet plans: 'I saw myself pushed into a siding.'[98]

It is certainly true that big-ship, big-gun men ruled at the *Marineleitung* in Berlin as they did at the British Admiralty, where it was assumed that the invention of an underwater sound detection device called 'Asdic' had rendered the submarine relatively harmless. However, there was a dedicated U-boat group in the German service; Dönitz certainly knew of their activities and had, according to his own account, joined the service after the war because of his enthusiasm for U-boats.

His most immediate concern on arrival was whether the *Emden* or the *Karlsruhe* would show up best at the Station Commander's inspection. He had every confidence in his crew—but as a perfectionist he was naturally afflicted with nerves. He need not have worried: the ship's company performed, as he recorded in his memoirs, 'magnificently'.[99] This is borne out in full by the Admiral's report on him:

Especially competent, energetic officer, cheerful in decision, of outstanding ability, quick power of perception and blameless character.

Tough, goal-conscious with clear recognition of the essentials, wholly given up to his profession, carrying his subordinates with him by example, with a sense of humour and much liveliness he had his ship in hand quickly after the commissioning and commanded her with great success. This showed in the specially good battle-readiness which

150

his leadership qualities, organizational talent, calm circumspection and power of resolution brought forth.

The crew and cadets made a very lively, soldierly impression, they carried the stamp of his personality. The appearance of the Commander and his company was a great success for the reputation of Germany.

Popular and respected by comrades and subordinates.

All in all a natural leader who deserves special observation.[100]

He started his leave almost immediately on July 17th. His sons Klaus, now fifteen, and Peter, thirteen, had written to him in January to say that as their summer holidays began at the same time as the *Emden*'s return they would all be able to spend five weeks sailing in the Baltic. Receiving the letter in Trincomalee, he had shown it to Admiral Rose, commenting that by July he would have been a year at sea and would far rather see German woods and meadows. 'No, Captain,' the Admiral had said, 'you do what your boys want.' There was nothing like a sailing holiday for experience in so many different directions. He had decided to take the advice; now he set off with the family in their yacht from Wilhelmshaven and through the Kiel Canal into the Baltic. He recorded that they were a close family; his daughter, Ursula agrees, 'very close'.

The cruise was not as long as anticipated. Raeder had arranged for him and an engineer officer, Thedsen, who was to join him in building up the new arm, to travel to Constantinople at the end of August to visit the Turkish U-school which had been started by Fürbringer, and where one of the top U-boat war 'aces', Valentiner, was continuing the German connection. At the end of July the arrangements were altered, however, and the two were ordered to Berlin on August 16th to travel on the 17th. No doubt he spent a nostalgic fortnight in Turkey; the *Breslau* had been sunk in the war, but one day he was invited to a meal aboard the *Sultan Yavus Selim*, ex-*Goeben*.

When he returned he immersed himself in preparations for his new task.

CHAPTER FOUR

Führer der U-boote

ON SEPTEMBER 21ST 1935, a week before he took over as chief of the first U-flotilla, Dönitz sent a paper to the fleet command about the organization of the new arm. He prefaced it with his idea of the function of U-boats in war:

> The U-boat is wholly and essentially an attack weapon. Its great action radius makes it suitable for operations in distant enemy sea areas. In consequence of its low submerged- and surface-speed its tactical mobility against fast forces is fundamentally excluded. Its employment will therefore in essence be only stationary.
> The operational mission of U-boats in war will be dependent on the war tasks of the Navy. In a war against an enemy who is not dependent on overseas supplies as a vital necessity, the task of our U-boats, in contrast to the World War, will *not* be the trade war, for which the U-boat in consequence of its low speed is little suited. The U-boat will be placed in a stationary position as close as possible before the enemy harbours at the focal point of enemy traffic. Attack target, the enemy warships and troop transports.[1]

This introduction makes it clear that he was not considering war against Great Britain at this time, but formulating his ideas in the context of the current mobilization plans for the two-front war against France and Russia—that is, the security of the Baltic and the German North Sea ports, together with offensive action against French Mediterranean warships and transports. As for his 'group' or 'wolf-pack' tactics, the paper has nothing to contribute, unless perhaps to induce a certain scepticism about his post-war claim that pack tactics sprang fully-formed from his mind on his assumption of the U-boat command.

The implication, especially of the third sentence, 'In consequence of its low submerged- and surface-speed its tactical mobility against fast forces is fundamentally excluded' is that he was not thinking of pack tactics at this stage, for his targets—warships and troop transports—were 'fast forces'. Moreover he used the singular, 'the U-boat will be placed before enemy harbours'. In view of his usually forward, ambitious way of presenting his views, it would be odd for him not to mention setting groups of boats before enemy harbours if that is what he intended to develop. Nevertheless the paper does not exclude that possibility. Although tactical mobility would be virtually impossible for submerged boats, thus for daylight operations against warships, it would not be ruled out for night surface attack, and later in the paper he makes it clear that he intended to train his force in surface attack.

The paper went on to put the development of 'attacking spirit' in the forefront of training, together with continuous sea-going to habituate commanders and crews to their proper element, particularly in the expected operational areas. This demanded that the flotilla should not be tied to its home port; he therefore asked for a support ship with the necessary equipment and accommodation for twelve U-boat crews—and 'numerous baths'.

It is in his remarks on practices with real torpedoes that his paper comes nearest to suggesting pack tactics. However, the most probable interpretation of this section is that it was simply about the efficient use of time by having all the boats do their attack runs on the same day. He also mentions the necessity for the flotilla to unite with the fleet for exercises on occasions; but again from the context it looks as if he meant to give his boats opportunities *against* the kind of forces they would be attacking in war rather than opportunities to act *with* the fleet.

The question cannot be resolved satisfactorily from his paper. It may be that the idea of two or more boats operating together as practised in the First War and ideas of submarines operating with the fleet were in such common currency that they did not need to be stated—simply tried out. Probably all that can be said is that anyone reading Dönitz's 1935 paper without knowing about subsequent developments would not have guessed that its author was about to develop a revolutionary new tactic. It is closely reasoned, but stictly conventional, strictly in the context of current planning.

He was congratulated on the report both by his immediate chief, Admiral Foerster, who allowed him a free hand for his training, and by Raeder. By this time eleven of the small 250-ton boats whose construction had been started in February had been completed and commissioned; some had been allocated to the U-school, and when he took over his command of the flotilla, named after a war ace, 'Weddigen', on September 28th, he received the salute of only three Commanders and crews. From such small beginnings came the developments which neither Raeder nor Foerster, and certainly not Dönitz himself, could have foreseen. Three days later he stepped up to the rank of full Post Captain (*Kapitän zur See*).

As always when taking over a new command he had already worked out a systematic training programme by which each crew learned progressively more complex skills; these schedules were communicated to all hands so that all knew what they were aiming for in each of the carefully graduated training periods: 'for instance every U-boat had to carry out 66 surface attacks and the same number of submerged attacks before proceeding in December 1935 to its first torpedo-firing practice.'[2] As always he led from the front; he and his flotilla engineer, Thedsen, the only men with operational experience in U-boats, donned the U-boat man's leathers and divided their time between the boats, guiding Commanders and control- and engine-room hands through the drills that had to become second nature before the tactical training could begin. The pace was hot and the boats were always at sea. The Commander of U 14, which joined the flotilla in January the following year, remembers: 'Mondays to Fridays eight attack exercises under water by day and six attack exercises on the surface by night. That was the upper limit of our physical and nervous capacity.'[3]

They were young men. Dönitz used their youthful energy and idealism and won their confidence with his powerful brand of personal leadership, enthusiasm and total commitment. His aims were not narrowly technical; he sought to instil in every crew a spirit of confidence in their weapon; this has been the hallmark of most great military leaders. In his case he had the particular difficulty of overcoming a 'recurring complex that the U-boat was, in consequence of the development of the British countermeasure, Asdic, an obsolete weapon'.[4] This feeling was, perhaps, a result of the training at the U-school; according to Dönitz they held Asdic in so much respect that boats were expected to fire their torpedoes from well outside the detection range of the escorts, 3,000 yards or more. Dönitz states in his memoirs that he on the other hand looked on Asdic as an unproved and overrated weapon with several limitations, and sought to develop an attitude for close attack where the chances of hitting were greater, 600 metres or so. His previously quoted paper makes it clear that

154

this was not his view when he took over the flotilla; in fact uncertainty about the range and effectiveness of Asdic influenced U-boat Commanders right up to the outbreak of war.

Nevertheless his own genuine belief in the power of the U-boat as an attacking weapon cannot be doubted, nor his success in communicating this to his Commanders and crews, together with 'a spirit of selfless mission-readiness'.[5] An essential part of this spirit which he sought to instil from the first was the feeling of belonging to a special or élite corps within the larger brotherhood of the service; one rather theoretical manifestation was his insistence that no U-boat man shaved while at sea, even on the short passages made by the small boats of the 1st flotilla.

At the end of his first year Foerster reported that he had seized hold of his task with verve:

> Through indefatigable work and personal instruction he has demanded so much from the U-flotilla 'Weddigen' in planned training that already in spring 1936 they were ready for employment on war tasks. Military and comradely spirit in the flotilla is above all praise.
>
> . . . In every respect a model officer of high value for the Navy. Attention must be paid to the fact that in his burning ardour he does not demand too much from his physical strength.[6]

Foerster also recorded that Dönitz had created useful foundations for the tactical employment of the boats; he did not say what these were, but everything Dönitz wrote after the war suggested they were group tactics. From the 1957 recollections of one of his Weddigen Flotilla Commanders cited in his memoirs it appears that these grew directly out of the strategic goals he set for the boats—finding and attacking enemy warships in the restricted waters of the Baltic—and the tactical lessons of his torpedo-boat days; indeed the former Commander stated that torpedo-boat doctrine was 'godfather' to U-boat pack tactics.

> It began with formation of reconnaissance- or lookout-patrols. On sighting the enemy the sighting boat, after signalling the enemy presence, attacked, the rest of the boats following into the attack . . .[7]

This was developed in countless exercises using different formations of reconnaissance lines and supporting groups until tactics fitting the characteristics of U-boats were developed. This description dovetails

155

neatly into the documentary evidence; it fits Dönitz's goals as described in his September 1935 paper, and also his first description of group tactics in a long paper he wrote in November 1937.[8] It is also the way that most 'inventions' or advances take place—a lateral jump by the prepared mind—serendipity—followed by unrelenting work. Others had made the lateral jump before Dönitz; that had been in the different context of trade war, however, and there are no documents to prove—or to disprove—Dönitz's claim in his memoirs that he came to the U-boat arm determined to try out group tactics.

One thing is certain: *his* pack tactic was not developed for war against trade: at the end of 1936 Dönitz still held to all his views expressed in the 1935 paper,[9] and when asked about U-boat types for the future he based his replies on a belief that the Mediterranean would be the centre of gravity for the U-boat war; since they were restricted in total tonnage by the naval treaty with England, he suggested the smallest boat suitable for the Mediterranean in order to get the largest *number* of them. These were the 626-ton Type VII which in an enlarged form for greater action radius was predominant in the Battle of the Atlantic. It is clear, therefore, that both the *Rudel* tactic and the boats that used it to such devastating effect were designed for quite different campaigns in different waters.

The first of the Type VIIs were already in service by the autumn of 1936 and Dönitz, who was given the title of *Führer der U-boote* (FdU) on October 1st, had begun training the nucleus of this 2nd flotilla alongside the Weddigen boats.

He had his chief holidays in the winter now, probably because this was the least suitable period for practical work in the Baltic. He had taken up skiing in the early '30s, travelling by himself to resorts in the South Tyrol; by this time he could afford to stay at good hotels.

Both his boys, who accepted without question that they would follow their father into the Navy, were now members of the *Hitler Jugend*; their elder sister, Ursula, who had been in the girls' equivalent, the *Bund Deutscher Mädchen*, during her final year at school had left directly after her *Abitur*; she recalls that she thought it all rather silly. Her mother was not a member of the Party, nor of course was Dönitz, for he was a member of the 'unpolitical' armed forces. The family, Ursula recalls, were about average in their allegiance to the National Socialist regime; they were like most other people in Germany.[10]

By this time she had met and become engaged to a naval officer,

156

Günther Hessler, whom she married in November 1937; her father heartily approved.

Hessler had served aboard the *Grille*, a support ship that had been used for clandestine training and testing functions, doubling as an official yacht. In this capacity Hitler had been a guest aboard. In general wardroom talk he had impressed Hessler enormously, not simply by his astounding command of technical naval detail, but by his breadth of reading and apparently effortless ability to speak knowledgeably on any subject that came up. Hessler's admiration for the Führer was not surprising. It was the general attitude throughout the service, particularly amongst the younger officers. When the *Reichsmarine* ensign was replaced by the swastika flag of the Third Reich in 1935 a week before Dönitz took command of the flotilla Weddigen, it was the occasion of fervent celebration.

By 1937 Hitler was hoist on the inexorable, hard logic of his policy. Immediately after taking power in 1933 he had electrified his service chiefs and a few days later his cabinet with the simple formula that for the next four or five years every measure was to be judged on whether it augmented the arms-bearing capacity of the German *Volk*. It was to be 'everything for the *Wehrmacht*. Germany's position in the world will be absolutely conditional on the German armed forces. The position of the German economy in the world also depends upon them.'[11] Economists might have told him that this reversed the conditions in the real world. His listeners, however, shared his beliefs; like him they had been brought up on power *Politik*, and it was only when practical difficulties crowded in after the first miracle years that doubt and argument surfaced. By this time he had consolidated his position through the Führer principle and it was too late to challenge his 'unalterable' decisions.

The economic facts he flouted were that single-minded concentration on rearmament sucked materials into the country and prevented the production of sufficient exports to pay for them, while reliance on public borrowing to finance inproductive war-spending laid the foundations for another bout of inflation. The problem was aggravated by the anarchy at the top: each of the three fighting services pursued its own programme in competition with the other two without co-ordination or consideration for the others' aims—indeed scarcely comprehending them.

157

By the beginning of 1936 the inevitable balance of payments crisis had arrived. Hitler's master economist, Schacht, now pleaded for a reduction in the armaments tempo in order to cut imports. The Führer went the other way, attacking the problem with a 'Four-year Plan' designed to make Germany largely self-sufficient in the most essential raw materials for war. It was a triumph of will over common sense. The resources to be hurled into the production of synthetic oil and rubber at costs far above the price of the real articles on the world market were bound to aggravate the crisis; his choice of Göring to mastermind the plan was another predictable disaster. It is interesting to speculate whether Hitler already realized that he was hedged in on a path leading to inevitable destruction. He could not turn back because the Party and the propaganda he had created crowded him on; ahead were the very dangers he had been determined to avoid but which his policy inevitably raised, above all the English danger hanging as threateningly over Raeder as it had over Tirpitz. Hitler's response was to press forward faster. It was a characteristic reaction: at crises throughout his political career he invariably committed himself to positions which admitted of no retreat, as if he feared that otherwise he might falter or turn back.

Raeder was already in difficulties over steel quotas, hence delivery dates for his new ships. Through 1937, while he played with the idea of adding a huge *ninth* battleship to the programme and arming her with a battery far outmatching the latest British *King George V* class, the steel position deteriorated and the delays in his construction programme grew longer. At the same time his worry about the possibility of Great Britain siding with France in any conflict—hitherto a taboo subject for official discussion because it was too painful to contemplate—came out into the open with an Operations Division study entitled 'The Tasks of Naval Warfare 1937/8'.[12]

That autumn Dönitz carried out the first large-scale exercises to test the group tactics on which he had been working; it is significant that a report he wrote afterwards called 'The Employment of U-boats in the Framework of the Fleet' started off on another tack altogether: 'The World War brought the realization that the U-boat is suitable for threatening the enemy sea communications, the enemy trade.'[13]

He went on to say that for a State whose lack of surface forces, bad strategic position and lack of colonial bases—all points forming the staple of German naval strategic thought—prevented any prospect of fighting for naval mastery, the U-boat would always be 'an excellent, perhaps the only means . . . effectively to threaten the vitally important enemy sea communications and under certain conditions to be able to damage them war-decisively'.

This is his first recorded endorsement of the U-boat for trade war since his appointment to the new arm; it marks a radical change from his thinking the previous autumn and from his original paper in September 1935. He is obviously dealing here with the possibility of England siding with France, and following the trend of current naval thought favouring trade war over the Tirpitz battlefleet doctrine which had been found wanting.

However, the entire paper, apart from these introductory remarks, was taken up with the tactical question of U-boats operating with surface forces, both as scouts able to remain off enemy bases unseen and report movements, and as attacking groups which could be positioned in the enemy's path. While these were essentially world war ideas, it is plain that a great deal of work had been done in communications. For instance, he already accepted that because of the U-boat's very limited range of visibility and communication facilities it was essential to control group operations from a command post ashore which could receive reports from all parts of the operations area and issue orders on the basis of the general picture; he did this from his command ship in Kiel during the Baltic exercise.

The other interesting point—looking back—is his attitude to aircraft. He was clear that in areas where a strong and continuous air patrol was maintained the manoeuvrability of the boats would decline and the group system would revert to simply taking up submerged waiting positions on the probable path of the enemy; however, he did not expect *continual* air patrols and thought that *passing* patrols would only limit manoeuvrability for a short time and not really affect the group system. This suggests he was looking back to his own war experience. It also reveals his habitually optimistic cast of mind, a determination that his arm and his system *would* prevail—entirely appropriate for a front-line leader, less so for an overall strategist. Like the rest of the service he was of course handicapped here by the Air Force chief, Göring's, jealous retention of everything that flew. The paper did have a section on U-boats working with aircraft, but without a naval air arm or proper co-operation with the Air Force it had to be largely theoretical.

The paper concluded:

159

The employment of U-boats in loose, but uniform, operational co-operation with the fleet is no longer a problem today. It offers considerable prospects of success.

The employment of U-boats in immediate [tight] tactical and battle unity with naval forces still falls down on the low speed of U-boats.

This employment can also be highly effective, however, so that it would be worthwhile to have *faster* U-boats suitable for practical tests.

German naval planning was in a transitional stage, anxious about Great Britain but concerned in practice with the two-front continental war; Dönitz's ideas were similarly divided; he was not yet an exponent of trade war as the chief concern of his boats.

The paper was dated November 23rd; this was just over a fortnight after a notorious meeting between Hitler and his service chiefs, at which the Führer displayed exactly the same ambivalence; it would be interesting to know whether Dönitz heard about the conclusions reached then—perhaps through his fleet chief—or whether his opening remarks about trade war were simply reflections of the new thinking about England within the service.

It seems likely that the meeting—usually known by the name of Colonel Hossbach, Hitler's Adjutant and author of a memorandum describing it—was provoked by Raeder. He had been issuing regular appeals for larger steel and other metal quotas for his programme since 1936; finally on October 25th 1937, he issued an ultimatum: unless he was allowed larger quotas he would have to cut his building back drastically to be sure of having at least a few modern ships available 'in a conceivable time'. Faced with this, Hitler called together his Army chiefs, Blomberg and Fritsch, Göring for the Air Force, Raeder and the Foreign Minister, von Neurath.

No doubt Hitler prepared the notes for his opening address to this group as carefully as he did for his public speeches. He started with the usual premise that Germany needed living space; like all his beliefs this was picked from a national stock of accepted ideas; his listeners would not have questioned it. Germany comprised over 85 million people which by its numbers and shut-in position in the centre of Europe represented an enclosed 'race-core' whose like was not to be found anywhere else. And he went on to outline his two-stage programme for expansion, first 'living space' in Eastern Europe, then overseas colonies and world power. Naturally there were risks:

160

German policy has to reckon with two hate-enemies, England and France, to whom a stronger German colossus in the middle of Europe would be a thorn in the eye, whereby both States would reject a further German strengthening as much in Europe as overseas . . . In the erection of German bases overseas both countries would see a threat to their sea communications and a security for German trade resulting in a strengthening of the German position in Europe.[14]

Finally, after detailing weaknesses in both British and French Imperial positions and glancing at the risks Frederick the Great and Bismarck had necessarily run in the cause of German greatness, he came down to cases:

Case 1—period 1943–45—after this time only a change to our disadvantage can be expected.

The rearmament of Army, Navy and Air Force would be approaching completion . . . with modern weapons . . . Should the Führer live it is his unalterable resolution, at the latest 1943/45, to solve the German [living] space question.

A further two cases were detailed in which a solution before 1943/45 might be expected: if France should be weakened by an internal political crisis or a foreign war.

From this lengthy preamble it is evident that Hitler realized that his plan for wooing England by holding back naval construction had little chance of success, or at the least there was a grave risk he would not be allowed to get away with his continental plan without British intervention. Nevertheless the plan was to proceed, rearmament was to be hurried on, particularly naval rearmament! This is evident from the second stage of the meeting, when Raeder was promised an increase in his steel quota from 40,000 to 75,000 tons; Krupp's mills were to be extended largely for this purpose. Here is another instance of Hitler forcing himself into an exposed position from which there could be no retreat, for naval building was the one area which was certain to force Great Britain into the opposing camp.

For Raeder, Hitler's speech must have come as confirmation of his own Tirpitzian world view, the practical ratification of his programme, a confirmation of the necessity for his long-term challenge to the Royal Navy. His only misgivings, again like Tirpitz's previously, were that he would not be allowed to complete his preparations before the outbreak

161

of war; he continually sought reassurance from Hitler on this point; Hitler continually reassured him.

It is tempting to see parallels between the 'Hossbach' meeting of November 5th 1937 and the Kaiser's meeting with his service chiefs in December 1912; both showed the boxed-in position to which a policy of massive rearmament for aggrandizement had brought the leadership, and the petulant, aggressive temper this provoked in the supreme leader. In the event both called the advance, and this seems to have had more to do with group psychology than with any rational balancing of arguments. At bottom both meetings were dominated by the intractable problem of Great Britain's role as continental make-weight.

There were essential differences between the two, however: the Army came out of the Kaiser's meeting convinced of its mission and able to command the lion's share of future defence increases, while the Navy was thrust aside; at Hitler's meeting Raeder got all he asked for. And whereas it was Tirpitz who sounded the warning to the Kaiser when von Moltke called for immediate war, it was the Army chiefs, Blomberg and Fritsche, who questioned Hitler's forward policy; they did not believe that the western powers would stand idly by for the preliminary stages of his drive for eastern living space, the incorporation with the *Reich* of the German-speaking peoples of Austria and Czechoslovakia. Raeder, on the other hand, does not seem to have questioned Hitler's aims, apparently satisfied with his assurances that he would not involve the *Reich* in a war with England before 1943.

Within five months of the 'Hossbach' meeting both Blomberg and Fritsche had lost their posts; Fritsche, like other senior Army officers, was contemptuous of the Party and increasingly fearful of the road down which its fanatic leader was forcing Germany. Such attitudes were not lost on Hitler; he could not tolerate men of independent judgement; his entourage had to perceive the truth as it dropped from his lips as uncritically as his unsophisticated followers in the Munich cafés. He arranged a homosexual scandal to unseat Fritsche while Blomberg hastened his own removal by marrying a former prostitute! Hitler took his functions upon himself by assuming the post of Commander in Chief of the Armed Forces. Next he replaced the professional Foreign Minister, von Neurath, with the amateur Ribbentrop, and his economic genius, Hjalmar Schacht—who told him the economy could not stand continuous rearmament—with a Party hack and uninstructed economic dabbler, Funk.

5a *(above)* The English Admiral commanding at Trincomalee, Ceylon *(right)*, is greeted by Dönitz *(left)* during the *Emden*'s visit

5b *(below)* Dönitz's cruiser *Emden* in 1934

6 C-in-C *Kriegsmarine*, *Grossadmiral* Raeder and his *Führer der U-boote*,
Kapitän zur See Karl Dönitz

7a *(left)* One of the major influences in Dönitz's life, *Vizeadmiral* von Loewenfeld in 1939

7b *(right)* Karl Dönitz in 1939

8a *(above)* Dönitz as BdU (his Flag-Lieutenant seated right) listening to the report of a U-boat Commander back from a war cruise in 1940

8b *(right)* . . . congratulating a Commander on his Knight's Cross

Of all the men who had either attended the 'Hossbach' meeting or, like Schacht, been concerned with its inevitable consequences, only Göring and Raeder remained. Göring, of course, had been one of the original Party faithful and was as personally corrupt as the Führer was fanatical. Of all the professionals whom Hitler had retained on his assumption of power, only Raeder remained; of all the key departments of State, Defence Ministry, Army, Police, Interior Ministry, Economics Ministry, Foreign Ministry, only one did not have to be purged—the Navy. A post-war taunt by Raeder that Dönitz was known in the service as 'Hitler-boy' indicated some lack of self-knowledge.

Shortly after Hitler had removed all professional constraints, completing the revolution of unreason and destruction in his own image, in mid-March 1938 he seized Austria with a combination of internal subversion, terrorism and threats. His propaganda chief, Goebbels, justified the annexation as saving Austria from chaos; completely fabricated stories of Communist disorder, fighting and pillaging in the streets of Vienna were broadcast in press and radio.

Dönitz had just returned from a month's skiing holiday at Selva in the South Tyrol with his daughter and son-in-law, Günther Hessler, when the tremendous news broke. No doubt he believed the stories put out by Goebbels for there was no other news to be read or heard. For the same reason he would have been unaware of the extent and frightfulness of the destruction and looting of Jewish property and the humiliations imposed on Viennese Jews by the triumphant young Nazi toughs who had engineered the *Anschluss*. Vienna had been a stronghold of anti-semitism, it was where Hitler had been infected. An American correspondent in the capital, William Shirer, saw groups of Jews of all ages and sexes rounded up by jeering Stormtroopers and made to clean the pavements on their knees; he heard of others forced to scrub out lavatories with the sacred praying bands, the *Tefillin*.

Dönitz's chief task as he returned, refreshed from his skiing, was to prepare for a large-scale test of his group tactics in spring exercises in the North Sea. Despite the hint in his November report that he may have heard something of the anti-British drift of the 'Hossbach' Conference, he was still working within the official framework of British neutrality in any immediate conflict. This is evident from a report he made on U-boat types just before the exercises; he declared the centre of gravity of U-boat operations in war as 'attacks on the French transports and sea communications in the Mediterranean . . .'[15] In the Atlantic he saw the

U-boat's task as attack on French sea communications and west-coast ports, in the North Sea the security of German traffic lanes. For these tasks he recommended the 626-ton Type VII boat as most suitable.

His paper went to Admiral Carls, who had taken over as Fleet Chief in October 1936. Like Foerster, Carls was mightily impressed with the leader of his U-boat arm: 'an excellent officer of iron will power, goal-oriented certainty and unwearying toughness . . . teacher, example and stimulus to his officers', deserving 'wholly special attention' and 'promising to become an outstanding leader in higher positions as well'.[16] In the report from which these remarks are extracted he had added to the usual description of Dönitz as 'tall and slim' the adjective 'straffe', which might be translated as 'taut', 'stern', or 'extremely upright'. All fitted!

On May 6th Carls forwarded Dönitz's paper on U-boat types to the High Command; in the meantime the exercises had taken place off the coast of Jutland; it is evident from his covering paper that Carls was thoroughly convinced about group tactics.

All tests point to the fact that *great numbers* of U-boats are required directly the individual disposition of U-boats (as in the World War) is dropped and a *planned disposition of groups of U-boats* striven for.[17]

Dönitz's own report after the exercises was quite clear on the point:

Combined action by *reconnaissance* (harbour-watcher, wireless repeater, touch-holder, escort- and reconnaissance-patrols) and *attack* groups has again been demonstrated as fundamentally correct.

In free sea areas more success is attained through such combined work than when each boat operates alone.[18]

He also reported that 'the question of communications between U-boats, and between the leadership (ashore) and U-boats is basically solved—short wave, long wave, periscope aerial'. The question of tactical command was not entirely resolved, however, since both a group leader in the operational area and a shore-based overall controller seemed necessary—the man on the spot with the knowledge of the actual conditions, the shore leadership with access to a more complete picture—and it was not certain how this dual system would function in war conditions.

It is the lot of the innovator to be thwarted. Dönitz was no exception. The Staff at High Command were against group tactics on the grounds that the wireless traffic necessary would forfeit surprise and aid detection of the boats by the enemy; meanwhile ideas for oceanic warfare with huge cruiser U-boats armed with heavy guns, virtually submersible surface raiders, were in the ascendant. Dönitz held that the U-boat was first and foremost a torpedo carrier and that to give it heavy artillery was to put it at a disadvantage by forcing it to the surface to fight. Some of the frustration of his running battle with the High Command shows through his reports at this period.

Meanwhile the whole orientation of naval policy changed. Since the *Anschluss* with Austria the second stage of Hitler's programme— Czechoslovakia—had been building up to crisis. The western half of this State was sandwiched between Germany and Austria and in the extreme west the German-speaking Sudetenlanders—now almost the only part of the 'shut-in race core' outside the boundaries of the *Reich*—were acting in concert with Hitler and Goebbels' Propaganda Ministry to produce the internal tension and fabricated excuses for action by the German Army that had characterized the move into Austria. Czechoslovakia had a defensive alliance with France, however, and the French government made it clear it would respect its obligations. Then on May 22nd, as it seemed the German Army was about to march, the British Ambassador in Berlin sought a meeting with Ribbentrop and delivered a personal message from the Foreign Secretary, Lord Halifax: if resort were had to force it would be quite impossible to foretell the consequences, 'and I would beg him not to count upon this country being able to stand aside'.[19] Hitler must have erupted in the same sense as the Kaiser when similarly checked by the British government in the Balkan crisis of December 1912—'The final struggle between the Slavs and Teutons will see the Anglo-Saxons on the side of the Slavs and Gauls!'

Whether on this occasion the Führer threw one of his uncontrollable rages, as he was said to have done later in the crisis, is not recorded. But on the 24th his naval Adjutant, Dönitz's former torpedo boat Commander, von Puttkamer, wired Raeder with an invitation to a meeting with the Führer on the 28th; with the message came proposals for a great acceleration of naval construction, particularly U-boats and large battleships, which left Raeder in no doubt that the target was Great Britain. What Hitler had suggested rather ambiguously at the 'Hossbach' meeting was now to be starkly confronted: the step-by-step approach to continental hegemony while wooing England was a chimera; it was necessary to build up such a threat, particularly with U-boats against supply lines, that Great Britain would be deterred from interfering with the continental plans; it was the predictable response of an international terrorist; it was also the tactic the Kaiser's Chancellor had attempted before the First War; Tirpitz's policy had come full circle; there was no way out of Germany's boxed-in position in the centre of the European land mass.

Raeder had reached similar conclusions on the political situation at least as early as the previous month—although of course England had always been in his long-term sights. At the 'wash-up' after the annual war game he had revealed to the Baltic station chief, Admiral Albrecht, 'I am convinced that today we have to reckon with a war *with France and with England*, as a result of which the fundamentals of naval operations will be radically altered.'[20] He had not taken steps to alter them; perhaps he still considered it too dangerous even to discuss the possibility officially. On the days immediately following Puttkamer's cable, however, he made that possibility official naval policy. And after the meeting with the other service chiefs on the 28th, at which Hitler affirmed his 'unalterable decision to smash Czechoslovakia by military action'—a meeting which Raeder had completely forgotten by the time he came to the witness stand at Nuremberg—he ordered his 1st staff officer, operations, to prepare a paper on the possibility of waging a naval war with Great Britain.

The paper, known after its author as the Heye *Denkschrift*, set out clear premises at the beginning: England's strengths were her commanding geographical position across Germany's exits to the oceans, and her strong battlefleet which Germany could not hope to match—her weakness was her dependence on overseas communications. From this it followed: 'The sea war is the battle over economic and military sea communication.'[21]

This was at the opposite pole to Tirpitz's doctrine of the decisive fleet battle; however, it too suffered from Germany's hopeless strategic position, for the commerce raiders and their tankers and supply vessels would have to break out and back through the blockade which the British could so easily set up across the Dover Straits and the northern North Sea. The situation could be eased, Heye pointed out, by the occupation of Holland, Denmark and Norway, yet this would be of tactical, not strategic, significance for they would still be *inside* the British blockade. The best solution was the acquisition of the whole northern coast of

France out to Brest, thus outflanking the Channel blockade and gaining free access to the Atlantic. This would also provide the *Luftwaffe* with bases from which to attack English Channel shipping and harbours, a vital adjunct to the Navy's war on commerce, hence 'in the case of war with England and France' it would be of 'outstanding value' if this were provided for in the land operations.

When it came to discussing the types of vessels necessary for the 'cruiser war' the paper showed just how far the naval staff in Berlin were from Dönitz's conceptions:

> There are grounds for assuming that the English counter-measures against U-boats, in the first-line (sound) detection, have reached an especially high standard. U-boats' attacks on English forces will therefore not be too successful. So long as no unrestricted U-boat war can be allowed, 'cruiser war' against merchant ships—if it is *only* conducted by U-boats—will have a limited effect. It comes down to the fact that the single U-boat by its nature does not come into question for 'cruiser war' on the high seas, but must be employed in a more or less stationary role.[22]

The paper recommended huge 'cruiser U-boats' armed with four 12·7-cm guns and a surface speed of 25 knots for commerce war on the high seas, but pointed out that once forced to dive U-boats had such a low speed they were at the mercy of the new detection device; the medium-sized torpedo U-boats which Dönitz favoured were listed under 'Other U-boats' whose chief operational area would be before enemy harbours and where traffic lanes converged. 'However, it is in precisely these areas that especially strong counter-measures are to be expected.' The conclusion was that in a U-boat war heavy 'losses should be reckoned with at some time after the outbreak as soon as the enemy counter-measures are organized and developed'.

Thus the U-boat arm had a fairly low priority in the paper; the highest priority was given to surface units, fast, long-range armoured cruisers supplemented by light cruisers, and to provide support for their breakthrough into the Atlantic a squadron of most powerful battleships. A naval air arm was seen as an 'unconditionally necessary' adjunct.

The paper was sent to the naval stations for comment. Dönitz's chief, Carls, took a positive view, apparently savouring the implications:

167

War against England signifies simultaneously war against the [British] Empire, against France, probably also against Russia and a series of overseas States, therefore against half to two-thirds of the whole world. It has inner justification and prospects of success only if prepared economically as well as politically and militarily and the goal is set for Germany to conquer the way to the ocean.[23]

Or as he put it in the same paper, 'The will to make Germany a world power leads of necessity to suitable preparations for war.'

Raeder approved the sentiments and when Carls ended his term as Fleet Chief, he was given a special liaison post with a staff committee set up to translate the philosophy of Heye's paper into a detailed fleet construction programme for the 'cruiser war' against England.

Looking back now, it is as difficult to understand Raeder at this crisis for his Navy as it had been for the British up to that time—outside the small Churchill–Vansittart circle—to comprehend the dark compulsions underlying German policy and the professions of peace and friendship with which Hitler and Goebbels clothed them. There are two parties to every misunderstanding: the British public, misled by their political and intellectual leadership about the true causes of the First World War, the stern necessity if one owns half the world to fight to protect it, seduced by liberal, socialist and pacifist propaganda to believe in their easy scapegoats—the armaments barons, the capitalist system itself—wishing only to prevent a repeat of the horrors of the trench war while retaining the even greater share of the world they had won, had been shut up in the reverse image of the fantasy inhabited by the German nation and so starkly revealed in Admiral Carls' paper—'the war . . . therefore against half to two-thirds of the whole world . . . has inner justification . . .'

There were numerous other parties to this cosmic misunderstanding, but any judgement on why the horrific sacrifice of the war was about to be rendered fruitless must take into account the hypocrisy and wishful thinking of the British and the other Western democracies as much as the *Realpolitik* of the Germans. Both sides had been brought up in their opposed convictions, both systems encouraged them and excluded the real world outside. Misunderstanding was inevitable and complete.

The other questions about Raeder concern his intelligence and moral courage; how much of either did he display at this abrupt turning point for his Navy? Already his building programme was lagging years behind schedule, affected not only by material shortages but by a host of technical problems inevitable in such a rushed start after the inactivity of the 'Treaty' years. Yet he now intended increasing the programme, and actually did so in January 1939 after the Führer had approved his staff committee's grandiose 'Z Plan' for huge battleships, armoured cruisers, aircraft carriers and 249 U-boats to be completed at various dates up to 1947. Not only was it impossible to complete the major units within the time limits without encroaching on the other service programmes and aggravating the already severe crisis caused by the war economy and the Four-year Plan, but the fuel required to drive such a fleet was more than Germany's total oil consumption for 1938—two-thirds of which came from abroad![24] The 'Z-Plan' was as much of a fantasy as the world-view which made it necessary.

This was apparent to the more intelligent officers, including Helmuth Heye, the author of the original staff paper. They did not question 'the great goal' before which Germany stood, only the rushed and risky method of attaining it. Time was needed if they were not to be held back by the superior forces encircling them.

Time was something Hitler entirely lacked; his war economy was leading inevitably to war: only thus could he rescue himself from the internal effects of the declining living standards and economic crisis about to become manifest, only by aggression could he secure the raw materials and production facilities the war economy devoured. Recognition of this apparently caused a few of the naval staff officers to harbour the kind of rebellious thoughts about Hitler and the regime that were apparent among more intelligent Army officers like the Chief of the General Staff, Beck. Whether this was ever much more than frustration at the insoluble problems caused by the new orientation of policy and revulsion at Germany's tarnished image in the world after fearful events like *Kristallnacht* in November, when Party members went on street rampages against Jews and Jewish property, is not clear. All that is certain is that Raeder co-operated actively and enthusiastically with the new anti-British policy as embodied in the 'Z-Plan'. This implies a severe attack of Utopian thinking worthy of his model, Tirpitz, or the kind of moral cowardice which had characterized the successive retreats of the Army leadership before Hitler and the National Socialist Party. Or perhaps it was the old blindness of ambition, combined with national hubris and renewed faith in the Führer after the western powers climbed down at Munich at the end of September that year and delivered Czechoslovakia 'bloodlessly' to the *Reich*.

Dönitz's views at this time are not known, but it may be assumed from all that he did and wrote that he was a good deal closer to Carls' than to Heye's position so far as faith in the Führer was concerned. Also there is no doubt that he saw the advantages of the new naval strategy for his own arm of the service. U-boats were quicker to build, used less raw material and were far cheaper than the huge 'balanced fleet' Raeder proposed; moreover they were the only class of vessel able to beat the British blockade before the Army reached the Atlantic. From now on he turned his energies and considerable force of personality and persuasion to bring these points to attention and change naval policy.

Besides his official efforts in this direction, he wrote a book that winter called *Die U-bootswaffe* (*The U-boat Arm*); it was published in early 1939. He was careful not to drop a hint of his development of group tactics for war on convoys, yet his remarks on U-boats working with the surface forces, taken together with a long section on commerce warfare, might have alerted anyone thinking about Britain's vulnerable merchant shipping routes. He started the section 'Employment of U-boats in Trade Warfare' thus: 'The destruction of the enemy trade, the attack on the enemy sea communications is the proper purpose of sea warfare . . .'[25]

Whether an inspired leap could have been made between these remarks and his later section on tactical co-operation between U-boats and surface forces, his section on night surface attack could not have been plainer; he spelled out in detail why the U-boat with its small silhouette was ideal for surprise torpedo attack by night and how rigorously his own arm had been trained in this tactic.

More interesting now is the insight the book provides into Dönitz's total commitment to the U-boat arm and to the warrior ethic of the service and current propaganda. The descriptive passages are written in heroic style foreshadowing his later Nazi speeches. The political and military-political views in and between the lines are naïve. On the World War, for instance, the U-boat campaign had 'brought England to the edge of the precipice' but had not been able to achieve decisive success because 'the homeland had become Marxist and capitulated'.[26]

Many passages are so over-written—to English eyes—as to suggest he had fallen completely under the mood of national hysteria provoked by Goebbels; his section on the U-boat's crew exemplifies what has been called the 'all male collective' of the Nazi movement with its cult of comradeship fostering 'a pervasive, though naturally unacknowledged

170

form of homosexuality'.[27] U-boat comradeship was described in idyllic terms, and one has the impression that the brotherhood found in a crew was to him a pure example of the larger brotherhood of the German *Volk*. Nothing could be more worthwhile than to be inside the charmed circle—working for the destruction of the hateful forces outside! Whether it was the noxious influence of the Party or suppressed feelings of inadequacy resulting from his experience with UB 68, or simply his own natural tendency to extremes, passages from the book suggest that Dönitz was more than a very competent U-boat leader by this time; he was a fanatic, as dangerous to his enemies as the fanatical Nelson had been to the French in a previous century. This would perhaps have been the most important message for any Englishman to have drawn in 1939. Naval Intelligence did not obtain a copy of the book until 1942, by which time the point had been made.

In the intervals of work and authorship, Dönitz found time to become a grandfather. Ursula produced a son who was named Peter. He was very tickled about this, and the fact that he was only 47 years old.

Instead of taking a winter skiing holiday early in 1939 Dönitz occupied himself with a war game based on supposed conditions in 1943—the year before which Hitler had assured Raeder on many occasions there would be no war with England. The purposes of the game: 'Atlantic war operations with U-boats, including combined operations between surface commerce raiders and aircraft with U-boats; employment of artillery—and fleet-U-boats.'[28]

The forces stipulated by the naval High Command were, on the 'Red' side, considerable detachments from the British Home and Mediterranean fleets and American and African station squadrons, twelve battleships and heavy cruisers, five aircraft carriers, 27 light cruisers and 100 destroyers, in support of five convoys—obviously British—two from Cape Town, one from the River Plate, one from the West Indies and one from Canada; on the 'Blue' side were fifteen torpedo U-boats, Type VII and Type IX (1,000 tons), two large fleet U-boats, two huge artillery U-boats, a minelaying U-boat and an armoured commerce raider with supply ship. This was a remarkably small force to try conclusions with convoys protected by the greater part of the Royal Navy and, according to the staff rules, the Royal Air Force when the ships came within range of bases in North Africa, France and the British Isles. The conditions were so unrealistic in view of the 'Z-Plan' building programme to 1943

171

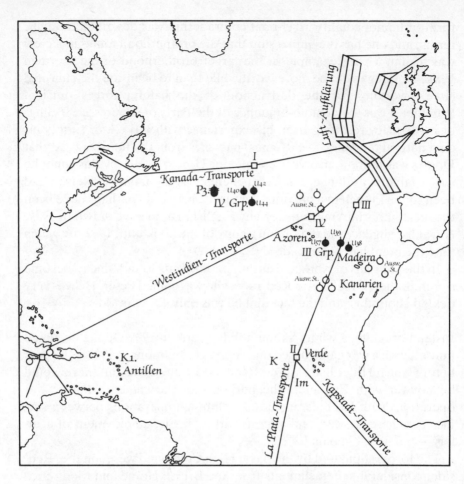

Dönitz's early 1939 war game against British Atlantic supply lines: five groups of three U-boats each are disposed to intercept convoys from Canada, the West Indies, the River Plate and Cape Town. The dark boats are the large Type IX, the others the medium Type VII B; P 3 is an armoured cruiser (*Panzerschiff*), *Luft-Aufklärung* anticipated British air patrols.

172

that one wonders how the staff arrived at them. The real interest lies in the tactics employed by the 'Blue', German side and the conclusions Dönitz drew from their inevitable failure to cause much damage.

The 'Blue' Commander arranged his torpedo U-boats in five groups of three, the northernmost group, together with the armoured cruiser, in mid-Atlantic on the Canada–Ireland shipping route and three groups about the Azores and Canaries to intercept the Cape Town and River Plate convoys. They were spread out in this way because the patrols expected around the British Isles, particularly air reconnaissance, were considered likely to restrict the boats' movements if they waited close in at the focal points of trade as in the First War. As a result the boats were spread too thin; three convoys got through without being sighted and only the second Cape Town convoy, which had joined the River Plate ships west of Cape Verde, was intercepted; the single U-boat which found these vessels kept radio silence so as not to give away her position before attacking, then called up the other two boats of her group; these were destroyed by the escort and the other groups were too far away to reach the spot. Dönitz commented, ' "Blue's" failure was not grounded in false dispositions but in the emptiness of the sea and the small numbers of boats, [and] in the low mobility and small reconnaissance area of the boats.'[29]

Despite the poor results, Dönitz managed to draw very positive conclusions. They were in fact a direct transposition to the war against trade of the lessons he had drawn from three years of training and exercises against warship targets. He pointed first to the altered conditions since the World War when no concentration of U-boats had been possible against the concentration of ships represented by a convoy, since radio had not been sufficiently developed. This was not true; W/T communication between U-boats acting together had been practised successfully in the Mediterranean and the English Channel in 1918;[30] perhaps he meant that no *shore* direction had been possible. In any case he continued with what was to become the *leitmotif* of his reports, '*concentration against concentration*'; this was the necessity that had caused the young U-boat arm to practise 'co-operative working' since its inception. And he went on:

The disposition of boats at the focal points of the seaways in the Atlantic has to follow these principles:

a) At least three boats form a group. Disposition of the boats in a breadth of some 50 and a depth of 100–200 miles.

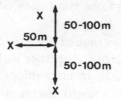

b) Further groups—according to the number of operational boats ready—disposed in the direction of the reported steamer way at some 200–300 miles.
c) Leadership of all groups basically through BdU [C-in-C U-boats] at home.
d) Enemy report by one of the boats of a group and all boats of this group attack the reported enemy independently without further orders.
e) Disposition of further groups on to this enemy through BdU.[21]

He went on to discuss co-operation between U-boats and surface forces and with the German Air Force in the eastern Atlantic, although the navigational and range difficulties here were enormous. If no surface forces were available he suggested that fast fleet U-boats would provide suitable reconnaissance for the groups. Nevertheless:

The *chief carrier* of the U-boat war *in the Atlantic* is the *torpedo U-boat*. The FdU is of opinion that we possess above all the most suitable types in the Type VII B and Type IX. Ninety continuously operational boats in total, thus at least some 300 of these types are necessary for successful operations.[30]

This figure of 300 boats necessary to bring the Battle of the Atlantic to a successful conclusion is quoted in most books about the Second World War. It is hard to see how Dönitz arrived at it; the conditions under which the war game was played and the almost complete lack of success of the Blue (German) side allowed no valid conclusions to be drawn, and for all the explanation in the paper itself the figure might have been drawn out of a hat. The arc covered by the U-boats in the game covered over 2,000 miles in extent; assuming three boats to a group, thus 30 groups to make up the 90 operational boats he wanted, and each boat in the group some 100–200 miles apart, they might have been expected to extend over the whole area, but not in the in-depth arrangement along the routes detailed in the paper.

It may simply be that 300 was a number he thought he might get away with; it was rather larger than the figure decided on by the 'Z-Plan' committee, but not extravagantly so!

He offered a crumb to the 'cruiser U-boat' enthusiasts in Berlin by suggesting that large artillery types had value for distant operations, proposing three operating in the South Atlantic and three in the Indian Ocean—thus a total of eighteen boats necessary to keep these six operational—together with three—thus altogether nine—large mine-laying boats, and ten operational fast 'fleet' U-boats of 2,000 tons, Type XII; these were both to work with surface forces and in reconnaissance off United States harbours. The idea here was for them to locate and hold touch with convoys bound from US ports to the British Isles and lead the groups waiting in mid-Atlantic to them. Whether Dönitz discussed the possible political consequences of this is not clear; there had been much earnest discussion since at least 1935 on the reasons why the United States had entered the World War.[32]

In his concluding remarks Dönitz reiterated the advantage of the modern U-boat over its First World War predecessor; able to receive intelligence, it did not have to wait and simply hope for a ship or convoy to turn up; it also had a new method of firing torpedoes which did not cause an upheaval of water to give away the boat's position, and the new electric torpedoes did not leave a line of bubbles. Against this was the British Asdic. However, he looked forward to a speedy solution to this problem—on what grounds is not clear. The last letter dated October 1938 in a file on the development of non-reflective materials which might be applied to U-boats to make them immune from sound detection stressed the huge difficulties.[33] He was evidently confident, nonetheless, for he wrote:

According to the English Press England apparently believes herself equal to the U-boat danger on the grounds of her detection apparatus. Our goal must be *under all circumstances to leave England in this belief.*

The sound-detection secure U-boat and also the co-operation of several U-boats on one convoy must be the greatest surprise for England.[34]

In the apparent acceptance of the inevitability of war with England, these are surely significant sentences. He concluded:

> By our geographical position . . . and inferiority to English sea power the U-boat is the means above all the battle means of our Navy which can be committed to the decisive battle against English sea communications by itself with the greatest *security*.

He therefore proposed the development of the U-boat arm 'with all means', and it is easy to read into this whole paper support for his later assertion that he foresaw the danger of war breaking out with Great Britain long before Raeder's huge balanced fleet was ready.

During the fleet's spring cruise that year Dönitz devised an exercise to test his group tactics for the war against trade in Atlantic conditions. It took place off the coast of Portugal and across the Bay of Biscay from the morning of May 12th to the evening of the 14th.[35] 'Blue' had fifteen U-boats, Type VII and IX as in the war game, and a surface raider represented by Dönitz's new Führer ship, *Erwin Wassner*, aboard which was the U-boat flotilla chief for the exercise. The target was a 'Gold' convoy represented by a tanker and a freighter; Dönitz's former Führer ship, *Saar*, represented the escort; she was inferior to the *Erwin Wassner* in speed, but supposed to outmatch her in artillery; during the course of the exercise the *Erwin Wassner* changed her spots to become an additional escort. The speed of the convoy was thirteen knots and the convoy Commander had complete freedom of manoeuvre provided he made good eleven knots along his intended route.

Naturally the conditions were somewhat artificial: the exercise had to be designed so that it was at least possible the convoy would be sighted or it would result in three days of fruitless cruising; so it was that the 'convoy' was started on a northerly course towards Ushant from 130 miles west of Lisbon and the Blue forces were placed in its path, four groups of U-boats arranged as outlined in Dönitz's war-game paper along the direction of advance of the convoy at intervals of some 200–300 miles and the 'commerce raider', *Erwin Wassner*, making long search sweeps. Perhaps the balance was weighted too heavily in favour of Blue; at any rate, despite unusually poor visibility of no more than five miles the convoy was sighted by the southernmost U-boat, U 46, at 12.05, barely four hours after the start. She signalled the position, course and

176

speed and attacked; later she was driven off and lost touch. The other three boats in her group, acting on her message, found the convoy again at dusk, but they too lost it because of poor visibility made worse by a head sea and spray.

During the night the Blue flotilla leader ordered his second group to patrol the expected path of the convoy on the latitude of Finisterre, and soon after daybreak one of these boats, U 37, regained touch and attacked. Again, worsening visibility and sea conditions allowed the convoy to escape. The flotilla leader now ordered his third group to patrol in the Bay of Biscay in the reported direction of advance; meanwhile the *Erwin Wassner* and the seven boats of the two south-ernmost groups which had been passed by the convoy steered for the same position at their best speed against heavy seas.

At 3 o'clock that afternoon *Erwin Wassner* came in sight of the convoy, and she was joined by two boats of the third group, U 34 and U 32, before the *Saar* drove her off to the west and she lost contact. The westernmost of this group, however, U 35, acting on her reports, found the convoy again at 7 pm. She held touch in exemplary fashion until nightfall, then attacked, keeping touch afterwards and enabling the *Erwin Wassner* to regain contact and attack the convoy at 3.00 in the morning before the slower *Saar* arrived back with her charges. At this point the *Erwin Wassner* changed sides to become an escort, and placed herself at the stern of the convoy at the limit of visibility, finding herself in the midst of the U-boats guided by the touch-holding U 35; she was 'repeatedly attacked with success. On the other hand the U-boats were at first forced to dive.'

By daylight on the 14th a pack of seven U-boats were either in sight of the convoy or in the close vicinity; by 7.45 am U 47 was able to attack from 500 yards, closing to 300 yards for a second attack ten minutes later. Torpedo attacks continued throughout the day; by the close of the exercise at 8.00 pm the convoy was surrounded by no less than thirteen U-boats. Dönitz commented: 'The convoy is thus beset by a pack of U-boats; numerous attacks already in the first night hours would render it unable to defend itself any further.'[36]

It is interesting in this respect that most of the torpedo attacks were made from 800 out to as far as 3,000 metres; really close attacks such as U 47's were the exception.

Naturally Dönitz drew the lesson he wanted from this highly successful demonstration:

The plain basic thinking of the battle against the convoy by U-boats is: essential effect against a *gathering* of steamers in convoy can only be realized when a *great number* of U-boats can be successfully set on the convoy.[37]

Someone, perhaps Admiral Boehm, underlined '*great number*' and wrote in pencil in the margin, 'Don't exaggerate!'
Dönitz's report continued:

This [great number of boats] is conditional on the U-boat in touch with the convoy *calling up* others. Then gradually ever more U-boats could come on to the convoy, its position would become ever more difficult, and also the strength relationship, the cover afforded by its *escort*, would become ever less, so that great losses from the convoy could be expected.[38]

He admitted by implication the artificially favourable disposition of the Blue U-boats in the exercise, and pointed to the difficulties of finding convoys in the broad spaces of the Atlantic—leading him back to the necessity for great numbers of boats, far more than were available at present, also to the proposal in his previous report for large, fast boats for reconnaissance purposes.

On the question of control, he considered the system developed for the Mediterranean also suited Atlantic trade war conditions; this was for the BdU at home to organize the general disposition of the groups in the seaways in the expected track of enemy convoys, while a local flotilla chief aboard a Führer U-boat would be in tactical control of all the groups in his area, for instance the North America–England route. This was because Dönitz considered that the BdU at home would not be able to exercise tactical control 'for want of milieu-knowledge', above all the weather position.

As for the possibility of the enemy taking bearings of the continuing wireless traffic necessary between the boats at sea, he had doubts about the accuracy they would obtain and also doubted the possibility of the convoys being able to call up reinforcements to meet the threat since the area of attack would be outside the range of coastal aircraft. He thought that the result would be attacks on the touch-keeping U-boat to drive it away. 'The FdU does not see this disadvantage as important; the military advantage of setting *several* boats on to one convoy is on the other hand so great that it justifies breaking radio silence.'[39]

Passing to tactics, he considered that the exercise had proved that it was possible for U-boats to hold touch at the borders of sight in Atlantic conditions, and pointed to the mast rangefinders on (war)ships as the greatest enemy of the touch-keeping U-boat. This is a significant remark in view of the developments on the way, and one wonders how much knowledge he had of secret German Navy radar experiments; certainly he became aware of them that summer of 1939 for he was involved in discussions about fitting two U-boats with a primitive radar ('*Dete-apparatus*'). The scheme was overtaken by events.[40]

It is interesting that in his report Dönitz foreshadowed exactly the tactics which convoys in the battle of the Atlantic would adopt, namely a sweep by escorts at dusk to shake off the touch-keeper, followed by a sharp alteration of course immediately after dark. He thought, however, that the 'sweeper' would be in grave danger from torpedo attack.

His conclusions were unequivocal:

The simple principle of fighting a convoy of several steamers with several U-boats also is correct.

The summoning of U-boats was under the conditions of the exercise successful. The convoy would have been destroyed.

It is necessary in this most important area for the U-boat war to gather wider experience through exercises in the Atlantic under the most realistic war conditions. (Security!)

Apart from providing the necessary tactical and operational knowledge such exercises would give the best warlike training for U-boat Commanders and crews.[41]

In contrast to his unbridled optimism, a memorandum from one of the leading U-boat experts in the German service, Rear Admiral Fürbringer, sounded a thoroughly pessimistic note at the time the exercise was in progress. He started with the premise that against the Royal Navy's material superiority only operational surprise would have any chance of success. In the World War the surprise had come too late—a reference to the unrestricted U-boat campaign; since then England had mastered that method with Asdic and today a U-boat war against England depended above all on whether it was possible to make U-boats Asdic-immune. All attempts to date had been unsuccessful. But if they were not made immune there was no prospect of success, hence no purpose in even beginning a U-boat war against trade, indeed it was 'irresponsible to commit the valuable U-boat crews' to such a war.

Short of the Asdic-immune boat, the only way of waging a successful campaign would be to destroy the convoy escorts, either with special torpedoes developed for the purpose or, since German surface forces were totally insufficient for the task, by employing a 'specially suitable weapon—the naval air arm'. And for success in war the foundations would have to be laid by the development of the right machines and tactical co-operation in peace. 'In a future war the tasks of the Navy and the naval air arm will be so interwoven that both must be welded into a unity by the outbreak of war if heavy failures are not to result.'[42]

In the light of history, this critique, both of U-boat and general naval policy, is rather more prescient than the optimistic determination that Dönitz as a capable and strong-minded 'Front Commander' indulged. Of course both mentalities have their place in any war machine; Raeder's machine failed under the severe pressures and huge difficulties imposed by the amateur in command of the *Wehrmacht*—Adolf Hitler— either to pay sufficient heed to the Fürbringers or sufficiently to control the Dönitzs. And Raeder, like Tirpitz before him, cannot escape a major share of the blame for allowing the bungling at the top; that indeed was the bargain that he, like Tirpitz, had struck for the sake of a greater and greater Navy.

Dönitz's answer to the bombshell was contained in a letter to Fürbringer's chief on the naval staff, Admiral Schniewind. It was in his tersest style:

It is clear that the attack on the English sea communications alone can have war-decisive effect in a naval war against England.[43]

This flat assertion was followed by all his usual arguments—the U-boat as the sole effective blockade runner in and out of the North Sea, the concentration of U-boats as the simple principle to combat the concentration of ships in convoys—'Then the English would experience the surprise demanded by Fürbringer!'—as, he went on, he had just demonstrated successfully in exercises in the Bay of Biscay!

He disagreed about the usefulness of the naval air arm in the open spaces of the Atlantic and thought that for the U-boats to carry special anti-escort torpedoes would be to limit their proper task, the elimination of merchantmen. He agreed that the Asdic-immune U-boat had not yet

180

been developed, but was confident that it *would* be in foreseeable time; the solution to this problem was of immense military importance. However, it is apparent that Fürbringer's ideas had not caused him to change his own views in any way at all, and one can deduce from the tone of the letter, and perhaps from the rounded signature and less violent crossing of the 'T', that he was extremely pleased with himself over the success of his 'pack' of U-boats in the exercise and more confident than ever.

The confidence was about to be tested, for Hitler had already lit the short fuse to war. On April 11th he had issued the directive for 'Case White', an attack on Poland at any time from September 1st 'to destroy Polish military strength and create a situation in the East which satisfies the requirements of defence'.[44] His stated policy was to limit the conflict to Poland, and he justified the practicality of this by the 'internal crisis in France' and the consequent restraint imposed on England. Perhaps this was a misjudgement on Hitler's part caused by his inflated opinion of himself after his series of easy victories over the western appeasers and the plaudits these had earned from the circle of admirers he had selected for his entourage. If this is the explanation it caused him to make a monumental psychological blunder; for it was just this series of easy victories and the lies which he had told on each occasion which ensured that the western powers could not give way again. If he did not perceive this his self-delusion was limitless. It is true that he was reported by a member of the German resistance to believe England 'degenerate, weak, timid' and 'without the guts to resist any of his plans',[45] but this is typical of the blustering tone with which he often concealed feelings of nervousness or inferiority; his actions do not bear it out.

However, once again he seems to have convinced Raeder, who, despite British and French guarantees to Poland, suggested in a staff memorandum that spring that the Polish conflict would be isolated. In his memoirs, written as a broken old man, he confessed that some officers did not share his view, and named Dönitz as one. This seems to be borne out by the fact that after he inspected Dönitz's U-flotillas on July 22nd that year he made a speech to the officers in which he told them he had the Führer's personal assurance that there would be no war with Great Britain in the near future.

'Do not believe that the Führer would bring us into such a desperate position, for a war with England would mean *Finis Germania*!'[46]

Nonetheless, Dönitz's apprehensions do not show in a paper he wrote at the beginning of July. This contained an ambitious proposal for building one or two U-boat repair ships and stationing them abroad. The rationale was that since the task of the U-boats in war would lie in the Atlantic and other distant areas it was necessary to train in these areas; this was not possible without repair and supply facilities which, in lieu of bases, could only be undertaken by specially equipped ships on station.

His conclusion leaves no room to doubt that he anticipated war with Great Britain within a few years, not within two months!

An essential part of the war against England will fall to the U-boats in the commerce war. In order to allow them to be committed suddenly and with the strongest effect immediately on the outbreak of war, *all* useful paths must be trodden. Amongst these lies the building of workshop ships.[47]

There is evidence that by this time he had convinced at least the U-boat department at High Command of the soundness of his views on the coming war; on August 3rd, the first staff officer (1 U), *Kapitänleutnant* Fresdorf, wrote a paper on U-boat types for the war against commerce whose conclusions might have been dictated by Dönitz.[48] Fresdorf was obviously not expecting war with England within a few weeks either! His analysis took into account German surface raider groups yet to be provided by the Z-Plan. He thought that these groups, which could only be beaten off by battleships, would force Great Britain to contract her supply lines—for shortage of capital ship escorts—into a single route across the North Atlantic. He believed the United States would act as a neutral 'middleman'; all supplies for England would be gathered in US ports then sent in convoys across a broad highway on which all British naval resources, above all aircraft carriers, would be concentrated. In this section he appears closer to Fürbringer than to Dönitz, pointing to the continuing uncertainty over how effective the British Asdic was, and to the probability that single U-boats would be forced under water by aircraft from carriers; hence they would be unable to use their surface speed to intercept convoys.

From these doubts he passed in one bound to the optimism of Dönitz's view that against a concentration of ships in a convoy it was neccessary to bring a concentration of U-boats! Further, that to overcome the difficulties of finding the convoys in the spaces of the Atlantic they must be located by special long-range, 25-knot boats stationed off the US assembly ports; these boats would then shadow the convoys when they sailed, continually reporting position and course so that attack groups could be positioned to intercept them over the last third of their journey. Fresdorf did not explain why these fast boats should be immune to the carrier aircraft threat he had spelled out in the earlier part of the paper; it might have been expected that their radio transmissions alone would have alerted the British, who would presumably do all in their power to shake them off. This possibility was not discussed; Fresdorf simply considered the number of boats required; he accepted Dönitz's figure of 300 torpedo boats Types VII and IX for the attack groups to operate in the eastern third of the Atlantic without any discussion, and accepted the need for Führer U-boats from which the area chiefs could exercise local tactical control; here he went far above Dönitz's figure, suggesting 20 Type XII boats simultaneously operational, thus a need for 60 of these boats in total. And for the 'cruiser' U-boats for reconnaissance off US harbours and for artillery and mining operations in distant sea areas, he suggested fifteen, thus a total of 45.

Since he also suggested smaller boats for North Sea and Baltic operations, and replenishment and 'tanker' U-boats to extend the Atlantic boats' endurance, the total fleet he envisaged was approaching 500 boats, a considerable increase on the Z-Plan and, as he pointed out, one that could not be met without increasing the number of building yards, nor indeed without personnel problems. He drew the logical conclusion that what the proposal amounted to was a renunciation of part of the surface element of the Z-Plan in favour of the U-boat arm. This ties in with Dönitz's advocacy of a U-boat alternative to the Z-Plan.

Hitler, meanwhile, had been working up his usual excuse for assault; this time it concerned the rights of the predominantly German inhabitants of Danzig, the port at the end of the 'Polish corridor' created by the allied powers at Versailles; events were following the same, sad course as at the end of July 1914 with the western governments trying desperately to douse the fuse of a European conflagration sparked in Berlin. Once again the vital decision was taken in Moscow. At the end of July the German Foreign Ministry had dangled a tempting proposition before Stalin: German policy was aimed at Great Britain, not Russia; Germany could offer Russia neutrality and a settlement of all questions between them from the Baltic to the Black Sea. At some time before August 12th the Soviet leader swallowed the bait, and his government declared themselves ready for a 'systematic discussion of all outstanding issues, including the Polish question'.[49] Hitler was jubilant: he had pulled off yet another master-stroke against his western enemies. After learning the outcome of a meeting on August 15th between his Ambassador in Moscow and the Soviet Foreign Minister, Molotov, he felt quite sure of it.

On the same day Dönitz, on six weeks' leave in Bad Gastein, was recalled by telephone. He arrived at Kiel on the 16th, and that afternoon took over from his chief of staff, Eberhardt Godt. Godt had been his adjutant in the *Emden*, had since taken a U-boat course and had joined his staff the previous year. The two made an excellent combination, Dönitz providing the fire and drive and inspiration, Godt the calm efficiency of the ideal staff officer who never pushed himself forward; they remained together until the very end. All that was missing from the team was a strong critical, analytical brain.

Dispositions for 'Case White' had been prepared long since; they provided for all boats not required in the Baltic against Poland and Russia to sail to waiting stations around the British Isles ready to attack British trade, should Great Britain honour her obligations to Poland. The next few days were taken up in getting the 35 immediately ready boats away and attending to unforeseen difficulties such as a shortage of operational torpedoes; Dönitz personally took his leave of all the Commanders before he sailed, commenting afterwards in his war diary, 'The very confident attitude of the crews deserves special mention. In my opinion it is a sign that the broad masses of the people have great faith in the government.'[50]

His own view of the chances of a World War at this time are difficult to guess; by the 21st he knew of the likelihood of a treaty with Russia, and this probably caused him to believe the Führer would pull off another miracle, as indeed the great majority of Germans believed. In any case on that date he transferred his command ship to Swinemünde, which seems to imply that he expected to be controlling eastern, not western operations; it had been agreed earlier that 'if Case White should develop into a major war the FdU will go to Wilhelmshaven with the *Erwin Wassner*'.[51]

On the other hand frustration at the lack of numbers of U-boats burns through the pages of the war diary he had started, and it is difficult to account for this solely in terms of a limited Polish operation.

By the 24th, after the announcement of the non-aggression treaty with Russia, and news that both England and Poland were mobilizing he must have anticipated war with the West; he asked the naval war staff in Berlin not to reduce the area now occupied by his boats when danger zones were declared for shipping, and he told them that zones extending only 200 miles west of England were not sufficient. He was informed that the zones had not yet been fixed! He then dictated a message to his Atlantic boats to give them the latest political developments; it was held up in Berlin; he wrote in his war diary: 'I do not agree with this. FdU must be able to give his boats general information as well as just the dry bones of orders if touch is to be maintained between leader and subordinates.'[52]

By this time fifteen boats, including U 37 with a flotilla chief aboard to take local tactical control, were on their way to Atlantic waiting positions Northabout around the Faroe Islands, an unnecessarily extended route in Dönitz's opinion but forced on him by the naval staff; the increased fuel expenditure meant that they would only be able to stay on patrol until mid-September. A further three boats were preparing to sail the same route, a flotilla of the small Type II boats were either on station in the North Sea or preparing to sail and fourteen others were in the Baltic. This comprised practically the entire U-boat force of 56 boats; it left nothing in reserve to take over the positions when the boats had to come in. This was a decision from Berlin. Also by this date, the 24th, the 'pocket battleships' *Graf Spee* and *Deutschland*, with their supply ships, were on their way to Atlantic waiting positions. It was a pitifully small force with which to take on the Royal Navy. '*Y-Tag*' for the attack on Poland was 48 hours away.

Hitler, however, had lost his nerve: the British government was evidently determined to support Poland despite the shock of the Russian treaty, and his ally, Mussolini, was not prepared to support him! He ordered a postponement of the attack and, calling the British Ambassador to the Chancellery, made a desperate effort to get back to the original first principles of his policy; he personally would guarantee the continued existence of the British Empire, even to the extent of placing the power of the *Reich* at the disposal of the British government.[53]

Besides re-opening the official dialogue, Hitler, at Göring's insistence, sent an unofficial go-between to London; this was a Swedish engineer named Dahlerus, an enthusiast for Anglo-German co-operation, who had made earlier forays in this field. Dahlerus saw the British Foreign Secretary, returned to Berlin the next day, the 26th, and at 12.30 the same night reported to Hitler in Göring's presence that Britain was going to stand by her obligations to Poland. By this time Hitler had worked out detailed proposals for how the British should help him gain Danzig peacefully! However, he went on, raising his voice, should there be war, *'Dann werde ich U-Boote bauen—U-boote—U-boote!'* and working himself into a paroxysm through which his words were scarcely distinguishable, he drew himself up and shrieked as if addressing a Nuremberg rally, *'Ich werde Flugzeuge bauen—Flugzeuge—Flugzeuge—und ich werde meine Feinde vernichten!'*[54] (I will build aircraft—aircraft—aircraft—and I will destroy my enemies!')

Dahlerus, stunned, turned to see Göring's reaction, but found him unmoved. Hitler grew calmer after the outburst and begged the Swede to tell him, since he knew England so well, why he (Hitler) had been unable to reach agreement with the British government. Dahlerus hesitated, then told him he believed it was due to lack of confidence in him and his government.

In the next few days the official replies from Great Britain, while absolutely firm on the guarantee to Poland, gave rise to hopes that there were areas for negotiation; a feeling that the political genius of the Führer had manifested itself once more seems to have passed down the line to Dönitz. The evidence is in his war diary. His frustrations at the lack of boats had culminated on August 28th in a determination to put the case for a rapid build-up of the U-boat arm personally to Raeder. He composed a long memorandum[55] reiterating all the points made in his previous reports about the unique suitability of the U-boat for the Navy's principal task—the destruction of British Atlantic communications—and the necessity for a force of at least 300 boats to carry this task to a successful conclusion—the magic number again, not analysed, flatly stated. There can be no doubt that he really believed that with 300 boats he could force Great Britain to her knees by himself; the single foundation for this was his development of group tactics, since that was the only real change in the U-boat's favour since the First World War. His paper ended with a plea to Raeder to build the arm up to this strength at the expense of other fleet units in the shortest possible time so that it could 'carry out its main task, that is to defeat England in war'. It was typed out and sent to Berlin on September 1st; he wrote in his war diary:

Certainly the memorandum is based on the assumption that there will not now be a war with England; but if it should come to such a war, the demands set out for the development of the [U-boat] arm with all means would be even more correct.[56]

The extraordinary thing is that while he wrote these words he knew the German assault on Poland was under way. It had been ordered by Hitler the previous day. Afterwards the former Commander of the Baltic Station, Admiral Albrecht, had told the Führer of his fear that England must be drawn in, to which the reply had been, *'Ich höre den Frieden-sengel rauschen'*[57] ('I hear the wings of the angel of peace'). Perhaps this delphic utterance had reached Dönitz, who had moved in the meantime with his staff to U-boat command headquarters West, a plain timber barracks on the outskirts of Wilhelmshaven. At 6.30 pm, one and a half hours after his arrival a message had gone out from the High Command to Atlantic U-boats in the sense of Hitler's directive that responsibility for opening hostilities in the west should rest unequivocally with England and France: 'No attacks against English forces except in self-defence or by special order.'[58] The boats were informed that hostilities with Poland would start at 04.45 the following morning: 'Attitude of western powers still uncertain.'

At the appointed hour on September 1st German soldiers dressed up by Admiral Canaris' *Abwehr* in Polish uniforms, provided the border 'provocation' that led to the planned 'counter-attack' by the *Wehrmacht*, and at 10.00 Hitler broadcast the news to the nation—and the world. Listening to him in Berlin, William Shirer had the impression that the Führer was 'dazed at the fix he had got himself into'[59] and a little desperate about it. No doubt he was; once again he had put himself into a position from which no retreat was possible, and this time he knew with the rational part of his mind the inevitable, momentous consequences.

They followed somewhat as they had on the first day of August 1914, although there was a delay in presenting the British ultimatum; this reinforced the impression in Germany that the Führer had worked another of his miracles. But eventually at 9 o'clock in the morning of the 3rd the ultimatum came; it gave Germany two hours to call off the attack and withdraw her troops from Poland. There was no reply. At 11.15 the British Prime Minister broadcast to the country, '. . . all my long struggle to win peace has failed'.[60] The uncoded signal had already gone out to the fleet: 'Total Germany'.

It was intercepted by the German Radio Intelligence Service, and minutes later Dönitz was handed a note of it in his operations room in the headquarters hut at Wilhelmshaven. He was stunned. After expecting war with England, then not expecting it, then thinking it must surely come to it, then beguiled by the delayed ultimatum and the propaganda machine into thinking perhaps the miracle had happened, assured by Raeder earlier that morning after news of the ultimatum that Hitler intended avoiding and would avoid war with England—suddenly to be confronted with it.

His staff officers observed his consternation. Holding the signal in his hand he paced back and forth apparently sunk deep in thought, repeating more to himself than to those following him with their eyes, *'Mein Gott! Also wieder Krieg gegen England!'*[61] ('My God! So it's war against England again!'). Then, as if suddenly rousing himself from his thoughts he made for the door with rapid steps.

He left the room and after half an hour came back, a changed Dönitz. 'We know our enemy. We have today the weapon [the new U-boat arm] and a leadership that can face up to this enemy. The war will last a long time; but if each does his duty we will win. Now to your tasks!'[62]

Raeder, presiding at his daily conference, suffered a similar shock when the news came. He too left the room. A silent man, he let his despair pour out in a memorandum which was filed for the record:

Today the war breaks out against England–France which, according to the Führer, we need not have reckoned with before about 1944 and which until the last moment the Führer believed he should prevent . . .[63]

He went on to detail the fleet he would have available under the Z-Plan had the war been postponed, as the Führer had told him it would be until 1944/45. Then, 'particularly with the co-operation of Japan and Italy', there would have been good prospects of defeating the English fleet and severing English supply lines, 'that is to say finding the final solution to the English question'. As it was, the *Kriegsmarine* was in no way prepared for 'the great battle' and 'could only show that it understood how to die with honour in order to create the foundations for later reconstruction'.

William Shirer was not far away in the Wilhelmplatz when the announcement came that England had declared war; the people standing about him in the late summer sunshine were silent. 'They just stood there

188

as they were before. Stunned. The people cannot realize yet that Hitler has led them into a world war.'[64]

In the Chancellery Hitler turned to a strangely subdued Ribbentrop. 'What now?'

CHAPTER FIVE

The Battle of the Atlantic

THE ORDERS TO the U-boats in waiting positions around the British Isles were to conduct their operations against merchant shipping strictly in accordance with Prize Law; this involved surfacing, stopping and searching ships, and when it was found necessary to destroy them, ensuring that the crew and any passengers got away in the boats and were close enough to land to find safety. These rules were adhered to, not from humane motives or because Germany had been a signatory to the treaty enshrining them—as she had—for they were manifestly unsuited to U-boat operations—but simply for political effect on neutrals. A staff paper dated 'beginning September 1939' makes this clear.[1] It started with the premise that an 'unrestricted' campaign with U-boats attacking without warning would bring a greater sinking rate than the Prize Rules allowed, but it would also bring conflict with neutrals.

However, the paper went on, the enemy was arming his merchant ships against U-boat attack; this fact should be used to work up a political propaganda justifying the treatment of *armed* merchant ships as warships – hence justifying their sinking without warning. As it was expected that all British merchantmen would soon be armed an 'unrestricted' campaign like that of 1917 could be brought in as it were by the back door. The main concern was with the most powerful neutral, the United States of America:

A tolerant attitude of the USA is not excluded in this case [sinking *armed* merchantmen without warning] since the American neutrality statute takes account of a possible special treatment for armed merchantmen. Further, in the World War there was no case of the torpedoing of an armed merchant ship, violating American law, about which the President of the United States protested.[2]

The cynical—or *real*—nature of German adherence to the Prize Rules is encapsulated in the conclusion of the paper:

The declaration of a war zone, as was done on February 4th 1915, is inexpedient because this measure simply announced the sinking without warning of *enemy* merchantmen in the indicated area. With the expected general arming of enemy merchantmen a situation will develop allowing the sinking without warning of all enemy merchantmen which, because of the release of armed merchantmen into the category of military targets, will be unobjectionable in international law.[3]

However sensible this staff appreciation, Raeder actually favoured the declaration of a blockade zone around England and an unrestricted campaign within it as the means of 'achieving the greatest damage to England with the forces to hand'.[4] Hitler still hoped to come to terms with England or France, however, by driving a wedge between them directly he had settled the Polish question, and would not agree to any such illegal action which might lead to an irreversible breach.

Dönitz, of course, did not make the rules; he simply carried out the policy decided in Berlin. At 2 o'clock in the afternoon of September 3rd he sent a message to his Forces, 'U-boats to make war on merchant shipping in accordance with operations order,' and noted in the war diary, 'This should exclude any misunderstanding as the operations are under the express orders for war on merchant shipping in accordance with Prize Law.'[5]

Nevertheless one of his Commanders, Julius Lemp, waiting in U 30 some 250 miles north-west of Ireland, was filled with such ardour to distinguish himself with a telling blow against England that he disregarded the orders. Sighting a large steamer approaching that evening on a westerly course, he intercepted and delivered a submerged torpcdo attack without warning.

The ship was the 13,581-ton Donaldson liner, *Athenia*, bound from Liverpool to Montreal with 1,103 passengers, including over 300 United States citizens; what Lemp was thinking about will probably never be known; from the range at which he fired his torpedoes it must have been impossible to have mistaken her for anything but a passenger liner—the number of lifeboats alone would have indicated this. Dönitz claimed in his memoirs that Lemp mistook her for an auxiliary cruiser; however,

191

1. Aufstellung: Spannungszeit bis 15·9·1939

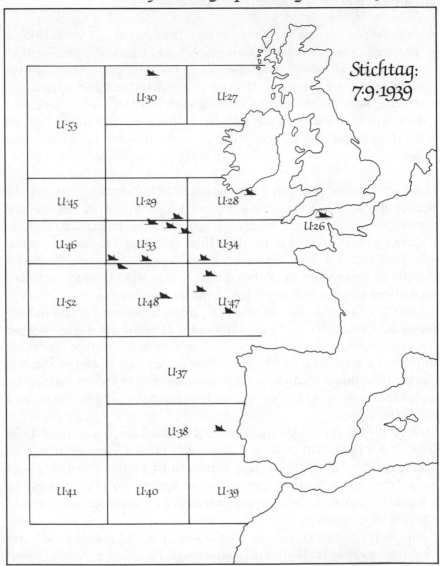

Stichtag:
7·9·1939

German chart showing areas of operation allocated to the Atlantic U-boats from the period of tension (*Spannungszeit*) in late August through early September 1939, and the positions of their victims after the outbreak of war. Note U 30's victim approximately 250 miles NW of Ireland—the *Athenia*.

she was not armed, it was evident from her position that she had sailed before the outbreak of war, and it was official German naval policy to give precisely the excuse Dönitz used to explain any breaches of international law!

One torpedo hit the port side of the liner, destroying the bulkhead between the engineroom and boiler room and hurling a huge column of water up the side. The explosion also destroyed the stairs to the third class and tourist class dining saloons—particularly unfortunate since the passengers were at dinner at the time. Most of the 112 who lost their lives were killed in the explosion or drowned because they could not get up on deck from the saloon. Lemp surfaced about 800 yards off the port side as the lifeboats were being manned; some eyewitness accounts suggest that he fired a single shell, others that another torpedo passed under the liner's bows—all agree that the U-boat's midship area was shrouded in smoke which was thought to be gun smoke. Then U 30 made away.[6]

According to Dönitz's war diary, news of the sinking picked up by the Radio Intelligence service did not reach U-boat headquarters until 10.35 the following morning. This seems a long time since it would not have required decoding. He noted: 'The orders given so far were checked again. It is inconceivable that they could have been misinterpreted.' In order to make absolutely certain, however, another signal was sent to all U-boats emphasizing that they were to operate against merchantmen according to Prize Rules. Hitler, alarmed at the possibility of another *Lusitania* incident bringing the United States in with the western powers, ordered that no action of any kind was to be taken against passenger ships, even if they were sailing in convoy. This went out just before midnight. No definition of passenger ship was given.

By this time Goebbels had been active: 'The *Athenia* must have been sunk in error by a British warship or else have struck a floating mine of British origin.'[7] This was broadcast on the afternoon of September 4th. Through the following days his inventions took wing, and the affair was soon shrouded in a fog of absurd distortion designed to confuse neutrals: Churchill had manoeuvred the incident in order to bring America into the war; the *Athenia* would still be afloat if she had had no Americans aboard; the British 'Ministry of Lies' had changed the British torpedo into a German one.

It is established beyond doubt that not a single German warship is near the Hebrides . . . if the *Athenia* had actually been torpedoed this

193

could only have been done by a British submarine . . . We believe the present chief of the British Navy, Churchill, capable even of that crime . . .[8]

Photographs reaching Germany of British ships which had gone to the scene to pick up survivors gave Goebbels the opportunity to claim—with pictorial evidence—that the liner had been sunk by Royal Navy destroyers. A telegram which had been sent to the Berlin shipping agent's offices on September 2nd, advising 'Do not forward passengers *Athenia, Aurania, Andania, Ascania* pending further advice' since other sailings had been cancelled and there might not have been room on these ships, was adduced as evidence that German citizens were not wanted aboard these 'death ships' in case they saw what the British were doing.

Had the affair with the *Athenia* not worked, then one of the other three 'prepared' ships would have been sunk so that Churchill would have his new '*Lusitania* case' to the order of the British Ministry of Lies.[9]

The treatment of the *Athenia* incident vindicated Hitler's and Goebbels' rule that the larger the lie the more likely it was to be believed; the American authorities and law courts and several American newspapers appear to have been confused until the evidence was finally produced at the Nuremberg trials. It is more interesting for the light it throws on the inevitable spread of corruption to all organs and levels of a totalitarian State. In this example Dönitz and his staff knew very well that U 30 was in the area in which the *Athenia* was sunk, and since it is inconceivable that they were unaware of the incredible stories being broadcast in the newspapers and on radio, they were, whether they liked it or not, accomplices to this deliberate campaign of lies. And it is a reflection of the way the Navy had been absorbed into the Nazi State that when U 30 returned towards the end of the month and Lemp confirmed that he had sunk the *Athenia* they became active accomplices. Dönitz and his staff carried out Raeder's instructions to swear the entire crew to secrecy, to have the boat's log doctored so that no mention of the episode appeared, and similarly to fabricate the headquarters record; the war diary entry for September 27th, when 'U 30 entered port', credited her with sinking SS *Blair Logie* and SS *Fanad Head*—'total 9,699 tons'!

* * *

Dönitz's belief that U-boats could throttle British supply lines if only there were enough of them, and his despair at the small force available on the outbreak of war reinforced his passionate conviction that a huge construction programme at the expense of the surface units of the Z-Plan had to be put in hand. He put this forcefully to Raeder again, this time offering himself as the officer best qualified to be in overall control to push the programme through. He realized, as he noted in the war diary, that it was wrong in principle to deprive the arm of its Commander just as his training and leadership was to be put to the test; 'on the other hand it is a fact that the operational activities of the arm will fairly soon be practically non-existent and control of it superfluous unless we succeed in building up quickly a numerically strong and effective U-boat arm'.[10]

After long telephone conversations with Raeder's chief of staff, Admiral Schniewind, who gave the High Command view that he could not be spared from his post at the front, he travelled to Berlin on the 7th to put his case to the C-in-C in person. Raeder was at the Chancellery, however, in conference with the Führer, and he had to be content with an assurance from the staff that the request would be put. His mood of frustration and determination to prove what his U-boats could accomplish is caught in a passage from his war diary that day:

> Only six to eight boats can be out at any one time at present (a third of the 22 Atlantic boats available). Only chance successes can be achieved with these. I consider it better to alternate periods with few boats in position with periods with as many as possible and then to score one great success, e.g. the destruction of a whole convoy. To achieve this, the ebb and flow of U-boats must correspond if possible to that of [enemy] merchant shipping.[11]

Besides capturing something of his intense desire for distinction, the entry illustrates his chief failure as a Commander, impatience and lack of proper evaluation of the enemy's situation or even of the probable consequences of his own action. Here the impatience was to test his 'group tactics' and score a 'great success'—yet by his own admission he had far too few boats to follow up any success achieved and he knew practically nothing of how the enemy were going to operate their convoys; finding them would be a matter of chance. Above all the surprise he hoped to inflict on England would be frittered away.

On the following day, the 8th, Schniewind phoned him to say that

Raeder did not want him to come to Berlin: an officer had been appointed to the post he wanted, and the C-in-C would explain his reasons for keeping him (Dönitz) in his front command in a personal letter.

There can be little doubt that Raeder retained him in command of U-boats because of the standard of high efficiency and devotion he had inspired in the arm. As the fleet chief, Admiral Boehm, reported that autumn, he had 'made the U-boat arm an outstanding instrument of war . . .'[12]

The first definite convoy sighting of the war was made by U 31 on the morning of the 15th; she reported ships steering west from the Bristol Channel. Dönitz ordered three other U-boats in the vicinity to close the position, entering in the war diary:

> They may have luck. I have hammered it into Commanders again and again they must not let such chances pass . . . if only there were more boats at sea now!
>   . . . The disposition of the next series of boats which *must* destroy a convoy is under constant consideration.[13]

He was disappointed on this occasion; although one other U-boat did find the convoy, the mass attack intended never developed. On the next day he sent a questionnaire to the Intelligence Service in order to obtain information on English trade routes.

Individual boats were scoring successes against ships sailing independently as they had in the First War, but he knew it could be only a matter of time before the convoy system was in operation on all routes; meanwhile his mine-laying U-boats operated close inshore, sowing mines at focal points of traffic.

On the 18th he received the best news to date; this was the sinking of the aircraft carrier, *Courageous*, by U 29. 'A glorious success,' he noted in the war diary, 'and further confirmation of the fact that English counter-measures are not as effective as they maintain.'[14]

Raeder visited his unpretentious headquarters in Wilhelmshaven that day to suggest the transfer of some U-boats to the Mediterranean; Dönitz strongly opposed the idea since he had so few boats anyway; he thought it wrong to remove those from the key area around the British Isles to make a long cruise south. Raeder, who was chafing quite as much as he at the opportunities missed by adhering to the Prize Rules, then told him of his plans for stepping up the war on trade by stages: before declaring an unrestricted 'danger zone' around the British Isles, he intended to declare a zone in which enemy ships only—not neutrals—would be liable to be sunk without warning. Dönitz opposed this idea too since submerged U-boats would have difficulty in identifying their targets in time to make their attack; in any case the British would presumably get around it by sailing their ships under neutral colours.

He was not averse to an unrestricted campaign in principle. The dangers for his boats of operating according to Prize Law were already becoming apparent. Nearly all boats had either come home or were on the return passage by now and several Commanders had reported merchantmen using their wireless when ordered to stop, as a result of which aircraft had appeared on the scene, sometimes while the prize crew was still aboard the merchantman. He considered that ships acting in this way were a part of the enemy anti-U-boat organization and should therefore be classed as warships and sunk; he sent a memorandum to Berlin to this effect on the 23rd. Raeder brought it to Hitler's attention on the same day and obtained his agreement. However, he could not move him on his other ideas for stepping up the war on trade. Hitler still hoped to drive a wedge between Britain and France and was concerned about American and neutral opinion generally; for instance it was decided that the notorious term 'unrestricted U-boat warfare' should be dropped from the vocabulary; when the time came to implement it 'the siege of England' would have better connotations while allowing equal 'freedom from having to observe any regulations whatever on account of military law'.[15]

The next day Dönitz sent a signal to all boats: 'Armed force should be used against all merchant ships using their wireless when ordered to stop. They are subject to seizure or sinking without exception.'[16] It was the first turn of the screw. Another was under consideration; it is described in a staff memorandum of two days earlier:

BdU intends to give permission to U-boats to sink without warning any vessel sailing without lights . . . In sea areas where only English vessels are to be expected, the measure desired by FdU can be carried out. Permission to take this step is not to be given in writing, however, but need merely be based on the unspoken approval of the naval operations staff. U-boat Commanders would be informed by word of mouth and the sinking of a merchant ship must be justified in the war

197

diary as due to possible confusion with a warship or auxiliary cruiser . . .[17]

Permission was granted on October 2nd. The memorandum is more important for the light it throws on the character of the German Navy than for the gradual introduction of 'unrestricted' U-boat warfare—which soon came in by other means. It is another example of the cynicism permeating every level of the service. It is also a pointer to the caution which has to be exercised when examining even documentary evidence for later, far more serious crimes against law and morality.

Poland had been beaten by this time, her ill-equipped armies out-classed by the German armour and the screaming Stukas of the *Luft-waffe*; a few centres of resistance still held out, but the end was very near. Behind the *Panzers* Himmler's special SS groups were rounding up and massacring Jews and resisters with extemporized bestiality, and the second stage of the total plan for Poland, the annihilation of the nobility, officers, priests, teachers, the educated and leaders of any kind and the degradation of the rest of the nation to the status of an illiterate mobile labour force for the German overlords was ready for when the Army had completed its task. Hitler's thoughts had turned west. Two days later he was back in Berlin, and on the 27th, as Warsaw surrendered, he startled his generals by telling them that the offensive against France must begin before the end of the year. He knew that time was not on Germany's side.

The next day he travelled to Wilhelmshaven to visit U-boat head-quarters and see the boats which had returned from their first war cruises. He had been surrounded by Army and Air Force men during the Polish campaign and Raeder wished to remind him of the Navy's existence. He could not have chosen a better venue: Dönitz seized the opportunity with verve, the hyperbole from his passionate beliefs masked by the dogmatic tone and *gravitas* of the expert as he explained his boats' performance to date and enormous potential for the future: the material and psychological effect of U-boats was as great as it had been in the First World War; it was not true that the enemy Asdic had mastered the threat; operational experience to date confirmed that the British escorts were not as effective as claimed. On the other hand the present U-boats had great advantages over their First World War predecessors, splash-less discharge of torpedoes which left no bubbles in their wake, above all long-distance wireless communication—and he launched into his favourite theme—allowing all boats in a given area to converge on convoys in that area, so meeting concentrations of enemy merchantmen with a concentration of attacking force; he had proved this practically in exercises in the Bay of Biscay.

And he went on, 'After consideration of all questions relating to U-boat warfare I am convinced that it is a means of inflicting decisive damage on England at her weakest point.'[18]

Again he returned to the number which had become fixed in his mind—300—'if this number of boats is available I believe that the U-boat arm can achieve decisive success.'

It was an impressive performance, quite untrammelled by scientific analysis and running contrary to every lesson of naval history, including those of the campaign in which he himself had taken part, but it left Hitler with the impression of a capable and forthright Commander. From the timber headquarters hut the Führer and his entourage, his chief of staff, Keitel, his naval adjutant, von Puttkamer, Raeder and now Dönitz, sped to the U-boat dock to see the weather-stained boats which had returned from British waters, and inspect their bearded crews— thence to the officers' mess, where he talked with the Commanders and lieutenants, including Schuhart of U 29 who had torpedoed the carrier, *Courageous*, and survived counter-attack by her destroyer escorts. The Führer's already favourable impression of the arm was enhanced; they were a tight brotherhood mirroring their chief's pride in their dangerous service—an élite with the confidence and ebullience of youth and recent successes and, now that the bogey of Asdic had been almost exploded, untroubled by too much doubt. As von Puttkamer wrote, Hitler 'carried back to Berlin an excellent impression of the leadership of the U-boat arm as well as of the liveliness and spirit of the crews'.[19]

In the days after the visit, with the last boats returning home, Dönitz pondered his next campaign; his conclusions remained typical of his conduct throughout the Battle of the Atlantic:

Goal must be to catch convoys and destroy them with a concentration of our few available boats. Finding convoys at sea is difficult. The boats must operate in areas of natural traffic convergence. This is the position south-west of England and in the Gibraltar area. The English area has the advantage of a shorter voyage. The patrols in the coastal area are however strong. . . . The Gibraltar area has the disadvantage

199

of a long route out. Since, however, the route cuts the shipping lanes success can be expected on the way. Gibraltar has the advantage of traffic. The weather position is more favourable than in the north . . . little information on patrols, . . . I have decided to send the boats against the Gibraltar traffic.[20]

He believed that success would depend upon a surprise appearance in strength, and since the boats would become ready and sail at different times, he decided to order them to waiting positions in the south-west approaches to the English Channel where they might find targets; when all were concentrated, he would order them to Gibraltar as a group with a flotilla leader in U 37 to take over tactical control when necessary. If the leader found conditions unpromising he would be authorized to order new dispositions.

Here are all the principles of surprise and concentration and probing for the enemy's weak points and trying to disperse the defence forces which were to become hallmarks of his Atlantic campaign, as familiar to his opponents in anti-submarine operations in London as to his own staff. Practically the only change was the abandonment later of the idea of divided control; it was found that the local flotilla chief could not remain on the surface—which was necessary if he was to exercise control—close enough to the actual operations; he had no advantage, therefore, over U-boat headquarters, and the concept of local tactical control was dropped.

A great success of the kind he had achieved theoretically in the May exercises with a convoy beset on all sides by U-boats, the escorts outnumbered or sunk and incapable of defending their charges eluded him on this occasion, but an equally dramatic blow he had been planning succeeded brilliantly. This was an old-fashioned operation by a lone U-boat against the British main fleet base at Scapa Flow in the Orkney Islands. It had been attempted twice before in the First World War; on both occasions the U-boats had been lost without scoring any success. Despite these precedents, on September 6th, three days after the start of the second round against Britain, Dönitz had called for the naval intelligence file on the fleet base;[21] it proved disappointingly incomplete. However, U 16 was in the Orkney area and her Commander spent some time reconnoitring the several entrances to the Flow; returning to Wilhelmshaven in late September, he reported his findings on enemy patrols, currents and the booms and blockships to be seen across the entrances. At about the same time Dönitz received a report from Admiral Canaris' *Abwehr*; a merchant skipper, who had called at the port of Kirkwall just north of Scapa Flow, a few days before the outbreak of war, had heard that the underwater defences at the eastern entrances to the Flow had been neglected.[22]

Heartened by both reports, Dönitz called for a *Luftwaffe* reconnaissance flight to obtain 'the most precise aerial photographs of all the individual obstacles blocking the entrances'.[23] He received an excellent set of prints on September 26th, and after studying them came to the conclusion that there was a seventeen-metre-wide passage between sunken blockships in the eastern entrance by Lamb Holm Island, which would be negotiable by a U-boat on the surface at slack water. Obviously this meant a night operation; the chief difficulties would be navigational, nevertheless it seemed that it might be done; furthermore it was found that on the night of October 13/14 both periods of slack water fell in the dark hours and the moon would be new, so lessening the chances of discovery.

The idea was worked up into a detailed plan and a Commander chosen, *Kapitänleutnant* Günther Prien, a tough extrovert with a zeal and competence matching Dönitz's own. On Sunday October 1st Prien and the Commander of U 16 were called in together to discuss the project over the charts and photographs. Finally Dönitz said to Prien, 'I don't want an answer now. Think it over and report back on Tuesday.'[24]

Prien was back the next day, his answer, as Dönitz must have known it would be, 'Yes'.

Strict secrecy was maintained, and when Prien took his boat, U 47, out on the 8th the crew had no idea of the mission on which they were embarked. They reached a position off the eastern entrance of the Flow on the 13th and spent the day submerged, waiting for slack water. When they rose that evening Prien was alarmed to see the sky bright with the radiance of the northern lights. Suppressing his doubts about going in with such brilliant visibility, he steered for the narrow passage between the blockships, scraping through, and entered the great basin of the Flow undetected soon after midnight. Casting about, he detected the silhouettes of two great ships, which he took to be the *Royal Oak* and *Repulse*, and steered for them, firing a salvo of three torpedoes at 4,000 metres. Only one of these hit, and that with so little apparent effect that he re-loaded and came in for a second attempt eighteen minutes later; this time two of the salvos struck the *Royal Oak*, igniting a magazine;

201

the battleship was torn apart in a thunderous explosion, then rolled over and sank, taking 833 officers and men with her.

Prien ran back for the Holm passage at full speed and succeeded in making his escape despite the now falling tide and the sweeps of the alerted guard ships. All in all it was a brilliant venture carried out with iron nerve, the hazard justified by success.

Much more was accomplished than the sinking of one old battleship and her valuable crew; correctly anticipating that whether or not Prien succeeded planned air attacks would force the Royal Navy to move base while the Flow was rendered more secure, Dönitz had sent minelaying U-boats to foul the Firth of Forth and Loch Ewe. Successes were scored in both areas; the new heavy cruiser, *Belfast*, and the battleship, *Nelson*, were badly damaged and put out of action for a period. Perhaps the greatest effect of U 47's success, though, was on the status of the U-boat arm within the Navy and within Germany. Hitler was 'beside himself with joy'[25] when the British Admiralty announcement of the loss of the battleship was intercepted; he had been briefed on the attempt by Raeder and he boasted to anyone who had occasion to see him at the Chancellery that day that the sinking was the work of a U-boat. Dönitz, who had been promoted Rear Admiral on October 1st, was advanced from *Führer*- to *Befehlshaber* (C-in-C)-*der U-boote* (BdU).

By the time U 47 returned, Prien and his men were heroes throughout Germany. Raeder and Dönitz were waiting to greet them on the quay, thronged with cheering crowds as a band played them in; when they had made fast, both Admirals went aboard and Raeder personally presented each member of the crew with the Iron Cross. Afterwards they were flown by aircraft of Hitler's flight to Berlin, and driven through streets lined with hysterical crowds to the Kaiserhof Hotel as the Führer's guests; from here they attempted to march through scenes of even wilder emotion across the Wilhelmplatz to the Reich Chancellery, but had to be rescued by the police. When they eventually arrived rather late Hitler shook hands with each of them, then after making a homely speech about his own time in the trenches, conferred on Prien the Knight's Cross. Later, after lunching at the Chancellery, they were paraded before a Press conference; one of the correspondents, William Shirer, noted Prien as 'clean-cut, cocky, a fanatical Nazi and obviously capable'.[26]

Prior to all this and further junketings that evening at which Goebbels basked in the reflected glory of the U-boat men, Hitler had given Raeder permission to take the first major step in the proposed escalation of the U-boat war on trade; any ship definitely recognized as enemy could be torpedoed without warning, and passenger ships in a convoy could be attacked after an announcement to that effect had been promulgated.

This was not as far as Raeder and his operations staff wished to go; 'certainly not only the enemy, but in general *every* merchant ship employed in supplying the enemy war economy with imports as well as exports' was their target.[27] This was a natural goal, but the chief interest of the brief which Raeder used for his meeting with Hitler lies in the attached draft of an announcement composed by his staff for the Führer to give out in order to justify the total campaign they required. This was composed by Heinz Assmann, number two in the operations division, and countersigned by the chief of the division, Fricke. It reveals that both these men were not simply convinced Nazis but exponents of the very essence of the system of lies and self-delusion on which it was founded. Goebbels could not have improved on the words they wished to put into Hitler's mouth:

My proposal for a just and secure peace such as is desired by all peoples has been turned down.

The determination of the enemy forces us to continue a war of whose absurdity every reasonable statesman responsible for the welfare of his people must be clear. The blood guilt for this crime is carried before the world and before history by the instigators of the war in power in England and France.

Our mortal enemy is England. Her goal is the destruction of the German *Reich* and the German people. Her method is not open war, but the mean and brutal starving out, yes extermination [*Ausrottung*] of the weak and defenceless not only in Germany, but in the whole of Europe. History proves it.

The head of the British government remained true to this historic attitude when on September 26th, before the lower House, he declared that the present siege of Germany by England by means of a naval blockade was no different from a siege by land, and it had never been the custom to permit the besieged free rations.

We Germans will neither allow ourselves to starve, nor will we capitulate . . .

203

The German government will use all measures to cut off every supply to Great Britain and France as, in the words of the British Prime Minister, is the custom in every siege.

Every ship without respect of flag in the battle area around England and France exposes itself from now on to the full dangers of war. The German government will maintain these war measures until there is a sure guarantee that England is prepared to live in peaceful and ordered co-operation with all the peoples of Europe.[28]

From a staff machine whose goals were to swallow up Nórway, Denmark, Holland, Belgium and the north coast of France to Biscay in order to defeat an enemy perceived as the chief obstacle to Germany swallowing up all the small nations of Eastern and South-Eastern Europe, this is a little ironic. The question of whether the staff actually believed it belongs not here but to a study of group psychology within secret societies. It is important here for the light it throws on the particularly dangerous secret society to which Dönitz belonged. These men were in the grip of fantasy; at the simplest level they hadn't the means to effect the siege of England and France, yet they were prepared to go off half-cock and alert their enemies.

The script is also interesting in psychological terms for its stress on England's 'base and unworthy' way of fighting—the First War 'hunger blockade' which had bitten deep into the German naval mind—and the concept of genocide, or *Ausrottung*, of the 'weak and defenceless' peoples of Europe. In the looking-glass world the naval staff inhabited, they ascribed to their enemies their own deepest convictions—as will appear. So, incidentally, did British and American naval officers, who swallowed the post-war myth of the decency of the German Navy. At all events the draft speech composed by Raeder's staff is one of the key documents for understanding Dönitz's mind and actions after he took power later in the war. As with Hitler, he was not different from those he led, rather he exemplified their convictions to an unusual degree and with unusual force of will.

Hitler, elated after his astoundingly quick victory over Poland, was nevertheless still constrained by considerations of neutral opinion and the German economy. Neither the totally unrestricted campaign for which Raeder was pressing, nor the absolute priority in materials which he needed for a massive U-boat construction programme, could be granted—the one because of the President of the United States—'the

Jew-loving Roosevelt'—who would have liked nothing better than to mobilize American opinion against Nazi Germany in the wake of another *Lusitania*—the other because of the Army's urgent needs for 'Case Yellow', the armoured assault on France.

Dönitz's standing orders to his U-boats at this time show the precise extent to which the United States was treated as a special case. Inside the area around England US ships were to be treated like any other neutral; outside the area though:

> While [US] ships and cargo must be treated in exactly the same way as all other neutrals, the crews and passengers must be shown greater consideration . . . US ships of all kinds . . . can be destroyed under Article 73 of the Prize Ordinance . . . Crew and passengers, however, are to be brought to safety before the destruction in exact observation of Article 74.
>
> The USA hate-propaganda should be given no occasion for the kindling of new sources of hate.[29]

Raeder continued to press his case for a completely unrestricted U-boat campaign doggedly at every audience through October and November. He seemed unperturbed by Hitler's failure to limit the war and as unconcerned for the strains on the German economy—visible as they were to every man in the street—as he had been when proposing the Z-Plan, unaware too it seems of the dangerous situation being created in the east as Russia advanced into the spheres of interest agreed in the Nazi-Soviet pact; looking at military and continental affairs from his world-oceanic eyrie, unchecked by any top-level cabinet or Chiefs of Staff committee, blindly following his Führer's star, he shut his eyes to the military, political and moral vortex into which the Fatherland was being sucked.

'No one expects anything of Raeder,' Ulrich von Hassell noted in his diary at this time. Hassell was one of those intelligent and sensitive Germans wracked by his nation's dilemma: the war could not be won militarily, the economic situation was critical, he was ashamed of being led by 'criminal adventurers' and revolted by 'the disgrace that has sullied the German name through the conduct of war in Poland, partly through the brutal use of air power, partly through the shocking bestialities of the SS, above all against Jews.' His diary entry continued:

The situation of the majority of clear-headed and reasonably well-informed people today while Germany is in the midst of a great war is truly tragic. They cannot wish for victory, even less for a severe defeat. They fear a long war and they see no feasible way out . . .[30]

Through October and November German propaganda, while concentrating on proving that the British arming of merchantmen, orders to merchantmen to ram U-boats, and radio signalling when attacked made them an arm of the Royal Navy, also carried the inference that it was suicidally dangerous for ships of any nationality to enter British waters; on November 24th the message was spelled out in an official warning to all neutral nations that 'in waters around the British Isles and in the vicinity of the French coast, the safety of neutral ships can no longer be taken for granted . . .'[31]

In fact neutrals had already been sunk without warning; 'unrestricted U-boat warfare' was already being waged *unannounced* as recommended in the naval staff appreciation at the beginning of the war. Dönitz's standing orders make this clear; No. 154 issued some time in November or early December ends:

Rescue no one and take no one with you. Have no care for the ships' boats. Weather conditions and the proximity of land are of no account. Care only for your own boat and strive to achieve the next success as soon as possible! We must be hard in this war. The enemy started the war in order to destroy us, therefore nothing else matters.[32]

The passengers and crews of destroyed ships, the boats, the weather conditions and nearness to land, all had to be taken into account under the International Prize Rules; in detailing them specifically as of no consequence, Dönitz was making it plain to his commanders that the Prize Rules no longer applied. The orders did have a section on the extreme care necessary when conducting war under the Regulations, but this only applied now to ships outside the large area around Britain and France extending as far as 20 degrees west into the Atlantic.

These orders of Dönitz's are revealing examples of his personality and method; they are full of the terse aphorisms with which he liked to put his message across; reading them one feels something of the flavour of his special brand of wholly-committed leadership. Here is Standing Order No. 151—presumably issued some time in November:

206

a) In the first-line attack, always keep attacking; do not allow yourself to be shaken off; should the boat be forced away or under water for a time, search again in the general direction of the convoy to regain touch, advance again! Attack!

b) When sighting convoys and other valuable targets on which other boats could also operate, without detriment to your own attack, as soon as possible and before your attack, signal [convoy position and course]; between your own attacks give touch-keeping signals.

c) When touch-keeping on convoys and when attacking do not worry about fuel consumption, so long as your return passage is guaranteed.[33]

The previously quoted order 154, marking the practical end of the Prize regulations, enjoined Commanders to 'attack with stubborn will until the destructive end is really accomplished!' and went on:

There are situations in attack when one could have grounds for giving up.

These moments or feelings must be overcome.

Never give in to self-delusion: I will not attack now or I will not stick stubbornly to it now because I hope, later, somewhere else to find something else. What one has, one has! Spare no fuel on such grounds![34]

The order went on to state that in war one was always further off than one imagined, especially at night—'therefore advance!' Shooting from close range was also safer since escorts did not drop depth charges in the close proximity of ships; furthermore, if forced to go deep it was easy to escape under the ships of the convoy where again one was safe from attack. After attacking in daytime, boats should refrain from going deep: 'Do not forget that surrendering oneself to the deeps makes one blind and the boat passive. Therefore attempt for as long as possible to remain at periscope depth', and again he repeated the injunction that if forced under by the possibility of being rammed or sighted by aircraft, all efforts had to be made to regain touch by making off afterwards at highest speed in the direction of the convoy.

The always aggressive, optimistic spirit of his orders is thrown into sharper light by the difficulties he was facing. He was still desperately short of boats; by the end of October he had lost seven from unknown causes, and these had not been replaced by new boats coming into service; he noted in the war diary that this 'must lead to paralysis of U-boat warfare if no means can be devised of keeping them [losses] down'.[35] Assuming that the losses must have been caused by boats being surprised on the surface in bad weather or damaged in surface action, he issued orders forbidding gun action: 'Ships are to be sunk by torpedo only.'[36]

Equally serious was an alarming number of torpedo failures. By the 31st October a note of desperation had crept into his war diary entries on this subject:

There is no longer any doubt that the Torpedo Inspectorate themselves do not understand the matter. At present torpedoes cannot be fired with non-contact [i.e. the newly-developed magnetic firing pistols] as this has led to premature detonations . . . *At least* 30 per cent of torpedoes are duds. They do not detonate or they detonate in the wrong place . . . Commanders must be losing confidence in their torpedoes. In the end their fighting spirit must suffer . . .[37]

By mid-December, after new magnetic pistols and new setting instructions had failed, the solution to the problem was as far from sight as ever; moreover defects in the boats themselves were showing up, in his opinion because he had not been allowed to dive them deeper than 50 m in peace training—added to which dockyard repairs were taking too long. 'The dockyard periods must be shortened by rigorous organization of the work. I will not tolerate the lack of organization which causes the boats to remain days longer in the yards . . .'[38]

He took a mere four days' leave at the end of the year, coming back to the same frustrating problems of lack of boats and a quite unacceptable rate of torpedo failures.

The confidence of commanders and crews is considerably shaken . . . I will continue to exert my whole influence to maintain the attacking spirit of the U-boats in spite of all the setbacks. We must continue to fire torpedoes in order to discover the causes of the defects and remove them. However, the unreserved faith of Commanders and crews in the torpedo can only gradually be gained by lasting technical improvements.[39]

Despite the high percentage of failure, individual Commanders were turning in good results; in February U 44 returned flying victory pennants which added up to 38,266 tons of merchant shipping sunk, 'the most successful patrol so far', Dönitz noted; later U 48 came back and reported 34,950 tons sunk, bringing the Commander, Schultze's, aggregate up to 114,510 tons, the first to top the 100,000-ton mark; he was awarded the Knight's Cross. The legend of the 'ace' was back and the competition between individuals for first place amongst the aces was on.

However, because of the very few boats available, it was impossible to realize Dönitz's dream of destroying a whole convoy by mass attack, indeed the British Admiralty anti-submarine department reported:

The outstanding point in anti-submarine operations has been the success of the convoy system against direct attacks by U-boats . . . Out of 146 ships sunk during the first six months by U-boats, only seven were in convoys escorted by anti-submarine vessels . . .[40]

And the report added somewhat prematurely, 'the U-boat has a marked antipathy against attacking convoys, preferring lone neutrals and stragglers'.

One aspect of Dönitz's pre-war training that was paying handsome dividends was the surface attack by night; in February this accounted for almost 60 per cent of total sinkings. This was noted in the anti-submarine operations room: 'The German aces, Prien and Schultze, are both reputed to attack during the dark and to rest during the day. This, however, has not altogether been borne out by Admiralty reconstruction of their cruises.'[41]

British interrogation of survivors from the U-boats destroyed also gave a somewhat different picture of Dönitz's men from that painted by German propaganda at the time and since; for instance, although the great majority of the crews were still volunteers, a shortage of experienced petty officers had already caused numbers of key men to be drafted into the arm without option. And not all Commanders were heroes to their crews; the 'somewhat aggressive and sullen' captain of U 63 was 'bitterly criticized' by both his engineer and junior lieutenant for irresponsibility in his handling of the boat. The interrogating officer reported, 'The officers and crew showed on the whole the usual Nazi mentality, but it was again noted that the older POs . . . were much less rabid than the younger men.'[42]

209

On the whole, however, there was a splendid morale in the U-boat arm, and the crews generally conformed to Dönitz's description of them as close communities bound by consideration and comradeship; William Shirer, doing a broadcast to America from aboard a U-boat in Kiel at the end of December, had been greatly impressed by the 'absolute lack of Prussian caste discipline. Around our table [in the boat] the officers and men seemed to be on equal footing and to like it.'[43]

In March the war on trade lapsed as Dönitz had to withdraw most of his boats to cover a planned invasion of Norway and Denmark. The occupation of these countries had been suggested originally by Raeder to protect the vital supplies of Scandinavian iron ore without which Germany could not continue the war; in winter when the Baltic froze, the ore was shipped from the ice-free port of Narvik down through Norwegian territorial waters. Of course, base acquisition was a factor in Raeder's proposal which Dönitz supported enthusiastically; Narvik and Trondheim were both suitable for the location of U-boat bases which would shorten the long passage into the Atlantic around the north of Scotland.

In early January the Scandinavian situation became suddenly urgent as *Abwehr* agents caught wind of Anglo-French plans to occupy Norway under pretext of helping the Finns against a Russian assault; on January 16th Hitler cancelled his planned western offensive and ordered preparations for the Scandinavian invasion. Dönitz was called to a Naval War Staff conference on February 5th and instructed to provide U-boat screens for the surprise landings that were to be made at points along the Norwegian coast from the Skagerrak up to Narvik. It was an undertaking of immense risk, hazarding not only the seaborne troops, but virtually the entire German Navy to the superior British fleet. It was also an ideal opportunity for the U-boats to carry out the group operations against enemy surface forces for which Dönitz had been preparing them for the first four years of his command, for there was no question that the Royal Navy would be drawn in in force. For this purpose Dönitz formed two attack groups in addition to the groups screening the fjords where the landings were to take place; a northern group of six boats was to lie in wait north-east of the Shetlands on the British fleet's assumed route towards Narvik while a group of three smaller boats waited closer in to Scapa Flow.

Misinterpretation of intelligence on the allied side resulted in the landings on April 8th and 9th succeeding virtually unopposed. But by an extraordinary coincidence a British plan to mine the Norwegian inshore route along which the ore passed, then to occupy the key ports of Stavanger, Trondheim, Bergen and Narvik if necessary, to pre-empt German retaliation, had been planned for exactly the same date; thus British troops and transports were already prepared and British landings at Narvik and elsewhere followed soon after the German landings. These, together with the British naval counter-attacks on the German forces, should have provided ideal conditions for the U-boats, but bad weather, the chances of war—in this case the discovery by British naval intelligence of a chart of the U-boat dispositions—and an increasing number of torpedo failures robbed them of success.

Dönitz's angry frustration poured out into the war diary:

19.4. All operational and tactical questions are again and again coloured by the intolerable state of the torpedo arm . . . In practice the boats are unarmed . . . Of 22 shots fired in the last few days at least nine have been premature detonations which have in turn caused other torpedoes fired at the same time to explode prematurely or miss . . .

It is an absurdity that BdU should have to be burdened with lengthy discussions and investigations into the causes of torpedo failures and their remedies . . .

Prien, who had already reported failures against anchored transports from close range, now reported that he had fired two torpedoes at the *Warspite* from 900 yards, which failed to detonate. Dönitz, refusing to endanger his boats any longer in these conditions, recalled them and rang Raeder in Berlin demanding satisfaction; Raeder set up a full-scale inquiry the next day. A month later Dönitz learned its findings:

. . . The facts are worse than could have been expected. I have been informed . . . that the correct functioning of the AZ [pistol] in peacetime was considered to have been proved by only *two* shots and these not even perfect. Such methods of working can only be described as criminal . . . The result is staggering . . . It is true that a splashless discharge has been developed but otherwise there is *nothing right with our torpedoes*. I do not believe that ever in the history of war have men been sent against the enemy with such useless weapons.[44]

211

It was not only the magnetic head that was at fault, but the mechanism of the impact head was so complicated that it too was prone to failure.

> I hope now for a pistol of the *simplest* type in which the striker will transfer the blow *immediately* aft and *not* as in ours . . . work from aft *forward* . . . I have therefore demanded that the English pistol be copied as quickly as possible . . . we will then abandon magnetic firing which in any case is becoming mythical with the enemy's increasing use of magnetic [degaussing] gear . . .

So the first nine months of the U-boat war ended in something like despair.

Early in the morning of May 10th Hitler started his assault on France with a *Luftwaffe* strike destroying over 300 planes on the ground; German armoured columns, skirting the heavily fortified Maginot line, rolled through Luxembourg and the Ardennes into Piccardy, and through southern Holland into Belgium; dive bombers and artillery softened resistance along the narrow spearheads of advance; the tanks swathed deep across the flat country, scarcely halting till they reached the sea, severing allied units and all supplies and communications. Within a fortnight the Low Countries and the Pas de Calais had been overrun, the British Expeditionary Force trapped between in a pocket around Dunkirk; momentary indecision, a too-confident belief in the power of the *Luftwaffe*, allowed the British to extemporize escape on their own element, the sea, then the *Panzers* regrouped and burst south and west across the Marne and the Seine. The lightning speed and apparently irresistible force of the assault ruptured French morale, long undermined by the same kind of political tensions that had wracked Germany before National Socialism.

As the *Panzers* closed around Paris, Mussolini threw in his lot with Hitler; a week afterwards the French government asked for an armistice, and on June 22nd it was signed in the railway carriage used for the signing of the German surrender after the First World War in the same spot in the clearing in the forest of Compiègne. Hitler's face at this moment of triumph was a study in scornful hate and exultation. By the monument there recording the downfall in 1918 of the 'criminal pride of the German Empire' he stood with hands on hips and legs wide apart, the picture of arrogance and contempt;[45] afterwards the monument was razed.

A similar euphoria was evident in the naval staff in Berlin. Even before the armistice was signed they were indulging the most extravagant fantasies of a world empire ruled by a vast Teutonic fleet. Fricke, supposedly chief of the 'operations' department, produced a memorandum on strategy after the 'won war' as early as June 3rd! All the peoples in the German-occupied countries, Norway, Denmark, Holland, Belgium and France, should be made *politically, economically and militarily* fully dependent on Germany'; France should be so militarily and economically destroyed and her population so reduced that she could never rise again to encourage the smaller States; overseas bases should be acquired in North and South America, Asia and Australia— and in Central Africa Germany should create a great colonial empire stretching from the Atlantic coast to the Indian Ocean; island groups in the Indian Ocean should be acquired as bases. Whether all this was in addition to the *Lebensraum* in Eastern Europe, the stated aim of Nazi policy, was not mentioned in the paper.[46]

The egregious Carls, now chief of Navy Group East, looked to a North European *Bund* of the smaller States and their colonies—Fricke added in the margin, 'The German part of Switzerland must come into the *Reich*'—and the division of France into small demilitarized German protectorates; 'if the war brings us decisive preponderance over Great Britain', he envisaged partition of the British Empire, and ceding Malta to Italy, Gibraltar to Spain, making the Suez Canal an international waterway without Great Britain and France, taking all rights in the Anglo-Iranian Oil Company and acquiring oceanic island bases necessary to secure these possessions.[47]

It would be tedious to detail all the daydreams which the most senior officers of the German Navy allowed to spill out on to memoranda and at least one world map showing the greater German *Weltreich* and its tributaries in blue opposing the red areas of the Anglo-Saxon empire controlled now by the United States of America. The intent was plain; it was the old Wilhelmine dream of gaining in one bound what had taken older empires centuries to achieve. It was fantastic, and the fleet programmes soberly and painstakingly worked out to Raeder's instructions were, like Tirpitz's future projections of old, on the one hand so monstrous and on the other so grounded in current technology as to represent so much waste paper.

Yet they serve a purpose; dreamlike, they provide a glimpse into the soul of the German naval staff. There was one vision imprinted there—

world mastery. To this everything was subordinate: economic reality, truth, morality and not least imagination to perceive that what they were striving for was a chimera. A sense of the ridiculous would have saved them, but humour and hubris are unsatisfactory bedfellows. Raeder and his staff stand revealed as crude, simple and humourless as villains of a comic strip seized with a master plan to hold the world to ransom.

There were, of course, reasons for their mood of super-confidence; most of the territory Heye had argued as necessary for oceanic strategy had been occupied; a huge arc of coast from North Norway down to the Atlantic coast of France was now available, and the Brittany ports especially were ideal for the war on communications since they lay so close to the western approaches to the English Channel. The only thing yet lacking was a fleet or the armaments capacity to construct one, for Hitler was now looking at his mortal enemy, Russia, and his priorities were for the tanks and aircraft necessary to strike *east*.

There were, however, U-boats. Dönitz lost no time in making a personal survey of the Biscay harbours to pick those most suitable for his boats and decide on a base. Lorient was his first choice, and just outside at Kerneval on the north bank of the river serving the port, hard by one of the eighteenth-century stone forts which guard the river entrance, he found a splendid château which he determined to convert into a command post. Work started immediately on the provision of fuel, supply and U-boat repair facilities at the port.

Meanwhile he had recommenced the attack on merchant shipping, at first with a single boat commanded by his first staff officer, Victor Oehrn, and once Oehrn had proved the new percussion pistols with a string of sinkings, he sent out a wave of thirteen boats. He formed these into two groups, 'Prien' and 'Rösing', and directed them against convoys reported by the Radio Intelligence Service, *B-Dienst*, which had cracked British operational ciphers before the war and was able to provide up-to-date information on rendezvous positions, courses and speeds. Thus on June 12th he had been able to position Group Prien on a Halifax convoy steering east at eight knots for a rendezvous five days later with its escort for the final leg home.

In order to give the boats if possible a chance to attack the day before the rendezvous in easier conditions they have received attack dispositions through which the enemy should pass at about midday June 16th. As good visibility is expected it is anticipated that an area of a

214

total breadth of 90–100 miles north and south of the enemy's course will be watched. Behind this screen of five boats there is a further boat on the enemy's course line, so it is to be expected that two boats for certain will be able to attack on June 16th even if the convoy passes the outer boat positions . . .[48]

At the same time he had distributed Group Rösing across the likely course of an important convoy of fast passenger ships, including the *Queen Mary* with 26,000 Australian and New Zealand troops, which was steering northwards up the West African coast.

Both these determined efforts to operate concentration tactics failed since the rendezvous position for the Halifax convoy was shifted and the fast passenger ships' exact route was never known. Despite these failures, stragglers and independents were picked off, individual boats attacked other convoys sighted, and sinkings that June rose to the highest monthly total of the war, 58 ships totalling 284,113 tons, of which Prien himself claimed 66,587 tons. Over 100,000 tons more were sunk by the *Luftwaffe*; mines, surface raiders and fast torpedo boats operating in the Channel and up the east coast of England brought the total to almost 600,000 tons,[49] the figure that von Holtzendorff in the First War had estimated would bring about the collapse of Great Britain inside five months; the estimate remained valid. As in the spring of 1917, it seemed that Britain stood close to disaster.

This was clearly perceived in the White House in Washington. Roosevelt was in a similar position with regard to majority US opinion as Churchill before Munich with majority British opinion. He realized that if Hitler made himself master of Europe and the British Empire fell, the United States would be the next target; already he had compromised American neutrality by supplying war material including escort destroyers which were on their way to England; now he declared his policy to be 'all aid short of war'; he could not move too far ahead of public opinion.

The first boat to take advantage of the supply facilities at Lorient was Lemp's U 30, which put in on July 7th. Others followed in the succeeding weeks, gaining something like a fortnight's extra time in the operational area by cutting out the long passage home and out around Scotland, thereby making up for the losses which were still exceeding new boats coming into service. The British reacted by re-routing convoys away from the south-west approaches and up to the North Channel between

215

Northern Ireland and Scotland. Dönitz moved the U-boats north in response. He also organized air reconnaissance from Brest with the local *Luftwaffe* Commander, but there were few suitable aircraft available and those could not venture across enemy air space to the northern approaches—besides which all the difficulties of co-operation, particularly the navigational ones which had been suggested in the few pre-war exercises, recurred and rendered the little assistance almost valueless. U-boat sinkings fell to just over 200,000 tons, the total from all causes to under 400,000 tons.[50]

Early in August U-boat facilities at Lorient were completed, and the number of available boats was boosted by a flotilla from the Italian Navy—for whom a base was prepared at Bordeaux. These were administered by Italian officers but came under U-boat HQ for operations; as they lacked experience Dönitz started them off in less patrolled areas such as the Azores. Then on the 15th of the month the unrestricted campaign which had been going on for months was at last given official expression by the proclamation of a complete blockade of the British Isles and a warning to neutrals that any vessel in the zone ran the risk of destruction.

Meanwhile the Propaganda Ministry had discovered another hero in *Kapitänleutnant* Otto Kretschmer, Commander of U 99; he had sailed into Lorient the previous week flying seven victory pennants representing 65,137 tons, the largest haul so far from a single cruise; in fact British Admiralty records credited him with under 40,000 tons—the discrepancy due in part to the fact that three of his victims were tankers in ballast and did not sink. Raeder flew to Brittany to confer on him the Knight's Cross.

Although Kretschmer claimed four victims from a convoy which he had followed westward until the escorts had left to rendezvous with inward bound ships, the problem of finding convoys remained the major difficulty of U-boat operations with such a small number of boats. Here is Dönitz's war diary entry for August 20th:

U-boats are being badly hampered off the North Channel by bad visibility and strong air patrols. The dispositions are being altered to give the boats a better chance of evading enemy surface- and air-craft. Formerly the boats were disposed in a north-south line so that as many as possible would cut the east-west steamer route. Now, however, the strong patrols force us to east-west lines with allocation of central points for boats. Thus they will have the chance of moving away from the coast with its naturally stronger patrols. The angle between the operational line of U-boats and the steamer track will be less favourable but this will have to be accepted for the sake of greater freedom of action for the boats . . .

Raeder was busy at this time with rushed and extraordinarily amateur preparations for an invasion of England code-named 'Sea Lion'; as the chief of Hitler's operations staff, General Jodl, said scornfully to his interrogating officer after the war, these 'were equivalent to those made by Julius Caesar'.[51] Whether Hitler ever took the preparations seriously is doubtful; according to his naval adjutant, von Puttkamer, he was half-hearted from the start, largely because of his constitutional horror of the sea, over which the operation had to be conducted.[52] Besides this was the question of Russia; both his crusade against Bolshevism and very natural fears for his chief sources of oil supply from the fields around the Black Sea diverted the major share of his attention east. Raeder knew this as well as anyone. At the end of July he had his operations staff draw up a memorandum on the question, and this paved the way to his acknowledgement that the question of oil supply was decisive, hence to his agreement to settle the question of England *via Moscow*.[53]

Despite this, and despite the total disruption of his building programme, Raeder loyally carried out Hitler's instructions to prepare for 'Sea Lion'. Part of the overall plan was for the U-boats to provide a screen to prevent Royal Naval forces entering the invasion crossing area, and to facilitate control Dönitz moved his headquarters to Paris; his was probably the only branch of the armed services and officialdom which had not set up shop there long since.

The stores of the French capital glittered like an Aladdin's cave after Germany with its shortages and rationing, and since the exchange rate for the occupation forces was fixed at the very favourable rate of 20 Francs to the *Reichsmark*, three Francs over the rate quoted on the Berlin Exchange, they could buy a surfeit of luxuries not seen in the *Reich* for many years and send them to their families. No doubt Dönitz took the opportunity; Ingeborg remained at home when he moved.

The block he took over for his staff quarters and operating centre was on the Boulevard Suchet, whose windows commanded a view of the Bois de Boulogne, a far cry from the timber hut overlooking the meadows outside Wilhelmshaven. Albert Speer, who visited him at another Paris headquarters he took over later in the war, described the refreshing lack of ostentation he found there compared with the extravagant style assumed by many of the conquerors; nevertheless it seems that Dönitz was not above corruption: thus one U-boat rating captured by the British in 1941 told his interrogator that Dönitz commandeered a hotel in Paris and requisitioned everything including 100,000 bottles of champagne, which were sold to his officers at about 1/6d a bottle and to non-U-boat personnel at 6/- a bottle. There were also unofficial sales to ratings, one of whom told his interrogator that he had celebrated his engagement by buying 20 bottles of champagne and sending them to his family, together with 40 pairs of silk stockings.[54]

Perhaps it was at this time that Dönitz conceived the idea of putting together a collection of sea paintings by old masters; certainly he acquired a collection during his time in France, as well as adding to his collection of carpets and engravings.

However Dönitz may have exploited the beaten enemy or turned a benevolent eye on his officers, particularly his commissariat officers, who did so, his self-discipline, attention to work and will to achieve re-sounding success with the U-boat arm remained unimpaired.

Every morning he rose early and stepped into his operations room promptly at 9 o'clock, where the staff under Godt waited for him before a large wall chart of the Atlantic operations area. The chart was brought up to date at 8 o'clock every morning; pins with coloured flags marked the positions of all U-boats; different-coloured flags marked the Italian boats, and the convoys were marked in another colour. After studying the positions for a moment, he would hear a report on the night's events, signals received, action taken, from the first staff officer; the second staff officer, A 2, would report on minesweeping and patrols along the routes used by the U-boats for leaving and returning to port; A 3 on intelligence received, virtually a record of *B-Dienst* interceptions of British traffic, although these were becoming progressively less useful since the British had woken up to the fact that their ciphers had been cracked, and had changed them; it was still possible to decrypt most messages but it took longer, rendering much of the information out of date and useful only for clues to the general British responses and routing patterns. Apart from these there were occasional reports from *Luftwaffe* reconnaissance flights, but the positions and courses were often inaccurate. Reports from agents in neutral countries were scarcely ever specific enough to be of use—in effect the intelligence department consisted of his own boats' sighting reports and the telephone line to *B-Dienst*.

218

Two other staff officers, A 4—communications—and A 5—statistics of successes and losses and odd questions not dealt with by the others—were heard, following which Dönitz and Godt considered the dispositions to be ordered for the day. With so few boats, each with such a small area of visibility and these few driven by aircraft patrols from the focal area off the North Channel it was impossible to provide anything like a complete survey of the approaches and it was usually a matter of trying to guess what the enemy would do next. Often during the day Dönitz could be seen sitting at his desk which faced the great wall chart, his glasses on his nose, staring up at the coloured symbols, deep in thought.

The same guessing game was being played in the U-boat tracking room in the complex below the Admiralty building in London. Here all U-boat sightings from ships and aerial reconnaissance, reports of ships sunk by U-boat and bearings of U-boat wireless transmissions obtained from the direction-finding (D/F) chain were plotted and analysed, Dönitz's intentions pondered, and predictions sent to the 'Trade Plot' nearby, where the evasive routing of convoys was planned. So far results had not been good; the German 'Enigma' ciphers had not been broken, the D/F chain, starved of funds before the war, was not yet sufficiently widespread to produce good 'fixes', the inter-war neglect of aerial reconnaissance training over the sea—like a similar neglect to develop effective weapons to destroy submarines from the air, or even a suitable aircraft for the purpose—was having the same effect that Dönitz was experiencing with *Luftwaffe* co-operation.[55]

Of the mistakes on both sides, British complacency since the development of Asdic, neglect of merchant shipping protection and inter-service in-fighting like that which bedevilled Hitler's High Command, was the more serious. It was proved that autumn as the U-boats suddenly got in amongst the convoys and Dönitz's training in group tactics brought its first rewards. The surprise he had hoped for was complete; for the U-boat men it was 'the happy time'; a growing list of aces vied with one another for highest place in the 'tonnage war', chief amongst them Kretschmer, 'the tonnage king' in U 99, Prien 'the bull of Scapa' in U 47 and their crew comrade Schepke in U 100.

20.9. U 47 made contact with an inward convoy . . . All boats sufficiently close . . . ordered to attack dispositions on the enemy course to operate in accordance with shadowing reports from U 47.

21.9 The first boat to contact the convoy, U48, sank two steamers and took over as shadower. During the day U 99 and U 100 attacked the convoy with success, U 65 without success.

22.9. In the morning U 100 was driven off by destroyers which had reached the convoy in the meantime. Because of accurate shadowing reports this inward convoy was attacked altogether by five boats which were originally up to 350 miles away from the point of first sighting. Thirteen ships were sunk. This success was achieved through 1) early interception of the convoy far to the west while the escort was still weak; 2) correct tactical behaviour of boats as shadowers and in disposition over a wide area; 3) fair weather . . .

The actions of the last few days have shown that the principles established in peacetime for using radio *in contact with the enemy* and training the U-boat arm to attack convoys were correct.[56]

A month later there was a far more shattering demonstration of 'wolf pack' tactics: on the night of October 16/17th, U 48 sighted a homeward bound convoy in the Atlantic, reported, then attacked, sinking two ships before being forced under by two of the escorts and losing touch. The following day U 38 sighted the convoy, reported, shadowed and attacked by night, sinking one and missing another ship before she too was forced deep. In the meantime Dönitz had ordered U 46, U 100, U 101, U 123 and U 99 to form a patrol line off the Rockall Bank in the probable track of the convoy, and it ran straight into this group on the evening of the 19th. It was bright moonlight—full moon had been on the 15th—and the ships were clearly visible as they steamed in eight columns with only two escorts ahead; the attacks started at 9 o'clock and reached a crescendo about midnight with the convoy beset from both sides, lit by flames from torpedoed ships and star shells thrown up continuously by the outnumbered and vainly circling escorts.

Kretschmer, who had worked into position ahead, then dropped back inside the escorts to attack the starboard line from close range, was actually inside the columns of merchant ships at one stage, whether by design or due to an emergency turn towards him is not clear; he was chased out by a freighter which turned to ram, but he returned an hour later and continued attacking repeatedly on the surface until 1.30 the following morning, finally loosing his last torpedo on a straggler just before 4.00; this was his seventh victim and he estimated their total tonnage as 45,000.

Of course it was impossible to check ships' names in the confusion of a night battle, and the actual total was six ships—since one did not sink and was finished off later by U 123—of altogether 28,000 tons.[57] Since the tendency was always to overestimate Dönitz received rather an exaggerated view of the success—great as it undoubtedly was. By chance on the following night another convoy was attacked by Prien and three other boats, Prien causing havoc from close range and claiming eight ships. Dönitz exulted: 'By joint attack therefore over three days seven U-boats with 300 men have sunk 47 ships totalling about 310,000 tons, a tremendous success.'[58]

The actual figures were 32 ships totalling 154,661 tons sunk by eleven boats; nevertheless it was a devastating blow, particularly since no boats had been lost in the entire four days' operation; Dönitz's conclusions must have appeared justified at the time:

1) The operations prove that the development of U-boat tactics since 1935, and the training based on the principle of countering the concentration of ships in a convoy by a concentration of U-boats attacking, was correct . . . 2) Such operations are only possible with Commanders and crews thoroughly trained for them . . . 3) Such operations can only be carried out if there are enough U-boats in the operations area. So far in the war this has only been the case from time to time. 4) The more U-boats there are in the operations area, the more frequently such operations will be possible . . . 5) Further, if there were more U-boats the English supply routes would not be left free after such attacks because, as today, nearly all boats have to return after using all their torpedoes. 6) Successes such as this cannot always be expected. Fog, bad weather and other conditions could nullify prospects from time to time. The main thing will always be the ability of the Commander.[59]

The successes of the autumn, which were focused largely into periods immediately after the hunter's moon, were partly due to the surprise achieved by a concentration of boats attacking and escaping on the surface where Asdic could not detect them and where they could outrun the slower escorts, partly to a shortage of escorts and aircraft and generally inadequate training; for instance, the escorts of Kretschmer's convoy had never worked together previously. Surprise was a diminishing asset, however, and it was inevitable that the devastating results would concentrate minds at the British Admiralty. They did. Moreover, it is apparent from the reports of the anti-submarine division that the problem was well understood and the remedies were to hand and only needed development. The October report for instance:

> Great efforts are being made to equip all convoy escorts with apparatus that will enable them to locate a U-boat on the surface at night outside visibility distance . . . This new equipment has also been fitted into the aircraft of coastal command and fleet aircraft. It will detect U-boats on the surface at a range of five miles and will be especially valuable for detecting U-boats on the surface at night . . .[60]

This was a primitive radar apparatus; teething troubles were being experienced by the first escorts fitted with it, but 'no effort is being spared to clear up these difficulties and it is hoped that ASV will soon become effective and its use by our ships universal.'[61] Of equal importance in the tactical field—what Dönitz might have called meeting the concentration of U-boats by a concentration of escorts—was training escort Commanders in team work. 'This it is hoped is being achieved by forming ships into groups, each under its own leader, each working as a team and sharing a common training.'[62]

The importance of aircraft in 'keeping down submarines who may be shadowing outside visibility distance in daylight and in locating U-boats that may approach in darkness' was recognized. And besides ASV radar, aircraft of coastal command were now being equipped with depth charges in place of the ineffective bombs they had been using against U-boats.

There was some time to go before these material and training changes could have effect; in the meanwhile the 'happy time' continued, consciously or unconsciously exaggerated tallies were notched up by a growing list of aces awarded the Knight's Cross, while the Propaganda Department raised them to national stardom.

For Dönitz it was a time of fulfilment. He had moved from Paris to the château at Kerneval outside Lorient after 'Sea Lion' had been called off in September; from the windows of the grand salon which let in the tangy smells of the foreshore and fish jetty immediately beyond he could see the open Atlantic; past the buoyed approaches, past the grey stone fort at Port Louis on the far bank the view stretched up the broad stream to the harbour of Lorient and the quays where the U-boats lay, and where construction workers of the Todt Organization had started building the foundations for massive concrete shelters to protect them from air attack.

Today one can stand at these great windows of the salon or immediately outside where Dönitz loved to pace, and look upstream to the overwhelming, fortress-like grey concrete monument to his aspirations, now housing part of the French submarine fleet, and cast back to the autumn and winter of 1940 when the whole of Western Europe lay under the conqueror and it seemed only a matter of time before Great Britain too bowed to the new Charlemagne—and imagine the mood of confidence mixed with frustration—for there were still far too few boats to bring about the decision—and sense the pride, hearing on the breeze the songs of aggressive young Germanhood.

There is an echo in the British interrogator's report of the first of the aces to be captured, Hans Jenisch of U 32, depth-charged to the surface on October 24th:

> The prisoners were all fanatical Nazis and hated the British intensely, which had not been so evident in previous cases. They are advocates of unrestricted warfare, and are prepared to condone all aggressive violence, cruelty, breaches of treaties and other crimes as being necessary to the rise of the German race to the control of Europe.
>
> German successes during 1940 appear to have established Hitler in their minds not merely as a God but as their only God. Maintaining that Germany is at present only 'marking time' until after the consolidation of a series of political victories and corrective 'adjustments' in the Balkans and elsewhere, they think at any moment deemed suitable a German attack on Great Britain would be overwhelmingly successful and profess to be amazed at the British failure to see the inevitability of our utter defeat at any moment convenient to Hitler.[63]

Nevertheless the strain of the Atlantic war was already telling. Dönitz's insistence on the quickest possible turn-round in port was the cause of some resentment, and the officers admitted that their nerves were being affected by continuous cruising. Moreover losses of boats, although by no means great, were already causing shortages of personnel; officers were being drafted from the surface fleet for short training courses, sent on one or two cruises under an experienced Commander, then given their own boat to command; ratings were being sent on shortened

223

promotion courses to fill gaps amongst the petty officers, while among the junior ratings of U 32 there were 'scarcely any who have volunteered for this branch of the service';[64] most were 'inexperienced youths with little or no training who had been drafted without option'.

Expecting the utmost from his officers and men at sea, Dönitz did his utmost for them on their return. A special train known as the *BdU Zug* expressed those going on leave to Germany via Nantes, Le Mans, Paris, Rotterdam to Bremen and Hamburg; those not going on leave went to rest camps known as 'U-boat pastures' to recreate; these were sited at holiday resorts like La Baule, well away from the bombing and war. Since all hands had U-boat allowances almost doubling their service pay, they could send home French luxury foods, wines and clothes sold to them at reduced prices in special shops for their use *and* paint the town red—as they did. Luxury hotels were requisitioned for the officers who relieved the enormous strains of their under-sea life with similar excess.

More important than material benefits or the adulation these men received constantly in the national media was the personal inspiration they had from Dönitz. He made a point of attending the passing-out parade of every training course and inspecting officers and men, looking each in the eye with his own 'clear, shining eyes'.[65] No one in the arm had not seen his commanding officer at close range, many had exchanged words; he had an extraordinarily retentive memory and he made it his business to remember what they told him; important family news such as births he wirelessed to the boats at sea. And he made it a point personally to attend as many departures and arrivals as his unremitting schedule allowed.

'*Heil* U 38!'

'*Heil, Herr Admiral!*' in unison from the bearded men lined in stained clothes on the deck, weeping rust.

Each felt his eyes as he walked down the rank with his extraordinarily upright bearing. He turned to address them: 'Men, your boat has sunk 100,000 tons in only three cruises. The credit for this excellent performance is due chiefly to your gallant Commander. *Kapitänleutnant* Liebe, the Führer has conferred on you the Knight's Cross, and it is my pleasure to hand it to you.'[66]

He was equally adept at the unexpected word or act of momentary inspiration. At one homecoming of a boat that had been out on many cruises later in the war, he stopped opposite one non-commissioned

Chief Engineer to ask him how many actions he had been in in the Atlantic. 'Ten or twelve' was the reply.

Dönitz tapped him on the shoulder, '*Ich schlage dich zum Ritter!*' ('I dub you a knight').[67]

This sort of behaviour would have been unthinkable for admirals of the old school like Raeder, as would his use of the familiar '*dich*'. Although reserved by nature, his burning commitment to the service and personal interest in everyone who belonged to it communicated itself to officers and men alike. They knew he would not tolerate anything but the best they could give, but they gave it from admiration—his staff officers say love—not from fear. That came later. He was known as '*Onkel Karl*' or '*Der Löwe*' (The Lion). Undoubtedly he possessed leadership charisma.

Leadership is, of course, a two-way process. These were young men, indoctrinated by Nazi propaganda, many of whom in old age are unable to admit any fault in their former BdU or in the cause for which they were prepared to give their lives. Reading the interrogation report on Jenisch's band of 'fanatical Nazis' who 'hated the British intensely' one is left wondering how much this was a reflection of the mood in Germany after the astounding successes of 1940, how much a reflection of Dönitz's own extreme attitudes and style of leadership. There can be little doubt it came from both; nevertheless these were young men with the ardour and idealism of youth, stunted by Nazi education, and the question must be posed, how much did *they* demand of him? How much was it their recognition of the iron leader for whom they had been prepared since their schooldays, how much his conscious or unconscious response to their idealism in his striving for high morale?

At all events there can be no doubt that the morale of the arm and the sense of belonging to an élite corps which had been his aim from the beginning reached full flowering in late 1940 and spring 1941. The British interrogator of the crew of U 70, rammed and sunk by a Dutch tanker in a convoy battle in February 1941, noted: 'The morale of both officers and men was high, there was no sign of war weariness and the usual undigested propaganda was repeated *verbatim ad nauseam*.'[68]

The following month U 100 was also rammed on the surface, her ace Commander, Schepke, killed as he stood on the bridge; his surviving crew 'showed high morale despite their shattering experiences (under depth-charge attack) and a common, unshakeable confidence in a German decisive victory this year'.[69] In the same action the top-scoring

225

ace, Otto Kretschmer, was forced to the surface and captured with his crew. The interrogating officer was impressed by their morale, teamwork and proficiency; his only criticism was of their

> . . . exaggerated idea of their importance and dignity; these inflated opinions were no doubt due to the extraordinary degree of public adulation to which they had become accustomed. Special aeroplanes and bouquets of flowers at railway stations had long since become part of their daily lives when ashore.[70]

Kretschmer himself was a more thoughtful character than some of his swaggering rivals, and better educated. He admitted to his interrogator that he had become weary of the war some time ago and latterly got no satisfaction from sinking ship after ship, and 'his political views were less extreme Nazi than had been assumed'. Equally interesting to the interrogator was his first officer, formerly Dönitz's Flag Lieutenant, Hans-Jochen von Knebel Döberitz, from a Junker family in East Pomerania. 'On the surface he seemed a very thorough Nazi, but actually he was rather ashamed of many of the Nazi methods and most of their leading personalities. He maintained a façade of loyalty towards the regime whereas in reality he was only loyal to his class and country . . .' The two midshipmen, who had entered the service in 1939, were both 'typical Nazis, immovably certain of a supreme German victory in 1941, and repeated the usual propaganda when discussing any subject'.[71]

That same month of March 1941 three other boats including Prien's U 47 also failed to report and were assumed lost—although it was not until April 26th that the three stars denoting a loss were placed against U 47 and Prien's death was admitted to the nation. He was probably Dönitz's favourite Commander, Kretschmer was another, and the loss of three top aces in the same month was a bitter blow; it is said that Dönitz's reserve and aloofness at this time betrayed to those close to him the depth of his feelings.

By early summer the *hubris* of the previous year was beginning to fade.

After the morning's work and lunch with his staff, Dönitz liked to take an hour's sleep. Then, accompanied by his adjutant and one or two staff officers he had invited, and with his young Alsatian dog acquired at the beginning of the war—named Wolf—he was driven in his Mercedes out into the countryside, where he walked for two hours or more. Striding out across the Breton fields—for it was still safe for German officers to do so—stopping sometimes to exchange a few words with locals, he tried to clarify his ideas by talking them out and drawing arguments from his staff. They knew he wanted their real opinions and responded openly; the exchanges became keen at times and astonishingly frank. He could sink into an evil mood when things were going badly or frustration and tension drew him taut, but on average days he liked nothing better than vigorous opinions and honest debate seasoned by chaff. The staff of a *Luftwaffe* general invited to lunch one day were astonished at the free style of the U-boat men with their chief, and the riposte and banter which bounced back and forth across the table.

Viktor Oehrn, who was with Dönitz either as staff officer or U-boat Commander throughout the war, recalls:

> Dönitz very seldom 'ordered'. He convinced, and because all that he wanted was very precisely considered, he really convinced. He sought discussion with everyone who had an opinion without regard to rank. Anyone who had no opinion, he soon left aside. He provoked his discussion-partners in order to learn the contrary arguments. *Then* he decided.[72]

Arriving back at the Kerneval Château, known on account of its small size for the function it performed as the 'Sardine tin', he would discuss new developments with the duty officer before the Atlantic chart, perhaps debating fresh dispositions with his chief of staff. Dinner, again with his staff, was at eight; the U-boat men lived on the best the French countryside and coastline provided, and Dönitz, although as disciplined in his eating and drinking as in every other aspect of his life—astonishingly as an Admiral he could still get into his midshipman's uniform—was no exception; he drank a glass or two of a good Bordeaux every day, never too much. Promptly at ten he retired to bed; even if he was entertaining guests he would rise and bid them a good night, '*Amüsiert Euch noch gut—ich gehe jetzt schlafen.*' ('Carry on enjoying yourselves—I'm off to bed.')[73]

There were exceptions to the full night's sleep he tried to obtain if an important convoy battle were taking place; then he and all the staff would be roused by the duty officer and would appear in the operations room in pyjamas and bath robes. The other exceptions were air raids; at the sound of the alarm everyone would go down to the sleeping quarters in a great concrete command bunker which the Todt Organization had sunk into the garden at the back of the Château. The bunker is still there, the walls of the operation room now bare and damp; open entrances without doors lead through white tiled shower and lavatory cubicles, their fittings torn away, and accommodation stripped of its original timber panelling and strewn with debris to the telephone exchange at the rear, where large copper terminals on the switchboard survive in testimony to the pre-electronic age in which this war was fought. Outside the front entrance to the bunker stand two magnificent magnolia grandiflora planted then. They are large now.

Dönitz kept as close as possible to the realities of the front in searching debriefing sessions with each Commander the day after the boat's return. He and his staff would listen in silence as the man gave his report, interjecting only if he wanted an explanation of a point, or if he thought something was being deliberately withheld; his skill in probing behind the stated facts was legendary, and for the less resolute the debriefing, which concluded with intensive questioning by Dönitz and Godt and perhaps other staff officers present, could be almost as much of an ordeal as the cruise itself; a few found wanting were transferred to other branches of the service, those who had made a successful cruise came out elated by their chief's satisfaction with their prowess.

However, he could not interview those who had the most valuable information about enemy tactics and counter-measures—those who did not come back; these simply failed to wireless in their position; the way in which they had met their end and the reasons could only be guessed from their last report and enemy announcements. As the losses continued, uncertainty gave rise to speculation about secret enemy detection devices, improved Asdic, a new and accurate system of dropping depth charges, fatal to any U-boat pinpointed by Asdic.[74]

Speculation about new detection devices was fed by the extraordinary way in which British convoys evaded U-boat patrol lines. This was remarked as early as April 1941: 'the impression is being gained that English traffic is deliberately routed around attacking groups'. Security precautions were taken in case the positions were being given away to the enemy by spies, the circle of those with access to operational details was cut to the minimum, the daily position report to other interested commands stopped. Still, as the boats were forced further and further west across the Atlantic by increasing numbers and effectiveness of British escorts and air patrols, the convoys evaded them. All the

228

sightings which led to battles were made fortuitously by lone boats, not by the deliberately positioned patrol lines of closely-spaced boats across their supposed tracks. By November it was clear this was no coincidence:

Coincidence alone it cannot be—coincidence cannot always work on one side and experiences extend over almost nine months. A likely explanation would be that the British from some source or other gain knowledge of our concentrated dispositions and avoid them, thereby running across only boats proceeding singly.[75]

The three ways they could get this information were by spies—everything had been done to exclude this possibility—or by deciphering radio messages—the experts in crypt-analysis at High Command considered this out of the question—or by 'a combination of U-boat radio traffic and reports of sightings'. Dönitz considered it impossible to investigate the third contingency because 'it is not known what information can be gained by the enemy from sighting reports and radio traffic (particularly the accuracy of D/F bearings).'[76] This problem had been a staple for discussions with his staff for months, yet no satisfactory answers had been found. On November 19th, he decided that 'perhaps closer co-operation with *B-Dienst* may help', and requested an experienced officer from the Radio Intelligence Service to join his staff to investigate the problem of how the enemy routed his convoys.

Here we are at the nub of the extraordinary amateurishness of the German war effort: Dönitz was conducting a campaign of vital importance, which would help to determine—if not as in his own view actually *decide*—whether the overwhelming naval power of the British Empire was to strangle or be strangled by the *Reich*—literally the most important question facing Germany; yet he was attempting to do so with a staff of half a dozen young U-boat men! They had not been trained to think scientifically, indeed their education had in most cases been seriously undermined by the Nazi control of schools. But if they had been natural geniuses their routine tasks and their demanding schedule at U-boat headquarters would have precluded serious analysis of the problems of this hide-and-seek war; thrashing them out in forays across the Breton fields was no substitute for thorough scientific analysis and proper organization of intelligence. Like Hitler's attempt to create an uneducated slave labour force of Poles and Slavs for the (to be conquered)

229

German East, it was an anachronism, an eighteenth-century way of war in a twentieth-century age of technology.

Dönitz was no more to blame for this than he had been in the torpedo fiasco, or in the continuing fiasco of *Luftwaffe* non co-operation. From the amateurishness at the head of the nation, chaos and corruption separated every organ of government and the armed services. It may be thought that it had taken the U-boat staff rather a long time to realize that patrol lines were not finding convoys, and for Dönitz to realize that it might 'perhaps help' to inject some expert analysis into the problem, yet that should not have been his job any more than it had been his job to find out what was wrong with the torpedoes. It was the system of command and analysis and co-ordination that had failed from the top as it had in Tirpitz's day. Dönitz was left fighting his war by his fingertips with little scientific assistance.

A glance at the British organization he was facing by this time indicates the scale of the German failure. At the top was the Battle of the Atlantic Committee, chaired by Churchill himself and consisting of the War Cabinet, the chiefs of the naval and air staffs and scientific advisers; the committee normally met once a week to consider overall progress in the campaign, and obviously from its composition had the power to allocate resources.[77] The day-to-day control of anti-submarine forces was concentrated chiefly in the Commander-in-Chief Western Approaches with his headquarters in Liverpool; here a 'Trade Plot' covering one huge wall of his operations room duplicated the trade plot in the Operational Intelligence Control which had moved from the underground complex below the Admiralty to a nearby 'Citadel'; this master plot was associated with the submarine tracking room, which was fed information from the nearby D/F plotting room and from aircraft and shipping at sea, and from the secret Code and Cipher School at Bletchley Park in Buckinghamshire.

In the early days the German Enigma machine ciphers had defeated Bletchley Park, but on May 8, 1941 an Enigma machine complete with the daily setting instructions and other secret material was captured from U 110 after she had been depth-charged to the surface by the combined attack of one of the new escort groups. It is interesting that this boat was commanded by Julius Lemp, who had sunk the *Athenia*; he was lost, but according to the British interrogation report, he was much respected and liked by his crew. Despite this, U 110 did not conform to Dönitz's ideal; the first lieutenant, 'narrow-minded, callous, brutal and a bully

230

as well as intolerant of any criticism of the [Nazi] regime which he ardently supported' was 'detested by the crew', and the junior lieutenant was apparently incompetent. Although nearly all the petty officers were experienced men, 'many of the ratings were raw and ill-trained and had been drafted into U-boats without option'. The interrogator concluded, 'It would seem there is real difficulty in manning U-boats,' and significantly, although morale was still high, 'conviction of Germany's ultimate victory was not quite so unshakeable'.[78]

In any case, capture of U 110's cipher apparatus enabled Bletchley Park to read U-boat traffic to the end of June—when the settings expired—and thereafter they were usually able to crack new settings within 48 hours and often more quickly. The information derived from this code-breaking—known simply as 'Ultra' to keep it secret—explains Dönitz's problems in locating convoys in the latter half of 1941, although not of course the earlier group failures.[79]

Presiding over the submarine tracking room was a former barrister with a keen brain, Commander Roger Wynn, RNVR. He had a staff of six—actually inadequate to deal with the flood of information coming in from all sources, but of course equal to the entire staff of Dönitz's headquarters, who had their normal executive duties to attend to. Wynn himself wrote a weekly appreciation of the U-boat war, and attempted to peer into Dönitz's mind and forecast his future moves; as he acquired experience of his opponent he was able to do this with remarkable accuracy.

As important as this co-ordinated intelligence web feeding operational command in the Atlantic battle was the intimate co-operation now established between Western Approaches Headquarters and the several Coastal Command groups of the Air Force who covered the sea area; it was this combination of air and sea forces which was pushing the U-boats ever more westerly; by June Dönitz was grouping his boats as far west as Newfoundland.

By contrast Raeder had been unable to break through Göring's jealous control of everything that flew, and at the beginning of the year Hitler himself had taken advantage of the Reichsmarschall's absence on holiday to place a small Air Force group under BdU's operational control; there had been few aircraft and those of the wrong type, but Dönitz had had 'great hopes that this co-operation will eventually lead to success.'[80] Already those hopes were dashed: the planes lacked the

231

endurance to keep contact for long, their navigators were not sufficiently accurate and their numbers had not been increased.

To add to his difficulties in reconnaissance the Italian flotilla had proved useless. It had been apparent before the end of 1940 that he could expect little from them; by May 1941 'in spite of attempts to increase their abilities by . . . taking Italian Commanders along with operational boats and training in the Baltic' he had come to regard them as incorrigibly unsuitable for Atlantic warfare.

They see nothing, report nothing or too late, their tactical ability is effectively nil . . . The Italians will be assigned an area between 47 30 and 53 N, and 15–25 W. Here they cannot adversely affect our own operations, on the other hand if they are only sighted without achieving any successes they may contribute by diverting traffic into the area of our own boats.[81]

He thought the real reason for the failure of the Italians had more to do with national character than with the refusal of the Supamarina (Admiralty) in Rome to permit training in German methods under German officers:

. . . they [Italian personnel] are not sufficiently hard and tough for this type of warfare. Their way of thinking is too sluggish and according to rule to allow them to adapt themselves clearly and simply to the changing conditions of war. Their personal conduct is not sufficiently disciplined and in the face of the enemy not calm enough. In view of this I am forced to dispose and operate the German boats without regard to the Italian boats.[82]

To add to his frustrations with the Italian ally, Hitler, who had had to send a German Army Corps to North Africa to stiffen Italian forces there, decided in August to offer Mussolini 20 U-boats to help him in the struggle to keep open the sea lines of communication to these forces! Despite Dönitz's urgent pleas that the Atlantic 'tonnage war' was the decisive task for his boats, he was ordered to send further waves down to the Mediterranean that autumn for there was danger of Italy crumbling altogether. As delays in the U-boat building programme caused by bottlenecks in materials and labour, together with losses of boats on operations, had left him with a fleet scarcely larger than in 1939, Dönitz was forced virtually to give up the battle in the Atlantic for a while. As compensation, his boats had striking successes against the Royal Navy in the Mediterranean, sinking both the aircraft carrier, *Ark Royal*, and the battleship *Barham*.

Hitler meanwhile had launched his assault on Russia. It has been represented as a great strategic mistake—impaling himself on the two-front war that had been the Kaiser's undoing; his choices were limited though, dictated as in 1939 by the necessities of his overheated war economy. Raeder's and Dönitz's view was, of course, that every re-source had to be poured into the defeat of Great Britain; yet short of a successful jump across the Channel which neither the generals nor the naval staff thought feasible without absolute air superiority and the exclusion somehow of the Royal Navy from the invasion route, this was bound to be a long-drawn-out process. In the meantime the Soviet Union, which was growing stronger by the month, held the tap on vital war materials, particularly oil and rubber which Germany could not get through the British naval blockade. Given the nature of Bolshevism and its unchanging goal of world revolution, it is not necessary to explain Hitler's desire for getting in his blow first simply by his long-standing ideological crusade against Communism; the feeling was sound on strategic and economic grounds. For if the Navy and *Luftwaffe* proved unable to force Great Britain's surrender in comparatively short time there would be real danger from the east.

The campaign was designed as another *Blitzkrieg* by the *Luftwaffe* and *Panzer* columns, which Hitler expected to bring about the utter downfall of the Soviet system in short time; on the eve of the assault, which was cloaked with the most brilliant campaign of deception, he was boasting that they would see 'at the latest in three months such a collapse as has not yet been seen in world history'.[83] It was not to be a simple territorial victory as had been achieved in the west, but a repeat of thc Polish operation, a repeat of what the Soviets themselves had been doing in the eastern states they had walked into since the Nazi-Soviet pact—the extermination of the enemy leadership class and culture. There was no place in this for out-dated soldierly notions of chivalry, Hitler had briefed his service chiefs—including Raeder—it was a struggle in which Bolshevism was to be eradicated for all time.[84] Commissars and other Soviet officials were criminals; they were to be summarily executed, and any civilian resistance broken with the utmost severity. 'One of the sacrifices which Commanders have to make is to overcome any scruples they may have.'[85]

Following this long briefing, at which none of the officers present raised a word in protest, or even question, a staff memorandum had spelled out the illegalities necessary: political leaders (Commissars) not executed summarily were to be segregated from other prisoners and exterminated at prisoner collection points or at the latest on passage through the transit camps. One of the operations staff officers minuted the draft, 'it remains to be seen whether a *written* instruction of this kind is *necessary*'[86]—calling to mind the naval staff memorandum that permission to sink without warning ships in areas where only English units were to be expected should 'not be given in writing, but need merely be based on the unspoken approval of the naval operations staff'.[87] When one considers Carls' memorandum about 'the war against half to two thirds of the whole world' and the British interrogator's report on the prisoners from Hans Jenisch's U-boat, who were 'prepared to condone all aggressive violence, cruelty, breaches of treaties and other crimes as being necessary to the rise of the German race to the control of Europe' one is brought against the terrifying reality of a nation thinking with its blood, in the grip of a wish to destruction—with honourable but as in all such cases relatively few active exceptions—in which individuals, Himmler, Heydrich—whose special squads were to follow the army into Russia to round up and dispose of the Jewish enemy at the heart of both Bolshevism and Capitalism—were simply the visible tips of a general will to revolt against the entire system of European civilization; it is a startling insight into the genie Hitler had uncorked, and which drove him mercilessly—the desperate *Weltanschauung* of a locked-in, continental people indoctrinated for generations with the idea of an amoral world, red in tooth and claw, in which only the fittest survived and all means were permissible for the desired end, a people who had cast off reason, marching through the dark forests of their tribal imagination.

For Carls' prediction was about to come true; since Roosevelt's declaration of 'all aid short of war' to Great Britain, the United States' productive capacity had been thrown into the scales against the *Reich* and the US Navy had formed escort groups to patrol a so-called US Security Zone without precedent in international law which was extended by stages over 2,000 miles into the Atlantic from the American seaboard! In September, after a meeting between Churchill and Roosevelt, the US Navy began to take part in convoying ships of all nationalities from US ports as far as Iceland with both surface and air escorts. Hitler stressed the importance of avoiding incidents which might provoke full and open hostilities from this undeclared war, but U-boat Commanders were faced with impossible tasks of recognition when attacking convoys in the north-west, and there must have been many incidents between US escorts and U-boats, had Dönitz not had to send the majority of his force to the Mediterranean; as it was, there were several skirmishes and in one at the end of October the US destroyer, *Reuben James*, was torpedoed and sunk.

By this time German armies in the east had been halted before Moscow by the Russian winter and their own lack of preparation for meeting it—another example of the amateurishness in every separated department of Hitler's machine. The lightning war had failed against the distances and sheer manpower of Russia; the stage of easy conquest was over; now it was to be a struggle for survival against the productive capacity and manpower potential of the three leading world powers.

Dönitz was to need all the strength of character and ability which, in his 1939 book, he described as the mark of the U-boat Commander, who 'alone must decide and act and fight out the inner battle to preserve in his heart despite all difficulties the will to victory to the last'.[88] In this battle he was to be remarkably successful.

On December 7th 1941 Japanese fleet aircraft struck the US naval base at Pearl Harbor. The news came as a surprise to Hitler although he knew of their intention to strike somewhere at some time and had made up his mind to support them if they attacked the United States. Now frivolously disregarding the huge financial and productive power of America and, according to his naval adjutant, von Puttkamer, blind to the realization that this power could be projected across the Atlantic, he gained renewed confidence in a victorious outcome to the war. His generals suffered from the same land-locked hallucination; his entire headquarters staff gave themselves up to 'an ecstacy of rejoicing'; the few who saw further 'became even lonelier'.[89]

Naval officers saw no more clearly than the generals: Carls, thinking in terms of combined operations with the new Japanese ally on an oceanic scale, exulted in a coming 'new division of the possessions of the world'.[90] The chief of Navy Group South broke into verse: 'Begone coward thoughts, defeatist wavering and womanly timidity . . .'[91] The

235

naval staff war diary carried a note of pain that the 'decisive blow' had been struck by the Japanese, not the German Navy.[92]

Some of the euphoria, at least on Hitler's part, was no doubt a release of the tension that had been building up in the undeclared Atlantic war; now he could clarify the position with Roosevelt. Nevertheless, Hitler was not without rare flashes of insight, and perhaps there was another reason for this burst of manic confidence; it is possible that even as he gave orders for lifting all restrictions on attacking US ships in the 'so-called Pan-American Safety Zone',[93] and cast about for reasons for presenting a formal declaration of war against the United States which would encourage his own people, he foresaw the end.

Dönitz had no such presentiments. He welcomed the removal of the restrictions against attacking American ships which gave him opportunity to strike in the formerly closed area along the eastern seaboard:

. . . an area in which the assembly of ships at the few points of departure of Atlantic convoys is in single-ship traffic. Here, therefore, is an opportunity of getting at enemy merchant ships in conditions which elsewhere have ceased almost completely for a long time. Further, in the American coastal area, there can hardly be any question of an efficient patrol, at least a patrol used to U-boats. Attempts must be made as quickly as possible to utilize these advantages, which will disappear shortly, and to 'beat the drum' along the American coast.[94]

This extract from his war diary for December 9th, two days before Hitler's official declaration of war on the United States, reveals the extent to which British defence against U-boat pack attack on convoys had tightened. In the early years he had looked for a 'great success, for instance the destruction of a whole convoy', now he was probing for a resounding success against *single* ships in a soft spot where the defenders would be inexperienced.

True to the principles of concentration and surprise which had marked all his probes in different areas, he asked High Command to release twelve of the large Type IX boats with the range for such distant operations, intending to send them straight to the American coast with instructions not to give away their positions by attacks until all were assembled and he gave the order. In the event he was only allowed to send half the force he had asked for, but when these boats reached their areas on January 13, and he sent the code-word *Paukenschlag*, the conditions were more favourable than he could possibly have expected, and the Commanders gathered an immediate, rich harvest.

The reasons for this second 'happy time' are not creditable to the US Navy. The first US naval mission sent to study British experience and methods had arrived in London in July 1940, a second in March 1941; since then a great deal of co-operation had been necessary between the staffs in the allocation of air and sea escorts and spheres of protection as the US Navy took over responsibility for convoys in the western Atlantic. Yet on January 13th 1942, five weeks after the German declaration of war, and after warnings had been received from the British submarine tracking room based on Ultra decrypts and other indications that Dönitz's boats were heading for the US coast, nothing had been done either in training, routing or command organization to take advantage of the experience the British had gained in the hardest school over three gruelling years.

It is not realized perhaps how much the US Navy, like the German, gained expansionary wind from jealousy of the Royal Navy, shading naturally in more aggressive US naval officers into active dislike of the arrogant pretensions and imperial manner of British naval officers. Whether Admiral Ernest J. King, the US C-in-C, was actively anti-British is not for debate here, but his attitude was undoubtedly that he was not going to play second string to the Royal Navy as the US Navy had in the First World War, and as Patrick Beesley puts it in his study of British operational intelligence, neither he nor his staff had anything to learn from 'a bunch of limeys'.[95] Since US naval operational intelligence was conducted rather like Raeder's from separate command bases without centralized co-ordination and his escort Commanders and pilots were about as experienced in anti-submarine work as their British counterparts had been in 1939, this was a mistake of criminal proportions.

The results are described in Dönitz's war diary; here is his note after the return of the first *Paukenschlag* boat, U 123:

The expectation of coming across much single-ship traffic, clumsy handling of ships, few and unpractised sea and air patrols and defences was so greatly fulfilled that the conditions have to be described as almost of peacetime standards. The single disposition of boats was, therefore, correct. The Commander found such an abundance of

237

opportunities for attack in the sea area south of New York to Cape Hatteras that he could not possibly use them all. At times up to ten ships were in sight sailing with lights on peacetime courses . . .[96]

Encouraged and surprised by the slow reaction of the Americans, Dönitz sent further waves of boats to take advantage of the easy pickings along the coast and as far south as the Caribbean and Gulf of Mexico, large Type IX's and even Type VII's with additional fuel drums stowed wherever space could be found; U-tankers—'milch cows'—planned long before the war and laid down in early 1940, were sent out with them to extend their time in the operational zone.

In March sinking figures rose to over half a million tons. Dönitz was promoted full Admiral—his third advance inside two and a half years and one of the quickest sprints through the flag ranks ever achieved in the German service. The propaganda department, in need of encouraging news, made the most of the U-boat achievements, the heroic crews and their dynamic chief; an official was even granted access to one of Dönitz's debriefing sessions. A Commander back from the US coast came into the operations room with his charts under his arm, saluted, and spread the charts on Dönitz's desk while making his report.

> Every single phase of the operation is discussed. Wireless messages and times are checked. No matter how successful the Commander has been, his operations Admiral is not satisfied before he is convinced that every torpedo and every gallon of oil was employed to the best advantage. While the Commander makes his detailed report, the staff officers are jotting down the observations the Admiral is making on this or that experience . . . Then the staff officers contribute from their own experiences. Finally the Admiral places his hand on the Commander's shoulders, 'Well done. I am glad you are one of us.'[97]

Despite the splendid results, Dönitz was experiencing much the same frustrations as in the earlier 'happy time' in British waters. This was not because of overall shortage of boats, for the numbers were at last rising satisfactorily—256 in service by February 1st, seventeen more commissioned that month and only two lost, bringing the total to 271 in March, of which 111 were available for operations—but because of their dispersal on other tasks ordered by Hitler or naval High Command, particularly in the Mediterranean and off Norway. Hitler expected an allied

238

landing in Norway to establish the 'second front' in Europe demanded by the Russians, and to cut his vital iron ore supplies, and he insisted on a large naval presence in the north including U-boats. Dönitz argued strenuously that this and other diversions from the 'tonnage war' constituted a serious misuse of the U-boats' unique capabilities. He gave the argument pure expression in a war diary entry on April 15th when dealing with a question raised about whether it was not more important to sink tonnage proceeding to England and the Mediterranean or other war theatres, rather than sink indiscriminately in American waters:

The enemy powers' shipping is one large whole. It is therefore immaterial where a ship is sunk—in the end it must still be replaced by a new ship. The decisive question for the long term lies in the race between sinking and new construction. However, the centre of the enemy's new construction and armaments is in the United States while England is so to speak the picket and sally port of the enemy powers in Europe. I am therefore grasping the evil at the root if I attack supplies, especially oil, at this centre. Every ship which is sunk here counts not only as a ship sunk but at the same time damages the enemy shipbuilding and armament at its inception . . .

I am therefore of the opinion that tonnage must be taken where it can be destroyed most reasonably—for utilizing the boats—and most cheaply—for losses, because it is incomparably more important to sink than to reduce sinkings by making them in a prescribed area . . . U-boat warfare must therefore continue to be concentrated on the east coast of America as long as counter-measures and the possibilities of success remain roughly as at present.[98]

His anxiety to strike hard with all available force was fully justified. With the formal entry of the United States the real tonnage war had begun. Roosevelt had announced a new building programme for eight million tons of shipping in 1942, ten million tons in 1943. Added to British Empire and neutral shipbuilding it was a formidable total to have to put on the bottom every month.[99] Moreover, Dönitz knew that sooner or later the US Navy would tighten up the protective system around her coasts and he would be forced back to convoy battles in the North Atlantic. Since one of the chief problems here was finding the convoys, a great number of boats were necessary. It was resolving itself into a competition between US and German productive capacity as much as between the training and resolve of the opposing crews.

The German economy seemed hardly in a position to compete. Earlier Hitler had ordered priority to U-boat construction and an increase to 25 boats a month, but the latest demands from the Russian and North African fronts had forced him to return priority to the Army. Meanwhile there were shortages everywhere: the latest report from the U-department, naval High Command, stated that the deteriorating dockyard 'worker situation and want of materials' made it doubtful if the U-boat building programme could be achieved. It continued in tones indistinguishable from Dönitz's own that today they faced a situation like that in the First World War when 'apart from the military-political failures of direction—despite greater successes finally the U-boat war was wrecked by too few boats'.[100]

Dönitz was forced into the opinion that if the building programme had to be curtailed for want of materials Type VII boats should be built in lieu of the larger types for two of them could be built for one Type IX, and it was *numbers* not size that would count when it came to searching for convoys again.[101]

In the meantime he made the most of the continuing favourable conditions on the US coast and in the Caribbean; what he called the 'potential' of his boats, the average tonnage sunk per boat per day at sea, continued to rise despite the long passage to the hunting grounds; by the end of April it had almost doubled to 412 tons, and his Commanders were 'all of the same opinion; that the American area will remain highly favourable for operations for several months'.[102] Added to this was an extraordinarily low loss rate in these waters, so that his numbers built up almost as well as if the production quotas had been met. By May 1st his nominal strength was 174 'front-boats'; although some were still on trials, the total number of boats in commission at this time was 295.

It was perhaps because of all this that he appeared in his most optimistic form when commanded to report to Hitler at his East Prussian headquarters, *Wolfschanze*, on the afternoon of May 14th. There he repeated his conviction that the U-boat war was a war against enemy tonnage, that American and British tonnage had to be 'regarded as one' and that it was 'therefore correct to sink ships wherever the greatest number of them can be sunk at the lowest cost—i.e. with the fewest losses'.[103] Sinkings from January 15th, the start of the US campaign, to May 10th amounted to 303 ships of a total 2,015,252 tons.

'However,' he went on, 'U-boat operations in the American area are also right from the point of view that the sinkings of the U-boat war are a race with merchant ship new construction. The American is the greatest enemy shipbuilder. His shipbuilding industries lie in the eastern States. Shipbuilding and ancillary industries depend mainly on oil fuel. The most important American oilfields lie on the Gulf of Mexico. Consequently the greater part of American tanker tonnage is in the coastal traffic from the oil area to the industrial area. In the period (15.1–10.5, 1942) we sank 112 tankers of a total 927,000 tons. With every tanker sunk the American loses not only the ship for transporting oil, but he experiences immediate damage to his *new* construction . . .'

And he concluded from the experience to date, 'I believe the race between the enemy new building and U-boat sinkings is in no way hopeless.'

His argument was that on the stated American figures it would be necessary to sink 700,000 tons a month to keep up with new construction, 'but we are already sinking these 700,000 tons per month now'—'we' meaning German, Italian, Japanese U-boats, airforces and mines. 'There is, therefore, already now an absolute decline taking place in the enemy tonnage. Moreover the building figures quoted are the maximum amounts ever mentioned by enemy propaganda. Our experts doubt if this goal can be achieved and consider that the enemy can only build about five million tons in 1942. Then merely 4–500,000 tons per month need to be sunk in order to prevent any increase. Anything above that cuts into the tonnage'. So Dönitz arrived back close to the 600,000 tons a month requirement of von Holtzendorff in the First World War. The experts' scepticism about American claims appears to have been based on tonnage launched in the first two months of the programme.[104]

He intended continuing operations in American water, he went on. 'One of these days the situation will change. Already there are signs that the Americans are making strenuous efforts to master the large sinking figures. They have raised a considerable air defence and are using destroyers and patrol craft around the coast. However, all these are inexperienced and do not present a serious threat at present. In any case the boats with their greater war experience are superior to the defence. The American fliers see nothing. The destroyers and patrol craft are mostly travelling too fast to locate the U-boats or they are not persistent enough with depth charges . . .'

He described how easily the situation could be changed if convoy were

241

instituted; when that happened he intended to resume operations in the Atlantic against the ocean convoys, but he believed this would be easier in the future because of the greater number of boats coming on line. 'Formerly the most difficult part of this warfare was locating [the enemy].'

His optimism stands in marked contrast to British assessments. Horrified as they were by the unnecessary losses off America, Wynn and the experts at the tracking room in the 'Citadel' were clear that, once instituted, convoy would 'master the menace in the Western Atlantic as it has done elsewhere and reduce our losses to a tolerable figure'.[105] Directly this situation was reached and U-boat losses started to rise 'we can definitely expect another change of strategy'; although it was impossible to predict exactly where Dönitz would strike, the answer to the threat was convoy with surface and air escorts equipped with radar.

It may be said that with an adequate and efficient air escort wolf pack tactics on a convoy should be impossible . . . we hope to achieve this beyond the reach of land-based aircraft by auxiliary carriers with the convoys.[106]

Dönitz, in his report to the Führer, was clear that losses would rise once they were forced back into convoy battles but did not appreciate that his group tactics were actually doomed if the enemy succeeded in providing full air cover; for one thing he didn't know that radar had been developed for aircraft—or for that matter for surface escorts. Suspicions were forming that some kind of location device was in use, but just what was not clear. This failure to read the signs of the last convoy battles of the old year and the ever-extending allied air cover can be seen in retrospect as the turning point of the U-boat war. For this was the time that the U-boat arm should have been striving for an improved U-boat with an underwater speed sufficient to catch up with convoys and reach an attacking position *after being forced under by aircraft sightings*. The pointers were all there; from 1940 onwards U-boats had been forced further and further out into the Atlantic by air reconnaissance and escort; on the basis of this experience it should have been plain that if the enemy found themselves in trouble in the mid-Atlantic gap still not covered by aircraft and if this were to result in the kind of monthly sinkings Dönitz needed, they would take the most strenuous efforts to rectify the situation.

These conclusions were not drawn. An experimental type with high

242

underwater speed had been under development by its inventor, Professor Walter, since before the war; a small prototype had been built, achieving 28 knots submerged in 1940, since when designs for a coastal type and a larger ocean-going boat had been prepared. But Hitler's allocation of priority to tanks and aircraft that January caused a radical reappraisal of all naval building and work on the Walter boats was stopped. Walter immediately travelled to Paris to seek Dönitz's aid; he was not disappointed; Dönitz was enthusiastic—naturally he wanted high speed under water—and pressed Raeder to continue development. As a result work was resumed on the coastal prototype in February, not, however, with any sense of urgency.

The Walter idea involved new technology; the high-speed underwater drive was provided by a fuel containing its own oxygen, whose combustion did not, therefore, exhaust the oxygen in the boat which the crew needed to breathe. Naturally there were problems with such a new concept, and the naval construction department believed these so serious the war would be over before they were solved; they were right. However, if the seriousness of the position facing existing boats had been realized the most urgent priority must have been given to the search for any means of gaining speed under water—not necessarily Walter's. Dönitz and his staff and the U-department in Berlin must share the blame for not perceiving this and not impressing it on Raeder and the naval staff.

They, for their part, were still day-dreaming, planning great three-way pincer movements across half the world, one thrusting south from the Caucasus and through Iraq towards the head of the Persian Gulf, another via North Africa through Alexandria and Suez to the Red Sea, while the Japanese fleet operated in the Indian Ocean to prevent supplies reaching the British in these areas; and assuming this strategic centre of the board was in their grasp—thanks to the exertions of the Army and their Japanese ally—they were making detailed plans for the *post-war* fleet necessary to hold it![107]

'These people dream in continents,' the Chief of the Army General Staff, Halder, noted in his diary after a conversation with Schniewind, Raeder's Chief of Staff.

> . . . they simply assume that according to the whim of the moment we can decide whether and when we will move overland from the Caucasus to the Persian Gulf or drive from Cyrenaica through Egypt

to the Suez Canal. They talk of land operations via Italian Africa to the east African coast and South Africa. They talk arrogantly about the problems of the Atlantic and irresponsibly about the Black Sea. One is wasting one's breath talking to them.[108]

Such at the crisis of a great war was the extent of the total breakdown of the German command organization.

Dönitz for his part was a front Commander whose strengths lay in personal leadership charisma, undaunted devotion and unquenchable optimism. It was not in his nature to take a negative view; consequently he brushed aside the threat from the increased efficiency of the British escort groups and air cover just as he had brushed aside Fürbringer's doubts about U-boat war on commerce in 1938. And although naturally supporting Walter's revolutionary boat, he was more immediately concerned to increase numbers of existing types to *find* the convoys in the battle about to be rejoined in the North Atlantic.

He also called for improved weapons, and here we reach a dark area matching the darkness that had fallen over Germany and the occupied territories of Europe. On January 3rd Hitler had discussed the strategic situation with the Japanese Ambassador, Oshima, in the presence of Ribbentrop. Coming to the war in the Atlantic, he had stressed the importance he attached to the U-boat campaign, and had said of US shipbuilding capacity that however many ships they built, one of their chief problems would be manning them.

'For that reason,' he went on, 'merchant shipping will be sunk without warning with the intention of killing as many of the crew as possible. Once it gets around that most of the seamen are lost in the sinkings, the Americans will have great difficulty in enlisting new people. The training of sea-going personnel takes a long time. We are fighting for our existence and cannot therefore take a humanitarian viewpoint. For this reason I must give the order that since foreign seamen cannot be taken prisoner, and in most cases this is not possible on the open sea, the U-boats are to surface after torpedoing and shoot up the lifeboats.'[109]

Oshima agreed with this and said the Japanese would be forced to use the same methods, as indeed they did. Dönitz denied ever having heard of this conversation or receiving this order, and the record of lives saved from the sinkings off the US coast suggests that he did not give such an instruction. Nevertheless, this conversation re-echoes down the later years of the U-boat war, and it was heard at this May 14th conference.

Prophesying that U-boat losses would increase once convoy battles were resumed, and stressing that it was therefore necessary to improve the U-boat's weapons against the enemy escorts, he said the most important development was an *Abstand* or non-contact pistol for torpedoes. This would have a more certain effect against destroyers than existing pistols but 'above all will accelerate the sinking of torpedoed ships'; this would result in 'the great advantage that in consequence of the very rapid sinking of the torpedoed ship the crew will no longer be able to be rescued. This greater loss of ships' crews will doubtless aggravate the manning difficulties for the great American building programme'.[110]

Both he and Raeder insisted at the Nuremberg trials that this reference to US manning difficulties was provoked by Hitler at the conference. There is nothing in the record to suggest this. The most likely explanation, perhaps, is that at some time after his discussion with Oshima Hitler did propose the elimination of survivors to Raeder who discussed it with Dönitz. Now Dönitz was proposing a legal and morally defensible method of gaining similar ends. ·

Step by step the necessities of submarine warfare and Germany's struggle against insuperable odds were increasing the pressure on him to move from accepted codes of warfare. It was but a step back from here to the barbarities of the Middle Ages—already being practised in the eastern campaign.

The savagery Hitler had unleashed in the east was now rebounding on the German people. German soldiers captured by the Red Army were being shot, beheaded, hanged upside down, burned alive. In the west, British area bombing raids against German and German-occupied cities were claiming hundreds of civilian victims; resistance movements in the occupied countries were mounting campaigns of harassment and assassination, which had led to a vicious cycle of reprisal and counter-terrorism. One captured rating from a U-boat based on Lorient told his British interrogator that he thought the shooting of hostages in reprisal for the killing of German sentries might whip up such feeling among the French that they would fall on and annihilate a number of garrisons.[111] Hitler decreed that all commands in France must have forces under their direct control; this compelled Dönitz to prepare a move back to Paris—'a regrettable step,' he noted, 'since the direct contact with the front, i.e. the personal touch between the commanding officer and the front boats and crews will not be possible to nearly the same extent . . .'[112]

The day after he wrote that entry a British raiding party attacked St Nazaire. No U-boats were lost, but it was obvious that a similar raid on Kerneval and the British could have had the entire staff of U-boat Command! He accelerated the move.

The building chosen for his second Paris headquarters was a modern apartment block on the Avenue Maréchal Maunoury. The switch-over from Kerneval took place at 10 am on March 29th.

This was two days after the first train-load of 1,112 Jews left Paris for Auschwitz, purportedly in reprisal for attacks on German servicemen in the capital; in truth it was the beginning in the west of the 'final solution' to the Jewish problem agreed at a conference chaired by Himmler's deputy, Reinhard Heydrich, at Wannsee, Berlin, on January 20th.[113] There is no reason why Dönitz should have known about this; it was a closely-kept secret and all his time and energy were devoted to the U-boat campaign. If the round-ups and deportations impinged somewhere at the periphery of his attention they would not have appeared anything out of the ordinary; similar episodes had been commonplace since the Nazis seized power. Some of his own U-boat men had served spells in concentration camps and suffered the *Gleichschaltung*, or reduction to the Nazi philosophy, meted out by the guards; others had suffered spells of hard labour in punishment camps; the ultimate deterrent was transfer to a punishment battalion on the eastern front.

Dönitz went on holiday with his family to Badenweiler that summer soon after his meeting with the Führer at the *Wolfschanze*; his daughter, Ursula, went too and took his grandson Peter. Her husband, Günther Hessler, had made his name as one of the ace U-boat Commanders, having returned from a cruise to the South Atlantic the previous summer with a bag of fourteen ships totalling 86,699 tons, a record for a single voyage which was never equalled.[114] Dönitz had called him to U-boat headquarters where he now served as first staff officer directly under Eberhard Godt.

By the time Dönitz and Hessler returned to Paris after the holiday the campaign against French Jews was in full swing. They were required to wear a yellow six-pointed star now on their left breast as in Germany and Poland; while it is doubtful if Dönitz would have chanced across any during his intensive daily round it is inconceivable that he would have remained unaware of the mounting scale of operations in the capital. Horror stories broadcast by the BBC must also have reached his ears; his staff listened for the serious purpose of gleaning information particularly about U-boats reported sunk. It is scarcely conceivable that anything as dramatic as the first accounts of the massacres of Jews in the east reported from July onwards were not drawn to his attention—unless the idea of mass murder was by then a commonplace in Germany. One rating from a U-boat sunk at the end of the previous year told his British interrogator that Germans had sterilized or shot so many Poles, he believed that if Germany lost the war a huge number of his countrymen would be sterilized in return—he understood that 20,000 British doctors had already been mustered for the purpose.[115] In the face of this kind of evidence it is apparent that not only Jews and Communists, but Germany itself was caught up in *Nacht und Nebel*—night and fog. To ask how Dönitz viewed the intensification of the internal war would probably be an irrelevance; his commitment to the struggle was absolute, and he made no difference between enemies outside or inside.

Early in September it was reported that British destroyers had machine-gunned survivors from the German minelayer *Ulm* in their lifeboats. Hitler's response suggests that Raeder and Dönitz had indeed rejected his earlier suggestion to shoot up shipwrecked survivors for he called for vengeance: 'An eye for an eye and a tooth for a tooth. We must straightaway declare that from now on parachuting airmen will be fired on and our U-boats will shell the survivors of torpedoed ships regardless of whether they are soldiers or civilians, women or children!'[116]

Raeder, told of his intention to take reprisals, immediately set up an investigation into the *Ulm* and similar cases. On the 13th, while the staff was still analysing the results, Hitler called for a report from Dönitz on the situation in the U-boat war:

14·18   13/9   20·15

Secret—Führer wishes *Befehlshaber der U-boote* to report soonest possible at Führerheadquarters on the position of the U-boat war.[117]

To gain an idea of Dönitz's state of mind and preoccupations at this time it is necessary to backtrack briefly. The easy successes on the US coast had come to an end during July when coastal traffic had at last been organized in convoys; although a few 'soft' areas of independent traffic remained around the West Indies for a few weeks more, Dönitz had been

247

forced back in his main attack to the North Atlantic. He had more boats by this time: on August 1st he was operating no less than 113 in the Atlantic out of a total 342 in service. His new tactic for the main theatre was to organize the newly-sailed boats in groups at about the limit of British air reconnaissance in the eastern Atlantic, from where they travelled slowly westwards, combing the probable convoy routes so that when they found a convoy they could fight it on its way across, refuel from a tanker in the west, reform off Newfoundland and comb back eastwards on the homeward leg.

By this time the potentially decisive threat of radar-equipped aircraft, noted by the British in April, had been forced in on all at U-boat Command. Boats on passage to and from the Biscay bases were being attacked by day and night, and often the first the U-boat lookouts knew of the danger was a searchlight trained on them from close astern as the plane which had located the boat by radar made its visual run in for the kill. An apparatus to detect the radar transmissions—actually a French device given to Dönitz gratuitously by the French Admiral Darlan—had been supplied to the boats to give them warning and time to dive, and Dönitz made urgent demands for aircraft to win command of the airspace over Biscay; the few he obtained were quite insufficient. By August 21st a note of desperation was evident in the U-boat Command war diary:

. . . the numerical strengthening of enemy flights, the appearance of a wide variety of aircraft types equipped with an excellent location device against U-boats have made U-boat operations in the eastern Atlantic more difficult . . . The enemy daily reconnaissance extends almost as far as 20° W and has forced a movement of U-boat dispositions far into the middle of the Atlantic since a discovery of the dispositions would lead to the convoys being re-routed around them. Besides daily reconnaissance it is now known that there are some especially long-range aircraft types which are used for convoy escort . . . As the war diary of 20.7 shows, this has made the operation of boats very much more difficult, in some cases no longer worthwhile. This worsening of the operational situation must, if continued, lead to insupportable losses, to a decline in successes and so to a decline in the prospects of success of the U-boat war as a whole . . .[118]

The entry concluded that despite all, and very heavy depth-charging by escort groups, 'resolute, confident mood unbroken through unshakeable faith in victory'.

This is not always the picture conveyed by British interrogations of survivors. 'A number of prisoners expressed doubts about the final success of the U-boat war',[119] one report noted. And as in the First World War the rapid increase in the number of boats had led to a tremendous dilution of experienced personnel; increasingly the ratings were raw, only briefly trained and in many cases unhappy:

> There is no doubt that large numbers of them [prisoners] speak with loathing of their service in U-boats, which they find very different from what propaganda had led them to expect. Some said they would never have joined the U-boat arm if they had known what active service was going to be like. This seems to imply that crews are not always drafted without option.[120]

An earlier report had described the situation of men called by their divisional officer to extend their service after the original period of four and a half years for which they had signed was up:

> Most did so and were more fortunate than those who did not and found the papers endorsed 'Left the Fatherland in the hour of need' when they took discharge at the end of the shorter period. This made it impossible to get a job. One prisoner repeatedly said, 'Once the Navy gets you, you are finished.'[121]

Despite these reports the exalted status the U-boat men enjoyed as a *corps d'élite* and the real dangers and hardships of the life did shore up morale to a remarkable extent.

Of Dönitz's own morale there was never any doubt. He used any successful operation to support his determination that the battle *could* be won, and when it seemed that the enemy's air mastery was about to reduce his boats to impotence—as in the following war diary entry in September—he sent urgent demands for planes or weapons to deal with it.

> Already on 1.9 at 0900 in AK 3726 [800 miles from England, 450 miles from Iceland] air escort appeared over the convoy. It was reinforced towards evening. By systematically forcing the boats under water it

249

made them lose contact at evening twilight, thus spoiling the best prospects for attack of all boats in the first four moonless hours of the night. The enemy made clever use of the boats' loss of contact to make a sharp leg so that touch was not regained until 03.00 and then it was no longer possible to get the boats of the group (except for two) near the convoy. The convoy operation had to be broken off in the morning of 2.9 as it no longer seemed possible for boats to haul ahead in face of the expected heavy enemy air activity, and on the other hand, because of the poor visibility there was too great a risk from aircraft with radar [*Funkortung*].

As the above sketch indicates, by increasing the range of their aircraft the English have succeeded in gaining air control over a great part of the North Atlantic with land-based planes and narrowing the area in which U-boats can operate without threat from the air . . .[122]

The day was approaching, 'BdU sees with extreme anxiety' when this situation would spread to all parts of the North Atlantic, 'the chief battleground of the U-boat.' Unless suitable counter-measures were taken, 'this would signify an unendurable reduction in prospects for success'.

As he had anticipated, U-boat losses were rising now that convoy battles had been joined again.[123] To make matters worse the naval staff had reconsidered the 'tonnage war' in the light of US shipbuilding performance and arrived at an astonishing figure for the total amount of shipping which it was necessary to destroy each month if there was to be any chance of winning—no less than 1·3 million tons or well over double the figure in Dönitz's May report to the Führer. Since calculations of the U-boats' performance January to August gave an average monthly sinking rate of only 400,000 tons—actually too low—the conclusion was: 'It is in the present state of affairs questionable whether such a high sinking rate can be achieved on a lasting basis.'[124]

The alternative to the pure 'tonnage war' Dönitz was fighting was the 'supply war' in which attacks would be concentrated on shipping proceeding to England or to a particular theatre; the paper concluded that the more the monthly sinking figure dropped below the required 1·3 million tons the more urgent it became to make the transition from the 'pure tonnage war to the supplies- and freight-war'.

On the same date, September 9th, Dönitz himself made two impassioned pleas to the naval staff for help. One was by teleprinter; it listed five episodes since June 14th in which enemy aircraft had 'caused premature abandonment of hitherto favourable U-boat operations against convoys'.[125] Noting that all these cases had occurred within the range of the Heinkel 177, he asked that the first squadron of these planes—which so far as he knew was in Germany and not at the Russian front—be sent to the Air Commander, Atlantic, to work with the U-boats.

The other was a paper drafted that week on the development of weapons for U-boats; he suggested that rockets being developed at Peenemünde should be adapted for his arm—specifically for submerged, remote-controlled firing against convoy escorts. More interesting than the proposal itself was the state of mind, the loneliness and agitation revealed by the paper:

> The U-boat arm today completes the third year of uninterrupted battle missions. It has remained in all the changes of the war always the chief weapon in the sea war, in the first line on grounds of its battle characteristics which allow it, not only to hit the enemy successfully, but also to exist in the face of a superiority in numbers and strength. If all forces are not used in the *first line* in order to keep the battle strength of the U-boats in the highest possible condition, the danger is clear that one day the U-boat will be crushed and eliminated by the defence forces.
>
> The German sea war direction will thereby have the only weapon which it can set effectively against the great sea powers struck from its hand. The BdU therefore requests anew that the question of the co-operation of the weapons departments of the High Command with the BdU be carefully examined and all possibilities for improvement of the armament of U-boats exploited.[126]

Such was the desperate situation of the U-boat arm—despite rapidly rising numbers—when Hitler commanded Dönitz to report to him on the position on September 13th. He was directing an unusual rescue operation when he received the summons. He had sent four large Type IX boats to probe for a soft spot off Cape Town, and on the way, just within the limits he had set for attacks—so as to preserve secrecy—one of these had sunk the British troop transport, *Laconia*. The U-boat Commander then discovered that the ship had been carrying 1,800 Italian prisoners of war, and he radioed U-boat Command for instructions. Dönitz was

251

confronted with a difficult choice—this was in the early hours of the 13th and one can imagine him and his staff officers hastily summoned in bath robes—to abandon the operation or to abandon the ally's men. Although there was obviously a strong political element in the choice, he claims in his memoirs that he made the decision himself—ordering all the Cape Town-bound boats and others in the area to break off their operations and proceed immediately to the rescue. Raeder approved his action and the naval staff arranged for Vichy French vessels to head for a rendezvous with the boats to take off survivors. Hitler was also informed; his naval adjutant, von Puttkamer, told Dönitz the Führer did not wish to see the Cape Town operation prejudiced, and the U-boats were under no circumstances to allow themselves to be endangered in the rescue operations.[127]

Hitler was at his Ukraine headquarters, *Werwolf*, at this time, personally directing the assault on Stalingrad which his generals, so he believed, had botched; he was furious with them all, demanding wholesale resignations and not on speaking terms with his two principal staff officers, Keitel and Jodl. Evidently the *Laconia* episode jerked him away from these immediate preoccupations, for it was that afternoon that von Puttkamer sent the wire summoning Dönitz to report on the U-boat situation.

Three days later a four-engined US Liberator aircraft from Ascension Island sighted U 156, the boat which had sunk the *Laconia*, towing four of the ship's lifeboats filled with survivors; in further demonstration of his mercy mission U 156's Commander displayed a two-metres-square Red Cross flag from the bridge. After circling awhile the aircraft made off. An hour later a second US Liberator appeared; she flew in low from the bow and dropped two bombs; while the lifeboats were hurriedly being cast off a third bomb landed in their midst and shortly afterwards a fourth bomb was dropped. By then another US aircraft had appeared, which also attacked, one of its bombs exploding deep immediately below the control room and causing damage. The boat was able to dive, however, and carry out repairs. Later she surfaced and radioed a report.

This message was received at U-boat headquarters shortly after eleven that night; again one can imagine Dönitz in pyjamas and bathrobe, with his staff officers—maybe they were still drinking nightcaps when they received the summons to the operations room. According to Dönitz's account a warm (*temperamentvollen*) discussion developed, in which his staff argued that continuing the rescue operation was wholly unjustifiable. Dönitz, however, was determined to finish what he had started, and he eventually closed the discussion with the words, 'I cannot put the people in the water now, I shall carry on.'[128] By 'the people' he meant the Italians, not the British; orders were sent that only Italians were to be retained aboard the boats, which were to proceed towards their rendez-vous with the Vichy French ships while taking every possible precaution against enemy counter-measures.

The war diary entry on the episode on the 16th concludes:

As shown by the report from U 156 the Commander did not believe the enemy would attack when he saw the Red Cross flag and the rescue attempts. This opinion is impossible to understand. It must be assumed that he was influenced by seeing hundreds of survivors fighting for their lives.[129]

So much for the facts; behind them, in the discussion at U-boat head-quarters that midnight continuing into the early hours of the 17th, lies the largest question mark over the U-boat war and Dönitz's claim to have fought cleanly; the details will probably never be known; only certain results emerge from *Nacht und Nebel* to feed conjecture.

Dönitz's own account is notable for its silence on whether he was in touch with Raeder or Hitler during that night; it leaves the impression, probably intentionally, that all the orders were issued on his own authority and discussion was confined to his own staff. It is inconceiv-able, however, that naval High Command was not informed, and in view of Hitler's earlier involvement and his anxiety that the U-boats should not be hazarded it is difficult to imagine that Führer headquarters was not also put in the picture. Hitler's nocturnal habits and love of diver-sions enabling him to work off a head of destructive emotion and take an active part make it easy to imagine him coming on the line personally to Dönitz—not difficult in that case to guess his mood or the trend of his instructions.

He had been wanting an excuse to attack survivors of torpedoed ships for the dual purpose of terrorism to deter neutral and American sailors and to cut down the numbers available to man new construction since at least January, when he had disclosed his ideas to the Japanese Ambassa-dor. Fresh life had been breathed into the subject by the apparent gunning down of the survivors from the *Ulm* and the interim results of the investigations and analysis instituted then had just come to hand, dated September 14th. These showed three cases when survivors of German destroyers disabled or sunk at Narvik during the Norwegian campaign had been fired on by the British as they attempted to reach the land, and numerous cases of the German survivors of transports off Crete being fired at and killed in the water during that campaign; one incident detailed was when a British submarine Commander allowed the Greek crew of a motor sailer, *Osia Paraskivi*, to take to the lifeboats:

> . . . and had then opened fire with aimed shots from short range at the remaining German officer and three other German soldiers in the water after they had abandoned ship until all four were hit and killed.[130]

The paper did point out that it was easy for survivors in the water to mistake shots at other targets for an attack on themselves, and in no case had any written or oral order to attack shipwrecked survivors been traced. It suggested therefore that before any retaliatory measures it should be considered whether these would not affect their own people more than the enemy; 'if the existence of such a German order became known the enemy propaganda would exploit it in a way, the consequences of which can hardly be estimated.'[131]

To suggest from Hitler's current preoccupation with shooting up survivors that the attack by US Liberators on boats involved in rescuing the *Laconia* survivors gave him just the opportunity he wanted, and that he immediately instructed Dönitz by telephone to issue orders to that effect is speculation; there is no documentary evidence or direct testimony. Nevertheless, the orders issued by Dönitz on September 17th make it probable that something like that happened.

Dönitz could not of course issue instructions to shoot survivors in lifeboats for the very reason given in the naval staff analysis: if discovered they would be a gift to enemy propaganda, and might redound on their own men captured. Apart from this there was the morale of his own forces, many of whom, despite the intense hate-propaganda to which they had been subjected, would have been shaken by such a cold-blooded instruction against accepted codes of sea war. Moreover, if the enemy then started reprisals the advantage would lie inevitably with them since they virtually controlled the seas and the sky above. And if U-boat crews were to expect that in addition to the increasing hazards of

254

depth-charge and air attack they would be subject to execution if captured it would be impossible to preserve their commitment to attack.

The orders he sent out at 21.00 on 17th September were, as recorded in his war diary:

To all Commanders:
1) All attempts to rescue members of ships sunk, therefore also fishing out swimmers and putting them into lifeboats, righting capsized lifeboats, handing out provisions and water, have to cease. Rescue contradicts the most fundamental [*primitivisten*] demands of war for the annihilation of enemy ships and crews.
2) Orders for bringing back Captains and Chief Engineers (issued previously) remain in force.
3) Only save shipwrecked survivors if [their] statements are of import-ance for the boat.
4) Be hard. Think of the fact that the enemy in his bombing attacks on German towns has no regard for women and children.[132]

The actual wording of the order was not necessarily exactly as this war diary entry summary; bearing in mind the policy of deception permeat-ing every level of the German services, exemplified in the *Athenia* case, in the clandestine abandonment of the Prize Rules and introduction of unrestricted warfare in the waters around England—'not to be given in writing but need merely be based on the unspoken approval of the naval operations staff'—not all documents can be taken at face value. How-ever, even in this record there are certain ambiguities which must have been deliberate. The evidence for this is contained in the mass of Dönitz's other orders and memoranda; all are written with crystal clarity; his staff officers attest the fact: '. . . all he wanted was very precisely considered . . . he sought discussion . . . then he decided himself . . .'[133] Moreover, as his communications staff officer, Hans Meckel, stated, 'Dönitz regarded his staff as the servants of the front Commanders; if a Commander said he did not understand his orders, Dönitz always blamed the staff for not making it clear.'[134] And there is ample evidence that the order was discussed at great length by the staff. When it became clear after the war that it was to be used in evidence against him at the war crimes trials, Dönitz said that both Godt and his first staff officer, Hessler, his son-in-law, had advised him not to send it. Both denied or claimed to have forgotten this.

255

The sentence which provoked the heat then and at Nuremberg was: 'Rescue contradicts the most fundamental demands of war for the annihilation of ships and crews.' It did not order the shooting of defenceless men, but any Commander so minded could read it as a licence to do so—any Commanders who believed—as all did—that they were fighting against powers determined to destroy the Fatherland, partition it, reduce its people to agricultural serfs, emasculate numbers of German men, powers who had already killed thousands of defenceless women and children and the old in saturation bombing raids, might take it as a green light for vengeance; any Commander with a brutal twist in his make-up, or immature men who doubted their National Socialist hardness and needed to prove it to themselves and others, and who questioned the strange wording and were given 'the unspoken approval' of the staff or the chief himself, *Der Löwe*, any of these might take it as a licence to massacre defenceless survivors.

The presumption must be that this was what Dönitz intended for, at about the same time, perhaps on the same day although this is not clear, another order, which was not noted in the war diary, pointed out the desirability of sinking the 'rescue ships' which were attached to most convoys for picking up survivors after U-boat attacks: 'In view of the desired annihilation of ships' crews their sinking is of great value.'[135]

In addition there is testimony from the chief of the 5th U-boat flotilla based at Kiel,[136] who was worried about the ambiguities in the orders and sought guidance from one of Dönitz's staff officers; for answer he was given two examples; the first was of a U-boat leaving on a mission from a Biscay port which sighted the shot-down crew of a British aircraft afloat in their rubber dinghy; unable to take them aboard because he was outward bound and every inch of space was utilized, the U-boat Commander left them. At the debriefing at the end of his mission he was reproached by the staff—or was he really perhaps reproached by the BdU?—for not attacking the crew if he could not bring them back for interrogation; for it was to be expected that in less than 24 hours the dinghy would be rescued by British reconnaissance aircraft and the crew would be returning to destroy U-boats.

The second example concerned the sinkings off the US coast, where because of the proximity to land a high proportion of the crews had been rescued; that was regrettable as the enemy merchant fleet consisted of crews as well as tonnage, and these crews were able to man the newly-built ships.

256

After this conversation the 5th U-flotilla chief took to explaining the orders in terms of these two examples if Commanders asked about the precise meaning when he briefed them before their missions. 'However,' he added, 'U-boat command cannot give you such an order officially—everyone has to handle it according to his own conscience.' He also told them that sinkings and other acts contrary to international law were not to be entered in the Log, but simply reported orally after returning to base.

It seems surprising that just at the very moment the naval staff was questioning the possibility of winning the 'tonnage war' with its demand for a constant 1·3 million tons of shipping to be sent to the bottom every month in the face of increasingly tough convoy defence which threatened, in Dönitz's words 'to crush and eliminate the U-boat', the U-boat staff should be adding to the war against shipping a ruthless campaign against enemy crews—in effect throwing overboard every seamanlike and moral code in pursuit of what must have begun to seem a hopeless cause.

There are three possible explanations: one concerns the personality and reaction to imminent defeat of Dönitz himself—and on that there should be sufficient material to form judgement; another concerns his response to possible direct orders from the Führer—of that too there is ample material from the final two and a half years of the war; and the third possibility is that the events were indeed connected: with the prospect of having to sink 1·3 million tons every month perhaps the only hope was to make it impossible to man the new ships sliding down the ways by the day, by the hour. Yet even this was an irrational response, for if convoy battles were becoming hard, the chances of U-boats being able to stay around on the surface for sufficient time to massacre survivors was remote in the extreme; the only results to be expected were against independent ships and these could only be found away from the main theatre where the battle would be won or lost. There seems little doubt, therefore, that whatever explanations are chosen the true answer lies in the realms of the irrational and the National Socialist vision.

In any case there can be no doubt that propaganda that autumn was concentrated on the manning difficulties the Americans were said to be experiencing. Dönitz himself participated; sometime at the end of September or beginning of October he made his usual appearance at the conclusion of a U-training course and made a speech which started with a confession of the recent decline in sinking figures. This was due to the

257

strength of enemy air cover, he said, but he saw the answer in new weapons; Hitler, with whom, he remarked, he enjoyed a good relationship, had personally assured him that the U-boats would be equipped with a new type of anti-aircraft gun before other arms of the services, then the successes of earlier times would be resumed.

Questioned by an officer about a newspaper report that the Americans were building a million tons of shipping a month, he expressed scepticism, saying that this was based simply on Roosevelt's announcement. He added that in any case the allies were having great difficulty manning their ships. Many allied seamen had been torpedoed more than once, and these facts spread and deterred others from going to sea. Apparently warming to the theme, he went on to say—according to the recollection of one young officer there—that losses of men affected the allies severely because of their shortage of reserves, consequently the stage had been reached where total war had to be waged at sea as on land. The crews of ships, like the ships themselves, were a target for U-boats, and he spoke of the possibility of seamen's strikes breaking out in the allied countries if the U-boat war were waged more vigorously. Those who thought these tactics harsh should remember that their families and their wives were being bombed.[137]

The combination of unfounded optimism backed up by a resort to the most ruthless, even desperate methods revealed here was a characteristic feature of Hitler's leadership, and it may be that Dönitz was under his spell already. He had made his report to the Führer on September 28th, accounting for his boast about the excellent relationship he enjoyed with him, and there are so many similarities between what Hitler said then and Dönitz's remarks to the U-training course as remembered by the young officer—who could not possibly have read the minutes of the Führer conference—as to suggest he was indeed closely following the Führer's line.

The record of Hitler's opening comments shows that, having expressed his great recognition of the achievement of the U-boats, he went on to express his conviction that the monthly sinking rate would remain so high that the enemy would be unable to keep pace by new building. He thought it impossible that the increases in production of the enemy yards would be as great as their propaganda represented.

'If it were possible for the enemy to launch ships' hulls at such a rate, they would still want for engines, auxiliary machinery, ancillary equipment and above all men to man these ships. With regard to the manning

258

problem,' he went on, 'it is very disadvantageous if a great part of the crews of sunk ships are always in a position to put to sea again in newly-built vessels.'[138]

He then passed on to the necessity of putting new technical developments into use as quickly as possible—after which Dönitz gave his report. He used it to press his previous requests for He 177s to dispute the allied air superiority, and managed to strike an optimistic note by suggesting that the Walter boat under development would revolutionize U-boat warfare. Raeder added that good progress had been made with the new *Abstand* firing pistol which would give the torpedoes such tremendous destructive power as considerably to increase the loss in human life.

It is interesting to speculate how far Raeder approved of Dönitz's recent orders to the U-boat Commanders, how far he understood their purport. It may be that one of the reasons for an increasing hostility between the two men marked from about this time was caused by a disagreement over the spirit of the orders; Raeder had compromised most of his ideals of honour before the Nazis, but it is possible he had a sticking point. That is speculation; there can be no doubt, from the documentary evidence, that the naval staff in Berlin was calling for a propaganda campaign to exploit allied manning problems at this time. Here is part of a recommendation by the section dealing with the question of reprisals after the *Ulm* affair; it was dated October 3rd:

. . . it is in the interests of the Axis powers, that in foreign countries the merchant navy personnel should be ever more deterred [*abgeschrekt*, or literally, 'frightened'] from submitting themselves freely to the risks to body and life associated with voyages in the enemy service.[139]

In view of the weight of evidence from such a variety of sources it seems that Dönitz and the U-boat staff had passed by this time over that blurred and indeterminate line separating the established western ethics of war from the barbarism of earlier ages. No sophistry about the inhumanity of war itself or the increasingly indiscriminate violence of mechanized war can obscure the fact that there was at that time a line and while it was not easy to distinguish it clearly, it was possible to tell on which side of it one stood. In view of the revolutionary character and hate- and destruction-inspired dogma of National Socialism, of Dönitz's own character and of

259

the fact that the allies themselves had passed across the line with indiscriminate slaughter of non-combatants from the air—a development pioneered by the *Luftwaffe*—the transition was probably inevitable at some stage; perhaps it is not surprising that it was crossed just as failure became a real possibility.

Dönitz's fears during August and September that his campaign stood on the brink of defeat from the air were not realized that winter. The 'Metox' radar-warning devices installed in the boats reduced the numbers surprised on the surface, and the increasing number of operational boats he was able to deploy—200 during October, of which over 150 worked in the North Atlantic—made it difficult for the convoys to evade them, particularly as fuel shortages forced the allies to direct shipping along the shortest therefore predictable great circle route; moreover, *B-Dienst* had recovered its earlier facility while the allied cryptographers found themselves temporarily defeated by the added complication of an extra encoding wheel being used in the German Enigma machines. Perhaps the chief reasons for the U-boats' continuing successes, however, were the exploitation of distant 'soft spots' off Cape Town and the Indian Ocean, and the diversion of allied resources from the Atlantic campaign into preparations for the invasion of French North Africa, code-named 'Torch'.

The landings took place on November 7/8th, taking Hitler completely by surprise. The previous week the results of the 'supply war' in the eastern Mediterranean had come as an equal shock; after eight days' fighting at El Alamein, his *Afrika Korps* general, Rommel, had been forced to retreat. The Führer had ordered him to stand firm: '. . . this will not be the first time in history that the stronger will must triumph over the big battalions'.[140] He had won a temporary stay, but as the US Army entered the European war in strength from the armada assembled for 'Torch', Rommel was in full retreat. Hitler was trying to come to terms with these disasters in his mountain hideaway, the *Berghof*, when a third surprise blow fell: the Russian armies encircled his forces fighting for Stalingrad. The war had turned. He no longer held the initiative in any theatre; he could only steel his generals to hold what they had.

By contrast with these shocks on land the U-boats notched up a record total that month. Dönitz's war diary entries revealed a new optimism: '. . . successes in November climbed to a new high and will probably amount to 900,000 tons. The time has come to regard these results in a true light and to give propaganda suitable guidance . . .'[141]

This result—actually an over-estimate by about 160,000 tons[142]—appeared to bring ultimate success within his grasp if only he could get sufficient new boats quickly enough, thus heightened his exasperation at the delays which continued to surround every aspect of U-boat building and equipping. He felt that he was battling alone against an indiarubber bureaucracy in Berlin run by big-ship men indifferent to or actively jealous of the feats of the U-boats.

> . . . the BdU requests a *single* department and a *single* person to be responsible for this fitting out (with a newly developed circling, FAT) torpedo . . . and the name of the person concerned is to be made known . . . As a result of these agreements not being kept, U-boats ready for action have been kept inactive for weeks and our naval command thereby caused a painful decline in the sinking of enemy tonnage; this is irresponsible and further delay insufferable.[143]

Raeder, for his part, found Dönitz's conceit and pushiness insufferable. Not only was he seeking to impose strategic decisions on the naval staff by constant stress on the North Atlantic 'tonnage war', oblivious, it seemed, to any other war theatres, but there was no aspect of the building, fitting out, repairing, experimental and development work on U-boats, or even the training of personnel which he was not trying to take over, reorganize and drive forward. He was forced to send him a written order forbidding him to deal in technical matters, to confine himself in future to operations. According to Wolfgang Frank, Dönitz's immediate response was to put through a call to Raeder's adjutant, 'Please inform the Grand Admiral that I cannot obey this order . . .' Then turning to his right-hand man, 'Well, Godt, if I were in Raeder's place I would probably sack the BdU for this; but we'll see what happens.'[144]

In fact he was in a stronger position than perhaps even he realized. The U-boat successes were almost the only gleams of light against the dark clouds now ringing the *Reich*. They glowed more strongly by contrast with the impotence of Raeder's costly surface units. Moreover, Dönitz's energetic, forthright personality and over-optimistic outlook suited Hitler better than Raeder's formality and somewhat inarticulate reserve. Although Dönitz had reported to Hitler on relatively few occasions, he

261

had made an impression and there were real grounds for his boast that he was on good terms with the Führer; Hitler, like other isolated tyrants, was always glad to hear opinions and, as Albert Speer noted, 'seek advice from people who saw the situation even more optimistically and delusively than he himself'.[145]

Above all, perhaps, in that byzantine atmosphere, Dönitz had more friends at court. One of these was Albert Speer, Minister for Armaments and Munitions and chief of the Todt construction organization; in his Armaments hat he had clashed with Raeder over plans to rationalize all ships and weapon production within his Ministry; in his Todt hat he had found Dönitz a sympathetic collaborator over the extension of the chain of U-boat bunkers to Bordeaux, Brest and St Nazaire—bunkers at Lorient and La Pallice had already been completed. No doubt he also formed the opinion that Dönitz approved his ideas for reform of naval production—anything that would provide more U-boats more speedily! When it came to his attention towards the end of the year that Raeder was having Dönitz's name censored from propaganda material and that the U-boat officers, reading the signs, were anxious they were about to lose their revered chief, he sought opportunities to influence Hitler in Dönitz's favour against the elderly C-in-C.[146]

Göring was another who was working against Raeder—although not in favour of anyone else particularly—in order to divert attention from the failures of the *Luftwaffe*. And Hitler's naval adjutant, von Puttkamer, who had commanded Dönitz's Führer torpedo boat in happier times, shared the mood of the younger generation of naval officers that changes were necessary in the old and rather dead wood at the top of the service. Certainly his memoirs, extremely guarded as they are, leave the impression that he admired Dönitz more than Raeder.

So it is not surprising that when a surface force headed by two heavy cruisers attacked an Arctic convoy with arms bound for Russia in the closing days of the year and was repelled in brilliant actions by the British escorts, Hitler vented his passion on Raeder, lecturing him for an hour and a half without pause on the history of the German Navy, the inglorious role of the fleet in the First World War, the mutinies and the revolution, above all on the uselessness of the big ships which needed small ships and aircraft to protect them rather than the other way around. He had decided to scrap them all and mount their heavy guns ashore; the naval staff were to examine the question of where they could be most usefully installed on land and to what extent the

U-boat arm could be expanded once the big ships were withdrawn from service.

Raeder withstood the onslaught in silence, then asked for a private audience and tendered his resignation. Hitler changed his tone at once, but Raeder's pride and no doubt weariness after years of battling for the service—vainly it now appeared—made him adamant. He asked that he might stand down on January 30th, the tenth anniversary of the inauguration of the Third Reich so that it would look as if he was retiring in the normal course to make way for a younger man. Finally Hitler asked him to recommend two suitable successors.

My Führer! . . . I regard as suitable in the first line Generaladmiral Carls and Admiral Dönitz . . . Generaladmiral Carls (58 years old) . . . I consider in view of his personality and comprehensive experience in the conduct of operations in other areas . . . especially suitable. His appointment would cause no friction since there would be no officer of merit to jump over. Admiral Dönitz is similarly suitable; his appointment would have the advantage of stressing especially the significance of the U-boat campaign as of war-decisive importance. The only disadvantage is the fact that Admiral Dönitz with his appointment as C-in-C would not be able to dedicate himself to the immediate conduct of the U-boat war to the same extent as formerly. Perhaps this disadvantage would, however, be alleviated by organizational measures. I beg you, my Führer, to make the decision.[147]

This seems an admirably objective assessment, considering his quarrels with Dönitz; in fact he never seems to have doubted the value of his over-zealous subordinate; at the height of their disagreements in November he had endorsed a glowing report by the fleet chief, Admiral Schniewind, with an equally generous tribute. Schniewind had reported on Dönitz as an officer endowed with 'superior intellectual gifts and special leadership qualities . . .' whose 'wide-minded, energetic and indefatigably tough' leadership had been fully justified by results; he had continued:

Strong, pithy and self-aware character who enjoys the highest respect inside his arm. The BdU sphere has been welded together by him into a tight, sworn war-community. In my opinion [he is] suitable in personality to rise to the highest positions of leadership.[148]

On November 1st Raeder had approved the report and added:

[He] has since the first day of the war directed the operations of the U-boats with the greatest general view, keenest deliberation and judgement constantly proved correct, and has thereby laid the foundations for the great successes. If the U-boat war proves able to bring about in essentials—as I am satisfied it will—the decision of the war, this will be primarily to the credit of the Admiral Dönitz.[149]

Hitler predictably chose Dönitz to succeed Raeder, not doubting that he would fall in with his ideas for scrapping the larger fleet units to concentrate all resources on U-boats, whose numbers had climbed by then over the 400 mark; at the end of the month 222 were operational; another 78—say four months' production—and the magic number of 300 front boats might be reached.

In his last war diary entry of the old year, Dönitz reiterated his credo:

The tonnage war is the main task of the U-boats, probably the decisive contribution of the U-boats to the issue of the war. It must be carried on where the greatest successes can be achieved with the smallest losses. It is necessary to draw the firmest conclusions from a clear recognition of this situation, namely the concentration of all possible forces on the main task while knowingly accepting the gaps and disadvantages this will cause elsewhere.[150]

A fortnight later at a conference in Casablanca, the allied leaders, knowing that the offensive strategy to which they were committed in Europe could not succeed until the threat to the North Atlantic supply routes was eliminated, decided to make the defeat of the U-boats their first priority.

And that month the report from the British submarine tracking room concluded:

Evasive alterations of route were employed tactically with success, but it should be appreciated that with the growth of the operational U-boat force and the consequently greater areas covered by their patrols—which sometimes appear to approach ubiquity—the use of this method is limited and may soon be outworn . . . The potentially annihilating superiority which the enemy, given a favourable strategic situation, might bring to bear on a convoy unlucky enough to be caught early on a homeward journey and far away from effective air cover cannot be appreciated by reference to any past experiences . . . the critical phase of the U-boat war in the Atlantic cannot be long postponed.[151]

CHAPTER SIX

The Grand Admiral

WITH HIS SUCCESSION as Commander-in-Chief on January 30th 1943, Dönitz was appointed *Grossadmiral*. this was the high-water mark of his life. He was 51, at the height of his powers; in Ingeborg he had a gracious hostess for the social duties that came with high office, and which despite himself he enjoyed. He could be proud of his two sons, both lieutenants in the élite U-boat arm; Peter just coming up to his 21st birthday was second watchkeeping officer in U 954 working up for its first war cruise; the elder, Klaus, prevented from front service perhaps by injuries to his head in a motorcycle accident in 1939, was on the staff of the 5th U-flotilla at Kiel; his son-in-law, the ace Günther Hessler, was first staff officer under his U-boat department chief, Godt.

Above all and filling his thoughts was the prospect of winning the war—virtually on his own! With the *Reich* now on the defensive everywhere, the U-boat arm, which he had decided to keep under his own direct control, was the sole means to victory. Success had seemed so close in November; over the last two months it had danced away tantalizingly; few convoys had been found, due chiefly to bad weather and the enemy using new routes and somehow sailing *around* the U-boat groups, although just how they had discovered his dispositions was not clear. Now at last he had the power to remedy this, he intended increasing the monthly production totals, cutting down the exasperating delays in the dockyards and so filling the North Atlantic that the enemy would be unable to avoid his patrol lines.

His mood and the ruthless practicality of his thinking showed in his first directive issued to the staffs within days of taking office; it could scarcely have provided a greater contrast to Raeder's methods:

1) It is a question of winning the war. Considerations of how the Navy should appear after the war have no value.

2) The sea war is the U-boat war.

3) All has to be subordinated to this main goal . . .[1]

He knew it was a race against time, but he believed recent experience showed that tactical surprise could still be achieved in the mid-ocean 'air gap'—narrow as this had become—and a concentration of boats could still overwhelm the surface escort and achieve decisive success.

It is easy to criticize this as a gross underestimation of the enemy's capacity, both in the air and in merchant shipbuilding, an even more serious misjudgement of their likely reaction if threatened with defeat in the Atlantic: they were bound then to concentrate all their dispersed resources on closing the 'air gap' to make the whole North Atlantic convoy route as impossible for U-boat operations as they had already made the western Mediterranean—as indeed he had prophesied the previous summer.

Nevertheless he was optimistic by temperament and there was really little alternative to the U-boat campaign; the surface fleet had been rendered virtually impotent by allied naval and air superiority; in the east the German armies were on the defensive, and within a day of his taking over as Supreme Commander, von Paulus' forces at Stalingrad surrendered to the Russians; in North Africa Rommel was being starved of supplies by sea, air and submarine assault on the transports, and neither the Italian surface fleet nor the Axis U-boats were able to prevent a huge Anglo-American build-up against him. In the air the *Luftwaffe* could not cope with the weight of the allied raids on the *Reich*, let alone hope to deliver a decisive blow of its own. The only offensive force left to Germany was the U-boat arm, and it was natural that it should be used in a desperate throw to break out of the circle of defeat.

Whether Hitler believed it could do so may be doubted. Probably he knew already with the rational side of his mind that the Third Reich was doomed; he had based his strategy in both west and east on lightning campaigns to smash his enemies before their rearmament programmes could tip the balance against him. Now, not only had the *Blitzkrieg* in the east failed, but the huge economic and industrial power of the United States had risen against him. There are signs that he was already preparing himself and the Party in the ideology of defeat; on February 7th, for instance, the day before the first conference Dönitz attended as naval C-in-C, he told a gathering of gauleiters that if the German people failed it would be because they did not deserve to win—in the elemental

267

struggle for survival between races, the Germans would have proved the weaker and the responsibility would not be his, nor the Party's![2] This was to become a familiar motif in the last months of the *Reich*. It was at night that this rational and logical side took over; to shut it out he talked to his aides or weary female secretaries far into the morning hours, but when at last he went to bed it prevented him from sleeping; he was forced to take sedatives. By day he could escape his doubts by attention to the small detail of the campaigns at his situation reports, and allow the irrational side of his nature to seize on any straws of hope presented.

It was here that Dönitz played such an important role; his optimism, his determination that the U-boats could and would succeed, his positive response to all difficulties, were exactly what the jaded Führer needed to feed his wilful self-deceptions. Moreover, Dönitz's great strengths as a leader, noted over the years by his superiors, his 'iron will-power, goal-oriented certainty and unwearying toughness . . . calm, circumspection and power of resolution . . .' his 'inner enthusiasm for his profession . . .' and 'absolute reliability . . .' impressed Hitler and won his immediate confidence. Hitler also recognized, with his sure instinct, that this taut-lipped professional would follow him, body and soul, with unquestioning devotion to the end.

Dönitz, for his part, tasting a fulfilment which because of his inner insecurity could never be complete without a fixed object to adhere to, saw in the person of the Führer, aged since Stalingrad with bent back and trembling hand and his formerly electric blue eyes rather dulled and protuberant, all that he had been taught and needed fervently to believe in; here was *the* man of iron will whose political and military genius had rescued Germany from internal chaos, Bolshevism and the hate-inspired dictats of the western powers. So, while he held to his own judgement in naval affairs, he never questioned Hitler's overall strategy or views— indeed he made them his own—and while exasperated often enough by the lack of co-ordination at the top of the three services he blamed this on personalities, particularly the gross sybarite, Göring, rather than the Führer system or the Führer himself.

It was from both their points of view an ideal relationship; Hitler needed assurance that—despite recent events—he was the man of German destiny—Dönitz needed to give him that utter faith and loyalty. And since Hitler distrusted all his generals as a class and Göring was a caricature of self-indulgence, it is natural that he seized on Dönitz as confident and adviser, and in view of Dönitz's ambitious and thrusting temperament inevitable that he responded ardently.

Can Dönitz have been so blind as to have no doubts? Could a man capable of such sensitive appreciation of the quiet culture of the Balinese or the contentment of the Javanese villagers, so appreciative of the fact that the native women did not scold their children and would have found hitting them inconceivable, never reflect that his own *Volk* were in hell and never ask himself whether it was not the ruling circle he had joined who had brought and were keeping them there? It could not have been ignorance. 'The tyranny, the terror,' Helmuth von Moltke had written the previous year, 'the loss of values of all kinds is greater than I could have believed possible a short time ago.'[3] He had estimated that a hundred Germans a day were being executed after civil trial or court martial and hundreds more being shot in concentration camps without pretence of a trial. The greater part of the population had been uprooted by conscription or forced labour and 'spread all over the continent, untying all bonds of nature and thereby loosing the beast in man'. Could Dönitz have accepted the very obvious effects of all this and the reports of the barbarities on the Russian front and the bestial treatment of, particularly, the Jews in the occupied countries as simply exigencies of a war necessary to save the Fatherland from Bolshevism? Certainly this is the impression he seeks to convey by total silence in all his writings. This very silence, however, is proof enough that he deliberately shut out all doubt: the question then arises, was it simply ambition or deep inner insecurity and the consequent need to cling to the image of what he thought he ought to be and ought to serve—as he had been indoctrinated all his life—that enabled or forced him to blinker himself so thoroughly? And was it the suppression of other more sensitive feelings that drove him to excess?

A simpler answer to questions about his moral blindness might be the corrupting effects of power and status. He moved into an imposing house built about the turn of the century—now the Institute for Experimental Therapy, University of Berlin—set back in spacious grounds in the suburb of Dahlem, Berlin, where many other Nazi bosses had their grand residences. It is interesting that this had been the parish of his one-time fellow-cadet in the class of 1910, subsequently fellow U-boat Commander, Martin Niemöller. Niemöller had taken Holy Orders after the war, and although an enthusiastic supporter of Hitler at the beginning, his later opposition had led to his incarceration in a concentration

269

camp; in 1943 he was still inside. His successors are clear that neither Dönitz nor Ingeborg were churchgoers during their time in Dahlem.

In addition to his splendid home, which was guarded by an SS company, Dönitz had all the other gleaming trappings of Nazi power, a large Mercedes staff car—escorted by SS guards when he travelled—a smaller car for Berlin, a private aeroplane and a train named *Auerhahn* with a restaurant coach and a sleeping coach with a conference chamber. And like the other top men he had his collections—the Persian carpets he loved, the heroic engravings, the sea pictures he had been acquiring in France. He also collected silver, antiques and *objets*, and had been presented by his flotillas in France with a priceless Gobelin tapestry which had adorned the wall of a château; the house in Dahlem was furnished with exquisite taste. How much all these came from his service pay, how much from the handouts with which Hitler was wont to retain the loyalty of his chief servants, or from the general corruption that welded the seams of the Nazi machine is quite unknown. He received a grant of 300,000 marks from Hitler on his promotion to Grand Admiral, but this was standard for equivalent ranks in all the services. Probably the question is not important; undoubtedly Dönitz's loyalty sprang from deeper wells than money or possessions; all who knew him describe him as upright and not out for personal gain—as one of his adjutants put it, 'the complete opposite of *Reichsmarschall* Göring'.[4]

He truly believed and acted on his first directive to his staff, which ran:

Our life belongs to the State. Our honour lies in our duty-fulfilment and readiness for action. No one of us has the right to private life. The question for us is winning the war. We have to pursue this goal with fanatical devotion and the most ruthless determination to win.[5]

His own devotion and habits of work remained uncorroded by his new status. He continued to retire early to bed and to rise early. His adjutant, *Korvettenkapitän* Hansen-Nootbar, who joined him that spring from torpedo boats so that he could inform him of the attitudes and needs of the surface fleet, describes him as the 'consummate "morning-man"'; he recalls being roused by telephone at between five and six in the morning and hearing Dönitz's voice.

'Hänschen, are you still asleep!'
'Jawohl, Herr Grossadmiral . . .'
'That's no good. I want you . . .'[6]

Dönitz used to tell him he had his best thoughts in the early morning.

He lost no time in getting rid of the senior officers identified with Raeder's policies, dismissing some like Carls and shifting others to front commands or to backwaters like education. 'The great seal cull', as it came to be known, caused bitterness among those axed, but it was undoubtedly necessary and brought an infusion of younger blood and practicality to areas where failure and fantasy had ruled.[7]

Some of his choices were not so happy, in particular perhaps his appointment of Wilhlem Meisel as chief of the naval staff. Meisel was a conscientious worker—who was not in the German Navy!—but lacked the imagination or personality to be much more than a transmitting organ for Dönitz's ideas. This suited Dönitz perfectly, but it was the worst possible relationship for naval decision-making. What Dönitz needed was a strong curb, an analytical and sceptical right hand with the toughness to oppose his own blood-reasoning. Whether he would have tolerated such a man for long is, of course, doubtful. The fact that he chose a man like Meisel for the key post at High Command is significant; probably this too stemmed from his insecurity; or it may be, as his adjutant, Hansen-Nootbar, believes, he lacked understanding of other men.

Since the sea war was now to be the U-boat war, he combined the office of BdU with his own post as C-in-C of the Navy, and had U-boat headquarters moved from Paris to Berlin, where the Hotel am Steinplatz in Charlottenberg was furnished for the purpose. He retained Godt as his effective chief of operations with the title of Admiral commanding U-boats and FdU; Hessler remained Godt's number one.

The *Kriegsmarine* was a vast concern by this stage of the war; it had the defence of scores of harbours and thousands of miles of coastline from occupied Scandinavia and the Baltic right around northern Europe and Biscay to the south of France, the Aegean and the Black Sea to look after; it was responsible for the protection of the shipments of iron ore and other vital metals down the Norwegian coast and across the Baltic, troop transport and supplies to the eastern armies, the security of blockade runners from Japan and Spain with equally vital commodities for the war effort; in the Mediterranean the Navy was working in co-operation with the Italian Navy in the struggle to keep open the supply lines to the *Afrika Korps*, now squeezed into a corner of Tunisia, and was fully engaged in the attack on allied supply lines. It was a hugely complex military, military-political and economic mosaic quite different

271

from the simple certainties of the Atlantic 'tonnage war'. He learnt this quickly, but in the beginning his concern was the battle in the Atlantic, his first overriding priority to boost U-boat production. He also intended to increase production of the only other potent weapon of offence, the *Schnell* (fast motor torpedo)boats which attacked shipping in the English Channel. The task was rendered particularly difficult since Hitler's reaction to the disaster at Stalingrad was to cut the Navy's already insufficient steel quota further to make more available for tank production, which he accorded the highest priority. A great part of Dönitz's energies, therefore—according to Hansen-Nootbar at least 90 per cent of his working time—was spent with the technical and construction departments.[8]

At first he seems to have agreed with Hitler's directive to scrap the big ships; already the surface fleet was being combed for more officers and men for the ever-increasing force of U-boats and his first plans included the phased de-commissioning of the major units to release yet more men and dockyard workers, whose shortage also contributed to the bottle-necks in construction. However, he soon came to appreciate Raeder's objections to this course which were persisted in by the naval staff: it would amount to an effortless victory for the allies, not only handing them a great psychological and propaganda success, but allowing them to release far greater forces, at present held back to cover the threat posed by the *Tirpitz* and the other big ships, for offensive operations against the German coasts and supply shipping, or to protect Atlantic convoys. Moreover the release of steel and manpower would be a mere drop in the ocean. Chiefly, though, it was the classic argument of the fleet 'in being' to tie up the enemy's forces which had been accepted by virtually every inferior fleet throughout the modern history of navies.

Dönitz's handling of these problems calls to mind those earlier reports of his 'ability and quick perception of essentials . . .' in staff appointments, and his deftness in dealing with other ministries. This was particularly noticeable in his handling of the Führer himself. In three apparently effortless stages he not only reversed the edict on scrapping the big ships, but turned the whole naval production situation round. The initial steps were taken during his first conference with the Führer on February 8th; Hitler agreed in principle that no more skilled workers engaged in U-boat construction or repairs should be called up for the Army; the next day he agreed that the big ships should be ordered out to battle as soon as a worthwhile target appeared, and that once out they

272

should be allowed to operate on the force Commander's initiative without any restrictions such as Hitler himself and the naval staff had imposed on earlier sorties. It is interesting that the British naval intelligence assessment of Dönitz's character led them to predict that his appointment as C-in-C would lead to the big ships being used to attack the northern convoys or to attempt a desperate break-out into the Atlantic.[9]

At his next meeting with the Führer on February 26th, Dönitz said that in his opinion the Archangel convoys with war supplies for Russia would make excellent targets for the surface forces and he considered it his duty, in view of the heavy fighting on the eastern front, to exploit this possibility to the full. To Hitler's disbelief he went on to propose the despatch of the *Scharnhorst* to reinforce the *Tirpitz*—both condemned in his earlier plans—in northern Norway for the purpose.

Hitler objected that he was strongly opposed to any further surface ship engagements since, beginning with the *Graf Spee*, they had led to one loss after another. 'The time for great ships is over. I would rather have the steel and nickel from these ships than send them into battle again.'[10]

There were strong grounds for this view; the Pacific war had demonstrated that the gunned surface warship had been mastered by air power, and German naval-air co-operation had not begun to meet the challenge. However, Dönitz countered by implying again that the previous failures of German surface units had been due to restrictions placed on the force Commanders.

Hitler denied that he had ever issued orders of that sort, and contrasted the lack of fighting spirit shown in the surface ships with the bitter fighting by German soldiers on the eastern front and said how unbearable it was to see Russian strength built up continually by the northern convoys.

Dönitz seized his chance: he would consider it his duty, instead of decommissioning the *Tirpitz* and *Scharnhorst*, to send them into action whenever suitable targets for them could be found.

After further discussion at which both stuck to their guns, Hitler said finally, 'We will see who is right. I will give you six months to prove that the big ships can still achieve something.'[11]

There was a price to pay for Dönitz's victory; as Michael Salewski, author of one of the few scholarly works on the German naval High Command, has pointed out, from that moment on Dönitz was under pressure to use the heavy ships in the way he had promised; their success

273

was in the nature of a wager struck between the two men, the stake the big ships themselves.[12]

In his efforts to gain more steel for the Navy, continuing through the spring, Dönitz fully convinced Hitler of the necessity for his expanded programme but there were so many other urgent priorities for the fighting in the east and so little steel that the matter was only fully resolved when he allowed Speer to take over naval construction. This was what Speer had been attempting to gain from Raeder; that Dönitz agreed to it—with suitable safeguards in the shape of a naval ship-building commission under his own nominee, Rear Admiral Topp—demonstrates his excellent sense of priorities. The scheme was fought through in the teeth of the naval construction department under Admiral Fuchs, whom Dönitz wanted to sack, but he could find no replacement for some time. While there was still a chance of rational production it proved itself: Speer had virtually the entire production resources of the *Reich* at his disposal and could exploit the materials and manpower in this vast empire better than individual services fighting their own corner. The measure also released Dönitz from one of Raeder's constant frustrations, allowing him to devote more time to operations.

The Battle of the Atlantic was now at its height; from Dönitz's point of view there were several disturbing developments. The first, noted in January, was the success with which the enemy routed his convoys around U-boat groups and the fact, confirmed by intercepts of allied U-boat disposition reports, that they had a very accurate knowledge of where the groups were. Hessler and the 1A Operations, *Kapitänleutnant* Schnee, made a detailed analysis of all the information probably available to the allies from bearings of U-boat wireless transmissions, sightings, radar contacts and U-boat attacks on ships, matched this with the allied reports and came to the conclusion that it was possible—except in one or two unexplained instances—for the enemy to have arrived at their precise knowledge by these means.

Dönitz's suspicion of treachery was strong, nonetheless, and every member of the U-boat staff at am Steinplatz was subjected to investigation within the department; this turned up indiscreet French liaisons but no traitor. Finally only Dönitz and Godt remained to be vetted. 'Shall I investigate you,' Godt asked, 'or will you investigate me?'[13]

Meanwhile, despite the conviction of the communications experts that

274

the enemy could not have broken the Enigma codes, Dönitz had ordered U-boats at sea to use the fourth rotor in their enciphering machine. It was a good move; the cryptanalyists at Bletchley Park had broken in again on the previous December 13th and the accurate situation reports were in fact based on decrypts.[14] The fourth rotor blacked them out for a while, but they soon broke in again. *B-Dienst* was reading the allied convoy routing signals at the same time and as the speed of both sides' decrypts varied randomly from a few hours to several days it is hardly possible to say which had the edge, nor is it important; this climax of the U-boat campaign was decided on other factors.

The most potent of these was manifesting itself to U-boat Command by a sharply increased rate of losses of boats on the way to or from their Biscay bases. The war diary for March 23rd noted:

> . . . between November 1942 and January 1943 enemy air activity against U-boats had little result but since February its effect has increased to an alarming extent. We cannot tell whether this is due to improved location gear or more suitable types of aircraft . . .

There had been suspicions for several weeks that a new type of radar location was being used since Commanders were reporting being attacked by aircraft at night or out of low cloud without any warning from their Metox radar search receivers now in use on all boats. It seemed as if the enemy had deliberately developed a location device working on frequencies outside the range of this warning apparatus.

These were indeed the first signs of a very short wave allied radar operating on a wave length of only 10 cm instead of the old 1·5 m, designed not to outwit the boats' receivers, but to gain greater range and definition. By these early months of 1943 the revolutionary set was being fitted to surface escorts as well as aircraft. As for the aircraft, the Boeings, Beaufighters, Liberators and Fortresses probing Biscay outmatched the few Junkers possessed by the Air Commander, Atlantic, who did not expect anything better in the near future. 'There will be further particularly painful losses,' Godt predicted.[15]

Yet, despite all difficulties it was still possible towards the end of March for Dönitz to believe that with more boats and a tremendous effort he could win. The latest battle in the North Atlantic had resulted in the biggest success ever for U-boat packs against convoys.

The operation had been set off by *B-Dienst*, on top form, supplying

U-boat Command absolutely current routing instructions for Convoy HX 229 eastbound off the US coast. On Dönitz's instructions other operations had been broken off and all boats in the area formed into three patrol lines, *Raubgraf* (robber baron), *Stürmer* (daredevil) and *Dränger* (Harrier) across their route. While the boats were speeding to their positions *B-Dienst* intercepted new allied routing instructions for the convoy and another nearby convoy, SC 122, which was also heading east; these were designed to steer the convoys around the northernmost *Raubgraf* line, which had revealed its presence by attacking a westbound convoy. The U-boat lines were now re-positioned and early in the morning of March 16th, U 603 of *Raubgraf* found herself in very heavy weather in the midst of one of the convoys. She reported and shadowed in exemplary fashion and U-boat Command ordered half the available boats towards her convoy, then after an intercept by *B-Dienst* suggested that the other convoy had passed, ordered all boats at full speed towards her position.

By dusk that evening seven boats were in contact, working their way ahead on the surface into attack positions, and at 10 o'clock U 603 herself opened the action from inside the escorts, scoring one hit. The other boats came in at half-hour intervals throughout the night, hitting another seven merchantmen although reporting rather more. The five escorts, meanwhile, who had to spend much of their time in rescue work, damaged two of the boats in depth charge attacks.

At the same time one of the *Stürmer* boats, U 388, heading towards the scene found herself in the midst of another convoy, actually SC 122, and attacked, scoring four hits. There was some confusion at U-boat Command about whether this was the second convoy or whether she had made a mistake in navigation, but the situation clarified during the next day, and orders were sent out distributing the boats roughly equally between the two convoys. Meanwhile reports of sinkings amounting to fourteen ships of 90,000 tons[16] and a further six damaged had induced high spirits at U-boat Command, where the staff had been up all night. Godt sent a jaunty signal to all boats in the style of his chief. Dönitz was in Italy at this time, but it is possible he dictated the order by telephone.

'*Bravo! Dranbleiben! Weiter so!*' ('Bravo! Keep at it! Carry on like that!')

The convoys were in the central Atlantic 'air gap' now but approaching the extreme limit of very long range Liberators stationed in

Northern Ireland, and one of these ordered out that morning reached the leading convoy, SC 122, and forced two of the shadowing boats to dive; she could not stay for long, however, and in the interval before the arrival of another aircraft, U 388 was able to work ahead into position for an underwater attack and she sank another merchantman. Similar underwater attacks were made on the original HX convoy which lacked air cover and three of whose escorts were attending merchantmen crippled the previous night; two more ships were sunk.

More and more boats were homing in meanwhile to both convoys but the appearance of Liberators shortly before dusk forced them to dive, and probably because the weather was still bad and the convoys made the usual dusk alterations throwing off the shadowers contact was not regained until the following day. By this time the actions were moving out of the 'air gap' and the boats were constantly forced to dive by the appearance of shore-based aircraft. They hung on nevertheless for another two days and nights, sinking another seven merchantmen until continuous air cover around the convoys made prospects hopeless. Before the operation was finally called off one boat was sunk when attacked by aircraft through squall clouds.

Analysing the results at U-boat Command it was noted that 'As in so many actions the surprise attacks on the first night were the most successful . . .'[17] but then owing to the appearance of land-based aircraft 'the U-boats from the second day on had a hard struggle'. Results were assessed as 32 ships totalling 186,000 tons and one destroyer sunk, and nine other ships hit. 'This is so far the greatest success obtained in a convoy battle and more gratifying in that nearly 50 per cent of the boats shared in it.' The Propaganda Ministry, badly needing good news, boosted the tonnage to 204,000 and early in April, as a further propaganda exercise, Hitler presented Dönitz with the oak leaves of the Knight's Cross in recognition of the triumph and the total March sinking figures of 779,533 tons (actually 627,300 tons) which closely approached the record set the previous November.

The actual results of the battle were 22 merchantmen of a total 146,596 tons sunk (no destroyer hit) against only one U-boat destroyed; the shock impelled both Roosevelt and Churchill to intervene personally; as a result more destroyers were made available for 'support groups' to reinforce the convoy escorts under attack, and more long-range Liberators were provided to close the 'air gap'. In this sense the U-boats' undoubted triumph in the four-days' battle, March 16–19th, hastened their ultimate defeat—for it seems that the allied chiefs of staff needed such a jolt to remind them of the Casablanca Conference decision that the defeat of the U-boats was their first priority.

In another sense, the balance was bound to tip against Dönitz at some stage, and the process was already well under way. On the very day that the U-boat Command war diary noted 'the greatest success so far obtained in a convoy battle'[18] the British Commander of the Western Atlantic defences, Admiral Sir Max Horton, wrote to a friend, 'I really have hopes now that we can turn from the defence to another and better role—killing them.' He went on:

> The real trouble has been basic—too few ships, all too hard worked with no time for training . . . The Air of course is a tremendous factor, & it is only recently that the many promises that have been made show signs of fulfilment so far as shore-based air is concerned, after three and a half years of war . . . All these things are coming to a head just now and although the last week has been one of the blackest on the sea, so far as this job is concerned I am really hopeful.[19]

The U-boats' successes had been made possible by the diversion of allied resources to the North African landings, the Pacific campaign and to bombing raids over Europe, aimed first at knocking out the U-boat bases and, when it proved impossible to penetrate the giant concrete shelters provided by Todt and Speer, to crippling German industry in the Ruhr. There were already more than enough long range Liberators to cover the whole North Atlantic convoy routes, and if a fraction of the effort devoted to these 'offensive' raids had been spent on the protection of convoys Dönitz's gloomy forecasts of the late summer of 1942 must have been fulfilled and a great many allied ships and lives saved—not to mention civilians in France and Germany who also paid the price for the mistaken bombing policy. In this sense the crisis in which the allies found themselves in the spring of 1943—and which Dönitz and most German authorities on the U-boat war have used to claim that the Atlantic battle was a close-run thing—was entirely self-induced. There was never a possibility that the U-boats which Dönitz was throwing into the attack could have cut the Atlantic lifeline; directly they threatened to do so, allied resources must have been re-allocated from so-called offensive operations to the defence of this vital artery, and since the contemporary German U-boat had been rendered obsolete by improved aircraft per-

278

formance and weaponry, his surface and group tactics by radar, this must have proved fatal.

U-boat Command misread the signs completely. It is not clear from the record whether this was due to wishful thinking, lack of imagination or failure to stand up to the pressures imposed by the chief, Dönitz. These pressures must have been immense; whatever may be said about his habit of consultation before taking decisions, great strength and confidence would have been needed to withstand the combination of fire and tenacity with which he pursued his goals, and the aura of experience and success and power surrounding him in his new rank. And there is no question that he was at this time focusing all his powers on winning the Battle of the Atlantic; thus at the end of March he issued guidelines for the staff in the form of twelve 'Commandments':

1) All measures must serve the winning of the war.
2) The 'Tonnage war' has the first rank. For this every effort must be made.
3) Of special importance is the battle against enemy location devices and the enemy air force . . .[20]

The next four commandments also concerned the tonnage war: U-boat building was to be increased, the *Schnell* boat arm enhanced, the *Luftwaffe* and the Japanese navy co-opted for the battle against merchantmen. Finally he addressed other areas: Tunisia had to be held, protection of German convoys improved, economy in manpower striven for, bureaucracy annihilated, decentralization and individual responsibility promoted.

It is clear from the order and wording of these guidelines that the threat from the air and the allied radar was appreciated; the danger was driven home in the first days of April as U-boat packs in the former happy hunting ground of the mid-Atlantic 'air gap' found themselves harried round the clock by trained support groups working in co-operation with escort-carrier-based planes and long-range Liberators, all equipped with high definition radar whose beams could not be detected by U-boats' warning sets. Still the staff at U-boat headquarters failed or refused to recognize the signs; of an HX convoy contacted by eight boats on April 4th, the war diary comment was '. . . very little success achieved, probably chiefly because of the inexperience of young Commanders'.[21]

That Dönitz's priorities remained unchanged is made clear by his report to Hitler on April 11th;[22] he started by admitting that the U-boat war had become 'difficult, losses high'—nineteen boats sunk in February, fifteen in March, six already in the present month:

On the other hand it is plain that the aim of the tonnage war must be under all circumstances to sink more than the enemy can build. Should we fail in this the enemy would continue to suffer a very great destruction of material but the gradual bleeding of enemy tonnage would not occur. My great anxiety therefore is that the U-boat war will fail if we do not sink more ships than the enemy builds.

He went on to say that he did not believe the enemy could stand a net loss of *100–200,000* tons a month for any length of time, and that German U-boats, *Schnell* boats and aircraft, together with Japanese forces, had to exert every possible effort to achieve this. He did not like to think that one day they might reproach themselves, 'we could have attained the goal of bleeding the enemy if only we had tried somewhat harder in the tonnage war'. And since many more U-boats were now needed to achieve the success of one boat in 1940, it was essential to increase U-boat building to the full extent of capacity so that 'the relationship between losses and new building will not be too unfavourable'.

It seems evident here that it is Dönitz who is putting the pressure on Hitler for increased efforts, not the other way around, and that in calling simply for more U-boats he was blinding himself to the very obvious signs that all he had feared the previous summer had now happened: air cover had been extended over the entire North Atlantic; prospects of success for U-boats *had* 'declined to an insupportable extent'.

Of course, Hitler was happy to agree with his reasoning; yet the increased construction he proposed demanded 30,000 tons of steel a month above the quota allowed, and the problem remained, he said, 'Where can the steel be obtained? Obviously in a totalitarian state I can order the required amount to be made available, but that would mean taking it from some other arm . . .'

After itemizing the urgent need for more tanks, aircraft, anti-aircraft guns, he said he would discuss the matter with Speer—as a result of which the Armaments Minister and Dönitz moved closer to a joint plan for naval construction.

It is this programme that demonstrates Dönitz's refusal to recognize the significance of recent convoy battles. The circumstances call to mind Fürbringer's May 1939 paper arguing that it would be irresponsible to commit valuable U-boat crews to trade war unless the boats had been rendered Asdic-immune and trained in intimate co-operation with the air arm; Dönitz's response then had been in the form of flat assertions: 'It is clear' that only an attack on English sea communications could have a war-decisive effect, the U-boat was the 'sole means' of accomplishing this, he was confident the Asdic-immune boat *would* be developed in foreseeable time, aircraft would not play a role in the open spaces of the Atlantic, it was not necessary to develop a special torpedo for use against escorts, above all his new group tactics, by providing a 'concentration of U-boats against the concentration of ships in a convoy', would give the English a surprise.

He had been right about the surprise, but the advantage had been thrown away. Now it was his boats which were being surprised from the air; he was urging the rapid fitting of anti-aircraft guns, the development of an acoustic torpedo for use against escorts, and he had set up a Commission of Scientists to find a solution to the new enemy location method, the search for a substance to render U-boats radar-immune high on the programme. But his overall response was precisely as it had been to Fürbringer: the U-boat was the sole means of forcing a decision; his pack tactics were correct: *Also dranbleiben! Weiter so!*

His new programme called for an increased building rate of existing types of boats, chiefly the medium Type VII, to 27 a month rising to 30 a month in 1944 and throughout 1945.[23]

Where in 1943 was his Fürbringer? This raises serious questions about his choice of staff at U-boat Command, particularly his chief of operations, Godt. A report by a team of British anti-submarine officers who interrogated Godt and members of the U-boat staff directly after the war brings these questions into focus; the overall impression the British gained was that 'we gave the U-boats more credit than we should have done for efficiency'; another impression was that 'in the main the U-boat officer lacks one vital attribute, imagination'.[24] The team was surprised at the very small organization at U-boat headquarters and the fact that there was no research department attached. It is possible to infer from their report that, like the crew of the cruiser *Emden* in 1934, U-boat headquarters staff 'carried the stamp of his [Dönitz's] personality'— were indeed an extension of his determination that his goal and his way were right and would prevail.

*   *   *

At the time of Dönitz's meeting with Hitler his son Peter was in the North Sea, three days out of Kiel on his first war cruise as second watchkeeper of U 954, also on her first mission; by coincidence, or the flotilla chief's sense of humour, her Commander enjoyed the name by which Dönitz was known in the service, *Loewe* ('Lion'). Over the next two days U 954 worked northwards, hugging the Norwegian coast, then struck out around the Faeroes into the open Atlantic and joined a group combing westwards. On April 21st she was ordered into action.

At 6 o'clock that morning U 306, patrolling in Group *Meise* off Newfoundland, had sighted an expected eastbound convoy, HX 234; U 954's group of seven boats was in a waiting position to the east and they were instructed by U-boat Command to proceed towards the position. They ran all day before gale force winds and high seas, through drifts of fog and snow, and that night the convoy, exploiting the conditions, shook off its shadower; contact was not regained for the whole of the next day during which the weather moderated, but U 306 picked it up again at seven in the morning of the 23rd, and reported so consistently that seven more boats were able to join. One of these was U 954; she succeeded in working her way into position for a submerged attack, and at 4 o'clock that afternoon scored a hit on a large steamer. If Dönitz was not at U-boat headquarters monitoring the progress of the battle, no doubt the good news was phoned through to him.

Aircraft appeared shortly afterwards, attacking several boats, forcing others down and so frustrating the looked-for mass attack that night. Aircraft were again patrolling the convoy the next day and although U 306 regained touch and continued reporting, allowing altogether fifteen boats to come up, all were beaten off. Meanwhile the wind rose to Force Nine from ahead, visibility fell to a quarter of a mile, and as intensified air activity was expected from Iceland the next day the operation was called off. Altogether nineteen boats had taken part, fifteen of which had followed the convoy over 700 miles, but the results were meagre: two ships only sunk, and in exchange one U-boat lost and others more or less damaged.

U-boat Command summed up the main reasons for the failure as 'variable visibility during the night. The Commanders, for the most part inexperienced and fresh from home waters, were unable to cope with these conditions . . .'[25]

The assessment made in the anti-submarine tracking room in London was more realistic: for some weeks the decrypts of U-boat transmissions had been suggesting 'incipient decline in morale amongst at least some U-boat crews'.[26] The latest battle was described as a 'remarkably feeble operation' by the boats concerned, who had made 'repeated and bitter complaints about the ubiquity and efficiency of the aircraft which were constantly with the convoy on April 24th . . .' The report concluded:

> The outstanding impression felt on reading recent U-boat traffic is that the spirit of the crews which are at present out on operations in the Atlantic is low and general morale is shaky. There is little doubt that BdU shares this impression for he has been comparatively restrained in expressing his none the less evident disappointment . . .

At the end of the month the anti-submarine report from the tracking room predicted that historians would single out April and May 'as the critical period during which strength began to ebb away from the German U-boat offensive'.[27] The prediction was based not so much on a dramatic fall over the month in the tonnage sunk, nor in the increased U-boat killing rate; it was

> . . . because for the first time U-boats failed to press home their attacks on convoys when favourably situated to do so. There is ground for a confident estimate that the enemy's peak effort is past. Morale and efficiency are delicate and may wither rapidly if no longer nourished by rich success.

Morale at U-boat Command and in the Biscay bases was already low.[28] The increase in surprise attacks by aircraft during the outward and homeward passage through the Bay and the increase in the number of boats lost, the lack of knowledge, in most cases, of how or why they were lost, the event indicated simply by a failure to report or reply to call signs and noted in the war diary as 'probably lost in . . .', all this fed speculation which bred rumours of secret weapons and bizarre ruses. The situation was horrific without imagined terrors: new aerial depth bombs, new devices for lobbing charges ahead of surface escorts, allowing attack while in good Asdic contact, a doctrine of persevering in attack for hours if necessary, which was made possible by extra vessels from the support groups now kept on station in mid-Atlantic to race to the aid of threatened convoys, above all the high standard of training and

283

the teamwork between the vessels of each escort group and between them and air escorts made life for U-boat crews almost unbearably difficult and dangerous.

We are unlikely ever to know the precise course of the discussions among the staff at U-boat Command, or whether it was proposed that the campaign be called off temporarily or swung to other theatres, and if so who put such views and how strongly. Undoubtedly there was much soul-searching. Undoubtedly Dönitz took part; undoubtedly he knew that his crews, his own son out there in U 954, were exposed to hazards that he and his fellow First War Commanders had never experienced. There is no trace of these internal debates in the war diary though, only a record of doomed attempts to combat the losses by equipping U-boats with AA batteries for instance, and sending them into Biscay as aircraft decoys like the first war 'Q' ships which lured U-boats to their death, or by organizing sailings in groups so that the total anti-aircraft battery of the group would protect them; all failed for the simple reason that the allies had command of the air and U-boats were not suitable craft to dispute it. There were small experiments with dispositions, increasing the distances between boats in groups, dividing groups into sub-sections spaced apart to make it more difficult for the enemy to plot their positions, or giving the outer boats instructions to make wireless signals to create an impression of an enormously extended patrol line. These were ineffectual responses to the scale of the threat hanging over the arm. The fundamental tactics remained unchanged for Dönitz's response was unchanged: more boats! It is ironic perhaps that in this month during which the battle turned decisively against him he had a daily average of 111 boats at sea in the Atlantic, rather over the '90 continuously operational boats' he had picked on in 1939 as necessary for success; such were the distances involved, however, and the difficulties of passage that only a third of these were in the operational area at any time.

By May 1st there were 425 boats in service; of these 118 were on trials and 67 in use for training in the Baltic, leaving a total of 240 available for operations; 207 of these were detailed for the decisive theatre, the North Atlantic, and 45 were actually grouped in the prime operational area south of Greenland.

Peter Dönitz's boat, U 954, was one of these; after the operations against HX 224 had been broken off she had been incorporated into a group *Star* ('Starling') which had been ordered after a westbound convoy; high steep seas in their face and driving snow squalls had prevented more than five of the group from actually sighting the convoy; U 954 had not been one of them. Two boats had been attacked and the others forced down by aircraft, after which contact had been lost and on April 30th the operation was called off; the summary in U-boat Command war diary for May 1st ended on a defiant note, 'this operation failed only because of bad weather, not because of the enemy's defences'.[29]

Meanwhile the groups were redisposed in three patrol lines to catch three more expected convoys. Only one of these was sighted, the westbound ONS 5, which was spotted by the northernmost boat of the *Star* line. However the weather was still so appalling that none of the other boats could find it and U-boat Command redirected the group southwesterly, forming them and other boats in the area—a total of 41—into separated sub-groups in the anticipated path of the convoy; the small groups were to mislead the allies whose very accurate U-boat disposition reports, intercepted by *B-Dienst*, were still thought to be compiled by radar sightings and bearings of wireless transmissions. The plan was to close the sub-groups up at high speed at the last possible moment, so foiling evasive routing and bringing the boats into two closely-spaced lines across the enemy's track.

It worked brilliantly, and this time fortune seemed to be on their side for continuous gales had scattered the convoy and forced three of the escorts to put back to refuel, yet the weather as the boats closed on May 4th was moderating sufficiently to make attack possible. However, the convoy had air cover from Canada and as the boats approached two were destroyed and others forced under. Contact was regained at eight o'clock that night, and as the groups homed in a fierce surface battle developed; the outnumbered escorts counter-attacked as they located the boats on their radar but were unable to devote sufficient time to the pursuit as they had to return to protect their charges; four ships were sunk from the main body and one straggler, and the next day a further seven were sunk in submerged attacks for the loss of a third U-boat. U 954 was not one of the successful boats.

A long range Liberator appeared in the evening, but could not remain long, and fifteen boats were able to gather in the vicinity, ready to strike after dark; in Berlin the staff waited confidently for reports of further sinkings. None came. Fog drifted up over the now calm sea giving the escorts with their radar sets inestimable advantages, and some 24 attacks

285

were beaten off without loss of another merchantman. In the course of these fierce and sudden actions six boats found themselves under gunfire from vessels they could not see, one was rammed and sunk by a destroyer which came at her out of the fog and the others were depth-charged after being forced under; three were lost in this way, bringing the total destroyed in the two days of the battle to six boats; five more were heavily damaged and twelve reported lesser damage.

This was recognized in the allied camp as the turning point; no force could sustain such a proportion of losses.

It was not regarded as such at U-boat Command; the war diary summary of operations concluded: 'This loss of six boats is very high and grave considering the short duration of the attack. The blame can be laid mainly on the foggy period . . .' and '. . . If fog had held off for six hours many more ships would certainly have been sunk . . .'[30] The surviving boats were given new patrol lines in the area or sent to replenish from two 'milch-cow' U-boats stationed in the unfrequented area further to the south; one of these was U 954.

One change was ordered, however; since it seemed that the larger Type IX boats were proving more vulnerable to bomb and depth charge attack on account of their more complicated structure, it was decided not to send any more into the North Atlantic, but to use them in more remote, less heavily-patrolled areas.[31] And on May 14th Type IX boats already operating in the North Atlantic were ordered to transfer their fuel to other boats and return home. It was the first sign of retreat.

Dönitz's refusal to admit even temporary defeat in the North Atlantic battle as a whole was not due to ignorance of the conditions faced by his Commanders at the front; after the summary of the ONS 5 battle in the war diary of May 6th under 'General Remarks', it was stated: 'Along with air activity, enemy radar location is the worst enemy of our U-boats . . .' and '. . . radar location is robbing the U-boat of its most important characteristic, the ability to remain undetected'. Then comes a passage reading very much as if Dönitz was the author:

All responsible departments are working at high pressure on the problem of again providing the U-boat with gear capable of detecting whether the enemy is using radar, they are also concentrating on a camouflage for U-boats against radar location, which must be considered the ultimate goal. A solution to at any rate the first problem may be of decisive importance for U-boat warfare . . .

Enemy air forces, the remarks continued, were already able to take over escort duties over almost the whole North Atlantic and it had to be expected that the only remaining gaps would be closed in reasonable time.

Air escort provided by a large number of planes operating over a fairly large area around the convoy has always forced our U-boats to lag hopelessly behind a convoy and prevented them achieving any successes, especially when air and naval escorts co-operated efficiently.

After noting the increased U-boat losses to aircraft in the Biscay approach routes and the increasing number of enemy surface escorts against which 'we as yet possess no really effective weapon' the remarks concluded: 'To sum up, the U-boat struggle is now harder than ever, but all departments are working full out to assist the boats in their tasks and to equip them with better weapons.'

The remarks demonstrate the failure at U-boat Command to react realistically to the crisis. It was not the fog of war and rush of events that obscured the field but emotional commitment. The U-boat was clearly recognized here as an obsolescent weapon against enemy counter-measures, 'robbed of its most important ability to remain undetected', its pack tactics rendered hopeless in the face of air cover. Instead of drawing the appropriate conclusions and making the strategic retreat that had been indicated for some time to enable the scientists and weapons departments to respond, more boats, more valuable, trained crews were to be hurled against the wall of the enemy defences in desperate, foredoomed attempts to find some small breach.

There can be no excuse. This was a campaign whose goal was ultimately numerical, to sink more tonnage than the enemy could build; Dönitz always expressed his aim in these terms, and avidly he studied the monthly statistics kept by the staff for trends. These trends now demonstrated that the battle could not be won with existing methods.

The vital figure was what Dönitz referred to as the 'U-boat potential', or the tonnage sunk per U-boat per day at sea. Since the average sea-days per boat never varied much from month to month, nor could they, given the fuel capacity of existing boats and the repair times at base, future monthly sinking totals could be predicted on just two of the variables, the number of boats and the 'potential'. The previous year the highest 'potential' had been 438 tons per boat per sea-day;[32] this had been in June while the boats were enjoying their 'happy time' off the US coast and Caribbean. Over the following months as convoy systems were organized in these areas, and Dönitz had been forced to return to the sterner task of fighting the North Atlantic convoys in the 'air gap' the 'potential' had dropped sharply to 256, 260, 229, 226; it rose briefly to 329 tons in the record month of November, then fell back to 139 in December—an average over the last six months of 1942 of 240 tons sunk per boat per day at sea. In the meantime the number of boats operating in the Atlantic had risen from 93 to 149.

Over the first four months of the present year, 1943, the 'potential' had dropped further: 129, 148, 230, 127—an average of rather under 160 tons sunk per boat per day at sea. Even assuming no further fall—a questionable assumption in view of the war diary remarks—it would take some 325 boats in the Atlantic to achieve a sinking rate of one million tons a month, and even this was at the lower end of Dönitz's goal; the naval staff estimate of the figure necessary to achieve victory was 1·3 million tons per month. Since all the other methods together, aircraft, *Schnell* boats, mines, Japanese and Italian forces, could not be expected to account for even 100,000 tons on present form, the U-boats had to do it virtually on their own. However, the U-boat loss rate over the past three months had averaged fifteen boats, and ten had already been lost in the first *five days* of May. Assuming that Speer managed to increase the monthly production figures to 27 as planned, a loss rate of fifteen would mean the fleet growing by only twelve boats a month and it would take between nine and ten months before the total 325 boats—necessary to sink a million tons—could be reached.

But over that nine or ten months some 140–150 boats and their now virtually irreplaceable crews would be lost. Meanwhile the enemy would be more than holding their own in shipbuilding capacity, and as a report of April 4th compiled from British sources had indicated, 87 per cent of merchant crews would be rescued from those ships that were sunk. [33]

It can be seen that the decision to carry on, if it was a decision rather than inertia or blind determination or more probably National Socialist 'will', was unscientific. Had the U-boat men been old-fashioned cannon-fodder, had there been a chance that, in Dönitz's rhetoric, 'putting forth a little more effort' and 'pressing home the attack' would have resulted in a decision in foreseeable time, had the U-boats been directly defending the homeland, the decision could be defended. None of these conditions obtained. The U-boats demanded scarce resources of steel and copper

288

and construction workers, the U-boat men were an acknowledged élite, the mettle of a good Commander as valuable and scarce a resource as the materials of which the boats themselves were made, and there was no glimmer of hope either in the statistics or the reports from the front that the battle could be won. Throwing more boats and crews away instead of husbanding them carefully while seeking new types and tactics and a new strategy was anachronistic folly. It is at this point that the flaws in Dönitz's qualities show up most vividly; it is at this point that we can look back to his 1938 and 1939 papers on U-boat strategy and tactics and his response to Fürbringer's critique and see that it was all there; he had not changed. The only difference now was that he had no curbs whatever. It is at this point, therefore, that the Führer system itself stands revealed as an anachronism.

Fresh boats from home and from the Biscay bases were directed, with the survivors of the recent battles, to form a 550-mile patrol line south of Greenland to intercept two expected eastbound convoys. Both these were routed around the danger area as revealed by Enigma decrypts, but *B-Dienst* put U-boat Command back in the game with equally rapid decrypts of the new routing instructions, and one of the convoys, HX 237, was found on May 9th.

Within half an hour the reporting boat had been located by an escort and forced under and contact was lost. U-boat Command instructed her group of seven boats to push on ahead in the path of the convoy 'with determination and on no account allow themselves to be shaken off'.[34] They followed the first part to the letter but aircraft from an escort carrier with the support group prevented them from carrying out the second part, and the convoy passed undetected. More brilliant work by *B-Dienst* allowed the boats to find it for a third time on May 11th and three stragglers were sunk, but the surface and air escort beat off attacks on the main body of ships and over that day and the next destroyed three of the seven attacking boats. On the 13th the operation was called off. U-boat Command commented:

> Right from the first day carrier-borne aircraft were sighted and later on the carrier itself. These and other land-based aircraft greatly hampered operations which finally had to be broken off because the air escort was too powerful . . .
> To sum up . . . it is almost useless today to attack a convoy escorted by a carrier with so few boats.[35]

U 954, meanwhile, had refuelled from the tanker, U 119, and returned to the operational area in the icy waters below Greenland. She was assigned to a new patrol line, *Donau* 1, which was positioned in the expected track of westbound convoys.

Dönitz's other main preoccupation at this time was the Mediterranean. He had been closely involved with this theatre from the beginning of his time as C-in-C, not only because the battle for North Africa hinged on the sea supply war, but also because he had become Hitler's trusted adviser, and the dangers threatening the southern flank had replaced the disasters on the Russian front as the Führer's chief preoccupation.

In March he had been sent to Italy to represent Hitler's views to Mussolini, an early indication of the confidence reposed in him. He had used the opportunity to obtain the *Duce*'s approval for the establishment of a small German staff in the Supamarina to improve the co-operation between the two Navies over the protection of North African transports, and in forceful but tactful discussions with the Italian naval chief, Admiral Riccardi, he had won a number of other important concessions; these included an agreement to supply convoy escorts with German AA guns and, the real object of this measure, *German-trained* gunners.[36]

The visit had seemed to mark a breakthrough in the strained relationship between the Axis Navies and he must have known as he reported back to the *Wolfschanze* that his reputation had risen with the Führer. He represented the pressing need for more aircraft since the supply battle was being lost largely as a result of allied air superiority; in the meantime he requested permission to send nine U-boats to the Mediterranean to release Italian submarines for the supply run—a remarkable change from his former attitude to diversions from the 'war-decisive battle in the Atlantic'! Hitler had agreed.[37]

Since then the allies had tightened their stranglehold and on May 1st Vice Admiral Ruge, whom Dönitz had appointed to head the German staff in the Supamarina, reported that the Italians had given up hope of saving North Africa and were turning their attention to the problem of defending Italy itself from anticipated allied assaults via Sardinia or Sicily. Dönitz's response was to tell Riccardi that the decision to hold the Tunis bridgehead was a matter for the supreme leadership; the Navy could not suddenly cease to co-operate while the other arms of the services 'fight and hold on in desperate positions'[38] and he virtually demanded the use of Italian cruisers for the supply run. When Riccardi refused he ordered the German naval command in Italy to send U-boats across loaded with drums of benzine for the forces. Since the three immediately available boats could only carry 13,000 gallons between them, the Supreme Commander, South, Field Marshal Kesselring—thanking him for the gesture—suggested this might not be a profitable use for the boats!

Dönitz persisted nonetheless, and on May 5th ordered both Ruge at the Supamarina and the German naval command to use all available forces 'without regard for future operations' to support the fighting soldiers and enable them to gain 'supremacy over the exhausted troops of the enemy'.[39] In isolation this order appears a remarkable misjudgement; viewed alongside his parallel misjudgement in the Atlantic battle and his precisely similar response it can be seen that Dönitz was not fighting with his head, but with his blood, behaving not as a rational Commander but as a National Socialist, convinced like Hitler that will-power and fanaticism would make up for numerical or technical inferiority.

This might be interpreted as the result of exposure to the atmosphere at Hitler's court, where since the shocking setbacks of the winter a new mood for extreme or 'radical' solutions had been evident. Goebbels and Speer were at the centre of the drive, the one using all the weapons of propaganda to whip up a 'backs to the wall' mood of fanatic defiance in the people, the other setting in motion a 'total war' economy. Dönitz's rhetoric on taking office—'Our life belongs to the State . . . The question for us is winning the war. We have to pursue this goal with fanatical devotion . . .'—was in the idiom of Goebbels' notorious public performance at the *Sportpalast* in Berlin on February 18th. Speer, who was present, called it the most effective arousal of an audience to fanaticism he had ever seen—as well he might, for the film of the audience's reaction shows him jumping up and leading the frenzy! 'Fanaticism', 'Total War', 'Victory despite . . .' were the codewords of the hour. Dönitz faithfully reflected them in every word and deed. Yet it is apparent from his service reports that he had been travelling a similar extreme, selfless, goal-oriented path and had held to it with 'indestructible toughness' throughout his career. He was not simply reflecting the new mood, he was part of it, and it seems evident that Raeder's dismissal and his succession were in fact manifestations of the new radicalism—as was his agreement with Speer in the teeth of the professionals of the old Navy to merge naval construction into the Ministry of Armaments.

The rise of the new spirit coincided with a dramatic decline in Hitler's health; this is not surprising since both stemmed from the same cause—defeat. The Führer had retired from his command headquarters on his doctors' advice to his mountain lair, the *Berghof* above Berchtesgaden. He had been suffering frightful headaches, stomach spasms and flatulence as well as a recurrence of trembling in his left arm and leg which had last affected him after his arrest and imprisonment in 1923. No doubt constant work and anxiety, sleeplessness and lack of exercise—for he believed he had a heart complaint and that physical exertion would prove fatal—and the drugs he was taking all played their part.[40] But underlying all the physical and personality changes noted by observers from this period was surely the overwhelming knowledge that he had lost control of events. He never admitted it, perhaps to himself least of all, and in the conscious exercise of his will against the material odds besetting the *Reich* he became more immovable in resolve, more suspicious, more impervious to argument, more subject to violent changes of mood, gloomily taciturn or overflowing with denunciations of his generals, his troops, his allies—never of his own cosmic misjudgements.

In this atmosphere no one who brought rational and analytical judgement to bear could have survived. It is a measure of Dönitz's natural affinities with the irrational nature of National Socialism that he not only survived, he prospered and grew to become Hitler's chief military and strategic anchor. It is significant too that after their preliminary skirmish over the usefulness of the big ships, Hitler never, so far as can be known, sought to interfere in the conduct of naval operations. Dönitz seemed to have given him every chance to do so by appointing a liaison officer at Führer headquarters whose task was to give detailed briefings on the everyday conduct of the war at sea—not simply highlights or disasters as in Raeder's time—but Hitler failed to take advantage of this opportunity to meddle as he meddled with his generals.

Hitler knew there was dissatisfaction amongst the military; arrests had been made at the *Abwehr*, the secret headquarters of resistance presided over by Admiral Canaris, and Himmler's agents were following a web of suspected treason leading to the highest levels of the Army. 'His opinion of all the generals is devastating,' Goebbels noted in his diary after a conversation with the Führer at this time; '. . . all generals are disloyal, all generals are opposed to National Socialism, all generals are reactionaries . . .'[41] The Navy was not implicated in treachery; Dönitz's single-minded devotion to the cause gave Hitler confidence it never would be; moreover, his consistently positive outlook and ardour to take on any and all responsibility in any field, combined with his unquestioning acceptance of the Führer's genius, demanded that Hitler in his turn play up to the role expected. With Dönitz he acted the wise elder statesman dextrously juggling world political and military complexities beyond the ken of mere military professionals; at the same time he drew strength from Dönitz's fire. Thus without the clash of argument each reinforced the other's cosmic delusions and, as von Puttkamer recorded, the two came in ever closer touch and were 'frequently together under four eyes'.[42]

This was already apparent by the time of the crisis over Tunisia; as allied troops entered Rommel's last major supply ports, Tunis and Bizerta, on May 7th, Dönitz was attending a Führer conference in Berlin. His determination to carry on the struggle to get supplies through by U-boat and small craft so long as a single soldier remained fighting was unshaken by the calamitous news of the day. Afterwards he caused a note to be entered in the naval staff war diary account of the conference—'The Führer was highly appreciative of the clear policy followed by the Navy'[43]—one of many such asides throughout the war diary that reveal his sense of importance at being at the centre of events and close confidant of the Führer, for instance: 'the example of Africa represents for him [the Führer] the most striking practical example of the correctness of the exposition by the C-in-C Navy'.[44]

Hitler's anxiety was not simply that Tunisia was about to be lost and the way opened for the allies to redeploy their forces in an assault anywhere along the southern flank of the continent, but that Italy itself was about to default and go over to the allies. He had faith in Mussolini, but smelled treachery among the Italian senior officers and civil servants. Similar reports were arriving on Dönitz's desk from his staff in Italy; they told of rampant defeatism among the population and the spread of mistrust of Germans. It was in these circumstances that Hitler sent him to Italy for a second time.

He took off from Berlin early on May 12th, arriving in Rome at 1 p.m. He was met by Ruge with the German naval attaché and the Commander of German naval forces in Italy, and over lunch in the Hotel Excelsior they briefed him on the ineffectiveness of the dual German-Italian staff system. So serious was the position, Ruge believed the only solution to be a transfer of the entire German naval operations staff in Italy to the Supamarina.

293

In the afternoon he met Admiral Riccardi and his staff and heard their plans for dealing with the allied assault they expected on Sardinia, then Sicily as stepping stones to the Italian mainland. Afterwards he gave them his ideas; the Axis was too weak to fight the invasion at sea and the whole problem came down to a successful defence on land; the Navy's task was to make the land battle possible by safeguarding the sea supply routes; the situation in North Africa where the troops had been defeated simply for want of supplies must not recur, and all available craft had to be pressed into service immediately to get as much material on to the threatened islands as possible—cruisers, small craft, even U-boats would have to be used.

'As transports?' Riccardi interrupted.

'Yes, because U-boats are not decisive in battle.'

Discussing the weakness in the air and the fact that it was now too late for many operations, Dönitz let slip a remark to the effect that it might have helped if the Italian fleet had been sacrificed earlier! Relations between the two sides were cool already; it was not a tactful observation and the translator apparently turned it into an attack on the honour of the Italian Navy. Riccardi flared up; Dönitz bristled in return and the meeting ended in a tense atmosphere which persisted throughout his stay in Rome.[45]

The following day he met the Italian military chief, General Ambrosio, repeating his rather surprising ideas for the employment of naval forces, and later in the morning expressed the same convictions in an audience with Mussolini: 'When the importance of transport is compared with fighting tasks the former takes precedence.'[46] The *Duce* showed more sympathy with the view than his senior Commanders. On the thorny question of co-operation between the Supamarina and the German naval staff in Italy, Mussolini agreed to a merger of the German operations staff with the small German liaison staff under Ruge.

The final act in the North African campaign was being played out that day as over 250,000 battle-hardened German and Italian troops surrendered to the allies, yet the Dictator impressed Dönitz with his amiability, confidence and calm. He even found comfort in allied bombing raids on the Italian mainland as he believed they would teach the Italian people to hate the British. If there was one Italian who hated the British, he said, it was himself.

'I am happy my people are now also learning to hate.'[47]

That afternoon Dönitz was driven to the Nemi Lake to see the old

Roman ships discovered there, then after returning and dining with the German Ambassador, von Mackensen, he had an evening conference with Kesselring. The Field Marshal believed Sicily a more likely target for the allied invasion than Sardinia, yet, he said, defensive preparations there were far from complete and the Italian naval forces too weak to play anything but a reconnaissance role. The desperate need was for more aircraft, but he believed the best way to relieve the situation was an offensive against the Iberian peninsula! This was an idea that Dönitz had been playing with for some time in order to gain bases for his U-boats outside the dangerous waters of Biscay. What he said to Kesselring about it is not recorded, but practical and positive as always he stressed, as he had to the Italian High Command, that the crux of the problem was supply: sufficient stores had to be transported to the endangered islands before the invasion if the battle which could not be won at sea was not to be lost on land. The problem of course, he added, was the leisurely manner in which the Italians were accustomed to working.

The following morning, May 14th, he had an early audience with the King of Italy, then flew from Rome to the *Wolfschanze*, to which Hitler had returned. After listening to his report of the conversations, Hitler asked him the key question: did he think the *Duce* was determined to carry on to the end? Dönitz replied that he certainly believed so, but of course he could not be sure, whereupon Hitler, who also believed so, launched into an exposition of his misgivings about the Italian upper classes. 'A man like Ambrosio would be happy if Italy could become a British Dominion today!'[48]

In an attempt to steer the talk into more practical areas which his conversation with Kesselring had reopened, Dönitz said he had been thinking over the plans to defend the Italian islands and had come to the conclusion that they would result in a costly and purely defensive operation which would not do anything to get the Axis out of its overall defensive posture. Furthermore the Anglo-Saxons, by clearing the Mediterranean—so regaining the direct route via Suez to and from the east—had in effect gained two million tons of shipping space.

'Which our trusty U-boats will have to sink,' Hitler interjected.

Dönitz had to reply that they were facing the gravest crisis in U-boat warfare. 'The enemy's new location devices are, for the first time, making U-boat warfare impossible and causing heavy losses—fifteen to seventeen boats a month—'

'These losses are too high,' Hitler cut in. 'It can't go on.'

Dönitz seized his opportunity, or perhaps he wished to sidetrack talk of losses for he had not been frank: they were running now at double the figure he quoted.

'At present,' he said, 'the only exit for U-boats is through Biscay, a narrow lane of the greatest difficulty for the boats, whose transit takes ten days. In view of this, the best strategic solution appears to be the occupation of Spain, including Gibraltar. This would constitute a flank attack against the direction of the Anglo-Saxon offensive, regaining the initiative for us, radically altering the situation in the Mediterranean and giving the U-boat campaign a broader base.'

The subject of Spain and Gibraltar had been thrashed out at Führer headquarters many times recently, and Canaris had travelled to Madrid twice to sound out Franco about the possibility of joining the Axis; he had been rebuffed, and Hitler had been forced to the reluctant conclusion that nothing could be done.

'We are not capable of such an operation,' he told Dönitz, 'because it would require first-class divisions. Occupation against the will of the Spaniards is not on. They are the only tough Latin people and would carry on a guerrilla war in our rear.'

Dönitz left the *Wolfschanze* immediately after the interview to return to Berlin; his plane touched down at the Tempelhof aerodrome at a quarter to eleven that night. Whether he then visited U-boat headquarters to check on the latest situation in the operations room is not recorded; probably he went straight home for there can be little doubt that his remarks to Hitler about the enemy location devices making U-boat warfare impossible were based on the latest information from Godt, probably acquired by telephone at Führer headquarters before presenting his report.

This revealed that in the most recent battle against a slow eastbound convoy one boat had been able to launch an underwater attack on the first day and sink two merchantmen, but all subsequent attempts by twelve boats out of 25 directed to the convoy had been beaten off by the escorts without further success and one boat had been destroyed; in fact two were destroyed in this battle, bringing the total number of boats lost in the half month to nineteen.

The explanation for the failure in the U-boat Command war diary was 'the numerical strength of the escort together with good conditions for location gear . . .' The enemy must have detected all the boats around the convoy and 'Since such a rapid detection of the boats has not previously occurred on such a scale it is not impossible that the enemy is working with a new type of efficient location gear.'[49]

The next day Dönitz, evidently deducing a decline in fighting spirit from the lack of success in recent battles, sent a message to all boats:

In his efforts to rob U-boats of their most valuable characteristic, invisibility, the enemy is some lengths ahead of us with his radar location.

I am fully aware of the difficult position in which this puts you in the fight with enemy escorts. Be assured that I have done and shall continue to do everything in my power as C-in-C to take all possible steps to change this situation as soon as possible.

Research and development departments within and without the Navy are working to improve your weapons and apparatus.

I expect you to continue your determined struggle with the enemy and by pitting your ingenuity, ability and hard will against his ruses and technical developments yet to finish him off.

Commanders in the Mediterranean and Atlantic have proved that even today the enemy has weak spots everywhere and that in many cases the enemy devices are not nearly so effective as they appear at first sight if one is determined, despite all, to achieve something.

I believe I shall soon be able to give you better weapons for this hard struggle of yours.

Dönitz[50]

No doubt he had convinced himself that effective weapons were on the way, but there was no basis in recent experience for the preceding sentence with its stinging implication that Commanders had not been showing determination. Read in conjunction with recent war diary entries it appears as a grotesque and inexcusable misjudgement, showing clearly once again that emotional commitment, or 'fanaticism', was overriding rational calculation.

Two days later *B-Dienst* deciphered routing instructions for an east-bound convoy, and an allied U-boat report diverting it south of the groups indicated in the report. From this it was deduced that the next convoy would be similarly routed and the groups *Donau* 1 and 2, a total of seventeen boats including Peter Dönitz's U 954, were ordered south-wards to form a patrol line across its probable track; new boats just

297

entering the operational area were directed to form another group *Oder* extending the line further south.

Shortly after midnight on the following day, thus in the early hours of May 19th the expected slow convoy, SC 130, ran into the line and was sighted by U 304, which reported and held touch. U 954 was close and by dawn she and another five boats had also found the convoy and were working into position for submerged attacks from ahead. The convoy made a 90-degree turn to the south, however, leaving them all trailing. They surfaced in order to make their way ahead on the new course out of range of the escort just as a Liberator of Coastal Command joined to provide air cover. U 954 was detected at once and attacked out of low cloud; the bombs dropped close either side of her, their explosion opening her hull and she sank, taking all hands with her.

The Liberator swept on, diving at another five boats, forcing them under, and calling surface escorts to the scene; these destroyed one boat by depth-charge attack, and damaged another. Through the morning more boats homed in to the convoy, but an escort group and three more aircraft were on the way and in sudden, fierce encounters during the early afternoon another three boats were destroyed, three were damaged so severely they had to drop out of the action and all the others were forced under so that when the convoy made the usual dusk alteration touch was lost. One boat reported sinking a 6,500-ton ship and damaging another; in fact no ships were hit.

The following day the convoy was located by hydrophone bearings of the propeller noises, but air cover was continuous and although the group attempted to close again any boats surfacing to gain position were attacked at once from low cloud. By midday it was perceived at head-quarters that the situation was hopeless and Dönitz called the operation off. The war diary summary noted:

> It was not possible to maintain contact and proceed in the vicinity of the convoy owing to continuous surprise attacks from low-lying cloud. These attacks are only explicable in terms of very good location gear which enables the plane to detect the boat even from above the clouds . . .[52]

This comment is extraordinary in view of the number of reports of just such surprise attacks over the past months. The summary went on to state that 'several boats also reported an efficient co-operation between aircraft and surface escort'. As to the casualties: 'The loss of U 954 in the vicinity of the convoy is taken as certain as this boat reported making contact when up to the convoy, possibly lost in underwater attacks.'[53]

Dönitz showed no emotion when he learned of his son's death. How he broke the news to Ingeborg cannot be known, but perhaps he left an avenue of hope that there might possibly have been survivors, for she refused to accept the loss as certain; in 1945 she searched lists of prisoners of war held in Canada and the United States in case he had been rescued.

Neither the failure in this battle, nor the disastrous result in numbers of boats lost and severely damaged, nor the confirmation of all the previous evidence that air cover and radar location made it virtually impossible for U-boats to close, let alone attack convoys, altered Dönitz's determination. When the next day *B-Dienst* supplied him with the route of another eastbound convoy, he directed the survivors of the battle to intercept, together with fresh boats, and sent the Commanders an extraordinary message:

> If there is anyone who thinks that fighting convoys is no longer possible, he is a weakling and no real U-boat Commander. The Battle of the Atlantic gets harder but it is the decisive campaign of the war. Be aware of your high responsibility and be clear you must answer for your actions. Do your best with this convoy. We must destroy it. If the conditions for this appear favourable, do not dive for aircraft but fight them off. Disengage from destroyers if possible on the surface. Be hard, draw ahead and attack. I believe in you. C-in-C.[54]

Arriving in the vicinity of the convoy the boats found conditions hopeless: there were two carriers with a support group in addition to the escort and continuous air cover made it impossible for a boat to surface without being attacked. Five more were destroyed before the operation was called off at 11 o'clock on that first morning, May 23rd. The war diary noted: 'The operation showed again clearly that at present with existing weapons it is not possible to fight a convoy under strong air escort . . .'[55]

Dönitz at last bowed to the inevitable:

> Losses, even heavy losses, must be borne when they are accompanied by corresponding sinkings. In May in the Atlantic the sinking of about

299

10,000 tons had to be paid for by the loss of a boat while not long ago a loss came only with the sinking of 100,000 tons. Thus losses in May have reached an intolerable level.[56]

It was thought that 31 boats had been sunk so far in the month; the true figure, including two lost in collision was 34. This 'intolerable' number and 'the lack of success in operations against the latest convoys', Dönitz continued, 'forced a temporary shift to areas less endangered by aircraft'. To keep the enemy in ignorance of this for as long as possible some boats were to be left in the North Atlantic; however they would be ordered to attack 'only under particularly favourable conditions, i.e. in the new moon period'. This lunatic reference, quite irrelevant in view of radar, must be a measure of the difficulty Dönitz found in admitting defeat. The withdrawal was being squeezed out of him as blood from steel, and he comforted himself with the idea it was a temporary deviation only:

> . . . It is however clearly understood that in future as in the past the main operations area of U-boats is in the North Atlantic and that the battle there must be resumed with all hardness and determination as soon as U-boats are given the necessary weapons for it.

The first step was to arm the boats with quadruple A.A. guns, and he expected that directly this was done, 'i.e. from the autumn, the battle in the North Atlantic can be resumed in full measure'. He ended his summary on a necessary but typically egotistical note:

> Meanwhile it is essential that the *morale* of the men should not be affected by these temporary defensive measures, a task which requires the full co-operation of the commanding officers as well as the personal touch of the C-in-C Navy.

He took the first step that day in a message addressed to all U-boat officers. He started by emphasizing the seriousness of the present position: although the Army and Air Force were fighting off heavy enemy attacks successfully on all fronts, this only represented defence against an enemy stronger in men and materials; it would not bring victory.

300

At present you alone can take the offensive against the enemy and beat him. The U-boat arm, by continuously sinking ships with war materials and supplies for the island must subdue the enemy by a continual blood-letting which must cause even the strongest body to bleed to death.

Each of you must be aware of this huge responsibility and each Commander after the cruise is answerable for the energy and hardness with which he has operated for the attainment of our great goal. I know that at the moment your battle out there is one of the sternest and most costly in losses because the enemy's new technical equipment is presently superior. Believe me, I have done and will continue to do everything to catch up with this enemy leap forward. Shortly the day will come when, with new and sharper weapons, you will be superior and will be able to triumph over your worst adversaries, the aircraft and destroyer.

In the meantime we must master the situation with the measures already ordered and a partial change of operations area. We will not, therefore, allow ourselves to be forced on the defensive, nor rest, but where opportunity offers, strike and strike and fight on with greater hardness and resolution in order to improve our striking force for the time, soon, when with improved weapons we conduct the decisive battle in the North Atlantic, the enemy's most sensitive area.

Then we shall be victorious, my belief in our arm and in you tells me so.

Heil dem Führer! Your C-in-C Dönitz[57]

Most of the developments with which Dönitz hoped to overcome his 'temporary' setback in the Battle of the Atlantic had been under way for some time. The crisis of the previous summer and his despairing messages to Berlin had provided the first real spur. At a conference called by Raeder at the end of September 1942 to decide how to respond to the increasing effectiveness of allied counter-measures, Dönitz had called for the development of a large Walter U-boat suitable for the Atlantic without waiting for trials of the small prototypes then under construction; the first was not due before the end of 1942. He had also stated a requirement for higher *surface* speed for the existing Type VII since it was the best sea boat in Atlantic conditions, and had particularly stressed the need to develop a weapon with which the U-boat could deal with its pursuer, the destroyer.[58]

By March 1943, when aircraft were recognized as the U-boat's chief enemy, he had turned his energies to the procurement of anti-aircraft guns and—again vainly—the co-operation of the *Luftwaffe* for the 'tonnage war'. At the same time Professor Walter had come up with the idea of giving U-boats extending masts through which they could suck in fresh air while travelling submerged at periscope depth. 'The increasing danger for U-boats from the air gave me this idea,' he told Dönitz, 'which is certainly not a new one . . .'[59] Development of this concept was to result later in the 'Snorchel' or 'Snort'.

In May, as it had become apparent that the real cause of the crisis in the U-boat war was the new enemy location device, Dönitz had concentrated all naval scientists on finding an antidote, relieving the Communications Experimental Department of all production tasks, and widening the search for a solution by tossing the problem to 'a select circle of research scientists, physicists and representatives of industry'.[60]

Meanwhile he had been working on a new building programme for the service as a whole to rectify the disastrous position inherited from Raeder, who had been unable to get sufficient steel or shipyard workers for any of his schedules. U-boats were of course at the heart of this plan, and as the individual boats' 'potential' had dropped and losses had increased so the numbers projected had been increased to make up for it. Now they stood at 40 a month, virtually double Raeder's best achievements during 1942. Since the plan was to run for five years the total number envisaged was 2,400! The programme was in fact an extension of the 'alternative' fleet plan he had proposed to Raeder in 1939, enlarged for the new scale of the war on commerce and the Navy's greatly increased defensive responsibilities, and was as far from the 'Z' Plan and the subsequent post-war 'balanced fleet' programmes dreamed up by Raeder's teams in the euphoria of 1940 as Dönitz's grasp of immediate essentials was from Raeder's Utopian approach. In its concentration on a single strategy it was in the tradition of the original 'Tirpitz Plan' for a battlefleet, although at the opposite pole: there was nothing in it larger than a destroyer, and few enough of those. It is most interesting perhaps as a mirror of Dönitz's own great strengths and fatal weaknesses. It was positive, practical in its concentration on small craft which could be built quickly and comparatively cheaply—and aimed at a clearly defined goal, yet it achieved its inner logic by cutting out or minimizing outside forces, in this case the enemy's proven ability to concentrate overall naval, air and technological superiority into effective anti-submarine defence.

There was also the question of Germany's own armaments and manpower capacity, for the plan, the largest ever seriously conceived by the German Navy, called for 50,000 tons of steel per month more than the existing quota, and made prodigious demands on manpower for the shipyards and crews which were quite as fantastic as Raeder's various essays—especially in view of the desperate needs of the other two services. It is significant that this point was raised at a conference of all construction and weapon department chiefs which Dönitz chaired on May 24th, the very day he was forced to withdraw from the North Atlantic. Would it not be better, since the enemy's air superiority was clearly 'the pivot of the present crisis', to renounce parts of the naval construction programme to release materials for building fighter air-craft?[61] The Navy had no business to be debating this question; it is a measure of the total lack of co-ordination at the top of the *Reich* that it was felt to be necessary. Dönitz's response was predictable: such a renunciation would mean either a reduction of the U-boat programme 'which did not come into question' or a reduction of the programmes of light forces, which would mean that one day the Navy would be unable to perform its escort and defensive duties. He would, however, reserve his decision pending further investigation.

Given his absolute commitment to U-boats as the sole offensive arm left to Germany and his habit of taking decisions on the basis of his goals without much regard for difficulties, the issue of the 'investigation' can hardly have been in doubt. He met Speer a few days later, who encouraged him in his demands, and at the end of the month he went to see Hitler at the *Berghof*, determined to press for the whole programme.

It was a remarkable meeting: Dönitz, who brought only failure, adopted his usual confident line and made radical demands; Hitler, who only three weeks earlier had been telling the Gauleiters of the great hopes he placed in the U-boat arm, took it all without a sign of reproach, fully agreed with all Dönitz had to say, and allowed him his vast programme without hesitation, let alone consultation with Speer or the other service chiefs. It was a perfect illustration of his trust in Dönitz and his eagerness to accept optimistic opinions, an epitome of how in the Führer system delusion fed naturally on itself, and how Dönitz's nat-urally positive approach, deployed skilfully for his own ends, had become one of the chief props for the ailing Führer.

Dönitz's great talent, which stemmed from his infinite capacity for self-delusion in pursuit of his own goals, was his ability to present plain and factual reports apparently concealing nothing, then to draw as it were from under this professional cover wholly optimistic conclusions. This technique was evident in the interview of May 31st. He started with an objective assessment of the failure of the U-boat campaign, the increase in the enemy's Air Force and—'the determining factor'—the new location device which had led to losses of 36 or even 37 boats in the month.[62]

'These losses are too high. We must conserve our forces now, otherwise we will only do the enemy's business for him.'

Therefore, he went on, he had withdrawn from the North Atlantic to an area west of the Azores, where he hoped to catch Gibraltar-bound convoys; as new U-boats became available he would send them to more distant areas in the hope that the aircraft there 'would not be equipped to the same extent with the new location device'. However, assuming U-boats would have 'protective weapons' by July, he intended to attack in the North Atlantic in the new moon period. The implications here were not defeat so much as a crisis forcing temporary redisposition. It is significant that the only statistical analysis he presented concerned where and how the boats had been lost—so far as that could be ascertained—not how much enemy tonnage it was necessary to sink, nor how much he expected to sink, nor how many boats would be necessary.

He went on to list the weapons needed before resuming full-scale attack in the North Atlantic; first was a receiver to intercept the beams of the enemy location device and give warning of attack; in the meantime he had ordered U-boats to operate at night on one electric motor so that, without the noise of the diesels, the lookouts would be able to hear approaching aircraft. He did not admit it but this so reduced speed as to make night surface attack 'in the new moon period' virtually impossible. Meanwhile work was under way to find means of jamming or dispersing enemy radar waves; experiments had already shown that it was possible to reduce conning-tower reflections by 30 per cent, he said, so cutting by a third the distance at which a U-boat could be located.

In addition conning towers were being rebuilt and fitted with four-barrelled machine guns for use against aircraft, and by October boats would definitely have an acoustic torpedo for use against escorts; this, however, would not be effective against an enemy making over twelve knots, for which reason every effort was being made to ensure that the

304

Zaunkönig acoustic torpedo, effective against ships moving at up to eighteen knots, would also be in service by the autumn.

'I shall discuss this with Minister Speer,' he went on, and asked for Hitler's support 'since I consider it absolutely necessary that the U-boats be supplied with the anti-destroyer torpedo before the favourable winter fighting season.'

Again he did not explain how, in the radar age, the long winter nights were 'favourable'. Nor did Hitler question him; he simply agreed that everything possible had to be done.

At this point, according to an account of the interview by Wolfgang Frank,[63] Dönitz glanced down at his notes. Frank was not there, only Hitler's chief of staff, Keitel, his naval adjutant, von Puttkamer, two other staff officers and the official stenographers; nevertheless it is likely there was a pause for Dönitz now took the offensive, cautiously at first—in his opinion *Luftwaffe* support for U-boats was inadequate and it was essential that Messerschmitt 410s be transferred to Biscay to shoot down the enemy patrols—but as Hitler sought to disassociate himself from mistakes in aircraft production, Dönitz thrust deeper: in his opinion suitable planes for naval warfare should have been constructed at the latest when the larger U-boat construction programme had been started.

Hitler, who was entirely responsible for not forcing Göring to allow Raeder the naval air arm he had wanted from the beginning, agreed.

'Undoubtedly,' Dönitz continued, 'the U-boats would have sunk very much more shipping over the past year if we had had naval aircraft.'

Hitler agreed.

'Even now it is not too late to give the Navy an air arm.'

Again Hitler agreed.

Dönitz launched into a scheme for starting a school for naval fliers at Gdynia in direct contact with the convoy training flotillas and the U-School so that they learned how to keep touch with a convoy, how to navigate and above all learned to speak the same language as the U-boats; Hitler was in full agreement. Then, according to Frank, he rose suddenly and began pacing with his hands behind his back. He might well have done. He was racked with anxiety over the possibility of an imminent Italian desertion to the allies—with all the dangers this held for his continental position and the vital Rumanian oil fields. The *Luftwaffe* meanwhile was not capable of stemming the allied mass raids devastating his industrial towns, yet here was his Navy chief wanting a separate air

305

arm with new designs of plane and more young men who were needed for Russia and Italy!

If he paced now, it was not with the arrogance of 1940; his left leg tended to drag, his left hand trembled uncontrollably in his right behind his bent back, his dulled eyes and pouchy skin told of the extraordinarily unhealthy life he led—as Speer was to realize later in conditions resembling those of a prisoner, scarcely ever seeing the sunlight or feeling the fresh breeze in the close rooms of his headquarters bunkers. His dark hair was sparser and flecked with white. Those who visited him only occasionally were shocked by the suddenness with which he was ageing.

Dönitz, trim and erect as ever, passed on to future prospects in the U-boat war. He quoted the U-boat 'potential' for 1940—1,000 tons sunk per boat per sea day—and for the end of 1942—200 tons—but avoided the present figure, simply saying it was impossible to foretell the extent to which U-boat war would again become effective.

'Nevertheless I am of the opinion that U-boat warfare must be carried on even if the goal of achieving greater successes is no longer possible, because the enemy forces tied up by U-boats are extraordinarily large. Jellicoe in his book described the forces the U-boats tied up in the First World War . . .'

'A let-up in the U-boat war is quite out of the question,' Hitler interrupted. 'The Atlantic is my first line of defence in the west and even if I have to fight a defensive battle there that is better than defending myself on the coasts of Europe. The enemy forces tied up by the U-boats are so extraordinarily large that even if we no longer have great successes, I cannot permit their release.'

Dönitz took the opportunity to press for his increased construction programme! He had an order form with him, previously agreed with Speer, listing 30 boats a month, and after saying that in his opinion they should now strive for 40 a month he handed it to Hitler for signature. Hitler obediently scratched out the '30', wrote '40' in its place and signed.

In such a casual way, without any analysis of the actual enemy resources the U-boat campaign was tying up or discussion of alternative options which might be open, huge German resources were tied up in a patently obsolete weapon.

Three days later Dönitz addressed his departmental chiefs again. His starting point was that continental Europe, 'which provides us with our food and raw materials must be held against attack from outside, and, I

306

am convinced, will be held'.[64] It was a significant change from his attitude on taking office only four months before.

He blamed the present crisis on the *Luftwaffe*'s failure to support the U-boats, and on the enemy's 'technical expedient', the location device; there was no doubt, however, that 'in the changing fortunes of war between attack and defence' they would once more gain the upper hand. They must put aside the old ideas of trying to manage as frugally as possible and work on a grand scale to force weapon development ahead. Then, the tonnage war would be resumed. It is evident, though, that he no longer believed it could be won; he repeated the arguments about tying up huge enemy resources and holding the war at a distance from the coasts of Europe.

He developed this idea afterwards in a memorandum,[65] and in discussion with the station Commanders and staff on June 8th stressed that since there was no possibility of the eastern campaign bringing victory the centre of gravity of armaments production had to be shifted to the Navy, which alone could affect the outcome of the war by striking at allied sea communications. Similarly the centre of gravity of the air strategy had to be shifted to the tonnage war.[66]

By this time detailed estimates of the manpower requirements for the programme had been worked out, and the following week Dönitz presented them to Hitler—altogether 335,000 men above the Navy's allocation of 103,000 for the coming year, and 141,800 extra shipyard workers. According to his own probably boastful account of the meeting to his staff on the following day, his demand had the effect of a bombshell at Führer headquarters.

'I haven't got them,' Hitler said. 'It is necessary to increase flak and night fighters to protect German cities, necessary to strengthen the eastern front—the Army needs divisions for the protection of Europe.'[67]

Dönitz warned him that if U-boat warfare were to cease the whole material strength of the enemy would be hurled against Europe and the coastal supply routes bringing in vital materials would be endangered, and he hammered the necessity of manning the expanded U-boat service . . . transferring officers from the Army and Air Force, increasing the number of naval officer candidates . . . it was his duty to point out the consequences of too small an assignment of men . . . until Hitler said that discontinuing the U-boat war was out of the question, he was to submit a list of the required numbers of men and when they were needed. Dönitz passed on to the question of shipyard workers, provoking Hitler

307

into another declaration: calling up men from the shipyards was out of the question.

Once again Dönitz had every reason to be pleased with his influence over the Führer; he appeared well on the way to a major shift of resources in favour of the Navy, and with it a major increase in his own standing in the highest councils of the *Reich*. Yet the real effects were less than they seemed at the time. This was particularly so for the new air strategy and the naval air arm he demanded; the reason was that despite 'quarrels' with Göring, which he made much of in his memoirs, he never forced a showdown with him directly or with Hitler. Hansen-Nootbar recalls that Göring's 'special relationship with Hitler' was always first on the agenda when Dönitz went to see the Führer, but he always came out without having broached the subject. 'I can't do it,' he would say, 'after all, it is not my job to interfere in the long-standing trust between Hitler and Göring. And so I left it.'[68]

As for his own relationship with the gross and gaudy *Reichsmarschall*, it was more successful than Raeder's—at least it produced a show of harmony—but there was no radical change of the kind that was needed, indeed the crisis in the *Luftwaffe* itself, and Hitler's constant interference probably precluded the scale of air co-operation necessary for worthwhile results. And in that bizarre court where the Führer held all power and jealously prevented the separate arms of the services and departments of State from knowing what the others were doing or what intelligence they were working on, Dönitz could not have gained his ends unless Hitler had been prepared to force the matter. He was not. Dönitz did not offer his resignation; he tried instead to extract specific aircraft for specific tasks and used them in local co-operation with naval forces, meanwhile rubbing along as best he could with the fat one.

Hansen-Nootbar recalls one argument between the two which ended when Göring unpinned the diamond-studded pilot's decoration from his exquisite uniform and handed it to Dönitz who to the delight of the officers watching them unpinned the U-boat decoration from his own service blue jacket and handed it to Göring. It was a typically nimble and appropriate response. Von Puttkamer gives a shorter version of this episode in his memoirs,[69] implying that from then on Dönitz made his way successfully with Göring. One is left wondering about the incident. Was it the force of Göring's personality and intelligence or the aura of his power and the long-established position he held in the Nazi hierarchy, or loyalty to the Führer perhaps, that caused Dönitz to respond as he did

308

and humour and get along with the *Reichsmarschall* in public while privately regarding him as a national disaster? When he and Hansen-Nootbar were alone they referred to Göring as 'the grave-digger of the *Reich*'.[70]

Dönitz meanwhile, with Hitler's agreement to his five-year naval building programme in his pocket, drove the organizational details of his planned hand-over of all construction to Speer's Ministry ruthlessly through the opposition of all departments. His argument was that they were engaged in an economic war with the sea powers, therefore a war of long duration, and the difficulties of gaining the necessary share of raw materials and labour which had crippled Raeder's efforts would increase. Indeed, he told his department chiefs on July 5th, the new programme was only practicable *with* Minister Speer; '*without* him meant *against* him'.[71]

He had a similar fight for new methods of building U-boats. His hopes for regaining the advantage in what he saw as the see-saw struggle between offence and defence were now placed chiefly in new types known as 'electro' boats. These had been proposed earlier that year as an alternative to the large Walter boat; they were to achieve high submerged speed by a combination of streamlined shape as pioneered by Walter, and vastly increased battery capacity in a deeper hull. Two classes were proposed, a 1,600-ton Type XXI for the Atlantic and a smaller Type XXIII for coastal waters. The Atlantic type, in which he was chiefly interested, had a designed underwater speed of eighteen knots for one and a half hours or twelve to fourteen knots for ten hours. This was not quite as good as the Walter boat promised but it had the advantage over Walter's scheme that the batteries could be recharged and, by using the Snorchel, recharged while submerged. Its chief advantage in the present circumstances was that it involved no new techniques and could therefore go straight into production.

This at least was what Dönitz and Speer hoped. The naval construction department expected to build two prototypes in the usual way first. Speer's technical director, however, came up with a proposal based on the American method of overcoming the merchant tonnage problem by prefabricating sections complete with fittings in factories, then transporting them to the shipyards to be welded together. Such a sudden break with traditional methods carried grave risk and demanded much skilled labour and investment in new plant at the yards; if successful, however, it promised to halve building times and, more important, by dispersing the

309

work, shorten the period between start and completion. It also meant that a good deal of the work could be done in factories far from the coast and out of range of enemy bombers. Undoubtedly, though, it was the prospect of getting the new types quickly and being able to take the offensive once more in the Battle of the Atlantic that made Dönitz decide on the 'radical' new method. Given his character and circumstances there could have been no other choice.[72]

'We'll get them!' he would say to Hansen-Nootbar—meaning the British—'We'll get them in the end! But first we must have the new boats!'[73]

His passion appeared to derive as much from the First War 'starvation blockade' as from the present position. 'He could not forget about the hunger blockade,' Hansen-Nootbar recalled; 'he said to me again and again and again that he wanted to undo what England had done in the First War. He wanted to starve out the English, not only physically, but in weapons and war materials.'

On the question of whether Dönitz hated the English, Hansen-Nootbar hesitated: 'I cannot unconditionally deny it,' and on another occasion, 'When he [Dönitz] talked himself into a frenzy, he would say, "A man must be able to hate".'

This phrase was common currency in Hitler's circle. Mussolini had said something very similar to him in Rome. Hate was a weapon in Goebbels' armoury—as indeed in the armoury of Germany's enemies; Churchill's hatred of Nazis was well known. The infamous allied mass raids on German civilians under cover of the euphemism of 'military targets' and the declaration by Roosevelt and Churchill in Casablanca in January that year that allied war aims were unconditional surrender provided more material for 'hate-propaganda'. Hate was in the air; there can be no doubt that a man of Dönitz's extreme temperament, who 'talked himself into a frenzy' on occasions, would have attuned to it—indeed the previous year's interrogation reports on 'fanatical Nazis who hated the English' suggest that it was nothing new to him.

On July 5th Dönitz was shown plans for the sectional method of constructing the type XXI boats by the man Speer had chosen to direct the programme; his mind was evidently made up by then—despite the continuing opposition of his own construction department—for he exclaimed, 'With this we begin a new life!'[74]

Three days later he was expanding on the 'successful' design of the 'electric' U-boat to Hitler at the *Wolfschanze*; it introduced entirely new possibilities to the U-boat war by allowing a rapid approach to convoys and evasive action under water without the need to surface.

'This will make all former enemy striving for counter-measures ineffective since the construction of escort vessels is based on the low speed of U-boats under water . . .'[75]

He went on to give similarly optimistic reports on other developments; by the end of July he expected to have an efficient radar warning set, and Professor Krauch of I. G. Farben had told him he was convinced he would soon find a material with 100 per cent absorption of radar waves; 'this will effectively nullify radar location'!

Until the convoy battle could be resumed he was using U-boats for minelaying so that the enemy's gain in tonnage could be held as low as possible. 'The goal must be for sinkings to keep pace with new construction, and this will be possible with the new U-boat'—which brought him back to the personnel problem: according to the latest report they would soon be facing a situation where Minister Speer was producing these new U-boats but there would be no one to man them. He needed 262,000 men by autumn 1944, 'and indeed young men'.

Hitler began to prevaricate, and although Dönitz stuck to his demands he failed this time to extract a firm promise. Finally Hitler suggested he investigate the possibilities of recruiting men from the occupied countries as the SS had done so successfully. He agreed to look into it; he would contact the *Reichsführer SS*, Heinrich Himmler.

Before he left he returned to the subject of the electric U-boat, again stressing the need to build with the utmost speed. Hitler absolutely agreed and, as Speer entered the room as if on cue, turned to him and said, 'The most important thing is the construction of this new boat.'

'Of that there is no doubt,' Speer agreed. 'We have already given instructions that the new boat is to take precedence over everything else.'

In the constant press of activity Dönitz did not lose sight of his duty to provide personal inspiration for the U-boat service. Although he could no longer see all returning Commanders, he continued to interview as many as he could, particularly those with special experiences or success to relate. According to Hansen-Nootbar his understanding approach was the foundation for the morale that was preserved through this difficult period of defeat. He insisted his Commanders 'spare neither criticism nor grievances, on the contrary he demanded they tell him just "where the shoe pinched."'[76]

311

The approach stemmed from genuine concern. He was always upset when a loss was reported, Hansen-Nootbar recalled; beneath the taut exterior was a heart which grieved for the men he had sent to their deaths. This may seem difficult to reconcile with his chilling request to Hitler for additional thousands of men for a so-far untried weapon—'and indeed young men'—but not perhaps if one remembers his lament for those who went down in UB 68 in 1918. Undoubtedly he operated on several levels.

Certainly there are tell-tale signs in Hansen-Nootbar's recollections that as a Grand Admiral he remained basically unsure of himself. For instance, he sometimes showed off the sea paintings he had collected in France to young officers who, because of their lack of background in this direction, were quite unprepared for the experience and consequently ill at ease. This tallies with his often showy reports to the naval staff about his relationship with the Führer, and comments about the 'rightness' of the course he was pursuing which were now turning up in the naval staff war diary as frequently as they had in the U-boat war diary.

And there is one telling remark after the visit of an officer whom Hansen-Nootbar commented on as a very clever man.

'Hänschen,' Dönitz interrupted, 'I have enough clever people. What we lack is men with stamina.'

The significance of this is that it was a stock idea from the Führer's collection. Throughout his adult life Hitler professed absolute contempt for educated men 'spoon-fed with knowledge' but ignorant of real life; it was one of the *motifs* of his monologues, particularly in adversity. After von Paulus' capitulation at Stalingrad, for instance, his denunciation had contained the phrase, 'In Germany there has been too much emphasis on training the intellect and not enough on strength of character.'[77]

Taken together with Dönitz's repetition almost *verbatim* of other ideas from Hitler's basic stock, particularly about the Jewish 'virus'—as will appear—the remark recalled by Hansen-Nootbar is further evidence of his uncritical acceptance of the transcendental genius of the Führer's mind. Those who have had a glimpse into that mind through the records of his table talk are bound to be surprised that the third-hand, usually silly nonsense emanating from it could ever have been mistaken for genius, and must wonder at the poverty of Dönitz's own mind after his education at Jena and Weimar, or at the strength of his emotional need for a cause and a father to serve—but they may not be surprised at his

312

actions as the National Socialist *Reich* fought savagely to preserve itself against the assaults from without and disaffection within.

For there was another Germany. It was small and virtually impotent. Nearly all the men of an age to resist effectively were at the front or in concentration camps or were Party members, nearly all women were so fully absorbed in war work or struggling to keep a home going that they had no energy left over, yet a core of brave men, nearly all under constant surveillance by Himmler's agents, sought to keep alive values that Goebbels had destroyed for the majority. It is no coincidence that they were Christians or intellectuals, their strength grounded in standards whose existence Dönitz and so many others denied. One of the leaders of this select circle, Helmuth von Moltke, wrote: 'The individual must be reawakened to an awareness of his inner commitment to values that are not of this world . . . Yes must be again yes, and no, no. Good must once again be an absolute, and evil likewise.'[78]

On July 9th news came of an allied invasion force heading for Sicily. Once again Hitler was taken completely by surprise. Dönitz ordered the German torpedo boats into action and pressed Riccardi to unleash the Italian fleet, held back for just this eventuality. Riccardi refused to commit his heavy units against the superior enemy, and as the allies landed and occupied the greater part of Sicily virtually unmolested Dönitz repeated his Tunisian performance, bombarding the Supamarina with personal requests, recommendations and operational suggestions—all to no effect. When an Italian flotilla sortied on the 15th it failed to find the enemy!

By the 17th he had become desperate and he suggested to Hitler that the Italian Navy be taken over. Hitler doubted if this was feasible.

At the next crisis the roles were reversed; as news came on the evening of the 25th that Mussolini had resigned and General Badoglio had taken over the Italian government, it was Hitler who temporarily lost his head and called for the radical solution of surrounding Rome with German parachutists, disarming the Italian forces and reinstating the dictatorship, and Dönitz, flying to him the next day, who counselled moderation. The change in Dönitz's attitude can probably be put down to the excellent intelligence he was receiving from his men in Rome, Ruge and the German naval attaché, Löwisch. Ruge reacted to Hitler's preparatory order to disarm the Italian services by sending an urgent report that such a measure would rouse the population and the greater

313

part of the Italian forces against them without any corresponding advantages.[79]

There is a brief account of the conference at which Dönitz showed this message to Hitler in the diary of Field Marshal von Richthofen, who had just flown in from Italy: '. . . Dönitz is moderate and sensible. Everybody else, especially Ribbentrop, just repeating whatever the Führer says.'[80] In fact Jodl and von Richthofen himself did their utmost to dissuade Hitler, who was convinced that Badoglio was already negotiating surrender to the allies. Finally the moderates won. Preparations for disarming the Italian forces were to go ahead, but were not to be put into effect until Italy deserted the cause. Dönitz ordered the necessary measures for securing the Italian fleet and merchantmen in such an eventuality; where this could not be done the ships were to be sunk.

During the crisis, which lasted throughout August, Dönitz was one of Hitler's most intimate advisers and supports. He spent days at a time at Führer headquarters, was present at most of the key conferences and the select discussions within the inner circle; he dined and breakfasted alone with the great man, or with Goebbels and Ribbentrop also present, or on another occasion in company with Himmler, Ribbentrop, Jodl and Rommel. Rommel's attitude at this stage was similar to his own, combining touching faith in Hitler with hatred of the Italians, who he considered had let him down. His diary entries and Dönitz's notes in the naval staff war diary reveal that the Führer for all his ravaged health and dull eye could still exert himself to flatter and had lost none of his persuasive power; both men obviously revelled in his good opinions; here, for instance, is the naval staff war diary entry for August 3rd when Dönitz requested permission to leave the *Wolfschanze* for Berlin: '. . . in view of the fact that the C-in-C Navy can return in short time the Führer reluctantly consents to his departure'.

In the continuous discussions over the Italian question he maintained a level-headed approach, but he was as fanatical about holding the bridgehead in Sicily as he had been for holding Tunisia to the last man, and continuing the U-boat war in the Atlantic; his reasons were identical: 'We are tying up considerable forces in Sicily, which if released to become available for new landings, will hang over us like a sword of Damocles. Therefore it is best we prevent new operations by binding the enemy's forces in Sicily.'[81]

More interesting than his strategic views was his political education,

314

for it was during this period in August when he was expecting Italy to break away from the Axis any moment that Hitler developed the idea of an inevitable split in the allied coalition against them! Quoting from history and drawing as he was wont on the wars of Frederick the Great, he pointed out to Dönitz how often during the darkest hours for a nation unexpected developments brought a sudden turn for the better. In this case, he said, 'the harder the war becomes for us, the more the divergent views of the allies will grow and reveal themselves'.[82] Already England's war aim of maintaining the balance of power in Europe had proved false; Russia had been so stimulated as to become a threat of a wholly new dimension. 'In future the onslaught from the east can only be met by a Europe united under German leadership,' and he added a significant rider, turning the clock back to his original strategic conceptions, 'This will also be in England's interest.'[83]

Dönitz agreed that England's vital concern to keep Russia from the Balkans and prevent her gaining access to the Mediterranean via the Dardanelles brought her directly up against Russia's aims, and concluded, 'Everything will depend upon our holding out stubbornly. We are much better off with regard to food than we were in 1918. In addition we have the great plus of the unity of the German people, our most precious possession, which must be carefully preserved.' He was referring to National Socialism, and this led him to a theme that was to preoccupy him for the rest of the war, 'I believe there are numerous groups among the German people who lack hardness and easily incline to criticism without being able to do better themselves or even to comprehend the whole picture.'

Was he speaking in general terms here, or did he have special knowledge of the resistance groups Himmler's agents were watching? Hansen-Nootbar recalls that Himmler tried very hard to establish a relationship with Dönitz in early 1943, sending him a spate of invitations. This was natural in the jockeying for power around the Führer's throne; Himmler would obviously have sought out the new favourite; noting his ardent National Socialism, it would have seemed an obvious ploy to court him with the shocking tales of disloyalty being uncovered in the higher reaches of the Army. That is speculation. Hansen-Nootbar characterizes the relationship between the two as 'good, or better described as correct'—yet 'correctness' was as close as anyone got to this reserved and coldly pedantic zealot.

Of Dönitz's attitude to Hitler there can be no doubt; it is caught at this

315

time by an extraordinary hand-written note he appended to the war diary account of the August meeting:

> The huge force which the Führer radiates, his unshakeable confidence, his far-sighted judgement of the situation in Italy have made it plain during these days what very poor little sausages we all are in comparison with the Führer, and that our knowledge, our vision of things outside our limited sphere is fragmentary. Anyone who believes he can do better than the Führer is foolish.[84]

This says much about Hitler's skill in keeping his professional chiefs in their separated boxes; it says more, probably, for his consummate ability, remarked from the beginning of his career, to seek out men who would surrender every critical and moral faculty to him. And yet it is possible to suggest other interpretations: could this passionate overstatement be a measure of the doubt surfacing in Dönitz's mind about the genius he had hitherto taken for granted? It may be significant that the naval staff officer responsible for keeping the naval staff war diary took a very different view about the divergent war aims of the allies, believing they would lead both sides to intensified efforts to destroy Germany and reap the rewards for themselves. In expressing himself so violently Dönitz was perhaps relieving his own doubts in characteristically tempestuous fashion.

Here we stray into forbidden territory, for such a reaction and the whole of his subsequent behaviour until Hitler's suicide could be explained in psychological theory as 'obsessional'—that is, single-mindedly following a path which the rational side of his nature was pulling *against*.

It would be possible to suggest any number of periods or incidents in his life which would fit textbook causes of 'obsession'; his childhood was ruled by a strict father—perhaps overstrict? His initiation into the Imperial Navy had been brutally strict, indeed the whole ethos of the Prussian *Kaiserreich* had pressed him into a tight mould which perhaps did not suit his character. Then there were the traumatic experiences of his twenties, the horrifying events accompanying the loss of his U-boat, the captivity about which he was reminiscing so bitterly fifteen years later, the naval revolutions and the collapse of all he had been brought up to believe in, his own experiences in the second series of revolutions after the Kapp *Putsch*, and finally and most recently his decision to encourage

316

his Commanders to act against shipwrecked survivors, cutting across all accepted codes. Any of these experiences might have affected such a deeply self-conscious personality as Dönitz to produce pathological obsessions.

Of course, it is not necessary to accept this explanation. His attachment to Hitler may have resulted from an emotional need for love and approval by an all-powerful father—a role once performed by von Loewenfeld, perhaps.

Even on a plain man's unanalytical level Dönitz's proven record for extreme duty-consciousness and goal achievement taken together with Hitler's development of a new war aim at this time provide sufficient explanation. The idea of continuing fighting until the enemy alliance split apart gave him justification and rationale for his fanatical commitment to the Führer and to a war which on any material assessment was already lost. His belief in Hitler's grasp of historical and political realities outside his own ken fuelled this determination.

It is interesting that a deeply pessimistic naval staff review of the war situation on August 20th, whose gist was that Germany had changed 'from the hammer into the anvil',[85] pointed to the necessity for showing the greatest consideration for the peoples of the occupied territories 'in order to guarantee their use for the war effort and to counteract the enemy propaganda, which we have nothing to oppose in the enemy countries'. It was this moral dimension that Hitler omitted in his historical/political analysis, and he omitted to heed it in practice. As the occupied peoples sensed the war had turned decisively against Germany and resistance movements supported by the allies increased their campaigns of sabotage, the security forces reacted with trained barbarism; meanwhile the obsessive drive to eliminate 'the Jewish bacillus' from Europe gathered renewed strength.

The situation was desperate enough without this hideous diversion. By the date of the staff memorandum Kesselring had made a strategic withdrawal from Sicily to mainland Italy. It is significant that this decision was made without informing Dönitz, who never changed his position about resistance to the last. In the east it was evident that the line could not be held against the Russian summer offensive; it could only be a matter of days before the Army of the Ukraine under Manstein was forced to retreat.

At sea U-boats were still being sunk at a murderous rate—37 in July —without in most cases finding any targets for attack. Not unnaturally

317

morale had declined, particularly among the more experienced petty officers and men. They saw Commanders, in many cases younger than themselves, who had been combed from the surface fleet or from the Air Force, subjected to a crash U-boat course and minimum sea time as watch officer or trainee Commander before being given their own boat. Inexperience was rendered more dangerous in many cases by ardour to gain distinction; such men, known as *Draufgänger* ('daredevils') or *Halsschmerzen* ('afflicted with throat trouble'—for the supreme mark of distinction, the Knight's Cross, was worn at the throat) were anathema to old U-boat hands, who volunteered in droves to serve with experienced Commanders, recognized as *Lebensversicherung* ('life-insurance'). Even these were not proof against the new scale of allied superiority. Three such Commanders who had been attached to the U-boat staff in Berlin to freshen the headquarters with the latest front experience were sent out in August to find out what was going on; only one returned.

Dönitz visited the bases to lend his personal authority to the fight for morale and, in 'pep' talks to the Commanders, he explained why they had to keep the seas even if they never sank a ship: by their very presence they were tying up some two million enemy personnel in the escort forces and shipyards.

One of these Commanders who survived wrote after the war:

> No more parties were given to celebrate the start of a campaign now; we just drank a glass of champagne in silence and shook hands, trying not to look each other in the eyes. We got pretty tough, but it shook us all the same. Operation suicide![86]

Meanwhile troops and guns and aircraft poured virtually unhindered across the Atlantic to Great Britain in preparation for the invasion of the continent. While most German intelligence estimates doubted if sufficient strength had yet been built up to cross the Channel before winter, there was no question about the allied air superiority, now being exploited in sustained mass raids on German cities. The effects outdid anything previously seen. Begun on the night of July 24–25th against Hamburg this new scale of bombing created uncontrollable fire storms which sucked in winds of cyclone strength, devastating vast areas and leaving charred, mutilated victims among the rubble and thousands more asphyxiated or drowned by burst water mains in shelters and cellars

318

beneath the smoking shells that remained. Speer compared the scenes to the aftermath of a major earthquake.

'Terror can only be broken by terror . . .' Hitler rasped in repetitive monologues after news of the raids. 'We can only stop this business if we get at the people over there . . .'[87] He authorized Speer to mass-produce the rockets under development at Peenemünde for use in bombarding London. Fighter aircraft to protect the *Reich* would have been a more profitable use of resources.

In early August Berlin came under air attack; Hitler ordered all women and children to be evacuated. Dönitz meanwhile made a tour of inspection of the shipyards at Hamburg after further raids, reporting to Hitler on the 19th; his impression was that industry would not be materially endangered by the bombing; he did foresee dangers to morale, though, and again he impressed the point on Hitler.

'Despite all willingness to work, the people are depressed, they see only the many reverses . . . I consider it urgently necessary for the Führer to speak to the people very soon. I believe it absolutely necessary. The entire German nation longs for it.'[88]

Hitler said he intended to do so—but he had to wait until the Italian situation clarified.

Dönitz went on to tell him how the people he had spoken to in Hamburg had asked him when Germany was going to retaliate and when the fighter aircraft cover would be improved. He had not told them, he said, giving as his reason that this would play into the hands of the enemy.

'I believe we should say to the German *Volk* that one insists on patient fortitude—that the German people cannot always demand to hear when and how things will improve and that if not told they have the right to throw in the towel. Then we show ourselves to be as the English consider us, who say *they* can endure air-raids because they are harder—the German is closer to the Italian in this respect. I believe, therefore we must seize the German through his pride and honour without making promises or raising hopes that cannot be fulfilled.'

He continued to hammer at this theme, saying that he kept telling his officers it was their solemn duty to inspire morale in the people—which brought him back again to the dangers of defeatism amongst 'educated circles', who were expressing opinions 'in a wise and important manner. These people see only a part of what is going on and not the overall picture'. This was a faithful echo of Hitler's constant diatribes against educated men.

Hitler listened intently to all he had to say and thanked him, but the suggestions had no effect. Now that the real world was collapsing around him, he refused to step outside the world of his imagination, which he preserved in the familiar distractions of briefings, conferences and consciously *gemütlich* tea parties with his Nibelung intimates beneath the massive concrete roof of his command headquarters in the East Prussian forest and refused to view the destruction outside.

Tragedy, meanwhile, struck the family of Dönitz's estranged brother, Friedrich. His home was in Berlin; his daughters had been evacuated to East Prussia, but he worked in the capital—at what is not clear—and was in his house in the suburb of Lichterfelde when it was set ablaze by incendiary bombs in a raid on the night of August 23/24th. He suffered third-degree burns and died on the 25th.

Finding that his name was Dönitz, the authorities contacted the Grand Admiral; whether they did so before Friedrich died, so giving the brothers a last chance to see one another, or whether he was in a coma or dead by the time Karl Dönitz was informed is not clear. It must be assumed that he went to the funeral on September 2nd; certainly Friedrich's wife, Erna, came to live at their house in Dahlem and the three girls spent their school holidays with him and Ingeborg for the rest of the war, bringing a touch of spring into his ever-darkening world.

On September 8th 1943 news came that the Italians had committed the treachery Hitler had long been anticipating by signing an armistice with the allies; the plans prepared for just this eventuality were put into effect and in a series of lightning moves Rome was surrounded, the Italian forces disarmed, Mussolini seized from internment and reinstated, and before the end of the month central and northern Italy had become a German province under a puppet government. The arrangements for taking over the fleet were not so successful; most of the heavy units escaped to the allies, who had begun their landings on mainland Italy five days before the armistice was made public; the greater part of the light forces and submarines also escaped although several were taken over according to plan.

Well-prepared and brilliantly executed as most of these moves were, they did nothing to alter the defensive posture of the *Reich*. In the east Manstein was withdrawing. Dönitz was instructed to use his forces in the

Black Sea to evacuate troops and assist in establishing the Crimea as the next 'fortress' to be held at all costs.

By this time criticism of the conduct of the war must have spread to the Navy itself; facts are difficult to establish, but the documents suggest that Dönitz's operations staff in Berlin did not see eye to eye with him, and disaffection may well have been spreading from those officers whose duties brought them in contact with wider affairs; among these in the juridical department of the Navy was Bertholdt, brother of Claus Count Stauffenberg who had recently joined the active resistance to Hitler. Whether the criticism chiefly concerned the hopeless strategic situation in which Hitler had placed the Fatherland, or the stains laid on the name of Germany by the crimes of National Socialism, or whether they also touched Dönitz's own 'fanatic' commitment to the regime and its strategy is not clear. It is evident he took them seriously though, for on September 9th he issued a 'Decree against Criticism and Complaints'.[89]

This started with a reminder of the 'stupendous successes' won in the early war years which had established the fundamentals for a successful conclusion to the war. Such times of attack were the high points of a soldier's life; times of defence and waiting were harder to endure, and it was such times that demanded above all strong inner conviction. This was being eroded however by the 'complainers' who spoke 'depreciatingly and without restraint about everything, and usually about things which were none of their business'. No one could see more than a small fraction of the totality of the war; it could, therefore, only be 'foolish, conceited or malicious people' who fancied themselves competent to criticize military and political measures they did not understand. He concluded:

> Complainers who broadcast their own miserable opinions openly to comrades or other *Volk*-mates, thereby weakening their will and assurance as soldiers, are inexorably to be called to account by court Martial for undermining the armed forces.
>
> The Führer has laid the basis for the unity of the German people through the National Socialist ideology. It is the task of all of us in this period of the war to secure this precious unity through hardness, patience and constancy, through fighting, work and silence.

The word 'silence' could simply have meant not complaining; in view of the stories of SS atrocities in the east which were circulating at all levels in

321

Germany,[90] and news about the extermination of millions of Jews being put out by the BBC and other forbidden stations, it probably had a more sinister implication.

It was of this time that a former petty officer from U 333 reminisced long after the war. Referring to the preferential treatment and extra comforts provided for U-boat crews on their return from the 'front', he spoke of his own boat's return from a war cruise in the summer of 1943. The men were presented with a wooden chest of watches from which to choose what they wished. The watches were all second-hand, all in working order; a few were watches for the blind. 'Then we knew exactly. That was too macabre. Nobody should say that he knew nothing. We knew at that time where they came from.'[91]

It is inconceivable that such a crate could have been sent from the death camps in the east to the Biscay U-boat bases unless Dönitz had arranged it with Himmler.

Lest this story be dismissed as hearsay from long after the event there is documentary and recorded evidence to prove that Dönitz attended the *Tagung*—or Convention—that autumn at Posen, when Himmler first revealed to a select audience of Reichsleiters and Gauleiters his final solution to the Jewish question. The convention was designed to boost the morale of the assembled Party bosses and inform them in particular about armaments production. Bormann and Himmler, who called the convention, had assembled a top-level team for the purpose: besides Dönitz, Albert Speer, five of his Armaments Ministry chiefs and the State secretary of the Air Ministry, *Generalfeldmarschall* Milch, took part.

It was not a pleasant group; Milch, for instance, was one of those lost souls who had had to overcome the knowledge that a part of his own blood was Jewish; he had found it necessary to obtain from his father a sworn affidavit that he (Milch senior) had always been impotent, and could not therefore have sired him, and from his mother that his real father was not Milch senior but another of unquestioned Nordic stock. It is noticeable there was no representative from the Army among the team of guest speakers; it was a Party occasion; only those dedicated to the Party and the Führer had been invited.

Bormann opened proceedings, after which the morning session was taken up with the speeches of Speer and his Armaments Ministry colleagues. They then took lunch and left—that at least is Speer's story, but as Himmler addressed him personally in the course of his own speech

322

9a *(right)* Grand Admiral Karl Dönitz, C-in-C *Kriegsmarine*, 1943. Compare this with his portrait as *Kapitän zur See* and FdU (**plate 6**) only four years earlier

9b *(below)* Relaxing with 'Wolf' in the grounds of his Dahlem, Berlin, home

9c *(below right)* On a walk with Günther Hessler, his three nieces and 'Wolf' in the country around 'Koralle'

10a The bomb-proof U-boat bunkers built at all Biscay bases

10b U-boats berthed in their bomb-proof concrete pens in Lorient

11a And out in the open Atlantic: U 175 meets her end

11b HMS *Starling* carrying out a depth charge attack in February 1944

12a With the Nibelungen: Hitler *(left)*, Göring *(foreground)*, Dönitz *(centre)*

12b In Rome, March 1943. The German Ambassador and Admiral Riccardi, Italian Navy C-in-C, are just behind Dönitz, Admirals Meendsen-Bohlken and Ruge behind them

in the afternoon it is not convincing.[92] Bormann reconvened the meeting at 3 o'clock, introducing the next two guest speakers from outside the Party circle, Milch and Dönitz. Milch then spoke for 65 minutes and after him Dönitz for 41 minutes, concluding shortly before 5 o'clock. *SA Gruppenführer* Wilhelm Scheppmann followed him, then at 5.30 the *Reichsführer SS*, Heinrich Himmler, rose to make the big speech of the day.[93]

Why he chose this occasion to reveal the secret of the extermination programme is not clear. Possibly it was because it had become the subject of speculation and dark rumour among those large sections of the German people in contact with men returning wounded or on leave from the east, or who listened to the BBC. On the other hand it may have derived from a conscious or subconscious urge to share his awesome responsibility and implicate the Party as a whole in the task for which the Führer had chosen him. It could also be interpreted as a subtle warning for them and for the German people as a whole of the consequences if the war were to be lost—a prospect now clear to all—giving them additional reason to act ruthlessly against any defeatism and disloyalty. For the same propaganda which espoused the necessity of exterminating Jews within German-occupied Europe raised the spectre of vengeance from Jews outside—namely 'International Jewry' operating from London, Washington and Moscow to destroy the German race. It is significant that he addressed himself in a key passage to the subject of vengeance.

Whatever the motives behind the speech, it is scarcely conceivable that Dönitz who had finished his own speech only half an hour before had left the hall by the time Himmler rose; this would have been a gross discourtesy to the *Reichsführer*, who ranked rather above a *Grossadmiral* in the hierarchy. There can be no reasonable doubt, therefore, that he heard all that followed.

What followed was a glimpse into the necessary and inevitable end-product of National Socialist ideology, that had focused from the first on the Jew as the single enemy; the shades and half-tones of the real world of infinite complexity had been seared away by Party propaganda, leaving only stark white and black—the honest German and the Jew. And since the Party had displaced God and for Christian morality substituted the law of survival there was in logic no constraint on action against this blood enemy. If Hitler and Goebbels were the supreme orators, Himmler was the supreme logician, and it was logic—in truth the logic of the asylum, for its premises were based on perceptions which bore no

323

relation to the real world outside—that he now expounded. All those who heard him became—if they were not already—fully certifiable inmates of the Party asylum.

> . . . I refer, in this closest of circles, to a question which you all, my fellow Party-members, have obviously addressed, which, however, has become for me the most difficult question of my life—the Jewish question. You all take it as self-evident and gratifying that in your *Gaus* there are no more Jews. All Germans—apart from a few exceptions—are also clear that we would not have endured the bombing, nor the burdens of the fourth and perhaps the fifth and sixth years of the war if we had this festering plague in the body of our *Volk*. The proposition 'The Jews must be exterminated' with its few words, *meine Herren*, is easily spoken. For him who has to accomplish it, it is the hardest and most difficult of all tasks . . .[94]

He spoke matter-of-factly, without emotion, although allowing himself some irony when he digressed for a moment to the question of the 'decent Jew'; from the number of people in Germany who had their 'decent Jew' it seemed there were more of these than the total Jewish population. He soon returned to the matter on hand, asking his audience never to speak of what he told them.

> We come to the question: how is it with the women and children? In this matter also I have resolved on an absolutely clear solution. That is to say I do not consider myself justified in exterminating the men—so to speak killing or ordering the killing—and allowing the avengers in the shape of the children to grow up for our sons and grandsons. The difficult resolution must be grasped—to cause this people to disappear from the earth. The organization for executing this mission was the most difficult task we have had. It was accomplished without—I believe I am able to say—our men or our Führer suffering injury to soul or spirit. This danger was very close. Between the two possibilities, either being too cruel and becoming heartless and not honouring human life, or becoming weak and by wavering losing nerve—the way between this Scylla and Charybdis is dreadfully narrow.

He passed on to the confiscation of the Jews' possessions, in which matter too it had been necessary to be absolutely consistent; all had to go

324

to the *Reich*'s Economics Minister for the benefit of the German people as a whole. From the beginning he had decreed the death penalty for any SS men taking even a Mark for themselves, and in the last few days he had signed—'I can say it calmly'—some dozen death sentences for his own men. He went on to promise that the Jewish question in occupied countries would be solved by the end of the year, after which there would only be a few solitary Jews left who had taken refuge; then only the question of the half Jews and those who had married Jews would remain to be 'sensibly and reasonably investigated, decided, then solved'.

He had, he confessed, had enormous difficulties so far as the economy was concerned. In Warsaw, for instance, one ghetto which had taken four weeks to clear—'Four weeks! We cleared out nearly 700 bunkers!'—had been a centre for the clothes trade.

'If one had wanted to reach in there in earlier times it would have been "Stop! Armaments work!" Naturally that had absolutely nothing to do with Party Minister Speer—you—' and one imagines him turning to the guest speakers—'certainly could do nothing about it. It is the area of alleged armaments work which the Party Minister Speer and I wish to cleanse together in the next weeks and months . . .

'With that may I conclude the Jewish question. Now you know your way about, and you will keep it to yourselves. Perhaps in some much later time one will be able to consider whether one should say something more to the German people. I believe it better that we—we as a whole—have done it for our people, have taken the responsibility upon ourselves—the responsibility for a deed, not simply for an idea—and that we take the secret with us to the grave.

'I come now to the problem of defeatism . . .'

Dönitz's and Speer's reactions to the revelation of the *Reichsführer*'s awesome commitment to the *Volk*—if indeed it was a revelation to them—can never be known. Both carried the secret to the grave. According to one of those present, Baldur von Schirach, an oppressive silence reigned while Himmler spoke; afterwards Bormann closed the meeting with an invitation to snacks. 'We sat speechless at the tables avoiding one another's eyes.'[95] According to Speer's recollections in his memoirs—recollections which did not extend to the content of Himmler's speech—the Gauleiters and Reichsleiters drank themselves into a stupor that evening, a sight which so disgusted him that the next day he asked Hitler to exhort them to moderation.[96]

Whatever the truth, it seems possible that the convention served to boost Dönitz's morale, for on the next day, October 7th, the order about rescue ships first promulgated the previous autumn was repeated over the signature of the FdU, Eberhard Godt, on behalf of the BdU, himself.

There is generally in every convoy a so-called rescue ship, a special ship up to 3,000 tons appointed to pick up the shipwrecked after U-boat attack. Most of these ships are equipped with aircraft and large motor boats and are strongly armed and very manoeuvrable, so that they have been described frequently by Commanders as U-boat traps. Their sinking is of great value in regard to the desired destruction of the steamers' crews.[97]

The care which had gone into the wording of this order in case it was discovered by the enemy is evident: the 'so-called' rescue ship was in reality a strongly-armed 'U-boat trap'; this justified the meaningful phrase at the end. But was it remotely likely in the desperate conditions of convoy warfare that Commanders would or could recognize or aim for specific ships?

The new U-boat campaign to wrest back the initiative in the North Atlantic had begun nearly three weeks before. The boats were armed with *Zaunkönig* acoustic torpedoes for use against the escorts, and increased flak armament for defence against aircraft. They also had a new receiving set called Hagenuk for detecting the allied radar beams. This had been developed because the old Metox warning set was believed to emit radiations which gave the U-boat's position away—a story planted by a captured English pilot. He had told his interrogating officers that the British hardly ever used radar in anti-submarine work since the (Metox) receiver radiation could be detected up to 90 miles away; aircraft simply homed in on this, using their radar in brief bursts to check the range!

While it was realized that the story might be a deliberate deception, it was felt necessary to act on it at once, and Commanders at sea had been instructed not to use their Metox; at the same time Dönitz had leaped to the conclusion, as he told Hitler, that the radiations could explain 'all the

326

uncanny and unsolved mysteries, for instance avoidance of U-boat dispositions, losses in the open seas'; future experience would prove whether the 'conclusion that Metox is responsible for a great part of our losses' was justified.[98] The episode shows how far behind the allies German radar scientists were and suggests that U-boat Command scarcely even comprehended the principles involved. Nor did Hitler; he was happy to agree with Dönitz that Metox 'radiations' probably accounted for the former losses.[99]

As boats carrying all the hopes for the renewed battle in the decisive theatre headed out towards the northern shipping lanes in mid-September, *B-Dienst* reported two westbound convoys, ONS 18 and ON 202, and the boats were ordered into a patrol line across their track. The signals were deciphered at Bletchley Park, however; a support group and shore-based Liberators were sent to augment the convoy escort, and on the 19th one of the Liberators sank U 341; the leading convoy was sighted on the same day and touch was held. Two boats made unsuccessful attacks that night, but battle was not really joined until the next night, by which time the second, faster convoy had come up into the same area. The boats had orders to use their acoustic torpedoes on the escorts first and they succeeded in damaging one frigate so badly that she had to be towed home; they also sank two merchantmen. Liberators from Iceland joined at dawn and one of these employing an acoustic torpedo under development at the same time as the German weapon sank a second U-boat; two other boats were damaged. That evening the pack evened the score by sinking two surface escorts with *Zaunkönigs*, but the fiercest battle took place on the fourth night when yet another escort was sunk, together with four merchantmen, for the loss of only one boat. By the next morning there was full air cover as the convoys reached Newfoundland, and the action was broken off.

The results of this four-days' battle were one destroyer and two smaller escorts sunk, one frigate severely damaged and six merchantmen, totalling 36,000 tons sunk, but the success reports reaching U-boat Command amounted to three destroyers and twelve merchantmen totalling 46,000 tons.[100] Dönitz was delighted and, encouraged in his belief that the anti-destroyer torpedo was the 'decisive' weapon and that the quadruple AA guns could counter the menace from the air, reported to Hitler on the 'successful' beginning to the new campaign. Hitler was equally delighted, spoke with 'unprecedented emphasis on the importance of the U-boat tonnage war, the only light in an otherwise dark situation', and stressed that U-boat warfare 'must be stepped up with all available means'.[101]

The gleam of light was short-lived. The boats, regrouped to catch reported eastbound convoys, missed them and three were destroyed by aircraft from Iceland. Regrouped again, they only succeeded in finding the escort for the next convoy, and although one destroyer was sunk with a *Zaunkönig* three more boats were lost to air attack. Dönitz, recently returned from the Gauleiters' *Tagung*, formed another patrol line with boats fresh from home and ordered them to stay on the surface when aircraft were sighted, fighting it out with their guns. The results were disastrous: in a five-day battle against two convoys whose own escorts were strengthened by a support group and shore-based Liberators, six U-boats were destroyed for the loss of only one merchantman. This time the lesson was heeded; U-boat Command war diary noted: 'A U-boat armed with 2-cm flak guns cannot stand up to a heavily-armoured large bomber or flying boat.'[102]

Yet the illusion of the first success with *Zaunkönig*s lingered on, and a new group named *Siegfried* was formed to find eastbound convoys; it is usually possible to deduce whether Dönitz was personally directing operations from the names given to the groups—*Siegfried* was undoubtedly one of his! The boats were ordered to proceed submerged by day to avoid detection and only to surface at night; still the convoys evaded them and three more boats were sunk. In an attempt to conceal the whereabouts of the patrol lines at the end of October the groups were split into three sub-groups, then on November 5th into five with one boat from each group stationed in advance in the expected direction of the convoy; still they found nothing. Finally new dispositions were formed south-east of Greenland with a number of groups of only three boats each, ordered to remain submerged by day and to surface and keep moving by night to confuse the enemy as to their whereabouts. Still they found nothing, still too many were themselves found and destroyed—in October 26 in all theatres, in November seventeen.

Meanwhile escort vessels had begun towing a noise-making 'foxer', under development previously as an antidote to just such a weapon as the *Zaunkönig*; these attracted the acoustic torpedoes away from the ship itself. In addition specialized escort groups had perfected a new tactic for use against deep-diving boats; it involved one 'directing' vessel fixing the position of the submerged boat by Asdic, while one or more of the other vessels of the group manoeuvred slowly and silently over it; when informed by the directing ship that they were in position these fired patterns of deep-set charges to sink in the track of the unsuspecting boat, which had no time to take evasive action before they were exploding around it. This 'creeping' attack proved so murderously effective no crews survived to report on it to U-boat Command.

For the second time that year the scale of losses in the North Atlantic reached crisis proportions without compensating successes, and in mid-November, barely two months after the start of the renewed offensive, Dönitz was forced to withdraw; again he moved the groups southwards towards the Gibraltar convoys, leaving the vital northern routes devoid of boats.

It was shortly before this, on November 10th, that naval operations staff laid a draft *Lagebetrachtung*, or general view of the war, before him.[103] It was even more pessimistic than the August *Lagebetrachtung*; German forces were everywhere so strained, reserves so short and the allied resources of personnel and material so superior that there was now no possibility of seeking a decision of the war by offensive action. Nor could any comfort be drawn from the situation in the east: the Japanese were in the same position as themselves, on the defensive and strained everywhere. In these circumstances the staff believed that the only way to regain freedom of action and avoid the series of continuing crises was to reduce the frontiers of occupied Europe by strategic withdrawals, and four areas were mentioned—the Crimea, the Baltic, the Aegean and northern Norway. Dönitz had objections to each, as he always had objections to any withdrawal anywhere; each objection was sound in itself; taken together they amounted to a policy of holding on everywhere until forced into involuntary retreat or surrender with huge and unnecessary losses of men and war materials. It was a negation of strategy.

Hitler was frozen in the same attitude. With no hope of an offensive thrust that could lead to victory, surrender not in his vocabulary, his aim had dwindled to holding the frontiers of 'Fortress Europe' with iron determination until the providence which had shielded Frederick the Great rescued him. It is possible therefore that Dönitz's conviction was that of a courtier echoing his master's views; certainly he was taking great pains to be present at the top councils at this period; he made frequent flights to the *Wolfschanze*, while there staying in a timber building Hitler had made available for him inside the defended perimeter; it was known as the *Haus der Marine* or *Haus Atlantik*. Besides providing

329

accommodation for him and his staff it was a useful venue for entertaining members of the clique around Hitler or other influential visitors to headquarters.

It would be wrong, however, to interpret his support for Hitler's policy as mere sycophancy. His skill in angling reports to present an optimistic picture under the guise of objectivity would have enabled him safely to oppose Hitler had he wished to do so; he proved this often enough in naval affairs; had he thought that a withdrawal anywhere was in the best interests of the Navy he could have found suitable arguments. He never did, and the records of his conferences with the Führer suggest that he was usually the first to express the view that one position or another must be held at all cost. The reason is probably quite simple: he still believed he could influence the outcome of the war decisively once the new types of U-boat with high underwater speed were available, but he needed time to put sufficient into commission and to work them up. This certainly coloured his attitude towards the Baltic region, vital for training. Probably, therefore, his vehement support for Hitler was in aid of the U-boat arm.

This is supported by his reaction to the November *Lagebetrachtung*. There was no necessity for him to echo the Führer's views in his own headquarters, but he expressed himself very bluntly when the draft was laid before him, as a result of which the staff, against their own judgement, trimmed the more negative aspects. This marked the final stage in the intellectual rift between Dönitz and his thinking departments.[104] No more overall *Lagebetrachtungen* were produced; the staff was reduced to a mere transmitting organ for his policy; since this was formed, as throughout his career, from a narrow concentration on his own goal with scant attention to the enemy's strengths or likely moves, and since his natural over-optimism was constantly reinforced during his visits to Führer headquarters, the Navy now finally departed from reality.

This coincided with a physical removal of Command headquarters to a new post in the open countryside some 30 kilometres north of Berlin, known as 'Koralle'. It was a complex of timber barracks inside a perimeter fence in a pine clearing rather similar to the various Führer headquarters; it had been started in July, but the move had been forced by the heaviest air attack to date on West Berlin on the night of November 22nd; the naval headquarters building on the Tirpitz Ufer was gutted by incendiary bombs, and overall naval command had to be transferred temporarily to Group North in Kiel. By the end of the month the transfer to 'Koralle' had been effected, however, and Dönitz, who made his home with Ingeborg in one of the only two stone buildings in the compound—the other was the Command *Zentral*—remained there until the closing stages of the war. His house was situated on rising ground, the windows commanding a splendid view of wooded and hilly country over which he liked to stride on long afternoon walks with his dog, Wolf, close members of his staff and in the school holidays his three young nieces.

He loved Wolf dearly; his first question of his adjutant after his return from Führer headquarters or one of the front command posts was always 'How is my dog?' Since he also loved children there is no doubt that these walks provided his chief, if not his only, relaxation from the increasingly severe strains of his position. Perhaps one of his remarks which his adjutant, Hansen-Nootbar, recalls from this time reveals something of those strains, 'Hänschen, there is nothing in the world more faithful than a dog. He believes in his master unconditionally. What he does is right.'[105] Hitler's closest and most constant companion was his wolf-hound, Blondi, and he was wont to make similar remarks about the wholehearted devotion of a dog to its master. Is this saying of Dönitz's yet another sign that he had fallen completely under the spell of the Führer, even to copying his remarks, or simply an indication that he, like Hitler, had doubts about the complete loyalty of his staff—or even about the correctness of the path he was following?

He never allowed such doubts to show—unless perhaps to Ingeborg and that can never be known. According to Hansen-Nootbar, she had a 'very balancing influence' on him. 'In my time he was often very agitated by the unfortunately negative events of the war; she understood how to calm him down—which was certainly not always easy.' Hansen-Nootbar was in a good position to judge since he lived with them virtually as a son of the house, taking his meals with them and in the evenings joining them for bridge—until after a short time Dönitz flung his cards down, 'It's not worth playing with you drips [*Flaschen*],' and announced he was off to bed.

Hansen-Nootbar found Ingeborg a delightful person—indeed he regarded it as his greatest good fortune to have known her; she had a wonderful head, although less fortunate perhaps in figure, tremendous charm, a good sense of humour and was immense fun—'quintessentially a lady', he recalls, and 'a personality I shall never, ever forget'. His view

331

of Dönitz was more reserved, and he thought he had little humour. This was not surprising perhaps at that cruel stage of the war: the first weeks at 'Koralle' coincided with shattering naval setbacks, one of which was final acceptance of defeat in wolf-pack tactics.

For the move southwards to attack the Gibraltar convoys in mid-November had brought no more success than achieved in the north, despite the fact that the co-operation of the local air group had been gained. Dönitz personally directed the first operation in the south—at least this is suggested by the name of the group formed, Schill, a hero of the German freedom fight against Napoleon, and by a most unusual wireless message to the group signed 'C-in-C'.

The action started on the 17th when a convoy of some 60 merchantmen was reported by air reconnaissance 400 miles from the Spanish coast steering north at seven knots; the boats were disposed in three patrol lines across its track and the next day the convoy ran into the southern line; one boat was rammed and forced out of the action, in return one of the escorts was hit by a *Zaunkönig* and disabled. Despite the strength of the defence, a boat under Werner Henke held on and sent touch-keeping reports, and at 10.45 that evening Dönitz sent the signal: 'Group Schill. Up to Henke! Beat them to death! [*Schlagt sie tot!*] *Oberbefehlshaber* [C-in-C].'[106]

This might have been the kind of hyperbole he was wont to employ in his *Feuersprüche*—or morale-boosting slogans—an interpretation which is supported by the fact that it went out as a personal message rather than one from U-boat Command. In its literal sense, however, it could only apply to the crews of the merchantmen and their escorts.

The escorts had been strengthened meanwhile; Bletchley Park had read the disposition signals, and a support group and air support had been sent to the convoy which from the 19th was protected by a double screen of nineteen warships and round-the-clock air cover. It was not surprising that the boats scored no further successes and during the following two night battles two boats were destroyed and a third the day after when the attack was called off. The merchantmen came through unscathed, the sole achievements of the 31 boats involved were the crippling of a sloop and two aircraft shot down on the last day.

There could be no reasonable doubt by now that the acoustic torpedo was not as effective as had appeared, and that pack operations were no longer feasible. Nevertheless, it was not until several more groups had been formed and had failed and several more U-boats had been lost that

332

group tactics were finally abandoned. Before this the size of the groups had again been reduced to just three boats—an interesting reversion to Dönitz's pre-war ideas. There was no instance of a convoy picked up by one of the three being found by either of its two fellows, so no point in continuing even this disposition, and on January 7th 1944 Dönitz was forced to the conclusion that henceforth his boats must patrol singly; as the U-boat war diary put it: 'one boat will now have to attack the whole escort and after discovery endure the enemy counter-measures alone'. The entry concluded: '*A successful mass U-boat campaign with existing types and those planned for the future is only possible if the boats are directed to the convoy by continuous air reconnaissance.*'[107]

It was a feature of Dönitz in defeat that he himself was never to blame. And of course there was a large scapegoat to hand in the *Luftwaffe* and its decadent chief. In a sense he was correct; the lack of a naval air arm, and the failure of the Air Force to devote sufficient resources to the sea war was a major factor in the defeat of his packs. Yet in view of the overwhelming air superiority of the enemy and the demands on the *Luftwaffe* from every embattled front and over the cities of Germany, it was a narrow view indeed that showed up Göring's failure to help the U-boats as an isolated phenomenon. The root of the trouble was Germany's inferior industrial capacity; this was exacerbated by the Führer system and the ever more arbitrary decisions of the Führer himself. Dönitz, the most successful of the current flatterers at court, had gained in the free-for-all that passed for decision making, thus contributing to the shortages in the air. Blaming the other services did not help, it simply increased the anarchy at the top. Besides this it was not simply *Luftwaffe* failure which had caused the defeat of his packs; the existing U-boat had been overtaken by allied technology.

Dönitz knew this; as he told Hitler on December 16th, the time for surface attack was over, in future it had to be submerged attack.[108] All his hopes now were pinned on the 'Electric' and Walter boats whose series construction in sectional form had been started at various inland factories without waiting for prototypes. Yet even these new types with high underwater speed would be useless, he explained, if they could not *find* the convoys, and he categorically demanded the production of Junkers 290 aircraft for the future U-boat war.

He returned to this theme three days later at the *Wolfschanze*, this time demanding the entire output of Junkers 290 exclusively for long-range naval reconnaissance. He also stressed the need for original research in high frequency detection, and said that he and Speer would make a report on this 'which would recommend removal of a large area of research from the direct control of the *Reichsmarschall*', Göring! Hitler fully agreed his points.

It is apparent again that Dönitz was not simply a courtier under the spell of the Führer. In naval affairs he took the offensive and was almost always successful—successful, that is, in extracting promises. Undoubtedly he was now one of the chief props of the Führer, therefore of the Nazi State; undoubtedly the Navy had gained thereby, but his commitment came from the heart not the head; his reports were carefully constructed to match every disaster with three or four pieces of hopeful news or, if news were lacking, optimistic opinion, yet this had always been his way of deceiving himself. He continued to deceive himself and Hitler because of his commitment to Führer and Fatherland—one and the same in his eyes—as well as to his own service and his U-boats especially.

This shows clearly through an important speech he made at a *Tagung* for Flag Officers just two days before his *Wolfschanze* meeting with Hitler; he began:

I am a strong adherent of the idea of ideological training. For what is it basically? Fulfilment of duty is a matter of course for the soldier. But the whole importance, the whole weight of duty fulfilled only emerges when the heart and the whole inner conviction are engaged. Then the effect of the fulfilled duty will be something completely different than if I merely fulfil my task obediently and loyally to the letter. It is therefore necessary for the soldier to put all his intellectual and spiritual powers and his willpower behind the fulfilment of his duty; this is where his conviction, his ideology, come in. Therefore it is necessary for us to train the soldier uniformly and comprehensively to adjust him ideologically to our Germany. Every dualism, every dissension in this training, every divergence or unreadiness implies a weakness under all circumstances . . .[109]

He carried on in this vein at some length; it was a nonsense to say that the soldier or the officer should be unpolitical; the soldier embodied the State, he was its representative, its outstanding exponent, therefore he had to put his full weight behind the State.

'We have to travel this path from deepest conviction. The Russians do.

334

In this struggle we can only hold our own if we follow it with holy ardour, with complete fanaticism.'

Then turning to the war situation, he reaffirmed his conviction that England had forced the war because she did not wish to allow Germany to become great. 'The Anglo-Saxon is the chief enemy—of that there is no doubt. Without the policy of the English the war would never have occurred.'

It was as clear as the sun, he went on, when the war came in 1939 it was going to be a long one. For they were opposed by two giant seapowers with all their potential for gradually developing strength from the resources of the world. Sea wars were economic wars, and lasted an extraordinary time. The Führer had employed the only correct strategy by acquiring the economic space to enable Germany to survive such a war. Europe was put in the bag, the east won essentially for economic reasons—so that they could survive and not, as in the First War, be forced under by blockade. Now the enemy was trying to squeeze this economic space and undoubtedly the position in the east was hard and serious; nevertheless it should not be forgotten that the other side had suffered monstrous losses, was tired and exhausted and lacked strength to capitalize its gains.

'We will deploy fresh forces and there is no doubt that the east will be held under all circumstances. I am an adherent of not giving up anything in the east that is not unconditionally necessary. I have strongly advised holding the Crimea—I have exerted my influence so far as I am able to. Because the Crimea protects the Balkans like a shield, we will hold the Crimea . . .'

So he reviewed the position on all fronts in line with official policy; the Russians would be contained; there was in any case plenty of space in the east, a long way for the enemy to drive before Germany itself was endangered. The position in the west, however, was different. The Anglo-Saxons would certainly attempt an invasion early next year; if they were to succeed and break through they would be close to the borders of Germany and the vital industrial regions of the Rhine and Ruhr; such a breakthrough had to be prevented under all circumstances.

'The Navy, lying off the coasts and manning the coastal fortifications will in such a case [invasion] have a task demanding the most fanatical and complete commitment in which there is no yielding—not a metre.'

Only thus would it be possible to defend the coasts successfully. And the enemy, once beaten back, would not try a second landing. This then was the 'war-decisive' battle.

'War-decisive'—*Kriegsentscheidend*—had been a *leitmotif* of German naval discussion from Tirpitz's time; it reveals a particular way of thinking, or perhaps the word itself directs thought along cataclysmic lines. But it was nonsense to talk in one breath of economic war and in the next of a 'war-decisive' battle. The problem is to decide how much of the speech Dönitz believed, how much was deliberate deception to counter the arguments of the 'defeatists'. He knew the overwhelming material/economic/manpower odds against the *Reich*; he had virtually said as much when he spoke of the two giant seapowers building up their strength gradually from the resources of the world. He knew Germany's strategic resources were strained beyond the limit; the heavy ships he had rescued from Hitler's decree could not be sent to sea for training because of oil shortage. Yet it is probable these considerations weighed with him as little as statistical considerations during the May crisis in the Battle of the Atlantic. It was not in the German military tradition to give up; it was not in the soldier's code to make individual judgements, only to obey his orders and do his duty. And the order from the Führer was to continue the struggle, opposing material odds with burning fanaticism until the enemy found the cost of destroying Germany too great or the allied coalition cracked. It was Dönitz's duty to inspire this fanaticism in his service. This was the purpose of the speech, and there can be no doubt from the esteem in which his name is held in naval circles that it touched a responsive chord in his audience and among naval officers generally; the seniors were determined the shame of the mutinies and the naval surrender should never be repeated, the younger ones, brought up in the fanatical atmosphere created by the Nazi Party, were conditioned to go down the path outlined with holy ardour, with complete fanaticism.

His speech begged every rational question about war strategy, about the necessity to regain control of the air over the *Reich* if there was to be any hope of defeating an allied invasion, of gaining air mastery over the Atlantic if there was to be any hope of renewing the U-boat war with success, above all perhaps where the reserves of men were to come from who were to plug the gaps in the eastern theatre, beat back the 'second front' in the west, man the necessary aircraft *and* the massive new fleet of the building programme 43. There is no reason, in view of his record, to put it all down to deliberate deception—unconscious self-deception and fanatical commitment played their part.

336

Certainly these two played a major role later that month when he sent the battlecruiser *Scharnhorst* out on a desperate gamble into the Arctic night. Probably this decision was also influenced by the nature of the deal he had struck with Hitler when he won the preservation of the big ships. He had said as much at the end of April: after a somewhat 'defeatist' appreciation by the northern command Admirals of the chances of a successful sortie, he commented that he, Dönitz, had done all he could to preserve the fleet from the Führer, but the question could only be resolved 'by bravely venturing a sortie and achieving success'.[110]

In fact Battle Group North, headed by the *Tirpitz* and *Scharnhorst*, had been playing a considerable role in allied naval planning without moving from their moorings; powerful naval forces and their escorts had been held in the north against an attempted break-out, and the Arctic convoys to Russia had been discontinued while attempts were made to destroy the force; the latest had been in September; midget submarines penetrated the fjord where the *Tirpitz* lay and succeeded in exploding charges beneath her which so damaged the main engines as to put her completely out of action. With the chief threat removed, the Admiralty had re-started the Arctic supply convoys to Russia in November, providing each with a close escort and a heavy covering force at a distance to deal with the *Scharnhorst* should she intervene.

So far as the Commander of Battle Group North, Admiral Kummetz, and his immediate superior in Kiel, Admiral Schniewind, were concerned, there was little prospect of this. Besides the damage to the *Tirpitz*, the cruiser *Lützow* had been sent home for refit with five destroyers, and only the *Scharnhorst* and five destroyers remained operational in the north. The main point, however, was that the almost perpetual darkness of the northern winter provided the worst possible conditions for a gun action by the German forces and the best possible conditions for enemy torpedo attack on a heavy unit such as the *Scharnhorst*. Moreover, German radar was inferior to British—as proved in the action of the previous December which had been the immediate cause of Raeder's downfall—and since radar transmissions could give away a ship's proximity German ships were wont to use their sets as little as possible if there was a chance of enemy forces in the area. Added to this was the difficulty, indeed virtual impossibility, of obtaining a clear picture from air reconnaissance during the dark and often severe conditions of the winter months—particularly as reliance had to be placed on whatever *Luftwaffe* planes were made available at the time.

337

Kummetz went on extended leave in November, and command of the battle group devolved on his destroyer Commander, Rear Admiral Bey. He was quite as sceptical of the chances of a successful sortie as his chief, and on November 22nd he concluded a report on the tactics he would employ if he were to be ordered out with a passage reminiscent of the words of another fleet Commander faced with an impossible task, the Duke of Medina Sidonia in 1588: '. . . thus the feasibility and the success of the convoy operation depends largely on luck and the chances of the enemy somewhat exposing himself or making great mistakes. From the experience of this sea war,' Bey went on, 'which despite the weakness of our forces has brought much good fortune, it is correct to hope that now too fortune will be on our side.'[111]

Despite the clearly expressed doubts of the Admirals who would have to carry out the operation, on December 2nd Dönitz's operational staff in 'Koralle' reaffirmed the official position that a sortie by the *Scharnhorst* in the winter months was both practicable and had prospects of success.

There can be few possible interpretations of this: either the Chief of Staff, Meisel, in his time noted as a *Draufgänger* ('daredevil'), was as emotionally committed to action as Dönitz himself and was determined to ignore—or was even ignorant of—the allied lead in radar and radar-controlled gunnery, or he knew that Dönitz was determined on this course and believed it impracticable to oppose him. He was either an irresponsible gambler or completely under Dönitz's thumb. The only other possibility is that the staff at 'Korrale' were aware of something Group North did not know, that time was running out for the big ships and unless they somehow proved their value Hitler would force their scrapping; that had been his 'unalterable decision' when Dönitz struck his bargain.

Probably there were elements of all three in the extraordinary staff appreciation. At all events, a fortnight later at the Flag Officers' *Tagung* Dönitz proclaimed his intent, 'should the opportunity arise for the battlegroup to strike I will under all circumstances go at the enemy'.[112] And two days afterwards at the *Wolfschanze* he told Hitler of his intention to attack the next allied convoy by the northern route with *Scharnhorst* and the destroyers if there were prospects of a successful operation. He had, he said, ordered additional U-boats to the Arctic.[113]

Three days later, on December 22nd, a report from aerial reconnaissance of 'about 40 ships including transports, escort vessels and presumed carrier. Course 0450, speed ten knots' was interpreted as a raiding force heading for the Norwegian coast and Battle Group North was put on six hours' notice. By the following day the force had been identified as a normal convoy to Russia; it was kept under air surveillance and a U-boat group was ordered to form a patrol line across its estimated track between the North Cape and Bear Island.

The question of using Battle Group North against the convoy now came to the fore. The final decision did not have to be taken until the morning of the 25th when the ships would be near the North Cape area; in the meantime the overall Commander, Admiral Schniewind, ordered air searches to gain 'certain news of a possible distant heavy escort group'. Only when and if such intelligence came in, he reported to 'Koralle', and if the prospects then appeared favourable, would he feel justified in ordering the sortie of the Battle Group. The naval staff concurred.

Dönitz was in Paris at this time, on his way to take part in the Christmas festivities at the U-boat bases. As he explained to Hansen-Nootbar, 'I must go to the front—that is where I belong. I must be with the troops. I must ever and always have an ear for my people.'[114] It was therefore at Admiral Krancke's Group Headquarters West that he received the *Luftwaffe* reconnaissance reports and appreciations of the situation from 'Koralle' via Schniewind at Group Headquarters North in Kiel. Krancke's first staff officer, Edward Wegener, noted his extremely serious attitude as he took the messages; in the mess after dinner he recalled Dönitz took no part in the general conversation; he was far away, immersed in his own thoughts.[115]

By midnight on Christmas Eve the position was still very uncertain. A wireless transmission from a British ship at sea had been plotted by three D/F bearings as coming from 200 miles west of the convoy; it had been assumed at Arctic Command in Narvik that this must be the position of the expected distant heavy covering force. The *Luftwaffe*, however, had failed to find such a force. The Narvik station pointed out to Schniewind in Kiel that weather conditions had precluded comprehensive reconnaissance, and there was no certainty that a support group was not in the area, hence the sortie of the battle group carried an element of risk. Schniewind was well aware of this, and while his summary of the situation shortly before midnight started with the proposition that no heavy support group had been located, it concluded that favourable conditions of weather, visibility and clarification of enemy strength were unlikely, 'prospects of major success improbable, the stakes high'.[116]

At 'Koralle' Meisel discounted these doubts and those expressed at Narvik just as he had discounted the earlier doubts of Kummetz and Bey; one of his comments suggests that he was indeed ignorant of the possibility of radar-controlled gunnery, for on a message from Bey pointing out that conditions would be against artillery action, he scribbled, 'Then the English cruisers could not shoot either!'[117]

In these circumstances Dönitz decided to cancel his trip to the bases and fly back to headquarters. Arriving some time after 2.30 in the afternoon of Christmas Day, he found the situation unchanged, no support group located and Meisel of the opinion that 'the long-awaited opportunity to bring the Battle Group to action' was upon them. As time was pressing, the preparatory order for a sortie, '*Ostfront*', had been sent out a few minutes before his arrival. This suited Dönitz's own determination; it was easy to find arguments of necessity: the convoy was obviously carrying war materials to Russia and the Navy had 'the opportunity of making an important contribution to the easing of the strained situation on the eastern front'.[118]

Once again the goal was occupying Dönitz's whole attention—and it must be assumed that in this case the goal had as much to do with Hitler's opinion of the big ships and the urgent need for some success after the second failure of the U-boats as of the situation on the eastern front. He ordered instructions for the sortie to be prepared by the operations staff. Later in the afternoon these were laid before him, and he set about stamping them with his own style.

The first paragraph ran, 'Enemy intends aggravating heroic struggle of our eastern armies with important convoy of supplies and arms for Russia.' He added, 'We must help.'

The second paragraph, '*Scharnhorst* and destroyers to attack convoy' he left unchanged, but hacked at the third: originally it read, 'Turn to account changing tactical situation. Greatest chance lies in superior artillery *Scharnhorst*. Therefore strive to bring it to action.' To the first phrase Dönitz added 'skilfully and boldly' then he inserted 'Fight not to be ended with half success. Opportunities seized to be pressed home' and at the end: 'Destroyers to engage as suitable.'

The fourth paragraph read, 'Break off on own judgement. Basically break off on the appearance of heavy forces.' He left this as it stood, then added a fifth and final paragraph, 'Crews to be briefed in this sense. I trust in your offensive spirit,' and ended *'Heil und Sieg!* Dönitz, *Grossadmiral.'*

During the time he was putting the order into shape the northern area weather report was received:

> Southerly winds increasing to gale force eight to nine, sea six to seven on the 26th, veering SW force six to eight, heavy SW swell. Mostly overcast with rain, visibility only occasionally ten miles, otherwise three to four miles . . . Barents Sea, snowfalls.[119]

This virtually ruled out prospects of success; the destroyers would be unable to use their speed in this kind of weather, indeed they would be hard put to keep the sea, effective aircraft reconnaissance would be impossible and an average visibility of three to four miles with the possibility of snowstorms made nonsense of the passage in the orders about using the superior artillery of the *Scharnhorst*.

Apparently none of these considerations affected Dönitz or the staff at 'Koralle'; the order was transmitted exactly as edited by Dönitz over three-quarters of an hour after receipt of the weather report. What was the mood then at nearly eight o'clock on Christmas evening? Had wine passed at dinner, had glasses been raised to the success of Battle Group North? Were Meisel and the other staff officers weary perhaps after the long vigil since the convoy was first sighted? Did the final transmission of the order represent a relief in tension or had tension relaxed as soon as Dönitz returned to assume full responsibility?

The battle group had sailed meanwhile, the crew of the *Scharnhorst* cheering wildly as they were told of the purpose of the mission; later as the big ship started heaving to the swell outside, most of them cooped up for so long in the smooth water of the fjord began to feel the torments of sea-sickness.

Admiral Schniewind in Kiel received Dönitz's attack order at nine minutes past eight. He had been in possession of the weather report for some time, and also an urgent request from Narvik Command to break off the operation. At eight-thirty he called up Meisel at 'Koralle' and told him of this, and that Air Commander Lofoten had ruled out reconnaissance on the 26th because of the weather, and he suggested abandoning the mission. Meisel made no comment, but passed the message to Dönitz. Shortly afterwards he rang back and told Schniewind that he had reported his remarks to the C-in-C who had nevertheless decided to carry on (*durchzuhalten*).

Schniewind, who had been Dönitz's immediate superior the previous year, was already composing a message explaining his anxieties. The deteriorating weather 'burdens the operation with too many unfavourable conditions. Sweeping success not to be expected. Therefore propose breaking off. In case total position nevertheless demands sortie, can only suggest sending *Scharnhorst* without destroyers to seek and seize convoy.'[120] At a quarter to nine, shortly after taking the call from Meisel, Schniewind passed the message over the teletype to 'Koralle'; the effect was heightened by the timing, so soon after Dönitz had reaffirmed his decision; no doubt Schniewind intended this; it was bold dissent and an indication of his extreme anxiety.

Whether his proposal to send the battlecruiser out without an escort was intended seriously—for he might have reasoned that the enemy destroyers would make just as heavy weather as their own—or whether it was intended to point up the foolhardiness of the mission will never be known, nor what discussions Dönitz now had, what advice he received, what pressures or habits of mind, what toughness or weakness, fanaticism or desperate optimism conditioned his decision. But his reactions at the crisis of the U-boat war and Italian campaigns should be borne in mind; he had never allowed rational considerations of profit and loss to affect his commitment to strike or to endure—*durchzuhalten*—whatever the odds. It is not necessary therefore to see the brooding figure of the Führer as the chief pressure on his mind during these critical hours. The decision he came to was in line with all his others, made with blood, not reason.

There was much deliberation nonetheless; it was three hours before Schniewind received his reply: the operation was to go ahead; if the destroyers could not keep the sea the question arose of the *Scharnhorst* working on her own as a commerce raider; this decision should be left to the force commander, Rear Admiral Bey. Schniewind could do no more. He passed this latest instruction to the battle group, now well out at sea.

As suspected at Narvik and Kiel, the signal intercepted by *B-Dienst* on Christmas Eve from 200 miles astern of the convoy had indeed been from the British distant covering force; this consisted of the new 14″-gun battleship, *Duke of York*, flying the flag of Admiral Sir Bruce Fraser, C-in-C Home Fleet, and the heavy cruiser *Jamaica*. The numerous signals to the German battle group and to and from the Air Commander, Lofoten, had alerted the Admiralty to the probability of the *Scharnhorst* coming out, and the executive signal, *Ostfront*, which Schniewind passed to Bey at 3.27 am had confirmed this belief;[121] consequently Fraser knew the *Scharnhorst* was at sea, and he was heading east at his best speed to interpose himself between the convoy and Bey's escape route home to Altenfjord. Also in the area was another support group of three heavy cruisers under Vice Admiral Burnett; this force was to the east of the convoy and was heading south-west to intercept Bey, who, unaware of the enemy closing from both sides, was heading north to get ahead of the merchantmen; Bey had a good idea of their position from earlier shadowing reports passed by one of the U-boats from the patrol line positioned across the convoy's track. So the forces converged through the night and early morning of the 26th.

By 7.30 am Bey considered he was close ahead of his prey and he detached his destroyers to search southwesterly. This was a departure from his original ideas for a convoy action, which envisaged keeping two destroyers with the battlecruiser; probably he was acting on Dönitz's latest instructions passed by Schniewind, difficult as these were to reconcile with the conditions in which he found himself. The convoy had been ordered to a more northerly course by Fraser and the destroyers failed to find it, but Burnett's cruiser group was closing, and just over an hour later the lone *Scharnhorst* was detected on the flagship. *Belfast*'s, radar at just under thirteen miles. Burnett held on a converging course until the battlecruiser was sighted visually at six and a half miles; Bey was not using radar—no doubt in order not to give away his presence—and had no idea of the enemy in the vicinity until star shells from the *Belfast* burst overhead; moments later he found himself under fire. He turned away at high speed, replying with his after turret, whose control officer had only the British gun flashes to range on.

Burnett followed, sending shadowing reports to Fraser, who ordered the convoy to steer due north. *B-Dienst* intercepted the signal and although they could not immediately decipher those from Fraser, they were recognized as operational instructions. Shortly before 10 am, Bey reported that he was under fire from supposed cruisers using radar. By this time the terrible suspicion had formed at 'Koralle', Kiel and Narvik that the operational instructions were from the Commander of the heavy covering force that had been feared. As the morning wore on and Burnett left the *Scharnhorst* in order to join the convoy, then found her again, and Fraser, still steering to cover the battlecruiser's route home, continued to direct operations, the suspicion hardened; after 1 o'clock it became virtual certainty as an aerial reconnaissance report was received of one large and several smaller units some 200 miles south-west of the *Scharnhorst* and her shadows. This could only be the distant heavy support group steering to cut Bey off from his base.

Dönitz's feelings may be imagined. Earlier intimations of disaster must have taken root now and he must have felt it very personally; he bore a very personal responsibility. He could only hope that Bey, who had reported a heavy unit amongst the cruisers engaging him and had therefore set course for home at full speed, would be able to shake off his followers. But as further *B-Dienst* intercepts came in it became clear that he was not doing so. Dönitz was spared nothing. It was not like the end of a U-boat which simply failed to report; throughout the afternoon he was able to follow the chase in detail through the intercepts of the enemy's signals and Bey's own signals down to its shattering climax.

Directed to the quarry by the cruisers, the *Duke of York* first picked up the *Scharnhorst* on her radar at 26 miles at 4.17 pm; Bey was still not using his radar and was quite unaware of the battleship as Fraser closed to six miles, then at 4.50 fired star shells and opened fire. Bey, caught by surprise for the third time that day, immediately turned away and the final stage of the chase continued easterly, the *Scharnhorst* gradually opening the range but suffering from the greater accuracy and weight of the radar-directed fire of the battleship. After a while her speed was reduced by underwater damage and Fraser's destroyers closed and scored several torpedo hits, further reducing her speed and ensuring her end. She continued the unequal contest as Fraser's forces closed for the kill, and proved again that German capital ships and German crews could endure fearful punishment. At 6.19 she signalled that she was surrounded by heavy units firing by radar-direction, and a few minutes later came Bey's last message, 'We shall fight to the last shell. *Heil* Hitler!'

Less than an hour later *B-Dienst* intercepted Fraser's signal to two cruisers to finish her off with torpedoes. Dönitz knew the worst.

The scenes as the blazing hulk of the battlecruiser finally slid below the seas at about 7.45 provided vivid demonstration that his call for fanatical loyalty had not gone unheeded. Hurrahs and shouts of '*Heil* our Führer!' sounded defiantly amongst the wreckage in the icy darkness as the British closed to rescue survivors—only 36 of whom out of a complement of nearly 2,000 were eventually saved.

The immediate consequence of the loss of the *Scharnhorst* was recognition that the enemy advances in radar technology had put paid to the big ships' chances of success just as they had put paid to the U-boats' surface tactics—a belated recognition, revealing again the essential amateurishness of the German naval staff, particularly, perhaps, of Dönitz and Meisel. Dönitz, Hansen-Nootbar recalls, felt the disaster 'extraordinarily deeply'; he made it his business nonetheless to slough off his personal responsibility.

With Hitler this was not difficult; from the initial reports of the action it was already clear that Bey had made a grave error in mistaking Burnett's cruisers for heavy ships. Dönitz was happy to reinforce this impression: It had been a 'tragic error'. Actually the position had been one for which the High Command had always striven: the battleship (*Scharnhorst*) had come up with the weaker cruiser escort. *Scharnhorst* had not been able to utilize the favourable situation, however, on account of the misjudgement of the position. Had she engaged the cruisers it was 'absolutely possible that the first phase would have gone in our favour'.[122]

He then appeared to contradict himself by pointing out the superiority of the enemy radar which 'enables the enemy to fight with success in the dark'. Hitler disregarded this; at all events he returned to a familiar theme: was not the real cause of the failures of the big ships, starting with the *Graf Spee*, the fact that they had sought escape rather than battle? Dönitz produced his trump card: in his orders to the *Scharnhorst* he had expressly stated that battle was to be pressed home, 'not ended with half success', and he followed this up with a typical piece of meaningless optimism: 'if the *Scharnhorst* had smashed the cruisers the whole operation would have proceeded more favourably, and she might perhaps have been able to get up to the convoy afterwards. Then the battleship *Duke of York* would very probably have come up too late to protect the convoy.' Then returning to his original proposition, the 'tragedy' came about through the false judgement aboard the *Scharnhorst*; it was 'especially tragic that the *Scharnhorst* actually came close to the target, the convoy, and was unable to use the favourable situation'.

He developed this theme later; since it had been proved that surface ships could not perform their primary function of preventing enemy landings because they could not operate without fighter cover, 'the idea of using the *Scharnhorst* during the Arctic night was basically correct'.[123] And since it was important to maintain strength in the north for strategic reasons, he suggested transferring the heavy cruiser, *Prince Eugen*, to Battle Group North.

Hitler made no objection. Undoubtedly he had won his wager over the usefulness of the big ships, but he made no reference to it now or later, and was content for Dönitz to dispose of the remaining heavy units as he wished. The fact was he needed Dönitz; he needed the support he invariably gave him over the strategy of holding on everywhere until . . . He needed the hopes he embodied of a renewed U-boat offensive with the new types of boat, and he needed the personal loyalty he brought to all questions. The conference in the wake of the *Scharnhorst*'s loss demonstrates above all that success was not a factor in Hitler's judgement of his Commanders, nor analysis, nor rational argument; the only things he looked for were unquestioned loyalty to his person and optimism; as he remarked when discussing another supreme optimist, Field Marshal Kesselring, 'my view is that without optimism you cannot be a military Commander'.[124]

It was more difficult for Dönitz to escape criticism from within the service, although this could not be open and could scarcely come from Meisel and other staff officers who had seemed equally eager to send the *Scharnhorst* out to prove the value of the big ships; they also had psychological reasons for shifting the blame. Nevertheless Dönitz trod warily. Bey, the obvious, indeed the only possible scapegoat, had died a hero's death fighting the ship to the end; he could not be blamed directly. Instead Dönitz blamed himself, not for sending Bey out on a fool's mission on insufficient intelligence with conflicting instructions to the evident disagreement of those most closely involved in Group North, but for not recalling Kummetz from leave. He had, he told a staff meeting on January 4th 1944, discussed the possibilities of such an operation with Kummetz and knew his intentions and knew that he would seize any opportunities with great energy. It would not have been necessary to issue him with directives—'for instance about breaking off the operation'. Later he laid stress on a passage in a report by Schniewind pointing to the fleet's lack of opportunity for sea-training as a cause of the failure.[125]

These oblique attempts to shift the blame reveal Dönitz once again as a man whose tough outer casing concealed terrible insecurity.

The year 1943 had been a hard one for Dönitz, as for Germany; one of his sons had been lost, his hopes in the Battle of the Atlantic twice dashed, his victory in preserving the big ships turned sour by the latest revelation of the Anglo-American technological lead which precluded offensive action by any of his forces except in remote peripheral areas. In contrast to the confident directives he had issued on taking office he could only hope now for new types of U-boats yet to be produced by Minister Speer; all he could offer his men to make up for lack of success and loss of initiative was increased fervour. On January 1st 1944 he issued an Order of the Day:

> To the Navy!
> An iron year lies behind us. It has made us Germans hard as no generation before us. Whatever fate may demand from us in the coming year, we will endure, united in will, steady in loyalty, fanatical in belief in our victory.
> The battle for freedom and justice for our people continues. It will see us pitted inexorably against our enemy.
> The Führer shows us the way and the goal. We follow him with body and soul to a great German future.
> *Heil* our Führer!
> Dönitz, *Grossadmiral* Commander in Chief of the Navy.[126]

He spent the first three days of the New Year at the *Wolfschanze*, as he noted in the war diary 'taking part in many discussions on the course of the war with some of the leading personalities as well as discussions in private with the Führer personally'.[127] One of the leading personalities was Albert Speer, and it was during these three days that Speer and Dönitz between them persuaded Göring that all radar research should be concentrated in Speer's Ministry—another sign of the close alliance between these two new men in the power struggle around the Führer. It would be too simple to suggest that the outcome of the war and the fate of the German people took second place to their manoeuvring for position, but there is no doubt that the worse the situation of the *Reich* became, the more Dönitz and Speer—and also Himmler—usurped the position of the old guard. Thus locked into the system, their reaction to the external and internal threats became more extreme as the danger increased. In Dönitz's case this meant binding himself and his service into the system as tightly as Himmler and the SS were already. This in turn meant tying the Navy to belief in the Führer's genius and ability to lead Germany to victory, however irrational both concepts had begun to seem.

It meant again rationalizing the irrational, cutting out all complexities, all divergencies, with ideological blinkers. On the material plane it meant knowing that this was an economic war and that the enemy's resources and potential were overwhelmingly superior, on the spiritual plane that crimes so unimaginable that they were not at first credited in the outside world were being perpetrated in the name of Germany— Jewry systematically exterminated, industry employing slave labour on a scale and with a pitiless, mindless cruelty not witnessed since the Pharaohs. Dönitz was aware of these things, yet by concentrating on the goal and the task he was able to prevent them from impinging at the level where decisions had to be taken.

The more they threatened to impinge—and it is ridiculous to suppose that anyone with the basic intelligence and sensitivity that Dönitz possessed was unaware of the strategic and moral impasse into which the *Reich* had been driven—the more Dönitz leant on his war-father, the pitiful wreck in the *Wolfschanze*, stooping even lower now under the unbearable weight of failure, his unhealthy face etched with the ravages of self-will, his left arm and leg shaking uncontrollably, disguising strategic impotence with calls to his Commanders to fight with 'bitter hatred'[128] against the enemies seeking to annihilate Germany. Thus Dönitz's New Year message in the wake of the *Scharnhorst* disaster, 'The Führer shows us the way and the goal. We follow him with body and soul . . .'

In February he called another *Tagung* for his Flag Officers, a sign of the dissatisfaction within the service; it was expressed on the day in a 'huge number of complaints' from the assembled officers. In his own concluding speech in which, he said, he came before them 'as always as a plain man', he did not attempt to deny that Germany stood on the defensive everywhere, but pointed to his Programme 43 which would provide a fleet of light forces 'in greater style than hitherto' and promised that the Navy would not always be on the defensive; for the service possessed the 'sole offensive means of our entire war direction'; this was, of course, the new type of U-boat; it would take the offensive to the enemy in a renewed 'tonnage war'.[129]

He went on to defend the Führer's policy of not giving an inch of ground in the east against those 'clever strategists' who thought they knew better, then came to the nub of his message, not the material but the spiritually important realities, the unity of the nation behind the Führer:

348

We have to guard this unity of our people which has proved itself in the National Socialist State to a degree previously unimaginable. It is the duty of every officer to do so and he who offends against this and so against his people must be smashed by me. I believe it to be necessary to train our young officer candidates who have to be in a position of command after a very short training period particularly in this aspect. They must be trained militarily, but above all will also be trained in such a way that as officers they have to be the unconditional guardians of the National Socialist State . . .

From the very start the whole of the officer corps must be so indoctrinated that it feels itself co-responsible for the National-Socialist State in its entirety. The officer is the exponent of the State. The idle chatter that the officer is non-political is sheer nonsense.

Towards the end of the month Hitler, who had begun to suffer severe pains in his eyes in addition to his other complaints, retired from the *Wolfschanze* to the *Berghof*, where he underwent a course of treatment and rest. He was still unfit when the time came for him to review the annual Heroes' Memorial Day parade in Berlin; more probably he didn't mean to come before the people—the real people he had led to disaster. It is a sign of the new order of precedence that he chose Dönitz to stand in for him—to the bitter chagrin of the old guard.

Dönitz was not a good public speaker. He was at his best in small groups where his burning sincerity and clear gaze compelled responding fervour; with large audiences he lacked the feel of Hitler or the conscious artistry of Goebbels; he came to them indeed as a plain man. Nevertheless it is evident that he worked hard over the speech he had to deliver after the parade for transmission on German Radio. Like Goebbels' recent speeches it was couched in Churchill's 'Dunkirk' idiom heightened with Party ideology. It was preceded by the heroic chords of Beethoven's *Coriolan* overture.

German men and women—for the fifth time in this war we remember our dead, the fallen heroes on all fronts, on land, in all seas and in the air. We remember the men, women and children at home slaughtered in the air terror. In deep reverence we honour their sacrifice and proudly mourn their loss.

Today everyone knows that we are faced with a merciless struggle of the greatest harshness and seriousness. The events of this war and the brutal aims of the enemy, which they have broadcast openly to the world, have shown us how it is. Our enemy forced this war on us. With ruthless and unscrupulous egoism, sanctimoniously professing the protection of Polish interests, they wished to veto Germany uniting with German brothers. The real reason was their fear of the power of the united German *Volk*; it was their recognition that our social community is the greatest ideological danger for their materialism and their degraded Jewish human enslavement. Without warning, therefore, but of necessity, they entered the war to exterminate our *Volk*.

Yet we know that we will endure this struggle of destiny. Thanks to a unique leadership which Providence bestowed on us in this mightiest struggle of history—the Führer, who leads us with foresight and broad vision, resolution and boldness, who cares for us indefatigably and carries his uniquely great burden forcefully and resiliently, will guide us surely through the battle for the existence of our *Volk*.

We will endure this war, thanks to the operational readiness and incomparable heroism of our soldiers on all fronts. In the last year the enemy attempted to break into our *Lebensraum* and that of our allies with great forces of men and materials. Nowhere has he gained a decisive breakthrough. What would have become of our German Fatherland, how would it be with our German *Volk* if the Führer had not spent ten years creating the *Wehrmacht*, which alone is in a position to counter the storming of our enemy into Europe. The flood of Bolshevism, which for the first time in this war, thanks to a systematic war-direction, has put its human and material resources to use on a grand scale, would have exterminated our *Volk* and eliminated European culture.

We will endure this battle of destiny, thanks to the hardness and resolution at home! We know about the quiet heroism of the millions of men and women who work selflessly at home for the defence and armament for the front. We know above all of the heroism of the areas of the homeland which, through the terror attacks, have become front areas, and whose people have shown an operational readiness and a toughness and dogged bearing comparable to that of the soldiers at the front. What would our homeland be today if the Führer had not united us in National Socialism? Divided in parties, permeated with the disintegrating poison of Jewry and vulnerable to it because we lacked the protection of our present uncompromising ideology, we would have succumbed long since to the burdens of this war and would have

350

been delivered up to the pitiless destruction of our enemy. We know, therefore, that every one of us must be the guardian of this priceless possession, this unity of our *Volk*, this unconditional loyalty to our Führer.

Every weakening from this—even the least—is a weakening of our power and a strengthening of the enemy's. The more decisively and unconditionally each of us affirms our National Socialist community and leadership, the more he can—since he is not checked or weakened by any duality within—throw his whole heart, his whole conviction into the fulfilment of his duty and so do great things.

In this unity between leadership, fighting front and *Volk* at home lies our huge force. In this unity we are invincible. With this unshakeable bearing, which the sacrifices and trials of this war still demand, we will wrestle a German peace, the peace of a proud *Volk*, welded together by necessity, with a new great future in a true National and Social community . . .[130]

He continued on these lines, concluding that the preservation of National Socialist unity was the best way to honour the fallen and the only way to ensure they had not died in vain. There could be no better thanks to the fallen than selfless 'loyalty to *Volk* and Führer'.

This was a pure expression of Nazi ideology; God had been displaced; in His stead was inscrutable Providence which had given the German *Volk* a protector—the father imagery used by Dönitz is surely significant—a far-seeing guide who cared indefatigably for each one of them and who would lead them through the struggle against the monstrous forces without to a great new German future. The reference to the 'poison of Jewry' was couched in much the terms that Himmler had used at the Gauleiters' *Tagung* in October—although of course these ideas were from *Mein Kampf*, and common currency.

Total commitment to the Führer carried with it total commitment to what, to the west of the National Socialist State, were regarded as crimes. Dönitz did not shrink from this, and there were no categories in which the German Navy did not play some part. Whether two transports which sailed from Black Sea ports with Jewish refugees for Palestine were sunk by German U-boats is uncertain[131]—they may have been the victims of Russian attack—yet there is no doubt that in January 1944 Admiral Kurt Fricke, Commander of Navy Group South, and a fanatical Nazi, proposed to the High Command at 'Koralle' that Jewish refugee

351

ships found at sea should 'clandestinely without the knowledge of our allies' be 'caused to disappear with their entire complements'. The naval staff referred the request to the Foreign Ministry![132] But that such a proposal could be raised and treated at headquarters as routine is evidence that Dönitz was far from the only naval officer who knew of the programme of genocide.

The Navy was also involved in terrorism, both against civilian shipyard workers and uniformed enemy units. The latter started under Raeder, who passed on a notorious 'Commando order' of Hitler's to all units in October 1942; this decreed that enemy forces engaged in 'so-called Commando operations . . . in uniform or demolition troops, with or without weapons, in battle or in flight are to be exterminated to the last man'.[133] The idea, as described by the naval staff in February 1943, after Dönitz had succeeded Raeder, was to 'act as a deterrent' so that those taking part learned 'that certain death not safe imprisonment awaits them'.[134] The order was classified top secret since it called for the 'shooting of uniformed prisoners acting on military orders even after they have surrendered voluntarily', but for deterrent value the deaths were to be published as resulting from the units' annihilation in battle. The naval staff memorandum concluded, '. . . after consultation with the C-in-C to ensure that all interested positions are clear about the handling of members of Commando units . . .'; it is thus virtually certain that the issue was brought to Dönitz's attention.

The first documented case concerning the Navy occurred in Raeder's time. A seaman from a two-man submarine or 'chariot' was caught in Norway in November 1942 after an abortive attempt on the *Tirpitz*. He was interrogated by naval officers, then passed back to the Security Services who had first captured him, the notorious SD, in whose hands he was shot in January 1943.[135] A more blatant example occurred in July 1943: the entire crew of a torpedo boat on a minelaying operation in Norwegian waters was captured on their boat in uniform and taken to the Bergen headquarters of the naval commander, South Norway, Admiral von Schrader. There the men were interrogated by naval intelligence officers, who concluded they were entitled to treatment as normal prisoners of war. Despite this, von Schrader decided that they came within the scope of the 'Commando order' and handed them over to the SD for treatment as 'pirates'. Early the following morning the men were taken to a rifle range adjoining a concentration camp and shot one by one; their bodies were loaded on a lorry and taken to the coast where they were guarded until nightfall, then placed in coffins with explosive charges attached; the coffins were taken out to sea, thrown overboard and the charges detonated under water 'according to the usual practice'.[136]

Dönitz, of course, had been involved in terrorism against merchant service crews for some time. The orders of September 1942, including the 'rescue ship' order sent out again immediately after the Gauleiters' *Tagung* in October 1943, with its reference to the 'desired destruction of the steamers' crews', were the visible signs of a secret policy. It is significant that after September 1942 Hitler, who waged the war with mounting 'bitter hatred' and calls for reprisals in every direction at every opportunity, never again mentioned slaughtering or taking reprisals against shipwrecked survivors, despite frequent discussions with Dönitz about the U-boat campaign. There can be no doubt about the reason for such an uncharacteristic lapse; he knew that behind Dönitz's ostensible orders to take captains, Chief Engineers, Chief Officers and navigators prisoner, lay secret instructions, given orally to Commanders, to annihilate survivors—so long as this did not endanger the boat.

In convoy battles this was out of the question, but in remote seas against independent ships there were opportunities. Not all were taken—it depended on the Commander—but the most notorious proven example occurred that year on Heroes' Memorial Day immediately following Dönitz's broadcast speech. The boat was U 852, the Commander *Kapitänleutnant* Heinz Eck, and the evidence comes from his trial immediately after the war.

Before his departure he was briefed in Berlin, according to his own account by 'the Commander of the U-boat flotilla'; his German defence counsel corrected this to BdU, and if correct this was of course Dönitz himself. Whether it was Dönitz or Godt, Dönitz's obsession with the importance of U-boat warfare, the only offensive means left to Germany, came into the talk Eck heard. He was then given detailed instructions for his mission by *Kapitänleutnant* Schnee at U-boat Command, who apparently warned him of the extreme danger from aircraft; he was also given a book full of standing orders, including those from September 1942 about rescue contradicting 'the most elementary demands of war for the destruction of ships and crews' and the 'Rescue ship' order.

It was Eck's first war cruise in command; he had transferred—according to his evidence 'volunteered'—from minesweepers in early

1942. He sailed from Kiel on January 18th 1944 bound for the Indian Ocean and, after passing out of the Baltic, made his way up the Norwegian coast and north of the British Isles to mid-Atlantic, then southwards, travelling on the surface only at night, submerging by day. It was a tense and strenuous passage, as is made clear not only by his own evidence, but by a U-boat Command war diary summary of the extraordinary mental and physical strain on crews at this stage of the war:

Boats must always be prepared for surprise attacks by enemy aircraft . . . their whole behaviour is therefore largely influenced by their radar interception gear, on which unfortunately only the fact of their location can be observed, not the type, distance or bearing of the locating enemy. When location is observed by night the boat will dive instantly on the assumption that it is an aircraft location. In many cases the hydrophones will then show that the boat is being located by a destroyer or corvette now approaching its diving position and forcing it on the defensive. It must in most cases endure depth-charging. If— learning by this experience—the boat remains on the surface after next finding she is located, she will perhaps have to suffer bomb-attack. In this case her behaviour is also wrong. Since at present radar interception gear cannot pick up all location frequencies . . . sudden attacks by naval or air craft often occur without previous warning.[137]

The summary concluded, however, that despite the 'harshness of the battle the bearing of commanders and crews remains above all praise: although aware of the heavy losses, although constantly pursued and weary, the U-boat man remains undaunted. Hard on himself, resigned to a hard fate, hating the enemy, believing in his arms and victory, he continues the unequal struggle'.

Such it must be assumed was the attitude of Eck and his officers when in the late afternoon of March 13th, after three weeks of travel sub-merged continuously by day, the steamer *Peleus* was sighted. Eck shadowed and after dark fired two magnetic torpedoes whose detonation broke the ship apart. She disappeared almost immediately but it was apparent from torch lights, whistles and calls among the wreckage that there were a number of survivors. Eck surfaced and took his boat among them, picking up the third officer and a seaman from one of the several rafts but apparently made no attempt to find the captain or other key personnel. After interrogating the two he had taken he allowed them back on their raft, then steered away.

He ran about half a mile, ordering machine guns, mauser pistols and hand grenades to be passed up to the bridge, then turned back. Approaching the rafts again he or his watch officer hailed one on which the chief officer was trying to gather survivors and ordered it closer; as it neared he gave the order to his bridge group to open fire, and the survivors found themselves under a hail of machine gun bullets. Then a signal lamp was trained on them and grenades were hurled, both at the raft and amongst men who had leaped into the water.

Eck repeated this treatment with the third officer's raft, then spent the rest of the night cruising amongst the wreckage, mainly timber beams and hatchboards on which other survivors were clustering, directing machine gun fire at them. The guns were manned during this time by his watch officer, Hoffmann—who also threw grenades—his engineer, Lenz, a petty officer, a seaman and, most extraordinarily, the U-boat's doctor, Walter Weisspfenig—all according to the evidence firing quite calmly without excitement over a period of at least five hours. Eck's defence at his trial was that he was attempting to eliminate all traces of the sinking so that his presence would not be discovered by aircraft which would hunt him down. Since he failed to sink a single raft, the wreckage was timber and the oil slick left by the steamer was bound to reveal the sinking to passing aircraft, the explanation was rejected by the court. The episode came down therefore to cold-blooded murder of defenceless survivors by a number of officers apparently in their right minds during a long period of darkness when the boat might have been speeding away from the area and towards her destination.

It is significant that after this long night the feeling among the crew was such that Eck felt it necessary to explain his actions to them; part of his talk contained the idea that if they were influenced by too much sympathy 'we must also think of our wives and children who die as the victims of air attack at home'.[138] This was of course the precise justification that Dönitz used in the September 1942 orders carried by Eck.

It must be assumed that Eck was acting on the ambiguities in this order or had received a specific order from Dönitz or Schnee at his briefing in Berlin to leave no survivors. Otherwise there was no sense in what he did, indeed it endangered his boat in an area known to be patrolled by aircraft based on Ascension Island and Freetown, Sierra Leone. If there was no superior order it follows, not only that Eck himself was an unnatural specimen but that his officers and his doctor—whose ethical code should have forbidden the taking of life and who therefore enjoyed privileged status under the Geneva Convention—were also natural barbarians.

The only reasonable explanation of an otherwise inexplicable act is 'superior orders'; this, however, could not be used in defence since the case of the *Llandovery Castle* tried in a German Court had established that superior orders were no defence for an obviously criminal act. Counsel were, therefore, in an impossible position; they circled round and round the question, raising it with each of the accused but letting it drop immediately without probing. Eck was asked if he had any secret orders not to be divulged to the crew; 'Yes,' he replied; he was not asked what they were.[139] Hoffmann said without being asked, 'I had complete trust in the Commander and the righteousness of his orders. I also knew that he had orders and instructions of a secret nature which were not known to me.' The doctor, Weisspfenig, and the petty officer who had fired a machine gun both testified that they knew the Commander had secret orders. No one was asked about the nature of these orders.

These men were on trial for their lives; therefore it would not be necessary to believe these muffled pleas of 'superior orders' if there were any other rational explanation for their conduct. But what other explanation can there be for so deliberate and senseless a massacre?

Perhaps the most significant speech came from a German expert on international law, Professor Wegner, who spoke for the defence; it was on the face of it a ridiculous, endlessly digressive and repetitive speech he gave, designed, it seemed, to show off his knowledge rather than guide the Court on the case. Yet amongst his meanderings the true difficulties shone through: the world had become a different place, too much had happened since the *Llandovery Castle* judgement: 'The psychology of a whole nation, not to say of the world, has changed . . .' He repeated the point later, and later still, 'an individual forming part of a public force and acting under the authority of the government is not to be held answerable as a private trespasser or malefactor . . .'

Finally, despairingly, he said, 'I wanted to make you understand what type of man Eck is. I cannot imagine that anyone will doubt the relevance of superior orders . . . If you apply the rules of the *Llandovery Castle* case as if nothing had happened at all you will not be doing justice to these men . . . I can only appeal to you not to apply an old law to a world which was in revolutionary chaos—to minds which have been changed by the irresistible force of new events.'[140]

Here was the nub of the matter. The Court, of course, could not take such abstract principles into consideration and Eck, his watch officer and his doctor were sentenced to death by shooting, the other accused to terms of imprisonment. Ten days before Eck was executed he was examined on behalf of Dönitz's defence counsel at the Nuremberg War Crimes Trials: 'Did you ever receive direct orders from Dönitz to shoot at shipwrecked survivors?'

'No.'

'Have you ever heard that orders had been issued either by Dönitz himself or in his name that survivors from wrecks or anything which might be held to save such survivors should be shot at?'

'Only now when I was in London did I hear through the British authorities that such orders really did exist.'[141]

He went to his death denying that Dönitz, and by implication any other officers at U-boat Command, had any part in his decision to massacre the survivors of the *Peleus*. Among the thousands in the U-boat service who found a hero's grave, the name Eck must have had special significance with Dönitz to his dying day.

Together with the construction of his new U-boat types, Dönitz's preoccupations in the first half of 1944 were with practical measures for preserving the European economic space and winning the time necessary to complete the boats in sufficient numbers. In the west this meant throwing back the Anglo-American invasion whenever and wherever it came. The surface fleet could not be considered for this since adequate fighter cover would be lacking, and it came down to minelaying off the enemy embarkation ports, minelaying and fortification along the coasts of Western Europe and, for attacking the landing forces at sea, U-boats—although why he thought the existing U-boat would be able to manage much better without fighter cover than surface units is difficult to understand. There were also midget submarines, manned torpedoes and other manoeuvrable explosive devices under development in a Small Craft division he had set up in 1943. He transferred a particularly inventive and forceful officer from Schniewind's staff to head this division, Vice Admiral Helmuth Heye; he was to be the *Kriegsmarine*'s Mountbatten.

While Heye set about his task with desperate energy and fanatical

357

commitment—for it was not expected he would be granted much time—U-boats were held in Biscay ports and in southern and central Norway in readiness to sortie at the first sign of the invasion forces. Dönitz issued the Commander with instructions that since, in case of invasion, the future of the German people depended upon them they should pay no regard to precautions which would be valid in normal circumstances; they should have only one goal before their eyes and in their hearts: *'Angriff—ran—versenken!'*—'Attack—forward—sink!'[142] He followed this two weeks later on April 11th with an order headed 'Reckless Attack':

> Every enemy vessel taking part in the landing, even if it only carries half a hundred soldiers or a tank, is a target which demands the full mission of the U-boat. It is to be attacked even if this carries the risk of loss of one's own boat.
>
> If it is a matter of approaching the invasion fleet no regard is to be had for danger such as flat water or possible mine barriers or any other considerations . . .[143]

In view of the powerful air and sea escorts to be expected around an invasion force this was a suicide order; in the event it was not enforced, so it should perhaps be regarded, like his similar decrees to naval units manning the coastal fortifications not to yield a metre of ground,[144] as exhortation to fanaticism rather than as a literal instruction.

In the east he continued, in opposition to the generals and his own operations staff, to support Hitler's policy of clinging on to the Crimea regardless; on March 20th Hitler asked him to write down his arguments for holding Odessa—near the base of the peninsula—so that the generals could see it was not only the Führer who was in favour of holding the area. Dönitz instructed his reluctant staff to prepare a document on these lines. His lack of realism was staggering; since this was how he always reacted to imminent defeat it is unnecessary to examine the rationalizations he put forward.

One of his preoccupations at this time of desperate manpower shortage was to ward off demands from the generals for naval personnel and construction workers engaged in his Programme 43. To the military the decisive struggle was on land in the east; when it came to invasion that too would be a land affair. In view of the Navy's inability to affect the issue at sea this was a reasonable standpoint and Dönitz was very conscious that Hitler's support was vital if he were to resist these demands and safeguard his long-term aim of taking the offensive to the enemy—something the generals could never do. He constantly explained the prospects for the renewed 'tonnage war' to Hitler in glowing terms, constantly demanded more men for training and construction, aircraft for reconnaissance or attack on carriers supporting enemy convoys; in return there was an obvious requirement to flatter and agree with the Führer's strategy; yet in view of his record who can say that he employed conscious deception? His own insecurity and, on the other hand, narrow, goal-oriented focus and fanatical drive are sufficient to account for his attitude.

It is certain, too, that National Socialist ardour distorted his vision. Whatever his mix of reasons for supporting Hitler's strategy, by April events had overtaken it. A Russian thrust forced withdrawal from Odessa. Dönitz's memorandum arguing the importance of this port for the defence of the area was now used against him by the General Staff anxious to abandon the Crimea before it was too late. He replied that only the Führer could comprehend the entire strategic picture, and retired to his invariable fall-back in defeat: if the Crimea were given up, 30 enemy divisions would be released to attack the Rumanian front.

He was still arguing on these lines when the local Commander began a withdrawal without the Führer's orders towards the fortress of Sebastopol, and he was arguing that 'bridgehead Sebastopol' must be held at all costs, when on May 9th Hitler was at last forced to give the evacuation order. The Navy, which had been ferrying in supplies up to the last moment, turned to evacuating the troops, and succeeded under difficult conditions in taking out over 30,000 including wounded; over 75,000 men and quantitites of arms were left behind.

It was shortly after this débâcle that Dönitz suffered another personal tragedy. At some time after the loss of his son, Peter, in U 954 he had taken advantage of a dispensation whereby senior officers could withdraw a son from the front; the idea, pure National Socialist theory, was to ensure that elements of the best blood survived to enrich the race— senior officers and Party members were by definition of the best blood. Klaus had, therefore, been sent to train as a naval doctor at a special course at Tübingen University.[145]

While still at Tübingen in May that year, Klaus visited naval friends serving in the 5th *Schnell* boat flotilla at Cherbourg. The flotilla was in the front line for reconnaissance sorties off the English south coast to report any signs of the invasion. Such a sortie was ordered on the night of May 13th during Klaus's visit and he went along for the ride in S 141 as guest of the commander. It was a calm night with haze and fog patches reducing visibility in places to 1,000 yards, and half an hour after midnight off Selsey Bill S 141's group of three boats came under fire from destroyers, themselves invisible. These were HMS *Stayner* and the Free French *La Combattante*.[146] While turning away S 141 received a hit from the French ship which put her steering out of action and, as she continued her turn towards the enemy, another direct hit which caused her to sink. Six survivors were rescued by the destroyers later; Klaus Dönitz was not among them.

According to interrogation reports on the survivors he was an epileptic and drowned after suffering a fit in the sea—a story which excited a Canadian intelligence officer who had been playing records of Karl Dönitz's speeches over and over again after detecting slight hesitations in his voice which he thought might be signs of epilepsy. This clinched it, he believed; Dönitz had a mild form of epilepsy known to the medical profession as *petit mal*, which Klaus had evidently inherited. Dönitz's daughter, Ursula, denies this. Nevertheless, if true the story might account for the fact that Klaus had been transferred to the shore staff of the 5th U-flotilla in mid-1942 without having made an operational cruise. Another reason advanced for this transfer was that the head operation necessary after his motorcycle accident rendered him unable to cope with the pressure changes induced in boats fitted with Schnorchel; this is certainly false since the Schnorchel did not come into use until 1944. The question is open; the medical records cannot be traced.

News that Klaus was not among the survivors reported by the British was phoned through to 'Koralle' in the morning of the 14th. Dönitz showed no emotion when he heard and continued work; Hansen-Nootbar noticed that he was not as collected as usual, however, and at the end of the morning U-boat conference he said, 'Hansen-Nootbar, I'm going to my wife now to tell her.'

'*Herr Grossadmiral*,' Hansen-Nootbar replied, 'may I remind you that the Japanese Ambassador, general Oshima and several staff officers are due for lunch at one o'clock . . .'

'I will call you,' Dönitz replied. 'I will leave the decision to my wife.'

A quarter of an hour later the call came. There was to be no change in the arrangements.

The guests arrived, eight to ten all told; Ingeborg played the hostess with all her usual poise and charm, and sitting between Oshima and a Japanese Admiral, kept the conversation going in French, which she spoke fluently. The mood was somewhat forced, but the visitors never learned of the loss of her second son. Afterwards Dönitz, Ingeborg and Hansen-Nootbar escorted them to the door and waved goodbye. A moment after they had driven off Ingeborg collapsed. Hansen-Nootbar was standing immediately behind and caught her as she fell. 'Never in my life,' he recalls today, 'have I met a woman who showed such bearing.'[147]

Klaus's body was washed ashore on the French coast later, his wrist-watch still ticking. He was buried in the German military cemetery near Amiens.

At the beginning of June, Dönitz and Ingeborg with his daughter and son-in-law and their family, Peter aged five, and a little girl, Ute, born the previous year, went on leave to Badenweiler again—a hillside resort in the Black Forest. Four days later he was woken by a telephone call in the early hours: the invasion had begun.

The allies achieved complete strategic and tactical surprise. Even systematic preparatory raids on coastal battery sites, airfields, gun batteries and inland communications in France had been regarded as a mixture of bluff and preparation for a later invasion; a memorandum to this effect prepared by Admiral Krancke, chief of Navy Group West, was on its way to 'Koralle' even as the huge armada of transports, support ships and escort vessels headed across the Channel. Nevertheless the Navy was the first service on that morning, June 6th, to realize that this was a major landing; by 11.15 when Dönitz, back at 'Koralle', chaired a conference on the situation, the staff had no doubt that, in the words of the war diary, 'the war has entered its decisive phase for Germany'.[148] The long-planned counter-measures were ordered—the U-boats held in the Biscay ports to sortie, the boats in southern and central Norway to come to instant readiness in case of enemy landings in that area.

By then it was far too late; in any case Bletchley Park had deciphered earlier messages to the U-boat bases and to Navy Group West and the allies knew Dönitz's plans and his orders for 'Reckless Attack' as precisely as the flotilla Commanders themselves. Massive sea and air counter-forces had been mobilized to prevent the boats getting into the Channel, let alone approaching the assault forces; they included escort carriers, no fewer than 286 destroyers, frigates and smaller anti-submarine vessels in trained escort groups, and in the west alone 21 squadrons of anti-submarine aircraft flying over Biscay and the Channel approaches in day and night patrols of such intensity that every square mile was covered at least once every half-hour. Against such a concentration the U-boats' task was practically impossible, certainly it was impossible to reach the operations area in time to have any effect in the decisive early stages, and none did.

Harried unmercifully as soon as they left their bomb-proof shelters, it soon became apparent that only those boats fitted with the Schnorchel, which had recently entered service, had any prospect of working into the Channel; the others were recalled. Those that continued dared not surface by day but had to creep along continuously submerged, never able to make more than 30 to 40 miles a day, their crews enduring constant tension and danger in physically debilitating conditions. Whenever the boat dipped below the correct Schnorchel-depth the valves shut and air for the diesels was sucked from inside the hull itself, reducing the pressure dramatically; exhaust gasses, too, were unable to escape if the water pressure outside became too great, and they were forced back into the engine compartment, half suffocating the men. Meanwhile carbon dioxide built up and the power available from the batteries fell.

So while allied troops, tanks, personnel carriers, fuel and stores of every description flowed along the short route between the Isle of Wight and the assault beaches in Seine Bay, establishing a decisive bridgehead, those U-boats fortunate enough to survive were far away, working painfully, infinitely slowly towards the scene. The majority were destroyed or so damaged they had to turn back; three reached the German-occupied Channel Islands, a feat justly described in the British Admiralty tracking room report as 'a heroic achievement'.[149] After nine days one boat, U 621, reached the Cherbourg peninsula; it sank a US troop landing craft, fired at and missed two US battleships, then started an equally slow and hazardous return passage. By the end of the month three more had reached the operational area and on the 29th one of these, U 984, scored the only significant success of the campaign by sinking four ships from a coastal convoy.

These delayed results, scarcely even reaching the category of pinprick compared with the size of the allied operation, were achieved at horrendous cost in loss and damage. Dönitz's orders to the commanders make it clear that he expected this during the attack on the invasion fleet, but it is apparent from the small number that succeeded in coming anywhere near the target that he grossly underestimated the forces that the allies would deploy in defence.

His light forces were scarcely more successful. Four destroyers which tried to break into the Channel from Brest on the night of June 8th were located by a British flotilla of eight and two were sunk; the other two escaped back to Brest damaged. Other light torpedo craft based on Havre and other Channel ports made night attacks on the flanks of the assault area and the convoys approaching it but seldom pierced the escort screen and in the first week sank only one destroyer, three small ships, three landing craft and a few smaller vessels. Air raids on their bases subsequently destroyed so many of them as virtually to rule out effective operations. Meanwhile the naval coastal batteries had been subdued by the preliminary aerial bombing, followed by a tremendous fleet bombardment by all calibres from battleships' main armament downwards, while the other hope, the midget craft which Heye was forcing through production, were not quite ready for action. The truth was that in the face of the enemy air mastery the *Kriegsmarine* was impotent to do much more than show it knew how to make heroic sacrifices.

By June 10th at the latest Dönitz had conceded that the invasion was successful: 'the second front is at hand'.[150]

The logic of this recognition was not pursued. Up to the invasion Dönitz had regarded the battle for the beaches as 'war-decisive'; all his hopes had been based on the assumption that the Anglo-American assault forces would be so mangled the allies would lose heart and recognize 'Fortress Europe' as impregnable. This would have released large German forces held in the west to reinforce the eastern front, guaranteeing the vital Baltic region and even permitting a counter-attack to repossess the Ukraine while his new U-boats came into operation and took such a toll of North Atlantic tonnage that the Führer could have negotiated terms from a position of strength. The converse of this rosy picture, however, was that once the second front was established, the *Reich* faced a drainage of manpower and materials west and east—and south to Italy—a steadily shrinking land base, dwindling economic resources and eventual certain defeat.

It was not in his nature to admit this, for one thing it would have meant admitting that his course had not been correct, his underestimation of enemy resources and overestimation of the power of commitment to National Socialism an error, for another it would have meant admitting defeat while there were still numerous avenues for optimism! The secret rocket weapons for bombarding London were ready for launch, Heye's small craft coming on to line, the 'revolutionary' U-boats due at the end of the year, the *Kriegsmarine* was still master of the Baltic, indeed the *Reich* was still master of the greater part of Western Europe. And there was always the prospect of the western allies waking up to what a Bolshevist-dominated Europe would mean, and a consequent splitting from the eastern partner. On the other hand was the certainty that in surrender or defeat they could look forward only to the partition of the German nation announced publicly by the allies, and for the German people unthinkable terrors in retaliation for the crimes committed in the east.

This raises the question of the effect knowledge of such crimes had on Dönitz's commitment to fight on to the bitter end. Himmler's reasons for revealing the extermination policy to the Gauleiters the previous October had probably included binding all members of his audience into the unholy compact, making it clear that all moral bridges had been burned and showing them that the only alternatives before them now were victory—or the rope. And it is significant that as tension about the allied invasion had mounted in May, Himmler gave similar addresses to audiences of generals—attended on one occasion by one of Dönitz's liaison staff at Führer headquarters, Vice Admiral Voss. Hitler also explained the extermination policy to them, answering his own rhetorical question whether he could have solved the problem more humanely, with the assertion that they were fighting a battle for existence;[151] should the enemy win, the German people would be exterminated, the upper classes, intellectuals and their children butchered in a programme organized by international Jewry.

In June after the invasion, Himmler addressed another group of Corps Commanders from the northernmost front in Finland, again spelling out the extermination programme; both he and Hitler used the argument Dönitz had employed on Heroes' Day: Germany could not have withstood the bombing terror if the Jewish virus had remained in the body of the people.

These disclosures to even wider groups occurred at a time when not only the external but also the internal dangers to the regime were growing fast. The military wing of the resistance, the only arm that could stage an effective *coup*, had grown in numbers and resolve since it had become plain that Germany was going down to defeat, and had gained a new leading spirit in Claus Schenk, Count Stauffenberg. Severely wounded in Tunisia, he had been appointed in October 1943 to the Reserve Army in Berlin as Chief of Staff to one of the principal conspirators, General Olbricht; here he helped complete plans for the assassination of Hitler and a military take-over of government. Himmler's security services, meanwhile, penetrated the civilian arms of the resistance, arresting leaders from time to time—including von Moltke in January 1944—but more concerned to watch and lay traps to trace the wider circles; by early summer Himmler had a good picture of the extent and aims of the movement. The conspirators knew this; they had further cause for haste in the imminence of the expected invasion, for it was felt that unless the Nazis could be displaced before an allied landing in Europe all political meaning would be lost. When the invasion caught them, too, by surprise, Stauffenberg wondered whether they should proceed. He was assured by General Beck, a founding member and leader of the military resistance, and by one of the younger leaders, General Tresckow, that it remained a moral imperative; they must prove to the world and to future generations of Germans that they were prepared to stake their lives for their convictions.[152]

It became clear, moreover, that the Gestapo net was closing. Himmler told Canaris, the *Abwehr* chief he had displaced, that he knew a military *coup* was being prepared, and dropped names of the military and civilian leaders, Beck and Goerdeler—no doubt expecting Canaris to pass the information on, as he did. In early July wholesale arrests of Communists, among them a close friend of Stauffenberg's, added to the pressure, for no one could resist Gestapo interrogation for long, and Stauffenberg felt personally threatened. He had been appointed Chief of Staff to the Commander of the Reserve Army, General Fromm, in June, a post that gave him personal access to Hitler, and on July 11th he attended a Führer Conference with a bomb concealed in his briefcase; finding Himmler not present he did not set it off. He carried the bomb to another conference a few days later, but again Himmler was absent and again he postponed the attempt—that at least is the usual explanation, although Speer records attending a Führer conference at the *Berghof* at this time with Himmler and Göring present.[153]

Just how much Himmler knew by then will never be known, nor how much he revealed to Dönitz, who was with Hitler for some of this time; he was at the *Wolfschanze* on July 9th, and after the daily situation

365

conference had taken lunch with Hitler, Himmler and several Commanders from the eastern front; he then followed Hitler to the *Berghof* and after the conference there on the 11th when Stauffenberg made his first aborted attempt, he had lunched with Hitler alone; on the next day he was Himmler's guest. Nothing is known of the conversations that took place. It is clear, however, that the situation for the *Reich* was critical; in the east the Russians had broken through on the central, Polish, front and threatened to push up to the Baltic, cutting off the Northern Army Group in Lithuania–Estonia; in the west the allies were establishing a material superiority via supply lines which neither Dönitz's few remaining forces nor the overstretched *Luftwaffe* could begin to threaten; at home 'defeatists' advocated either a pact with the west against the Bolsheviks or a pact with Stalin against the Anglo-Saxons; the General Staff advocated withdrawal; military revolt was imminent.

Hitler's attitude to all this is known from his remarks during the conferences and fragments of his conversations the following month—on land to raise fifteen new blocking divisions for the east by combing the *Luftwaffe* and *Kriegsmarine* for men, placing these under the nominal command of Himmler, and not giving an inch anywhere—at sea to attack the enemy supply lines and warships fanatically: 'Should the enemy lose six to eight battleships in the Seine Bay it would have the greatest strategic consequences'[154]—in the air to challenge the enemy mastery with a great fighter production programme—in overall war strategy:

> The time is not right for a political decision. I think during my life I've proved many times I can win political success. I don't have to explain to anybody that I won't pass up such an opportunity. But it is childish and naïve to expect that at a time of grave military defeat the moment for favourable political action has come. Such moments come when you are having success.[155]

Dönitz's attitude is also clear from his conference remark he echoed this strategy and assisted in creating the make-believe on which it floated; as he had for Tunis and Sicily and the Crimea, he echoed the Führer's calls for resistance to the bitter end;[156] he had learnt nothing from the former disasters inflexibility had brought. As for his personal loyalty to the Führer and the Nazi creed, this had been made clear in every recent speech and directive.

Nor can there be any doubt about the National Socialist ardour of the third member of this circle, Heinrich Himmler; there is room for doubt about his attitude to the current situation though. He was the most powerful figure in the *Reich*, in control of the internal terror that alone preserved the state from chaos, and of all external intelligence agencies; these provided him with a picture of the real world outside and access to lines of communication with both enemy blocs; in addition he had in the *Waffen-SS* a private army indoctrinated with fanatical loyalty as the true bearer of the National Socialist revolution, the natural rival and potential usurper of the field-grey forces under the old aristocratic officer corps, which now appeared to be splitting apart in 'defeatism' and 'disloyalty'. Himmler was personally ambitious, absolutely ruthless and, as Hitler was wont to repeat, 'ice-cold in crises—every time it got really bad he became ice cold'.[157] He was also capable of rationalizing any means of personal advancement as necessary for the attainment of National Socialist ends. It is not fanciful to suggest that such a man, so steeped in Nazi mythology as to carry out genocide as a moral imperative, might have regarded the martyrdom of Hitler in the same light. Goebbels took this view at the end.

Himmler's later actions leave no doubt that he regarded himself as the Führer's natural successor, and believed that with Hitler out of the way the western allies might be prepared to make peace with him as the leader of Germany. To conclude from all this that he knew of Stauffenberg's intent—although not the full extent of the organization behind him—and allowed him his head is not justified on the evidence nor, however, is it ruled out. For there can be no doubt that he gained most from the attempt, the conspirators lost all, and the old guard of generals was finally broken.

At whatever level he was playing, he needed Dönitz and the *Kriegsmarine*, and probably he told him during their talks at this time of the latest strata of disloyalty he was uncovering in the Army. Dönitz's reaction may be imagined; certainly he stood shoulder to shoulder with the *Reichsführer SS* after Stauffenberg's bomb went off.

According to the naval staff war diary, Dönitz had intended spending July 20th and 21st at the *Wolfschanze*, but on learning that Mussolini was due there on the 20th, he postponed his visit until the 21st—according to Hansen-Nootbar because the *Duce*'s arrival would curtail his time for discussion with the Führer. On the morning of the 20th—again according to Hansen-Nootbar[158]—he tried to call Führer headquarters, but could not get through for some time; when at last he did get through, the report

367

he received was not clear this must refer to the period immediately after 12.42 when the bomb Stauffenberg had fused and left under Hitler's map table during his morning situation conference went off. Dönitz could not have been calling up about this since no news of the event leaked for some time; only Himmler, in his headquarters some fifteen miles from the *Wolfschanze*, had been informed, and he immediately left by car for the scene.

It may be that Dönitz was trying to get through to his liaison officer at Führer headquarters, *Kapitän zur See* Assmann in answer to an urgent wire Assmann had sent him late the previous evening.[159] On the other hand, Hansen-Nootbar's account from memory 40 years after the event may simply be wrong.

It is more reasonable perhaps to follow the naval staff war diary account, which states that Dönitz received an urgent call from the Admiral at Führer headquarters at about 1.15 telling him to come at once, but giving no reason. This would have been soon after Himmler had arrived at the *Wolfschanze* and about the time or shortly before a phone call was put through by Himmler's adjutant to his Berlin headquarters to summon a team of detectives to investigate the explosion. Dönitz's attempts to get through to Führer headquarters, recalled by Hansen-Nootbar, might have taken place after this as he tried to find out the basis of the enigmatic call. He would not have been able to get through then since the *Wolfschanze* exchange was shut down for the next two hours to prevent news of the attempt emerging.

In any event, he and Hansen-Nootbar took off in his plane one and a half hours later, arriving at Rastenburg airfield at 4.45, where he was met by one of his staff officers and given the first account of the attempt as they were driven the short distance to Führer headquarters. The explosion had been tremendous, wrecking the timber conference hut and killing and wounding several near the Führer who, however, had been stretched out across the heavy map table and had escaped with slight burns, bruising and burst ear-drums; he had recovered sufficiently to meet the *Duce* when he had arrived in his special train at four that afternoon and had immediately taken him on a tour of the still smoking scene of his miraculous escape.

Himmler had nosed out the culprit by this time—not a difficult task since Stauffenberg had left the conference chamber shortly before the explosion that morning just as he was due to make his report, and had then made a hasty exit from the headquarters compound and driven to the airfield at Rastenburg; his car had been checked out through the first guard-post minutes after the explosion; the fact that he managed to get through two posts manned by SS at this time is surprising. In any case there could be little doubt of his guilt. And in Himmler's mind there seems to have been no doubt about the guilt of his immediate superior, General Fromm, for reports were coming in from Berlin that made it clear the attempt was part of a *Putsch* to seize power organized at Fromm's Bendlerstrasse headquarters. Before leaving for Berlin himself, at about the time Dönitz's car was heading for the *Wolfschanze*, Himmler obtained a commission from Hitler as Commander of the Reserve Army in place of Fromm, and phoned orders to his Berlin headquarters to have Stauffenberg arrested. The SS Colonel and two detectives assigned this task were too late at the airport, so went to the Bendlerstrasse and walked into the nest of conspirators, where they themselves were arrested.

It was about this time that Dönitz joined Hitler and his guest the *Duce* for a bizarre tea party which has been described often. Göring and Ribbentrop were also present, having driven there after hearing the news, as were several permanent members of the entourage including Bormann and Keitel; all were naturally anxious to congratulate the Führer on his miraculous escape and assure him of their own loyalty and conviction that this dramatic exposure of treason would mark a turning point in the war; with the internal sabotage of the generals lanced, the nation united would prove invincible. Dönitz and Ribbentrop apparently led the attack on the generals, furiously resisted by Keitel, and during the mutual recriminations, in which Göring joined, Dönitz turned on the *Reichsmarschall* and relieved his long-repressed feelings about the *Luftwaffe*'s failure to support the Navy. Hitler sat quietly through the shouting, cotton wool protruding from his damaged ears, popping coloured lozenges into his mouth until someone mentioned the Roehm plot and the blood purge of 1934, when he rose, suddenly galvanized into frenzy, and with bulging eyes screamed vengeance on the traitors who had dared attempt to frustrate the providence which had chosen him to lead the German people. The surrounding quarrels were silenced by the power of the rage consuming him; apparently he continued, pacing with foam flecking his lips for an hour until interrupted by a telephone call from Berlin. That, at least, is the outline of the scene described by one of Mussolini's entourage, who thought he was in the presence of a madman.[160]

In Berlin, meanwhile, the *coup* had run into trouble; the conspirators had been off to a slow start because the pre-arranged signal that Hitler was dead had not been sent from the *Wolfschanze*. They also failed, for some reason, to take over the telephone exchange and radio stations, and Goebbels in Berlin was able to call the *Wolfschanze* and talk to Hitler in person. Afterwards he broadcast an announcement that, despite an attempt on the Führer's life, Hitler had received no injuries beyond light burns and bruises. This went out over the air throughout Europe at about 6.45.

Meanwhile Goebbels had connected Hitler on the telephone with the Commander of the battalion sealing off the government quarter for the conspirators. This was the call that broke the Führer's manic raving. The grating voice, no doubt harsher after its recent exercise was unmistakable, and after receiving instructions to restore order and shoot anyone who tried to disobey, the Guards Commander swung his force against the rebels.

At Führer headquarters Hitler slumped back into his chair, suddenly spent. 'I am beginning to doubt if the German people is worthy of my genius. No one appreciates what I have done for them'—a remark that was true so far as the tea circle was concerned, although not in the sense intended. All hastened again to assure him of their loyalty, Dönitz recounting the heroic feats performed by the Navy. He was soon recalled to more urgent matters: a call came through from Admiral Krancke in Paris, who wanted assurance that the Führer was alive; he had just received an order sent out in the name of a retired Field Marshal, von Witzleben, claiming that Hitler was dead and he, von Witzleben, was the new C-in-C of the armed forces. Dönitz told him Hitler was very much alive, and that no orders were to be obeyed unless from himself or the *Reichsführer SS*. He then set about composing a proclamation, which went out at 8 o'clock:

Men of the Navy! The treacherous attempt on the life of the Führer fills each and every one of us with holy wrath and bitter rage towards our criminal enemies and their hirelings. Providence spared the German people and armed forces this inconceivable misfortune. In the miraculous escape of our Führer we see additional proof of the righteousness of our cause.[161]

This was an accurate summary of Hitler's own feelings about his escape.

Dönitz ended with a call to rally round the Führer 'and fight with all our strength till victory is ours'.

Hitler had decided he would broadcast to his people that night, and he suggested that Dönitz should follow him. Dönitz called Hansen-Nootbar and told him to sit down and write a short speech for him 'not too long, short and pithy—you know how', then he phoned 'Koralle' and instructed his staff to promulgate a decree from Keitel to all naval Commands: no orders from Witzleben, Fromm or Hoepner were to be obeyed, only those from Keitel or Himmler; he followed it with his own instructions at 8.50, again to be issued immediately to all group headquarters:

a) Military *Putsch* by a clique of generals (Fromm, Hoepner) b) *Reichsführer SS* named Commander of the Reserve Army c) Navy ordered to state of readiness d) Orders from Army Command not to be executed, only orders of C-in-C Navy or other Flag Officers e) Demands of the *Reichsführer SS* to be complied with. Long live the Führer! C-in-C Navy.[162]

When he came to collect the radio address Hansen-Nootbar was preparing he threw it away in disgust and said he would do it himself. A recording van was hastening towards the *Wolfschanze* from Königsberg, some 70 miles away, and the Führer's forthcoming speech was announced at intervals between continuous Wagner excerpts. There could have been no more appropriate background to the events now taking place in Berlin. The conspirators in the Bendlerstrasse were overpowered by loyalists from within the building as the Guards battalion cordoned it off outside; Fromm who had refused to lend his authority to the revolt after speaking on the telephone to Keitel during the afternoon now, to prove his loyalty, had the four leading members of the conspiracy taken down to the courtyard and executed by firing squad, while the nominal head of the government-to-be, General Beck, was allowed to take his own life. Fromm then rang through to Führer headquarters.

Hansen-Nootbar answered; Fromm asked to speak to Keitel, but when told this Keitel shouted he did not wish to speak to that bastard, 'Tell him I'm in a meeting with the Führer!' a refrain taken up by everyone else Fromm asked for; Hansen-Nootbar eventually had to note down the message himself; it was that Fromm had ordered a street Court

371

Martial and the following officers had been sentenced to death and executed: General Olbricht, Colonel Stauffenberg, Lieutenant Haeften (Stauffenberg's adjutant), Colonel Mertz von Quirnheim. When Hansen-Nootbar came in to the assembled chiefs and read this out, there was an explosion of 'growling rage', particularly against Fromm; no doubt it was felt he was attempting to cover his tracks. This testimony[163] to the unsavoury mood at Führer headquarters that night adds authenticity to the stories of the earlier scenes at the tea party.

The one capital where the conspirators enjoyed decisive success was Paris; a dedicated band around the military Commander of the city, von Stülpnagel, had set the operations in motion that afternoon, and as dusk fell some 1,200 SS and Gestapo were surrounded and imprisoned in their barracks without a shot fired; their chiefs were taken and held separately. Whether any of Admiral Krancke's staff in Paris knew of the intended *Putsch* beforehand is not clear; the late Admiral Wegener, then first staff officer, Navy Group West, has stated that when an obscure wire was shown to him earlier that afternoon he had told the officer of the watch to take it to the Admiral, then he beckoned to the rest of the staff and took them riding in the Bois de Boulogne.[164] It was obvious a *Putsch* was taking place, and he did not wish to be involved in action against the *Putschists* which Admiral Krancke, a convinced Nazi, would assuredly order. By the time he returned from the ride it was clear that Hitler was still alive.

This was the decisive factor for the man on whom responsibility for the spread of the revolt in France rested, Field Marshal von Kluge, Commander Army Group West. He had already told von Stülpnagel that with the Führer still alive he could not support the *Putsch*. At about 11 o'clock the Paris conspirators heard of the collapse of the Berlin revolt from a call Stauffenberg made immediately prior to his arrest; there was nothing for them to do then but to prepare themselves for arrest or suicide.

Admiral Krancke provided a postscript to the Paris failure, indicating the mood of the Navy. Learning that the Paris SS had been arrested, he made repeated calls to von Kluge and Stülpnagel, demanding their release, finally threatening to use his own forces for the purpose. Whether this was a considered bluff is not clear—most of his small force were wireless specialists, and neither he nor anyone else wanted Germans fighting Germans in the centre of Paris; perhaps he banked on this; certainly when Stülpnagel was told of the threat he reluctantly ordered the release of the prisoners. It was two o'clock in the morning.

The revolt had failed. It was another twelve hours though before Dönitz relaxed the Navy's state of readiness.[165]

He himself remained at the *Wolfschanze* throughout the 21st, issuing another proclamation:

Men of the Navy! Holy wrath and extravagant fury fill us over the criminal attempt which might have cost the life of our beloved Führer. Providence wished it otherwise—it has sheltered and protected the Führer in order not to abandon our German Fatherland in its fateful struggle.

An insane, small clique of generals, who have nothing in common with our armies, conspiring in lowest treachery to our Führer and to the German people instigated the murder with cowardly disloyalty. For these villains are the tools of our enemies, serving them in characterless, cowardly and false cleverness.

In reality their folly is limitless. They believe that by the removal of our Führer they can free us from our hard but unalterable struggle of destiny—failing to see in their blind and anxious narrow-mindedness that by their criminal act they would have delivered us up defenceless to our enemies. The extermination of our people, the enslaving of our men, hunger and nameless misery would have resulted. Our *Volk* would have experienced an unspeakable time of endless misfortune, much crueller and harder than the hardest time the present war can bring us.

We will deal with these traitors appropriately. The Navy stands true to its oath, in proven loyalty to the Führer, unconditional in readiness for battle. Take orders only from me, the C-in-C of the Navy, and your own Commanders, so that errors through false instructions will be impossible. Destroy ruthlessly anyone who reveals himself as a traitor.

Long live our Führer, Adolf Hitler![166]

Three days later he joined his name to that of Keitel and Göring in offering Hitler the adoption of the Nazi salute in all arms of the services 'as a sign of their unbroken loyalty to the Führer and the close union between the armed services and the Party'.[167]

Meanwhile a blood purge was under way, more horrifying and sadistic than anything the Party had yet descended to as it wreaked hideous revenge on its hated class enemy. Within three weeks the first show trial took place in the Peoples' Court in Berlin, presided over by a turn-coat former Communist leader, Roland Freisler: von Witzleben, Hoepner, Peter Count Yorck von Wartenburg—a friend of von Moltke's and member of the resistance from the beginning—and other leading *Putschists* who had not taken their own lives were verbally assaulted and humiliated by this ambitious proselyte; despite his extraordinary rantings Yorck succeeded in making the moral case for the resistance: 'What is fundamental and linking all these problems together is the State's totalitarian hold on the citizen, excluding the individual's religious and moral obligations before God.'[168]

The sentence of death was implicit in Freisler's proceedings, only the manner may have been in doubt, and that not for long; immediately after he had pronounced, all the accused were taken to Plötzensee prison, and in a low-ceilinged dungeon, lit dazzlingly by studio bulbs and reflectors, they were hanged one by one from meat hooks while a cine camera in the corner recorded their agony *pour encourager les autres*. Other trials and barbarous executions followed; the numbers are not known with any certainty, but the tale of vengeance and martyrdom continued up to the last weeks of the war, extending, as Hitler had promised in his frenzied outburst at the *Wolfschanze* tea party, to the traitors' families; their young children were placed in the care of National Socialist Welfare organizations, given new surnames and denied all news of their parents' fate.

It is interesting that in the Navy itself only three officers were arrested, one of them Stauffenberg's brother, Bertholt, who was the conspirators' legal adviser; another was 1c in the headquarters operations staff; his special duty during the *Putsch* was to observe Dönitz and if necessary arrest him. Probably there were others who were sympathetic to the plotters, at least in the thinking departments of the service, and especially those whose duties gave them access to uncensored intelligence from outside, but given the known extreme views of the C-in-C Navy and the majority of Flag Officers, these had little chance of taking an active part.

On August 24th, Dönitz called his Flag Officers together at yet another *Tagung* to explain to them and through them to the service as a whole the events and lessons of the attempted *coup*. It is evident that he had been briefed by Himmler or his chief agent, Kaltenbrunner, for his opening remarks reveal a wide knowledge of the extent of the conspiracy not available from trial reports; he began by reciting with deep cynicism the rebels' ideas: once the Führer had been removed, both the 'Anglo-

Saxons and the Russians would be convinced that our aggressive spirit had disappeared . . . we would at once be granted an honourable peace without partition',[169] whereupon a new government would institute immediate freedom of expression, press freedom, restoration of individual rights, removal of special courts, opening of concentration camps and so on. It is interesting that he did not include in this catalogue the punishment of war criminals although the members of the resistance had long considered it 'absolutely essential for the restoration of the rule of law, and with it peace in Germany and the community of nations' that the many crimes committed during the war should be punished,[170] and therefore deemed it 'necessary to establish a retrospective German law'. They had defined a war criminal as anyone 'who orders a criminal action or who, in a responsible position, instigates the crime, or who spreads general doctrine or instructions of a criminal character . . .'[171] There can be no possible doubt from Dönitz's remarks at this *Tagung* of August 24th alone that he came into this category.

Having given his summary of the conspirators' aims, Dönitz poured scorn on their methods as 'laughable and historically uninformed'; they had believed they had only to say the word and without any attempt to seize the communications, the radio stations, telephone exchanges and telegraph offices, the government would fall. The truth about this failure is not so simple as he made out; some aspects remain a mystery today. He poured similar scorn on the conspirators' intentions to free concentration camp inmates:

> They had apparently imagined that only worthy citizens who were unpopular with the present state were inside, not realizing that 99 per cent of the inmates are habitual criminals serving an average five years' term of imprisonment, which the former State allowed to run around freely until they committed their next murder, sex crime or act of violence, and of whose incarceration we today cannot be thankful enough for the safety of our families and our whole public life . . .

Here he demonstrably overstepped the facts as he knew them. He had heard Himmler at the 1943 Gauleiters' *Tagung* speak of the '50 to 60,000 political and criminal criminals . . . in the concentration camps', who together with 'approximately a further 150,000, among them a small number of Jews, a great number of Poles and Russians and other rabble in the concentration camps' were employed by Minister Speer for his 'vitally important tasks'.[172] Dönitz was, of course, working closely with Speer on the naval construction programme and knew that his colleagues' slave labourers were not murderers and sex offenders; within three months he was calling for 12,000 of them to supplement the shipyard workforce!

As his final shot at the 'narrow-mindedness . . . and monstrously uneducated presumption' of the conspirators, Dönitz revealed they had intended subordinating the *Kriegsmarine* to the General Staff of the Army!

He went on to summarize the overall situation: there were two possibilities before them; the first was to capitulate as the General Staff clique had wished; he outlined the consequences—disarmament, the destruction of all war production, a prohibition on the possession of aircraft and U-boats—in short, although he did not say so, a return to the position after the First World War. The Russians would create a Communist government immediately and remove all members of those classes which would oppose it. 'In addition millions of us would be freighted to the east in order to rebuild . . . because certainly the east was destroyed by us. That these millions of men, our whole labour force, would not see the homeland again is similarly self-evident.' Therefore, he concluded, capitulation did not come into the question.

Again some doubts about his real thoughts and motives occur. Certainly there was everything to fear from Stalin, whose treatment of the officer class, clergy and intelligentsia in occupied countries and bloody purges within Russia were notorious; certainly he believed that the British had started the war in order to destroy Germany and that Churchill and Roosevelt would fulfil their pledge to partition the Fatherland; but he also knew that an Anglo-Saxon occupation would carry none of the terrors of a Russian occupation, and by the date of his address the western allies had broken out of their bridgehead and advanced as far as the line of the Seine; Paris was being liberated as he spoke. With his intimate knowledge of the conspiracy as revealed in this talk, he probably knew that the western Commanders, Rommel and von Kluge, both of whom had been in the plot, had long since conceded defeat and hoped to secure an armistice with the Anglo-American enemy, which alone might allow Germany to hold her eastern front against Bolshevism. This was an alternative he did not mention, though—which leads to the conclusion that this part of the address was deliberately dishonest, the highly coloured picture of the terrors of

Russian occupation deliberately misleading propaganda, and one is again left with the question of whether this falseness arose from his indestructible commitment to his soldier's goal, in this case to the continuation of the fight as commanded by the Führer, or whether guilt and complicity in war crimes branded as punishable by fellow Germans of the resistance played an equal part.

The only other possibility, he went on, was 'fanatical further fighting'. There was no half-way house; compromise was 'false and impossible'. And he repeated his frequently expressed conviction that any 'deviation from this fanatical and resolute struggle' implied a weakness, anyone who deviated 'in the last from the National Socialist State' weakened the State's unity and resolution, hence the war effort; finally, 'anyone who expresses the least defeatism weakens the will to resistance of the people and must in consequence be ruthlessly annihilated'.

The soldier had no right to question whether an order to fight had purpose; the calling and task of the soldier was to fight; were each man or group to start questioning whether his orders made sense it would shake the profession of arms to the foundation and signify the dissolution of the *Wehrmacht*. In this, of course, he was correct; in explaining it, though, he was surely explaining the great responsibilities invested in military leadership—in those who were listening to him, above all in himself as Supreme Commander. Naturally he argued afterwards and to the end of his life that he, too, was simply a soldier carrying out the orders of his C-in-C, the Führer, Adolf Hitler; naturally he wished to believe that any Commander, like Beck, Rommel or von Kluge who exercised independent judgement, hence broke his oath of loyalty to the Führer, was a miserable traitor, for in doing so he passed on his own responsibility. But whether at the time he made this speech his subconscious and very human desire was to cast off responsibility, or whether he was impelled more by the doctrines of unreason, hate and destruction that informed National Socialism is, of course, not revealed by the record.

It is possible that he was simply out of his depth. He had been brought up to unconditional loyalty as a soldier; his language expressed it on this occasion:

It is false if the officer, who derives his position and his honour from the State, and who in good times serves willingly, now in evil times, in place of hard and unswerving fighting, becomes doubtful and turns to politics, which is certainly not his affair. He should leave politics to people who understand them better than he. So each soldier has to fulfil the tasks of his position regardless. So our calling and our fate is to fight fanatically, and bound up with it is the task for each of us to stand fanatically behind the National Socialist State and unconditionally to bring up the troops accordingly.

This was the essence of the Prussian code; it cannot be challenged on general grounds. The questions are, surely, had his perceptions been so narrowed by early indoctrination, was his capacity so limited that he could not reinterpret general propositions in the light of specific circumstances, or was he using the argument of unconditional loyalty to escape awesome responsibilities? Did he feel himself too deeply involved in the crimes of the regime to turn back? Was he simply unbalanced? Or was the need for a war-father his master emotion?

    . . . Then came the man who inscribed all these virtues of the soldier on his banner. It is self-evident that we, as we pledged our soldiers' oath to him, pledged also to stand with our whole soul and heart behind this man. It is a nonsense to believe that one can station a *Wehrmacht* in a void. The *Wehrmacht* must fanatically adhere to the man to whom it has sworn loyalty, because otherwise, if this fundamental law of a *Wehrmacht* is not understood and despite the oath inner opposition is reserved against the man who embodies all these virtues and has executed and impressed them, such a *Wehrmacht* founders. What then would we expect? To whom should we then submit ourselves with our whole soul? In the final analysis this is the fundamental reason for the failure of these sections of the General Staff. They have not adhered to the Führer with their whole soul.

    It is therefore necessary to recognize this situation clearly, there is in this most bitterly serious battle of destiny only fanatical adherence to this man and this State. Each deviation is a laxness and a crime. I would rather eat earth than that my grandson should be brought up and become poisoned in the Jewish spirit and filth, and that the cleanness of today's public art, culture and education, which we now all regard as obvious—and the changes which would become clear if we were suddenly to see things from the former times—should come into Jewish hands again.

This sentiment brought him back again to the need for those listening to stand unequivocally behind the Nazi State, and to indoctrinate their men in this spirit, 'not with fine speeches, but by showing fanatical ability to die. Whoever neither wants to nor can do this cannot be a senior officer or troop Commander and must disappear'.

He passed on to an optimistic assessment of the overall war situation; the *Putsch* had cleared the air extraordinarily—indeed it would have been a blessing if it had occurred six months earlier. The leadership and spirit of the armies in the east was now wholly different; Guderian—who had been brought back as the new Chief of the General Staff—was giving clear, strong, optimistic leadership, the *Panzer* divisions were being deployed offensively to smash the enemy thrusts instead of in passive defence. Additional divisions were being raised at home—Himmler's *Volksgrenadiere* or Peoples' Army; production was rising; the fighter aircraft programme was on schedule despite enemy harassment; by September—echoing Hitler's remarks—they had the possibility of the mastery of German air space. The U-boat programme was proceeding unchecked, Heye's Small Craft Division was of great significance. He ended by calling for the maintenance of the Navy's striking power and a high standard of training.

He was not the only leader to adopt blinkers: Speer, whose armaments production figures were indeed rising astonishingly, exaggerated his future output and the effect this could have on the situation, especially in the air; re-reading his words at this time after the war he found himself horrified by the recklessness he had shown, and felt 'something grotesque' about his efforts to persuade serious men that supreme exertions might still bring success.[173] Himmler overestimated the effect of National Socialist ardour in his new Peoples' divisions for the eastern front, and of his own committed leadership in place of the 'defeatist and obstructionist generals' of the old guard. Goebbels encouraged Hitler's hopes of miraculous intervention while stepping up propaganda for total war, self-sacrifice in daily life as in battle, and the rooting out of all traitors and defeatists—Dönitz's address might almost have been composed by him, even to the remarks on the cleaning up of public art, one of the Propaganda Minister's important accomplishments.

The final months of the war from autumn 1944 until Hitler's suicide in April 1945 below the ruins of the Chancellery raise all the questions about Dönitz's character in starkest form. His performance was fanatical in the strictest sense. The *Wehrmacht* was forced to withdraw from one 'vital' position after another, German cities were reduced to spectral ruins standing in wastes of rubble, allies and friendly neutrals deserted the *Reich*, raw material sources were blocked, coal and oil supplies cut to a fraction of the amounts necessary to maintain even a one-front war, the homeland invaded, morale in the west collapsed and in the east civilians with reason fled the Red terror; Ribbentrop, Goebbels, Himmler each in their different ways came to terms with the inevitable and extended peace feelers to the enemy, Speer set himself the task of sabotaging Hitler's 'scorched earth' policy so that when the end came the German people would not be denied all means of subsistence—but Dönitz, practically alone among the top leadership, cleaved straight, scorning any 'deviation' from the course set by the Führer, seemingly intent only to prove that when the waters finally closed over the tortured ruins of the Third Reich the ensign of the *Kriegsmarine* would still be flying, he himself beyond reproach by his Führer or posterity.

The really remarkable thing about his performance is that it never changed. Had he been a rational leader subject to rational considerations, there must have come a point during this steady erosion of Germany's position when attitudes appropriate in January 1943, when he had taken over from Raeder, became totally inappropriate. Dönitz never perceived this in Hitler's lifetime, or if he did never acted on it. In 1943 it was still possible to believe in the Führer's political and strategic genius, still possible to hope that more U-boats or new types of U-boats might yet snatch victory from the sea powers, hence still everything to fight for. Two years later none of these assumptions was valid. It was plain to all officers—and of course the generals had seen it long since—that Hitler's 'strategy' was a disaster, and it was clear that even if the new U-boats did all that was expected of them they would never have the *Luftwaffe* support vital to their success; moreover by the end of 1944 it was clear that there would not be enough of them to affect the situation before industry was brought to a standstill, the country occupied.

No one was in a better position to assess the situation than Dönitz himself; he had seen the débâcle at close quarters and witnessed one after another of the Führer's promises come to nothing—even Goebbels at the end was entering in his diary 'we have heard it all so often before that we can no longer bring ourselves to place much hope in such statements'[174] of Hitler's; he had heard Hitler vilifying one scapegoat after another for failures for which he was responsible, had seen the

380

alarming deterioration in Hitler's already ruined physical and mental condition; during the final months when he was spending two or three days every week, sometimes longer, at Führer headquarters, he was reporting to a bowed and shaking figure whom shocked newcomers described as prematurely senile. Yet neither the form nor the manner of his commitment altered in any way. He seized on any scrap of hopeful news to weave an optimistic forecast; if there were no good news he invented something; in December, during one of his private conversations with Hitler he said he had decided to send ten to fifteen German naval officers to Japan so that they could study fleet operations on a large scale, experience which could be used later when it came to rebuilding the German fleet;[175] on New Year's Day 1945 he produced an article from *Picture Post* alleging weak construction in American Liberty ships![176] Two days later he assessed the prospects for the latest weapon from Admiral Heye's Small Battle Units, the *Seehund* midget U-boat carrying two underslung torpedoes: 'Assuming that from the 80 *Seehund* U-boats planned per month, only 50 come into operation, then 100 torpedoes will be carried to the enemy; with 20 per cent hits that gives a sinking figure of some 100,000 tons . . .'[177]

After a *Seehund* sortie towards the end of the month when all boats were forced back to base by the weather or technical defects without reaching the target area, he reported that despite the lack of success the operations were of the highest value as 'all the teething troubles which might never have shown up under test in the Baltic have shown up in the severe conditions in the Hoofden and can thus be corrected . . .'[178]

Of course, the chief hope which he held out before the Führer's exhausted gaze to the last rested in the new Type XXI U-boats. By mid-February, by extraordinary exertions, Speer's teams had succeeded in launching over 100 of these and 49 of the smaller Type XXIII boats. It is interesting that Dönitz preceded his report on their future use with a summary of conventional U-boat operations, virtually returning full circle to his first thoughts on U-boats in September 1935 when he became FdU; then he had written that their low speed virtually excluded use against fast forces, they would therefore be used in stationary mode before enemy harbours; now he said that 'old-type' U-boats had little chance of success in mobile warfare, hence it was best to station them outside ports.[179]

Afterwards Hitler stressed the great importance for the overall war situation he attached to the revival of the war at sea with the new boats.

Dönitz reacted enthusiastically: the new Type XXI could travel all the way from Germany to Japan without surfacing; all the apparatus presently employed by the sea powers to maintain their mastery could now be circumvented—the new boats could be expected to be very effective. But he pointed out that the nub of the matter was the construction problem; the yards needed priority rating for personnel, coal and steel.

By this date the coalfields and industries of Silesia had been overrun by the Russians who had reached the Oder river; the western allies were attacking the Ruhr, whose output had already been reduced to a fraction of the previous year's peak by concentrated bombing, and armaments production was only being maintained at all by expedients and the consumption of existing stocks of components. Dönitz's remarks on priority bore no relation whatever to possibility or reality.

At the end of the month he was reporting to Hitler again on the revolutionary qualities of the new U-boats 'against which the mighty sea power of the Anglo-Saxons is essentially powerless'.[180]

Goebbels noted in his diary, '. . . what a fine, imposing impression is made by Dönitz. As the Führer told me he is the best man in his arm of the service. Look at the invariably gratifying results he has achieved with the Navy . . .'[181] On March 13th after another discussion with Hitler, Goebbels wrote:

The Führer wishes to make a renewed attempt to stabilize the fronts. He hopes for some success in the U-boat war, particularly if our new U-boats come into action which for the moment they have not yet done. What a difference between Dönitz and Göring. Both have suffered a severe technical setback in their arm of the service. Göring resigned himself to it and so has gone to the dogs. Dönitz has overcome it . . .[182]

A week later Goebbels was recording that although reproaching Göring, Hitler would not appoint a new C-in-C for the *Luftwaffe*. 'From many quarters Dönitz is being proposed for the post and I think this proposal is not too wide off the mark.'[183]

There is no doubt that Dönitz's bearing in the crisis was everything he was demanding from his subordinates, unquestioning loyalty, unquenchable optimism, selfless, indefatigable zeal and eagerness to take on any responsibility. He was performing exactly as all his service reports indicate he had throughout his career. Already he had taken over the transport and supply of coal throughout the *Reich*, a task he had proposed himself for in January after the allied devastation of the Ruhr and inland communications had brought chaos. Since then he had extemporized a system of canal barges assisted by narrow-gauge field railways around danger spots or locks which had been destroyed. No difficulties were too great for him to find solutions. If Himmler needed additional troops, Dönitz combed men from his naval garrisons; if the Army wanted river bridges destroyed, he sent detachments of naval frogmen and mining experts from the Small Battle Units; when the RAF destroyed dams with bombs set to explode against the walls at depth it was to Dönitz that Hitler turned for a defensive solution.

To the very end he maintained an air of imperturbable confidence and reliability. One young officer, Gerhardt Boldt, whose task it was to lay out maps for Hitler's daily situation conferences, recalls a day in January 1945 when he placed them in the wrong order. Guderian, starting his report on the eastern front with the southern sector as was customary, realized that the map he was pointing to was of the northern area and stopped in mid-sentence, glaring at Boldt; Hitler, too, looked him over with an 'indescribable glance' before sinking back wearily, and the rest of the assembled company stared at the unfortunate young officer, now stammering in confusion as if he had committed treason.

> Only Grand Admiral Dönitz smiled at me and, saying a few consoling words, lifted the pile of maps and requested me with a nod to lay them out again in the correct order. I conceived a lasting affection for the Admiral as a result of his kindness.[185]

During regular visits to his men at the front and in the training divisions, Dönitz left the same impression of confidence and determination which marked his performance at Führer headquarters. The late Admiral Wegener recalled accompanying him on an inspection of sailors and supply staff at Gdynia in the closing months of the war; the men were morose, but as Dönitz went along the lines looking each in the eye they straightened, visibly regaining their pride.[185]

One U-boat Commander training crews for the new boats recalled Dönitz coming round every three months or so, making rousing speeches, invariably ending with the resolve to 'pursue this war until victory is achieved'. Afterwards he would spend the evening in the officers' mess. 'I often sat next to him, and he always left me with the same impression of a reliable and energetic man perfectly confident that final victory *would* be achieved. He met all criticisms by short, clipped references to ultra-modern boats that could do fabulous things . . .'[186] He argued that if he, with his close contacts with the Führer, could not judge the situation, nobody could, and echoing Hitler's repeated— repeatedly falsified—promises he assured them that if they could just hold on they would see a complete turn of the tide in Germany's favour. 'Whenever he visited us, he left us feeling better.'[187]

He maintained his armour-plated confidence and inspring mien to the end, the very model of a Prussian soldier in adversity. Yet a model of leadership appropriate for a time of hope in victory or succour is inappropriate when there is no possibility of either. And while loyalty is the bedrock of soldierly virtue, to a leader who has proved himself unworthy it is the basis of evil. Hitler had proved himself unworthy, as decent judges of character had known from the beginning. Having blamed everyone but himself for his cosmic political and military mis-judgements, at the end he blamed the German people, rationalizing his refusal to accept responsibility for the fate of those he claimed to lead with the dictum that they had proved the weaker in the struggle of races, hence could not expect and did not deserve to survive. Keeping faith with such a leader meant acquiescing in the ever-mounting slaughter of the German people in whose name he was exhorting his men to fight. Of all the multitude of deceptions which Dönitz perpetrated on his service— and no doubt on himself—this was the ultimate.

The causes lay deep in his personality, but it was the system he served and the history and tradition of the German Navy that shaped his responses. Scheer and Hipper and von Trotha had attempted a similar deception at the end of the First War when they planned the suicide sortie of the High Seas Fleet to preserve the honour of the service; that had precipitated the naval mutinies which Dönitz and every officer of his generation resolved should never recur. It was also possible to rational-ize *Heldentod*—hero's death—as in the First War, as necessary to gain the Navy honour for posterity and so ensure its future rebirth. This hardly accorded with political or economic reality, but neither had any place in naval education. The majority of naval officers at the time seem to have had much the same feelings as Dönitz.

Behind the naval tradition was the Prusso-German philosophy that condoned any deception for the good of the State; taken to its ultimate by the Nazis it became a system of lies in which Dönitz was inextricably bound. The ultimate lie that the forces of the State must continue fighting for the people was inherent from the beginning in the totalitarian deception that the people were no more than collective units of the State without right to independent personality.

On a personal level there were equally powerful forces acting on Dönitz, one an individual trait, his refusal to admit that he was wrong, his compulsion to take every opportunity to assert that his course had been correct. He had espoused the Nazi doctrine, probably as early as any serviceman, had affirmed not only his soldier's loyalty to the Führer in countless speeches and directives, but had made it clear that he had given him his 'whole soul'; he had reacted to the assassination attempt with 'holy wrath and extravagant fury' against the 'criminal traitors'; could he six to eight months later have altered course 180° and declared *himself* a traitor? Probably this never came in question; he was wholly emotionally committed.

Another force which can hardly be overestimated is the conviction and repetition with which he was assailed at Führer headquarters. There were no dissentient views there. He lent his own inner fires to the doctrines of hate and destruction repeated endlessly, his own confidence to the group certainties rising in the stale air of those Nibelung gatherings. Towards the end, as Speer recalled, it had become pure nihilism: 'We leave the Americans, English and Russians only a desert.'[188] There is ample proof from his speeches and other utterances that Dönitz was prepared to repeat the most extreme tenets of Hitler's and Goebbels' creed; there is no reason to suppose he was unresponsive to this ultimate 'logic'.

There were significant moments during the final months when he was confronted with opportunities to break out and use individual judgement. One was in February 1945, when Speer, according to his memoirs, drew him aside during a situation conference revealing the disastrous military position on all fronts and said that something had to be done.

'I am here to represent the Navy,' Dönitz replied curtly, 'All the rest is not my business. The Führer knows what he is doing.'[189]

On another occasion in March Guderian drew him aside to enlist his support for his own repeated pleas to Hitler to withdraw the northern army in Kurland, now encircled and only supplied by the Navy; he believed Hitler's decision to hold on could be traced back to Dönitz's concern for maintaining naval mastery in the Baltic. This time Dönitz agreed to intervene; he had, it was true, repeatedly represented the necessity of holding Kurland, chiefly for reasons of U-boat training, but now the task of supplying the Army there and evacuating wounded and refugees had become the greatest strain on the service; he told Hitler this and supported Guderian's evacuation plan. According to the naval staff war diary, Hitler agreed with him on the naval argument, but 'described at length the reasons [for holding on], all based on land strategy'. According to Gerhardt Boldt, who witnessed the scene, Hitler rose slowly at Dönitz's unexpected intervention, made a few dragging steps about the room, then spat out his reply in a harsh voice.

'I have already said that repatriation of the Kurland troops is out of the question. I cannot abandon the heavy equipment. Moreover, I must take Sweden into account.'[190]

Ever present in the background to these and no doubt other moments when Dönitz may have been asked or even felt tempted to question policy were Hitler's repeated denunciations and threats against 'defeatists'; there was also Führer order number one which laid down that no one had the right to reveal information from his own service sphere to other departments; all information and views had to pass upwards to the Führer who alone might be in possession of the complete picture. And as Hitler reminded Guderian, failure to comply with this fundamental law constituted treason; there were fearful proofs of the punishments meted out for treason in the wake of the July assassination attempt. And the coarse, scarred features of Himmler's principal lieutenant, the giant Kaltenbrunner, head of the Security Central Office, were seldom absent from Führer headquarters during these final months of the war. Terror had always been the buttress of the system; it was needed now more than ever and must be added to the powerful forces distorting the environment in which Dönitz was moving. Whether his attitude at the end came as much from the push of fear of getting out of line, or knowledge of complicity in crimes for which the allies had promised to exact atonement, as from the pull of his need for an all-powerful father and all-embracing creed to which he could commit himself—reinforced by the convictions of the brutal group with whom he consorted day after day in the final months—there is no doubt that the manner in which he carried on performing his duty with fanatical commitment while the *Reich* and all rational hope crashed around him represented a growing separation from reality. Nor can it be doubted that he was aware of it at some level, which he managed to exclude from judgement, for directly

386

he learned of Hitler's death he dropped from his fantasy plane with an abruptness which astonished those closest to him.

The documentary record from autumn 1944 suggests that his way of excluding reality was by increasing his already over-loaded working day and exaggerating his normal goal-oriented methods. He had always tended to discount factors interfering with his aims; now he banished outside events completely, concentrating on solving problems within his own sphere *in vacuo*; his solutions were practical and worked out in immaculate detail, but they did not key into what was happening outside. They represented so much lost motion.

The construction programme was an example. On September 29th he wrote a memorandum calling attention to the fact that losses of naval units had outstripped new building since the summer by 60 craft; if this continued the Navy would be unable to fulfil its tasks, and he concluded therefore that the programme in its entirety should be accelerated.[191] Since the original grand plan had already been set back by severe material and personnel shortages, aggravated by his own *additions* such as the Small Battle Units and extra minesweepers, and disrupted by allied bombing and sabotage in the occupied territories, since it competed for ever scarcer resources with the other armed services, this was pure fantasy. He continued to press for the complete augmented and accelerated programme, however, refusing to consider any reduction— 'We yield not a finger's breadth'—[192] and in November had the satisfaction of gaining Hitler's approval. This was worth as little as the detailed and practical proposals with which he backed his arguments. The resources were not available. Before the end of January all surface shipbuilding had stopped for lack of coal.

One of the practical measures he had proposed was to boost the shipyard labour force with 12,000 concentration camp inmates. He also suggested steps to deal with poor performance and sabotage in Danish and Norwegian yards. It was absolutely senseless, he wrote, to expend costly raw materials and scarce foreign exchange in these yards 'if, for example, out of eight newly-built ships in Denmark, seven will be destroyed by sabotage'.[193] If new measures to be taken by the Security services proved ineffective, he suggested:

Because in other places measures of retaliation against whole work shifts in which sabotage occurred have proved effective and, for example, in France yard sabotage was completely suppressed, the possibility of using similar measures in the northern yards should be considered.

Through the employment of the personnel concerned (wholly or in part) as concentration camp workers not only would their performance increase 100 per cent, but the loss of their formerly good earnings would be a considerable discouragement to sabotage, since this is probably conducted by enemy agents only with the silent acquiescence of the workers.

Two months later, on January 23rd, after even the pretence of continuing the building programme had been abandoned, he raised the proposal again in a small group consisting of Hitler, Ribbentrop, Göring, Keitel, Jodl, Lammers and Bormann after the daily situation conference at Führer headquarters, recording the result: 'The Führer decides to resort to energetic measures as advocated by C-in-C Navy.'[194]

Extension of the slave-labour system to the northern shipyards was a brutal measure to propose to fulfil a programme that was plainly impossible; to repeat the proposal after surface shipbuilding had come to a halt was pure fanaticism; the springs of fanaticism lay within, but the record of these conferences in the final months of the war leaves no doubt that he was playing up to and for the Führer—Professor Salewski even suggests that the whole charade of memoranda and proposals about the construction programme was no more than image-building to prove his capacity for endurance.[195]

'Military qualities don't show themselves on a sand model,' Hitler repeated often, 'in the last analysis they show themselves in the capacity to hold on, in perseverance and determination . . . fanatical determination.'[196] Dönitz had no need to prove he possessed these qualities; he had shown them throughout his career and especially perhaps during his time as C-in-C Navy, yet it is evident he felt the need to reaffirm them continually to Hitler. Again and again, with childish eagerness to please, he brought little episodes which might reflect credit on his Navy or himself to the Führer's attention. After the collapse of a vital bridge over the Rhine at Remagen—too late to prevent the passage of US troops—he described to Hitler 'the repeated attempts by Navy detachments to destroy the bridge under the most dangerous conditions'.[197] He not only made hugely over-optimistic and groundless predictions for future U-boat warfare at the end, but when reporting actual results explained how much better they would have been if only they still had the Biscay ports, a futile observation, which he repeated in early April with the Russians practically at the gates of Berlin. The war diary recorded: 'C-in-C Navy points out how great our chances for successful U-boat warfare would be now if we still had the Biscay ports.'[198]

Similarly he brought to Hitler's notice the fanatical spirit of Admiral Hüffmeier, recently appointed Chief of Staff to the Commander of the Channel Islands. When Hüffmeier suggested in November 1944 that a programme of drastic confiscation and severely reduced consumption would enable the islands to be held until the end of 1945, he commented on the soundness of the appointment of 'this energetic personality'.[199] In March 1945 he commended the Admiral to Hitler again for his inspiring leadership, later reporting the reply to his own congratulatory telegram: 'Vice Admiral Hüffmeier hopes he will be able to hold the Channel Islands for another year.'[200] A few days later, after differences of opinion in the channel Islands Command about whether or not the forces should hold out to the last man, the garrison Commander was relieved, and Hüffmeier appointed to the post; Hitler then ordered that all fortress Commanders in the west should be naval officers. 'Many fortresses have been given up,' he said, 'but no ships were ever lost without fighting to the last man.'[201]

This finally was what Dönitz's fanaticism was reduced to. All other rationalizations had been stripped away by this date, March 26th: there was no prospect of fighter production erecting the 'roof over Germany' which according to his new adjutant, Walter Lüdde-Neurath, had sustained his hopes through the autumn. Instead Germany was being destroyed from the air. Central Berlin was under ceaseless 1,500-bomber saturation raids which had forced Berliners into a troglodyte existence. Hitler had taken up residence in a catacomb of bunkers 55 feet below the Chancellery, where he sought with the aid of a single switchboard and a radio telephone link to Army headquarters to hold up his disintegrating empire by will power. It was to this unhealthy concrete warren that Dönitz reported day after day.

There was no prospect either of the new U-boats becoming operational in time. Rumours of other 'secret weapons' with which Goebbels had boosted morale successfully for a while were plainly unfounded. Churchill and Roosevelt had not, it seemed, woken to the danger of Bolshevism overrunning Europe; the break-up of the alliance which Hitler and Goebbels had predicted had not happened; the allies

389

were calling for unconditional surrender in terms that left no doubt of their brutal intent. On the other hand, German forces were running out of arms and fuel. Systematic production had come to an end; Speer was concentrating on saving what he could from Hitler's 'scorched earth' policy for life after the war, miraculously escaping the fate that would have been meted out to any general expressing his openly 'defeatist' opinions. 'His viewpoint is that it is no function of war policy to lead a people to a hero's doom,' Goebbels had entered in his diary two weeks before, '. . . and that this was stressed absolutely explicitly by the Führer himself in *Mein Kampf*.'[202]

Everyone knew the war was lost; the roads from the east were clogged with refugees; pathetic columns trekked through Berlin on their way westwards, leaving frozen corpses among the rubble. In the west civilian morale had sunk, according to Goebbels, 'very low, if it has not already reached zero'.[203] Soldiers had been deserting in droves for a long time. Confronted with the figures of those reported missing in February Hitler had declared he would abandon the Geneva Convention: 'If I make it clear that I have no consideration for prisoners, but will deal with them ruthlessly without regard for reprisals, many [Germans] will think seriously before they desert.'[204] He had been urged to do this previously by Goebbels in retaliation for the bombing terror, and to make it known that captured allied aircrew would be shot out of hand. He had put it to Dönitz, asking his opinion. Dönitz had consulted his legal department, reporting back the next day that the disadvantages of such a step would outweigh the advantages, and 'it would be better in any case to keep up outside appearances and carry out the measures believed necessary without announcing them beforehand'.[205] This had been the common view in the Führer bunker; it remained so; even Bormann supported it.

Balked, Hitler instituted a system of itinerant Courts Martial to root out defeatism in the upper levels of the *Wehrmacht*. They had powers to investigate and execute Commanders found guilty of withholding full commitment. Other methods were in use to keep the troops up to the mark; SS General Schörner's way with deserters was described to Hitler by Goebbels on March 13th: 'They are hung from the nearest tree with a placard round their neck saying, "I am a deserter. I have refused to defend German women and children and have therefore been hung." '[206]

In this bloody finale, as Hitler and Goebbels, cornered and with no hope of escape, turned savagely on anyone not prepared to hate and to throw away his life for them and the continuation of the failed cause for a few more weeks, Dönitz gave fanatic support. His *Schnell* boats, U-boats and midget craft under Admiral Heye continued desperate sorties against allied supply convoys in the North Sea and around the British Isles, taking fearful punishment from the concentrated air-sea defence, and in the case of the midget craft from the weather, scoring only isolated successes, chiefly by minelaying, which could not affect the course of the allied advance by even a day. When fuel shortage forced the abandonment of operations by the few remaining *Schnell* boats in mid-April, the midget craft kept up the hopeless struggle. Whether or not they went out in the spirit of suicide mission as many did, that was usually the result. The units had been rushed through design and production too quickly and for the very different task of defending the coasts against allied landings; the young crews were trained in fanaticism; some performed feats of endurance, some navigating by their wrist watches simply lost themselves, others were picked up fast asleep in their craft, the great majority never returned.

U-boat crews, too, suffered heavy and increasing losses in these last weeks; Dönitz had predicted they would in early March, and on April 7th he explained to Hitler again that there was such a concentration of anti-U-boat forces in the operational area around the British Isles that once a boat disclosed its position by attacking it was often lost, for its low underwater speed did not permit escape.[207] Altogether 25 were lost around the British Isles or on passage during the month, a further eleven in areas as far distant as the US east coast and the Indian Ocean; this was over a third of the 100 or so boats operational at the beginning of the month, and for this just thirteen allied merchantmen were sunk. Meanwhile so many of the new Type XXI boats were destroyed or damaged by allied air raids on Hamburg and Kiel that eventually only one sailed for an operational cruise at the beginning of May.

The real task of the Navy was in the Baltic, supplying the armies in Kurland and East Prussia and giving supporting fire in coastal operations. Meanwhile officers and men from administration and specialist branches, others from coastal batteries not immediately threatened were combed to form naval infantry divisions to stiffen the fronts or relieve regular garrison troops for front-line duty. Dönitz worked closely with Himmler and Hitler in these attempts to relieve the shortage of soldiers. On April 14th he offered Hitler 3,000 young men from the Navy to operate with light packs and bazookas behind enemy lines in the west.[208]

The men had no training for the task; it was a desperate idea and appears even more extraordinary in retrospect when it is realized that at this time German forces in the west were being manoeuvred in careful defiance of Hitler's orders, to open a corridor through which US armour might speed to reach Berlin before the Russians—an opportunity that was not realized. As for the eastern front, Guderian had broken openly with Hitler over his senseless strategy a fortnight before and had been sent on 'extended leave'. Himmler, in eclipse because of the alleged failure of his SS regiments in the south-east and his own failure as a general in Pomerania, was trying to make up his mind about opening armistice negotiations through Sweden. Speer, of course, was working openly against Hitler's destruction orders; as Goebbels recorded in his diary on March 27th, 'Speer is continually saying that he does not intend to lift a finger to cut the German people's lifeline . . . The Führer uses extraordinarily hard words about Speer . . .'[209] Dönitz, therefore, was practically alone in his continuing unswerving commitment to the struggle.

What that meant in human terms may be judged by his decrees during this final month of the war. The men of the Navy were as subject to demoralization as the rest of the population; those sent out in U-boats had more reason than most to wonder why they should sacrifice themselves for a plainly lost cause, especially those experienced petty officers and ratings ordered to boats with young, fanatically indoctrinated officers. For any who proved recalcitrant there were punishment battalions on the eastern front, where conditions were as unpleasant and death as certain as in U-boats. Courts Martial for cowardice and summary hanging for desertion by the notorious naval police, known as *Kettenhunde*—'chain-dogs'—from the chains of office they wore around their necks, provided powerful inducement to loyalty. Dönitz personally encouraged the most savage measures; here is the final paragraph of a secret decree he issued on April 7th:

We soldiers of the *Kriegsmarine* know how we have to act. Our military duty, which we fulfil regardless of what may happen to right or left or around us, causes us to stand bold, hard and loyal as a rock of the resistance. A scoundrel who does not behave so must be hung and have a placard fastened to him, 'Here hangs a traitor who by his low cowardice allows German women and children to die instead of protecting them like a man.'[210]

One wonders whether Hitler suggested this measure of Schörner's, or whether it was by then a commonplace. Hitler issued a similar proclamation a fortnight later before the final battle for Berlin. Dönitz's order was carried out ruthlessly as men from the naval infantry divisions, finding themselves armed with Dutch or even Russian rifles and with little ammunition, or expected to face armour with hand weapons, or simply infected with the current hopelessness, joined deserters and refugees trudging west to surrender to the British and Americans.

Generalizations about the state of morale are not possible, however; it varied widely. Those officers and men engaged in obviously worthwhile missions, supplying and supporting the Army in the Baltic and evacuating the wounded, performed selflessly to the end; the élite of the experienced U-boat men, training in the Baltic for the new type of boat, appear to have preserved morale; they were the fortunate ones; they had survived the worst of the Atlantic battle, had been held back from the more desperate missions in the last year when a boat was not expected to survive more than three war cruises, and they knew that when they were sent out they would be in boats whose high underwater speed would allow them to elude their pursuers. On the other hand there were naval garrisons waiting with nothing to do except think, where morale sagged; on Heligoland in the final weeks several officers and men of Marine-artillerie Division 122 and Marine Flak Division 242 actually arranged to give the island up to the British; their wireless messages were intercepted by the Security Services, however, and early in the morning of April 18th, the day they had arranged to raise a white flag on the Flak control tower as a signal to the British, an SS detachment came out from the mainland in three *Schnell* boats, and rounded up and executed the mutineers—an indication of the continuing close co-operation between Dönitz and Himmler. The corpses were interred in an unmarked mass grave outside Cuxhaven.[211]

It is in any case evident from Dönitz's drastic decrees that the Navy had its share of 'defeatists' and what he called 'intellectual weaklings'. On April 11th, almost a fortnight after British and US air strikes against Hamburg and Kiel had destroyed 24 U-boats, including nine of the new Type XXI's, damaged a further twelve and destroyed or seriously damaged three of the six remaining heavy surface units in use in the Baltic operations, he issued a long explanation of why they had to keep on fighting;[212] this repeated the dire predictions about the results of capitulation he had made after the assassination attempt of July 1944,

393

and it is interesting that this time he included the areas 'occupied by the Anglo-Saxons' in his warning: Germans would be drafted as 'work slaves' to all enemy countries—above all of course to Russia. 'Or does anyone think that the Anglo-Saxons will start a war with the Russians on behalf of these men?'

In the Russian-occupied area those elements in all classes liable to resist Bolshevism would be exterminated, but in the Anglo-Saxon areas, too, National Socialists would be violently removed; the intellectual weaklings who now thought about capitulation would be the first to be done away with or freighted off as work slaves; why, he did not explain.

I turn against the irresponsible and short-sighted weaklings who say 'If we had not had National Socialism all this would not have happened.' If we had not had National Socialism we would already have had Communism in Germany, further unemployment and political chaos. Without the rearmament which the Führer brought us Germany would have been trampled over by the Russians in their expansionary push to the west . . .

I turn against the clever people who say we should have avoided the war against Russia in 1941. Had the leadership done that, then the unweakened Russians would have rolled over us long since at a time that suited them. Then these same clever people would have said, 'Yes, the leadership should have prevented it with a timely attack on Russia . . .'

Having next turned himself against dilettante strategists who said that the armies should have withdrawn to Germany in good time, he came to a point that really undermined his case for those with eyes to see; it implied that the war was irretrievably lost. The armies should not have retired, he said: 'Quite the contrary. In this war with such far-ranging weapons as the Air Force, extent of space is decisive in order to hold the enemy as far as possible from the home area and home armaments industry.'

Since Germany's last heavy industrial area, the Saar, had been over-run the previous month, it was a dangerous argument, but he went on in the same vein: '. . . The closer the ring becomes, the greater the enemy pressure on the defence and the greater the effect of the enemy on the remaining area . . . had the whole *Wehrmacht* fully grasped these problems it would have been better.'

394

Did he really believe this, or are the muddled arguments and un-finished explanations a sign of his determination somehow to find rationalizations for the course he had pursued? And after months of closest proximity to Hitler and the few ugly men from his past with whom he now surrounded himself, hearing the expressions of hate and frustration which extended to their own people, could he have believed his next words about the Führer? The answer may be yes. It is impossible to know the extent of his self-deception.

The Führer knows more about the mood of the German people and has given more thought and heartfelt care to the tasks of leadership arising from it than any one of us soldiers. I know that because I see it daily . . .

Alone for years the Führer clearly recognized the danger threatening from Bolshevism. Therefore he did away with our disunity and monstrous unemployment, made us powerful in defence and attempted to enlighten Europe. On the other side stands this hate-blinded Churchill, the gravedigger of English power, who entered the war in order to preserve the balance of power and to pledge himself to the freedom of the small nations. What now remains of this balance of power, and where has the freedom of the small nations gone? Poland and all the other small States of Eastern Europe are provinces of Bolshevik Russia. At the latest in a year's time, perhaps even this year, Europe will learn that Adolf Hitler is the single statesman of stature in Europe. Therefore all negative brooding is unfruitful and objectively incorrect. Because it is born of weakness it cannot be anything else, since cowardice and weakness make one stupid and blind . . .

And he came to the most breathtaking deception; it was only through 'hard endurance' that they could profit from the military and political possibilities to hand. Of the military possibilities, nothing could be said 'without disclosing our immediate intentions to the enemy'; of the political possibilities: 'I should like to say: the blindness of Europe will be torn away one day, bringing psychological help for Germany and with it political possibilities. If we give ourselves up beforehand it is too late for these possibilities. Then we are dead and they are no use any more.'

This passage sounds as if it was lifted straight from Hitler's lips, for Field Marshal Kesselring was briefed by Hitler in the same sense on the next day, April 12th; Kesselring gained the impression that Hitler still expected to be saved; he talked of a coming great victory against the Russians on the Oder, of a new Army he was raising to defeat the western allies, of new secret weapons, and of the coming split between their eastern and western enemies.[213] It was to this last 'political possibility' that Hitler and Goebbels really clung. Hitler spent long periods sitting staring at a portrait of Frederick the Great which went everywhere with him, dwelling on that moment in the Seven Years' War known as the 'miracle of the house of Brandenburg'; this was when Frederick, in an impossible position, ringed by enemies and in despair, was saved by the sudden death of the Tsarina of Russia and a subsequent untying of the alliances against him. Goebbels had taken to reading Hitler extracts from Carlyle's biography of the Prussian hero.

Later that evening, April 12th, a monitored BBC news flash revealed that President Roosevelt had died. Goebbels rang through ecstatically to the Chancellery bunker: '*Mein Führer*, this is the miracle of the house of Brandenburg . . . this is the turning point . . .'[214] Hitler seized on the news hysterically, summoning Speer and Dönitz so that he could tell them himself. 'Who was right! The war is not lost,' his words tumbled out in excitement, 'Read this! Roosevelt is dead.'[215] According to Dönitz's adjutant, Lüdde-Neurath, his chief was not impressed. 'Dönitz replied soberly that in his opinion a favourable outcome for Germany was not to be expected for the time being.'[216] This hardly accords with Dönitz's usual contortions to keep in the Führer's good books, nor with the views on the current situation expressed in his decree only the day before; indeed, if Lüdde-Neurath's account is correct it suggests he employed conscious deception in the decree. There is no reason to accept this however. Lüdde-Neurath's memories, like all others from this period, reveal quite naturally a rather more selective instinct than most recollections.

Returning now to the decree to the Navy of April 11th, Dönitz, having dispensed in the first part with the rationale of the continuing struggle, turned to more basic verities; he demanded that all Flag Officers and Commanders 'clearly and plainly tread the path of soldierly duty', and that all act ruthlessly against any Commander not so doing. If a Commander believed he lacked the spiritual power to do his duty he was to declare it immediately, whereupon he would be reduced to the ranks so as not to be burdened with the tasks of leadership. Thus Dönitz came to what was for him surely the blood-reasoning that overrode analysis:

396

The honour of our flag on board is sacred to us. No one thinks of giving up his ship. Rather go down in honour. That is self-evident to all of us. Exactly so in the land battle. Should it come to the point of having to defend our naval bases, so according to the Führer's order, the place is to be defended to the end. It is then victory or death. The Commander who lacks the spiritual strength for this and wants to weaken has the duty, according to the Führer's order, to question his troops and surrender command to a harder warrior.

The *Kriegsmarine* will fight to the end. Some day its bearing in the severest crisis of this war will be judged by posterity. The same goes for each individual. Earlier deeds are wiped out if, in the decisive hour for which he is a soldier, he fails. Or does anyone believe that the enemy respects one who in cowardice capitulates? Certainly he welcomes him, but he will despise and treat him accordingly.

He then produced a sentence which encapsulates the extraordinary gap between the world he inhabited and, for example, Speer's: 'We must be clear that we have to be the exponents of the will to life of our *Volk*.' Finally he concluded there were no situations which could not be improved by heroic bearing; it was certain that the opposite signified 'dissolution, chaos and inextinguishable shame'.

The striking remark, surely, was his preceding appeal to the judgement of posterity—'the same goes for each individual'—for it applied above all to Dönitz himself. Rarely indeed are individuals tested to the extent and under the pressures that he was tested in these final weeks of the war. And interpretation of the result, as revealed in these April decrees, provides a key to understanding his character that can be applied backwards to the whole of his career.

Interpretations will differ; 'the honour of the flag', 'victory or death' are powerful ideas for which countless numbers have given their lives throughout history. And of course Dönitz had always argued and continued to argue to the end that it was no part of a soldier's duty to question his orders or decide whether there was a purpose in fighting, therefore no part of his duty—certainly not in the Führer system—to question the Führer's orders and the purpose on which they were based. Here is the nub of interpretation for it was the Führer and the Führer system to which he was nailing his colours, and the severity of his ordeal was caused by the fact that he was being tested as a man in a system which relegated men to 'no more than a part, a member and a functionary of the

State'. The words come from the declaration of the German resistance to Hitler, most of whose leaders had been wiped out by this time; this went on to describe the main features of the system as 'the formation of an authoritarian political will, which imposed itself by means of propaganda and violence'.[217]

It is evident that Dönitz had selected himself as one of the chief exponents of the system by his encouragement and support for Hitler. Leaving aside any comment on the system or whether he supported it for personal ambition or through emotional commitment, it is evident that the judgement of posterity which he sought must be recorded in the context of the system, that is of an 'authoritarian political will which imposed itself by propaganda and violence'. Such a system automatically denies principles of loyalty and honour—for who is to tell whether these too are not propaganda? Anyone as close to the Führer and his principal lieutenants for as long as Dönitz who remained unable or unwilling to distinguish between propaganda and closer approximations to the truth must by the same token have been unable to distinguish between loyalty and treason, honour and dishonour; this may have been his misfortune and it may be posterity's judgement, for it seems to accord with what he was doing—had been doing for some time; stripped of fine words, he was harnessing the natural idealism of his young men for a plainly lost cause and sending them out to die to please a tyrant whose egomania was so monstrous he was prepared to sacrifice the entire nation for himself—a precise inversion of what he was demanding from his people.

That Dönitz was a perfect exponent of his system is evident from his next secret decree, issued on April 19th. It concerned an idea close to Hitler's heart, the promotion of petty officers and men who proved themselves leaders by their 'inner bearing and firmness' in difficult situations. And he gave an example:

In a prisoner of war camp for the men of the auxiliary cruiser *Cormoran* in Australia, a petty officer as camp senior, systematically and unsuspected by the guards, did away with Communists who came to his attention amongst the crew. This petty officer is certain of my full recognition for his resolve and his execution. I shall promote him with all means on his return because he has proved he is suitable as a leader.[218]

There were more men like this in the Navy, he went on; he expected

398

all senior officers to take prompt and active measures to advance them.

By April 19th 'Koralle' was almost a ghost camp. Dönitz had ordered the evacuation of the headquarters staff to a new command post at Plön in the north during March, since the expected Russian breakthrough from the Oder towards Berlin must endanger 'Koralle'. He remained with a small personal and communications staff in order to keep in touch with Hitler, whom he visited in the bunker every day; since the opening of a tremendous Russian offensive on the 16th, however, he had put his staff on an hour's readiness to move, and that evening feeling suddenly uneasy, he ordered evacuation. They left shortly before midnight, a small convoy on the road for Berlin, and in the early hours of the 20th set up a makeshift command post in his house in Dahlem—just as Marshal Zhukov's tanks, breaking out of the Oder bridgehead, rolled past his abandoned headquarters.

Later he and Lüdde-Neurath were driven to the Chancellery as they had been every day that week, past the empty windows of burned-out blocks, threading through rubble, around anti-tank barricades manned by youths of Goebbels' newly-recruited *Volkssturm*, slowing for crowds of refugees heading listlessly westwards with bicycles and handcarts or prams with a few belongings. Groups of women and a few girls with wan, tired faces queued outside food shops listening to the thunder of the Russian guns and the shell bursts in the centre of the city. Goebbels had sought to stiffen resistance with tales of Red Army atrocities, and for once had not embroidered the truth; it had been necessary to tone it down. Today was April 20th, Hitler's birthday and a public holiday; the women's eyes reflected fear for the immediate future.

The façade of the new Reichschancellery still stood; inside, the grand marbled and columned reception halls were bare; timber joists and partitions shut off areas damaged by bombs, but great cracks were visible in the ceilings and windows whose panes had been blown out were blanked with cardboard; thin light from others filtered through masonry dust. From outside the multiple shock of bombs was added to the noise of the Russian bombardment as the city came under another daylight raid. Passing through check-points manned by SS guards armed with machine guns, Dönitz and Lüdde-Neurath came to the wrought-iron stairway leading down to the Führer bunker. Lüdde-Neurath records that he reached the bottom just as Hitler emerged from his private quarters. It was his 56th birthday; he looked an old man, 'broken, washed-up, stooped, feeble and irritable'.[219]

All members of the higher leadership were present that afternoon to pay their birthday respects; Hitler received them one after another in order of seniority in his small living room; what passed between him and Dönitz is not known, although afterwards at the daily situation conference, when he was urged by most of those present to leave Berlin before it was too late to fly south to continue the fight from the *Berghof* he charged Dönitz with the defence of North Germany; for it was apparent that the country was about to be cut in two by the meeting of the US and Russian armies in the centre.

The next day, as Lüdde-Neurath prepared the move to the northern headquarters, Dönitz visited the Chancellery bunker again. It was assumed there that everyone would be flying south to the *Berghof* at any moment since the Red Army was closing a ring around the city; time was running out fast and Dönitz was advised to leave; he gained Hitler's permission to do so. What was said, what his feelings were as he took his last leave of the Führer he had served with undeviating loyalty is not known. Speer described Hitler in these last days as almost senile with dragging footsteps and a quavering voice, whose once immaculately kept uniform was 'stained by the food he had eaten with a shaking hand'.[220] The increased shaking and trembling of the left side of his body, especially his hand and arm, was remarked by Gerhardt Boldt, who described his movements as ever more shambling, his posture more bent.[221] To Speer he gave the impression of someone whose purpose had been destroyed, who was going through his routine by habit. Did Dönitz still regard him as *brav und würdig*, the only statesman of stature in Europe? After the capitulation he told his US interrogator that Hitler was a man with an abundance of good heart; 'his mistake was perhaps that he was too noble', too loyal to colleagues 'who had not deserved it'.[222] Perhaps he had to believe something like this.

Was he moved now by the sight of what Hitler had become, was he reinforced in his hatred of the enemy who had done this to his warfather? Or was he, perhaps, simply relieved that he could go away and be his own master in the north? Did Hitler attempt to act up for the last time to the role of wise and imperturbable elder statesman expected by his devoted *Herr Grossadmiral*?

The answers to such questions would be interesting, for after he arrived at his Plön headquarters and added the administration of the

400

northern area to his naval tasks, he continued on his straight path of absolute loyalty. Whether he did so from unshaken faith in the genius of the Führer or because of his service training in obedience, which must have seemed the single solid thing to hold on to in the strong currents pulling towards chaos and disorder, whether he believed Hitler's predictions about the fate of the German race at the hands of the victors, as he appeared to, or feared for his own fate at a war crimes tribunal, or whether as before he buried himself in his wide-ranging new tasks to avoid making ultimate decisions, he was probably as little aware then as we can be now. One thing undoubtedly haunting him was the memory of 1918. Mutiny had to be avoided at all costs; this was a powerful reason for his anxiety to send naval detachments to plug the gaps in Himmler's SS regiments and in these final days he sent Hitler more and more men for the defence of Berlin. Mutiny bred in idleness; employment had to be found for the men who were released from sea-going duties almost daily by the reduction of his surface and U-boat fleet through allied air strikes on the naval bases.

Whatever his mix of reasons, he refused to listen to civilian ministers and the *Gauleiter* through whom he conducted the civil administration when they urged him to open negotiations with the British—the nearest of the western allies—in order to release forces to hold off the Russians. This was what the General Staff of the Army had advocated for a long time, and what Himmler, who had also come to the northern area, was now attempting to bring about through the Swedish Red Cross. Dönitz apparently cut short all discussion on these lines by saying that no one had the right to deviate from the course set by the Führer,[223] and he echoed Hitler's views on the destruction of the German people that must follow capitulation.

In rejecting the idea of a separate peace he was actually closer to reality than the civilians who advised it, much closer than Himmler who was attempting it; for one thing, the allies had made it clear they would accept nothing less than unconditional surrender, and there were no military possibilities of forcing a change of attitude; for another, operational control of the armies was still at least nominally in Hitler's hands, more importantly there were still diehard generals including the Commander in his own northwestern area, Field Marshal Busch, who would have rejected an order from anyone but the Führer; consequently an independent initiative must have produced chaos and Germans fighting Germans. This had been Dönitz's criticism of the July plot; it was even more valid for him now since although vested with plenary powers in his own area, he had no force unconditionally loyal to him except the Navy, which was neither trained, nor for the most part armed for fighting on land. He was in a far tighter position than he had been in Berlin; then it had been at least theoretically possible for him to have acted with Guderian, Speer and Himmler to force Hitler to accept defeat and its consequences. Whether it would have been practically possible in that charged atmosphere in the ominous shadow of Bormann, Kaltenbrunner and Fegelein is a different matter, but in any case he had shown he was only intent on gaining Hitler's favour and feeding his delusions; the others could have expected nothing from him.

The real problem about his attitude in the north was his relationship with Himmler. At the height of his power Himmler had regarded himself as Hitler's natural successor. The legal heir, Göring, was in eclipse; Lüdde-Neurath recalls being told that when Himmler was Dönitz's dinner guest at the *Haus der Marine* in October 1944, an alleged remark by Göring, '*Donnerwetter!* if the assassination had succeeded I would have had to handle things!', had brought shouts of laughter. Then Himmler, suddenly serious, had turned to Dönitz: 'However, one thing is certain, *Herr Grossadmiral*. The *Reichsmarschall* will in no wise be the successor.'[224]

Now Himmler had also fallen from favour, yet there was no doubt of his internal power, nor of his astonishing belief in himself as the natural successor; this was strengthened on April 23rd when Göring was officially stripped of all his offices after sending a message from his southern headquarters which Hitler misconstrued as an attempt to usurp his authority. Himmler's peace feelers were based on the assumption that he would be accepted by the western powers as Head of State. And yet Dönitz's appointment as Führer of the northern sector obviously moved *him* into line for succession. Himmler must have known, moreover, that Dönitz had been spoken of as a possible successor in some quarters in the Reichschancellery at about the time he was being mooted for Göring's job as chief of the *Luftwaffe*.[225] Dönitz, for his part, knew that he could not maintain internal order in his domain without Himmler—which of course Himmler also knew. The situation was extraordinarily delicate.

Just how it worked out in practice is not clear. Dönitz and his apologists afterwards sought to obscure the connection between him and the *Reichsführer SS* in order to distance the Navy from the most notorious organ of Nazi criminality. Yet the two worked closely together, as they had to if total chaos was to be prevented; according to the Commander of Himmler's bodyguard, *SS Obersturmbannführer* Heinz Macher, his chief visited naval headquarters at Plön every morning during these final days.[226]

Naturally they speculated on the succession. Hitler had made his decision not to leave the capital on April 22nd, the day after Dönitz saw him for the last time. The decision was encouraged by Goebbels who was determined to stage a grand Wagnerian finale in the blazing ruins of the city as his last service for the Führer and posterity. The circumstances in which Hitler announced his decision to stay must also have been well known to Dönitz and Himmler since they were the subject of sensational rumour among the operations staff of the High Command, now moved to a temporary headquarters at Neu Roofen, near Rheinsberg, some 60 miles north of Berlin. Hitler's two chiefs of staff, Keitel and Jodl, who had been sent to direct military operations from this command post to instructions dictated from the Chancellery bunker, had witnessed the extraordinary scene. It had started at the daily situation conference; Hitler, raving about treason and disloyalty, his face alternately dead white and suffused with colour, his voice cracking, had slumped back in his seat sobbing and admitting for the first time that the war was lost. 'I shall shoot myself.'[227]

This was hardly Wagnerian, more a simple uncurbed child's ego-tantrum, an exposé of his whole career. It is inconceivable that Himmler had not been fully briefed, and since it was evident that Berlin could not hold out for many days, the question of what would happen when the Führer departed the scene came up frequently in discussion. Dönitz apparently expressed his willingness to serve in a government headed by Himmler. Despite this he was unaware of Himmler's approach to the western powers—at least he expressed complete ignorance when he was asked about it in a call from High Command headquarters, Neu Roofen, on April 28th.[228] A monitored foreign bulletin had just revealed the astounding news there and the fact that the proposals had been rejected on the grounds that surrender must be to the Soviet Union as well. After the call Dönitz contacted Himmler and half an hour later—at 5.20 pm— the *Reichsführer SS* called Neu Roofen to say the news was false!

By this date Dönitz's determined optimism appears to have deserted him; a visit to Keitel's headquarters the previous day, April 27th, had revealed the extent of military disintegration;[229] Commanders in the north were making their own decisions, troops and civilian refugees were flooding westwards with but one thought, not to fall into the hands of the Bolsheviks, and it was evident that the Russian advance from the Oder could not be held. He knew already the precarious fuel and armaments situation; once Mecklenberg was overrun vital stocks of food and ammunition would be lost, and it would be literally impossible to continue the fight; moreover Berlin was encircled—the Russians had joined hands with the Americans to the south of the city—and as noted in the High Command war diary, 'the end of the battle for the *Reich* capital is beginning'.[230]

According to his son-in-law, Günther Hessler, Dönitz returned from Neu Roofen convinced that resistance would soon be impossible, therefore futile, and that there would be no successor to Hitler after the fall of Berlin. He told Hessler in confidence that he proposed to surrender the Navy—presumably after Hitler's death—and, to remove any stain on the flag, seek his own death in battle.[231] According to this account Hessler asked whether it would not be better for him to stand with his authority behind the preservation of order in the dissolving situation, but he replied that the collapse would be so complete it would imply the loss of all values, and it might be important in the future for Germans to know that there had been men with the courage to draw the right conclusions without thought of self. He then dismissed Hessler, told him to regard himself as the head of the family and take care of his wife and daughter.

Lüdde-Neurath records Dönitz making a very similar statement to 'a close circle' two days later: his own death in battle would expiate any charges of cowardice or treachery that might otherwise attach to the Navy in surrender.[232] These accounts ring true as they express both the propaganda emanating from the Führer bunker at the time and the orthodox military view that those who had signed the armistice in 1918 had been traitors. They are also explicable in terms of an inner crisis as reality forced its way into his hitherto impervious world of unconditional loyalty.

On the evening of the 28th the news of Himmler's peace offer to the west was brought down to the Führer bunker by an official of the propaganda ministry who had picked up a Reuter's flash from San Francisco. It was the ultimate sensation—'*der treue* Heinrich' a traitor! Hitler released his feelings of rage and impotence in another frenzied outburst, shambling through the bunker corridors and thrusting the report at anyone he found. He ordered the immediate execution of Himmler's lieutenant, Fegelein, then went into a room where his new chief of the *Luftwaffe*, Ritter von Greim, was recovering from wounds suffered while flying in to the capital to receive the appointment! Hitler ordered him to fly out immediately to Dönitz's headquarters and have Himmler arrested and, his voice quavering with hysteria, liquidated.

Greim, on crutches, was helped up the steps from the bunker, driven a short distance in the glare of the burning city to a waiting light plane, where he and the aviatrix, Hannah Reisch, who had shared his perilous journey in, took off along the wide avenue leading to the Brandenburg Gate—*with* the wind to fox the Russian gunners—just clearing the heroic statuary above.[233] While they were escaping Hitler prepared for the penultimate ceremony in his staged departure, marriage to his long-time mistress, Eva Braun. A champagne reception followed the formalities, then at about two o'clock in the morning of the 29th, Hitler retired to dictate his political testament. He disassociated himself from all responsibility for the war and the millions who had died and suffered; this was the work solely of 'international finance conspirators' of Jewish blood or working for Jewish interests. And after affirming his commitment to end his life in the capital of the people to whom, he said, he had given every thought and act over the past three decades, he consigned Göring and Himmler to the outer darkness for their secret negotiations with the enemy:

> In order to give the German people a government of honourable men to fulfil the duty of continuing the war with all means, I, as Führer of the nation, name the following members of the new Cabinet: Reichspresident, Dönitz; Reichschancellor, Dr Goebbels; Partyminister, Bormann . . .[234]

In the long list of ministerial posts that followed Dönitz was also named as War Minister and as C-in-C Navy. Since Hitler combined in his own person the posts of President and Chancellor, and since he knew that Goebbels, whom he was appointing Chancellor in the new government, was resolved to die with him in the bunker, it appears he intended Dönitz to take over all his own authority as Führer; this is also evident from Dönitz's appointment as War Minister. How long the idea had been gestating is not clear. It is usually held that the decision to appoint Dönitz was only made after Himmler's defection, yet Himmler had been out of favour for some time and it was Dönitz whom Hitler had appointed to

405

take command of the northern area when it seemed that he himself might be flying south. In any case there can be no doubt that Dönitz's appointment was the result of the support, fanatical loyalty and indefatigable will to win over every obstacle he had shown during his time as C-in-C Navy.

Hitler's resolve to stay in the *Reich* capital was in keeping with decisions he had made throughout his career; it placed him in an exposed position from which there was no retreat; it was, for the last time, victory or death. Yet he still clung to the hope of victory, and late that evening, the 29th, sent an anguished message to Keitel, who had been forced by the Russian advance to move his command post further north to Dobbin, near Krakow, asking where the relieving armies were, and when they were going to attack. Keitel, after long consideration, replied with the truth: the 12th Army was held and could not come to the relief of the capital; the 9th Army was surrounded. This was sent early on the 30th;[235] it was taken in the bunker as proof of further treason, and Bormann despatched a message to Dönitz accusing Keitel of allowing the forces around Berlin to stand idle for days, and urging him to act ruthlessly against traitors. He ended that Hitler was still alive and conducting the defence of Berlin from the Chancellery in ruins.

Dönitz had received the new *Luftwaffe* chief, on crutches, and his intrepid mistress the previous day, and had been told that he must arrest Himmler; now he was required to act ruthlessly against Keitel and the High Command. The situation was plainly impossible and if, as Lüdde-Neurath states, he now talked of seeking death in battle it was indeed the only solution to the conflict between loyalty and impotence. To make matters worse, the *Gauleiter* of Hamburg, Kaufmann, had determined to avoid further destruction and loss of life in his already devastated city by surrendering it to the British, if necessary leading his people against any German forces ordered to prevent this. The problem of Hamburg came high on the agenda of his conference with Himmler that day—at all events Lüdde-Neurath states that during the meeting he worked on a wire to be sent to Kaufmann;[236] the message is interesting in showing that despite everything Dönitz was keeping his head and his usual excellent sense of priorities: it stated that the chief task of the military leadership at present was to save German land and people from Bolshevism; for the latter purpose it was essential to keep open a gate to the west across the partition lines between occupation zones agreed by the allies at Yalta, vital therefore to defend the line of the Elbe (thus Hamburg) against the

406

west. The destruction resulting here would be recompensed a thousand-fold by the saving of German blood in the east; therefore this was the best contribution that he, Kaufmann, and Hamburg could make to the 'destiny struggle' of the German people. '*Heil* Hitler!'

It is probable that another reason for this plea to Kaufmann was the hope that if the British could be prevented from advancing to the full extent of their 'zone' as agreed at Yalta, and they saw the Russians sweeping into the territory from the east, it might trigger the expected break in the alliance; at all events this hope was still very much alive at Keitel's headquarters at Dobbin, where Jodl was saying that fighting had to be continued 'in order to win political time'—translated in the High Command war diary as 'a split between the Soviets and the western allies'.[237]

In Berlin, meanwhile, Hitler, confronted with reports of Russian tanks only a few blocks from the Reichschancellery, and knowing that there were no relieving armies on the way, finally gave up hope. Shortly after 3.00 that afternoon, he and his new wife made their farewells to the bunker residents then retired into his private quarters to execute their suicide compact; they arranged themselves at either end of a small settee; he clamped his teeth over a poison capsule and more or less simultaneously pulled the trigger of a Walther pistol placed to his right temple, she bit into her poison capsule as she heard the shot. Some minutes later shocked aides entered the chamber, after which the two bodies were carried up to the shell-pocked Chancellery garden and cremated according to his previous instructions.

Some two hours later Bormann sent Dönitz a message usually re-garded as intentionally ambiguous, since it made no mention of Hitler's death:

> *Grossadmiral* Dönitz. In place of the former *Reichsmarschall* Göring, the Führer appoints you, *Herr Grossadmiral* as his successor. Written authority on the way. You should immediately take all measures which the current situation requires. Bormann.[238]

This was received at Plön at 6.35 pm. It was Dönitz's first intimation of Hitler's choice of successor. He was stunned. Speer, who had come to Plön to discuss matters, was present when Lüdde-Neurath handed him the message, and he too was surprised; according to Lüdde-Neurath it took him a moment or two to recover and offer his congratulations. The question then was, how would Himmler take the news! Obviously it was necessary to take precautions, and after sending a radio message to Himmler's headquarters asking him to come at once to Plön, Lüdde-Neurath sought out *Korvettenkapitän* Ali Cremer, a U-boat ace of daring and charisma, who was commanding the detachment of U-boat men guarding the naval headquarters. 'He won't like our chief becoming the Führer's successor,' Lüdde-Neurath said, 'We must be prepared for anything.' They surrounded the headquarters building with armed men, having them hide behind trees in order not to arouse the *Reichsführer*'s suspicions.[239]

This was a gross underestimation of Himmler's nose for trouble. He had just returned to headquarters from his meeting with Dönitz, the chief of his personal bodyguard, Heinz Macher, recalled years later. It had taken a long time because of the constant allied air attacks along the roads, and as soon as he saw the message he said, 'Macher, this I don't like. We've just left him. Something must have happened. Please take enough men.'[240]

Macher, a battle-hardened, highly decorated veteran of the killer SS division, *Das Reich*, picked 36 men, 'the most piratical, bravest and most experienced warriors to be had in the whole of Germany'! They left with the *Reichsführer* on the return journey to Plön in a column of open Volkswagens and armoured troop carriers, arriving in darkness with only the faintest moon illuminating the blacked-out buildings. Macher immediately sensed that something was wrong, and went out first alone; walking up the path, he saw a lone officer coming to meet him, the glint of a Knight's Cross at his throat; this was Cremer. Macher half-turned and, making out Cremer's men hiding by the trees behind, thought to himself, 'Oh God, those poor bastards! We'll blow them away with the greatest of ease.'[241]

There was no bloodshed, however; Himmler was escorted to Dönitz's room and the two were left by themselves while Macher and two SS adjutants were entertained by Lüdde-Neurath and Cremer in a canteen next door. What was said at the meeting will never be known. Himmler did not live long enough to tell the story, Dönitz's account is brief and melodramatic; he had, he wrote, taken the precaution of hiding his pistol with the safety catch off under some papers on his desk. He handed Himmler the message form and asked him to read it, watching his face as he did so. It expressed great surprise, dismay, and became very pale. Then Himmler stood, bowed and said, 'Allow me to be the second man

408

in your State.' Dönitz told him there was no question of this; he had no use for him—after which Himmler left. It was one o'clock in the morning.[242]

Whether or not Himmler adapted himself to the situation as quickly and thoroughly as the story implies cannot be known; it is not impossible; he was a man of limited intelligence whose career had been built on the foundation of the Führer's absolute authority. Once that foundation was removed it is likely he would have felt lost and have offered his services to the man the Führer had chosen to succeed. It is inconceivable, however, that Dönitz responded so brusquely. He had been co-operating closely with Himmler and whatever he thought or felt could not afford to alienate him and the ruthless fighters and police forces under his command; had he been in the strong position his story implies he should have arrested and executed him the previous day when von Greim and Hannah Reisch gave him Hitler's instructions to do so. Instead, at his next meeting with the *Reichsführer SS*, according to Lüdde-Neurath's account, he had discussed Hamburg and probably other security matters in the usual way.

Whatever they said to each other it was not the short interview Dönitz described; they talked through the night while in the canteen the adjutants drank quantities of Hennessy brandy together. Macher recalled it was sunrise before they parted and his companions had breakfast at Plön and met Ritter von Greim and Hannah Reisch, who were still there, before they started back.

The time Himmler arrived the previous evening is not known; it is not possible to say whether he was there when Lüdde-Neurath phoned through to the military High Command headquarters and summoned Keitel and Jodl to Plön as soon as possible; this call was logged at 10.15 pm.[243] It is not even possible to state definitely that he had arrived by 1.22 am when Dönitz sent a reply to Bormann, but it must be assumed he had—indeed Dönitz records Himmler *leaving* at one o'clock. It is almost certain, therefore, that this message to Bormann went out during their long discussion. Dönitz and Lüdde-Neurath both omitted it from their accounts, but it suggests that Dönitz's former ideas of capitulation with the Navy and seeking his own death in battle had altered since hearing of his appointment as Hitler's successor.

Close colleagues like Godt had noticed a dramatic change in him after receipt of the message. Almost certainly this can be ascribed to clarification of the chaotic command structure; he had been in the impossible position of responsibility virtually without power; now he had supreme authority. As he recorded later, 'A weight fell from my heart.'[244]

> *Mein Führer!* My loyalty to you will be unshakeable. I will therefore undertake further attempts to relieve you in Berlin. If fate nevertheless compels me to lead the German *Reich* as your appointed successor, I will conduct this war to an end befitting the uniquely heroic battle of the German *Volk*. *Grossadmiral* Dönitz.[245]

Bormann replied from the bunker at 7.40 am:

> *Grossadmiral* Dönitz. Testament in force. I will come to you as quickly as possible. Until then, in my opinion, withhold publication. Bormann.[246]

This reached Dönitz, who must have been hollow-eyed from lack of sleep, shortly before 11.00 that morning. May 1st. He ordered a thorough investigation by the legal department of the authenticity of the message with its implication that Hitler was dead, and when the results proved positive, assumed the office of Führer of what remained of the Third Reich.

Shortly after 3 o'clock that afternoon a last confirmatory message arrived from the Chancellery bunker:

> *Grossadmiral* Dönitz. Führer died yesterday 1530. Testament of 29.4 transfers to you the office of Reichspresident, Dr Goebbels the office of Reichschancellor, *Reichsleiter* Bormann the office of Partyminister, Reichsminister Seyss-Inquart the office of Foreign Minister. On the orders of the Führer the testament has been sent out of Berlin to you, to Field Marshal Schörner and for preservation for publication. *Reichsleiter* Bormann intends coming to you today to clarify the position. Form and time of announcement to the troops and public is left to you. *Confirm receipt.*   *Goebbels   Bormann.*[247]

CHAPTER SEVEN

The Last Führer

DÖNITZ WAS PRODUCT as well as last leader of the Third Reich; inevitably, therefore, he opened his account with a gigantic lie. This concerned the manner of Hitler's death. He knew it was suicide. Hitler had told both Speer and Ritter von Greim that he intended to take this course since he could not risk being wounded and captured to be tried and made sport of by the enemy. Undoubtedly Dönitz was told this by both men. It was clear, too, from the last message from Goebbels and Bormann that he had committed suicide, for they had used the word *verschieden*—deceased; if he had died in battle they would unquestionably have used *gefallen*.

While Dönitz had been talking to Himmler in the early hours of May 1st, Speer had been working on a draft announcement of the succession, starting, 'The Führer has remained in Berlin fighting against Bolshevism. . . . We hope that after his death . . .'[1] If adopted, such a formula would have served propaganda and the facts. It was not sufficiently stirring for Dönitz.

German radio that night prepared the people for a 'serious and important mesage' with excerpts from Wagner and Bruckner's seventh symphony, then at three minutes past ten, following rolls of drums, came the announcement, Adolf Hitler, in his command post, fighting to his last breath against Bolshevism, *'für Deutschland gefallen ist'*. Dönitz's address immediately afterwards reinforced the message:[2]

German men and women, soldiers of the German armed forces! Our Führer, Adolf Hitler has fallen. In deepest grief and respect the German people bow. He early recognized the frightful danger of Bolshevism and dedicated his being to this struggle. At the end of this, his struggle, and his unswerving direct life's path, stands his hero's death in the capital of the German *Reich*. His life was a unique service for Germany. His mission in the battle against the

Bolshevist storm-flood is valid for Europe and the entire civilized world.

The Führer has appointed me as his successor. In consciousness of the responsibiiity, I take over the leadership of the German *Volk* at this fateful hour . . .

His first task, he went on, was to save German men from the advancing Bolshevik enemy; it was only for this purpose that the military struggle had to be continued; so long as the British and Americans hindered this they too had to be fought. He praised his listeners for what they had achieved in battle and borne in the homeland and asked them to help him by maintaining order and discipline. 'Only thus will we mitigate the suffering which the coming days will bring to each one of us, and prevent collapse,' and he ended, 'If we do what is in our power God will not abandon us after so much suffering and sacrifice.'

The appeal to trust in God was a striking departure from Nazi philosophy. Could it be that a residual core of belief, to be found perhaps in most sailors who have witnessed His wonders and felt their own puniness in crisis, was surfacing in him at this ultimate crisis? Or was he advised that the majority of the people had turned against the 'brown pest' of Nazism which had brought them to their present condition? Or was it simply that Providence seemed too impersonal a concept to rescue Germany from the misery it had brought?

Afterwards Dönitz issued an order of the day to the *Wehrmacht*:

German armed forces! My comrades!

The Führer has fallen. True to his great idea to preserve the peoples of Europe from Bolshevism, he committed his life and found a hero's death. With him, one of the greatest heroes of German history has gone. In proud respect and grief we lower the colours before him.

The Führer has appointed me as his successor as Head of State and as Commander in Chief of the armed forces. I take over command of all arms of the services with the intention of continuing the battle against the Bolshevists until the fighting forces and the hundreds of thousands of families of the German east are saved from slavery or destruction.

Against the English and Americans I must continue the fight for as far and as long as they hinder me in the execution of the battle against the Bolshevists.

412

The position demands from you, who have alrady performed such great historical deeds, and who presently long for the end of the war, further unconditional commitment. I demand discipline and obedience. Only by execution of my orders without reservation will chaos and collapse be avoided. Who now avoids his duty and thereby brings death or enslavement to German women and children is a coward and a traitor.

The oath of loyalty which you gave to the Führer is now due from each one of you to me as the Führer's appointed successor . . .[3]

This was his trump card over Himmler, and the chief reason he had had Bormann's message from the bunker examined by his legal department, who had taken sworn statements from the communications personnel. The loyal oath had an inner significance as potent as flag or Fatherland. He ended: 'German soldiers, do your duty. It is for the life of our people!'

The military situation as he made this appeal was catastrophic: the greater part of the Fatherland and the capital had been overrun; resistance was confined to his own small area in the north, including the peninsula of Schleswig-Holstein and German-occupied Denmark, and a completely separated southern area under the overall military command of Field Marshal Kesselring, including western Czechoslovakia, the mountainous southern region of Bavaria and what remained of Mussolini's puppet state in northern Italy. There were two separated and beleaguered armies on the Baltic coast, one in Kurland, the other in East Prussia now confined to a narrow coastal strip around the Gulf of Danzig; neither had any hope of holding out for long; the only question was how many men could be evacuated to the west before they had to surrender to the Red Army. The only other significant areas outside Germany and Denmark where the German writ still ran were western Holland and Norway.

The position could not be conveyed in simple territorial terms, however; the *Luftwaffe* was virtually grounded for lack of fuel and the western allies had total command of the air over land and sea; moreover, the process of disintegration of the German armed forces, weary of continuing an apparently purposeless struggle, had reached an advanced stage; more and more Commanders were making their own decisions to lead their units west to surrender to the British and Americans; as the High Command war diary put it that day, 'Hitler is dead and in these last

413

hours of the war each German is understandably only striving not to fall into the hands of the Russians.'[4]

This constituted a genuine dilemma. Germans in the east were reaping at the hands of the Red Army what Hitler and the SS had sown: rape and crucifixion, hideous slaughter of all ages and sexes were no fictions of propaganda, nor, in view of what Speer and his collaborators had done for the sake of German war production, was the fear of enslavement just an emotive stimulus to continuing the struggle. Dönitz and his advisers had every reason to believe it would be a reality, and his remarks a few days later about the consequences of surrendering the eastern armies— hence the German civilians they were shielding—were not rhetoric: 'No German of honour could associated his name with this [capitulation]. The curse of millions would outlaw his name and history would brand him a traitor.'[5]

It is evident from his decisions from his first day in office that other reasons for continuing the struggle, notably because it was the will of the Führer, or to prevent the dishonour of capitulation and the brand-mark this would stamp on his name for evermore, appeared to fall away miraculously at the news of Hitler's death. It was an extraordinary transformation: Speer, who witnessed it from close quarters, recalls, 'The objectivity of the trained officer [now] came uppermost. From the first hour Dönitz was of the opinion that we had to wind up the war as quickly as possible.'[6]

Speer had undoubtedly played a part in this sea-change; he had been a frequent visitor to Plön during the past few days, and before that his behaviour and attitude must have shown Dönitz there were other views with, perhaps, as much validity as Hitler's. The uncharacteristic pessimism into which he had sunk over the past two or three days probably owed as much to inner conflict between Speer's brand of realism and his own brand of loyalty to Hitler as to the impossible command structure in his area. It had been the outward sign of inner ferment; finally Hitler's death released him from the spell of nihilism.

It would probably be wrong, however, to trust too far to Speer's and also Lüdde-Neurath's recollections about an immediate decision to wind up the war as quickly as possible. The adviser who had more influence over him at this stage was Jodl, whose intelligence and military judgement he respected. Jodl still believed that the inevitable break between the eastern and western enemies might be engineered in these final days before all was lost. And Dönitz, for all the scepticism he had shown

414

about this idea in his April decree and for all his later denials, must have thought it inconceivable that the western powers could remain blind to the Communist threat, now that the Russians were poised to storm over the zone boundaries agreed at Yalta. The attempt to stall for 'political time' pulled in the same direction as the necessity to rescue as many troops and German civilians as possible from Kurland, East Prussia and Czechoslovakia, hence his decision to continue fighting the western powers.

In view of the war weariness of the population and a majority of his forces, and the vulnerability of both to slaughter from the air, it was a dangerous game, and only possible under sanction of the severest penalties. He had never shrunk from that. Just as young sacrifices to the Führer dangled from trees and lamp posts in central Berlin, so grisly offerings spread among the trees on the plain of Mecklenberg and in Schleswig-Holstein.

It was on this night of May 1st, after hearing Dönitz's voice on the radio, 'Our Führer, Adolf Hitler, has fallen . . . but the fight must go on . . .' that Heinrich Jaenecke and other young naval ratings fresh from school sprang out of the windows of their barracks and away over the fields:

We wanted to allow the Grand Admiral to conduct his war to the end alone. We came through villages in which deserters hung from the trees. The farmers warned us against the naval *Jagdkommandos*: 'They are worse than the SS, they do you in without asking questions . . .'[7]

Besides summary lynchings by the *Kettenhunde*, juridical sentences of death passed by naval courts for mutiny and desertion continued to be carried out.[8]

The next day, May 2nd, Himmler arrived at Dönitz's headquarters and was invited to lunch.[9] He brought news that Gauleiter Kaufmann was still intent on surrendering Hamburg without a fight; this enraged Dönitz; if everyone acted on their own, he said, there was no point to his office, and he agreed to Speer's offer to drive to Hamburg to talk it out with Kaufmann. At this stage it seems, therefore, he was still intent on holding off the west to gain political time. During the afternoon, however, it was discovered that both British and US forces had stormed from the Elbe right across the base of the Schleswig-Holstein peninsula to the Baltic coast, a move ordered by the Supreme Commander in the west, General Eisenhower, to prevent the Russians taking the Schleswig-Holstein peninsula. This removed the political reason for continuing the fight against the Anglo-Saxons in the north and Dönitz decided to try a strategy of local capitulation—again favoured by Jodl who was at Plön that afternoon for a situation conference. The idea was to get around the allied refusal to accept anything but unconditional surrender on all fronts, while still buying time to continue the rescue of the easterners. He decided to send *Generaladmiral* von Friedeberg—whom he had appointed C-in-C Navy after his own assumption of supreme power— as head of a delegation to the British Commander, Field Marshal Montgomery.

The brief he drew up for the mission was:

Strive to save as many German soldiers and civilians as possible from Bolshevism and enslavement. Therefore withdrawal of Army Group *Weichsel* [from the eastern front] into the Anglo-Saxon power sphere. Preservation from destruction and starvation of the men gathered in the Schleswig-Holstein area. Provision of medical supplies in these areas. Preservation of major places from destruction by bombardment. In addition strive to find formulae for preserving Central and North Europe from further chaos.[10]

The latest allied advances made it imperative to move his headquarters further north, and he arranged to meet von Friedeberg to give him his instructions on his way that day; meanwhile Jodl had instructions phoned through to Kaufmann explaining that it was not now intended to defend Hamburg; German forces would disengage over the Elbe without fighting.

The site Dönitz had chosen for his next and last command post was the Navy cadet school at Mürwik, near Flensburg, at the far north of the Schleswig-Holstein peninsula, and he drove there that evening with the man he was appointing his Foreign Minister, Count Schwerin von Krosigk; a noble from an ancient family, von Krosigk had been a Rhodes scholar at Oxford before the First War, becoming for a while a convinced Fabian Socialist, had reverted to more natural conservative colours during the Republic, then served Hitler faithfully as a finance minister— for example settling the sums Jews were required to hand over after their property had been savaged in the notorious *Kristallnacht* rampage—

while remaining apparently a devout Christian and friend of the leading members of the German resistance—an epitome of the moral collapse of old Germany. He and Dönitz had to dive for the ditch during the journey as they were strafed by low-flying aircraft and no doubt they passed wrecked and burning vehicles and drove by crowds of civilian refugees interspersed with troop detachments trudging silently from the enemy.[11] It was not until nine that evening that they reached the bridge over the Kiel Canal where von Friedeberg was waiting.

Quarters had been arranged for Dönitz aboard the modern motor passenger ship, *Patria*, berthed in Flensburg harbour, and the following morning, May 3rd, Speer joined him for breakfast aboard. Keitel and Jodl had travelled to Flensburg in the early hours to set up their headquarters there, as had Himmler. Whatever Dönitz had said to him during their long night session, the *Reichsführer SS* still attended at his headquarters in the full panoply of office, travelling in a retinue of high SS officers and bodyguard in convoys of staff cars; moreover, he believed, or said he believed, he would become Dönitz's Chancellor, and was still included or included himself in policy discussions. Speer, for instance, obtained permission from Dönitz that morning to broadcast a speech to the German people to rouse them from despair and lethargy and encourage them to start the work of reconstruction necessary for their livelihood after the war. Himmler accosted him, according to his memoirs, in the transmitting studio and objected to the proposed speech on the grounds that it would give the enemy the idea they were prepared to give up without a fight, whereas he believed that they should bargain for concessions with the enemy, using occupied Denmark and Norway as bargaining counters. An SS officer acted as liaison at Dönitz's headquarters and the implication of the story is that, whatever Speer and others said subsequently about Himmler wandering about in a fantasy world at this time, he was still in the governing circle working closely with Dönitz. This is confirmed by the fact that as reports came in that day of increasing war weariness, the commanding general Northwest, Field Marshal Busch, was charged with maintaining order in Schleswig-Holstein, while Himmler retained responsibility for all other areas.[12]

At ten that morning Dönitz conferred with the Party chiefs of Norway and Denmark, together with the Supreme Commanders of German forces in both countries, and his own military and civilian advisers, Keitel, Jodl, von Krosigk and Speer. Himmler's view that Denmark and

Norway were valuable bargaining counters was strongly represented; so were the extreme views still held by many officers that Dönitz should move his headquarters to one of the Scandinavian countries, or south to Prague, to lead the fight to the bitter end in the spirit of Hitler's last stand in Berlin; Dönitz had already been reproved by Busch for acting against Hitler's intention in seeking local capitulation; at this conference the military not only took the view that resistance should be continued outside Germany, but the Commander in Denmark, General Lindemann, spoke of 'the last decent battle of this war'.[13] It was left to the civilians to argue against such staggering irresponsibility. They pointed to the further destruction of German lives, industries and communications, the plight of the wounded and the refugees streaming into Schleswig-Holstein from the east, the shortage of medical facilities, the certainty of partisan risings behind the lines and the probability that Sweden would intervene militarily if they were to make a 'frivolous' stand in the north.[14]

Dönitz, uncertain how the negotiations with Montgomery would turn out, reserved his decision; in the meantime he sent Godt and Hessler to Norway to report on the situation, which presumably means that he had not ruled out the possibility of moving there. Meanwhile he ordered the evacuation of refugees and wounded from Schleswig-Holstein into Denmark and had all available forces deployed to defend the peninsula along the line of the Kiel Canal. That afternoon he received the *Reich* Commissioner for Holland, Seyss-Inquart, who had made the journey in a *Schnell* boat; again he could only reserve his decision about continuing the fight until the outcome of von Friedeberg's negotiations was known; he did, however, instruct Seyss-Inquart not to carry out inundations or demolitions, another sign that despite the delusions and atavistic lust for destruction still gripping many about him, he was taking rational decisions from a viewpoint rather closer to his civilian than to his military advisers.

The idea of area surrenders had already been agreed in principle by the allies, consequently von Friedeberg's mission met with more success than Dönitz probably expected. Montgomery would not accept the surrender of the forces fighting on the eastern front, however, and when von Friedeberg told him that no German would willingly surrender to the Russians, for they were savages and he would be deported to Siberia, he was cut short; 'The Germans should have thought of all these things before they began the war.'[15] The terms he demanded were unconditional surrender and the handing over of all arms in the north-western area, including Holland and Denmark and the islands.

Von Friedeberg returned to Flensburg that evening and his report was considered in a conference early the following morning, May 4th; since the terms fulfilled the prime requirements of halting the destruction in the north while allowing continuation of the struggle to save Germans from the east, there was little disagreement; concern was shown by the military about the stain on the honour of the *Wehrmacht* if arms and ships were handed over to the enemy intact, and Jodl argued for the retention of 'trump cards' such as Holland and Heligoland. Dönitz took the rational view though and von Friedeberg was sent back to Montgomery with authority to sign the terms demanded.

Dönitz's conversion was shown by three other instructions that day; an order was sent to the garrison Commander on Rügen that he was not to defend the island against the Russians, but to evacuate as many men as possible, then surrender, another order forbade destruction or scuttling of ships,[16] and what must have been the most difficult order of all went out to his U-boat Commanders to surrender their boats. This came as such a surprise after his recent edicts about fighting to the last that many seem to have wondered at first whether the enemy had penetrated the cipher system and faked the message.[17]

My U-boat men!

Six years of U-boat war lie behind us. You have fought like lions. A crushing material superiority has forced us into a narrow area. A continuation of our fight from the remaining basis is no longer possible.

U-boat men! Undefeated and spotless you lay down your arms after a heroic battle without equal. We remember in deep respect our fallen comrades, who have sealed with death their loyalty to Führer and Fatherland.

Comrades! Preserve your U-boat spirit, with which you have fought courageously, stubbornly and imperturbably through the years for the good of the Fatherland.

Long live Germany!   Your Gr. Admiral.[18]

Stunning as such a message from 'the Lion' appeared, most officers must have felt extraordinary relief; it is certain their crews did. A few officers, like Schnee in command of one of the two Type XXI boats to have put out on operations in the very last days, probably felt cheated; Schnee made a dummy attack on a convoy to satisfy himself that he could approach and escape undetected, before heading back for Norway. The Commander of one of the smaller Type XXIIIs made a real attack and sunk a merchantman three days later, the last 'success' of the campaign that had started with the sinking of the *Athenia* so long ago. Some made for neutral harbours, two crossed the Atlantic to Argentina, five made for Japanese waters, most returned home or to allied ports.

For those already at home, preparations had been made for scuttling when the code-word *Regenbogen* was issued. According to Lüdde-Neurath it never was; two U-boat commanders called to see Dönitz about the matter that night, he wrote, but he told them that the Grand Admiral was not available; he also let slip a remark that he knew what he (himself) would do under the circumstances. This was taken as the signal to go ahead and a number of boats in the bases were scuttled.[19] This tale must be treated with caution, particularly as the cease-fire was not due to come into force until 8.00 on the morning of the 5th, by which time the deed had been done. However, it is apparent there was a good deal of confusion. One officer received the code-word *Regenbogen* at between 3.00 and 5.00 in the morning of May 5th, but by the time he had arrived to carry it out, the order had been countermanded. When he and one of his comrades decided they would scuttle their boats in any case, he was warned by his chief that he would be shot if he did so.[20]

The probability is that, whoever issued the code-word, Dönitz later sent a countermanding order. Certainly after the local armistice came into force at 8 o'clock there is ample evidence that he was not prepared to jeopardize it by breaking either the letter of the spirit of the terms. When a fanatical Party member started using Radio Wilhelmshaven that morning to call for opposition to the armistice and resistance to the end, he ordered energetic action against him, and strict orders were sent out later that day banning the *Werwolf* organization which had been set up to continue resistance on partisan lines in occupied Germany.[21] Officers also seem to have been bound on their word of honour not to scuttle their vessels.[22]

He had no intention of giving up the struggle to save the easterners, however; all naval and merchant shipping that was still serviceable was engaged in a massive 'Dunkirk' operation to bring back soldiers and refugees from the Baltic coast, and his orders to the troops fighting in southern and central areas remained uncompromising: 'Anyone who selfishly thinks only of his own safety and that of his unit makes the rescue of the whole [from Bolshevism] impossible. He is a traitor to the German people and will be dealt with accordingly.'[23]

The overall Commander in the south, Field Marshal Kesselring, had been forced to sign an armistice in the Italian theatre shortly after Dönitz's assumption of power, but Eisenhower let him know that any attempt to negotiate a local ceasefire with US forces in Germany while continuing to fight against the Russians would fail. Von Friedeberg was sent to Eisenhower's headquarters to try and change his mind, but he received the same answer: surrender must be unconditional and on all fronts simultaneously, including the Russian. When his report reached Flensburg on the morning of May 6th, Dönitz sent Jodl to try his hand.

Jodl flew to Rheims with a strong brief: it was Dönitz's intention to conclude the war as rapidly as possible; however, he was not prepared to sign his eastern armies into slavery, nor would it be possible for him to do so since 'no power on earth' could force the troops facing the Russians to lay down their arms so long as any escape route remained to the west. Therefore, even if he were to agree to unconditional surrender on all fronts he would be unable to enforce it; he would then be represented as a treaty breaker and the treaty would be void. It was to request aid in solving this dilemma that he (Jodl) had come to the Americans.[24]

How much hope was placed in this appeal to the humanitarian sentiment of the west is impossible to determine. The US forces had recently liberated the concentration camp at Buchenwald, and no secret was made of the shock and disgust induced by the sight of the inmates. General Patton, visiting the camp, had been so struck he had given instructions that the entire population of the neighbouring city of Weimar should also visit it to see for themselves the horrors perpetrated in their name. Von Friedeberg was given copies of the service paper, *Stars and Stripes*, containing pictures of the heaped corpses there and the walking skeletons who so closely resembled them to take back to Flensburg. It was not a good time for appeals to sentiment. Jodl soon realized this. General Bedell Smith, acting for Eisenhower, accused him of playing a dangerous game. The war had been lost when the Rhine was crossed, yet the German leadership still counted on a split between the allies; it had not occurred and a one-sided armistice with the western powers was totally impossible. He brushed aside Jodl's arguments about the troops not obeying orders to lay down their arms, and gave him an ultimatum: either he signed today or negotiations would be broken off,

421

bombing recommenced and the allied lines would be closed to troops from the east seeking surrender. He was given half an hour to decide.[25]

When Jodl reported this response back to Flensburg, together with his own opinion that there was no alternative to signing, it was evident the end had come: Jodl had always been the sternest opponent of unconditional surrender; if he could see no other way, there could be none. After a conference late that night he was sent an answer at 1.30 in the morning of May 7th: '*Grossadmiral* Dönitz gives full authority for signing terms as communicated.'[26]

In Rheims victory parties were already under way. The wheel had turned full circle. Did Dönitz think of a message he had received in his headquarters hut on the outskirts of Wilhelmshaven shortly before noon on September 3rd, 1939, 'Total Germany'?

At 2.30 that morning Jodl signed the terms of unconditional surrender in all areas to come into force at midnight on May 8th.

It is impossible to determine how many troops and refugees were saved from the Russians during the eight days Dönitz managed to prolong the fighting; a figure of some two million is often given. If so, this includes all those troop detachments and refugees who made their way overland from the eastern fronts on their own initiative. So far as the rescue operations at sea were concerned the figure of two million applies to those transported over three months between January and the capitulation; many more were evacuated in the following weeks and others continued to make their way back from the southern areas, where fighting against the Russians and partisans went on, as Dönitz had predicted, long after the ceasefire. Many more went into Russian captivity.

Whatever the figure, it is certain that no balance can be struck between those saved from the east and those killed in the continued fighting or summarily executed for desertion; nor can the terror and spreading chaos of those final days ever be measured. There are only the subjective impressions of individuals—Heinrich Jaenecke for instance, whose war ended in a meadow in Holstein when he saw an approaching British jeep with four soldiers inside wearing webbing belts.

A deep feeling of liberation, of freedom arose. In a second everything, the whole dreadful edifice of fear and destruction in which we had lived, collapsed. It was ended. We lay in this meadow in Holstein and

422

looked at one another. The tears ran down our cheeks, then we laughed until we were hoarse. It was the happiest moment of my youth.[27]

After the capitulation Dönitz had no idea of what the allies intended doing with him and the 'government' he had assembled from former ministers; his uncertainty was reflected in his last speech to the German people on May 8th, in which he announced the unconditional surrender and urged everyone to face the difficult times ahead with 'dignity, courage and discipline'.[28]

Already, however, his guidelines were clear; they were to distance himself and his administration from the crimes of the Nazi Party, to represent the Germany services as having fought heroically with no stain on their honour, their leaders as unpolitical soldiers who had simply done their duty. Preparations on these lines had been underway for months in the various services; incriminating documents had been weeded, although not always very efficiently because of the difficult conditions.

As a part of the show, on May 6th dismissal notices had been drawn up for the most notorious Nazi leaders, including Goebbels—whose suicide with his wife in Berlin after her macabre murder of their five children in the bunker was not yet known. Himmler was the most difficult case; his forces had been an integral part of the recent fight against internal chaos, and probably Dönitz felt he owed him loyalty from their relationship in better days. At all events he received him at 5.00 in the afternoon of the 6th to give him the news personally that he was stripped of all his offices.

There can be little doubt that Himmler was prepared for this, and that the two men had made previous preparations, for a large number of the SS officers gathered around the *Reichsführer* at Flensburg were soon, if not already, furnished with papers as naval petty officers or ratings and the uniforms to go with them. When Himmler, apparently in the best of humour—and it must be assumed that this was after his meeting with Dönitz—gave them their last order to 'dive for cover in the *Wehrmacht*'[29] they lost no time in doing so. One was Rudolf Höss, the notorious Commandant of the Auschwitz extermination camp; he became boatswain's mate Franz Lang with orders to report to the Navy Intelligence School on Sylt;[30] the rest of his section also 'dived' into the *Kriegsmarine*. It is inconceivable that this could have happened without Dönitz's knowledge and agreement—yet it was a risk. In view of the efforts that were to be devoted to clearing the Navy of complicity in the crimes of the Party one wonders whether this last service for the *Reichsführer* was done from loyalty to him and the Party he represented, or because he knew too much to be trifled with. In this connection Heinz Macher, chief of Himmler's bodyguard, tells an intriguing story of a naval party sent to arrest his chief about this time:

> . . . a hand-picked naval troop came very near our quarters. I just lined up my men, grim-faced warriors to be sure, and then I said to these naval people, 'Take a look at them!' and that was that![31]

Whether this was Dönitz's idea, or that of his administration, attempting to distance themselves from the architect of the concentration camp atrocities, or whether it occurred earlier as a result of Hitler's orders via von Greim and Hannah Reisch to liquidate Himmler for treachery, it would have been to the advantage of many if the *Reichsführer SS* had 'disappeared'. As it turned out they need not have worried. In this ultimate crisis Himmler proved far from the ice-cool exemplar of Nordic virtues that Hitler had portrayed. He neither led his men in a last fight they had been expecting against the invading hordes of the 'Jewish Capitalist' and 'Jewish Bolshevik' conspiracy, nor, seeing the collapse of the ideals for which he had steeled himself to sacrifice so many millions of men, women and children, did he sacrifice himself; he shaved off his moustache, adopted a black eye-patch and a false name and wandered southwards with a few other high SS officers also in disguise. When eventually they walked into a security patrol he announced himself as Heinrich Himmler then, apparently upset by a question about Belsen concentration camp, bit on the phial he carried in his mouth and died a grotesquely protracted and humiliating death as his captors struggled to prevent him swallowing the poison.

Dönitz and the members of his administration showed up in little better light; the single exception was Albert Speer. His motives have been questioned, nevertheless he is the only one to have left any visible record of having understood the scale of the moral catastrophe and to be prepared to take his share of the responsibility.

The physical destruction of great parts of the nation and the financial and social disintegration were beyond description: William Shirer, arriving in Berlin a few months later, found the city 'destroyed almost beyond recognition', the 'conquering people who were so brutally arrogant and so blindly sure of their mission as the master race when I departed from here five years ago', now 'broken, dazed, shivering, hungry' as they foraged among the ruins.[32]

Such was the physical plight of the people; only Speer, apparently, saw their moral plight, and the moral legacy they would leave to future generations of Germans. He was the only one to call for an administration not formed wholly of men tainted with the guilt of the regime and to offer his own resignation, the only one to be able to escape from the mental gaol of the Third Reich and see it from the outside.

Dönitz's reaction could have been predicted from his career—*he* had not been wrong; Göring for his voluptuous life and gross failure with the *Luftwaffe*, Ribbentrop for his failure to understand either the British mind or foreign policy, Raeder for not building U-boats instead of battleships and, when he had built them, not building them fast enough— these were his favourite scapegoats. He himself had only followed the path of his soldier's duty to the uttermost; furthermore, if he had had enough U-boats at the start, he *would have won*!

No doubt these were very human reactions to guilt and disaster, but they hardly matched the scale of events. The truth is that had he been of a stature to rise to the challenge now confronting Germany, he would not have been where he was, Hitler's successor, nor of course would any of the members of his administration have kept their places or even probably their lives. Speer, again, was the exception. The contortions this powerless government now put itself through while the occupation authorities—concerned to restore some semblance of ordered life to the people—left them alone to hold daily conferences and write notes to one another in the schoolrooms at Mürwik were pitiable.

Here is the chief of the naval justice department, Eckhardt, in a memorandum on May 12th:

Our western enemies have always declared during the war, and explicitly affirmed in the preliminaries to the capitulation, that their aim was directed towards the restoration of law in the relations between peoples. Our enemies therefore . . . will not expose themselves to the reproof before the world that they, despite attaining their alleged war aims, now employ the very same methods, whose elimination was the only purpose for their conduct of the war.[33]

This was the bedrock of the government's attitude to the occupying powers; as Jodl expressed it to his department on May 15th:

All objections and complaints are to be based on international law.

Unfortunately we have never used the weapon of law. We have broken the law, as it has been represented to us by the enemy side. But we have not worked with the law, through which we would have been able to attain infinitely more than through might.

The attitude towards the enemy powers must be:

They have conducted the war for the sake of the law. Therefore we wish to be handled according to the law.

We must continually point out international law to the allies . . .

We should stress to the allies the point at which our compliance in matters of the capitulation treaty ceases, that is, if our honour should be attacked.

For the rest, we want the Allied Control Commission to come to the conclusion that we are proceeding correctly; thereby we will gradually gain their trust. Then, once the ground of our loyalty is prepared, the *Grossadmiral* will go to Eisenhower in order to discuss questions about the future with him.[34]

It is not so much the cynicism of these 'guidelines' issued by men who had consciously waged war against every system of law, national or international, moral or Christian, who had carefully weighed the disadvantages against the advantages of *publicly* leaving the Geneva Convention, not so much the lack of any feelings of guilt or shame—for of course they were creatures of an amoral society: it is the failure to learn that is terrifying. These are the 'guidelines' for a straight replay of 1919, 1920. . . . After the most devastating defeat in the history of nations, these men who had thrown overboard every principle for the sake of victory, whose only moral value was success, in overwhelming defeat *learnt nothing*!

It is only in the light of these 'guidelines' that much of what otherwise seems petty concern over rank insignia, the wearing of medals, saluting and flags, with which Jodl and Dönitz occupied themselves excessively, can be understood. It was a deliberate campaign designed to play up to the peculiar psychology of the victors, to project themselves as normal soldiers subject to the normal usages of international conventions, to separate themselves from the Party which had so obviously violated the

426

law, and so find grace and be accepted into partnership with the occupying powers *over the future of the Fatherland*—so ensuring the continuation of their ideal of the German State; for Dönitz this was National Socialism—no doubt without the grosser abuses—as in 1919 it had been the *Kaiserliches Reich*. It was for this reason he did not take the title of Führer; Jodl explained to his department: 'In all discussions with the allies *Grossadmiral* Dönitz should be referred to as Supreme Commander of the *Wehrmacht* and not as Head of State.'[35]

Dönitz's proclamations have to be interpreted in the same light; there was no more talk of the 'spreading poison of Jewry'—although it had now presumably filled the land—no more references to eating earth rather than allowing his grandson to be brought up in the 'Jewish spirit and filth', no more calls for fanatical adherence to National Socialism, only a concern for honour, dignity and pride for what the *Wehrmacht* had achieved in five years of heroic struggle. 'We have nothing to be ashamed of,' he said in an order about the attitude to be adopted by soldiers to the occupying powers issued on May 11th, and rather than rushing to them: '. . . we have to allow our former enemies to come to us, then meet them with decency and courtesy.

'We stand without a spot on our honour as soldiers and can with justice appear full of pride and honour.'[36]

Certainly any other advice would have meant giving way to despair; naturally he had to strive to preserve morale, and of course the shadow of 1918–19 hung over his every action. It is true, too, that he achieved his aim; a British Admiralty mission visiting Flensburg on May 21st–24th reported, 'The German armed forces, both naval and military, appeared to be in good shape with good morale, and there was no visible sign of demoralization.'[37] This was the impression received by countless others who visited the area; the morale of the U-boat arm appeared especially high. It was very different from 1919 and evidence that his methods of indoctrination, ruthless punishment and, on the other hand, untiring personal concern for his men had been effective. Nevertheless, he had not been faced with the same problems of idleness in the big ships; breakdowns in discipline had occurred before the capitulation and the men whom the allies saw were survivors, most of whom, probably, had hardly expected to survive; they had every reason to be thankful that it was over and they had ended in the western camp. Whatever the truth about this difficult question, there is no doubt that behind and between Dönitz's carefully chosen words to preserve morale stood the clear aim

427

of separating the armed forces from the Party in the eyes of the occupying powers—a 180-degree turn from the course he had been pursuing for two and a half years!

The most urgent part of this task was to distance everyone from the atrocities in the concentration camps. The spirit in which this was attempted is conveyed in Jodl's statement to his department on May 15th: 'The *Grossadmiral* intends to issue an order in which he dissociates himself sharply from the outrages [*Auswüchsen* or, literally, 'excrescences'] of the concentration camps.'[38]

Dönitz drew up the order the same day; it decreed that all persons who had contravened the laws and basic principles of justice and morality in the treatment of prisoners in the concentration camps were to be tried by The *Reich* court of justice and sentenced under the current disciplinary code. Von Krosigk, acting as his chief minister, sent this decree to Eisenhower with a covering letter asking him to allow the *Reich* court to be charged with this task. The German people, he wrote, had no knowledge of conditions in the camps since they were completely sealed to the outside world, and everything inside was carried on in the highest secrecy. 'Even leading German personalities had no possibility of instructing themselves about the actual conditions . . .' The German people 'unanimously and indignantly repudiated the mistreatment and cruelties' which were 'simply incompatible with their fundamental principles and moral feelings'.[39]

The worthlessness of both decree and covering letter is apparent; Dönitz and von Krosigk had allowed the chief architect of the camps to escape without seriously attempting to bring him to justice, and large sections of his entourage, including the Commandant of Auschwitz, were even then masquerading in naval uniform, while the *Reich* court was a simple tool of the State, whose most savage sentences over the past year had been reserved for men who had intended to act against the perpetrators of the crimes of the regime which both Dönitz and von Krosigk had supported. Eisenhower took no action; the letter was not even answered. In 1969 Dönitz wrote, 'Apparently the allies then regarded us as unsuitable to prosecute these crimes in German courts.'[40]

Three days after drawing up the decree, he issued an order of the day to the *Wehrmacht*, announcing his 'horror and regret' at finding out about the inhuman conditions in the camps. The millions of German soldiers and members of the *Waffen SS* who had 'fought honourably and cleanly' had known nothing of these things and they rejected them with horror. And he announced his intention of bringing to trial any who had 'soiled the honourable uniform of the German soldier'.[41] It is as difficult to find genuine outrage and remorse in this as in the previous decree and covering letter. They were declamatory, stamped by a desire for self-justification and intended to convey to the occupying powers a picture of the 'immaculate' fighting forces on the one hand, and on the other a few criminal Party officials.

The other chief aim of the government was to assist the break between the eastern and western occupation powers, still anticipated at any moment—for then the west would need Germany to hold the line against the Bolshevik engine of expansion; this reasoning was sound as events were to prove—if a little premature; but the corollary that the west would turn to them (Dönitz's administration) as the legitimate government, and that the German people could only be welded together to resist a force as strong as Bolshevism by an equally uncompromising ideology—National Socialism—showed once more a total misconception about the moral forces Nazi Germany had unleashed, and an extraordinary blindness to the genuineness of the revulsion felt in the west.

For the members of the government were locked into their past; unable to take a fresh look at their country in the light of defeat, they followed old patterns of thought and behaviour like rats trapped in a maze. Perhaps it was a natural human reaction, perhaps it was why they had reached the top in the National Socialist State, but it is chilling to see in the voluminous memoranda and proposals drawn up—for some reason not entirely clear, in an effort to 'overwhelm the Allied Control Commission'[42]—no trace of remorse, no doubts about what had occurred under the Third Reich, no questions about the means to an end which had so obviously backfired—except for Jodl's assertion that they would have done infinitely better by using 'the weapon of the law'! Whatever the reasons, there was no recognition—apart from Speer's—of the crying need to atone for crimes past western imagination, to turn away from the system that had made them possible, to restore individual freedom of thought, hence rights and justice and the meaning of language itself, building dissent into the structure. It is only necessary to list these things to realize why no one thought of them; they were of the opposite polarity to National Socialism and simply beyond comprehension.

So Dönitz, who in any case had to live up to what was expected of him, *der Löwe*, by his troops—many of whom were more extreme than he—twisted and turned to regain along the familiar paths of deception and guile what had been lost by armed might, literally turning the clock back to 1919. Here is Eckhardt again, on May 17th:

> . . . the psychological cause of the failure to pacify the world after the First War lay essentially in the feeling of the German people after the war that they were unjustly treated by the allies. Our enemies cannot be told early and urgently enough that if our western enemies again, as in 1918, camouflage their real plans for destruction under the high ideas of right and justice, it will lead in foreseeable time at least in the English and American parts of Germany, as in 1918, to chaos and injustice . . .[43]

This noxious distortion, which still finds currency in the west, was translated by Jodl into simpler terms:

> After the First World War we suffered hunger and need. The result was a turn to National Socialism. If they, as allies, wish to achieve even starker hunger by their measures after this war, then there will be a reaction. Consequence: turning to Communism, and indeed the Germans already have some impulse [in that direction].[44]

Dönitz played this theme for all it was worth in a discussion with the US Chief of the Allied Control Commission, General Rooks, on May 17th, and on May 20th he invited both Rooks and his British number two, Brigadier Foord, to talks at which he pressed the case again with even greater urgency. He contrasted the friendly way in which the Russians were carrying out both reconstruction and rehabilitation in their zone—playing German music, offering the people cigarettes and sweets and hope—with the strict non-fraternization enforced in the western zones. In the west, he said, it was apparently assumed that the German people were all criminals; the newspapers were full of reports about concentration camps, which the German people knew were 'largely exaggerated and were propaganda';[45] the talk was all of war-criminals, when everyone knew this was untrue. Here Dönitz was guilty of a flagrant lie and, because it was so obvious, of a gross tactical error.

He went on, 'All sections of the German people and the *Wehrmacht*, even those formerly strongly Anglophile, are now rapidly turning away from you towards Russia. The primary reason is this mistaken, ideologically inspired determination to destroy National Socialism root and branch. In my view this is a time of decision for the political future of Western Germany. If you continue to treat the German people as you have done so far, they will turn to Russia, and Stalin will undoubtedly seize his chance.'[46]

He pointed to the fact that he, himself, was being attacked continually in the Anglo-American press, something which had never happened even during the war and the 'fierce but fair' U-boat campaign. Despite the obvious tactical errors of playing down the atrocity stories as 'propaganda' and attacking the de-Nazification programme, his views evidently impressed General Rooks, for he repeated the arguments about a probable swing towards the Russians to the head of the Admiralty mission then visiting Flensburg, who reported them home.[47]

Dönitz must have known by now that his time was running out. There was an air of desperation about these efforts to force his views on the Control Commission, as about his determination to preserve the façade of an administration that had no power outside the school buildings in which it met. He had long since lost his military High Command chief, Keitel, summoned to Eisenhower's headquarters never to return; he had been arrested. Two of the civilian ministers had gone the same way, leaving no word. His wife, Ingeborg, who had been working for the Red Cross at Malente, near his previous command post at Plön, had not come with him to Flensburg; facing the enmity of anti-Nazi Germans she assumed her maiden name and later went to stay with Frau von Lamezan on the Lamezan smallholding near Neumünster in Holstein.[48] Yet Dönitz, in immaculate uniform, was driven every morning the quarter of a mile or so from his quarters to the naval school in a large, armoured Mercedes which Hitler had given him, there to convene the daily 'cabinet' conference. Speer coined the phrase 'tragedy had turned to tragi-comedy'.[49]

On the afternoon of May 22nd Lüdde-Neurath received a telephone call from the Control Commission summoning Dönitz, Jodl and von Friedeberg to the liner *Patria*—which General Rooks had taken over—at 9.45 the following morning. When he was told this Dönitz said curtly, 'Pack the bags.'[50]

If Dönitz realized that this was the end for his government—as he surely did—he must also have realized that the text of an address to the officer corps which lay in his desk would be found by the allies. He left it

431

there; it must be assumed he intended it to be found—as it was. It was sent to Naval Intelligence, London, and from there a translation went out to the First Lord of the Admiralty, First Sea Lord, the War Office, the Air Ministry, Washington, Ottawa and a variety of other commands.[51]

The first section was a detailed review of the situation on his own assumption of power at the end of April, and his actions to deal with it, couched in his habitual style of self-justification. Thus: 'This agreement with Montgomery enabled us to avoid complete capitulation and hence to save thousands of German lives in both the west and the east'—it is interesting that he did not claim 'millions'. And of the final surrender: 'I found myself being coerced . . . I had therefore to decide to capitulate. But there was something gained and that was that General Jodl, by clever negotiation, had at least delayed the capitulation by 48 hours.'

Jodl had had no choice; the timing, like the other terms, had been dictated by Eisenhower. This first part of the address might perhaps be compared with Hitler's political testament. The second part was evidently for current allied consumption; he would have been gratified to know that when the Director of British Naval Intelligence circulated the translation on August 11th, he wrote in a covering letter 'Attention is particularly invited to paragraphs 15, 16 and 17 . . .'[52]

15. Comrades, it must be clear to all of us that we are now fully in the enemy's hands. Our fate before us is dark. What they will do to us we do not know, but what we have to do we know very well. We have been set back a thousand years in our history. Land that was German for a thousand years has now fallen into Russian hands. Therefore the political line we must follow is very plain. It is clear that we have to go along with the western powers and work with them in the occupied territories in the west, for it is only through working with them that we can have hopes of later retrieving our land from the Russians.

This must surely have been a direct appeal to the west to recognize him as a leader who would keep Germany in the western camp against the swing towards the east of which he had warned. The sting in the tail was timeless, and he repeated it as he reiterated the message to the occupation powers stressed in all his previous speeches:

16. Our fight against the British and Americans can be viewed with pride and glory. We have nothing to be ashamed of. What the German armed forces and the German people accomplished and withstood during these six years has happened only once in world history. Such heroism has never before been displayed. There are no spots on our honour. It is therefore useless to set ourselves against our former enemies. What really matters is that they are here with us and you must treat them with civility and politeness. We must remain loyal to the terms of the unconditional surrender . . . It is wrong for anyone to believe that he must continue the war wherever he can . . . that would destroy the entire policy of the State which is based on the hypothesis that the land taken from us by the Russians must once again be restored to us . . .

And he concluded with an urgent appeal to preserve the greatest boon of National Socialism—'the unity it has given us'.

There was no officer to greet his party when they arrived punctually at the pier the next morning, no guard to salute, only a posse of importunate reporters and photographers. There was no doubt any longer about what awaited them. Dönitz mounted the *Patria*'s gangway, Jodl and von Friedeberg following, and they were led to the liner's bar, serving as a waiting room. Five minutes later General Rooks entered, followed by Brigadier Foord, a Russian representative and an interpreter; waving the three Germans to chairs arranged along a table, the allied officers sat opposite.

'Gentlemen,' Rooks began, 'I am in receipt of instructions from Supreme Headquarters, European Theatre of Operations, from the Supreme Commander, General Eisenhower, to call you before me this morning to tell you that he has decided, in concert with the Soviet High Command, that today the acting German government and the German High Command, with the several of its members, shall be taken into custody as prisoners of war. Thereby the acting German government is dissolved . . .'[53]

The head of the British Admiralty mission to Flensburg was aboard the *Patria*. He reported:

Admiral Dönitz conducted himself with much dignity; the other two appeared nervous. The only comment after General Rooks had announced the decisions of the Allied High Command was made by

433

Admiral Dönitz, who said, 'Words at this moment will be superfluous.'[54]

German naval officers had been confined to their quarters that morning, British tanks had taken up positions in the streets and a detachment of troops surrounded the Mürwik police buildings where Dönitz and the members of his administration were brought under guard, each with one case of personal belongings. They were gathered into a waiting room and from there called one by one into an adjacent room to undergo a body search for poison phials; sitting silently on benches against the walls, they watched the different reactions as each returned from his humiliating ordeal. Afterwards Dönitz, Jodl and Speer were led out into a courtyard whose surrounding roofs were lined with machine guns to face a battery of press and newsreel photographers. Later they and their baggage were bundled into trucks and driven in a long, armoured convoy to the airfield.

One man who did not go with them was von Friedeberg. He had been behaving in a nervously excited way all morning, as the head of the Admiralty mission noted. It is probable the past had much to do with his agitation, and that he was a victim of the all-powerful legend of the 'stab-in-the-back' by the Novemberlings' who had signed the armistice after the First War; on this occasion he had signed and was answerable to posterity. At all events, arriving back at his quarters to collect his belongings, he had asked the British officer escorting him for permission to write to his wife. After writing the letter, he went to the bedroom where his 22-year-old son was packing his things; he was followed by the British officer, who thought he was acting 'somewhat peculiarly' and walking unsteadily.

He then requested to use the bathroom and I agreed provided he left the door open. I followed him to the bathroom and he entered rather slowly, then suddenly closed the door and turned the key. I called the escort and we immediately forced the door, which took approximately fifteen seconds . . . On my entering he was heaving by the washbasin; he half-turned round and fell into the bath backwards, striking his head on the bottom of the bath . . .[55]

A doctor was called, but von Friedeberg was dead by the time he arrived; he confirmed suicide by poison, then the body was carried

434

into the bedroom and laid out on the bunk beneath a picture of Dönitz.

A German seaman friend of the Admiral's servant called in and stayed about half an hour talking to him. They drank a small quantity of wine and removed their own Swastika badges and appeared somewhat pleased, saying, *'Nazi kaputt!'*[56]

Late that afternoon Dönitz and his ministers were ordered aboard a freighter aircraft and, sitting on crates along the sides with their cases between them, were flown off, they knew not where. Arriving eventually at Luxembourg, they found their plane surrounded by a cordon of US soldiers armed with machine pistols; they were taken under close guard to army trucks, as Speer described it like desperadoes in a gangster movie, then driven through the countryside to a hotel at Bad Mondorf, where they saw through the glass doors like a spectral vision of the Third Reich, Göring and most of the Party and SS leaders, Army chiefs and ministers they had last met in the bunker in Berlin.

If any had previous illusions about their fate, they could have retained them no longer. The allies had announced in October 1943 that those who had committed war crimes would be pursued if necessary 'to the uttermost ends of the earth' to be delivered to their accusers 'in order that justice may be done';[57] for weeks the western press had been baying for this promise to be honoured, and there could be no doubt why the leadership—or what remained of it—had now been gathered together again; the only questions concerned the nature of the trials and punishment ahead.

These questions also exercised the allies; there was no problem for Stalin: managed trials and executions were staples of Communist policy, but there were serious scruples and differences of opinion in the western camp. This is not the place to argue the 'legality' of the War Crimes Trials, but since this is challenged, particularly by apologists for Dönitz and the military leaders, some of the criticisms must be touched on. First, of course, any trials of Germans by the allies took the character of condemnation of the vanquished by the victors, hence were wide open to the charge of being simple retribution, not law, or as Dönitz claimed 'a continuation of war by other means'. According to his defence Counsel, *Flottenrichter* (Captain, legal branch) Otto Kranzbühler, his attitude about this remained unchanged throughout.[58] This could have been

435

predicted; there is no reason to pay attention to his opinion or to Kranzbühler's since he had publicly endorsed the nauseating mockeries of the Nazi Peoples' Courts after the 20th July attempt, and Kranzbühler had practised law for a regime that knew no law but might. Their attitude is revealing, however, in its self-justificatory tone and failure to accept a morsel of responsibility, even after hearing and seeing the terrible evidence produced at the trials.

The criticism has validity on other grounds, for of course none of the victorious powers was free from war guilt. Stalin's hands were red with the blood of millions, including all the Polish officers massacred in the Katyn Forest; Churchill and Roosevelt had sanctioned the slaughter of civilians by endorsing the euphemistically-termed 'area bombing', and before the trials began Truman, Roosevelt's successor, had ordered the wholesale immolation of the citizens of Nagasaki and Hiroshima. Should they and their military advisers have been charged as well? More interestingly, perhaps, were these means justified by the ends because they had been victorious, Nazi means not justified because they had failed? This was Nazi doctrine. Dönitz could not in logic complain of his treatment.

Another criticism that exercised many legal minds was that the political charges on which the German leaders were to be arraigned, for instance conspiring to wage aggressive war, had not been recognized crimes in any formal sense at the time they were committed, hence the law would have to be retrospectively enacted to enable them to be tried. This cut across the most fundamental principle of law in the western democracies, one that is enshrined in the constitution of the United States. They also strained definition; what was 'aggressive war'? All nations have to plan to take war to their enemies to defend their own interests.

These criticisms do not seriously concern Dönitz's case, since although he was charged on the count of waging aggressive war, the most serious charges against him related to ordering the slaughter of survivors from torpedoed ships, promulgating Hitler's 'Commando order', thereby the killing of prisoners who had surrendered, and by virtue of his position in the highest leadership being an accessory to the policy of exterminating the Jews. These were crimes in the laws of all nations and in international law, and there was nothing remotely *ex post facto* about them.

Yet another objection heard endlessly was that he—like everyone bar the Führer—was simply obeying orders. Dönitz applied this particularly

436

to himself as a military man; if soldiers weighed every order on moral and legal grounds—without in most cases having sufficient information—the military profession would quite obviously be impossible. This objection was valid for his campaign of unrestricted U-boat warfare—naturally he had to obey higher authority—but again it did not and could not apply to the more serious charges against him; even a German Court in the highly-charged atmosphere of 1921 had ruled that 'superior orders' were no defence for acts that were plainly criminal. As for the argument that Germany was a totalitarian state, the judgement of the US Military Court in the case of General Milch disposed of it in short time: those who 'abjectly placed all power in the hands of one man' had to accept the bitter with the sweet. By accepting attractive and lucrative posts under a chief whose power they knew to be unlimited, they ratified in advance every act, good or bad; they could not say at the beginning 'The Führer's decisions are final' then exculpate themselves from barbarous inhumanities by saying, 'Oh, we were never in favour of those things.'[59] Dönitz's inflammatory outbursts against 'the Jewish spirit and filth' made him a high accessory to genocide; they were not made on the orders of the Führer, but sprang from his own convictions.

There were other doubts about the constitution and validity of any Court set up to administer international law. On the other hand were the positive arguments for setting a precedent. Horror at the extent, variety and brutishness of the crimes that had been committed was genuine; to western minds brought up on justice and fair play in a democratic, humanitarian tradition, what had occurred in Nazi Germany was simply incomprehensible. Whether or not 'humanitarianism' was a hypocritical cover for exploitation, as German professors had been arguing for decades, it moulded opinion; the British crusade against the slave trade during the nineteenth century had been as genuine an expression of idealism as Abraham Lincoln's speech at Gettysburg. Yet Speer and Himmler had reintroduced slave labour into Europe on a scale and with a cruelty defying the imagination.

Elements of vengeance there were too in the call for justice; was that wrong? 'Lord, how long, how long shall the wicked triumph?' the Psalm runs, 'They break in pieces thy people, O Lord . . . they slay the widow and the stranger and murder the fatherless. Yet they say the Lord shall not see . . . O God, to whom vengeance belongeth, show thyself . . .'[60]

There were however stronger deeper longings even than vengeance— a heartfelt desire for a better ordering of international relations and an end to the curse of war; as one of the British prosecutors, Sir David Maxwell-Fyfe, put it, 'most men at the close of the war wanted a better world'.[61] The movement to try the Nazi war leaders was closely related to the movement to establish new instruments of international law and justice through a United Nations Organization. It was widely felt that Germany, Italy and Japan had deliberately sabotaged the United Nations' predecessor, the League of Nations, and that precedents and law had to be established to render a repetition of the events of the 1930s impossible for the future. It may be argued that this was naïve, or even another example of *vae victis*—an attempt to propagate the stupidly sentimental doctrines of the western victors at the expense of the *Realpolitik* of the vanquished—but it should never be dismissed as hypocrisy, least of all by those who held office under the Nazis.

Undoubtedly the chief reason the Nazi leaders were tried was founded on common sense: to let them go free after what had occurred would have been a greater dereliction and offence than to enact retrospective laws or upset other principles of the western legal system; as *The Times* put it as recently as 1983, 'There are times when a higher law must override the details of man-made law.'[62] This was such a time; the allies could feel confident they were representing the collective conscience of mankind.

In addition the testimony and evidence produced at the trials provides a huge body of irrefutable documentary proof to deter Nazi apologists and nationalist historians—although it has failed to do either completely—and direct mankind to an appreciation of what even the most civilized human beings are capable of under totalitarian rule.

Nuremberg, once venue of the Nazi orgies of militarism, where regiments shouted 'We are strong and shall grow stronger!', was chosen as a symbolic setting for the trials of the major war criminals. The town itself had been reduced to rubble by mass air-raids; an occasional statue, the bell tower of a church, the prison building were virtually all that remained intact of the once lovely, winding medieval streets.

The prisoners, Göring, Hess, Ribbentrop, Ley, Frank, who had imposed the reign of terror in Poland, Seyss-Inquart, his assistant who had been transferred to do the same for Holland, and Fricke, ex-master of Bohemia and Moravia, Speer and his chief recruiter of slave labour, Sauckel, the Gestapo chief Kaltenbrunner, who appeared later, the anti-Jewish pornographer, Streicher and his 'intellectual' equivalent,

438

Rosenberg, Fritsche, Goebbels' Minister for Radio Propaganda, the former conservative politicians, von Papen, von Neurath, and the economist Schacht, his successor Funk, whose Ministry had accepted the gold extracted in the death camps, von Schirach, who had exploited the idealism of youth, and the military men, Keitel, Jodl, Raeder and Dönitz who had served the *Nibelungen* and spoke of honour—all were held in individual small cells on the ground floor of the jail.

Each cell was furnished with a steel cot at one side of the door, a lavatory bowl without seat or cover at the other side, a straight chair and a small table, on which the prisoners could keep writing materials, family photographs and toilet articles; the other few personal possessions they retained had to be laid out on the floor. Natural light was provided by a high, barred window, artificial light by a bulb and reflector fitted into a grille in the door; this remained alight all night, although turned to a dim position, so that the guards stationed around the clock at each cell door could observe their charges, who had to sleep in such a way that hands and face could be seen at all times. No ties, belts, braces, shoe-laces or string were permitted, and the prisoners had to shuffle as they walked in unlaced shoes. Cell inspections were carried out frequently, the prisoners being forced to strip and stand in a corner while bedding and belongings were searched. Once a week they bathed under supervision.

Their reactions to this tumble to the status of criminals were observed by two US psychiatrists, Douglas Kelley and G. S. Gilbert, assigned to study them—for there was so little understanding in the western democracies of the nature of the enemy they had been fighting that the German leaders were widely regarded as deranged. Dönitz, Kelley wrote, 'got along quite well' with the rigours of his new life 'through his own sense of humour. Everything—the seatless toilet, K-rations, even an occasional bad night's sleep—was twisted into some sort of a joke'.[63]

He impressed both psychiatrists as a man of intelligence, integrity and ability. While Raeder and the two military men retained their habitual 'cold formality' towards the Americans Dönitz exercised the adroitness and flexibility in relationships that had served him well throughout his career; he was soon on friendly terms with them, and working hard at his task of distancing himself from the Party, playing the plain salt who had known nothing of the nasty businesses going on under the stones in other corners of the *Reich*! With Kelley, who had to conduct his interviews through an interpreter, he succeeded completely: 'Dönitz', he wrote, 'was bitter in pointing out that his seven days of Führership netted him nothing except an opportunity to hang with the other German criminals—a situation not humorous even to him.'[64]

The Americans served to break the monotony and tension of the prisoners' solitary conditions, and amused them with games called Rorschach inkblot tests; these consisted of asking each one individually what he saw in various shapes looking as though they had been made by spilling ink on a prep-school exercise book and folding the page over, then quizzing them on their answers. It must have added to the Germans' puzzlement that they had lost the war. The games continue to provide amusement; a recent replay of the results revealed to the psychologists analysing the inkblots no difference between the Nazi top brass and average middle-class Americans; two thought the Nazis were civil rights' leaders, one thought they were psychologists! Dönitz's results seem to have been lost, but surely he could have seen only U-boats.

Gilbert and Kelley also administered the Wechsler-Bellevue adult intelligence test, compensating for differences in German culture and vocabulary, and allowing in their results for average mental deterioration with age. It is interesting that apart from Streicher, all were found above average intelligence, but none came into the highest mental categories; Schacht came top by virtue of heavy age-weighting with 143 points, Seyss-Inquart next with 141, and Göring and Dönitz were equal third with a very respectable 138, confirming the impression both had already given the psychiatrists by their attitude and speaking ability.[65]

When eventually the Court, described as the International Military Tribunal, was ready to sit, and the charges had been formalized, Gilbert took his copy of the indictment to each of the prisoners and asked them to sign it with their comments. The result was a succinct record of the attitudes and poses adopted[66]—thus Göring: 'The victor will always be the judge and the vanquished the accused'; Speer: 'The trial is necessary. There is a common responsibility for such horrible crimes, even in an authoritarian system'; Keitel: 'For a soldier, orders are orders'; Frank: 'I regard this trial as a God-willed World Court, destined to examine and put an end to the terrible era of suffering under Adolf Hitler'; Streicher: 'This trial is a triumph of world Jewry'; Raeder refused to comment; Ley, despite the security precautions, managed to commit suicide.

Dönitz had previously told Kelley that he had been picked by Hitler as his successor because all other candidates were either dead or in disgrace, and he was the only one left to whom the *Luftwaffe*, Army and Navy would pay attention; also it was felt he was the one who could most easily bring about peace, which he had done as fast as possible, yet now as Hitler's successor the Americans wanted to hang him. 'This seems to be an example of American humour.' He condensed this on Gilbert's charge-sheet: 'None of these indictments concerns me in the least—typical American humour'[67]—remarks which Sir David Maxwell-Fyfe characterized as 'perhaps the most extraordinary of all'.[68]

The trial opened on November 20th. The prisoners were taken from their cells one by one under close guard to a lift up to the courtroom where they were seated in two rows along benches opposite the Judges' dais. Behind them armed US military police with white belts and helmets stood alert to ensure that no poison or other aids to suicide passed from the defence lawyers.

When William Shirer, anticipating the moment he had been awaiting 'all these black, despairing years' entered the courtroom the prisoners were in their places. He found his first sight of them in their changed condition indescribable. Shorn of their former glittering symbols of power, 'how little and mean and mediocre' they looked. At the left of the lower row, Göring was scarcely recognizable in a faded *Luftwaffe* uniform shorn of insignia; he had lost weight and reminded Shirer of 'a genial radio operator on a ship'.[69] Above him at the left of the second row Dönitz sat wearing a civilian suit and looking 'for all the world like a grocery clerk. Hard to imagine him as the successor of Hitler'; next to him Raeder looked 'a bewildered old man'.

The Court bailiff barked and the prisoners, assembled lawyers, Press men and spectators rose for the entrance of the judges in black robes, Lord Justice Lawrence, who was to preside, and Sir Norman Birkett; the US Attorney General, Francis Biddle, and Judge John H. Parker of North Carolina; the French Judge Donnedieu de Valres, his fellow countryman, M.le Conseiller Robert Falco, and the two Russian Judges, appropriately in uniform with decorations. When they had ascended to their places, Justice Lawrence rapped for silence.

'The trial which is about to begin is unique in the history of jurisprudence in the world . . .'

The morning session was occupied with details of the first two counts of the indictment, conspiracy to commit crimes against peace and humanity, and the planning and initiation of wars of aggression in violation of international treaties. During the recess the defendants took lunch in the courtroom and so were able to greet and talk to one another for the first time since their imprisonment. In the afternoon the other two

441

counts were read out, war crimes, including 'murder and ill-treatment of civilian populations of or in occupied territories and on the high seas . . .', and crimes against humanity including 'deliberate and systematic genocide, viz. the extermination of racial and national groups . . .'[70]

The charges against Dönitz were participating in the conspiracy and preparations for aggressive war set out in the first two counts, and that 'he authorized, directed and participated in the war crimes set forth in Count Three of the Indictment, particularly the crimes against persons and property on the high seas'.[71] The British prosecution, bringing these charges, believed they had a virtually impregnable case, particularly on the third count; no formal orders to murder shipwrecked survivors had been traced, but they were hardly to be expected from experienced staff officers; on the other hand they had a witness from the U-boat arm prepared to testify that Dönitz had publicly encouraged action against survivors, and a senior officer who would testify to his interpretation of the dangerously ambiguous orders of September 1942 as licence to attack survivors. They also had the entry in the BdU war diary detailing these orders, and Dönitz's rambling and unsatisfactory explanations under interrogation. The Admiralty transcript runs:

DÖNITZ: 'We have in all the years leading up to this particular event acted exactly in the opposite sense to the one laid down in this statement [the September 1942 *Laconia* orders]. That is what matters. This particular incident of the *Laconia* distressed us so very very deeply because it showed that in the very rare cases where we could possibly do rescue work, then we were even being murdered from the air.'
INTERROGATOR: 'That may be, but I still say that the language in this extract is contrary to the reason which you state, which is, as I understand it, that the safety of the submarine required that no efforts be made, but still you provide here that the orders concerning the bringing in of Captains and Chief Engineers of these vessels, still stands.'
DÖNITZ: 'That is an addition that is meant rather in a theoretical sense, because actually in no case, in no instance was it carried out, for the *Laconia* incident, which happened a very few days before the entry in the diary, shows how we acted. We were in a situation where in an infinitely greater number of cases we could do nothing, and in a very,

442

very slight number of cases we could do something, and in these cases then we would subject ourselves to the bombings from the air.

'. . . I lost in one month 42 U-boats only by the airplanes . . . I was obliged to give such an order to prevent the U-boats from being killed by the old orders of rescuing . . . This message was ordered only by me. I remember that Captain Godt and Captain Hessler were against this telegram. They told me that expressly, because they said that that can be misunderstood, but I said I must tell that now to these boats to prevent the losses in this one per cent. I must give them a reason so they don't feel obliged to do that.

'. . . I am completely and personally responsible for it because Captains Godt and Hessler both expressly stated that they considered the telegram as ambiguous, or liable to be misinterpreted . . .'

INTERROGATOR: 'I would like to ask you, why was it necessary to use the language that I read to you before, that the most primitive demands for the conduct of warfare by annihilating ships and crews are contradicted by efforts to rescue members of the crews?'

DÖNITZ: 'These words do not correspond to the telegram [i.e. only to the war diary summary]. They do not in any way correspond to our actions in the years of 1939, '40, '41 and '42 as I have plainly shown you by the *Laconia* incident. I would like to emphasize once more that the Captains Godt and Hessler both were violently opposed to the sending of the telegram.'[72]

Pressed again on the wording in another interrogation a few weeks later, just before the trial, he replied:

DÖNITZ: 'I had never given this order if I hadn't had the *Laconia* incident, see. Then I saw the time coming when I had to give the order, "You are not allowed to go to the surface at daytime at all." . . . Godt and Hessler told me, "Don't make this wireless, you see; one day there can be a wrong appearance about it. There can be a misinterpretation of that." And then I told him I must, I think, in the reality take measures. I wished to prevent my U-boats being bombed when they saved. That was the whole thing of it, you see . . .'

INTERROGATOR: 'Why did Godt and Hessler say this telegram might be subject to misinterpretation?'

DÖNITZ: 'That's a very right question from your side. The misinterpretation is the political side of the thing, you see. The Nationals. They

443

were quite sure nobody thought of a thing like that. But these points why I am sitting now here and have to speak with you—I couldn't think in 1942 that I would have to talk it over with you, you see. I only wish to tell the U-boats the other side . . . I was under great pressure . . .'[73]

His admirable determination to shield his former chief of operations and his son-in-law was reciprocated by them and the entire officer corps of the *Kriegsmarine*, which closed ranks solidly. An elaborate clandestine network for assisting his and Raeder's defence by finding documents and providing testimony and technical advice was organized under cover of the minesweeping service which the allies had set up with German naval personnel, and a weekly courier service was run between the Hamburg headquarters and Nuremberg by a young U-boat officer under cover of an automatic washing machine service![74]

On the second day of the trial, the chief US Prosecutor, Justice Robert Jackson, made the opening speech; he built up a devastating picture 'of the racial hatreds, of terrorism and violence and of the arrogance and cruelty of power' symbolized by the 'twenty lost men' in the dock. Probably the twenty considered it propaganda; for most, the first real jolt came in the afternoon of November 29th, when a film was shown of the concentration camps entered by US troops. In his opening address Jackson had warned that the proofs to come would be disgusting and cost those in the courtroom their sleep. Now they were told that no one was allowed to leave 'unless they become sick'. Special fluorescent lights had been built into the ledges of the dock and, as the courtroom lights went out, these illumined the faces of the prisoners with an eerie glow. The psychologists had stationed themselves one at each end of the rows to note the reactions.

The film started with scenes of prisoners burned alive in a barn. Gilbert noted:

. . . Frank swallows hard, eyes blink trying to stifle tears . . . Fritsche watches intently with knitted brow, cramped at the end of the seat, evidently in agony . . . Göring keeps leaning on the balustrade, not watching most of the time, looking droopy . . . Funk now in tears, blows nose, wipes eyes, looks down . . . Speer looks very sad, swallows hard . . . Funk crying now . . . Dönitz has head bowed, no longer watching . . .[75]

Shots of the piled dead in a slave labour camp were followed by scenes of crematorium ovens, a lampshade made from human skin, a woman doctor describing experiments on female prisoners at Belsen . . .

By this time Dönitz's head was buried in his hands.

As the film ended and the lights went on there was a stunned silence; Justice Lawrence forgot to adjourn the session; the Judges simply rose and left without a word.

After the prisoners had been returned to their cells, the psychiatrists visited them one by one. Reactions differed wildly: Fritsche burst into tears as soon as the door closed, so did Funk. Speer said he was more than ever resolved to acknowledge a collective responsibility and absolve the German people from guilt. Göring pretended indifference. Frank cried with rage, 'To think that we lived like kings and believed in that beast! Don't let anyone tell you they had no idea . . . They didn't *want* to know.' Raeder said he had hardly heard of the concentration camps before. Keitel said he was ashamed of being a German, 'It was those dirty SS swine . . .'

Dönitz trembled with emotion, his words tumbling out in mixed English and German, 'How can they accuse me of knowing such things? They ask why I didn't go to Himmler to find out about the concentration camps, why that's preposterous! He would have kicked me out just as I would have kicked him out if he'd come to investigate the Navy! What in God's name did I have to do with these things? It was only by chance that I rose to a high position, and I never had a thing to do with the Party.'[76]

In December he and the other military men on trial were defended from an unexpected quarter: the U.S. *Army and Navy Journal* apparently ignoring the war crimes and crimes against humanity in the indictments, accused Justice Jackson of attempting to discredit the profession of arms. The *Chicago Tribune* had made more intemperate attacks on the whole idea of the trials earlier. Dönitz naturally learnt of this support from his defence lawyer, and it is probably significant that his efforts to present himself as a simple sailor pledged to the Christian West were directed from now on at Americans.

The Prosecution documents against Dönitz were put in by Colonel H. J. Phillimore on January 14th; of the *Laconia* orders he submitted, '. . . The wording is of course extremely careful but to any officer of experience its intention was obvious and he would know that deliberate action to annihilate survivors would be approved under that order.

'You will be told that the order, although perhaps unfortunately

445

phrased, was merely intended to stop a Commander jeopardizing his ship by attempting a rescue, which had become extremely dangerous as a result of the extended coverage of the ocean by allied aircraft . . .'[77] However, if this had been the case, Phillimore asserted, the wording would have been very different.

He called *Oberleutnant zu See* Heisig, who had sworn an affidavit that he had heard Dönitz announce to his U-boat training course in October 1942 that the manning problem was the Achilles heel of the allied merchant service, and that the time had come to wage 'total war' at sea against crews as well as ships. After he had given similar testimony in the witness box, Kranzbühler rose to cross-examine, asking him first how he had come to make his original statement.

'I made the statement in defence of my comrades [Eck's officers] who were put before a military court in Hamburg and sentenced to death for the murder of shipwrecked sailors.'

Kranzbühler tried to find out whether he had been told, before he made the original statement, that the death sentence on Eck and his officers had been confirmed; Heisig could not remember.

'Since you have knowledge of the circumstances,' Kranzbühler went on, 'do you maintain that the speech of Grand Admiral Dönitz mentioned in any way that fire should be opened on shipwrecked sailors?'

'No, we gathered from his words and from his reference to the bombing war, that total war now had to be waged against ships and crews. That is what we understood and I talked about it to my comrades on the way back to the *Hansa*.'

'Did you speak about the point with any of your superiors at the School?'

'I left the School the same day. But I can remember that one of my superiors, whose name to my regret I do not recall, once spoke to us about this subject and advised us that if possible only officers should be on the bridge ready to annihilate shipwrecked sailors should the possibility arise or should it be necessary.'

Kranzbühler could hardly have been expecting such a damning answer. 'One of your superiors told you that?'

'Yes, but I cannot remember in which connection and where.'

Kranzbühler turned to the U-boat standing orders, asking whether these mentioned anywhere that shipwrecked sailors or their rescue apparatus were to be fired on.

'The standing orders did not mention that. But I think one can assume this from an innuendo of Captain Rollmann, who was then officers' Company Commander—a short time before that some teletype message had arrived containing an order prohibiting rescue measures and demanding that sea warfare should be fought with more radical, more drastic means.'

'Do you think that the prohibition of rescue measures is identical with the shooting of shipwrecked sailors?'

'We came to this—'

'Please answer my question. Do you think these two things are identical?'

'No.'

'Thank you.' Kranzbühler sat down.[78]

The following day Phillimore called *Korvettenkapitän* Karl Möhle, who had been chief of the fifth U-boat flotilla at Kiel from 1941 to the capitulation, and had briefed outgoing Commanders; he had found the *Laconia* orders ambiguous, and on his next visit to Dönitz's headquarters had discussed them with one of the staff officers there, *Kapitänleutnant* Kuppisch. Kuppisch was unavailable to testify since he had been lost later in the war. According to Möhle, Kuppisch had given him two examples of action to be taken—against shot-down aircrew in a rubber dinghy, and against survivors from ships sunk in US waters.

Asked how he briefed Commanders on these orders, he replied that he read the message to them without comment.

'In a very few instances some Commanders asked me about the meaning of the order. In such cases I gave them the two examples that headquarters had given me. However, I added, "U-boat Command cannot give you such an order officially. Everybody has to handle this according to his own conscience."'

'Do you remember an order about entries in Logs?'

'Yes, sir. At the time, the exact date I do not remember, it had been ordered that sinkings and other acts in contradiction to International Conventions should not be entered in the Log but should be reported orally after return to the home port.'[79]

Kranzbühler rose to cross-examine, and took him through each sentence in the orders, asking after each whether he saw an instruction there to kill survivors; Möhle found it in the one explaining rescue as contradicting the most elementary demands of war for the destruction of ships and crews.

447

'Does that sentence contain anything as to the destruction of ship-wrecked persons?'

'No, of crews.'

After ascertaining that Möhle had not spoken to Godt or Dönitz himself about the orders, Kranzbühler asked him whether he knew that the story of the aircrew in the rubber dinghy was just the opposite of that he had given. 'The Commander was reprimanded because he did not bring home these fliers even if it meant breaking off the operation.'

To appreciate the absurdity of this suggestion it is only necessary to consider the difficulty of the ten-day passage across Biscay with the ever-present danger of aircraft, and to imagine Dönitz's face if a commander had then come back with four airmen! However, the reason for Kranzbühler's desperate essay became apparent as he reminded Möhle of U-boat standing order 513, stating that every effort was to be made to take prisoners from aircraft and destroyers for interrogation purposes.

'Did you notice,' he went on, 'and try to clarify a contradiction between these orders concerning the rescue of aircrew in every case and the story you passed on about the destruction of aircrew?'

'No. Because in the order of September 1942 it also said that orders about the bringing in of ships' Captains and Chief Engineers remained in force.'

'Did you hear of any instances where a U-boat brought in Captains and Chief Engineers but shot the rest of the crew?'

'No.'

'Do you consider it at all possible that such an order can be given—that is that part of the crew should be rescued and the rest of the crew should be killed?'

'No, sir. One cannot make such an order.'

Re-examined by Phillimore, Möhle said he took the orders to mean that something further than abstaining from rescue was implied, 'only it was not actually ordered, but was considered desirable'.

'What were the actual words you used when you passed that order on to the Commanders?'

'I told the Commanders in so many words, "We are now approaching a very delicate and difficult chapter, it is the question of the treatment of lifeboats. The BdU issued the following radio message in September 1942"—I then read the radio message in full. For most of those present the chapter was closed . . . In some few instances the Commanders asked, "How should this order be interpreted?" Then as a means of interpretation I gave the two examples which had been related to me at U-boat command. "Officially such a thing cannot be ordered, everybody has to reconcile this with his own conscience."'

'Do you remember any comment being made by commanding officers after you had read the order?'

'Yes, sir. Several Commanders, following the reading of this radio message, said, "That is very clear, but damned hard."'[80]

From the moment the surviving Nazi leadership had been reunited in the Palace Hotel at Bad Mondorf, Dönitz as the Führer's nominated successor, and Göring as former heir apparent, had been circling one another warily in matters of precedence. This had been interrupted during the period of solitary confinement; since they had been joined again in the dock Göring had shown by force of personality and uninhibited defiance towards the prosecution that he was the natural group leader, and by mid-February, Dönitz, according to Gilbert's diary, had fallen into his pattern of undignified courtroom behaviour.[81]

Since it was evident the 'fat one' was trying to terrorize the rest into supporting Hitler and the Nazi myth, even to the extent of threatening to incriminate them in his own evidence unless they took the Party line, the prison authorities moved against him, banning communication within the prison and segregating the prisoners into five dining rooms for lunch. The arrangements were carefully devised: Dönitz was put in with the three elder conservatives, von Papen, von Neurath and Schacht, to allow their obvious disillusion with Hitler and the Party to work off on him and, it was hoped, wean him from his exclusive concern with his soldier's honour. The others were similarly grouped in patterns of influence. Göring had to take his lunch on his own.

Discussing the new arrangements with Speer a few days later Gilbert remarked that he had thought of putting Dönitz in with him. Speer replied that it was better as it was because even he felt somewhat inhibited when Dönitz was around.[82]

A Russian-made atrocity film was shown on February 19th, even more terrible than the US one, and over the following days survivors from death camps gave their dreadful evidence. 'Didn't *anybody* know *anything* about *any* of these things?' Kranzbühler asked Dönitz in Gilbert's hearing at the end of one harrowing session. Dönitz shook his head and shrugged sadly.[83]

At lunch in the 'elders'' dining room at the end of the month Gilbert was encouraged to hear Dönitz accepting the idea that the German people had been betrayed, and felt that the new arrangements were working well. What Dönitz was probably doing was continuing the campaign he had begun with Rooks and the address to the officer corps left in his desk at Flensburg to establish himself as a staunch 'Westerner': the Germans, he said, must have the feeling that they were being treated fairly if they were to be won over to co-operation with the west.

At the beginning of April Keitel was called to the witness stand; Jodl fumbled uneasily with his papers; Dönitz tapped nervously on the dock. When the former chief of Hitler's staff started taking the line that he was a soldier and had simply been carrying out his duties, Göring turned round to Dönitz and said contemptuously, 'The little weakling!' and later, 'The little white lamb! If he hadn't been in sympathy with National Socialism he wouldn't have lasted a minute.'[84]

Midway through the month Höss, the former Commandant of Auschwitz, was called to give evidence. He had been captured almost a year after he first dived for cover into the *Kriegsmarine* and just two days after inadvertently breaking his poison phial. He described the production-line arrangements for separating out able-bodied Jews and exterminating the rest at the rate of 2,000 to 10,000 a day, afterwards extracting valuable items like gold teeth and rings from the corpses and sending them melted down to the *Reich*'s Economics Ministry. Approximately two and a half million had been disposed of during his time.

Afterwards both Göring and Dönitz told Gilbert that Höss was a South German, not a Prussian.

Later in the month, after Rosenberg had given evidence about his 'master race' theories, Dönitz confided to Gilbert that Rosenberg had his head in the clouds. 'I have no doubt that he would not hurt a fly, but there is also no doubt that these propagandists were really responsible for paving the way for these terrible anti-semitic acts. It's too bad Hitler isn't here. He did so much of all that's discussed here.'[85]

They passed on to the question of whether Kaltenbrunner had known as little as he had claimed in the witness stand a few days before, after which Dönitz returned to the theme he had broached earlier, the Russian danger to Germany; it was not in America's interest to allow Russia to control Europe; he would like to talk with some sensible American official after the trial.

Towards the end of the month Streicher took the stand; Gilbert noted signs of obvious embarrassment in the dock as the obscene old man,

13a Dönitz aboard the *Patria* (Jodl seated on his right, von Friedeburg on his left) is informed by US General Rooks that his government is dissolved

13b . . . and under arrest—here outside the police station, Flensburg-Mürwick
13c *(inset)* Speer, Dönitz, Jodl

14a In the dock at the Nuremberg War Crimes Tribunal: Dönitz *(standing)*, Raeder *(seated beside him)*, *(in front)* Göring *(in dark glasses)*, Hess, Ribbentrop

14b *(right)* 'Number Two' serving his time in Spandau jail, Berlin

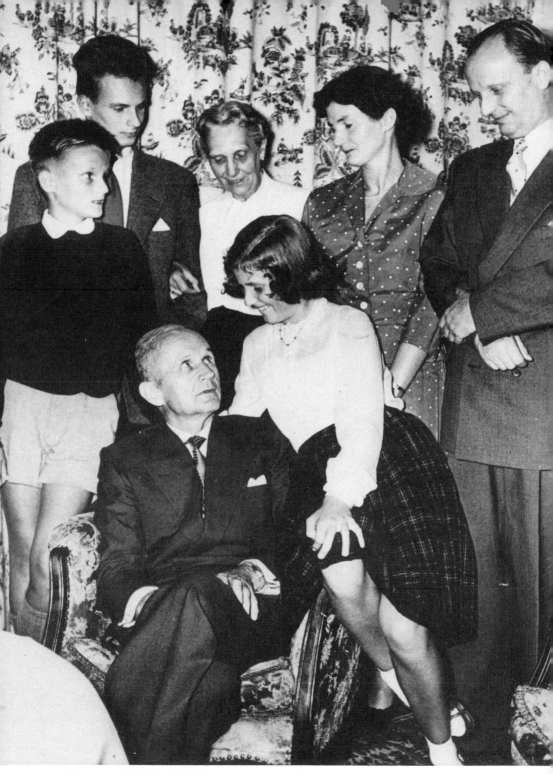

15 Dönitz with his surviving family after his release from Spandau in 1956:
standing from right, Günther Hessler *(son-in-law)*, Ursula Hessler *(daughter)*,
Ingeborg *(wife)*, two grandsons and *(seated)* granddaughter

16a Dönitz in 1972

16b *(below)* 'Old Comrades' at his funeral in Aumühle, January 1981

describing himself as the scourge of Jewry, denied any knowledge of the extermination policy.

That evening in his cell Dönitz told Gilbert he didn't want to know or say anything about these dirty politics and propaganda. His officers would not have touched Streicher with a pair of tongs, and he was glad his case was coming up soon and he was being represented by an upright example of a clean-cut young German naval officer who would present his case simply and honestly.[86]

His turn came in the afternoon of May 8th. Taking the stand, he repeated after the President, 'I swear by God—the Almighty and Omniscient—that I will speak the pure truth—and will withhold and add nothing.'

It was a somewhat meaningless oath to administer to a Nazi; he repeated it in German, then in answer to Kranzbühler's first question about his career began to establish his credentials as a simple professional sailor.

'Ich bin seit 1910 Berufssoldat, Berufsoffizier seit 1913.'[87]

Kranzbühler led him through his conduct of the U-boat war and the prosecution allegation that Hitler had ordered him to act against survivors. He replied that he had never had either a written or a verbal order from Hitler on these lines, but during a conference on May 14th 1942 Hitler had asked him whether some action could not be taken against the rescue ships which were succeeding in picking up a large percentage of allied crews.

'What do you mean by action taken?'

'At this discussion, in which Grand Admiral Raeder participated, I rejected this unequivocally and told him that the only possibility of causing losses among the crews would lie in the attack itself, in striving for a faster sinking of the ship through the intensified effect of weapons . . .'

Kranzbühler passed to the orders of September 1942; Dönitz maintained these were simply non-rescue orders; there was no intention to attack survivors.

'Firing on these men is a matter concerned with the ethics of war, and should be rejected under any and all circumstances. In the German Navy and the German U-boat arm this principle, according to my firm conviction, has never been violated, with the one exception of the Eck affair. No order on this subject has ever been issued in any form whatsoever.'[88]

451

During lunch he was reminded that it was the anniversary of the capitulation.

'That is why I am sitting here,' he replied drily. 'But if I had to do it all over again I don't know that I would have done it any differently.'

'Even if you knew then what you know now?'

'Oh, since then I have become a hundred thousand years wiser. I mean just knowing and thinking what I did *then*, I couldn't have acted any differently.'[89]

On the witness stand again afterwards, he was asked to explain the wording of the final sentence of his *Laconia* order.

'That sentence is, of course, in a sense intended to be a justification. Now the prosecution says I could quite simply have ordered that safety did not permit it [rescue]—that the predominance of the enemy's Air Force did not permit it—and as we have seen in the case of the *Laconia*, I did order that four times. But that reasoning had been worn out. It was a much-played record, if I may use the expression, and I was now anxious to state to the Commanders of the U-boats a reason which would exclude all discretion and all independent decisions of the Commanders. For again and again I had the experience that for the reasons mentioned before, a clear sky was judged too favourably by the U-boats and then the U-boat was lost—or that a Commander in the role of rescuer was in time no longer master of his own decisions, as the *Laconia* case showed. Therefore, under no circumstances whatever did I want to repeat the old reason which again would give the U-boat commander the opportunity to say, "Well, at the moment there is no danger of air attack"—that is I did not want to give him a chance to act independently . . . nor did I want to say "If somebody with great self-sacrifice rescues the enemy and in that process is killed by them then that is a contradiction of the most elementary laws of warfare." I could have said that too. But I did not want to put it that way and therefore I worded the sentence as it now stands.'[90]

It is interesting to note the subtle differences between this sophisticated explanation in reply to Kranzbühler, and his earlier answers to interrogating officers. The chief difficulty with the explanation, however, is that it is not possible to reconcile his stated wsh 'to exclude all discretion and all independent decisions' from his Commanders and at the same time expect them to bring in Captains and other officers, as the orders also stipulated.

Kranzbühler pointed out this inconsistency to him.

452

'There is,' he replied, 'a great difference in risk between rescue measures for which the U-boat has to stop and men have to go on deck and a brief surfacing to pick up a Captain, because while merely surfacing the U-boat remains in a state of alert, whereas otherwise the alertness is completely disrupted.'

Also there was a military purpose in taking Captains, for which he had orders from the High Command.

Asked about Möhle's misunderstanding of the order, he took full responsibility on himself as its author, but said that Möhle was the only person who had doubts about it, and regretted that he had not communicated those doubts to him since everybody had access. If there had been any consequences of his doubts 'I would of course assume responsibility for them'. Referred to the case of Eck, he said that Eck had stated under oath he knew nothing of Möhle's interpretation or doubts; he had acted on his own initiative and his aim had been to remove wreckage, not to kill survivors.

'Do you approve of his actions, now that you know of them?' Kranzbühler asked.

'I do not approve of his actions because as I said before in this respect one must not deviate from military ethics under any circumstances. However, I want to say that *Kapitänleutnant* Eck was faced with a very grave decision. He had to bear responsibility for his boat and crew and that responsibility is a serious one in time of war. Therefore, if for that reason that he believed he would otherwise be spotted and destroyed . . . if he came to this decision for that reason, then a German Court Martial would undoubtedly have taken it into consideration. I believe that after the war one views the events differently and does not fully realize the great responsibility which an unfortunate Commander carries.'

'Apart from the Eck case did you, during the war or after, hear of any other instances in which a U-boat Commander fired on shipwrecked people or liferafts?'

'Not a single one.'

Referred to the cases of the *Noreen Mary* and *Antonico* where, according to the prosecution, men had been fired at in boats, he replied that he had a great number of similar reports about the other side, but had always treated them with scepticism since shipwrecked people could easily believe they were being fired on, although the shots were actually directed at the ship itself. And he concluded from the fact that the

453

prosecution had only two examples that he was correct in assuming the Eck case the only real instance during the war.

Afterwards Kranzbühler turned to the conspiracy charges; Dönitz explained that his own dealings with Hitler had been strictly limited to his own sphere; it had been one of Hitler's peculiarities only to listen to a person about matters which were that person's express concern. He had had no knowledge of the internal policy of the SS or SD, and he had never received an order from the Führer which in any way violated military ethics. 'Thus I firmly believe that in every respect I kept the Navy unsullied down to the last man until the end.'

Asked whether he ever considered breaking with the Führer or attempting a *Putsch* he denied it hotly.

'The German nation was involved in a struggle for life and death. It was surrounded by enemies almost like a fortress. And it is clear, to keep the simile of the fortress, that every disturbance within would without doubt have affected our military might and our fighting power. Anyone who therefore violates his loyalty to his oath to plan or try to bring about an overthrow during such a struggle for survival must be deeply convinced that the nation needs such an overthrow at all costs and be aware of his responsibilities. Despite this every nation will judge such a man as a traitor . . .'

He went on in this vein until he was cut short by the President for making a political speech. He was then taken through the closing weeks of the war when he had learned of his surprise appointment as Hitler's successor; he described how he had come to appoint von Krosigk as his chief minister:

'I did this because in a chance discussion which had taken place several days before I had seen that we held much the same view, the view that the German people belonged to the Christian West, that the basis of future conditions of life is the absolute legal security of the individual and of private property . . .'

He explained his earlier 'fanatical' Nazi speeches as necessary to keep up morale, since the collapse of the eastern front would have meant that German women and children would have perished, and he went on to describe the Navy's tremendous efforts to rescue the refugees from the east. 'The very existence of the German people in this last hard period depended above all on the soldiers carrying on tenaciously to the end.'[91]

At the luncheon adjournment Göring leapt up in delight. 'Ah, now I feel great for the first time in three weeks. Now we finally hear a decent German soldier speak for once.'[92]

Even Frank told Gilbert that Dönitz was speaking like a fine officer because after all orders were orders. Speer who had been stung by Dönitz's reference to traitors, snapped back, 'Of course—orders for the destruction of the German nation are immaterial! Just follow orders, that's all!'[93]

The cross-examination began in the afternoon of May 9th; the British prosecutor, Sir David Maxwell-Fyfe, tried to draw an admission that Dönitz had known about the slave labour Sauckel imported and Speer used for his armaments programme. He denied all knowledge; during his conferences with Hitler and Speer the system of obtaining workers was never mentioned; he had been interested only in the number of U-boats he received.

'You tell the Tribunal you discussed that with Speer and he never told you where he was getting the labour?'

'Yes, that is my answer and it is true.'

Drawing his attention to the number of chiefs of the armed services and departments of State who attended the situation conferences Maxwell-Fyfe suggested that he had played as full a part in the government of Germany as anyone apart from Adolf Hitler himself. Dönitz denied it. Only the happenings of the past 24 hours were discussed at the conferences, and no one, neither Speer nor himself, nor anyone else, had an overall picture. The only one who had a complete picture was the Führer.

'Well, I won't argue with you, but I suppose, defendant, you say—as we have heard from so many other defendants—that you knew nothing about the slave labour programme, you knew nothing about the extermination of the Jews and you knew nothing about any of the bad conditions in the concentration camps. I suppose you are going to tell us you knew nothing about them at all, are you?'

'That is self-evident since we have heard here how all these things were kept very secret; and if one bears in mind that everyone in this war was pursuing his own tasks with the maximum energy then it is no wonder at all. To give an example I learned of the conditions in concentration camps—'

'I just want your answer for the moment. I want you to come to a point which was well within your knowledge, and that is the order for the shooting of Commandos which was issued by the Führer on 18th October, 1942 . . .'[94]

Dönitz replied that he had received a copy of this order as a front Commander; it did not concern his sphere of activities, and when he became C-in-C a few months later he had so much to occupy him he had not gone into the question. The memorandum arising out of a staff discussion about it in February 1943, a fortnight after he had taken office—one of the documents submitted by the prosecution—had not been placed before him.

That ended the day's sessions. Gilbert visited him in his cell in the evening and Dönitz asked him what he thought of his defence. The American replied that it was noticeable the military men were still refusing to say anything against Hitler even if they knew he was a murderer.

Dönitz replied that he had not been given a chance to say there was a black side which he didn't see.[95]

The next morning he was pressed again about the Commando order, and the shooting of the torpedo-boat's crew under its authority; the man directly responsible, Admiral von Schrader, had shot himself when he received orders to proceed to England. Dönitz continued to maintain he had not seen the order as C-in-C and had given it no consideration. He was then shown the document in which he had called for 12,000 concentration camp workers to be used in the shipyards. He explained that because of his urgent need of shipping space to evacuate refugees from the east he had called for suggestions as to how they might overcome the sabotage problem and get more ships.

'I received suggestions from various quarters outside the Navy, including a suggestion that repair work might be speeded up by employing prisoners from the concentration camps. By way of justification it was pointed out that in view of the excellent food conditions such employment would be very popular. Since I knew nothing of the conditions and methods in the concentration camps I included these proposals in my collection as a matter of course, especially as there was no question of making conditions worse for them, since they would be given better food when working. And I know that if I had done the opposite I could have been accused here of refusing these people an opportunity of better food. I had not the slightest reason to do this as I knew nothing about any concentration camp methods at the time.'

'Are you telling the Tribunal that when you ask for and may have got

12,000 people out of concentration camps, who work alongside people not in concentration camps, that the conditions inside the camps remain a secret to the other people and all the rulers of Germany?'

'First of all I do not know whether they did come. Secondly if they did come I can well imagine that they had orders not to talk, and thirdly I do not even know what camps they came from . . .'[96]

He was asked about the proposals he had made for collective penalties against whole working parties in the shipyards in order to stop sabotage. Again he referred to 'agencies outside the Navy'; they had suggested to him that measures for exacting atonement had been effective in France; he had since learnt that the measures proposed meant the withdrawal of rations issued by the management of the shipyard!

Maxwell-Fyfe passed on to his conduct of the U-boat war, suggesting that in the first year, out of 241 ships sunk by U-boat, at least 79 had been attacked without the warning necessary under the Conventions. Dönitz said he could not check these figures; the sinkings were not illegal, however, since the British had armed their merchant ships and had given them instructions to ram U-boats and to report their positions by wireless; they were therefore combatants and a part of the Navy's intelligence system. Moreover, England acted in exactly the same way, as did other nations.

The questioning passed to Hitler's anxiety to act against crews, and the orders Dönitz had issued. He was pressed on how the orders to bring in Captains and Chief Engineers could be reconciled with his explanation of the *Laconia* order—the aircraft danger.

'You know perfectly well,' Maxwell-Fyfe said, 'that in order to find the Captain or Chief Engineer, the U-boat has got to go around the lifeboats or wreckage and make enquiries: "Where is the captain?" And you know very well that the usual practice in the British Merchant Navy was to hide the Captain and prevent them finding out who he was. Is that not the practical position that had to be met, that you had to go around the lifeboats asking for the Captain if you wished to bring him in?'

Dönitz stuck to his previous reply to Kranzbühler that 'the risk of taking one man aboard was much less so far as time was concerned and would not limit the crash-diving ability of the boat', and that there was a military aim in seizing the Captain and 'as is always the case in war, a certain risk would have to be taken'. Moreover the significance of that order was not great as the results were always so poor.

'This order, if you want to construe it like this and take it out of

457

context,' he went on, 'militates against your contention that I wanted to destroy these people; because I wanted to take prisoners, and if I wanted to kill somebody first, then I certainly could not have taken him prisoner.'

He was reminded of Heisig's evidence about his remarks to the training course. He agreed that the German press had been full of the US shipbuilding programme at the time.

'But the argument I am suggesting to you,' Maxwell-Fyfe interrupted, 'was that the building programme would be useless if you could destroy or frighten off sufficient Merchant Navy crews. That is the point in Hitler's conversation and that Heisig said you said. Did you say that?'

'I have always taken the view that losses of crews would make replacement difficult, and this is stated in my war diary together with similar ideas, and perhaps I said something of the kind to my midshipmen.'

He was shown the 'Rescue ship' order. 'I just want you to look at the last sentence: "In view of the desired destruction of ships' crews their sinking is of great value . . ." It is continually pressing the need for ships' crews.'

'Yes of course, but in the course of fighting . . .'

He was questioned about Möhle's evidence: 'Are you telling the Tribunal that Commander Möhle went on briefing submarine Commanders on a completely mistaken basis for three years without any of your staff or yourself discovering this? You saw every U-boat Commander when he came back.'

'I am sorry that *Korvettenkapitän* Möhle, being the only one who said he had doubts in connection with this order, as he declared here, did not report this right away. I could not know that he had these doubts. He had every opportunity of clearing up these doubts and I did not know, and nobody on my staff had any idea, that he had these thoughts.'[97]

This is, of course, an incredible answer when taken together with Hansen-Nootbar's recollection of his methods of debriefing, his insistence that Commanders tell him all their worries and criticisms.

Maxwell-Fyfe drew his attention to the cases of the *Noreen Mary* and *Antonico*, and he repeated his contention that statements from men in lifeboats had to be treated with scepticism, and these were the only two cases in five and a half years of war.

'Yes, and of course for the two and a half of those years that the submarine Commanders have been shooting up survivors you are not likely to get many cases, are you? I just want to ask you one other point—'

'U-boat Commanders,' Dönitz interrupted, 'with the exception of the case of Eck, have never shot up shipwrecked persons. There is not a single case. That is not true.'

'That is what you say.'

'In no case is it proved. On the contrary they made the utmost efforts to rescue. No order to proceed against shipwrecked people has ever been given to the U-boat force with the exception of the case of Eck and for that there was a definite reason. That is a fact.'[98]

He was taken on to the faking of the U 30's Log after the sinking of the *Athenia*, which he represented as the only case in which a Log Book had been altered, then to his speeches about the necessity for ideological training in the Navy. He defended his words on the necessity to preserve national unity and morale. When asked the meaning of 'the spreading poison of Jewry' in his Heroes' Day talk, he replied, 'I meant that we were living in a state of unity and that this unity represented strength and that all elements and all forces—'

'No, that is not what I asked. What I am asking you, what did you mean by "the spreading poison of Jewry"? It is your phrase and you tell us what you mean by it.'

'I could imagine that it would be very difficult for the population in the towns to hold out under the heavy stress of bombing attacks if such an influence was allowed to work, that is what I meant.'

'Well now, can you tell me again, what do you mean by "the spreading poison of Jewry"?'

'It means that it might have had a disintegrating effect on the people's power of endurance, and in this life and death struggle of our country I as a soldier was especially anxious about this.'

'Well now, that is what I want to know. You were the Supreme Commander and indoctrinated 600,000 to 700,000 men. Why were you conveying to them that Jews were a spreading poison in party politics? Why was that? What was it that you objected to in Jews that made you think they had a bad effect on Germans?'

'That statement was made during my Memorial Day speech on Heroes' Day. It shows that I was then of the opinion that the endurance, the power to endure of the people, as it was composed, could be better preserved than if there were Jewish elements in the nation.'

'This sort of talk, "Spreading poison of Jewry", produced the attitude of mind which caused the deaths of five or six million Jews in these last few years. Do you say that you knew nothing about the action and the intention to do away with and exterminate the Jews?'

'Yes, of course I say that. I did not know anything about it, and if such a statement was made then that does not furnish evidence that I had any idea of any murders of Jews. That was in the year 1943.'

'Well, what I am putting to you is that you are joining the hunt against this unfortunate section of your community and leading six or seven thousand of the Navy in the same hunt . . .'

'Nobody,' Dönitz interrupted, 'among my men thought of using violence against Jews, not one of them, and nobody can draw that conclusion from that sentence.'[99]

The prosecution did not have the text of his speech at the Flag Officers' *Tagung*, in which he had referred to eating earth rather than allowing his grandson to grow up in 'the Jewish spirit and filth', since 51 of the 52 copies distributed had been 'weeded' from the files, nor did they have the war diary entries referring to Admiral Fricke's contemplated action against Jewish refugee ships since these, too, had been 'weeded'.[10] Had they been in possession of these, Dönitz could hardly have maintained that none of his men thought of using violence against Jews.

He was then questioned on the decree of April 1945 in which he had praised the petty officer in the prisoner of war camp in Australia, who had surreptitiously got rid of Communists. His explanation was that he had been told there had been an informer in the camp who passed on information to the enemy, on the strength of which U-boats were lost; consequently the senior man in the camp had decided to remove the informer as a traitor. That was what he had been advised and what he would prove with a witness. Asked why he had not put that in the decree but had referred to Communists in the plural, he said there may have been intelligence reasons for not divulging it.

When Gilbert visited his cell in the evening Dönitz asked him what he thought now. He had shown he was on the side of the west; he had said that Germany belonged to the Christian West. And he went on to tell Gilbert how a US Admiral among the spectators had passed a message to Kranzbühler to say that he considered Dönitz's naval warfare beyond reproach.[101]

'I told Kranzbühler to tell him,' Dönitz went on, 'that the Russians have been trying to get hold of the technicians who have been working

460

on our new U-boat—the one that can go around the world without surfacing.'

Gilbert said that would make it look as if he were trying to play the west against the east for personal advantage.

He realized that, Dönitz replied, and for that reason had changed his mind about Kranzbühler passing the message. 'But *you* ought to tell him,' he urged Gilbert. 'It is your duty. Ever since the armistice the Russians have been trying to get hold of these technicians and experts on the X-boat [the Walter boat]. And do you know why? Because it has a cruising range all round the world without surfacing for recharging the batteries—and it is foolproof against any weapons—even the atomic bomb! And if Stalin is as generous as I believe he is in these matters it will be a simple matter for him to build a few thousand of these U-boats, and then he will control the seas of the world. And what will you do against a U-boat that never has to surface? Now I have imparted this information to you, it is your duty to inform that admiral because six months from now I will say that I told you about it, and you don't want to carry it around in your heart.'[102]

It seems possible that Kranzbühler had been informed on the Navy courier link that former SS men who had dived into the service at the end of the war were being recruited by US Intelligence for anti-Communist operations. At all events Gilbert thought to himself that for an honest soldier who condemned dirty politics, this was a clever move.

Admiral Wagner, who had been Dönitz's personal liaison with the High Command during the last year, was called to the stand after Dönitz. He said he had been a prisoner of war with Heisig at the time the latter had made the statement recounting Dönitz's speech to the U-boat course; Heisig had told him then that he had learned from his interrogators that one of Eck's officers, Hoffmann, had testified to hearing a speech by Dönitz in the autumn of 1942, which he had considered was a demand for killing shipwrecked survivors. Heisig had been told, 'If you confirm this testimony of Hoffmann's, you will not only save Eck and Hoffmann but also two others who have been sentenced to death . . . Of course you will thus incriminate Grand Admiral Dönitz but the material against Admiral Dönitz is of such tremendous weight that his life has been forfeited anyway.' Wagner went on to say that Heisig had also told him, without any prompting, that at the time he heard Dönitz's speech he had been deeply distressed. He had just returned from witnessing the terrible

461

consequences of a bombing raid on Lübeck; his mind was set on revenge for these brutal measures and Heisig considered it possible that his emotional state might have influenced his interpretation of the speech.

Later Wagner confirmed Dönitz's story about the spy in the Australian prisoner of war camp; asked why in that case the word Communists in the plural had been used, he thought the only explanation was that the true state of affairs had to be concealed from enemy intelligence. He denied that Dönitz had been considered a fanatical Nazi—'he was carrying on his duties as a soldier to the end'.[103]

Cross-examined by Colonel Phillimore on his testimony about Heisig, he was asked whether he knew that Eck and the others had been executed before the conversation he described took place.

'No, I just found it out now.'

'At any rate the witness Heisig knew it before he gave his evidence, did he not?'

'Obviously not. Otherwise he would most likely have told me about it—'

Phillimore read him an extract from the questions put to Heisig showing that he had been told that the death sentence had been carried out.

'I can only say, in that case he told an untruth to me.'[104]

This pitiable attempt by a senior officer to cast doubt on Heisig's evidence suggests the weight attached to it in the German camp. It is noticeable, too, that Wagner referred to the allied bombing wherever possible in his evidence, insinuating the *tu quoque*—or 'you too'— principle by the back door.

On May 14th Admiral Godt took the stand. He insisted under cross-examination that he did not remember that he and Hessler had tried to stop the *Laconia* orders being sent.

'I suggest to you now,' Phillimore said, 'that this order was very carefully drafted to be ambiguous deliberately so that any U-boat Commander who was prepared to behave as Eck did was entitled to do so under the order, isn't that right?'

'That is an assertion.'[105]

After him Hessler came to the stand and described how as a U-boat Commander in the early years of the war he had given survivors their exact position and course to the nearest land and assisted them with water and medical supplies. He too denied having tried to dissuade Dönitz from sending the *Laconia* orders. Pressed by the President, he said, 'We talked it over just as we discussed every wireless message drafted by us. As time went on, we drafted many hundreds of wireless messages so that it is impossible to remember what was said in each case.'[106]

This answer is hard to square with Dönitz's own account in his memoirs ten years later of the circumstances in which the order was drafted. 'There was a very *temperamentvoll* discussion in my staff.'[107]

Raeder took the stand next; he explained that his pre-war notes about building 'against' England had meant using England as a yardstick. He had been thoroughly taken in by Hitler, he said, and as his former Chief of Staff, Schülte-Monting, later confirmed, had never believed in his intentions to attack. Asked about the Führer's assertion in his presence that he would 'smash' Czechoslovakia, he replied that Hitler had wanted to smash lots of things! He admitted he had known the *Athenia* had been sunk by a U-boat, but as Schülte-Monting explained afterwards, placed the State's interest—not to have complications with the United States—above newspaper articles.

For Dönitz the low point in his examination probably came when the prosecution tried to put in an affidavit Raeder had made while in captivity in Russia immediately after the war. This was not read in court, but Dönitz had an opportunity to see it and was not flattered. Raeder had said that relations between the two of them were very cool since Dönitz's 'somewhat conceited and not always tactful nature did not appeal to me', and that mistakes 'resulting from his personal viewpoint, which were known to the officer corps, soon became apparent, to the detriment of the Navy'. He had gone on to accuse Dönitz and Speer of casting aside tried and tested methods at a critical moment, and said Dönitz's political inclinations had produced difficulties: 'His last speech to the Hitler Youth, which was ridiculed in all circles, earned him the title of "Hitler-boy" Dönitz.' He then said Dönitz had hardly been qualified to become C-in-C—a remark very difficult to reconcile with his own recommendation in 1943![108]

Dönitz appeared glum and annoyed after reading all this, and relieved his anger when Gilbert visited his cell in the evening, accusing Raeder of being a disillusioned old man jealous about the increased U-boat construction that he and Speer had achieved.

Annoyed as he was, Dönitz had every reason to be overjoyed at another development that day; Fleet Admiral Chester Nimitz, formerly

C-in-C US naval forces in the Pacific, had delivered an answer to a questionnaire from Kranzbühler: in accordance with an order from the Chief of Naval Operations in Washington late on December 7th 1941, he wrote, he had ordered unrestricted submarine warfare against Japan from the first day of the war; moreover it had become general practice not to attempt rescue of survivors unless it could be done without prejudice to the execution of the mission.

'Do you know what he said?' Dönitz exulted at lunch the next day. 'He conducted *unrestricted warfare* in the whole Pacific from the first day after Pearl Harbor! It's a wonderful document!'[100]

Two days later von Schirach came to the stand and denounced Hitler in forthright terms as the greatest mass murderer of all time, perpetrator with Himmler of the darkest blot on German history. In the 'elders'' lunch room afterwards, the politicians agreed he had been absolutely right. Gilbert asked Dönitz if he did not agree too. 'Of course,' he replied abruptly and said nothing else.

The next evening Gilbert pressed him on the point; he agreed it was true, but thought von Schirach had been covering up too much. It was the Nazi leaders who had started the whole business and the soldiers who had done nothing but their duty were the sufferers. He went on to tell Gilbert how he had brought up his own children as Christians, and they had remained so despite joining the Hitler Youth, which he knew had been anti-Christian; 'The two sons I lost in battle were good Christians and good soldiers. So was I. So are your Admirals. We are the same type.'

And he returned to his favourite theme: the politicians had caused these disgusting crimes, but now the soldiers had to sit in the dock and share the blame.[110]

Towards the end of June Speer went to the stand and made his intended statement about the leadership's common responsibility for the crimes of the Third Reich, although he stopped short of admitting his own knowledge of the extermination policy. Afterwards he told Gilbert that his admission of a common responsibility was causing great consternation among the others.[111]

The final prosecution speeches began towards the end of July. Dönitz could have taken little comfort from the US Prosecutor's description of him as promoting 'the success of the Nazi aggressions by instructing his pack of submarine killers to conduct warfare at sea with the illegal ferocity of the jungle', nor with the sting in the tail, which charged all the professional men, politicians and military, with betrayal.

'It is doubtful if the Nazi master plan could have succeeded without the specialized intelligence which they so willingly put at its command . . . Their superiority to the average run of Nazi mediocrities is not the excuse. It is their condemnation.'[112]

After him the British Prosecutor asked if Dönitz was ignorant of the crimes of the regime when he addressed to a navy of some 600,000 men a speech on the 'spreading poison of Jewry', and circulated Hitler's directive, 'terror should be met by terror' at the time of the shipyard strike in Copenhagen, asking for 12,000 concentration camp workers and recommending collective reprisals.[113]

The French Prosecutor pointed to Dönitz's 'indisputable adherence to the criminal policy of the system.' He said among other things, 'The officer is the representative of the State. This talk about non-political officers is sheer nonsense.'[114] Finally the Soviet Prosecutor said that his British colleague had proved the guilt of Dönitz and Raeder so convincingly he would not dwell on the Grand Admirals; he did, however, call for 'the last head of the Hitlerite government' to be among 'the first to pay the penalty for all those crimes which have led to the trial'.[115]

This was a very reasonable call. However, Kranzbühler and Dönitz probably took comfort from the fact that, despite the hard language, none of the speeches had referred to the most dangerous charge to his personal account—ordering the shooting of shipwrecked survivors. Justice Jackson had come nearest to it, but his use of the term 'illegal' might well have referred to the unrestricted campaign, and that, as Fleet Admiral Nimitz had agreed, had been the US policy in the Pacific from the beginning; it had also been British policy in the Skagerrak area from May 1940.

When he came to make his final statement to the court at the end of August, Dönitz said he considered his conduct of the U-boat war was justified, and he 'would have to do the same again'. His subordinates had carried out his orders in complete confidence in him and in their legality and no subsequent judgement could deprive them of their belief in the honourable character of the struggle for which they had made such sacrifices. Of the Führer principle, he admitted that 'if in spite of all the idealism, all the decency and all the devotion of the German people' it had led to such results, it must be wrong 'because apparently human

465

nature is not in a position to use the power of this principle for good without falling victim to the temptations of power'.

Finally, '. . . my life was devoted to my profession and thereby to the service of the German people. As the last C-in-C of the German Navy and the last head of State, I bear responsibility towards the German people for everything which I have done and left undone.'[116]

It was a neat move towards Speer's position without committing himself to knowledge of or responsibility for crimes.

Raeder was equally concerned to stress the 'cleanness and decency in battle of the *Kriegsmarine*' which stood 'before this Court and before the world with a clean shield and an unstained flag'; he could only explain the repeated attacks on the Navy and himself as the result of the Prosecution being 'unqualified to judge soldierly honour'.[117]

The period of about a month between these final statements and the judgements was one of tense depression amongst the prisoners; several just lay on their cots staring at the ceiling, and as the days passed even Göring grew nervous and uncharacteristically quiet. Dönitz probably clung to the hope he had gained from Nimitz's statement and a feeling perhaps that his efforts to place himself firmly in the western camp and explain the dangers if the Russians obtained the secrets of the Walter U-boat might pay off. That is speculation.

The judgements were delivered on October 1st. For Dönitz, 'The evidence does not show that he was privy to the conspiracy to wage aggressive war.' Nevertheless 'from January 1943 Dönitz was consulted almost continually by Hitler' and the evidence showed he was 'active in waging aggressive war'. Of the unrestricted U-boat campaign, 'In the actual circumstances of this case the Tribunal is not prepared to hold Dönitz guilty'; of the *Laconia* orders, 'The Tribunal is of the opinion that the evidence does not establish with the certainty required that Dönitz deliberately ordered the killing of shipwrecked survivors.' The orders were, however, 'undoubtedly ambiguous, and deserve the strongest censure'.

He had permitted the 'Commando' order to remain in force, but claimed he knew nothing of the MTB crew being turned over to the SD and shot; his call for 12,000 concentration camp inmates for the shipyards had been a suggestion; he had no jurisdiction over the shipyards, and did not know whether they had been procured. His attitude to breaking away from the Geneva Convention had been: 'It would be better to carry out the measures considered necessary without warning and at all costs to save face with the outside world.'

Dönitz claims that what he meant by 'measures' were disciplinary measures against the German troops to prevent them surrendering, and his words had no reference to measures against the allies. Moreover this was merely a suggestion, and that in any event no such measures were ever taken either against the allies or Germans. The Tribunal does not, however, believe this explanation. The Geneva Convention was not, however, denounced by Germany. The Defence has introduced several affidavits to prove that British naval prisoners of war in camps under Dönitz's jurisdiction were treated strictly according to the Convention, and the Tribunal takes this fact into consideration in regarding it as a mitigating circumstance.

He was found 'Not Guilty' on the first count of the indictment, 'Conspiracy to wage aggressive war', but 'Guilty' on the second and third counts, 'Waging aggressive war' and 'War crimes'.[118]

It is extremely difficult, if not impossible, to discover from the language on what grounds these guilty verdicts were brought. In the circumstances in which he found himself in 1943, waging 'aggressive war' could hardly be considered a crime. As for 'War crimes', if the evidence was insufficient to convict him of ordering the killing of survivors—and it is most unlikely that he ever gave a direct order to this effect—and he was not held responsible for the murder of the MTB crew under the 'Commando' order, nor for what happened in the Danish shipyards, and his encouragement to anti-semitism in a speech to the nation was not even mentioned in the judgement, what was left? Only the 'ambiguous' orders about survivors for which he received the 'strongest censure'. If Heisig's and Möhle's evidence meant anything—and it is difficult to see why they, against the grain of the entire officer corps working for Dönitz's acquittal, should have invented it all—he had incited his men to kill survivors, the 'ambiguities' in his orders had been criminal, and he bore prime responsibility for the murder of the crew of the *Peleus*—to take one proven instance. For this there could have been only one sentence.

Sentences were pronounced that afternoon. The prisoners were taken up one by one in the lift to the courtroom to hear their fate. Gilbert remained below to note their reactions as they came down. First was Göring; he was evidently fighting an emotional breakdown as he answered Gilbert: 'Death'.

When it was Dönitz's turn to put on the headphones in the court, he heard himself sentenced to ten years' imprisonment. He removed the

467

headphones, banged them down, and walked quickly to the door, apparently very angry.[119] But to Gilbert he seemed not to know quite how to take it.

'Ten years—well, anyway I cleared U-boat warfare—your own Admiral Nimitz said—you heard it—'[120]

If he was a little confused it was not surprising. The judgement and sentence do not fit; they read like the result of an inept committee compromise. There can be no doubt that the Russians wanted Dönitz's head, so did the British, therefore the questions concern the attitude of the American and French Judges. Did politics as well as justice inform their judgement? If not, on what basis was the sentence pronounced? It is known that the US Judge, Francis Biddle, said that he thought Dönitz should have been acquitted; perhaps ten years was the best compromise they could reach. Apart from three acquitted, von Papen, Schacht and Fritsche, it was the lightest sentence of all.

Of one thing there can surely be no doubt; tried with the evidence and insights available today, he would have joined Göring, Ribbentrop, Keitel, Jodl and the rest of the twelve condemned to death by hanging.

Seven 'major' war criminals remained in the cells at Nuremberg after the executions had been carried out; besides Dönitz there were Hess, Funk and Raeder, all sentenced to life imprisonment, Speer and von Schirach, twenty years, and von Neurath—found guilty on all four counts—to fifteen years. Speer, agonizing over questions of guilt and responsibility, found himself the odd man out, positively disliked by Raeder, Dönitz and von Schirach for his attitude at the trial. On December 6th—according to the illegal diary he kept on scraps of paper—this came out into the open. As they were cleaning the corridor Schirach, breaking the non-communication rule, jeered at him for his assumption of total responsibility, which even the Court had rejected. Speer saw the other five nodding in agreement.[121]

Was it only the question of shared responsibility that irked the others? It is more likely they felt him to be a hypocrite. They knew he had been as aware as they themselves of the extermination policy, of which he had denied all knowledge; they considered his attitude in the witness stand an opportunist posture to save his neck. Dönitz certainly believed this. He and Speer had been friends; Speer was the only one in the dock, according to Kranzbühler, with whom his client was on the familiar '*du*'

468

terms. Kranzbühler could never understand this, believing Speer to be a pure opportunist; after a long time Dönitz had come to share his opinion.[122] It is difficult to explain Speer's moral turmoil—after he had unburdened himself of his feeling of shared responsibility—without assuming a deeper layer of guilt than anything he admitted to.

In March the following year the rules banning communication were relaxed during the periods for exercise in twos in the prison yard. Speer and Dönitz seem to have repaired their relationship to an extent as they sometimes walked together. One morning Dönitz said to him with aggressive suddenness that the trials had made a mockery of justice—if only because the judging nations would not have acted any differently. Speer felt it was futile to try and persuade him of the moral legitimacy of the verdicts since Dönitz was 'unable to see the magnitude of the horror'. But assuming, as it must be assumed on the evidence, that Dönitz recognized his good fortune in escaping with his neck, his words sound rather as if they sprang from a compulsion to justify himself.[123]

On July 18th the prisoners were woken at four in the morning and told to prepare for a move; this was the long-expected transfer to Spandau prison in West Berlin, a maximum security jail which had been a collecting point for political prisoners *en route* to the concentration camps from the start of the Nazi regime. Arriving at the castellated red-brick building inside a high wall and outer security fence the same morning, the seven were made to strip and were led, naked, to the surgery to be examined by doctors from each of the four, formerly allied nations, then searched for secreted poisons. Afterwards in the Chief Warder's room they were told they would henceforth be known as numbers, and were shown seven piles of numbered clothing which, the Warder made a point of telling them, had been worn by concentration camp inmates. They consisted of underwear, a coarse grey shirt, tattered brown convict's trousers and jacket, a convict's skull cap and sandals. The prisoners went to collect them in the order they had entered the room; Dönitz was 'number two', Raeder 'number four', Speer 'number five'—and so they remained to the prison authorities to the end of their time. Hess, who was destined to stay longest, was 'number seven'.

The prison rules, which were read out to them, forbade communication either between themselves or with their guards without permission; Dönitz was probably one of the first to break this when he asked a guard how many other prisoners were in the jail. After some hesitation the reply came: 'None.' Escorted through a steel door that clanged shut behind them, they came into the wide corridor of the inner cell block, and were locked into alternate cells, an empty cell between each. These were similar to the ones they had left at Nuremberg with a single, high barred window and a grille in the door and rudimentary furniture. Soon after Dönitz heard the key turn in the lock, he sat down at the small table and began a letter to his wife:

'*Meine Ingeliebste*, we are in Spandau. I may write two letters in six months and may receive the same number . . .'[124]

He asked her to send him a hairbrush and soap, and told her he could receive a visit lasting a quarter of an hour every two months. 'I must say I will never acknowledge my sentence as just or internationally sound . . .' Nevertheless, he continued, the ups and downs of life could not change their own values. He ended '*Dein Junge*' ('Your boy').

There began for each of the prisoners a renewed struggle to preserve minds and bodies from the isolation and lack of incident, or even news of the outside world—for they were forbidden papers or magazines and during their visits their relations were not allowed to tell them anything apart from personal matters. Dönitz may have found it easier than the others; he had less time to go, he had always been dedicated to a more or less spartan regime of disciplined work, above all he still had much to live for. For he believed that the German people might turn to him as the legitimate Head of State.

The naval officers' organization which had contributed to his defence at Nuremberg was actively co-ordinating a propaganda drive to clear the stigma of war crimes from his name and elevate him into a national hero who had saved millions in the east from the Russians. What connections they may have had with extreme right-wing organizations planning a neo-Nazi State with Dönitz as the Führer's legitimate successor—as alleged by the journalist Jack Fishman in *Seven Men of Spandau*—is not clear. But whether or not there was any serious planning, Dönitz certainly considered himself the legitimate Head of State!

Ingeborg evidently believed this too. She told Jack Fishman that her husband had the right to the highest position in the land and would be 'ready to take the wheel' if certain influential people were to ask him.[125] Some of her answers to his questions suggest intimate knowledge of Dönitz's defence at Nuremberg; asked for instance whether her husband had not asked Himmler about the concentration camps, her reply was almost identical to his own: certainly not; he always maintained that one department was not justified in questioning another on the basis of

470

rumour; he would have thrown anybody out who had questioned him about the affairs of the Navy.

From her answers at this and other interviews, it does not seem she felt any more shame or guilt for the stains brought on Germany by the regime her husband had served than Dönitz himself. She seemed more concerned at her loss of status and the disappearance of all the possessions they had collected: the priceless Gobelin tapestry, the sea paintings, the Persian carpets, 60 copper engravings, silver and plate which had been crated and stored with relations of Admiral Heye's on an estate near Zulfeld in Holstein had been looted by a British Colonel of the Parachute Regiment.

'I don't want anything to do with the British,' she told one intelligence officer, 'they are thieves,' and she produced photographs of the interior of the Dahlem house showing the carpets which the Colonel had stolen.[126] Another complaint was that the British had frozen her bank account and she was receiving only the pension of a *Kapitän z. See* for her husband.

This was something which angered Dönitz. The reason given by the authorities was that he owed his promotion above that rank to Hitler; he regarded this as an insult and quite untrue since he would have become an Admiral in any event; 'I became the Supreme Commander of the Navy at the most critical time of the war,' he told von Neurath, the elder statesman in whom most of the prisoners confided. 'I had the thankless task of bringing the war to a finish and now all the government can do is give me a Captain's pension for my wife . . .'[127]

Relationships between the prisoners naturally fluctuated, but von Neurath and von Schirach were the two with whom Dönitz consorted most on their exercise walks and at other times when the 'western' guards relaxed the no-communication rules; with the Russian guards it was always difficult to snatch a few words together. The hostility Dönitz felt for Raeder since reading his Moscow statement came to the surface from time to time, as did the dislike which he had conceived for his former friend, Albert Speer. Speer records one of these occasions that December. The two of them were talking while sweeping the corridor, when he made an inadvertent remark, presumably about Hitler, and was immediately taken to task by Dönitz.

Speer concluded that 'for all his personal integrity and dependability on the human plane', Dönitz had not revised his view of Hitler in any way, and he wrote in his diary that evening, 'To this day Hitler is his

471

Commander in Chief.' It was probable, he considered, that a large proportion of the generals and the German people thought in the same way, and would never realize what had actually happened.[128]

Here Speer hits on the predominant characteristic of the attitude Dönitz displayed in all his writings and everything he said to the end of his life. Speer's explanation was that Dönitz retained a 'naïve loyalty such as I had only at the very beginning'. He, of course, had greater opportunity to observe him than anyone, but it has to be asked whether he was right. Dönitz was certainly obsessive, but he was not unintelligent and the strongest influence on him during his time in Spandau, as during the talks in the 'elders' dining room during the Nuremberg trials, was von Neurath, a representative of the old Germany in which Dönitz had been brought up and in whose service he had been conditioned. Von Neurath's disillusion with the Nazis was genuine and arrogant in its detachment; 'For all of you,' he told Speer one day, 'it's just Hitler and the Third Reich that have perished.'[129] It is difficult to believe that this sense of the disaster the Führer's criminal amateurishness had brought upon Germany and its good name did not rub off on at least the rational layers of Dönitz's mind.

This being so, his protestations of loyalty, like his assertions that the victor nations would have done just the same if the positions had been reversed, and his repeated statements that he would do it all over again and no differently, sound like desperate self-justifications for the course he had followed and the crimes he had condoned and perpetrated. Even without that compulsion to self-justification which was a part of his character, it is difficult to see how he could have faced the charges on his conscience other than by denying to himself the possibility of acting differently—that is 'disloyally'. What other recourse had he if he thought of Eck and his officers than to insist to himself that he had been following his soldier's duty when he indoctrinated them in fanaticism?

Speer, still tortured with doubts, came to a similar conclusion about himself; it suddenly seemed to him that he had heard no word more frequently than 'loyalty' in the Third Reich, and he asked himself whether it had been 'no more than the rag we used to cover our moral nakedness'.[130]

The seasons passed. The prisoners had been given the opportunity of taming the wilderness that had grown up behind the cell blocks during their first summer, and had welcomed the chance. The space had been

472

turned into the 'Garden of Eden'—after the British Foreign Secretary!—in which each had his area for growing vegetables for the kitchens; Speer, as a special dispensation, grew flowers and constructed a rock garden. Dönitz, probably for the first time since his early schooldays, had an opportunity to devote himself to the simple satisfying tasks of growing things; he specialized in tomatoes and became characteristically obsessive, sometimes achieving 40 or 50 fruits on a single plant—transparently delighted when anyone counted them in his presence.

He found a renewed interest in nature, the night sky, the birds and insects he saw and the mice which swarmed in the garden. He put lupin seeds outside their holes and watched them come out to take them. 'It is remarkable,' he wrote to Ingeborg, 'how in the absence of normal distractions, one remembers all that has gone before. Things that really meant something to one become clearer, among them the many songs learned as a child.'[131]

As spring came round again he thought of his sons; he had pictures of them both in the centre of a collection of family photographs on the small table in his cell.

On the 20th March, my dear Ingefrau, our thoughts will be united, thinking of our dear, brave Peter. It was a bitter time in Bitterstrasse [Dahlem]: Peter missing at sea, and everything was so serious, heavy responsibility and nothing to lighten our affairs . . .'[132]

Even here, though, his thoughts could not stray far from the inevitability of his course; it would have been better, he went on, if his views (about building U-boats instead of a surface fleet) had been accepted in time. 'That is where the tragedy in my affairs lies.' Is it possible that Speer was right? Did Dönitz never realize what had happened—apart from defeat—and what he had shared in? Or is this cry in his most intimate correspondence another sign of the deep cover he had imposed on his thoughts?

To outward appearance Speer was right. He heard him one day in February 1949 lecturing von Neurath excitedly in the garden about the shortage of U-boats at the beginning of the war, insisting that if he had had the number he had demanded England would have been forced to her knees by 1941. Speer watched the old aristocrat as he listened with polite interest to Dönitz's agitated voice.[133] Almost five years later Dönitz received via an 'illegal' channel an extract from the British official history of the war at sea, which suggested that Germany's failure to build up a large U-boat fleet at the beginning had been a vital error. Enormously pleased, Dönitz repeated again and again, according to Speer's diary, that he intended to bring this up 'in the full light of publicity' once he and Raeder were free.[134]

The reference to Raeder being free was caused by the hope, shared by all the prisoners, that they would soon be released. News of the Cold War, the blockade of Berlin, and the re-arming of West Germany by the western allies, had reached them through the clandestine channels of communication each now had, and seemed finally to make nonsense of the Nuremberg judgements and their own incarceration. Dönitz appears to have convinced himself that he and Raeder at any rate would be let out since it would be impossible to re-establish the *Wehrmacht* if their new allies were holding high-ranking officers in Spandau. Also he knew that his friends outside were doing their utmost for him in representations to the West. Whatever the Americans may have wished, the Russians were adamant that all seven were going to serve their appointed terms to the last day, and on December 6th 1952, Dönitz received a letter from Kranzbühler, still his legal adviser, that he should count on serving his full sentence. His hopes were not permanently stilled; they continued to burst out afresh at any apparently hopeful news.

Early the following year rumours of an attempt by a neo-Fascist group to lift him from Spandau and place him at the head of a new West German government brought brief excitement. Speer took the opportunity to cast a fly. Dönitz rose beautifully; he had nothing to do with the attempt, he said; he would disassociate himself from it publicly if only they would let him out. Moreover he condemned Hitler's system. 'But I am and will remain the legal Head of State. Until I die.'

Speer, who knew his convictions on this score, pretended surprise. 'But there has been a new head of State—'

'He was installed under pressure from the occupying powers,' Dönitz contradicted, and insisted that until all political parties, including the neo-Nazis, were allowed to operate, whether he liked it or not, his own legitimacy remained.

'It has become an obsession with him,' von Neurath said.[135]

He received an unexpected boost for the idea in April 1953 when a research organization, the *Allensbacher Institut*, published the results of a survey of opinion on formerly prominent people. Dönitz received a note from his son-in-law, Günther Hessler, to say that he had topped the pole; 46 per cent of Germans had a good opinion of him, only seven per cent a bad opinion; Schacht ran him close with 42 per cent of good opinions. Göring had 37 per cent and Hitler was still well thought of by 24 per cent—indeed only 47 per cent had a bad opinion of him!

At the time he was apparently thinking of himself as a future Head of State, the other side of Dönitz's nature manifested itself in dreams of caring for orphans or animals in need. 'I think I shall start a kindergarten when I get out,' he is reported to have said, 'a mixed one for puppies as well as children.'[136] It seems he was serious about this, for after his remark had appeared in print in the series Jack Fishman had written about Spandau, Dönitz commented, 'My wife is trying to dissuade me from it because I'm too old. She may be right.'[137]

That his personality was not fully integrated is suggested by his relationship with the guards; for periods he would act the Grand Admiral, ostentatiously preserving his distance, at others he sought companionship and engaged them in long talks. He was constant in his hostility to Speer, though—to such an extent that Speer began to suspect that he planned his quips at night 'since he is not very witty'. He also preserved his coolness towards Raeder, which was fully reciprocated; both Grand Admirals, however, joined forces against Hess, whose self-pity, constant, unseemly cries for attention, refusal to co-operate in the work they all had to do and generally muddled manner cut across their military ideas of behaviour. 'He has to be trained and treated harshly,' Dönitz remarked in the presence of the guards after one incident in 1955.[138]

He preserved his own habits of daily exercises, and early to sleep. He read more than he had ever been able to—according to his letters mostly history, astronomy, biology and a few novels, and according to Jack Fishman he greatly enjoyed C. S. Forrester's 'Hornblower' books, and Jack London's adventures, particularly those concerning dogs. According to one of his former adjutants, von Knebel Doeberitz, who saw much of him after he was released, he read the 'King' plays of Shakespeare with great intensity—one imagines with practical insight into the power struggles, favouritism and corruption at Court. He was also preparing his own memoirs, the details of which were being worked on by former members of his staff outside; his son-in-law had particularly good opportunities since he had been commissioned by the British Admiralty to write a history of the U-boat war.

The prison routine—the early-morning processions to the washroom, sweeping the corridor, always in the same order established in the first few days, Speer and Schirach at the sides, Dönitz with his favourite broom following in the centre leaving little piles for Funk with the dustpan and Hess with the brush to sweep them in—the gardening, the changing guards according to which of the four Powers was on duty— rolled on in unbroken succession; even the brief and tantalizing glimpses of his family became routine. The U-boat Association paid for Ingeborg's trips to Berlin; often she was accompanied by Ursula and her children, but since only one adult and one child were allowed in together, they took two months' visiting allowance on successive days. He loved seeing his grandchildren, but the conditions were not conducive to intimacy or even relaxation: the visitors were separated from him by a wire mesh, and a translator listened to every word in case current affairs or other forbidden topics were discussed. After one visit from his wife, Speer reported him returning with the words, 'It was very pleasant, almost intimate. Only the Russian interpreter, the French *sous-chef*, a guard and one or other of the directors alternately were present.'[139]

However much each of the prisoners worked to preserve his sanity, the restraints and constant small humiliations imposed on such formerly active and extraordinarily ambitious men took their toll. Speer records one incident in the tenth year of their captivity which illustrates this perfectly. Funk, who had grown some sunflowers in his garden area, was ordered to remove them as they interfered with observation. The instruction caused an emotional outburst: Schirach hacked the heads off the flowers in his own area, Dönitz attacked his rows of beans; the guards watched incredulously.[140]

This 'prison psychosis' explains some of Dönitz's extraordinary hostility to Speer—that at least was Speer's charitable comment years afterwards: 'Dönitz was of choleric disposition and this tendency was strengthened during his imprisonment, so that he was unable to control many sharp remarks.'[141] The experience certainly bit deep, for after he left Spandau he said nothing about it even to his family; as his daughter, Ursula, said, 'The curtains came down.'

After a constant series of raised hopes that the changed political constellation or Kranzbühler's efforts would gain him early release— followed always by bitter disappointment—finally on May 24th 1955, the tenth anniversary of his capture, he felt certain he would be going home; so did Kranzbühler, former U-boat officers and a posse of reporters and photographers who waited outside the gates. The British director who had watched a film of the Nuremberg trial at the end of April—since when his attitude towards the prisoners had grown markedly cooler—merely informed him that time in prison before the trial was not counted; he would have to wait another year and a half. Dönitz protested indignantly, but to no avail.

Von Schirach remarked that since he repeatedly maintained the trial and sentence were unlawful, he was being inconsistent in arguing that his sentence had been completed!

Von Neurath had already been allowed home because of his advanced years and poor health; that autumn the other old man, Raeder, was allowed home on the same grounds. Finally, a year later, tension mounted among the prisoners as Dönitz's time approached—again. He himself grew quieter and more inclined to fits of melancholy, although from time to time, according to Speer, he emerged to play the Grand Admiral and presumptive Head of State again, informing the others that the Powers were devising a procedure for dismissing him that would not attract attention, and that he and Kranzbühler would work for their release once he was out.[142]

On what was expected to be his last day, September 30th 1956, he said to Speer that he wanted to discuss something with him; it turned out to be the question of whether Speer had recommended him as Hitler's successor during his last visit to the Führer bunker in Berlin. Speer told him—according to his account—that he had not; a direct recommendation to Hitler was usually counter-productive; he had simply answered questions about how he, Dönitz, was managing in the northern area. 'Extremely well,' he had told Hitler. When Göring was deposed a few hours later he had had the feeling that Dönitz would be appointed. 'But it wasn't I who proposed you.'

Dönitz said he had to know for his memoirs. Then, suddenly hostile, he accused him of being to blame for his imprisonment and the loss of eleven years of his life.

'What did I have to do with politics? But for you, Hitler would never have had the idea of making me Head of State. All my men have commands again. But look at me! Like a criminal. My career is wrecked.'[143]

Speer, stung, retorted that Dönitz had 'slandered, disparaged and ostracized' him for ten years. Now he wanted him to hear something: 'You and the others here have endlessly talked about honour. Every other word you or Schirach utters is dignity, bearing. This war killed

477

millions of people. More millions were murdered in the camps by those criminals. All of us here were part of the regime. But your ten years here perturb you more than the 50 million dead. And your last words here in Spandau are—your career!'[144]

Dönitz did not leave a record of his time in prison, nor did the others; moreover he told his niece after the publication of Speer's recollections that he had not and would not read them; it is not possible, therefore, to check Speer's account. Probably it was coloured by the hostility he had endured from Dönitz and the others, possibly it was distorted by his own 'prison psychosis', and his guilt feelings; the story might even be a fantasy like those Dönitz dreamed up to put down his enemies and present himself in a favourable light. Yet the attitudes depicted are surely correct: there are too many other indications of Dönitz's concern to present himself as an honourable sailor to doubt the attitude ascribed to him here—indeed it appears to have been one of the chief aims of the memoirs he busied himself with directly he left prison.

It was not quite his final word. After supper that evening he shook each of his fellow prisoners by the hand and bade them farewell; he was visibly moved when he came to Speer. Later Speer heard him weeping in his cell. It was not until towards the end of his own sentence that he realized the pressures that caused 'strong-nerved Dönitz' to weep quietly during the last hours of his imprisonment.[145]

Dönitz was kept until the stroke of midnight; when he was taken up to collect his possessions, the Russian director said, 'Sign here, number two,' and when he had done so, 'so that ends that, Admiral Dönitz.'

Ingeborg had been working as a nursing sister in a Hamburg hospital while Dönitz was in Spandau, and struggling to remake a home in rented rooms on the ground floor of a villa in Aumühle; it was a large house, not unlike the one they had possessed in Dahlem, set amongst trees and shrub-bordered lawns in this quiet residential town outside Hamburg, but the flat itself, consisting of two main rooms, was somewhat gloomy and scarcely fitting the status of a Grand Admiral. It was a pleasant spot though, convenient both for the U-boat reunions in Hamburg and Kiel and for walks in the surrounding countryside and forest, and this was where he settled after a brief holiday in Badenweiler, surrounding himself with books and pictures of ships and U-boats and old comrades, buying engravings from time to time to replace those looted by the

British. His pension had been raised to that of an admiral, two grades below his former rank, so, while not wealthy, he was never short of money.

His first task was to produce his memoirs, and he was soon hard at work on the detailed material supplied mainly by his son-in-law, who had access to the archives captured by the British. The book appeared two years later under the title *10 Jahre und 20 Tage* (*Ten Years and Twenty Days*); it was, as was to be expected, concerned exclusively with his activities as a naval officer. The first 328 pages detailed his development of the *Rudel* (pack) tactic before the war and the various phases of the Battle of the Atlantic up to the spring of 1943, ending with a conveniently abbreviated quotation from Captain Stephen Roskill's official *History of the War at Sea*; instead of completing Roskill's sentence, 'After 45 months of unceasing battle of a more exacting and arduous nature than posterity may easily realize, our [allied] convoy escorts and aircraft had won the triumph they so richly deserved', he cut it after 'may easily realize' and finished in his own words, 'the tremendous sea- and air-defences of both the greatest seapowers, above all on the basis of the new detection methods, had crushed the U-boat war.'[146] A small enough change perhaps—it might even be said substituting one side's propaganda for the other's—nevertheless fundamental in its revelation of the spirit of self-justification pervading the whole book; there are countless similar instances.

The next 54 pages opened simply: 'After my appointment as C-in-C,' with no discussion of how this came about, and dealt with the various theatres of the sea war in seven sub-sections—the Mediterranean, Black Sea, Baltic and so on. His treatment of the loss of the *Scharnhorst* in the 'northern area' is particularly revealing. He omitted the crucial question of radar altogether; Burnett's cruiser squadron appears to have found the *Scharnhorst* in the wastes of the Arctic night by eye, and to have shadowed her by eye, and the same for the *Duke of York* and the final gun action. Admiral Bey's message when breaking away from the cruisers that he was under 'radar-directed fire from a heavy unit' was the sole reference to this absolutely vital aspect of the battle. In the run-up to the decision to send the battlecruiser out in the first place, he omitted the suspicious message from 200 miles astern of the convoy which turned out to have been from the *Duke of York*, and the weather forecasts of gales and snowstorms, depicting what was really a gamble of extreme hazard as a simple operation on which all were agreed: 'In my opinion and in

479

that of the Fleet Command and the naval High Command this was a great chance for the *Scharnhorst*.'[147]

Most disgraceful of all was a subtle attempt, like the one he had made in the aftermath of the action, to shift blame to the shoulders of Admiral Bey; since Bey had been unable to make a report and explain his decisions, he wrote, it was not known whether the battle could have been handled in 'other or better ways', and therefore one could not criticize, 'only raise questions', which he proceeded to do.[148]

After his glance at the naval aspects of the various theatres of war came five pages on the July 20th plot. This, he wrote, had to be seen free from present political prejudices. The mass of German people at the time stood behind Hitler; 'one had no inkling of the facts known to the resistance, which induced them to act'.[149] Even without the knowledge since gained from the archives this was a truly breathtaking statement; the plotters' legal adviser came from within his own service! It would have been better for his reputation if he had omitted the sentence and dealt with the affair on the practical basis of the internal chaos which must have resulted if the plot had succeeded—as he proceeded to do.

As for his feelings towards the plotters now, if they knew of the outrages 'which today we all know', he could not dispute their motives. At the time, however, the Navy had not had the same contacts with Hitler as the generals, since Hitler personally conducted the land battles, whereas the sea war was something foreign and uncanny to him. Moreover, the Navy had not seen what many generals and army staff officers had seen of Himmler's activities behind the lines in the east. Any tolerably informed person might have asked him what naval officers in the Baltic bases had been doing when the Jews were rounded up and deported from there, what indeed he and his officers in Paris were doing when that city had become the centre for deportation of French Jews. But a more fundamental question from the point of view of the rational prosecution of the war was, did Army and Navy officers have no contact even at the highest level? The whole section is an insult to the intelligence of his readers—although not, it seems, to many reviewers of the English-language edition in Great Britain and America.

There followed 26 pages on the U-boat war from May 1943 to the end. The staggering sacrifices of men and materials during this period he justified chiefly on the grounds of the huge allied resources that would otherwise have been released for the offensive against German coasts, sea traffic and civil population, also because morale would have collapsed if they had broken off the campaign and it would have been difficult to re-start afterwards with the new boats. He ended this section with Churchill's tribute in his *History of the Second World War* to the stubbornness and implacable courage with which the U-boats had fought to the very end.[150]

The remaining 42 pages of text were taken up with the final months of the war; it was the allies' demand for unconditional surrender, and their plans for the partition and destruction of the German nation, that had been responsible for the German continuation of the war to the bitter end; as for himself, he had considered the rescue of Germans from the east as his first priority, and here he followed his former adjutant, Lüdde-Neurath, whose *Regierung Dönitz*, published in 1950, had already pointed to the disastrous consequences that would have over-taken the armies in the east had they laid down their arms in mid-winter.[151] Dönitz did not mention his own support for Hitler's deter-mination to hold the Baltic areas to the last—the real reason why so many troops were in the east and why the evacuation had to be carried out under such gruelling conditions. The legend of the rescue of millions of easterners had been prepared by his adherents; he only had to confirm it, and of course he did.

His account of the final April days in command of the northern area was concerned chiefly to distance himself from Himmler. His story of their midnight meeting on April 30th after he had been appointed Hitler's successor is reminiscent of the fantasies he had indulged in in his 1934 account of his Hindenburg Award journey. He had passed Himmler the telegram from Berlin with the curt instruction to read it, and after the SS chief's servile response, bowing and asking to be his second man, had simply told him he had no use for him!

Coming next to his radio message to the German people in the evening of May 1st, he completely omitted the first section giving the news that Hitler had died a hero's death 'fighting to the end against the Bolshevik storm flood . . .' Similarly he omitted the opening section from his order of the day to the *Wehrmacht*, that with the death of Hitler they had lost 'one of the greatest heroes of German history . . .'[152]

It would be tedious to list all the half-truths, evasions and downright lies with which the volume is replete—even about the actual course of the U-boat war; it was designed for two main purposes: to justify his own handling of the U-boat arm and, in the later stages, the Navy; and to present himself as an upright and honourable naval officer who had

481

known nothing of anything else taking place in any other areas. Speer, reading it in his cell in Spandau, felt it 'the book of a man without insight. For him, the tragedy of the recent past is reduced to the miserable question of what mistakes led to the loss of the war. But should this surprise me?'[153]

Later Speer wrote that he was becoming more and more puzzled why Dönitz systematically obscured his personal relationship to Hitler, and the high esteem in which Hitler held him. Contrary to the story he himself had told him on the last day in Spandau, Dönitz asserted in the book that Speer had proposed him as the successor, presumably to strengthen his claim that he had no personal relationship with Hitler. 'Dönitz maintains he had no inkling of Hitler's esteem for him. Hadn't it ever struck him that he was one of the very few men awarded the distinction of an armoured Mercedes weighing some five tons? Or that during the last months of the war Hitler forbade him to use an aeroplane? . . .'[154]

Of course Speer knew exactly what Dönitz was doing in his memoirs, and these published diary excerpts were presumably in retaliation for the hostility he had experienced since Nuremberg.

Dönitz was kinder to Raeder than his attitude in Spandau had suggested; he made much of his own call for a U-boat alternative to the 'Z-Plan' before the war, but did not make it a personal matter, no doubt to preserve a united naval front against the politicians; Raeder also brought out his memoirs at about this time and did not say what he had really thought of Dönitz! It is an open question which of the two Grand Admirals produced the more deliberately dishonest volume.

Whether Dönitz still hoped that a turn of the political wheel might reinstate him in his legitimate position as Head of State is difficult to say. He talked of it. When his former adjutant, Hansen-Nootbar, visited him in 1958, they went for long walks as of old and discussed the question, but Hansen-Nootbar could not make out whether he really wanted to involve himself in politics;[155] Dönitz did say that he believed he meant more to the German *Volk* than they admitted, but this may well have been to impress his former subordinate. The *Wirtschaftswunder* had transformed West Germany by this time. Prosperity and old bourgeois values, which he and everyone else in 1945 had thought would never rise again, had blossomed; few wished to remember the immediate past. He was of that past; probably he realized it.

He attended dinners and numerous functions organized by the various naval and U-boat associations, received old comrades at his flat, gave interviews and corresponded with historians and others interested in naval affairs from all over the world, but it is probable that he realized his active days were over.

In 1962, in May, his tragic month when he had lost both sons and the U-boat war, and indeed the war itself, Ingeborg died, and the final lonely phase of his life began. He had become a Christian, and he had a large carved wooden crucifix placed over the grave: Christ, as he told his pastor, was the only one to whom, finally, he could adhere.[156]

As he grew older, he dwelled more and more in his grand early years, and began work on another volume of memoirs to cover this period. The volume came out in 1968 as *Mein wechselvolles Leben* (*My Changeful Life*). Whereas at the end of his first volume of memoirs he had been concerned to separate himself and the Navy from the criminal side of the regime, in this later volume, no doubt encouraged by many expressions of disgust with the Nuremberg trials from former enemies, he turned his concluding chapter into an attack on the Nuremberg process in general, his own sentence in particular. Relying on the vagueness of the wording in the judgement, he defended himself on three points which, he suggested, had been used to convict him of war crimes: these were the 'Commando' order, which had not concerned him when it first appeared, and of which, he wrote, he had heard no further word during his time as C-in-C; his suggestion that concentration camp inmates be used in the shipyards, which he explained in the same terms as he had used at Nuremberg; and finally the charge concerning his attitude to the Geneva Convention, which again he defended in the terms he had used at his trial. He made no mention of the 'severe censure' that had been passed on the ambiguity in his *Laconia* orders, and came to the conclusion that the judgement against him had been unjust on every point: 'It was evidently on political grounds that I had to go behind bars.'[157]

Making all allowance for his personal difficulty in admitting he had been wrong on any point at any time, and the huge difficulty anyone in his position would have had in acknowledging the barbarities he had been a party to, it is still hard to square this aggressively unrepentant attitude with the huge Christ crucified he had erected over his wife's grave.

He repeated exactly the same line in another volume he wrote at this time under the title *Deutsche Strategie zur See im zweiten Weltkrieg*, changed in later editions to *40 Fragen an Karl Dönitz* (*40 Questions to*

Karl Dönitz). Here he quoted from the many letters he had received from former enemy countries; typical was one he cited from the British military historian, J. F. C. Fuller, who apparently considered the judgement against him 'a flagrant travesty of justice resulting from hypocrisy'.[158] Whatever may be said of the more political aspects of the charges, particularly the difficult question of 'aggressive war'—which it seems from the rest of the letter probably concerned Fuller most—it cannot be said too often that the victors had every right to try individuals for war crimes and crimes against humanity. The law and the machinery were well established and to suggest—if Fuller and the others whose letters Dönitz quoted had indeed suggested—that genocide, the murder of captured prisoners on land and the massacre of shipwrecked survivors at sea, to all of which Dönitz was party, were not illegal at the time the acts were committed is plainly nonsense.

Dönitz was equally happy to cite the opinion of his former enemies about his strategic and tactical conduct of the war at sea; he quoted the British First Sea Lord, Admiral of the Fleet, Lord Cunningham, writing in the *Sunday Times*, that 'Karl Dönitz was probably the most dangerous enemy Britain has had to face since de Ruyter', and that 'it was extremely fortunate for us that his advice was so little heeded by his political leaders',[159] and Stephen Roskill in his official history: 'The small total [number of U-boats] available early in the year [1942], combined with diversions to unprofitable purposes, now seems to have been a decisive factor in the Atlantic battle.'[160]

Here we are at the nub of the real question about Dönitz's career and historical importance: could his U-boats have brought Great Britain to her knees if his strategy, of concentrating all naval resources on the U-boat arm and the Atlantic theatre, had been adopted? Like all historical 'ifs' this is not a question that can ever be answered. It is no good trying to deduce the tonnage that would have been sunk during 1941 by calculating how many U-boats could have been produced in the time available, how many crews could have been trained, then multiplying the total available for operations by the actual U-boat 'potential'—or tonnage sunk per U-boat per day at sea. Likely British reactions to mounting losses have to be put into the equation. For had the U-boat campaign looked as if it were about to strangle the British Isles, it must be doubted if it would have taken so long for the Royal Navy to have trained support groups, doubted if the Royal Air Force would have been allowed to misuse its bombers over Germany instead of protecting merchant shipping. Surely, too, the supply routes would have been concentrated as foreshadowed by *Kapitänleutnant* Fresdorf's paper in 1939, into a single highway across the North Atlantic from New York, which would have been made the focus of all other routes, and the vast agglomeration of shipping would have been protected by the whole strength of the Royal Navy, including aircraft carriers, for the passage across the 'air gap'. In short, if the British Admiralty had realized that all German naval resources were being concentrated on the U-boat Battle of the Atlantic, it must have responded with a similar concentration on defence in this area. Common sense and naval history alike suggest that had it done so it would have contained the threat. And if it had begun to look as though it might not, would the United States have stood by passively and watched the penultimate stronghold of the free world go under? There was plenty of uninformed isolationist sentiment around, but Roosevelt, at least, was under no illusions about Hitler's long-term designs and the danger to America from a Nazi Germany triumphant.

On the German side, quite apart from the effects on the *Luftwaffe* and *Panzer* divisions of such a concentration of resources on the U-boat arm, there was the essential weakness of contemporary U-boats—their low underwater speed. It was not necessary for the British to destroy them, only to force them under so that they lost contact or lost the ability to gain position for attack. To assume that the Royal Navy and Air Force would not or could not have combined to accomplish this is to fall into the very trap that Dönitz constantly fell into, of ignoring or underestimating the reactions of the opponent. Nor should it be forgotten that the decisive step in radar research, the discovery of the magnetron permitting 'centimetric' radar, had been made at Birmingham University by February 1940, and therefore all German efforts to step up the U-boat campaign would have been racing British efforts to develop and equip escorts and escorting aircraft with centimetric radar—against whose magic eye the U-boats had no counter.

It may be, therefore, that Dönitz's assertion that he would have beaten Great Britain if only he had been given 300 U-boats at the beginning—a formula which he continued to repeat against all historical arguments that war against trade alone had *never* succeeded in the long history of naval warfare—was as large, although unconscious, a deception as his insistence that he had been an unpolitical naval officer.

As for the new Electro boats, these were potentially dangerous, but

485

without *Luftwaffe* support they would have found it as difficult to find targets as the conventional boats, and they had other disadvantages which would have prevented them having more than nuisance value against the allied concentration of sea and air power.

In the early 1970s the past began to catch up with Dönitz. German naval historians had formerly been in the van of academic nationalism, prepared, like Raeder and Dönitz, to bend facts and distort, fake and suppress evidence for what they conceived as the good of the State. Now a new wave of German historians sought truth. Amongst them Volker Berghahn exposed the grandiose ambitions behind the Tirpitz plan, Jost Dülffer exposed Raeder's role in the Weimar Republic and the early years of the Third Reich, Gerhard Schreiber exposed the red thread linking Tirpitz and Raeder, the drive to world mastery, Michael Salewski exposed Dönitz's total identification with the Nazi State.[161]

Meanwhile in America, Professor Erich Goldhagen published evidence that Himmler, during his speech at the Gauleiters' *Tagung* in Posen in October 1943, had addressed an aside to Speer, who must, he asserted, have been present and thus have learned about the extermination programme.[162] Speer published a reply saying that he had left Posen after lunch that day, and while Himmler may have thought he was present during his speech in the afternoon, there had been so many in the hall he could not have identified who was and was not there! During this disclaimer, no doubt on purpose, Speer listed all the speakers at the *Tagung* and the times they had spoken—in the fateful afternoon session, Dönitz. For good measure he gave the opening words of Dönitz's speech.[163]

Dönitz must now have felt himself under threat from all sides, particularly as denouncements of the U-boat strategy that had caused such heavy losses in the latter stages of the war were appearing in popular works in Germany. It is not surprising, therefore, that when a BBC television team visited him in 1973 in the course of making a series of programmes on the U-boat war, he would not make any spontaneous statements, took out books from the huge collection that lined his walls to verify anything he said, and refused to be drawn on Hitler, in the words of the producer, 'as if terrified he would be whipped back into Spandau'.[164] His extraordinarily suspicious attitude struck the producer as bordering on persecution mania. One thing he was happy to talk about, however, was his strategy and tactics; he was proud of having

486

evolved an 'unbeatable strategy' for the defeat of England, and could have done it, he said, had it not been for political animals like Göring and Bormann.

Ludovic Kennedy, who was making the programme, recalled his first impression as being, 'how small he was, in repose like a wizened nut, in conversation like a virile old ferret'.[165] He had written out some fifteen pages, partly in English partly in German, in reply to the two questions it had been agreed he would be asked in front of the camera; he read them out as if addressing 'the furthest sailor on the longest parade ground in the Third Reich'. The essence of it was that if he had had the 300 U-boats he had asked for in the beginning, 'I think we would have won the war by 1942'. Kennedy visited him on another occasion after the release of the 'Ultra' secrets revealing how the allies had cracked the U-boat code; when he told Dönitz of this, Kennedy had the impression he did not believe him.[166]

The British television team formed the impression of an austere old man accustomed to a frugal existence, dapperish but rather frail; the Cambridge historian, Jonathan Steinberg, another of the many visitors to the Aumühle flat, felt himself in the presence of someone from the lowest circle of Dante's inferno, where all are frozen to ice. He came to life only twice during the interview, on the first occasion showing great anger that he had had to go to war on two occasions with the wrong weapons, and deploring the shortage of U-boats he had had to work with, the second time when he came to the subject of the *Scharnhorst*, again growing heated and justifying his decisions over her last sortie at great length.[167]

Photographs of him from the period convey an impression of a man peering out suspiciously from inside his skull as if haunted by the past and wondering whether it was going to blow up beneath him; perhaps the Judges at Nuremberg had sentenced him to a crueller fate than those who were hanged.

Undoubtedly he was retreating into himself. His daughter, Ursula, recalls how he seemed to recover physically from his ordeal in Spandau, but as time went on it had become evident he had not recovered in spirit. Even before Ingeborg's death he had become intolerant of any differences of opinion; growing deafness did not make him any easier, and the Hessler family visits to Aumühle became more infrequent. She had the impression in the later years that he was quite glad to be left alone again when they had gone. They tried to get him to have a housekeeper but it was impossible to discuss anything with him, and he continued to make do with a Prussian woman who came three times a week.[168]

His youngest niece, Brigitte, may have provided some of the brightest moments of his final years. She came to see him first after a break of over 25 years in about 1970, and he was visibly moved by the reunion.[169] After that she made visits from time to time, and he would take her out to eat at one of the local restaurants where he was a well-known figure, greeted by young and old alike, and talk to her of his younger days and of her father, his brother . . . and of those uncomplicated times of striving in his profession, the finest there was:

'. . . an officer of the best conceivable military qualities, of exemplary service outlook and the fullest devotion to his duty . . . a good comrade and, despite a serious outlook on life, full of hearty merriment . . . lively and energetic, an excellent soldier, decided in action, clear and confident in word and deed . . . a very popular comrade . . . As father of three children he had a considerable economic struggle against the exigencies of the time . . . A tough, brisk officer of indestructible leadership capacity, always at his post, placed high demands on himself . . . thoughtful, also inclined to be very critical of himself . . . high-minded, of good culture, jolly in social intercourse, ambitious . . . possessed much verve and knew how to get on with his men. Extremely duty-conscious and energetic . . . to the needs and cares of officers and men he brings an extremely warm heart . . . always ready to help . . . *Korvettenkapitän* Dönitz is an officer with strong personality who deserves special observation and promotion . . .

'. . . His strong temperament and inner verve frequently affected him with restlessness and, for his age, imbalance. Must, therefore be brought to take things more calmly and not set exaggerated demands, above all on himself . . . Ambition and the endeavour to distinguish himself remain outstanding characteristics . . . A strong personality of great knowledge and ability who will always give outstanding performances . . .

'Then the English staff officer wrote on a piece of paper the number of my previous boat, UC 25, and the name of the fat English steamer I had turned over in the Sicilian naval harbour of Port Augusta, and shoved the paper to the Admiral. I was amazed how well these people were in the picture. They knew exactly who I was . . .

'I have also never seen the brown women scold their own children and certainly not hit them—that would be to them, with their strong, animal natural child-love, quite inconceivable . . .

'In my dreams I saw your small band, you, Jeschen, first, climbing the steep way to heaven's gate . . . There in the distance in beaming, rosy morning light you saw the high, mighty fortress of heaven with turrets and pinnacles thrusting in the clouds. Yes, heaven's portals were opened wide to you because you could not give more to your *Volk* than you have given!

'. . . an excellent officer of iron willpower, goal-oriented certainty and unwearying toughness . . . teacher, example and stimulus to his officers . . . promising to become an outstanding leader in higher positions . . .'

By the 1970s it is probable he had convinced himself of his innocence of war guilt—it is possible, of course, that he had convinced himself even before the end of the Nuremberg trials—and his greatest disappointment—after the failure of his U-boat campaign—was the failure of the efforts made on his behalf with the Federal Government and with the former allied powers to clear his name. The campaign flickered for the last time in 1976 with the publication of *Dönitz at Nuremberg; a reappraisal*. It was not a reappraisal; no new evidence was produced. After the third of Michael Salewski's volumes on the wartime naval High Command had come out in 1975 a reappraisal could only have been highly damaging—which is perhaps why the American editors finally brought out the book when they did some twenty years after they started the project. On the other hand, it is possible they were not aware of the evidence which had been surfacing since Nuremberg, which rendered their extraordinary mix of overstated and usually uninformed opinions more valueless than they would have been at the start of the campaign.

Undoubtedly it brought great pleasure to Dönitz and to the old comrades in the naval and U-boat associations who had been working to raise him to the highest pedestal as an officer of 'unexcelled ability' who had 'offered his person and sacrificed his future to save the lives of many thousands of people'—to quote from the book's extraordinary dedication to him.[170]

He signed a copy for Brigitte in an unsteady hand, and hoped that the government, when they saw it, would permit him a State Funeral. He told the pastor in whose Church he prayed every Sunday that there was no doubt of his support for the Federal Republic. He would have on his coffin the black, red and golden flag.

By the autumn of 1980 he was obviously failing; almost deaf, practically blind and with the little strength left in his frail body visibly ebbing, he was taken unwillingly to hospital. No recognizable illness could be detected; he seemed merely to have run his course. After a few weeks, on November 20th, his wishes were granted and he was taken back to his flat in Aumühle, where he was cared for by nurses.

His former staff officers and old comrades, who had worked for his defence at Nuremberg, raised funds for Ingeborg to visit him at Spandau, petitioned the powers for his release, built a legend around his name and honoured and comforted him after his release, remained loyal to the end. His morning post was read for him as, neatly dressed and conscious as ever of his duty, he sat in a chair by his telephone with a glass of white Vermouth before him, and shouted replies, which were typed and sent. Towards Christmas, men from the *Deutscher Marinebund* came to his flat and sang him carols and the old sea-songs he loved, *Kameraden, wann sehen wir uns wieder?*—'Comrades, when shall we meet again?' He received them afterwards in his book-lined room and shook each by the hand. 'You have made me very happy.' Then he retired to the bedroom where pictures of his father and his wife and children were arranged on a chest of drawers beneath a carved wooden crucifix.[171]

He seldom found the strength to leave his bed during these final days. As one of those closest to him put it, his life waned like a candle flame which becomes very small before finally it extinguishes.[172]

The flame flickered out quietly at about ten minutes past seven in the evening of Christmas Eve.

The old comrades, as bitterly disappointed as he had been at the refusal of the Bonn government to grant him a State Funeral, or even to permit uniforms to be worn at any private funeral, made their own arrangements to pay their last respects at the Bismarck Memorial Chapel in Aumühle on January 6th 1981.

Finally, after the crowds have departed the churchyard, one stands before the great carved Christ crucified, crowned with snow, thinking of his last pronouncements, 'My position would have been completely different if I had not been Hitler's successor. But no one asks me today,

490

"What would have happened had Himmler been appointed to my position in the last days of the *Reich*? . . . I did everything humanly possible in a chaotic time.'[173]

Or perhaps his final words were contained in a letter dictated in halting English in February 1971, only to be opened and published after his death:

> British people!
> When we lose war, You lose with us!
> True enemies, red Russia and Communism, are now on your door!
> After the war, you judge us: why?
> I know, so well as you, that not any true was in accusation, if you except struggle against Hebrews!
> Times are very dangerous: it is necessary to joint and to fight together against the enemies of God and Europe!
> We are right to help you: remember, we are brothers!
> When you will read this letter I will be in Peace: with me they will be all the heroes . . . british, french, german.
> UNITE AND SAVE EUROPE!
> Truly yours
> Dönitz[174]

To be buried under the flag of the Federal Republic and admit publicly that the central tenet of Nazi world philosophy had been wrong was a long way for Dönitz to have travelled. How far had he come in private? Was it personal loss and imagined injustice that had turned him to ice—as Speer thought, a man without insight? Or had he recognized his years of power for what they were, the blood-seal of his nation's pact with the Anti-Christ? Did such a perception rush in perhaps during those last moments on Christmas Eve immediately before he stood before the judgement seat of Christ?

References and Notes

The following abbreviations have been used in references:

A/S R	British Admiralty monthly anti-submarine reports.
BA/MA	*Bundesarchiv-Militärarchiv*, Freiburg, West Germany.
F/*Vorträge*	C-in-C, *Kriegsmarine*, reports and discussions with the *Führer*.
Hindenburgreise	Unpublished typescript in diary form by Karl Dönitz of his Hindenburg Award travels.
IMT	International Military Tribunal; evidence and documents presented at the trials of the major war criminals, published Nuremberg, 1948. English-language edition.
IWM	Imperial War Museum, London.
KTB	War diary, referenced by command and date of entry only as sufficient for archival location. Thus:
BdS KTB	war diary, *Schnell*-boat Command.
BdU KTB (earlier, FdU KTB)	war diary, U-boat Command.
OKW KTB	war diary. Armed Forces High Command (the entries here all from J. Schultz: *Die Letzten 30 Tage*, Stuttgart, 1951).
1/Skl KTB A	war diary, Naval War Staff Operations Division.
U 39 KTB	war diary, U 39 for 1917 (archival ref: PG 61587).
MGM	*Militärgeschichtliche Mitteilungen* (journal)
Nat. Mar.	National Maritime Museum, Greenwich, England.
Nav. Lib.	Naval Library, Ministry of Defence, London.
P/Akte	personal records of Grand Admiral Karl Dönitz (PG 31044).
PG number	archival reference given to captured German naval records by the British.
PRO	Public Record Office, London (Kew Gardens).
Raeder Akte	personal file of Grand Admiral F. Raeder (PG 34004).
Saville	A. W. Saville; *The Development of the German U-boat arm, 1919–1935*, unpub. PhD, Washington Univ., 1963.

493

ONE *Ich hatt' einen Kameraden*

1 Address published in *Marine Rundschau*, 1/1981, pp. 1–2
2 H. Jaenecke in *Stern*, Jan. 9, 1981, p. 61
3 See Pastor H.-J. Arp's address in Dönitz: *Dokumentation*, pp. 16–20
4 Jaenecke above ref. 2
5 A. Schnee: *'Abschied vom Grossadmiral'* in *Schaltung-Küste*, Feb. 1981

TWO *The Imperial Naval Officer*

1 *P/Akte*
2 Dönitz: *Wechselvolles*, p. 18
3 ibid., p. 8
4 Frau Fidelak to author, 18.3.1982
5 Dönitz to Frau Dönitz from Spandau prison, cited Fishman, p. 192 (All these letters now apparently not extant)
6 Frau Fidelak to author, 18.3.1982
7 G. Sandhofer: *Dokumente zu militärischem Werdegang des Gr.admls Dönitz*, in MGM 1/1967, p. 60
8 Dönitz: *Wechselvolles*, p. 9
9 v. Bülow, p. 270
10 McClelland, p. 168
11 ibid., p. 181
12 Dorpalen, p. 149
13 ibid., pp. 149–50
14 v. Bülow to Richthofen, 26.7. 1899, cited P. Kennedy: 'German World Policy and the Alliance Negotiations with England, 1897–1900' in *Journal of Modern History*, vol. 45, 4/1973, p. 618
15 P. Kennedy: 'The Kaiser and German Weltpolitik' in Röhl & Sombart, p. 148: see also P. Kennedy: *Anglo-German Antagonism*, pp. 361 ff.
16 Dönitz: *Wechselvolles*, p. 13
17 ibid., p. 22
18 Frau Fidelak to author, 12.12.1982
19 Dönitz: *Wechselvolles*, p. 17
20 ibid., p. 18
21 ibid., p. 20
22 ibid., p. 19
23 ibid.
24 Herwig: *Luxury Fleet*, p. 117
25 Herwig: *Naval Officer Corps*, p. 55
26 ibid., pp. 40–1
27 Dönitz: *Wechselvolles*, p. 24
28 Frau Fidelak to author, 25.2.1982
29 Dönitz: *Wechselvolles*, p. 25
30 ibid., p. 33
31 ibid., p. 25
32 Dönitz: *40 Fragen*, p. 9
33 ibid.
34 Herwig: *Naval Officer Corps*, p. 66
35 Naval Attaché Reports, Jan. 29, 1914, Nav. Lib., Ca 2053
36 Bebel's letter enclosed in Angst to Tyrrell, Sept. 24, 1910, PRO ADM 116 940B
37 See Berghahn: *Tirpitz Plan*
38 Capt. H. L. Heath (Nav. attaché, Berlin) to E. Goschen, Aug. 6, 1910, PRO ADM 116 940B
39 Capt. Dumas to F. Lascelles, Aug. 6, 1908, PRO ADM 116 940B
40 Dönitz: *Wechselvolles*, p. 32
41 ibid., p. 33
42 ibid., p. 23
43 ibid., p. 38
44 Dec. 3, 1912: cited v. Tirpitz, Vol. I, p. 361
45 Three separate accounts of this meeting are in J. Röhl: 'Admiral v. Müller and the Approach of War, 1911–1914' in *Historical Journal* XII, 4/1969, pp. 661 ff.

46 See for instance P. Kennedy: 'The Kaiser and German Weltpolitik' in Röhl & Sombart

47 Dönitz: *Wechselvolles*, p. 50

48 ibid., p. 53

49 v. Hase, p. 3

50 Dönitz: *Wechselvolles*, p. 61

51 *P/Akte*

52 Dönitz: *Wechselvolles*, p. 68

53 Berghahn: *Approach of War*, p. 140

54 See ibid., pp. 116 ff.: Fischer, pp. 34 ff.

55 See Berghahn: *Approach of War*, p. 152; Röhl: *Delusion*, p. 31

56 Berghahn: *Approach of War*, p. 186

57 See K. Jarausch: 'Bethmann-Hollweg's Calculated Risk, July 1914' in *Journal of Central European History*, March 1969, pp. 54–5

58 V. Berghahn & W. Deist: '*Kaiserliche Marine und Kriegsausbruch 1914; Neue Dokumente . . .*' in MGM 1/1970, p. 45

59 Memo. by Pr. Lichnowsky, Berlin, Jan. 1915; cited Röhl: *Delusion*, p. 83

60 Berghahn & Deist, above ref. 58, p. 46

61 Dönitz: *Wechselvolles*, p. 72

62 Hopmann to v. Tirpitz, 20.7.1914; cited Berghahn & Deist, above ref. 58, pp. 53–4

63 ibid.

64 Dönitz: *Wechselvolles*, p. 72

65 ibid., p. 73

66 ibid., p. 74

67 July 31, 1914: cited Balfour, pp. 350–51

68 Dönitz: *Wechselvolles*, p. 74

69 cited Appendix: Grey

70 v. Müller diary, Aug. 1, 1914; cited Röhl: 'Admiral v. Müller . . .', above ref. 45, p. 669

71 Dönitz: *Wechselvolles*, p. 77

72 ibid., p. 82

73 Report of detached service, H.M.S. *Gloucester*, Aug. 28, 1914, PRO ADM 137 3105

74 Adml. Limpus diary, Aug. 11, 1914, Nat. Mar. (uncatalogued)

75 Manten, p. 45

76 Corbett, vol. I, p. 360

77 Dönitz: *Breslau*, pp. 14–17

78 Dönitz: *Wechselvolles*, p. 96

79 Corbett, vol. I, p. 71

80 Dönitz: Breslau, pp. 130–31

81 Manten, p. 166

82 ibid., p. 115

83 Dönitz: *Breslau*, pp. 119–20

84 Dönitz: *Wechselvolles*, p. 101

85 *P/Akte*: *Beurteilung*, Aug. 1915

86 Dönitz: *Wechselvolles*, p. 102

87 Dönitz: *Breslau*, pp. 147–8

88 ibid., pp. 150–51

89 ibid., p. 153

90 ibid., p. 156

91 Manten, p. 264

92 Dönitz: *Wechselvolles*, p. 106

93 *P/Akte*: *Beurteilung*, 18.9.1916

94 quoted Dönitz: *Wechselvolles*, p. 107

95 *P/Akte*: *Beurteilung*, Nov. 25, 1916

96 v. Holtzendorff memo., Dec. 22, 1916, cited Scheer, p. 249

97 ibid.

98 ibid., p. 252; see also Corbett, vol. III, pp. 345–6

99 Forstmann, p. 51; see also Herzog & Schomaekers

100 Forstmann, p. 99

101 ibid., p. 40

102 ibid., p. 59

103 Neureuther & Bergen, p. 90

104 ibid., p. 103

105 Kerr to Jackson, June 8, 1916; cited Marder, vol. III, p. 276

106 Forstmann, pp. 49–50

107 ibid., p. 63

108 U 39 KTB, 15.2.1917, 1H 30m Nm.

109 Forstmann, pp. 65–6

110 U 39 KTB, 15.2.1917, 1H 45m Nm.

111 Forstmann, p. 64

112 ibid., pp. 57–8

113 ibid., p. 108

114 Marder, Vol. IV, p. 102 for actual figures; Scheer, p. 261 for German estimates

115 Duff's minute, April 26, agreed by Jellicoe; see Marder, IV, p. 159

116 Forstmann, p. 92

117 ibid., pp. 97–8

118 Spindler, vol. V, p. 166

119 U 39 KTB, 5.8.1917, 11H 9m Vm.

120 ibid., 11H 10m Vm.

121 Forstmann, p. 104

122 U 39 KTB, 9.8.1917, 3H 15m Nm.

123 *Hindenburgreise*, p. 2

124 U 39 KTB, Sept. 18–Okt 14, 1917, endorsement on report

125 *P/Akte*: *Beurteilung* Dec. 1, 1917

126 Dönitz to Forstmann, Feb. 1943; cited Herzog & Schomaekers, p. 72

127 Dönitz: *Wechselvolles*, p. 109

128 Marder, vol. IV, p. 277 for actual figures; Scheer, p. 261 for German estimates

129 Spindler, vol. IV, pp. 567–8

130 from ibid., vol. V, p. 182

131 Dönitz: *Wechselvolles*, p. 114

132 Spindler, vol. V. p. 183

133 ibid., p. 217

134 Interrogation of UB 68 prisoners, PRO ADM 137 3900

135 Interrogation of Captain of UB class boat, Mar. 23, 1918, PRO ADM 137 3900

136 Herzog: *60 Jahre*, p. 171

137 ibid., p. 173

138 This description from Dönitz: *Wechselvolles*, pp. 118–19, and Dönitz, *10 Jahre*, pp. 7–8

139 Nav. W. O. Bohrmann's account in interrogation of UB 68 prisoners, above ref. 134

140 Dönitz: *Wechselvolles*, pp. 119–20

141 Interrogation UB 68 prisoners, above ref. 134

142 ibid.

143 *Hindenburgreise*, p. 114

144 ibid., pp. 113–14

145 ibid., and Dönitz: *Wechselvolles*, p. 127

THREE *Towards the Second World War*

1 Dönitz: *Wechselvolles*, p. 130

2 Frank: *Sea Wolves*, p. 13

3 Kelley, p. 106

4 Herwig: *Naval Officer Corps*, p. 260

5 See Horn: also Herwig; *Luxury Fleet*, p. 254

6 See Bird, p. 42

7 v. Trotha to Kap. Michaelis: BA/MA Nachlass N 164, vol. 6, 39; cited Bird, p. 265

8 Dönitz: *10 Jahre*, p. 10

9 ibid.

10 v. Trotha, 9.1.1919: cited Dülffer, p. 29

11 Dönitz: *Wechselvolles*, p. 133

12 *P/Akte*: *Qualifikationsbericht* Aug. 1, 1921

13 Bird, p. 76

14 Dönitz: *Wechselvolles*, p. 135
15 Cited Bird, p. 86
16 Bird, p. 102
17 Comments on Marschall's *Winterarbeit*, PG 33383
18 Rössler, p. 121
19 *P/Akte*: *Qualifikationsbericht* Aug. 1, 1921
20 *P/Akte*: *Beurteilung*, Nov. 1, 1923
21 Judgement of the German Supreme Court in the *Llandovery Castle* case, cited Cameron, p. 178
22 ibid., p. 180
23 ibid., p. 181
24 *P/Akte*: *Beurteilung*, 2.11.1924
25 *Gedenkschrift* III, M 503/4 BA-MA Meerscheidt-Hüllessen; cited Bird, p. 15
26 See Bird, p. 200
27 *P/Akte*: *Beurteilung* Nov. 1, 1925
28 Cited Wheeler-Bennett, pp. 65–6
29 Saville, pp. 230–40
30 See G. Schreiber: '*Zur Kontinuität des Gross- und Weltmachtstrebens der deutschen Marineführung*' in MGM 2/1979, pp. 136–8; also Dülffer, p. 88
31 *P/Akte*: *Beurteilung* Nov. 1, 1927
32 Frau v. Lamezan to author, 8.8.1982
33 This section Frau Hessler to author, June 1981
34 See Saville, pp. 292–8
35 Dönitz: *40 Fragen*, pp. 21–2
36 See Bird, pp. 153, 198–200
37 Dönitz: *Wechselvolles*, p. 166
38 *P/Akte*: *Beurteilung* 22.9.1928
39 Dönitz: *Wechselvolles*, pp. 152–3
40 Dönitz: *40 Fragen*, p. 22
41 IMT, Doc. 1463-PS
42 *P/Akte*: *Beurteilung* Nov. 29, 1929
43 *Hindenburgreise*, p. 105
44 See Bird, p. 287

45 ibid.
46 *P/Akte*: *Beurteilung* Nov. 1930
47 Dönitz: *40 Fragen*, p. 22
48 *P/Akte*: *Beurteilung* Nov. 1, 1931
49 IMT, vol. 13, p. 314
50 IMT, vol. 28, p. 260
51 ibid.
52 Dönitz: *40 Fragen*, p. 34
53 ibid.
54 Speech in Mannheim, 5.11.1930; cited Dülffer, p. 219
55 See Dülffer, pp. 218 ff.; also Gemzell, pp. 265 ff.
56 Dönitz: *40 Fragen*, p. 33
57 v. Roon, p. 26
58 Dönitz: *40 Fragen*, p. 33
59 *Kap*. Schuster: '*Vortrag von Führern der SS, SA und des Stahlhelm . . . in Kiel*,' Mai 5, 1933; cited Bird, p. 286
60 *P/Akte*: *Beurteilung* Nov. 1, 1932
61 *Hindenburgreise*, p. 108
62 ibid., p. 115
63 ibid., p. 6
64 ibid., p. 44
65 ibid., p. 43
66 ibid., p. 24
67 ibid., p. 26
68 ibid., pp. 28–9
69 ibid., pp. 34–5
70 ibid., p. 97
71 ibid., p. 42
72 ibid., p. 55
73 ibid., p. 56
74 ibid., p. 15
75 ibid., p. 118
76 ibid., p. 9
77 *P/Akte*: *Beurteilung* Nov. 1, 1933
78 Dönitz: *Wechselvolles*, p. 170
79 See Dülffer, pp. 566–7; also Saville, p. 545

80 *Raeder Akte: Gespräch mit dem Führer im Juni 1934:* see also Deist, p. 75

81 ibid.

82 *Raeder Akte: Gespräch mit dem Führer am 2.XI.34*

83 Dönitz: *Wechselvolles*, p. 197

84 Ludecke, p. 461

85 J. Steinberg to author, Feb. 1983

86 See Dönitz: *Wechselvolles*, p. 174 for suggestion that he was briefed

87 ibid., p. 175

88 ibid., p. 176

89 ibid., p. 193

90 Saville, pp. 613–16

91 *P/Akte: Beurteilung*, Nov. 1, 1934

92 See Saville, p. 618

93 Sir J. Simon to King George V, Jan. 19, 1935; cited Haraszti, p. 22

94 Br. naval staff memo. 'Anglo-German Naval Discussion', CAB 24/222; cited Haraszti, p. 103

95 ibid.

96 F.O. memo. to Br. Amb., Berlin: PRO ADM 116/3378–8678; cited Haraszti, p. 137

97 See for instance in *Raeder Akte*: '*Besprechung beim Führer und Reichskanzler am 27.3.35*: 'The Führer returns to the question of the conference . . . Germany claims full sovereignty and builds in the framework of its demands as it thinks necessary . . . According to the will of the Führer the *naval construction plan will be carried out according to plan* . . . Motto: Act and keep quiet. For the rest, it is England above all in the picture.'

98 Dönitz: *10 Jahre*, pp. 12–13

99 Dönitz: *Wechselvolles*, p. 197

100 *P/Akte: Beurteilung* Nov. 1, 1935

FOUR *Führer der U-boote*

1 B.Nr.Gkdos 65, *Organisation der U-Boote Waffe*, Sept. 21, 1935, signed Dönitz. PG 34443

2 Dönitz: *10 Jahre*, pp. 19–20

3 V. Oehrn to author, May 31, 1982

4 Dönitz: *10 Jahre*, p. 18

5 ibid.

6 *P/Akte: Beurteilung* Nov. 1, 1936

7 Cited in Dönitz: *10 Jahre*, p. 23

8 '*Die Verwendung von U-booten im Rahmen des Flottenverbandes*', signed Dönitz, 23.11.37. PG 33970

9 See Dülffer, pp. 387 ff.

10 Frau Hessler to author, June 1981

11 See IMT, Doc. D 806, vol. 35, pp. 529–31

12 *Fr. Kap.* Heye, cited Dülffer, p. 440

13 : 'Die Verwendung von U-booten . . .' above ref. 8

14 IMT, Doc. 386-PS, vol. 25, p. 407

15 FdU B Nr. 110 gkdos, *Neue U-bootstypen und Aufschlüsselung weiterer U-bootstonnage*, signed Dönitz, 10.4.38. PG 33390

16 *P/Akte: Beurteilung* Nov. 1, 1937

17 B.Nr.Gkdos 360 A1, *Aufschlüsselung neuer U-bootstonnage und neuer U-bootstypen*, signed Carls, May 6, 1938. PG 33390

18 FdU B Nr. G 1395 A1, *Erfahrungsbericht über die FdU-Übungen*, signed Dönitz, May 18, 1938. PG 33390

19 Cited Thorne, p. 109

20 Cited Dülffer, p. 461

21 *Seekriegsführung gegen England*, Oct. 25, 1938. PG 34181; cited Salewski, vol. III, p. 30

22 ibid. Clause 13

23 Cited G. Schreiber: '*Zur Kontinuität des Gross- und Weltmachtstrebens der deutschen Marineführung*, in MGM 2/1979, p. 126; see also Dülffer, p. 486

24 See Deist, p. 90

25 Dönitz: *U-bootswaffe*, pp. 68–9

26 ibid., p. 70

27 Grunberger, p. 384

28 Anl. zu FdU Gkdos 180 von 13.4.39, *Bericht über FdU Kriegspiel 1939*, signed Dönitz. PG 33390

29 ibid., p. 5

30 See Herzog: *60 Jahre*, pp. 170–72

31 *FdU Kriegspiel* . . . above ref. 28, p. 7

32 See, for instance *Die Diskussion über das Thema Wilson und den Eintritt Amerikas in den Krieg*, Berlin, 23.3.1935 (PG 33970), at which O. Spindler spoke and numerous naval officers, not Dönitz, attended

33 BN 1882/38 Gkds, *Versuche über S-Abwehr*, signed Fischel, Oct. 11, 1938. PG 33389

34 *FdU Kriegspiel* . . . above ref. 28, p. 13 *Schluss*

35 FdU B Nr. G 2186, *Bericht über die Geleitzugübung des FdU*, signed Dönitz, May 30, 1939. PG 33390

36 ibid., p. 5

37 ibid.

38 ibid., p. 6

39 ibid., p. 10

40 See Rössler, p. 197

41 *Geleitzugübung des FdU* . . . above ref. 35, p. 12

42 *Denkschrift*: '*Welche Entwicklungs-Aufgaben und welche operativen Vorbereitungen müssen heute zur Führung eines U-boots-Handelskrieges gegen England in alle erste Linie gestellt werden*', signed Fürbringer, May 17, 1939. PG 33390

43 FdU B Nr. 213 Gkdos *an den Kont. adml.* Schniewind, signed Dönitz, 23.5.1939. PG 33390

44 Cited in *Führer Conferences on Naval Affairs*, H.M.S.O., 1948, p. 1

45 Goerdeler to Br. F.O., Jan. 1939, from information supplied by Schacht; cited Astor, p. 46

46 Interrogation of Adml. E. Godt, Flensburg, July 31, 1945. Nav. Lib.

47 FdU B Nr. Gkdos 263: *Werkstattschiff für Stationeirung und Ausbildung von U-booten in ausserheimlichen Gewässern*, signed Dönitz, 4.7.1939. PG 33390

48 1/Skl 1U 1552/39, *U-bootstypen für den Handelskrieg*, signed lu, 3.8.1939. PG 33390

49 Aster, p. 300

50 FdU KTB 21.8.1939

51 ibid., 18.8.1939

52 ibid., 24.8.1939

53 See Aster, p. 357

54 Dahlerus' evidence to IMT, vol. 9, p. 481

55 FdU *Denkschrift*: *Gedanken über den Aufbau der U-bootswaffe*', 1.9.1939

56 FdU KTB 1.9.1939

57 Adml. E. Wegener to author, June 1981

58 FdU KTB 31.8.1939

59 Shirer, *Berlin Diary*, p. 159

60 Cited Aster, p. 389

61 Dönitz: *40 Fragen*, p. 49

62 V. Oehrn to author, May 31, 1982. A fuller version in Dönitz: *40 Fragen*, pp. 49–50

63 *Aufzeichnung* 3.9.1939, 1 Skl. Teil C VII. PG 32183

64 Shirer: *Berlin Diary*, p. 161

499

FIVE *The Battle of the Atlantic*

1 *Gedanken über den Einsatz der deutschen U-bootswaffe*, dated '*Anfang September*', 1939. PG 33970

2 ibid., p. 3

3 ibid., p. 8

4 Ch. of naval staff to For. Ministry, Berlin, Sept. 3, 1939; IMT Doc. D-851, vol. 35, p. 547

5 FdU KTB 3.9.1939

6 *Athenia* file, PRO ADM I 9760

7 Br. monitored broadcast from Cologne, 13.40 BST Sept. 4, 1939, PRO ADM 199 140

8 Cited in PRO ADM 199 140

9 Lehmann, p. 30

10 FdU KTB 8.9.1939

11 ibid., 7.9.1939

12 *P/Akte: Beurteilung* 19.10.1939

13 FdU KTB 15.9.1939

14 ibid., 18.9.1939

15 F/*Vorträge*, Sept. 23, 1939. PG 32182

16 FdU KTB 24.9.1939

17 IMT Doc. C-191, vol. 13, p. 356

18 FdU KTB 28.9.1939

19 v. Puttkamer, p. 24

20 FdU KTB 1.10.1939

21 Farrago, p. 189

22 ibid., p. 190

23 Dönitz: *10 Jahre*, p. 68

24 Frank: *Enemy Submarine*, p. 34

25 v. Puttkamer, p. 24

26 Shirer: *Berlin Diary*, p. 190

27 Skl. *Denkschrift: den verschäftigen Seekrieg gegen England*, Oct. 15, 1939. PG 32611; cited Salewski, vol. III, p. 73

28 ibid., pp. 92–3; *Anlage* 3

29 Standing Order, No. 1; cited IMT Doc. 642-D, vol. 35, pp. 264–5

30. v. Hassell: *Vom Andern Deutschland*, pp. 92–3

31 Cited IMT, vol. 13, p. 260

32 Cited IMT, Doc. 642-D, vol. 35, p. 270

33 ibid., p. 266

34 ibid., p. 269

35 BdU KTB 23.10.1939

36 ibid., 27.10.1939

37 ibid., 31.10.1939

38 ibid., 14.12.1939

39 ibid., 21.1.1940

40 A/S R Jan/Feb., 1940, vol. 1, p. 107

41 ibid., p. 104

42 ibid., p. 132

43 Shirer: *Berlin Diary*, p. 215

44 BdU KTB 15.5.1940

45 See Shirer: *Berlin Diary*, p. 331

46 1 Skl. 3.6.1940, signed Fricke; cited Salewski, vol. III, pp. 105ff.

47 14.6.40, signed Carls; cited ibid.

48 BdU KTB 12.6.1940

49 Roskill, vol. I, p. 615

50 ibid., p. 616 gives 195,825 tons for U-boat sinkings; A/S R July gives 213,938 tons

51 Jodl interviewed by Cdre. G. R. G. Allen, May 21–4, 1945, PRO ADM 1 18222

52 v. Puttkamer, p. 38

53 See *Betrachtungen über Russland*, by Fricke, July 28, 1940; cited Salewski, Vol. III, pp. 137ff.; also *Denkschrift* signed Raeder, Feb. 25, 1942; cited Salewski, vol. III, p. 273

54 A/S R Sept. 1941, vol. IV, p. 295

55 See Beesley, pp. 26–8

56 BdU KTB 20–22.9.1940

57 See Herzog & Schomaekers, pp. 100–2

58 BdU KTB 20.10.1940

59 ibid.

60 A/S R Oct. 1940, vol. II, p. 74
61 A/S R Nov. 1940, vol. II, p. 113
62 ibid.
63 ibid., p. 156
64 ibid., p. 164
65 Hans Meckel (formerly A4 U-boat HQ Staff) to author, June 24, 1981
66 Frank: *Sea Wolves*, p. 63
67 Adml. E. Wegener to author, June 24, 1981
68 A/S R March 1941, vol. III, p. 137
69 A/S R April 1941, vol. III, p. 202
70 ibid., p. 209
71 ibid., p. 210
72 to author, May 31, 1982
73 Frau Hessler to author, July 29, 1982; the previous description of Dönitz's typical day chiefly from Hans Meckel, formerly A4 U-boat HQ staff, to author
74 See for instance interrogation survivors of U 110, A/S R June 1941, vol. III, p. 333
75 BdU KTB 16.11.1941
76 ibid.
77 See Roskill, vol. I, p. 364
78 All quotes from A/S R June 1941, vol. III, p. 327–32
79 See Beesley, p. 95
80 BdU KTB 7.1.1941
81 ibid., 6.5.1941
82 ibid., 12.12.1940
83 v. Puttkamer, p. 44
84 See Warlimont, pp. 160–62; also Irving, pp. 222 ff.
85 Halder's note of Hitler's final words in Warlimont, p. 162
86 Warlimont, p. 164
87 See p. 197
88 Dönitz: *U-bootswaffe*, p. 132
89 Warlimont, p. 208
90 Cited Salewski, vol. I, p. 511
91 ibid.
92 1/Skl. KTB A 7.12.1941
93 BdU KTB 9.12.1941
94 ibid.
95 Beesley, p. 107
96 BdU KTB 7.2.1942
97 Dr K. Silex in *Deutsche Allgemeine Zeitung*, transl. in A/S R March 1942, vol. V, p. 163
98 BdU KTB 15.4.1942
99 1/Skl. KTB Teil C VIII 9.1.1942. PG 32194
100 1/Skl. KTB Teil C IV, Skl. U la, *Auswirkung der Arbeiterlage und des Rohstoffmangels auf die Führung des U-bootkrieges*, Jan. 22, 1942. PG 32174
101 ibid., p. 27
102 BdU KTB 30.4.1942
103 F/*Vorträge*, May 14, 1942. PG 32187
104 See OKM Abt. Wi Wr 1171/42 gk, *Die Wehrwirtschaftliche Lage des Auslands*, p. 6 in 1/Skl. KTB Teil C XII, 23.4.1942. PG 32210
105 A/S R April 1942, vol. V, p. 177
106 ibid., p. 179
107 See Salewski, vol. II, pp. 72ff. 'The Great Plan'; also Salewski, vol. III, pp. 287ff. '*Lagebetrachtung der Skl.*', 20.10.42; also G. Schreiber: '*Zur Kontinuität des Gross- und Weltmachtstrebens der deutschen Marineführung*' in MGM 2/1979, pp. 127ff., 142f., 147ff.
108 Halder's diary, June 12, 1942: cited Warlimont, p. 229
109 IMT Doc. D-423, vol. 5, p. 219
110 F/*Vorträge* May 14, 1942. PG 32187
111 A/S R Nov. 1941, vol. IV, p. 295
112 BdU KTB 26.3.1942
113 See Marrus & Paxton, p. 226; also Pryce-Jones, p. 131

114 Herzog & Schomaekers, p. 308
115 A/S R Nov. 1941, vol. IV, p. 295
116 Trevor-Roper: *Table Talk*, p. 696
117 1/Skl. KTB Teil C IV. Telegram 13.9.1942. PG 32174
118 BdU KTB 21.8.1942
119 A/S R Jan. 1942, vol. V, p. 52
120 ibid.
121 A/S R Oct. 1941, vol. IV, p. 226
122 BdU KTB 3.9.1942
123 Total U-boat losses to Aug. 24, 1942: 105 boats, 4.9 percent. of the front boats; 3,803 officers and men lost. From Summary of U-boat losses, 24.8.1942. *Anlage zu* 1/Skl. U la Gkdos 3221/42; 1/Skl. KTB Teil C IV. PG 32174
124 3 Abt. F.H. B Nr. 85/42 gKdos Chefs: *Einfluss der Schiffsversenkungen*, Sept. 9, 1942, p. 4; 1/Skl. KTB Teil C IV. PG 32174
125 BdU 3764 Gkdos: *Beeinträchtigung U-bootskriegsführung durch feindliche Luftwaffe*, 9.9.1942. PG 32174
126 BdU B Nr. Gkdos Chefs 349 A 4: *Waffenentwicklung für U-boote*, signed Dönitz Sept. 9, 1942, p. 3. PG 32174
127 Dönitz: *10 Jahre*, p. 250
128 ibid., p. 253
129 BdU KTB 16.9.1942
130 1/Skl. la 22792/42 gKds, den 14.9.42, p. 2 in 1/Skl. KTB Teil C VIII. PG 32194
131 1/Skl KTB A 14.9.1942
132 IMT Doc. D 650, vol. 35, pp. 304ff.
133 V. Oehrn to author, May 31, 1982
134 Hans Meckel to author, June 24, 1981
135 Atlantic op. order No. 56, Oct. 7, 1943, repeating an order of autumn 1942: IMT Doc. D-663, vol. 25, pp. 338ff.

136 Affidavit of *Korv. Kap*. Möhle, July 21, 1945: IMT Doc 376-PS, vol. 25, pp. 395ff.; also Möhle's testimony, IMT vol. 5, pp. 233ff.
137 Affidavit of P. J. Heisig, Nov. 27, 1945: IMT Doc. D-566, vol. 35, pp. 161–2; also Heisig's testimony, IMT vol. 5, pp. 223ff.
138 F/*Vorträge*, Sept. 28, 1942. PG 32187; also copy of this discussion '*zur Kenntnis und weiterer Veranlassung übersandt*', signed Schulte-Monting, Oct. 3, 1942 in 1/Skl. KTB Teil C IV. PG 32174
139 1/Skl. KTB Teil C VIII, 3.10.1942. PG 32194
140 Cited Warlimont, p. 268
141 BdU KTB 30.11.1942
142 Herzog & Schomaekers, p. 307; Nov. sinkings: 117 ships of total 737,665 tons
143 BdU KTB 14.12.1942
144 Frank: *Sea Wolves*, pp. 146–7
145 Speer: *Erinnerungen*, p. 257
146 ibid., p. 285
147 Raeder to Hitler, 14.1.1943: cited G. Sandhofer; *Dokumente zu militärischem Werdegang des Gr.admls Dönitz*, in MGM 1/1967, p. 80
148 P/*Akte: Beurteilung* July 1, 1942
149 P/*Akte: Beurteilung* Nov. 1, 1942
150 BdU KTB 31.12.1942
151 A/S R Jan. 1943, vol. VII, p. 5

SIX *The Grand Admiral*

1 Feb. 5, 1943; cited M. Salewski: '*Von Raeder zu Dönitz*' in MGM 2/1973, p. 146
2 See Irving, p. 483
3 v. Roon, p. 376

4 J. Hansen-Nootbar to author, July 1982

5 Feb. 5, 1943; cited M. Salewski: *'Von Raeder zu Dönitz'* in MGM 2/1973, p. 146

6 J. Hansen-Nootbar to author, July 1982

7 See Salewski, vol. II, p. 245

8 J. Hansen-Nootbar to author, July 1982

9 Hinsley, p. 531

10 F/*Vorträge* Feb. 26, 1943. PG 32188

11 v. Puttkamer, p. 53

12 See Salewski, vol. II, p. 238

13 F. Lynder to author, Nov. 1982

14 See Beesley, pp. 176ff.

15 BdU KTB 23.3.1943

16 For this battle see Roskill, vol. 2, pp. 365ff.; also Middlebrook, p. 206; also Jacobsen & Rohwer, pp. 289ff.

17 BdU KTB 20.3.1943: 'Final remarks on Convoy 19'

18 ibid., 23.3.1943

19 Adml. Sir M. Horton to Adml. Darke, 23.3.1943; cited Chalmers, p. 188

20 March 31, decree: cited Salewski, vol. II, p. 278

21 BdU KTB 7.4.1943

22 F/*Vorträge*, April 11, 1943. PG 32188

23 See Salewski, vol. II, pp. 630ff.

24 Capt. G. H. Roberts, RN report on interrogations of *Adml.* E. Godt, Kapt. G. Hessler and others, May 1945: PRO ADM 1 17561

25 BdU KTB 25.4.1943

26 Admty. Tracking Rm. Report, April 19, 1943: cited Beesley, pp. 180–1

27 A/S R April, 1943, vol. 7, p. 184

28 See Capt. Roberts' interrogation of *Kap.* G. Hessler, May 1945: PRO ADM 1 17561

29 BdU KTB 1.5.1943

30 ibid., 6.5.1943: 'Summary on Convoy No. 36'

31 ibid., 5.5.1943

32 1/Skl. KTB Teil C IV. PG 32174

33 1/Skl. KTB A 4.4.1943

34 BdU KTB 9.5.1943

35 ibid., 13.5.1943: 'Summary on Convoy No. 38'

36 See Salewski, vol. II, p. 260

37 F/*Vorträge*, March 18, 1943. PG 32188

38 See Salewski, vol. II, p. 265

39 ibid., p. 266

40 See Carr, pp. 142 ff.

41 May 10, 1943: cited Warlimont, p. 313

42 v. Puttkamer, p. 54

43 1/Skl. KTB A 7.5.1943

44 F/*Vorträge*, April 11, 1943. PG 32188

45 See Ruge, p. 237: see also F/*Vorträge*, May 14, 1943. PG 32188

46 ibid.

47 ibid.

48 ibid.

49 BdU KTB 14.5.1943

50 ibid.

51 Jacobsen & Rohwer, p. 305; Roskill, vol. 2, p. 376; Middlebrook, p. 323

52 Bd U KTB, 20.5.1943

53 ibid.

54 Cited Hinsley, p. 571

55 BdU KTB 23.5.1943

56 ibid., 24.5.1943

57 ibid.

58 Skl. B Nr. 62/42: '*Über die am 28.9.42 beim Ob-d-M durchgeführte*

Besprechung betr. Entwicklung des U-Boots und seiner Waffen . . .', Oct. 7, 1942, in 1/Skl. KTB Teil C IV. PG 32174

59 Prof. Walter to ObdM, 19.5.1943, referring to his March 2, 1943 visit to the director of construction, Dr Fischer, in PRO ADM 1 17667

60 1/Skl. KTB A 17.5.1943

61 ibid., 24.5.1943

62 F/*Vorträge*, May 31, 1943

63 Frank, *Sea Wolves*, p. 177

64 *Niederschrift über die Ansprache des ObdM an die Hauptamts- und Amtschefs am 2.6.43*; KTB Ca BA/MA. PG 31747; cited Salewski, vol. II, p. 633

65 *Denkschrift des Chefs der Skl.* 8.6.43; cited Salewski, vol. III, pp. 359 ff.

66 *Besprechung der Oberbefehlshaber in Berlin*, June 8, 1943; cited Salewski, vol. II, p. 311

67 F/*Vorträge*, June 15, 1943

68 J. Hansen-Nootbar to author, July 1982

69 v. Puttkamer, p. 55

70 J. Hansen-Nootbar to author, July 1982

71 1/Skl. KTB A 5.7.1943

72 Final decision promulgated Aug. 13, 1943; see Rössler, p. 216

73 J. Hansen-Nootbar to author, July 1982

74 Speer: *Erinnerungen*, p. 286; but see a later date for sectional construction in Rössler, pp. 214 ff.

75 F/*Vorträge*, July 8, 1943

76 J. Hansen-Nootbar to author, July, 1982

77 Cited F. Gilbert, p. 18

78 Cited v. Roon, p. 225

79 Ruge, p. 241

80 Irving, p. 549

81 F/*Vorträge*, July 28, 1943; similar remarks repeated at Führer conferences through August

82 Cited Salewski, vol. II, p. 372

83 F/*Vorträge*, Aug. 9–10, 1943

84 ibid.

85 *Lagebetrachtung der Skl.*, Aug. 20, 1943; BA/MA KTB Ca Case 280. PG 31747; cited Salewski, vol. III, p. 371

86 Schaeffer, p. 128

87 F. Gilbert, p. 40

88 F/*Vorträge*, Aug. 19, 1943

89 KTB B V, BA/MA III M 1005/8 1Skl. 273629; cited Salewski, vol. II, p. 638

90 See for instance Ruge, pp. 240–1

91 Statement of Diesel Maat of U 333 to F. Lynder, witnessed K. Behnke, 14/15.11.1978 in Berlin. Photocopy in author's possession

92 See Speer's rebuttal of the charge in Reif, pp. 395 ff., 404 ff.

93 ibid., p. 396

94 Smith & Peterson, pp. 169 ff.

95 B. v. Schirach: *Ich Glaubte Hitler*, Hamburg 1967, p. 269; cited Reif, p. 389

96 Speer: *Erinnerungen*, p. 341. In 1973 E. Goldhagen pointed to this passage in his memoirs as proof of his attendance at the Posen convention; Speer then said he had mistaken the occasion at which the Gauleiters became drunk, and produced sworn statements that he had driven away from Posen at lunchtime, thus before Himmler's speech; '*Antwort an E. Goldhagen*' in Reif, pp. 395 ff.

97 IMT Doc. 663-D, vol. 25, pp. 338 ff.

98 F/*Vorträge*, Aug. 19, 1943

99 See also BdU KTB 23.8.1943, 'VI General'
100 See Roskill, vol. 3, pt. 1, pp. 38 ff.; also BdU KTB 20.2.1944; Appendix: summary of U-boat campaign
101 F/*Vorträge*, Sept. 24, 1943
102 BdU KTB 20.2.1944; Appendix: summary of U-boat campaign
103 See Salewski, vol. III, pp. 372 ff.
104 ibid., p. 373
105 J. Hansen-Nootbar to author, July 1982
106 Wireless log, U 515, Nov. 17, 1943
107 BdU KTB 7.1.1944
108 *Fernschreiben*, cited Salewski, vol. II, pp. 508–9
109 *Gr.adml. Dönitz Schlussansprache auf die Tagung für Befehlshaber der Kriegsmarine in Weimar*, 17.12.1943; printed in IMT Doc. 443-D, vol. 35, pp. 106 ff.
110 1/Skl. KTB A 26.4.1943
111 BdK KTB 22.11.1943; cited Salewski, vol. II, p. 332
112 IMT Doc. 443-D, vol. 35, p. 109
113 F/*Vorträge*, Dec. 19–20, 1943
114 J. Hansen-Nootbar to author, July 1982
115 Adml. E. Wegener to author, June 1981
116 Cited Salewski, vol. II, p. 337
117 ibid., p. 338
118 1/Skl. KTB A 25.12.1943
119 Cited Salewski, vol. II, p. 339
120 Mar. Gr. Kdo. Nord/Flotte KTB 25.12.43, 20.46 *Uhr*; cited Salewski, vol. II, p. 340
121 See P. Beesley, pp. 213 ff; also Humble, pp. 184 ff; see Humble pp. 187 ff. for a blow-by-blow account of the action from the British side
122 F/*Vorträge*, 1.1.1944
123 ibid., 12.4.1944
124 Cited Irving, p. 578
125 See Salewski, vol. II, p. 343
126 IMT Doc. 2878-PS, vol. 31, p. 250
127 F/*Vorträge*, 1–3.1.1944
128 To his Commanders in Italy, June 28, 1944; cited Irving, p. 202
129 *Ansprache des ObdM vor den Oberbefehlshabern*, 15.2.1944; printed IMT Doc. 640-D, vol. 35, pp. 238 ff.
130 Speech printed in *Völkischer Beobachter*, 14.3.1944
131 See analysis in Rohwer
132 Mar. Gp. Süd KTB 29.1.1944 (pp. 121–22) Absatz IV; cited Rohwer, p. 50. These two pages had been extracted from the KTB found in the archive captured by the British – proof of archival 'weeding' towards the end of the war. Rohwer cited from another copy of the KTB deposited with the BA/MA. The Foreign Ministry's ruling on Adml. Fricke's request was also 'weeded' from the archive, but the note of the request itself can be seen in 1/Skl. KTB A 25.1.1944 (p. 457). PG 32073
133 Stevens, p. 8
134 Skl. li 446/43 gKdos. Chefs, *Behandlung von Saboteuren*; printed IMT Doc. 178-C, vol. 35, pp. 770 ff.
135 Stevens, p. 32
136 ibid., pp. 76–8
137 BdU KTB 1.3.1944, Enclosure 'e' to 'U-boat situation report'
138 Eck's cross examination, in Cameron, p. 58
139 ibid., p. 62
140 ibid., p. 103
141 ibid., p. 139
142 OKM 2/Skl BdU op. 1961 gKdos, 27.3.1944, KTB C 11b, BA/MA III M 1012/8; cited Salewski, vol. II, p. 415

143 ibid., pp. 415–6; see also Dönitz; *10 Jahre*, p. 414

144 See Salewski, vol. II, p. 414

145 Br. Naval Intelligence file on Karl Dönitz, based on interrogation of survivors from S 141. The records at Tübingen University are not sufficiently complete to trace Klaus's entry

146 BdS KTB 13.5.1944

147 J. Hansen-Nootbar to author, July 1982

148 1/Skl. KTB A 6.6.1944

149 June 19, 1944; cited Beesley, p. 30

150 1/Skl. KTB A 10.6.1944

151 See Irving, p. 631

152 Manvell & Fraenkel, p. 82

153 See Speer: *Spandau*, p. 191

154 F/*Vorträge*, June 29, 1944

155 Aug. 31, 1944; cited F. Gilbert, p. 105

156 See F/*Vorträge*, July 9 and 11–13, 1944

157 July 25, 1943; cited F. Gilbert, p. 44

158 J. Hansen-Nootbar to author, July 1982

159 See Salewski, vol II, p. 46

160 See Trevor-Roper: *Last Days of Hitler*, pp. 35 ff.; also Manvell & Fraenkel, pp. 110 ff.

161 F/*Vorträge*, July 20–21, 1944

162 ibid.

163 J. Hansen-Nootbar to author, July 1982

164 Adml. E. Wegener to author, June 1981

165 See F/*Vorträge*, July 20–21, 1944

166 IMT Doc. 2878-PS, Vol. 31, pp. 250–51

167 ibid.

168 Cited v. Roon, p. 277

169 *Flottenkommando* B Nr. gKdos 411/44 Chefs, *Ansprache Dönitz vom* 24.8.1944. PG 48609. It is interesting that of 52 copies printed, only one has been found in the archives.

170 1st draft of Kreisau Circle's 'German participation in the punishment of war criminals', 14.6.1943; cited v. Roon, pp. 340–1

171 2nd draft of above, 23.7.1943, cited ibid., p. 343

172 Himmler's 'Posen' speech; Smith & Peterson, p. 168

173 Speer: *Erinnerungen*, p. 378

174 March 13, 1945; Trevor-Roper: *Goebbels Diaries*, p. 125

175 F/*Vorträge*, Dec. 3, 1944

176 ibid., Jan. 1, 1945

177 ibid., Jan. 3, 1945

178 ibid., Jan. 25, 1945

179 ibid., Feb. 17, 1945

180 ibid., Feb. 28, 1945

181 Feb. 27, 1945; Trevor-Roper; *Goebbels Diaries*, p. 1

182 March 13, 1945; ibid., p. 128

183 March 20, 1945; ibid., p. 181

184 Boldt, p. 48

185 Adml. E. Wegener to author, June 1981

186 Schaeffer, p. 146

187 ibid.

188 Speer: *Erinnerungen*, p. 434

189 ibid.

190 Boldt, p. 35

191 *Denkschrift*, Sept. 29, 1944, BA/MA Case 280. PG 3174; cited Salewski, vol. III, p. 382

192 1/Skl. KTB A 3.11.1944

193 *Denkschrift*, Nov. 14, 1944; cited Salewski, vol. III, pp. 394–5

194 F/*Vorträge*, Jan. 23, 1945

195 Salewski, vol. II, p. 522

196 Dec. 29–30, 1944; cited F. Gilbert, p. 178
197 F/*Vorträge*, March 18, 1945
198 ibid., April 7, 1945
199 ibid., Nov. 1, 1944
200 ibid., March 12, 1945
201 ibid., March 26, 1945
202 March 13, 1945; Trevor-Roper; *Goebbels Diaries*, p. 124
203 March 21, 1945; ibid., p. 195
204 Fragment Hitler conference, end Feb./beginning March, 1945 in Univ. Pennsylvania Library
205 F/*Vorträge*, Feb. 20, 1945
206 March 13, 1945; Trevor-Roper: *Goebbels Diaries*, p. 127
207 F/*Vorträge*, April 7, 1945
208 ibid., April 14, 1945
209 March 27, 1945; Trevor-Roper: *Goebbels Diaries*, p. 250
210 *Geheimerlass des Gr.admls Dönitz*; SSD MBKO 6611; *Gltd. Plan 'Paula' Ost*; IWM
211 See F. Lynder: '*7 Helgoländer narrten Hitler*' in *Bild am Sonntag*, Berlin, 2.5.1965
212 *Geheimerlass des Gr.admls Dönitz* v. 11.4.1945; KMA 25641/45, IWM
213 See Irving, p. 792
214 See O'Donnel, p. 117
215 Speer: *Erinnerungen*, p. 467
216 Lüdde-Neurath, pp. 21–2
217 Goerdeler: 'Declaration for publication after the revolt against Hitler had succeeded'; cited Gaevernitz, p. 109
218 *Ostseebefehl* Nr. 19 *von* 19.4.1945. IWM
219 Lüdde-Neurath, p. 27
220 Speer: *Erinnerungen*, p. 474
221 Boldt, p. 82
222 July 21, 1945; 14.00 Hrs, Schuster File, National Archives, Washington
223 See Salewski, vol. II, p. 544
224 Lüdde-Neurath, p. 38
225 See ibid., p. 39
226 H. Macher to F. Lynder: photocopy of interview in author's possession
227 See, for instance, Boldt, p. 118
228 OKW KTB 28.4.1945
229 See Lüdde-Neurath, pp. 23, 33
230 OKW KTB 27.4.1945
231 See account based on conversation with G. Hessler in Steinert, pp. 58–9
232 Lüdde-Neurath, p. 41
233 O'Donnel, p. 184
234 Cited, for instance in Lüdde-Neurath, pp. 120–21
235 OKW KTB 29, 30.4.1945
236 See Lüdde-Neurath. pp. 34, 125
237 OKW KTB 30.4.1945
238 Cited, for instance, in Lüdde-Neurath, p. 126
239 Ali Cremer to F. Lynder
240 H. Macher to F. Lynder
241 ibid.
242 Dönitz: *10 Jahre*, p. 346. In an earlier statement published in Lüdde-Neurath, pp. 86–7, Dönitz said Himmler stayed an hour discussing his position; he had fantastic ideas about his 'resonance' in the West. Lüdde-Neurath gives the time of Himmler's departure as 2.30 am.
243 OKW KTB 30.4.1945
244 Dönitz: *40 Fragen*, p. 164; see also Steinert, pp. 62–3
245 OKW KTB 1.5.1945
246 Cited Lüdde-Neurath, p. 126
247 Cited ibid.

SEVEN *The Last Führer*

1 Steinert, p. 133
2 OKW KTB 1.5.1945
3 ibid.
4 ibid.
5 ibid., 6.5.1945
6 Speer: *Erinnerungen*, p. 495
7 H. Jaenecke in *Stern*, Jan. 9, 1981, p. 61
8 See Steinert, p. 145
9 Speer: *Erinnerungen*, p. 493
10 OKW KTB 2.5.1945
11 See Speer: *Erinnerungen*, p. 496; also Steinert, p. 140
12 Steinert, p. 145
13 ibid., p. 144
14 ibid.
15 ibid., p. 147
16 OKW KTB 5.5.1945
17 Schaeffer, p. 163
18 Cited Lüdde-Neurath, p. 131
19 Lüdde-Neurath, p. 67 (of 1st edition)
20 'The Scuttled U-boats' in *Law Reports of the Trials of War Criminals*, HMSO, 1947, vol. I, pp. 55 ff.
21 OKW KTB 5.5.1945
22 'The Scuttled U-boats' above ref. 20, p. 58
23 OKW KTB 7.5.1945
24 See ibid., 6.5.1945
25 ibid.
26 ibid., 7.5.1945
27 H. Jaenecke in *Stern*, above ref. 7
28 OKW KTB 8–9.5.1945
29 Höss, p. 148
30 ibid.
31 H. Macher to F. Lynder
32 Shirer: *End of a Berlin Diary*, p. 131

33 OKM 1/Skl. I/i 1157/45 v. 12.3.45; OKM *Allgemeine Akten Mai* 1945 BA/MA III M 15; cited Salewski, vol. II, p. 559; also OKW KTB 12.5.1945
34 OKW KTB 15.5.1945
35 ibid., 12.5.1945
36 ibid., 11.5.1945; see also Steinert, p. 193
37 Report of Admty. Mission to Flensburg, May 21–24, 1945; PRO ADM 1 18222
38 OKW KTB 15.5.1945
39 See Dönitz: *40 Fragen*, p. 147
40 ibid., p. 149
41 See ibid., pp. 148–9
42 Jodl to his dept.: see OKW KTB 12.5.1945
43 OKM 1/Skl. 1239/45 v. 17.5.45; cited Salewski, vol. II, pp. 560–61
44 OKW KTB 16.5.1945
45 Steinert, p. 262
46 ibid.
47 Report of Admty. Mission, above ref. 37
48 Frau v. Lamezan to author, 1.4.1982
49 Speer: *Erinnerungen*, p. 499
50 Lüdde-Neurath, p. 109
51 N.I.D. 1/G P.3: Address by Dönitz found in his desk, May 23, 1945, translated by N.I.D., sgd. E. G. N. Rushbrook, D.N.I., Nav. Lib.
52 ibid.
53 Lüdde-Neurath, p. 154
54 Report of Admty. Mission, above ref. 37
55 H. Davies, Capt. 1 Cheshire Reg., 'Suicide of *Adml*. v. Friedeburg', Appendix 'C' to 159 Infantry Brigade Letter 26/1 A of May 29, 1945, PRO ADM 228 55
56 ibid.

57 D. Maxwell-Fyfe in Cameron,
p. xvi
58 O. Kranzbühler to author, 6.5.1982
59 Cited Best, p. 292
60 Psalm 94
61 D. Maxwell-Fyfe in Cameron,
p. xiii
62 Leader, Feb. 8, 1983
63 Kelley, p. 108
64 ibid.
65 G. Gilbert, p. 19
66 ibid., pp. 1–2
67 ibid.
68 D. Maxwell-Fyfe in G. Gilbert,
p. x
69 Shirer: *End of a Berlin Diary*,
pp. 93–4
70 IMT vol. 1, pp. 40 ff.
71 ibid., p. 78
72 Interrogation of *Gr.adml* Dönitz
by Lt. Col. T. S. Hinkel, Oct. 22, 1945;
IMT Doc. 865-D, vol. 35, pp. 611–14
73 ibid., pp. 615–16
74 See Salewski, vol. II, p. 579
75 G. Gilbert, pp. 29–30
76 ibid., p. 31
77 IMT vol. 5, p. 221
78 ibid., pp. 226–8
79 ibid., pp. 230–37
80 ibid., pp. 240–45
81 G. Gilbert, p. 93
82 ibid., p. 94
83 ibid., p. 101
84 ibid., p. 144
85 ibid., pp. 163–4
86 ibid., p. 185
87 IMT (Germ. ed.) Bd. XIII, p. 276
88 IMT (Engl.) vol. 13, pp. 272–3
89 G. Gilbert, p. 197
90 IMT vol. 13, pp. 277–8
91 ibid., pp. 290–307
92 G. Gilbert, p. 199
93 ibid.
94 IMT vol. 13, pp. 323–9
95 G. Gilbert, p. 200
96 IMT vol. 13, pp. 343–4
97 ibid., pp. 382–5
98 ibid., 392
99 ibid., pp. 392–3
100 See above Section 6, ref. 132
101 See G. Gilbert, pp. 201–2
102 ibid.
103 IMT vol. 13, pp. 450–74
104 ibid., p. 497
105 ibid., p. 548
106 ibid., p. 557
107 Dönitz: *10 Jahre*, p. 252
108 Cited G. Gilbert, p. 207
109 ibid., p. 210
110 ibid., p. 218
111 ibid., p. 247
112 IMT vol. 19, pp. 416–18
113 ibid., p. 521
114 ibid., p. 554
115 ibid., p. 597
116 IMT vol. 22, pp. 390–91
117 ibid., p. 393
118 IMT vol. 1, pp. 310–14
119 *Evening News* (London), Oct. 1,
1946, p. 12c
120 G. Gilbert, p. 272
121 Speer: *Spandau*, p. 25
122 O. Kranzbühler to author, 6.5.1982
123 Speer: *Spandau*, pp. 30–1
124 Fishman, p. 21
125 ibid., p. 103
126 F. Lynder to author, Nov. 1982
127 Fishman, p. 122
128 Speer: *Spandau*, pp. 81–2
129 ibid., p. 193
130 ibid., p. 192
131 Cited Fishman, p. 194
132 Dated March 14, 1948, cited ibid.,
p. 195

133 Speer: *Spandau*, p. 121
134 ibid., p. 217
135 ibid., p. 220
136 Fishman, p. 158
137 Speer: *Spandau*, p. 239
138 ibid., p. 271
139 ibid., p. 216
140 ibid., p. 277
141 A. Speer to author, 3.5.1981
142 Speer: *Spandau*, p. 430
143 ibid., pp. 296–7
144 pp. 297–8
145 ibid., pp. 288, 430
146 Roskill, vol. 2, p. 377, and Dönitz, *10 Jahre*, p. 344
147 Dönitz: *10 Jahre*, p. 368
148 ibid., p. 366
149 ibid., p. 393
150 ibid., p. 422
151 Lüdde-Neurath, p. 20
152 Dönitz: *10 Jahre*, pp. 437, 438
153 Speer: *Spandau*, p. 333
154 ibid., pp. 334–5
155 J. Hansen-Nootbar to author, July 1982
156 H-J Arp's address at Dönitz's funeral; Dönitz: *Dokumentation*, p. 17
157 Dönitz: *Wechselvolles*, p. 215
158 Cited Dönitz: *40 Fragen*, p. 188
159 ibid., p. 69, citing the *Sunday Times* (London), Jan. 25, 1959
160 ibid., p. 75, citing Roskill, vol. 2, p. 104
161 See their books listed in Bibliography; also G. Schreiber above, Section 3, Ref. 30
162 E. Goldhagen in *Midstream*, July, 1973, N.Y., reprinted in Reif, pp. 383 ff.; see also Schmidt, pp. 231 ff.
163 A. Speer, '*Antwort an Erich Goldhagen*' in Reif, pp. 395 ff.
164 T. Broughton (BBC-TV) to author, March 22, 1981
165 L. Kennedy in *The Spectator* (London), Jan. 3, 1981
166 ibid.
167 Steinberg to author, Feb. 1983
168 Frau Hessler to author, June 1981
169 Frau Fidelak to author, 25.2.1982
170 Thompson & Strutz
171 This paragraph from A. Schnee: '*Abschied vom Grossadmiral*' in Schaltung-Küste, Feb. 1981; M. R. Beer: '*Was wäre geworden, wenn Himmler die letzten Tage bestimmt hätte?*' in *Die Welt*, Dec. 27, 1980; crucifix detail from Frau Fidelak to author, 25,2,1982
172 M. R. Beer in above ref. 171
173 ibid.
174 Letter in possession of *The Times* (London), was not published

Bibliography

S. Aster: *The Making of the Second World War*, Deutsch, 1973

M. Balfour: *The Kaiser and his Times*, Cresset, 1964

P. Beesley: *Very Special Intelligence*, Hamish Hamilton, 1977

V. Berghahn: *Der Tirpitz Plan*, Droste (Düsseldorf), 1971

———*Germany and the Approach of War in 1914*, Macmillan, 1973

G. Best: *Humanity in Warfare*, Weidenfeld, 1980

K. Bird: *Weimar, the German Naval Officer Corps and the Rise of National-Socialism*, Amsterdam, 1977

G. Boldt: *Hitler's Last Days*, Sphere, 1973

B. v. Bülow: *Imperial Germany*, Cassell, 1914

J. Cameron (ed.): *The Peleus Trial*, Hodge, 1948

W. Carr: *Hitler, A Study in Personality and Politics*, Arnold, 1978

W. Chalmers: *Max Horton and the Western Approaches*, Hodder, 1954

J. Corbett: *Naval Operations*, Longman revised ed., 1940

W. Deist: *The Wehrmacht and German Re-armament*, Macmillan, 1981

K. Dönitz (in chronological order): *Die Fahrten der Breslau im Schwarzen Meer*, Ullstein (Berlin), 1917 (and with T. Kraus, *Die Kreuzerfahrten der Goeben und Breslau*, Berlin 1918, the same text)

———*Die U-bootswaffe*, Mittler (Berlin), 1939

———*10 Jahre und 20 Tage*, Athenäum (Frankfurt), 1958 (references here from 1963 ed.) (English-language ed. entitled, *Memoirs*, Weidenfeld, 1959)

———*Mein wechselvolles Leben*, Musterschmidt (Göttingen), 1968 (references here from revised ed., 1975)

———*Deutsche Strategie zur See im zweiten Weltkrieg*, Bernard & Graefe (Munich), 1969 (references here from 4th ed., 1980, entitled *40 Fragen an Karl Dönitz*)

———A collection of funeral encomiums and notices entitled *Dokumentation zur Zeitgeschichte: Grossadmiral Karl Dönitz*, Deutscher Marinebund, 1981

A. Dorpalen: *Heinrich von Treitschke*, Yale UP, 1957

J. Dülffer: *Weimar, Hitler und die Marine*, Droste (Düsseldorf), 1973

L. Farrago: *The Game of Foxes*, Hodder, 1972

F. Fischer: *Germany's Aims in the First World War*, Chatto & Windus, 1967

511

J. Fishman: *The Seven Men of Spandau*, W. H. Allen, 1954

W. Forstmann: *U-39 auf Jagd im Mittelmeer*, Berlin, 1918 (references here taken from British Admiralty translation in PRO ADM 137 3842)

W. Frank: *Enemy Submarine*, Kimber, 1954 (references here from NEL paperback ed., 1971)

————*The Sea Wolves*, George Mann, 1953

G. Gaevernitz: *Revolt against Hitler*, Eyre & Spottiswoode, 1948

C.-A. Gemzell: *Organisation, Conflict and Innovation*, Stockholm, 1973

F. Gilbert: *Hitler Directs his War*, OUP, 1950

G. Gilbert: *Nuremberg Diary*, Eyre & Spottiswoode, 1948

E. Grey: *Twenty-Five Years*, Hodder, 1925

R. Grunberger: *A Social History of the Third Reich*, Weidenfeld, 1971

E. Haraszti: *Treaty Breakers or Realpolitikers?*, Boldt (Boppard am Rhein), 1974

G. v. Hase: *Kiel and Jutland*, Skeffington, 1923

U. v. Hassel: *Vom Andern Deutschland*, Atlantis (Zurich), 1946 (Engl. ed. entitled *The von Hassell Diaries*, Hamish Hamilton, 1948)

H. Herwig: *Luxury Fleet: the Imperial German Navy 1889–1918*, Allen & Unwin, 1980

————*The German Naval Officer Corps*, OUP, 1973

B. Herzog: *60 Jahre deutscher U-Boote, 1906–1966*, Lehmann (Munich), 1980

B. Herzog, G. Schomaekers: *Ritter der Tiefe, Graue Wölfe*, Welsermül (München-Wels), 1976

F. Hinsley: *British Intelligence in the Second World War*, HMSO (London), 1981

A. Hitler: *Mein Kampf*, NSDAP (Munich), 1942 ed.

D. Horn (ed.): *The Private War of Seaman Stumpf*, Frewin, 1969

R. Höss: *Kommandant in Auschwitz*, (Berlin), 1958

R. Humble: *Fraser of North Cape*, Routledge, 1983

D. Irving: *Hitler's War*, Hodder, 1977

H. Jacobsen, J. Rohwer: *Decisive Battles of World War Two, the German View*, Deutsch, 1965

D. Kelley: *22 Cells in Nuremberg*, W. H. Allen, 1947

P. Kennedy: *The Rise of Anglo-German Antagonism, 1860–1914*, Allen & Unwin, 1980

E. Lehmann: *Wie Sie Lügen*, Nibelungen (Berlin), 1940

W. Lüdde-Neurath: *Regierung Dönitz*, Musterschmidt (Göttingen), 1953

K. Ludecke: *I knew Hitler*, Jarrolds, 1938

E. Manten: *Der Krieg zur See; Die Mittelmeer Division*, Berlin, 1928

R. Manvell, H. Fraenkel: *The July Plot*, Bodley Head, 1964 (references here from Pan paperback ed., 1966)

A. Marder: *From the Dreadnought to Scapa Flow*, OUP, 1961–70

M. Marrus, R. Paxton: *Vichy France and the Jews*, Basic Books (NY), 1981

C. McClelland: *The German Historians and England*, Cambridge UP, 1971

M. Middlebrook: *Convoy: The Battle for Convoys SC 122 and HX 229*, Allen Lane, 1976

K. Neureuther, C. Bergen (eds.): *U-Boat Stories*, Constable, 1931

P. O'Donnel: *The Berlin Bunker*, Pan paperback ed., 1975

D. Pryce-Jones: *Paris in the Third Reich*, Collins, 1981

K.-J. v. Puttkamer: *Die Unheimliche See*, 1952

E. Raeder: *Struggle for the Sea*, Kimber, 1959

A. Reif: *Albert Speer*, Bernard & Graefe (Munich), 1978

J. Röhl: *Delusion or Design?*, Elek, 1975

J. Röhl, N. Sombart (eds.): *Kaiser Wilhelm II, New Interpretations*, Cambridge UP, 1982

J. Rohwer: *Die Versenkung der jüdischen Fluchtlingstransporter . . . im Schwarzen Meer*, Bernard & Graefe (Frankfurt), 1965

G. v. Roon: *German Resistance to Hitler*, Reinholdt (London), 1971

S. Roskill: *The War at Sea*, HMSO (London), 1954

E. Rössler: *The U-Boat*, Arms & Armour Press, 1981

F. Ruge: *In Vier Marinen*, Bernard & Graefe (Munich), 1979

M. Salewski: *Die Seekriegsleitung, 1939–1945*, Bernard & Graefe (Munich), 1970–75

H. Schaeffer: *U-Boat 977*, Kimber, 1952

Admiral Scheer: *Germany's High Seas Fleet in the World War*, Cassell, 1920

M. Schmidt: *Albert Speer: Das Ende eines Mythos*, Scherz, 1982

.W. Shirer: *Berlin Diary*, Hamish Hamilton, 1941

————*End of a Berlin Diary*, Hamish Hamilton, 1947

B. Smith, A. Peterson: *Heinrich Himmler, Geheimreden 1933–1945*, Propyläen (Berlin), 1978

A. Speer: *Erinnerungen*, Propyläen (Berlin), 1969 (English ed. entitled *Inside the Third Reich*, Weidenfeld, 1970)

————*Spandau, The Secret Diaries*, Collins, 1975

A. Spindler: *Der Krieg zur See; der Handelskrieg mit U-booten*, Vol. 4 Berlin 1941, Vol. 5 Frankfurt 1966

M. Steinert: *Capitulation 1945*, Constable, 1969

E. Stevens (ed.): *The Trial of von Falkenhorst*, Hodge, 1949

H. Thompson, H. Strutz: *Dönitz at Nuremberg, a Reappraisal*, Amber (NY), 1976

C. Thorne: *Ideology and Power*, Collier Macmillan, 1965

A. v. Tirpitz: *Politische Dokumente: der Aufbau der deutschen Weltmacht*, Berlin, 1924

H. Trevor-Roper: *The Last Days of Hitler*, Macmillan, 1947 (references from 4th ed., 1974)

H. Trevor-Roper (ed.): *Hitler's Table Talk*, Weidenfeld, 1953
————(ed.): *The Goebbels Diaries, The Last Days*, Secker & Warburg, 1978.
W. Warlimont: *Inside Hitler's Headquarters*, Weidenfeld, 1964
J. Wheeler-Bennett: *The Nemesis of Power*, Macmillan, 1967

Select Index

515

518

520

230–1, 237, 242, 248, 264–5, 283, 286, 362; support groups, 277, 283–4
Ruge, *Adml*.: 290–3, 312
Russia: 29–30, 38–40, 43, 48–52, 57–9; Soviet, 140, 152–3, 168, 183–5, 205, 210, 239, 335, 340, 336, 376–7, 382, 392, 394–6, 399–400, 404–7, 412, 415–18, 421–2, 430–3, 460–1, 466, 468, 470–1; German attack on, 214, 233–5, 273, 306, 315

SA: 106, 127, 130, 139
St. Nazaire: 246, 262
Salewski, M.: 273, 388, 486, 489
Sauckel, F.: 438, 455
Schacht, H.: 129, 158, 162–3, 439–40, 449, 468, 475
Scheer, *Adml*.: 93, 97, 384
Schepke, *Kap.Lt.*: 219, 225
Schirach, B. v.: 325, 439, 464, 468, 471, 476–7
Schleicher, *Gen.* v.: 117, 130, 139
Schnee, *Korv.kap.*: 7, 9, 274, 353, 355, 419–20
Schniewind, *Adml*.: 180, 195, 243, 263, 337, 339, 341–3, 346
Schörner, *SS Gen.*: 390, 393, 410
Schrader, *Adml.* v.: 352, 456
Schultze, *Korv.kap.* O.: 84, 96, 148
'Sea Lion': 216, 222, 233
Serbia: 29, 39–40
Seyss-Inquart, A.: 410, 418, 438, 440
Shirer, W.: 163, 187–8, 202, 210, 424–5, 441
Slave labour: 348, 388, 414, 437–8, 445, 455
Snorchel: 302, 360, 362
Souchon, *Adml.*: 41–6, 49, 51, 94
Spain, 271, 295–6
Speer, A.: 217, 262, 274, 280, 288, 291, 303, 305–6, 309–11, 319, 322–5, 334, 347, 365, 375–6, 379–81, 385, 390,

392, 396–7, 400, 402, 407, 411, 414–15, 417, 424–5, 431, 434–5, 438, 440, 444–5, 449, 455, 463–78, 482, 486, 491
Spindler, A.: 111–12, 114, 118
SS: 127, 130, 139, 198, 311, 321, 347, 367, 392–3, 408, 414–17, 423–4, 428, 435, 445, 454, 461
Stalin, J.: 183, 366, 431, 435–6, 461
Stauffenberg, B. v.: 321, 374
Stauffenberg, C. v.: 365–9, 372
Steinberg, J.: 144, 487

Tactics: see U-boats
Tirpitz, *Gr. Adml.* v.: 15, 20, 24–5, 29–30, 37–40, 62, 73, 95, 97, 99, 109, 128, 158–62, 166, 169, 180, 213, 230, 302, 336
Torpedo failures: 208–12, 230
Treitschke, H. v.: 13–14, 24, 72, 105
Tresckow, *Gen.*: 365
Trotha, *Adml.* v.: 95–9, 384
Turkey: 36, 38, 40, 45–52, 89, 112, 118

U-boats: campaign 1st world war, 60–5, 72–4, 78–9, 284; campaign in 2nd world war, 61, 64, 72, 190ff., 457, 480–81, 484–6; 1st 'Happy Time', 219–26; 2nd 'Happy Time', 236–47, 287–8; convoy battles, 196, 214–5, 219–21, 249–51, 275–90, 296–9, 327–9; morale, 153, 155, 184, 208–10, 223–26, 231, 249, 263–4, 354, 393, 427; decline in morale, 283, 300, 318; new types, 242–4, 259, 301, 309–11, 330, 333, 363–4, 379–84, 389–91, 461, 485–6; potential, 1st war, 64, 2nd war, 240, 287–8, 302, 306, 484; night attack tactics, 101–2, 119–20, 170, 209, 220; pack tactics, 84, 101–3, 119–20, 152–3, 155–60, 164–5, 170, 172–82, 195–6, 200, 209,

Index of Ships and U-boats

Ships